Revenue Statistics 2021

THE INITIAL IMPACT OF COVID-19 ON OECD TAX REVENUES

1965-2020

OECD
BETTER POLICIES FOR BETTER LIVES

This document, as well as any data and map included herein, are without prejudice to the status of or sovereignty over any territory, to the delimitation of international frontiers and boundaries and to the name of any territory, city or area.

The statistical data for Israel are supplied by and under the responsibility of the relevant Israeli authorities. The use of such data by the OECD is without prejudice to the status of the Golan Heights, East Jerusalem and Israeli settlements in the West Bank under the terms of international law.

Please cite this publication as:
OECD (2021), *Revenue Statistics 2021: The Initial Impact of COVID-19 on OECD Tax Revenues*, OECD Publishing, Paris, *https://doi.org/10.1787/6e87f932-en*.

ISBN 978-92-64-63303-2 (print)
ISBN 978-92-64-56735-1 (pdf)

Revenue Statistics
ISSN 2522-7696 (print)
ISSN 2522-770X (online)

Photo credits: Cover © some of the graphic elements in the main cover illustration were adapted from Freepik.com.

Corrigenda to publications may be found on line at: *www.oecd.org/about/publishing/corrigenda.htm*.

Foreword

This annual publication provides information on tax levels and tax structures in OECD countries. It was prepared under the auspices of the Working Party on Tax Policy Analysis and Tax Statistics of the Committee on Fiscal Affairs and is published under the responsibility of the Secretary-General of the OECD.

Acknowledgements

Revenue Statistics 2021 has been produced by the Organisation for Economic Cooperation and Development (OECD)'s Centre for Tax Policy and Administration (CTPA) under the auspices of Working Party No.2 on Tax Policy Analysis and Tax Statistics (WP2) of the Committee on Fiscal Affairs. The authors of this edition were Michelle Harding, Nicolás Miranda and Michael Sharratt. The special feature was written by Michelle Harding, Nicolás Miranda and Jingjing Xia.

The authors would like to thank colleagues in the OECD for their invaluable comments and practical support in finalising the publication, including David Bradbury, Karena Garnier, Natalie Lagorce, and Violet Sochay in CTPA; John Mitchell, Bettina Wistrom and Jorrit Zwijnenburg in the Statistics and Data Directorate; and the Statistical Editors and Content Management Team in the Press and Communications Directorate. Stephanie Coic in the Development Cooperation Directorate (DCD) designed the cover. The authors would also like to thank WP2 delegates and their colleagues working in national administrations for their input and comments.

Table of contents

FIGURES

TABLES

Additional chapters

Two additional chapters are available on line only at: https://doi.org/10.1787/6e87f932-en

- Chapter 5. Detailed country tables
- Chapter 6. Tax revenues by subsectors of general government

Follow OECD Publications on:

http://twitter.com/OECD_Pubs

http://www.facebook.com/OECDPublications

http://www.linkedin.com/groups/OECD-Publications-4645871

http://www.youtube.com/oecdilibrary

http://www.oecd.org/oecddirect/

This book has...

StatLinks
A service that delivers Excel® files from the printed page!

Look for the *StatLinks* at the bottom of the tables or graphs in this book. To download the matching Excel® spreadsheet, just type the link into your Internet browser, starting with the ***https://doi.org*** prefix, or click on the link from the e-book edition.

Executive Summary

In 2020, the average OECD tax-to-GDP ratio rose by 0.1 percentage points to 33.5%, against the background of the COVID-19 pandemic. Although nominal tax revenues fell in most OECD countries, the falls in countries' GDP were often greater, resulting in a small increase in the average tax-to-GDP ratio.

In this publication, taxes are defined as compulsory, unrequited payments to the general government or to a supranational authority. They are unrequited in that the benefits provided by governments to taxpayers are not normally allocated in proportion to their payments. Taxes are classified by their base: income, profits and capital gains; payroll; property; goods and services; and other taxes. Compulsory social security contributions (SSCs) paid to general government are also treated as taxes. Revenues are analysed by level of government: federal or central; state; local; and social security funds. Detailed information on the classifications applied is set out in the Interpretative Guide in Annex A.

Tax levels in 2020

Across OECD countries, tax-to-GDP ratios in 2020 ranged from 17.9% in Mexico to 46.5% in Denmark. Between 2019 and 2020, the OECD average tax-to-GDP ratio increased from 33.4% to 33.5%, with increases in country tax-to-GDP ratios seen in 20 OECD countries and decreases in 16:

- An increase in tax-to-GDP ratios from 2019 to 2020 is observed in 20 of the 36 countries for which preliminary 2020 data is available. The increase in the tax-to-GDP ratio was largest in Spain (1.9 percentage points (p.p.)), largely due to an increase in revenues from SSCs as a share of GDP due to nominal revenues from SSCs falling by less than nominal GDP. The second largest increase was in Mexico (1.6 p.p.). Iceland was the only other country with an increase of more than one percentage point.
- The largest fall was seen in Ireland (1.7 p.p.), due to a fall in VAT revenues following the temporary reduction in VAT rates in 2020 and the impact of the COVID-19 pandemic in decreasing economic activity. Smaller falls in personal income taxes, SSCs, property taxes and excises also contributed. Other large decreases were seen in Chile (1.6 p.p.) and Norway (1.3 p.p.). Thirteen other countries had decreases of less than one percentage point.

Across the last decade, 30 OECD countries reported higher tax-to-GDP ratios in 2020 than in 2010, with the greatest increases in the Slovak Republic and in Greece (6.7 and 6.5 percentage points, respectively). Among the remaining eight countries, tax levels in 2020 were more than five percentage points lower than in 2010 in Ireland and more than three percentage points lower in Norway.

Initial impact of COVID-19 on OECD tax revenues

A special feature in this publication looks at the initial impact of the COVID-19 crisis on tax revenues across the OECD, considering both the impact of the economic crisis and policy changes put in place to support businesses and households. It looks at changes in nominal taxes and nominal GDP, as well as changes for different tax types, to understand what drove the increase in the OECD average tax-to-GDP ratio and which tax types were the most affected.

It finds that the tax policy measures implemented to support households and businesses have often directly reduced revenues via deferrals or reductions in tax liabilities, enhanced tax credits and allowances and temporary or permanent reductions in tax rates. The sharp reduction in economic activity due to lockdowns and other restrictions has also reduced labour force participation, household consumption and business profits, further affecting tax revenues. However, government support measures may have indirectly bolstered affected revenues insofar as they were successful in reducing job losses and business closures. These support measures have therefore contributed to the weaker nominal falls in tax revenues than were seen during the global financial crisis of 2008-2009.

The special feature concludes that direct taxes on income were more strongly affected by the crisis than indirect or property taxes. In 2020, personal income taxes (PIT) and SSCs saw an increase in tax revenues, on average across the OECD; whereas corporate income taxes (CIT) saw the largest decrease, albeit smaller than that observed during the global financial crisis. No change was seen in property taxes or VAT as a share of GDP, on average, and a small but widespread decrease was seen for excise revenues, particularly from fuel use due to mobility restrictions.

Tax structure in 2019

In 2019, the latest year in which final data is available for all countries, SSCs amounted to the largest share of tax revenues in the OECD, at just over one-quarter (25.9%), on average. Together with personal income taxes (23.5%), these two tax types amounted to nearly one-half of tax revenues in OECD countries. Value Added Tax (VAT) accounted for a further one-fifth of total revenues (20.3%). Other consumption taxes and taxes on corporate income accounted for smaller shares of tax revenues (12.3% and 9.6% respectively), with property taxes (5.5%) and residual taxes accounting for the remaining share.

Since 2018, the average share of income taxes in total tax revenues has remained steady at 34.0%. This was largely due to an increase in the share of personal income taxes of 0.4 p.p. being offset by a fall in corporate income taxes of the same magnitude. By contrast, the average share of tax revenues from taxes on goods and services decreased by 0.2 p.p. in 2019: although VAT revenues were unchanged at 20.3% of total revenues, taxes on specific goods and services fell.

Changes by level of government

On average, subnational governments received a slightly higher share of tax revenues in 2019 relative to 2018. The central government's average share of revenues in 2019 fell from 53.3% to 53.0% of general government revenue in federal countries and from 63.3% to 63.2% in unitary countries. In federal countries, 25.4% of tax revenues were received at subnational level on average (ranging from 5.2% in Austria to 49.3% in Canada), with roughly two-thirds of revenues being received by state governments and one-third by local governments. In unitary countries, the share of local government revenues was 10.9% on average, ranging from less than 0.8% in Estonia to 35.5% in Sweden.

Introduction

The purpose of this annual publication is to provide internationally comparative data on tax levels and tax structures in member countries of the OECD. The taxes imposed in each country are presented in a standardised framework based upon the OECD classification of taxes and its Interpretative Guide as contained in Annex A to this Report.

The data for the Report has, for the most part, been provided by Delegates to Working Party No.2 on Tax Policy Analysis and Tax Statistics of the Committee on Fiscal Affairs. The OECD acknowledges the co-operation of the International Monetary Fund, whose classification of tax revenues — although in a number of respects less detailed — is in many respects similar to that of the OECD.[1] The most important of the other classifications currently in use is the System of National Accounts (henceforth referred to as SNA) and the European System of Integrated Economic Accounts of EU member states (henceforth referred to as ESA), which is primarily an elaboration of SNA, though differing from it in certain respects. Subject to a few exceptions, SNA/ESA figures can be reconciled with the figures in the present Report, since SNA criteria and definitions have been adopted unless the contrary is specifically indicated.

The material is organised in six chapters. Chapter 1 summarises tax trends of the past 50 years focusing in turn on tax-to-GDP ratios (section 1.1), tax structures (section 1.2) and taxes by level of government (section 1.3). Section 1.4 discusses the impact of alternate treatments of non-wastable tax credits and section 1.5 provides information on financing of social security-type benefits. This year's issue also carries in Chapter 2 a special feature on "The initial impact of COVID-19 on OECD tax revenues". Chapter 3 contains a set of comparative statistical tables for years 1965-2020. Chapter 4 provides country tables with tax revenue and tax-to-GDP ratios broken down by selected tax categories and by level of government for years between 1990 and 2019 (section 4.1).[2] Two memorandum tables show how countries finance their social benefits, and report taxes and social security contributions paid by general government (section 4.2). Chapter 5, which is available on line only provides statistical tables with a detailed breakdown of tax revenues by country for years between 1965 and 2019 (section 5.1). Two memorandum tables show how countries finance their social benefits, and report taxes and social security contributions paid by general government (section 5.2). Chapter 6, which is also only available on line, attributes tax revenues to general government by the following sub-sectors: central, state; local and social security funds. It contains a set of tables with a detailed breakdown of tax revenues by country for years between 1975 and 2019 (section 6.1).

Notes

[1] See IMF, *Government Finance Statistics Manual 2014* (Washington D.C.: International Monetary Fund, 2014).

[2] Because of space limitations, data are shown for selected years between 1965 and 2019. Data for years not shown are available online.

1 Tax revenue trends 1965-2020

Chapter 1 provides information on trends in tax revenues in OECD countries, including changes in tax-to-GDP ratios, tax structures, taxes by level of government, non-wastable tax credits and financing of social security-type benefits.

Revenue Statistics 2021 presents detailed internationally comparable data on tax revenues of OECD countries for all levels of government. The latest edition provides final data on tax revenues in 1965-2019. In addition, provisional estimates of tax revenues in 2020 are included for almost all OECD countries.[1]

Box 1.1. Revenue Statistics in OECD Countries – definitions & classifications

In *Revenue Statistics 2021*, taxes are defined as compulsory, unrequited payments to the general government or to a supranational authority. Taxes are unrequited in the sense that benefits provided by government are not normally in proportion to their payments.

In the OECD classification, taxes are classified by the base of the tax:

- Income and profits (heading 1000)
- Compulsory social security contributions paid to general government, which are treated as taxes (heading 2000)
- Payroll and workforce (heading 3000)
- Property (heading 4000)
- Goods and services (heading 5000)
- Other (heading 6000)

Much greater detail on the tax concept, the classification of taxes and the accrual basis of reporting is set out in the OECD Interpretative Guide at Annex A of *Revenue Statistics 2021*.

All of the averages presented in this summary are unweighted.

Tax-to-GDP ratios

Tax ratios for 2020 (provisional data)

New OECD data in the annual *Revenue Statistics 2021* publication show that on average, tax revenues as a percentage of GDP (i.e. the tax-to-GDP ratio) were 33.5% in 2020, an increase of 0.1 percentage points (p.p.) of GDP relative to 2019. The small increase in the OECD average tax-to-GDP ratio in 2020 occurred against the backdrop of the COVID-19 pandemic, which led to widespread falls in both nominal tax revenues and in nominal GDP; the reason for the increase is that in most countries, GDP fell by more than nominal tax revenues. Chapter 2 of this publication provides more information on the changes in tax revenues for each country, including for different types of taxes. The tax-to-GDP ratio increased in 20 of the countries for which 2020 data are available and decreased in 16; on average, the decreases and increases were of a similar magnitude (0.7 p.p.).

Figure 1.1. Trends in tax-to-GDP ratios, 1965-2020p (as % of GDP)

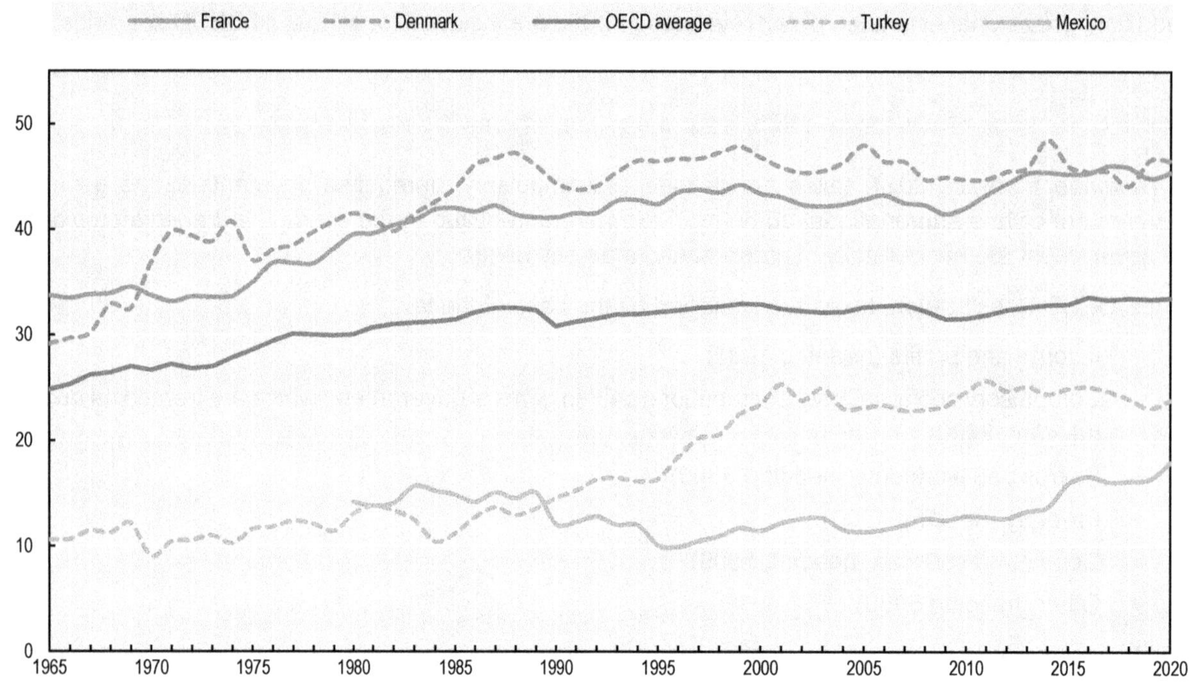

Notes: Data for 2020 are preliminary. The OECD average in 2020 is calculated by applying the unweighted average percentage change for 2020 in the 36 countries providing data for that year to the overall average tax to GDP ratio in 2019.
The 2016 OECD average tax-to-GDP ratio includes the one-off revenues from stability contributions in Iceland. Without these revenues included, the OECD average tax-to-GDP ratio in 2016 would have been 33.2%.[2]
Source: Table 3.1.

StatLink https://stat.link/5mtqjw

Table 1.1. Revenue Statistics: overview

	Tax revenue as % of GDP				Tax revenue as % of total tax revenue in 2019						
	2020p	2019	2018	2000	1100 Taxes on income, individuals (PIT)	1200 Taxes on income, corporates (CIT)	2000 Social security contributions (SSC)	4000 Taxes on property	5111 Value added taxes	Other consumption taxes[3]	All other taxes[4]
OECD - Average[1]	**33.5**	**33.4**	**33.5**	**32.9**	**23.5**	**9.6**	**25.9**	**5.5**	**20.3**	**12.3**	**2.8**
Australia	..	27.7	28.5	30.5	42.0	17.1	0.0	9.8	11.7	14.6	4.7
Austria[2]	42.1	42.6	42.3	42.3	22.6	6.4	34.9	1.3	18.0	9.5	7.3
Belgium[2]	43.1	42.7	43.9	43.8	26.5	8.7	31.0	8.0	15.6	10.1	0.0
Canada	34.4	33.8	33.5	34.7	36.0	12.3	13.9	11.4	13.3	9.5	3.6
Chile	19.3	20.9	21.1	18.8	7.2	23.4	7.3	5.5	39.9	13.2	3.7
Colombia	18.7	19.7	19.3	15.7	6.8	24.0	9.5	9.1	29.6	13.3	7.7
Costa Rica	22.9	23.6	23.2	21.1	6.1	11.9	34.2	1.9	18.5	16.3	11.1
Czech Republic	34.4	34.8	35.0	32.3	12.7	10.1	44.2	1.2	21.6	10.2	0.0
Denmark[2]	46.5	46.6	44.2	46.9	52.1	6.7	0.1	4.3	20.1	10.2	6.5
Estonia	34.5	33.5	33.0	31.1	16.5	5.5	35.0	0.6	26.7	15.7	0.0
Finland	41.9	42.3	42.4	45.8	29.0	6.0	27.9	3.4	21.7	12.0	0.1
France[2]	45.4	44.9	45.9	43.4	20.7	4.9	33.0	8.7	15.9	11.6	5.1
Germany	38.3	38.6	38.4	36.4	27.4	5.2	37.9	2.9	18.2	8.4	0.0
Greece	38.8	39.5	40.0	33.4	15.2	5.6	30.8	7.7	21.3	18.6	0.8
Hungary	35.7	36.5	36.8	38.5	14.2	3.5	32.0	2.6	26.1	18.5	3.1
Iceland	36.1	34.8	36.4	35.9	41.0	5.9	9.2	6.0	22.9	9.4	5.6
Ireland	20.2	21.9	22.4	30.8	31.7	14.0	16.8	5.7	19.6	11.3	1.0
Israel	29.7	30.2	30.8	34.8	20.9	10.1	17.4	10.2	23.9	12.0	5.6
Italy	42.9	42.4	41.7	40.5	25.8	4.6	31.2	5.7	14.7	13.6	4.3
Japan	..	31.4	31.6	25.3	18.8	12.0	41.1	8.2	13.2	6.5	0.3
Korea	28.0	27.3	26.7	20.9	17.5	15.7	26.7	11.4	15.7	10.1	2.8
Latvia	31.9	31.2	31.1	29.1	20.8	0.5	30.6	3.0	27.7	17.3	0.0
Lithuania[2]	31.2	30.3	30.2	30.8	23.9	5.1	31.8	1.0	26.1	12.1	0.0
Luxembourg[2]	38.3	38.9	39.5	36.9	23.9	15.2	27.7	9.8	15.0	8.4	0.1
Mexico	17.9	16.3	16.1	11.5	20.8	20.1	13.8	2.0	23.4	14.3	5.7
Netherlands	39.7	39.3	38.8	36.9	21.6	9.4	34.2	3.8	18.2	12.5	0.2
New Zealand	32.2	31.5	32.2	32.5	39.5	12.4	0.0	6.2	30.3	8.4	3.2
Norway	38.6	39.9	39.4	41.7	26.0	14.7	26.5	3.2	21.6	7.9	0.1
Poland[2]	36.0	35.1	35.1	32.9	15.1	6.3	37.6	3.6	22.6	13.9	0.9
Portugal	34.8	34.5	34.7	30.9	18.4	9.0	27.8	4.1	25.4	14.4	0.8
Slovak Republic	34.8	34.6	34.2	33.6	10.9	8.8	43.4	1.2	21.0	14.0	0.8
Slovenia	36.9	37.2	37.3	37.7	14.2	5.3	42.2	1.7	21.6	14.9	0.1
Spain	36.6	34.7	34.7	33.0	22.7	6.0	35.3	7.1	18.7	10.2	0.0
Sweden	42.6	42.8	43.8	50.0	28.7	7.0	21.4	2.2	21.3	7.0	12.5
Switzerland[2]	27.6	27.4	26.8	27.0	30.6	11.4	23.7	7.7	11.2	8.6	6.8
Turkey	23.9	23.1	24.0	23.5	16.3	7.9	31.4	4.2	18.1	20.9	1.2
United Kingdom	32.8	32.7	32.9	32.8	27.6	7.0	19.7	12.4	21.3	11.5	0.4
United States	25.5	25.0	24.9	28.3	41.1	5.4	24.5	11.5	0.0	17.5	0.1

1. 2020 provisional average calculated by applying the unweighted average percentage change for 2020 in the 36 countries providing data for that year to the overall average tax to GDP ratio in 2019.
2. The total tax revenue has been reduced by the amount of any capital transfer that represents uncollected taxes.
3. Calculated as 5000 Taxes on goods and services less 5111 Value added taxes.
4. Includes 1300 Unallocable between personal and corporate income tax, 3000 Taxes on payroll and workforce and 6000 other taxes.

StatLink https://stat.link/0pljx5

Country tax-to-GDP ratios in 2020 varied considerably (Table 1.1), both across countries and since 2019. Key observations include:

- Denmark had the highest tax-to-GDP ratio in 2020 (46.5%), and with the exceptions of 2017 and 2018, in which France was higher, has had the highest tax-to-GDP ratio of OECD countries since 2002. France had the second-highest tax-to-GDP ratio in 2020 (45.4%). Mexico had the lowest tax-to-GDP ratio (17.9%).
- Of the 36 countries for which data for 2020 are available, the ratio of tax revenues to GDP compared to 2019 rose in 20 and fell in 16.
- Between 2019 and 2020, the largest tax ratio increase was in Spain, at 1.9 percentage points of GDP. This was largely due to an increase in revenues from social security contributions as a share of GDP (1.5 percentage points), following a smaller fall in SSC revenues than in GDP (see chapter 2 for more information). The second largest increase was in Mexico (1.6 p.p.), with increases in all major tax types both in nominal terms and as a share of GDP. Iceland was the only other country with an increase of over 1 p.p. (Figure 1.2).
- The largest fall in the tax-to-GDP ratio between 2019 and 2020 was in Ireland, at 1.7 p.p.. The decrease in Ireland was in large part due to a fall in VAT revenues following the temporary reduction in VAT rates in 2020 and the impact of the COVID-19 pandemic in decreasing economic activity. Smaller falls in personal income taxes, social security contributions, property taxes and excises also contributed.
- Decreases of over one percentage points were also seen in Chile (1.6 p.p.) and Norway (1.3 p.p.). In Norway, the fall was due to a sharp decrease in corporate income tax revenues (3.5 p.p.), due to temporary changes in the Petroleum Tax Act to help oil and gas companies execute planned investments as well as the opportunity to offset losses in 2020 against taxed surpluses from the previous two years. This fall was offset by increases in all other major tax types.

Over the last decade, the OECD average tax-to-GDP ratio was higher in 2020 than in 2010, when it was 31.6% of GDP on average. Across countries, the tax-to-GDP ratio was higher in 2020 than in 2010 in 30 countries. The largest increase was seen in the Slovak Republic (6.7 percentage points) and in Greece (6.5 p.p.); increases of over 5 percentage points were also seen in Korea, Spain, Japan (2019 data) and Mexico. Decreases since 2010 were seen in the remaining eight countries. The largest fall has been in Ireland, from 27.7% in 2010 to 20.2% of GDP in 2020, largely due to the exceptional increase in GDP in 2015, although the tax-to-GDP ratio has continued a slower decline since 2015. The next largest decrease was seen in Norway (3.2 percentage points), largely due to falling corporate income tax revenues (Figure 1.2).

Changes in the tax-to-GDP ratio are driven by the relative changes in nominal tax revenues and in nominal GDP. From one year to the next, if tax revenues rise more than GDP (or fall less than GDP) the tax-to-GDP ratio will increase. Conversely, if tax revenues rise less than GDP, or fall further, the tax-to-GDP ratio will go down. Therefore, the tax-to-GDP ratio does not necessarily mean that the amount of tax revenues have increased in nominal, or even real, terms.

Figure 1.2. Changes in tax-to-GDP ratios, p.p., 2019-20p and 2010-20p

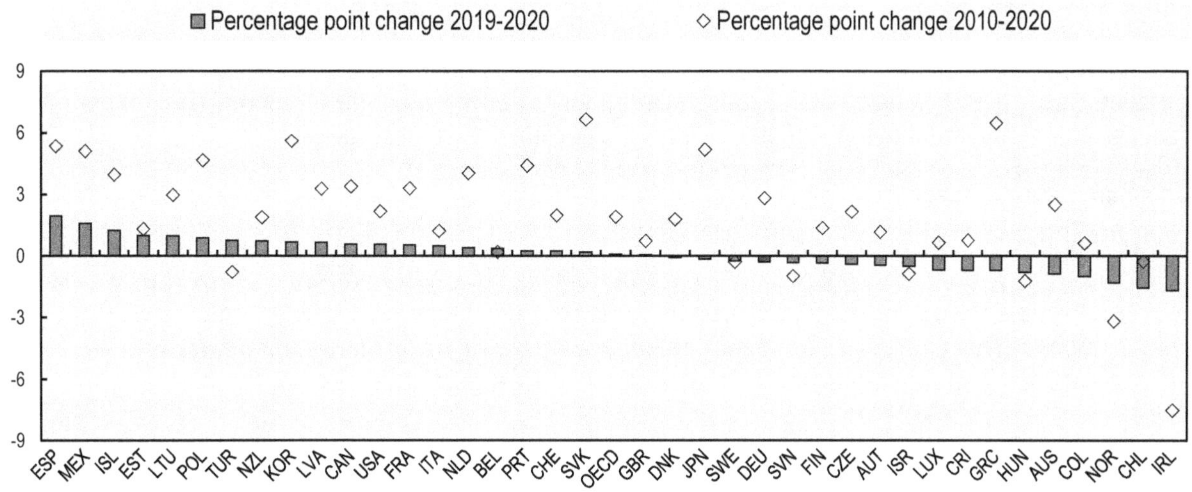

Note: Preliminary data for 2020 was not available for Australia and Japan. For these countries the comparison shown is 2018-2019 and 2010-2019 data.
Source: Secretariat calculations based on Table 3.1.

StatLink https://stat.link/9fv3h6

In 2020, 20 OECD countries experienced an increase in their tax-to-GDP ratio relative to 2019. However, this was due to an increase in nominal tax revenues in only six of these countries. In the remaining 14 countries where tax-to-GDP ratios increased in 2020, both tax revenues and GDP fell (with GDP falling further). Of the 16 OECD countries that experienced a decline in their tax-to-GDP ratio in 2020, only Denmark had higher levels of tax revenues in nominal terms than the preceding year and this increase was slightly less than the increase in nominal GDP. Eleven of these countries saw declines in both nominal tax revenues and in nominal GDP, with tax revenues decreasing further; and the remaining four countries (Ireland, Chile, Hungary and Luxembourg) saw decreases in nominal tax revenues compared to increases in nominal GDP. (Figure 1.3). In Figure 1.3, changes between 2018 and 2019 are shown for Australia and Japan, where the tax-to-GDP ratio is not available in 2020. In both countries, nominal tax revenues decreased while GDP increased, leading to falls in the tax-to-GDP ratio.

Box 1.2. Methodology: the tax-to-GDP ratio

The tax-to-GDP ratios shown in *Revenue Statistics 2021* express aggregate tax revenues as a percentage of GDP. The value of this ratio depends on its denominator (GDP) as well as its numerator (tax revenue), and that the denominator – GDP – is subject to historical revision.

The numerator (tax revenue)

- For the numerator, the OECD Secretariat uses revenue figures that are submitted annually by correspondents from national Ministries of Finance, Tax Administrations or National Statistics Offices. Although provisional figures for most countries become available with a lag of about six months, finalised data become available with a lag of around one and a half years. Final revenue data for 2019 were received during the period May-August 2021.
- In thirty-five OECD countries the reporting year coincides with the calendar year. Three countries — Australia, Japan and New Zealand — have different reporting years. Reporting year 2018 includes Q2/2018–Q1/2019 (Japan) and Q3/2018–Q2/2019 (Australia, New Zealand) respectively (Q = quarter).

The denominator (GDP)

- For the denominator, the GDP figures used for *Revenue Statistics 2021* are the most recently available in September 2021. By that time, the 2019 and 2020 GDP figures were available for all OECD countries.
- Using these GDP figures ensures a maximum of consistency and international comparability for the reported tax-to-GDP ratios.
- The GDP figures are based on the OECD Annual National Accounts (ANA – SNA) for the thirty-four OECD countries where the reporting year is the actual calendar year.
- Where the reporting year differs from the calendar year, the annual GDP estimates are obtained by aggregating quarterly GDP estimates provided by the OECD Statistics Directorate for those quarters corresponding to each country's fiscal (tax) year.

The average shown in this publication is an unweighted average for all countries in which data is available. The 2020 provisional average calculated by applying the unweighted average percentage change for 2020 in the 36 countries providing data for that year to the overall average tax to GDP ratio in 2019. The historical series for the OECD average shown in this publication is lower than that shown in previous editions due to the inclusion of Costa Rica in the OECD average for the first time in this edition, after Costa Rica became an OECD member in May 2021.

Figure 1.3. Relative changes in nominal tax revenues and nominal GDP (%), 2019-20p

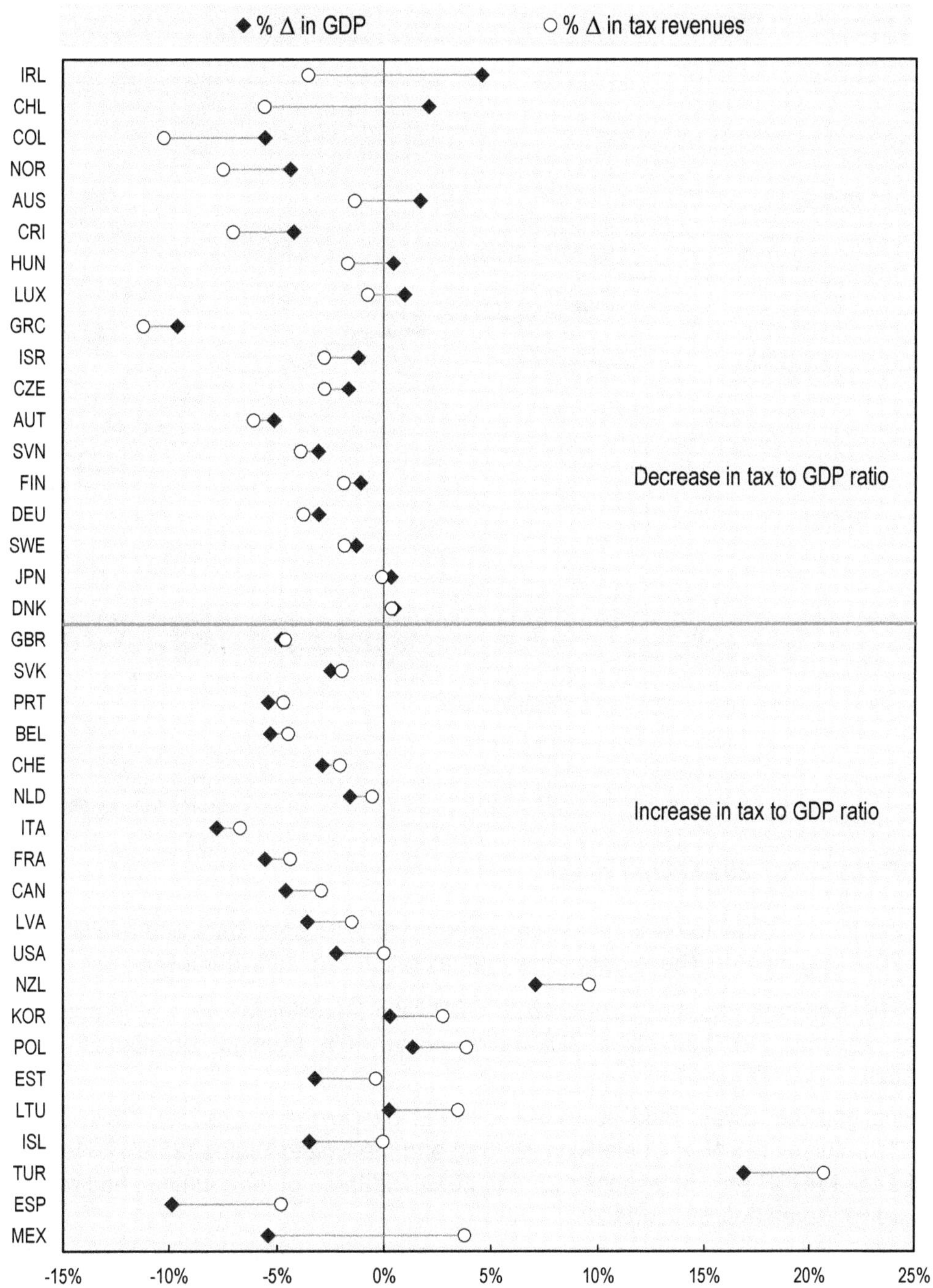

Note: Data for Australia and Japan show the change between 2018 and 2019, as preliminary data for 2020 was not available for Australia and Japan.

Source: Secretariat calculations based on chapter 4 (tax revenues) and table 3.19 (GDP).

StatLink https://stat.link/x5vajk

Figure 1.4. Tax to GDP ratios in 2019 and 2020p (as % of GDP)

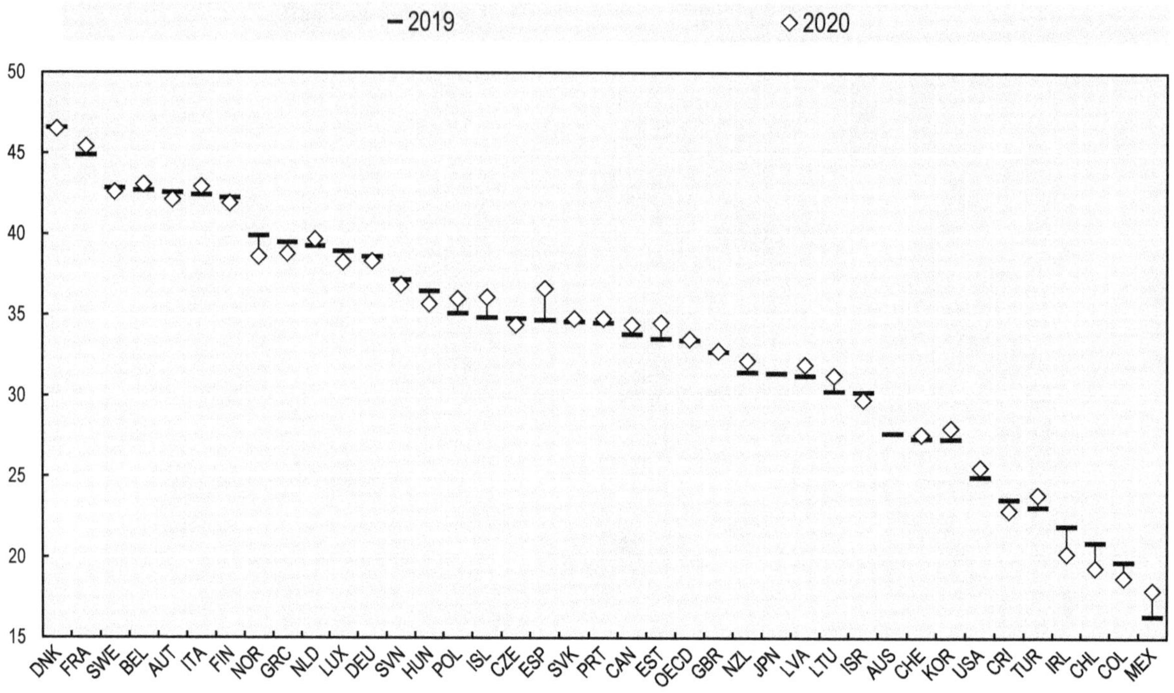

Note: Preliminary data for 2020 were not available for Australia and Japan.
Source: Secretariat calculations based on Table 3.1

StatLink https://stat.link/ny8ltj

Tax-to-GDP ratios for 2019 (final data)

The latest year for which tax-to-GDP ratios are based on final revenue data and available for all OECD countries is 2019 (Figure 1.4). These data show that tax ratios vary considerably across countries:

- In 2019, Denmark had the highest tax-to-GDP ratio (46.6%), followed by France (44.9%). Five other countries also had tax-to-GDP ratios above 40% (Austria, Belgium, Finland, Italy and Sweden).
- Mexico had the lowest ratio at 16.3% followed by Colombia (19.7%), Chile (20.9%), Ireland (21.9%), Turkey (23.1%), Costa Rica (23.6%) and the United States (25.0%). No other countries had a tax-to-GDP ratio of less than 25% in 2019 and three other countries had ratios below 30% (Australia, Korea and Switzerland).
- The tax-to-GDP ratio in the OECD area as a whole (un-weighted average) was 33.4% in 2019. In 2018, it was 33.5%.
- Relative to 2018, overall tax ratios rose in 18 OECD member countries and fell in 20.
- The largest increases in the tax-to-GDP ratio was in Denmark (2.4 p.p.). There were no other increases over one p.p..
- The largest reductions were in Iceland (1.6 p.p.) and Belgium (1.2 p.p.).

Between 2018 and 2019, the fall in the average tax-to-GDP ratio were driven by decreases in revenues from corporate income taxes and excise taxes (0.1 p.p. each), offset by an increase in personal income tax revenues (0.1 p.p.).

Table 1.2. Tax structures in the OECD area, selected years (unweighted average as % of GDP)

Per cent

	1965	1990	2000	2007	2010	2015	2017	2018	2019
Total tax revenue	24.8	30.8	32.9	32.9	31.6	32.9	33.4	33.5	33.4
1000 Taxes on income, profits and capital gains	8.7	11.5	11.5	11.7	10.2	10.9	11.2	11.3	11.3
of which:									
1100 Taxes on income, profits and capital gains of individuals	6.8	9.0	8.3	7.8	7.2	7.9	7.9	7.9	8.0
1200 Taxes on income, profits and capital gains of corporates	2.1	2.3	3.1	3.6	2.7	2.8	3.0	3.1	3.0
2000 Social security contributions (SSC)	4.5	7.1	8.4	8.2	8.6	8.8	8.9	9.0	8.9
3000 Taxes on payroll and workforce	0.3	0.4	0.4	0.4	0.4	0.4	0.4	0.4	0.5
4000 Taxes on property	1.9	1.7	1.7	1.7	1.6	1.8	1.9	1.8	1.8
5000 Taxes on goods and services	9.4	9.9	10.8	10.6	10.5	10.8	10.9	10.8	10.8
of which:									
5111 Value added taxes	0.7	5.1	6.3	6.5	6.4	6.6	6.7	6.7	6.7
5121 Excises	3.5	2.5	2.8	2.6	2.6	2.5	2.5	2.4	2.3
6000 Other Taxes	0.1	0.4	0.2	0.2	0.2	0.2	0.2	0.2	0.2

Note: Percentage share of major tax categories in GDP. Data are included from 1965 onwards for Australia, Austria, Belgium, Canada, Denmark, Finland, France, Germany, Greece, Iceland, Ireland, Italy, Japan, Luxembourg, the Netherlands, New Zealand, Norway, Portugal, Spain, Sweden, Switzerland, Turkey, United Kingdom and United States; from 1972 for Korea; from 1980 for Mexico; from 1990 for Chile, Colombia and Costa Rica; from 1991 for Hungary and Poland; from 1993 for the Czech Republic and from 1995 for Estonia, Israel, Latvia, Lithuania, the Slovak Republic and Slovenia. The figures for the 2016 OECD average include the one-off revenues from stability contributions in Iceland.
Source: OECD (2021), "Revenue Statistics: Comparative tables", *OECD Tax Statistics (database)*.

StatLink https://stat.link/hsnkpw

Tax ratio changes between 1965 and 2019

Between 1965 and 2019, the average tax-to-GDP ratio in the OECD area increased from 24.8% to 33.4% (an increase of 8.6 percentage points, with the difference due to rounding) (Figure 1.1).

Before the first oil shock (1973 to 1974), strong, almost uninterrupted income growth enabled tax levels to rise in all OECD countries. In part, tax levels rose automatically through the effect of fiscal drag on personal income tax schedules. From 1975 to 1985, the tax burden in the OECD area increased by 2.9 percentage points. After the mid-1970s, the combination of slower real income growth and higher levels of unemployment apparently limited the revenue raising capacity of governments. But during and after the deep recession following the second oil shock (1980), countries in Europe saw tax levels rise further, to finance higher spending on social security and rein in budget deficits.

After the mid-1980s, most OECD countries substantially reduced the statutory rates of their personal and corporate income tax, but the negative revenue impact of widespread tax reforms was often offset by reducing or abolishing tax reliefs. By 1999, the average OECD tax-to-GDP ratio had risen to 33.0%, the highest recorded level at that time. It fell back slightly between 2001 and 2004, but then rose again between 2005 and 2007 before falling back following the global financial crisis in 2008 and 2009. Taking these changes together the average tax level in the OECD area increased by 1.3 percentage points between 1995 and 2019 (Figure 1.1).

The OECD average conceals the great variety in national tax-to-GDP ratios. In 1965, tax-to-GDP ratios in OECD countries ranged from 10.6% in Turkey to 33.7% in France. By 2019 the corresponding range was from 16.3% in Mexico to 46.6% in Denmark. The trend towards higher tax levels over this period reflects the need to finance a significant increase of public sector outlays in almost all OECD countries.

Tax structures

Tax structures are measured by the share of major taxes in total tax revenue. In 2019, the tax structures of OECD countries varied. Seventeen countries raised the largest part of their revenues from income taxes (both corporate and personal), ten countries raised the largest part of their revenues from SSCs, and 11 countries raised the largest part of their revenues from consumption taxes (including VAT). Taxes on property and payroll taxes played a smaller role in the revenue systems of OECD countries in 2019, both on average and within most countries (Figure 1.5).

Figure 1.5. Tax structures in 2019 (as % of total tax revenue)

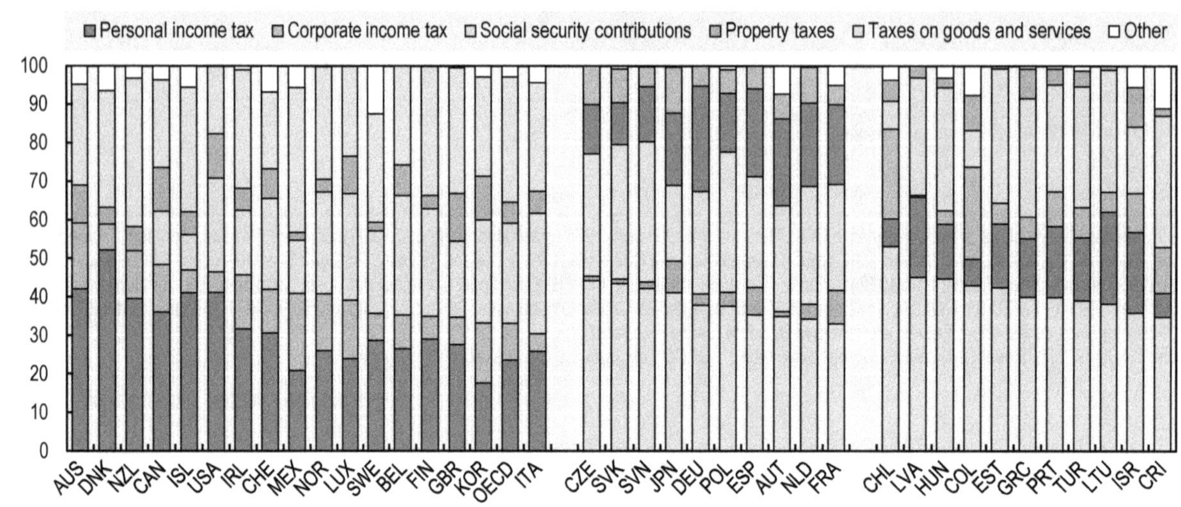

Note: Countries are grouped and ranked by those where income tax revenues (personal and corporate) form the highest share of total tax revenues, followed by those where social security contributions, or taxes on goods and services, form the highest share.
Source: Secretariat calculations based on data in chapter 4.

StatLink https://stat.link/h3m41g

While on average tax levels have generally been rising, the tax structure or tax 'mix' has been remarkably stable over time. Nevertheless, several trends have emerged up to 2019 – the latest year for which data is available for all 38 OECD countries. These trends are discussed further below.

Taxes on income and profits

On average, in 2019, OECD countries collected 33.1% of their tax revenues through taxes on income and profits (personal and corporate income taxes taken together). Taxes on personal and corporate incomes remain the most important source of revenues used to finance public spending in 17 OECD countries, and in ten of them – Australia, Canada, Denmark, Iceland, Ireland, Mexico, New Zealand, Norway, Switzerland and the United States – the share of income taxes in the tax mix in 2019 exceeded 40%.

Figure 1.6. Trends in tax structures (1965-2019, as % of total tax revenue)

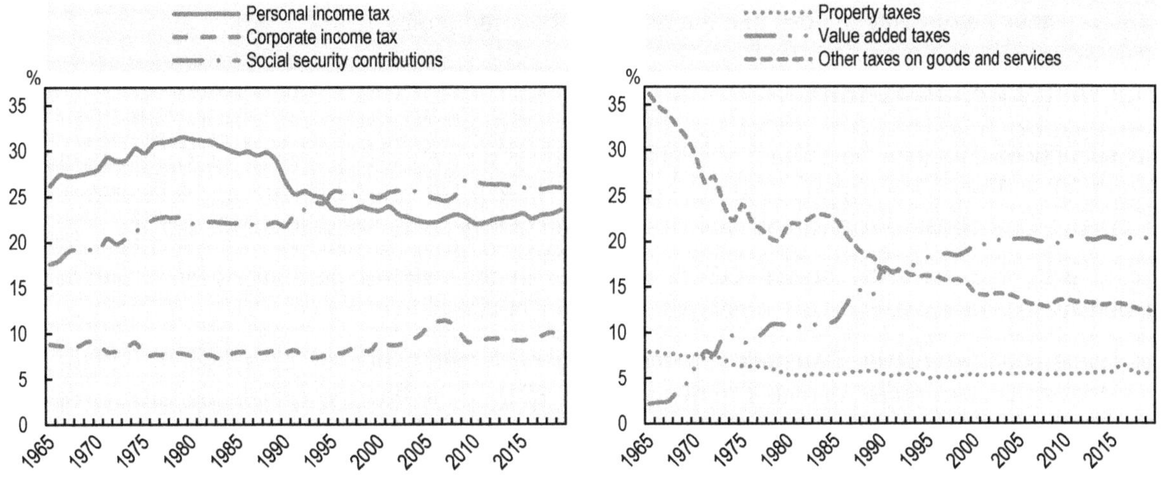

Note: The OECD average tax revenue in 2016 from main categories includes the one-off revenues from stability contributions in Iceland. This predominately affects the average revenues from property taxes, as a percentage of total tax revenues, in that year only.
Source: Secretariat calculations based on tables 3.8 to 3.14.

StatLink https://stat.link/96lkj0

Within taxes on income and profits, the share of PIT and CIT varies:

- Revenues from personal income taxes are 23.5% of total taxes on average in 2019 compared with around 30% in the 1980s. About two percentage points of this reduction can be attributed to the impact on the average of a number of relatively new entrants to the OECD from Eastern Europe and Latin America for which tax revenue data is only available from the 1990s onwards. These countries tend to have relatively low personal income tax revenues and high revenues from social security contributions or corporate income taxes, but this impact is observed in the post 1990 data only.
- The variation in the share of the personal income tax between countries is considerable. In 2019, it ranged from a low of 6.8% in Colombia to 42.0% in Australia and the United States, and 52.1% in Denmark (Figure 1.5).
- Corporate income tax revenues represented between 7% and 9% of total tax revenues, on average, throughout the period 1965 to 2003. They then increased to a high of 11.3% in 2007, before dropping to 9.0% in 2010, directly after the financial crisis. They remained at between 9.0% and 10.0% of total revenues until 2018, and dropped back to 9.6% of revenues in 2020.
- The share of the corporate income tax in total tax revenues varied considerably across countries from less than 5% (France, Hungary, Italy and Latvia) to over 20% in Mexico (20.1%), Chile (23.4%) and Colombia (24.0%) in 2019. Apart from the spread in statutory rates of the corporate income tax, these differences are at least partly explained by institutional and country specific factors, for example:
    - the degree to which firms in a country are incorporated,
    - the breadth of the corporate income tax base, for example some narrowing may occur as a consequence of generous depreciation schemes and of tax incentives,
    - the degree of cyclicality of the corporate tax system, for which one of the important elements are loss offset provisions,

- the extent of reliance upon tax revenues from the exploitation of oil and/or mineral deposits, and
- other instruments to postpone the taxation of earned profits.

Social security contributions

Social security contributions as a share of total tax revenues on average across the OECD accounted for 25.9% in 2019. They were highest in the Czech Republic and the Slovak Republic (44.2% and 43.4%, respectively). In contrast, Australia and New Zealand do not levy social security contributions.

There is also wide variation across OECD countries in the relative proportions of social security contributions paid by employees and employers (Figure 1.7):

- Nine countries (Chile, Denmark, Greece, Hungary, Israel, Lithuania, Luxembourg, Poland, and Slovenia) raise more revenues from employee SSCs, whereas the remainder raise more from employer SSCs.
- The highest share of employee SSC revenues are found in Lithuania, at 24.2% of total revenues. Germany, Greece, Hungary, Japan, Poland and Slovenia also have employee SSC revenues of over 15% of total tax revenues. Denmark had the lowest share, at 0.1% of total revenues. Apart from Denmark, only Estonia had revenues from employee SSCs of less than 5% of total revenues.
- The highest share of employer social security contribution revenues are found in Estonia, at 33.3% of total revenues. The Czech Republic (28.3%), the Slovak Republic (26.3%) and Spain (26.0%) also had employer SSC revenues of over 25% of total tax revenues. Denmark and Chile had the lowest shares, at 0.03% and 0.2% of total revenues respectively.
- The highest share of self-employed or non-employed social security contribution revenues are found in the Netherlands and Poland, at 7.8% and 7.3% of total revenues respectively.

Figure 1.7. Composition of social security contributions, as % of total social security contributions, 2019

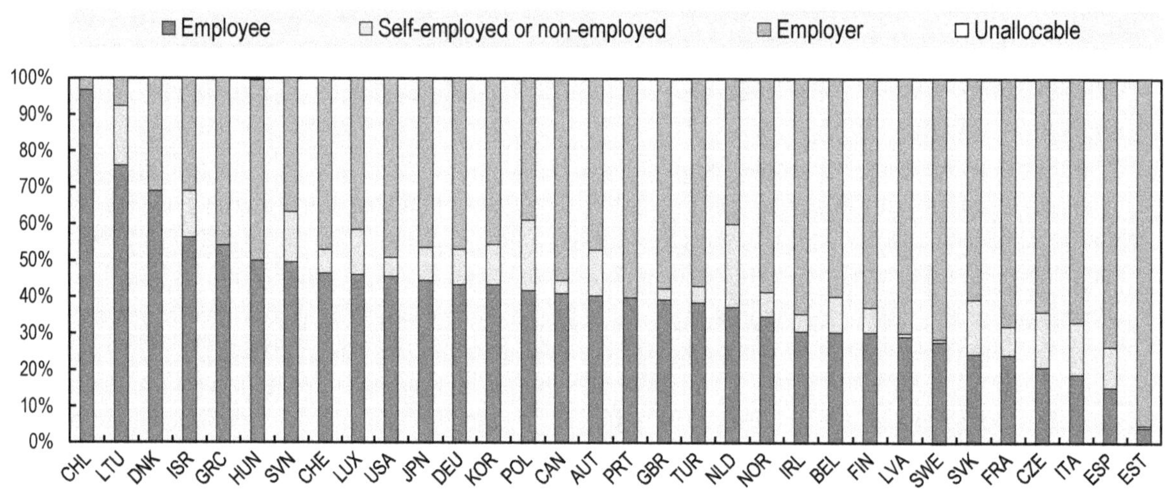

Note: Australia, Colombia, Costa Rica, Iceland, Mexico and New Zealand are not included within figure 1.7. Although Colombia, Costa Rica, Iceland and Mexico collect social security contributions, disaggregated data is not available. New Zealand and Australia do not levy social security contributions.
Source: Secretariat calculations based on data in chapter 4.

StatLink https://stat.link/e5z2hn

Property taxes

Between 1965 and 2019, the share of taxes on property fell from 7.9% to 5.5% of total tax revenues on average across the OECD (Figure 1.6). Canada, Israel, Korea, the United Kingdom and the United States had property tax revenues that amounted to more than 10% of total tax revenues. By contrast, property taxes accounted for less than 1% of total revenues in Estonia and Lithuania.

Consumption taxes

- The share of taxes on consumption (general consumption taxes plus specific consumption taxes) fell from 38.4% to 32.6% between 1965 and 2019 (Figure 1.6).
- During this period, the composition of taxes on goods and services has fundamentally changed. A fast-growing revenue source has been general consumption taxes, especially the value-added tax (VAT) which is imposed in thirty-seven of the thirty-eight OECD countries.[3]
- General consumption taxes presently account for 21.0% of total tax revenue, compared with only 11.9% in the mid-1960s. In 2019, the vast majority of this was from VAT (20.3% of total tax revenues) (Figure 1.6)
- The substantially increased importance of the value-added tax has served to counteract the diminishing share of specific consumption taxes, such as excises and custom duties.
- Between 1975 and 2019 the share of specific taxes on consumption (mostly on tobacco, alcoholic drinks and fuels, as well as some environment-related taxes) have almost halved from 17.7% to 9.5% of total revenues. In 2019, excises were the largest single category of total revenues in this heading, accounting for 7.2% of total revenues (Figure 1.8).
- Rates of taxes on imported goods were considerably reduced across all OECD countries, reflecting a global trend to remove trade barriers.
- Nevertheless, countries such as Costa Rica, Estonia, Greece, Hungary, Latvia, Lithuania, Mexico, Poland, Portugal, the Slovak Republic, and Slovenia (between 11-15%) and Turkey (19.3%) still collect a relatively large proportion of their tax revenues through taxes on specific goods and services.

Figure 1.8. Share of general consumption tax revenues (left panel) and specific consumption revenues (right panel) as % of total revenues, 1975-2019

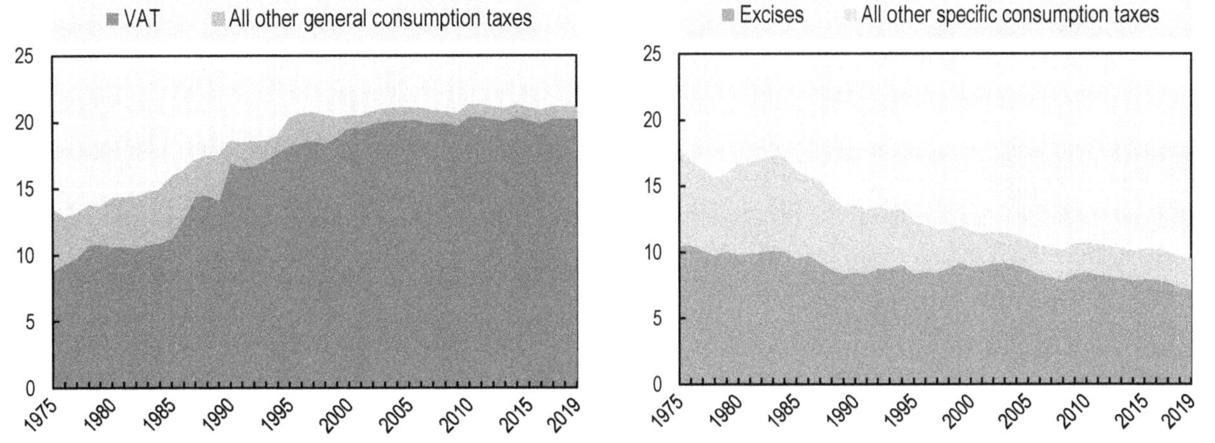

Note: The unweighted average for each year includes all countries which report revenue in the categories shown in that year. The OECD averages for 2016 include the one-off revenues from stability contributions in Iceland.
Source: Secretariat calculations based on chapter 4.

StatLink https://stat.link/38uvak

Taxes by level of government

This section discusses the relative share of tax revenues attributed to the various sub-sectors of general government in 2019. The different sub-sectors are:

- Central government
- State government (federal and regional countries only)
- Local government
- Social security funds
- Supranational authorities (EU countries only)

The guidelines for attributing these revenue shares to the different levels of government are based on the final version of the 2008 System of National Accounts. These guidelines are discussed in the special feature S.1 in the 2011 edition of OECD *Revenue Statistics*.

Revenues of sub-national governments in federal and unitary countries

Eight OECD countries have a federal structure. Among these countries, central governments received 53.0% of total revenues in 2019 on average. The second-highest share of revenues on average was received by social security funds, which are a sub-sector of general government, at 21.4% of total revenues, followed by 17.7% at the state level and 7.7% at the local level (Table 1.3). However, within countries there was considerable variation around these means:

- In 2019, the share of central government receipts in the eight federal OECD countries varied from 29.3% in Germany to 80.8% in Australia.
- In 2019, the share of the states varied from 2.0% in Austria, 4.1% in Mexico and 10.6% in Belgium to 39.5% in Canada. The share of local government varied from 1.7% in Mexico to 14.6% in the United States and 15.7% in Switzerland.
- Between 1975 and 2019 the share of federal government revenues declined by over fourteen percentage points in Belgium and by between five and six percentage points in Canada and the United States.
- The share of federal government revenues increased in Austria by around 13 percentage points. There was little change in Australia and Mexico.
- Of the seven federal countries with social security funds, five increased the share of revenue between 1975 and 2019. The exceptions were Canada and Mexico, where the share slightly declined between 1975 (1980 for Mexico due to data availability) and 2019.

Colombia and Spain are classified as regional rather than unitary countries because of their highly decentralised political structure, and have very different compositions by level of government. In Colombia, the share of central government receipts was 73.0% in 2019, with regional governments receiving 5.0% of total revenues and local governments receiving 12.5%. In Spain, the share of central government receipts in 2019 was 40.2% compared with 15.4% for regional governments and 9.2% for local governments.

Table 1.3. Attribution of tax revenues to sub-sectors of general government as % of total tax revenue, federal countries

Per cent

	Supranational			Central government			State or Regional government			Local government			Social Security Funds		
	1975	1995	2019	1975	1995	2019	1975	1995	2019	1975	1995	2019	1975	1995	2019
Federal countries															
Australia	..	..	..	80.1	77.5	80.8	15.7	19.0	15.6	4.2	3.4	3.6	0.0	0.0	0.0
Austria	..	0.4	0.4	51.7	64.7	65.0	10.6	1.8	2.0	12.4	4.1	3.2	25.3	29.0	29.4
Belgium[1]	1.4	1.0	1.0	65.3	60.1	50.8	..	1.8	10.6	4.4	4.8	4.9	28.8	32.2	32.8
Canada	..	..	..	47.6	39.1	41.7	32.5	37.1	39.5	9.9	9.8	9.8	10.0	14.0	9.0
Germany	1.2	0.6	0.5	33.5	31.4	29.3	22.3	21.6	23.8	9.0	7.4	8.5	34.0	39.0	37.9
Mexico	..	..	..	..	73.9	80.4	..	2.8	4.1	..	1.5	1.7	..	21.8	13.8
Switzerland1	..	..	..	30.7	31.7	35.7	27.0	24.0	24.9	20.3	17.5	15.7	22.0	26.8	23.7
United States	..	..	..	45.4	41.4	40.2	19.5	20.0	20.6	14.7	13.3	14.6	20.5	25.2	24.5
Unweighted average	1.3	0.7	0.6	50.6	52.5	53.0	21.3	16.0	17.7	10.7	7.7	7.7	20.1	23.5	21.4
Regional countries															
Colombia[2]	..	..	..	..	63.2	73.0	..	5.5	5.0	..	8.6	12.5	..	22.7	9.5
Spain[2]	..	0.8	0.6	48.2	51.1	40.2	..	5.0	15.4	4.3	8.6	9.2	47.5	34.6	34.5

1. The total tax revenue has been reduced by the amount of any capital transfer that represents uncollected taxes.
2. Colombia and Spain are not constitutionally federal countries, but both have a highly decentralised political structure, with high autonomy of their territorial entities.

StatLink https://stat.link/ml07h4

The remaining twenty-eight OECD countries have a unitary structure. In these countries, an average of 63.2% of revenues were derived at the central level, with 25.5% accounted for by social security funds. A further 10.9% were raised by local governments. Among unitary OECD countries:

- The share of central government receipts in 2019 varied from 32.6% in France to 93.1% in New Zealand.
- The local government share varied from 0.8% in Estonia to 35.5% in Sweden.
- Between 1975 and 2019 there have been shifts to local government of 5 percentage points or more in six countries – France, Iceland, Italy, Korea, Portugal and Sweden. Shifts of 5 percentage points or more in the other direction occurred in three countries – Ireland, Norway and the United Kingdom.[4]
- Between 1975 and 2019, there were increases in the share of social security funds of 7 or more percentage points in four countries – Finland, France, Japan and Korea and corresponding decreases in four other countries – Italy, Norway, Portugal and Sweden.

Table 1.4. Attribution of tax revenues to sub-sectors of general government as % of total tax revenue, unitary countries

Per cent

	Supranational			Central government			State or Regional government			Local government			Social Security Funds		
	1975	1995	2019	1975	1995	2019	1975	1995	2019	1975	1995	2019	1975	1995	2019
Unitary countries															
Chile	..	..	..	..	89.9	85.6	..	..	..	..	6.5	8.3	..	3.6	6.1
Costa Rica	..	..	..	..	65.5	57.8	..	..	..	..	1.6	3.0	..	33.0	39.2
Czech Republic	..	..	0.4	..	57.7	54.4	..	..	..	..	0.9	1.0	..	41.4	44.2
Denmark[1]	1.0	0.5	0.3	69.1	68.2	73.9	..	..	..	29.8	31.3	25.7	0.1	0.0	0.0
Estonia	..	..	0.6	..	84.3	82.0	..	..	..	..	0.8	0.8	..	14.9	16.6
Finland	..	0.4	0.4	56.0	46.6	48.9	..	..	..	23.5	22.3	22.8	20.4	30.8	27.9
France[1]	0.7	0.7	0.4	51.2	42.5	32.6	..	..	..	7.6	11.0	13.6	40.6	45.8	53.4
Greece	..	0.6	0.5	67.1	66.3	66.2	..	..	..	3.4	2.0	2.4	29.5	31.0	30.9
Hungary	..	..	0.4	..	63.8	62.7	..	..	..	..	2.5	5.8	..	33.6	31.2
Iceland	..	..	..	81.3	79.2	71.7	..	..	..	18.7	20.8	28.3	0.0	0.0	0.0
Ireland	2.3	1.5	0.6	77.4	83.1	82.5	..	..	..	7.3	2.7	2.0	13.1	12.7	15.0
Israel	..	..	..	..	79.7	74.7	..	..	..	..	6.4	7.9	..	14.0	17.4
Italy	..	0.4	0.4	53.2	62.7	57.0	..	..	..	0.9	5.4	11.4	45.9	31.5	31.2
Japan	..	..	..	45.5	41.2	35.5	..	..	..	25.6	25.2	23.5	29.0	33.6	41.1
Korea	..	..	..	89.0	69.2	56.0	..	..	..	10.1	18.7	17.3	0.9	12.1	26.7
Latvia	..	..	0.5	..	43.5	50.5	..	..	..	..	19.5	19.3	..	36.9	29.7
Lithuania[1]	..	..	0.9	..	71.7	66.1	..	..	..	..	2.3	1.1	..	26.1	31.8
Luxembourg[1]	0.8	0.4	0.7	63.6	66.4	67.6	..	..	..	6.7	6.5	4.8	29.0	26.6	26.9
Netherlands	1.5	1.3	1.1	58.9	56.0	61.2	..	..	..	1.2	3.1	3.4	38.4	39.5	34.2
New Zealand	..	..	..	92.3	94.7	93.1	..	..	..	7.7	5.3	6.9	0.0	0.0	0.0
Norway	..	..	..	50.6	57.6	84.5	..	..	..	22.4	20.0	15.5	27.0	22.4	0.0
Poland[1]	..	..	0.6	..	61.2	49.3	..	..	..	..	8.5	12.6	..	30.3	37.6
Portugal	..	0.8	0.5	65.4	72.3	65.8	..	..	..	0.0	5.4	7.2	34.6	21.5	26.6
Slovak Republic	..	..	0.4	..	62.6	55.5	..	..	..	..	1.3	1.8	..	36.1	42.3
Slovenia	..	..	0.4	..	50.5	48.9	..	..	..	..	6.2	8.9	..	43.3	41.7
Sweden	..	0.4	0.3	51.3	46.9	51.9	..	..	..	29.2	30.9	35.5	19.5	21.8	12.3
Turkey	..	..	..	..	75.1	59.5	..	..	..	..	12.8	9.2	..	12.1	31.4
United Kingdom	1.0	1.0	0.5	70.5	77.5	74.6	..	..	..	11.1	3.7	5.2	17.5	17.8	19.7
Unweighted average	1.2	0.7	0.5	65.2	65.6	63.2	..	..	..	12.8	10.1	10.9	21.6	24.0	25.5

1. The total tax revenue has been reduced by the amount of any capital transfer that represents uncollected taxes.

StatLink https://stat.link/819lsn

Composition of central and sub central revenues

Figure 1.9 shows the revenues from each major category of tax revenue for central and sub central governments. For federal and regional countries, the sub central level includes revenues received by both state and local governments. Figure 1.9 demonstrates that:

- Central government revenues in almost all OECD countries are predominantly derived from income and goods and services taxes, with a negligible share from property taxes.
- At the subnational level, revenue from property taxes provides a much larger share of revenues than at the central level, and accounts for over 90% of revenues in four countries (Israel, Ireland, Greece and the United Kingdom).
- By contrast, the share of income taxes and goods and services taxes is lower at the sub-central level, the exceptions being Finland, Luxembourg and Sweden, where over 90% of sub-central revenues are derived from income taxes.

Figure 1.9. Composition of revenues of federal or central government (left) and sub-national government (right), 2019

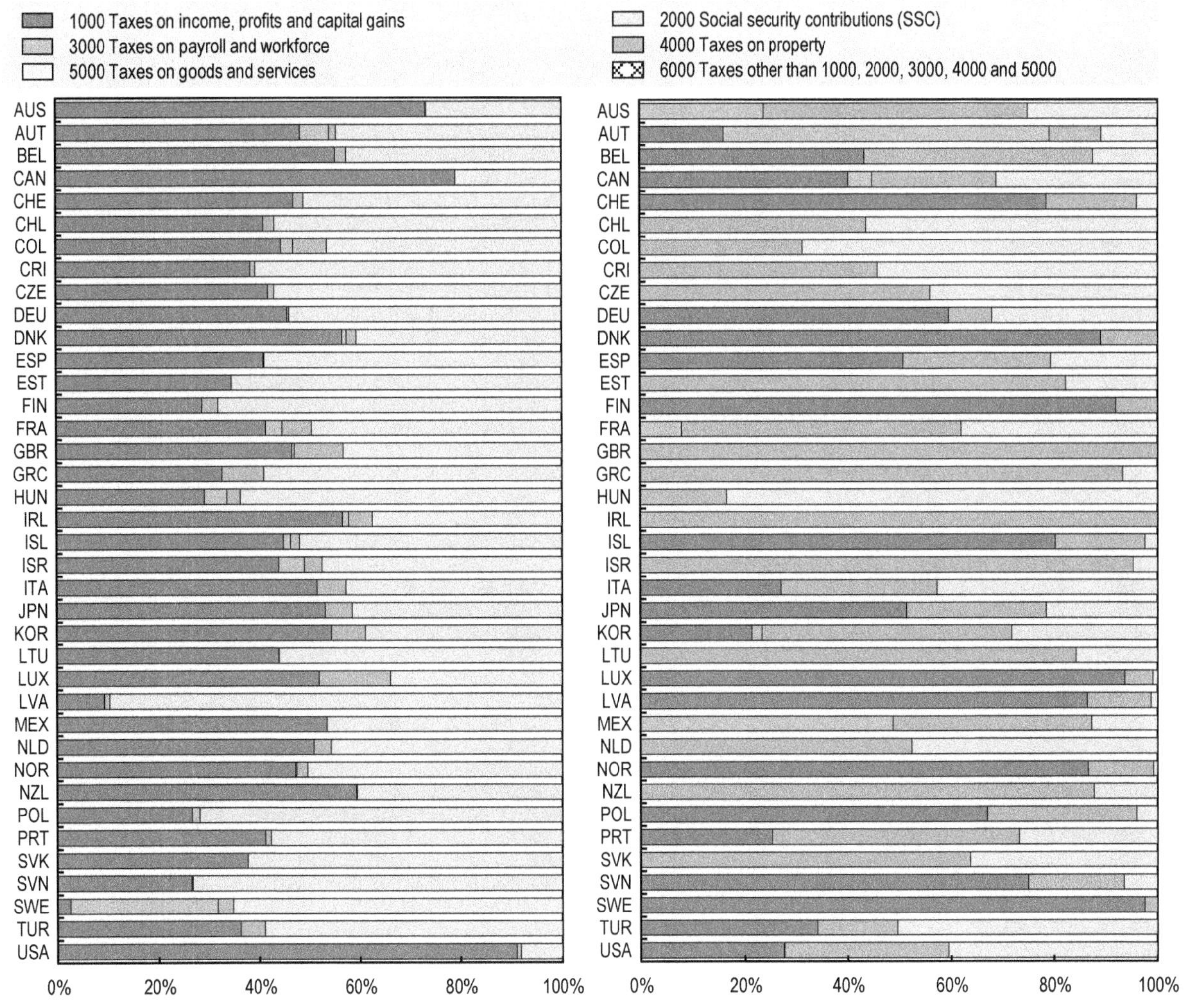

Note: The left-hand panel (a) refers to only those taxes which are classified as central government taxes. Social security contributions paid to social security funds are excluded. The right-hand panel (b) refers only to those taxes which are classified as sub-central taxes (local and (where relevant) state taxes). Social security contributions paid to social security funds are excluded.
Source: Secretariat calculations based on tables 3.16 to 3.18.

StatLink https://stat.link/r9wy2o

Revenues paid to a supranational authority

The twenty-two EU member states that are also members of the OECD collect taxes on behalf of the European Union (EU), as did the United Kingdom prior to 2020. These taxes primarily consist of customs duties and Single Resolution Fund contributions.[5] Both taxes are collected on behalf of the EU by national tax administrations and are included in the total tax figures under headings 5123 and 5126 at the SUPRA level of government. In addition, they are shown as a memorandum item separately from the main figures since they represent a tax imposed by the EU and collected by national administrations.[6]

Table 1.5 shows the level of taxes collected on behalf of supranational governments in EU countries that are also OECD members, divided into those countries in the Euro area and other EU member countries.

Table 1.5. Levies collected on behalf of the European Union, as % of GDP

Per cent

	2000	2005	2010	2014	2015	2016	2017	2018	2019	2020p
Euro area										
Austria, total supranational	0.2	0.1	0.1	0.1	0.2	0.2	0.2	0.2	0.2	0.2
of which: Customs duties	0.2	0.1	0.1	0.1	0.1	0.1	0.1	0.1	0.1	0.1
of which: SRF contributions	..	..	..	..	0.1	0.1	0.1	0.1	0.0	0.1
Belgium, total supranational	0.4	0.4	0.4	0.3	0.4	0.4	0.4	0.4	0.4	0.4
of which: Customs duties	0.4	0.4	0.3	0.3	0.3	0.4	0.4	0.4	0.4	0.3
of which: SRF contributions	..	..	..	0.0	0.1	0.1	0.1	0.1	0.1	0.1
Estonia, total supranational	..	0.2	0.2	0.2	0.2	0.2	0.2	0.2	0.2	0.2
of which: Customs duties	..	0.2	0.2	0.2	0.2	0.2	0.2	0.2	0.2	0.2
of which: SRF contributions	..	..	..	..	..	0.0	0.0	0.0	0.0	0.0
Finland, total supranational	0.1	0.1	0.1	0.1	0.1	0.1	0.1	0.1	0.2	0.2
of which: Customs duties	0.1	0.1	0.1	0.1	0.1	0.1	0.1	0.1	0.1	0.1
of which: SRF contributions	..	..	..	..	0.0	0.1	0.1	0.0	0.1	0.1
France, total supranational	0.1	0.1	0.1	0.1	0.1	0.2	0.2	0.2	0.2	0.2
of which: Customs duties	0.1	0.1	0.1	0.1	0.1	0.1	0.1	0.1	0.1	0.1
of which: SRF contributions	..	..	..	..	0.0	0.1	0.1	0.1	0.1	0.1
Germany, total supranational	0.2	0.2	0.2	0.2	0.2	0.2	0.2	0.2	0.2	0.2
of which: Customs duties	0.2	0.2	0.2	0.2	0.2	0.2	0.2	0.1	0.1	0.1
of which: SRF contributions	..	..	..	..	0.1	0.1	0.1	0.1	0.1	0.1
Greece, total supranational	0.2	0.1	0.1	0.1	0.2	0.2	0.2	0.2	0.2	0.2
of which: Customs duties	0.1	0.1	0.1	0.1	0.1	0.1	0.2	0.1	0.2	0.2
of which: SRF contributions	..	..	..	..	0.1	0.1	0.1	0.1	0.0	0.1
Ireland, total supranational	0.2	0.1	0.1	0.1	0.1	0.2	0.1	0.1	0.1	0.1
of which: Customs duties	0.2	0.1	0.1	0.1	0.1	0.1	0.1	0.1	0.1	0.1
of which: SRF contributions[1]	..	..	..	..	..	0.1	0.0	0.0	0.0	0.0
Italy, total supranational	0.1	0.1	0.1	0.1	0.3	0.2	0.3	0.2	0.2	0.2
of which: Customs duties	0.1	0.1	0.1	0.1	0.1	0.1	0.1	0.1	0.1	0.1
of which: SRF contributions[2]	..	..	..	..	0.1	0.0	0.1	0.1	0.0	0.1
Lithuania, total supranational	..	0.2	0.2	0.2	0.3	0.3	0.3	0.3	0.3	0.3
of which: Customs duties	..	0.2	0.2	0.2	0.3	0.2	0.2	0.3	0.3	0.3
of which: SRF contributions	..	..	..	..	0.0	0.0	0.0	0.0	0.0	0.0
Latvia, total supranational	..	0.2	0.1	0.2	0.2	0.2	0.2	0.2	0.2	0.1
of which: Customs duties	..	0.2	0.1	0.2	0.2	0.2	0.2	0.2	0.1	0.1
of which: SRF contributions	..	..	..	..	0.0	0.0	0.0	0.0	0.0	0.0
Luxembourg, total supranational	0.1	0.1	0.0	0.0	0.1	0.2	0.2	0.3	0.3	0.3
of which: Customs duties	0.1	0.1	0.0	0.0	0.0	0.0	0.0	0.0	0.0	0.0
of which: SRF contributions	..	..	..	..	0.1	0.1	0.2	0.2	0.2	0.3
Netherlands, total supranational	0.4	0.3	0.3	0.4	0.4	0.4	0.4	0.4	0.4	0.4
of which: Customs duties	0.3	0.2	0.3	0.3	0.3	0.3	0.3	0.3	0.3	0.3
of which: SRF contributions	..	..	..	..	0.1	0.1	0.1	0.1	0.1	0.1
Portugal, total supranational	0.2	0.1	0.1	0.1	0.1	0.2	0.2	0.2	0.2	0.2
of which: Customs duties	0.1	0.1	0.1	0.1	0.1	0.1	0.1	0.1	0.1	0.1
of which: SRF contributions	..	..	..	..	..	0.1	0.1	0.1	0.1	0.1
Slovak Republic, total supranational	..	0.1	0.2	0.2	0.1	0.2	0.2	0.2	0.2	0.1
of which: Customs duties	..	0.1	0.2	0.2	0.1	0.2	0.2	0.2	0.1	0.1
of which: SRF contributions	..	..	..	..	..	0.0	0.0	0.0	0.0	0.0
Slovenia, total supranational	..	0.1	0.2	0.1	0.2	0.2	0.1	0.1	0.1	0.2
of which: Customs duties	..	0.1	0.2	0.1	0.1	0.1	0.1	0.1	0.1	0.1
of which: SRF contributions	..	..	..	..	0.0	0.0	0.0	0.0	0.0	0.0
Spain, total supranational	0.2	0.2	0.1	0.2	0.2	0.2	0.2	0.2	0.2	0.2

	2000	2005	2010	2014	2015	2016	2017	2018	2019	2020p
of which: Customs duties	0.1	0.2	0.1	0.2	0.2	0.2	0.2	0.2	0.2	0.1
of which: SRF contributions	..	..	..	..	0.1	0.1	0.1	0.1	0.1	0.1
Non-euro area										
Czech Republic, total supranational	..	0.2	0.2	0.2	0.2	0.2	0.2	0.2	0.2	0.1
of which: Customs duties	..	0.2	0.2	0.2	0.2	0.2	0.2	0.2	0.2	0.1
Denmark, total supranational	0.2	0.2	0.2	0.2	0.2	0.1	0.1	0.1	0.1	0.1
of which: Customs duties	0.2	0.2	0.2	0.2	0.2	0.1	0.1	0.1	0.1	0.1
Hungary, total supranational	..	0.1	0.1	0.1	0.1	0.1	0.1	0.1	0.1	0.1
of which: Customs duties	..	0.1	0.1	0.1	0.1	0.1	0.1	0.1	0.1	0.1
Poland, total supranational	..	0.1	0.1	0.1	0.2	0.2	0.2	0.2	0.2	0.2
of which: Customs duties	..	0.1	0.1	0.1	0.2	0.2	0.2	0.2	0.2	0.2
Sweden, total supranational	0.2	0.2	0.2	0.1	0.1	0.1	0.1	0.1	0.1	0.1
of which: Customs duties	0.1	0.1	0.2	0.1	0.1	0.1	0.1	0.1	0.1	0.1
United Kingdom, total supranational[3]	0.2	0.2	0.2	0.2	0.2	0.2	0.2	0.2	0.2	0.2
of which: Customs duties	0.2	0.1	0.2	0.2	0.2	0.2	0.2	0.2	0.2	0.1

Note: SRF figures may differ slightly from those published on the SRB website. These differences are primarily due to timing. Details on these revenues for each country can be found in chapters 4 and 5.

1. In 2016 the figure includes the 2016 payment of 99.12 and also a payment of 75.89 which was due in quarter 4 of 2015 but was paid in quarter 1 of 2016. The figures in this table were reported by the Central Statistics Office and are gross amounts and therefore due to adjustments will differ from the figures reported on the SRB website, which are net figures.

2. The "Bank contribution to the unique European Resolution Fund" amount includes not only the European but the National resolution fund, as required by Eurostat classification.

3. Supranational taxes reported by the United Kingdom continue to be reported for 2020 in Revenue Statistics as in previous years. From 2021, at the end of the Brexit transition period, this will come to an end and taxes subsequently introduced by the United Kingdom will be reflected in the appropriate tax category at the national or subnational levels of government, as appropriate.

Source: *Revenue Statistics 2021*, supplemented by discussions with delegates.

StatLink https://stat.link/3q54hw

In 2019, the combined total of payments collected for the EU was highest in Belgium and the Netherlands, at over 0.4% of GDP. Levels above 0.2% of GDP were also seen in Estonia, Greece, Lithuania, Luxembourg, Spain and Germany. All other EU countries that are also members of the OECD collected revenues on behalf of the EU equivalent to between 0.1 and 0.2% of GDP. In all countries except Finland, France and Luxembourg, customs duties were the majority source of these revenues.

Non-wastable tax credits

There are two kinds of tax credits that apply to income taxes (both personal and corporate):

- Non-payable or wastable tax credits are those that can only ever be used to reduce or eliminate a tax liability. They cannot be paid out to either taxpayers or non-tax payers as a benefit. They are, therefore, the same as a tax allowance or relief.
- In contrast, payable or non-wastable tax credits can be partitioned into two parts. One part is used to reduce or eliminate a tax liability in the same way as a wastable tax credit. The other part can be paid directly to recipients as a benefit payment, when the benefit exceeds the tax liability.

The OECD methodology for classifying non-wastable tax credits is set out in paragraphs 25 and 26 of the *Interpretative Guide*. This states that only the part of a non-wastable tax credit that is used to reduce or eliminate a taxpayer's tax liability should be subtracted in the reporting of tax revenues. This is referred to as the 'tax expenditure component' of the credit. In contrast, the part of the tax credit that exceeds the taxpayer's tax liability and is paid to that taxpayer is treated as an expenditure item and not subtracted in the reporting of tax revenues. This part is referred to as the 'transfer component'.

Table 1.6. Effect of alternative treatments of non-wastable tax credits, 2019

	Non-wastable tax credits in billlions of national currency			Total tax revenue in billions of national currency			Total tax revenue as a percentage of GDP		
	Total value	Transfer component	Tax expenditure component	Net basis	Split basis (per current guidance)	Gross basis	Net basis	Split basis (per current guidance)	Gross basis
Australia	10.0	6.6	3.5	543.0	549.5	553.0	27.3	27.7	27.8
Austria[1]	0.3	0.1	0.2	169.1	169.2	169.4	42.5	42.6	42.6
Belgium[2]	1.1	0.2	0.9	203.2	203.4	204.3	42.7	42.7	42.9
Canada[3]	18.2	14.2	4.0	767.0	781.2	785.2	33.2	33.8	34.0
Chile[4]	278.8	200.6	78.2	41 025.5	41 226.1	41 304.3	20.9	21.0	21.0
Czech Republic	39.9	7.8	32.1	2 006.1	2 013.9	2 046.0	34.6	34.8	35.3
Denmark[2]	3.1	0.2	2.9	1 080.1	1 080.3	1 083.2	46.6	46.6	46.7
France[2]	35.4	18.5	16.9	1 075.7	1 094.1	1 111.0	44.1	44.9	45.6
Germany	45.2	15.9	29.3	1 325.4	1 341.3	1 370.6	38.2	38.6	39.5
Iceland	3.6	3.0	0.6	1 059.0	1 061.9	1 062.6	34.7	34.8	34.9
Ireland	0.4	0.0	0.4	..	78.1	78.5	..	21.9	22.0
Israel	1.3	0.0	1.3	428.5	428.5	429.9	30.2	30.2	30.3
Italy	10.4	1.4	8.9	758.2	759.6	768.6	42.3	42.4	42.9
Luxembourg[2, 5]	0.2	..	..	..	..	24.7	..	..	38.9
Mexico	50.6	1.3	49.4	3 994.4	3 995.7	4 045.0	16.3	16.3	16.5
New Zealand	2.8	1.4	1.4	98.4	99.8	101.2	31.0	31.5	31.9
Norway	4.2	3.4	0.8	1 420.7	1 424.1	1 424.9	39.8	39.9	39.9
Slovak Republic[5]	0.3	..	..	..	..	32.5	..	..	34.6
Spain	2.6	1.4	1.1	430.1	431.6	432.7	34.6	34.7	34.8
United Kingdom[6]	25.3	21.4	3.9	704.2	725.6	729.5	31.8	32.7	32.9
United States	256.0	153.0	103.0	5 183.5	5 336.5	5 439.5	24.3	25.0	25.5

Note: In Revenue Statistics, the tax revenue data are reported on a split basis, unless indicated otherwise.

1. The children's tax credit is not regarded as a tax credit in Revenue Statistics and is treated entirely as an expenditure provision.
2. The total tax revenue has been reduced by the amount of any capital transfer that represents uncollected taxes.
3. Some non-wastable tax credits cannot be split into the transfer and tax expenditure components. Their total values have been added to the transfer component.
4. In *Revenue Statistics*, the tax revenue data for Chile are reported on a net basis.
5. In *Revenue Statistics*, the tax revenue data for Luxembourg and Slovak Republic are reported on a gross basis.
6. Please note that the non-wastable tax credit data for the United Kingdom is on a cash basis and includes estimates in some years. Please see the footnotes in the table for the United Kingdom in chapter 5 for more information.

StatLink https://stat.link/7okx2n

Table 1.6 provides information on the non-wastable tax credits in 2019 for those countries reporting them in the *Revenue Statistics 2021* (though it may be that some countries with non-wastable tax credits do not appear in the table). It shows the amounts of the non-wastable tax credits and their two components together with the results of using the figures to calculate tax revenue values and the associated tax-to-GDP ratios. Table 1.6 also shows two alternative treatments:

- The 'net basis' which treats non-wastable tax credits entirely as tax provisions, so that the full value of the tax credit reduces reported tax revenues, as shown in columns 4 and 7.
- The 'gross basis' is the exact opposite, treating non-wastable tax credits entirely as expenditure provisions, with neither the transfer component nor the tax expenditure component being deducted from tax revenue, as shown in columns 6 and 9. This is the approach followed by the GFSM and the SNA.

Table 1.6 shows that, with some exceptions, the choice of method for reporting non-wastable tax credits has only a small impact on the ratio of total tax revenue to GDP. For the countries with available data, the differences between the ratios on a net basis and on a gross basis are one percentage point or more in only France, Germany, the United Kingdom and the United States, and between half a percentage point and one percentage point in Australia, Canada, Czech Republic, Italy, New Zealand.

Financing of social security-type benefits in OECD countries

A memorandum item[7] in *Revenue Statistics 2021* describes the financing of social security-type benefits in OECD countries. Unlike social assistance benefits, which are funded from general government revenues, social security-type benefits are funded via contributions to social security or to private insurance schemes, or by other earmarked sources of funding. These sources of financing include:

- Earmarked financing from tax revenues:
  1. Social security contributions (SSCs, category 2000 in the OECD classification)
  2. Other taxes earmarked for social security-type benefits
- Earmarked financing from non-tax revenues:
  3. Voluntary contributions to the government (VCG)
  4. Compulsory contributions to the private sector (CCPS)

Figure 1.10 shows the relative contribution of each of these sources to financing for social security-type benefits in OECD countries, based on data provided by countries for inclusion in the memorandum item in *Revenue Statistics 2021*.

Figure 1.10. Composition of earmarked financing for social security-type benefits, 2019

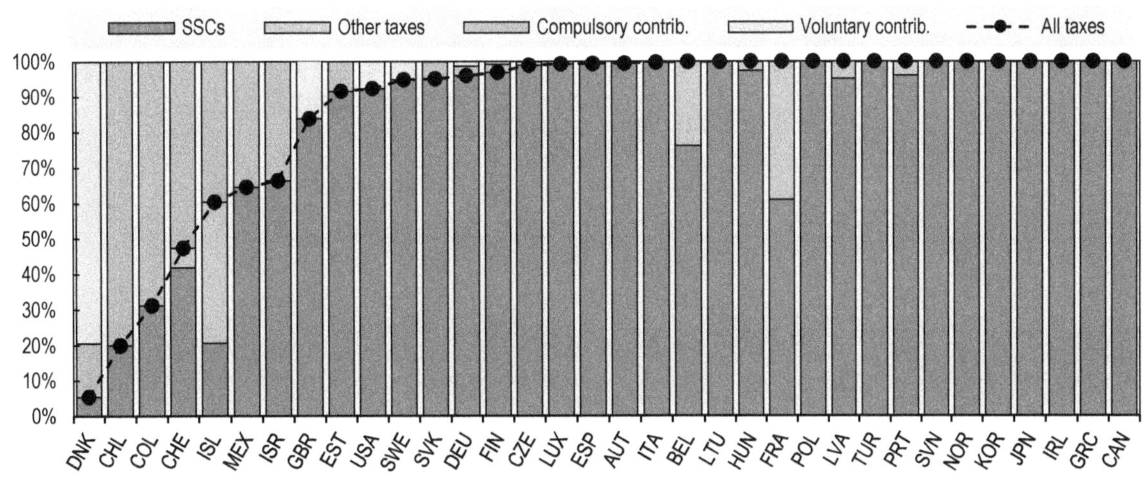

Note: Two countries (Australia and New Zealand) provide social benefits via social assistance rather than via social security, so are not included in the table. In addition, Costa Rica and the Netherlands are also not included in the figure as complete data on contributions were not available in Revenue Statistics. The figures for Denmark should be interpreted with care as the level of social security-type benefits is very small compared to the level of social assistance benefits. Further, there may be borderline issues in some countries when distinguishing between quasi-compulsory and voluntary schemes.
Source: Secretariat calculations based on chapter 4.

StatLink https://stat.link/odvl36

Taxes represent the largest source of earmarked financing for social security-type benefits, predominantly via social security contributions. Together, SSCs and other earmarked taxes account for over 90% of the financing of social security-type benefits in 26 OECD countries and 100% in 11 countries. In the remaining nine OECD countries that provide this data, compulsory contributions to the private sector play a larger role, at 80.0% in Chile, 68.8% in Colombia and 52.6% in Switzerland, with smaller shares in Iceland, Mexico and Israel. Few countries received significant shares of voluntary contributions: only in the United Kingdom and Denmark do these exceed 10% of financing.

Figure 1.11 shows tax-to-GDP ratios (as in Table 1.1 and Figure 1.4) both *exclusive* of earmarked funding for social security-type benefits (i.e. tax-to-GDP ratios *less* SSCs and other earmarked taxes) and *inclusive* of all non-tax earmarked financing for social security-type benefits (i.e. tax-to-GDP ratios - including SSCs and other earmarked taxes - *plus* compulsory contributions to the private sector and voluntary contributions to government).

Countries with the largest share of social security-type schemes financed by non-tax earmarked contributions are Switzerland (8.2% of GDP), Chile and Iceland (6.1% in both cases), which materially affects their rankings:

- Switzerland has a relatively low tax-to-GDP ratio among OECD countries, at 27.4%, but its combined ratio is above halfway in the OECD distribution;
- Iceland has a tax-to-GDP ratio of 34.8%, in the top-third of OECD countries, and a combined ratio of 41.0%, which is the eighth-highest in the OECD.
- Chile has the third-lowest tax-to-GDP ratio and the sixth-lowest combined ratio.

Figure 1.11. Tax-to-GDP ratios and earmarked social security financing (% of GDP, 2019)

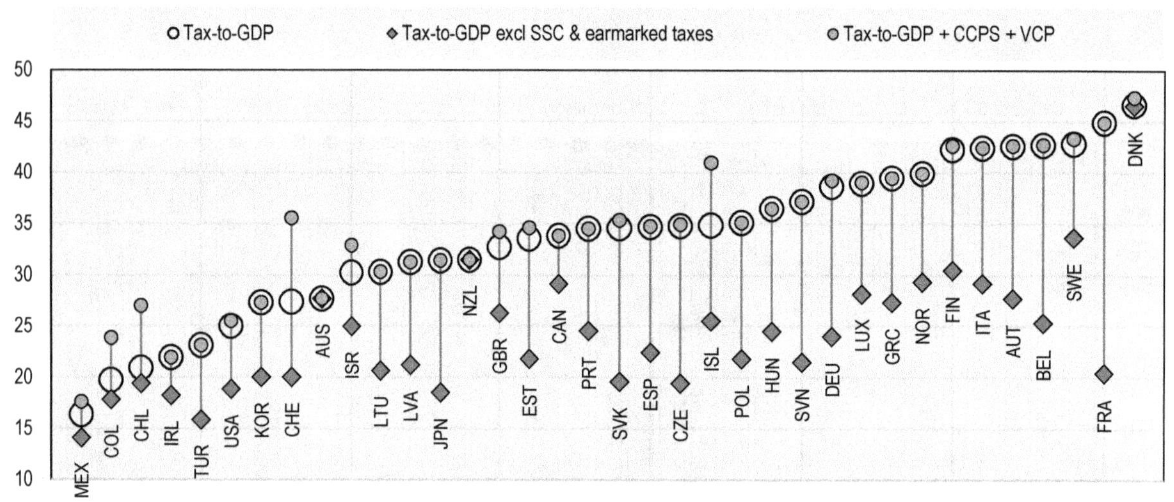

Note: Costa Rica and the Netherlands are not included in the figure as complete data on social security financing in both countries were not available.
Source: Secretariat calculations based on data in chapter 4.

StatLink https://stat.link/zlgu06

Excluding earmarked financing for social security benefits from the tax-to-GDP ratio does not affect Australia, Denmark and New Zealand, where benefits are funded out of general taxation. Figure 1.11 highlights that the largest share of earmarked funding for social security-type benefits is seen in France, at 24.5% of GDP, as indicated by the difference between the highest and lowest points on the figure.

Belgium, Iceland, the Slovak Republic and Switzerland have the next highest shares, at between 15% and 18% of GDP.

Notes

[1] Provisional 2020 figures are not available for Australia and provisional figures on social security contributions in Japan are also not available as at the time *Revenue Statistics 2021* was published.

[2] In 2016, Iceland received revenues from one-off stability contributions from entities that previously operated as commercial or savings banks and were concluding operations. The revenue from these contributions led to unusually high tax revenues for a single year and consequently, Iceland's tax-to-GDP ratio rose from 35.1% in 2015 to 50.3% in 2016, before dropping to 37.1% in 2017. This led to an artificial high in the OECD average tax-to-GDP ratio in 2016 of 33.6%. Without these one-off revenues in Iceland, the OECD average tax-to-GDP ratio would have been 33.2%, an increase of 0.3 p.p. relative to 2015.

[3] The terms "value added tax" and "VAT" are used to refer to any national tax that embodies the basic features of a value added tax by whatever name or acronym it is known e.g. "Goods and Services Tax" ("GST").

[4] For 1975, please see Table 1.4 of *Revenue Statistics 2021*.

[5] The Single Resolution Fund (SRF) has been in place since 2015 and countries in the Eurozone are required to make SRF contributions under the Single Resolution Mechanism (Regulation (EU) No 806/2014). Contributions are paid on an ex-ante basis and contributions are transferred from the national authorities to the SRF. So far, contributions have been collected for the years 2015 to 2020.

[6] In addition, EU civil servants pay income taxes and social security contributions directly to the EU. These revenues are not included in the data or total tax revenues in this publication as they are not paid to or collected by a national government. However, for two of the countries with the highest number of EU civil servants (Belgium and Italy), a memorandum account at the end of the respective country table in Chapter 5 provides information on the scale of these payments.

[7] The financing of social security-type benefits is shown in Table 4.77 on a comparable basis (percentage of GDP) and in Table 5.39 on a national currency basis.

2 The initial impact of COVID-19 on OECD tax revenues

Chapter 2 examines the initial impacts of COVID-19 on tax revenues in OECD countries. It uses preliminary data on revenues by tax type to further examine the impact of the pandemic on personal and corporate income taxes, social security contributions, property taxes, VAT and excises, considering changes in nominal terms and as a share of GDP.

Introduction

The COVID-19 crisis has significantly affected OECD countries, leading to a contraction in the economy and a worsening of inequality, with particularly severe effects for lower income households and other vulnerable groups. COVID-19 has also reduced tax revenues in two-thirds of OECD countries both via support measures provided through the tax system and through the flow-on impact of the economic crisis on revenues. When coupled with falls in non-tax revenues, the cost of support measures delivered outside the tax system, and increases in health and social expenditure, government fiscal positions have significantly deteriorated. OECD governments borrowed USD 18 trillion from the markets in 2020, equal to almost 29% of GDP. Compared to 2019, this was 60% more in absolute terms and 12 percentage points higher as a share of GDP (OECD, 2021[1])

However, unlike the global financial crisis (GFC) and despite the widespread falls in nominal tax revenues, the pandemic has not resulted in sharp falls in OECD tax-to-GDP ratios. This chapter uses preliminary data for 2020 to explore the initial impact of the crisis on tax revenues, the relationship between changes in tax levels and in GDP, the types of taxes most affected by the crisis, and similarities and differences with revenue changes in the first year of the GFC.

Overview: changes to total tax revenues, GDP and the tax-to-GDP ratio

Impact of COVID-19: changes in 2020 relative to 2019

As highlighted in chapter 1, the average OECD tax-to-GDP ratio increased by 0.1 p.p. in 2020 relative to 2019. Increases in the tax-to-GDP ratio were observed in 20 out of 38 OECD countries (Figure 1.2). However, the increases in tax-to-GDP ratios occurred despite falls in nominal tax revenues in 31 OECD countries between 2019 and 2020, with an average fall (across all countries for which data are available) of 2.1%. Although nominal tax revenues fell in most OECD countries, nominal tax revenues fell by less than nominal GDP in 14 of these countries (Figure 1.3), leading to an increase in their tax to GDP ratios. Therefore, while taxes represented a higher share of total GDP in 2020 than in 2019, this is due to GDP (the denominator) in most countries shrinking by more than tax revenues (the numerator) during the COVID-19 crisis.

Figure 2.1 shows the relative falls in nominal taxes and nominal GDP between 2019 and 2020 for all OECD countries. Only five OECD countries had increases in both tax revenues and GDP (Denmark, Korea, Lithuania, Poland and Turkey), with all but Denmark having larger increases in nominal tax revenues than GDP and thus an increase in their tax-to-GDP ratios. Including these five countries, eleven countries experienced increases in nominal GDP and six had increases in nominal tax revenues. The remaining 25 OECD countries experienced falls in both GDP and tax revenues, with the consequent impact on their tax-to-GDP ratio depending on which of the two components fell most.

Figure 2.1. Changes in nominal tax and nominal GDP, 2019-2020

Year-on-year % change

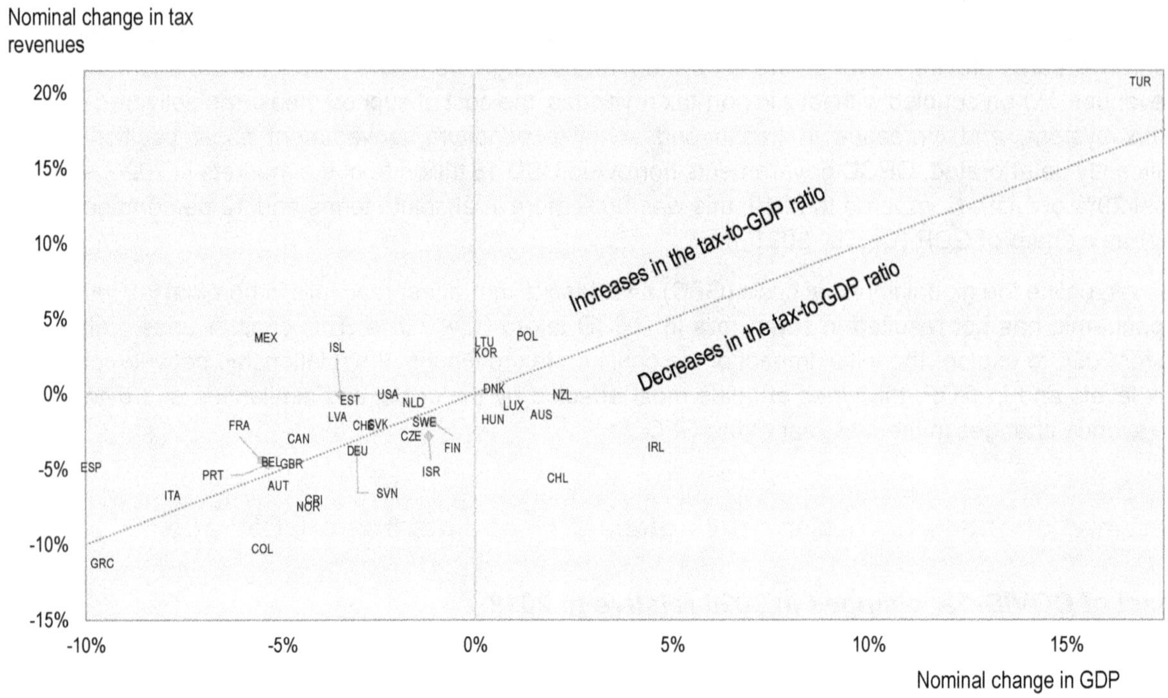

Note: Data for 2020 are preliminary and should be interpreted with caution; please see Box 2.1 for more details. Data for Australia and New Zealand show the change between the fiscal years 2018 and 2019 (as both countries report tax revenues on a fiscal year basis that includes Q2 of 2020 in the 2019 fiscal year); data for Japan are not included as data on SSC revenues is not available. See Box 2.2 for more information. The diagonal line across the graph represents the point at which the change in tax revenues and in GDP were of the same magnitude and therefore the point at which the tax-to-GDP ratio remained unchanged. Countries above the diagonal line had increases in their tax to GDP ratios; countries below it, had falls.
Source: *Revenue Statistics 2021* and authors' calculations.

StatLink https://stat.link/p3b1fm

How does the impact of COVID-19 on tax revenues compare to the GFC?

The COVID-19 crisis led to widespread falls in GDP in OECD countries in 2020 (Figure 2.1). Before 2020, the most recent global economic crisis faced by OECD countries was the GFC. In 2008, overall economic growth remained positive in most OECD countries, although growth rates fell sharply in the fourth quarter, leading to negative annual growth rates, in real terms in approximately one-third of OECD countries. In 2009, the impacts of the GFC spread, with all OECD countries except Australia, Colombia, Israel, Korea, New Zealand and Poland recording strong negative real GDP growth between 2008 and 2009. The (weighted) OECD average GDP growth rate in 2009 was -3.4%, compared to 0.3% in 2008 and 3.0% in 2010 (OECD, 2021[2]).

Box 2.1. Cautions in interpreting findings based on preliminary data for 2020

The indicators used in this chapter are based on preliminary data provided for the year 2020 as part of the data collection round for this year's edition of *Revenue Statistics*. Normally, the publication does not place emphasis on these preliminary data as they are subject to revisions in future years that can affect the magnitude, and less commonly, the direction, of change between the last two years of data. However, due to the interest in the tax revenue impacts of the COVID-19 pandemic, this special feature uses the indicators to provide an initial snapshot of what has happened to tax revenues during the crisis. Therefore, while the data should be treated with caution and the scale of the conclusions may be revised in future editions, they nonetheless present an important insight into the impact of COVID-19 on tax revenues across OECD countries.

Many important macroeconomic indicators, including Gross Domestic Product (GDP), are subject to revisions. Initial estimates are usually released around one to two months after the reference period, aiming to strike a balance between the accuracy and timeliness of the results, in order to properly support economic analysis and decision-making. In most countries, more complete and detailed data become available over time and National Statistical Offices (NSOs) progressively revise their estimates to further improve their accuracy. To obtain more insight in the role of revisions, the OECD is frequently conducting studies into the size and direction of revisions across OECD countries, the latest in 2018.

As a consequence of measures put in place by governments to reduce the spread of the Coronavirus (COVID-19), many NSOs have been facing unprecedented collection, compilation and methodological challenges. Challenges include those of a conceptual nature, for example, the appropriate treatment of education and other government services that were temporarily closed, severely diminished or switched to a virtual format. In addition, practical challenges, such as an inability to collect certain data sources or a significant decline in response rates of business and household surveys, inevitably affected data quality. Consequently, the initial estimates released during the pandemic may be subject to larger and more frequent revisions than normal.

That said, the compilation of GDP estimates involves a large number of data sources, many of which are non-prescriptive. As a result, NSOs have often been able to find alternative or proxy data sources to assist in overcoming specific data gaps. In many cases, these temporary, but often more timely, data sources could be confronted and balanced with the existing methodology to maintain the quality of many national account outputs including GDP. Furthermore, the international statistical community developed additional guidance on how to cope with specific challenges as put forward by the pandemic, for example on how to record specific government support schemes and how to deal with seasonal adjustment during the pandemic. Therefore, while revisions may be slightly larger than normal, these additional efforts of the statistical community helped to minimise the severity of the revisions.

The pandemic may also have affected the accuracy of Revenue Statistics. Whereas tax authorities themselves have continued to provide the relevant information as normal, several countries provided extensions to their reporting entities during the pandemic which may have affected the initial estimates. In those cases, the data may be liable to larger than normal revisions. The preliminary data for 2020 may also be subject to larger than normal revisions due to the support measures introduced by governments to support households and businesses in the crisis, including the widespread use of tax deferrals, extension of filing deadlines and increased flexibility with the treatment of tax losses. Finally, if tax revenues are recorded when the tax liability is determined, rather than when the economic activity takes place (i.e. a pure accrual approach), there may be a lag or mismatch between the timing of the change in economic activity and the recording of tax receipts. This is particularly relevant when an economic shock takes place and when loss carry-back provisions are introduced or extended.

Source: OECD Statistics and Data Directorate, country inputs and authors' contributions.

Relative to the GFC, the COVID-19 pandemic led to a more severe global recession in the short term, but is expected to give rise to lower losses in the medium-term. In 2020, global GDP declined by about 3.5% while OECD GDP declined by about 4.8% in real terms,[1] significantly larger than the global contraction of 0.5% and the OECD contraction of 3.4% in 2009 (OECD, 2021[2]). The contraction was particularly pronounced in the second quarter of 2020, where OECD economies contracted by 11.6% (year-on-year growth rate based on seasonally adjusted volume data), a much sharper decline than the 4.7% observed in the first quarter of 2009 (the quarter most affected by the GFC). Despite the strong short-term economic shock in 2020, medium-term losses for global output are expected to be smaller than the GFC (IMF, 2021[3]). Global output in 2024 is anticipated to be approximately 3% lower than the projection made before COVID-19, while the downward adjustment was almost 10% after the GFC. This is mainly because the finance and banking sectors were at the centre of the GFC and had strong interconnections with the rest of the economy (IMF, 2021[3]). The smaller persistent shock of the COVID-19 pandemic is reflected in the V-shaped recoveries of global manufacturing in both advanced and developing countries in the second half of 2020, which were not seen during the GFC (IMF, 2021[3]). Nevertheless, there is an element of uncertainty in the current crisis due to the evolving nature of the pandemic, which could affect the global economic recovery.

Another difference between the GFC and the COVID-19 pandemic is the countries and sectors affected. The GFC spread across countries via the interconnected finance and banking sectors. Advanced countries were at the epicentre of the crisis and bore the brunt of its impact, while most developing countries were less affected and recovered more quickly (Kose, Sugawara and Terrones, 2020[4]). During COVID-19, emerging market and developing economies are expected to suffer more, partly because they are less financially equipped to provide sufficient support to mitigate the negative impacts: countries with larger pandemic-related fiscal responses tended to experience smaller losses (IMF, 2021[3]). While the finance and banking sectors were most affected during the GFC, the impact of COVID-19 pandemic fell predominantly upon contact-intensive service sectors such as tourism and hospitality. As a result, countries that are more reliant on these service sectors, such as small island states, have experienced greater losses.

The COVID-19 pandemic is both a health and an economic crisis that has affected the vast majority of the population, especially the poor and vulnerable, smaller businesses and the self-employed. Fiscal support from national governments in response to the pandemic has been much stronger than during prior crises. Global fiscal support amounted to USD 13.8 trillion in 2020, of which USD 7.8 trillion represented additional spending or foregone revenues and USD 6.0 trillion represented equity injections, loans, asset purchases or debt assumptions, guarantees and quasi-fiscal operations (IMF, 2021[5]). By contrast, the aggregate amount of fiscal stimulus packages from G20 economies[2] was around USD 820 billion in 2009 (IMF, 2009[6]). In addition, due to the different territorial impact of the pandemic, sub-national governments have played a more important role in developing differentiated responses and providing support for local needs. For example, measures regarding masks, business closures, lockdowns and vaccination programmes have been designed and implemented in close coordination with sub-national governments in many countries (OECD, 2021[7]).

The impact of the two crises on revenues has also differed, although between them, the two crises account for most of the falls in nominal tax revenues seen in OECD countries since 1995 (Figure 2.2). On average, the OECD tax-to-GDP ratio fell by 0.7 p.p. in 2009, driven by larger falls in tax revenues (an average of 5.3%) than in GDP (Table 2.1). Tax-to-GDP ratios fell in 29 OECD countries: in 20 of these countries, because tax revenues fell further than GDP; in seven, because tax revenues fell while GDP rose; and in the remaining two countries, because tax revenues increased more slowly than GDP. By contrast, in 2020, tax-to-GDP ratios fell in 18 countries: in 11 of these, because taxes decreased more quickly than GDP; in six, because taxes decreased while GDP rose; and in one (Denmark) because tax revenues rose marginally more slowly than GDP (Table 1.3).

Figure 2.2. Changes in nominal tax and nominal GDP, all years

Year-on-year % change

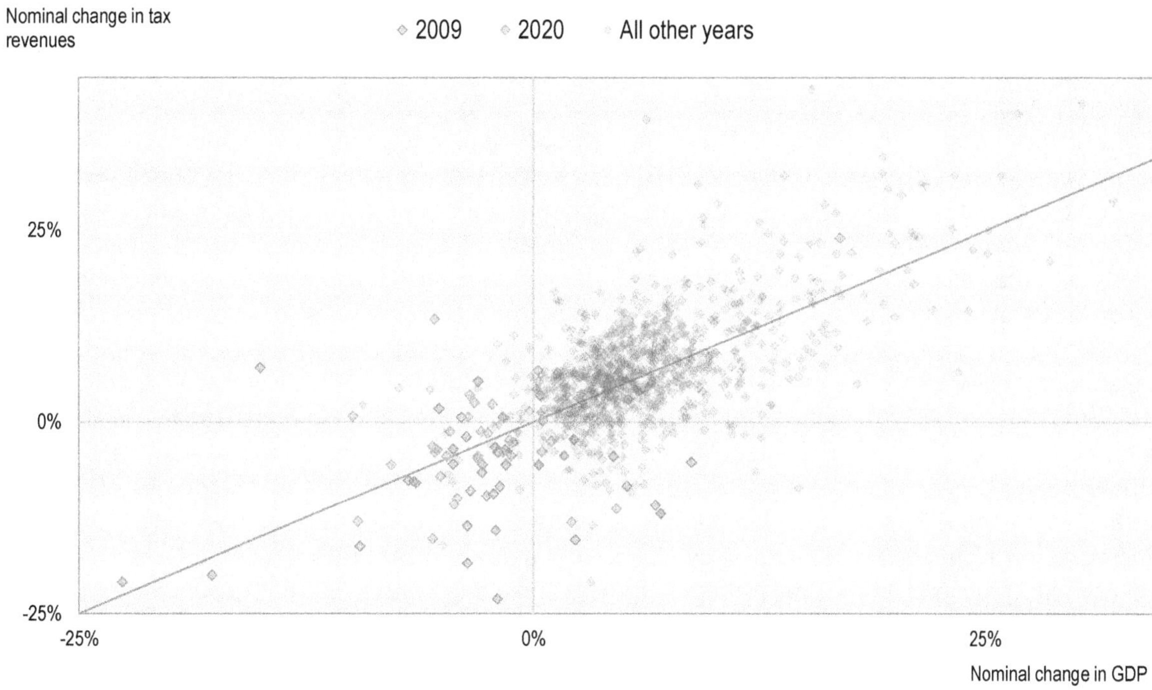

Note: Data for 2020 are preliminary and should be interpreted with caution; please see Box 2.1 for more details. Outliers have been excluded to improve the readability of the figure.
Source: *Revenue Statistics 2021* and authors' calculations.

StatLink https://stat.link/6cfqyt

Table 2.1. Comparison of changes in nominal tax and nominal GDP

Year-on-year % change

		Mean	Lower quartile	Median	Upper quartile
Tax	2009	-5.3	-7.2	-4.4	-2.4
	2020	-2.1	-4.6	-2.1	-0.4
GDP	2009	-2.7	-4.3	-2.4	-0.1
	2020	-2.1	-4.7	-2.7	0.3
Tax/GDP	2009	-0.7	-1.3	-0.5	0.1
	2020	0.0	-0.6	0.0	0.6

Note: Data for 2020 are preliminary and should be interpreted with caution; please see Box 2.1 for more details. The mean tax-to-GDP ratio in 2020 in this table differs from that shown in the other chapters in the report due to the use of the 2019 fiscal years for Australia and New Zealand in this chapter, for the reasons explained in Box 2.2.
Source: *Revenue Statistics 2021* and authors' calculations.

Impact of the COVID-19 crisis on different tax types

COVID-19 has affected tax revenues through a variety of avenues. The tax policy measures implemented to support households and businesses have often directly reduced revenues via deferrals or reductions in tax liabilities, enhanced tax credits and allowances and temporary or permanent reductions in tax rates. The sharp reduction in economic activity due to lockdowns and other restrictions have also reduced labour force participation, household consumption and business profits, further affecting tax revenues. However, government support measures may have indirectly bolstered affected revenues insofar as they were successful in reducing job losses and business closures.

Use of support measures and key economic changes influencing revenues

In relation to labour taxation, many countries introduced a range of tax reforms to support households, most of which included a revenue cost. The most common measures were administrative, including the full or partial deferral of personal income tax (PIT) and social security contribution (SSC) payments and waiver of interest and penalties (Figure 2.3). Tax filing deadlines were extended in many countries and a few countries accelerated refunds. These deferrals largely created differences in the timing of tax payments and may also lead to greater revisions in future years. A second common measure was the extension or introduction of new tax allowances and credits, either available to all taxpayers, or more commonly, targeted toward workers most heavily affected by the pandemic. Increased relief for teleworking expenses and provisions for the self-employed were also used in a few OECD countries. Thirdly, a few countries implemented PIT rate cuts or changes in tax thresholds. Typically these reduced tax liabilities for those on low incomes. For example, Australia increased the thresholds for lower income earners, a reform which had been planned prior to the crisis, while Austria reduced the lowest PIT rate and extended the application of the top PIT rate until 2025. On the other hand, several OECD countries implemented tax rate increases for high-income earners via the creation of a new top tax bracket and the Czech Republic moved from a flat to a progressive tax system. Finally, roughly one-quarter of OECD countries introduced timebound SSC waivers, often targeted to the most affected sectors or regions (OECD, 2021[8]; OECD, 2021[9]).

In addition to measures within the tax system to support households, job retention schemes including short-time work and wage subsides were used extensively across OECD countries during the crisis. Many countries introduced new schemes or extended the provisions available under existing schemes in response to the crisis and uptake was significant: in April 2020, around 20% of employees in the OECD were supported via these schemes (OECD, 2021[10]). These schemes protected employees' wages and jobs, with positive implications for PIT and SSCs in the longer run and, in many (but not all) countries, payments to employees under these schemes were also taxable, artificially pushing up PIT and SSC revenues for these countries in 2020 (OECD, 2021[9]).

The economic crisis also affected PIT and SSC revenues. The pandemic led to a sharp rise in unemployment, particularly during quarter two. Although this increase reversed throughout 2020, unemployment levels remained higher across the OECD at the end of 2020 than in 2019. Labour force participation decreased in all countries, while the average number of hours worked by employees reduced significantly. These job losses and reductions in hours were concentrated in the most heavily affected sectors and among low-income earners, whereas the change in employment, hours worked and income were considerably less pronounced for higher income workers (OECD, 2021[10]).

Tax measures to support business liquidity and cash flow were also widely used in 2020, affecting corporate income tax (CIT) revenues. Common measures include:

- Deferrals of tax payments, filing extensions and flexible tax payment plans, applied in over 70% of OECD countries (Figure 2.3). Several OECD countries suspended or reduced prepayments of CIT, often targeted toward SMEs, and refunds of advance payments and CIT credits were accelerated in many jurisdictions. A handful of OECD countries, including Korea, Italy and Portugal provided limited tax waivers for SMEs and the self-employed (OECD, 2021[8]).
- Cuts to statutory corporate income tax (CIT) rates were limited and OECD rates remained relatively stable. A few countries continued with planned decreases of the statutory tax rate (e.g. Colombia and France) while others introduced targeted rate reductions for small businesses (e.g. Chile and Hungary).

- Several countries introduced provisions to improve business liquidity, including tax measures to reduce rental costs in Italy, France, Korea and Spain. Several countries temporarily increased the threshold for low-value asset write-offs to promote liquidity and investment.
- Changes to loss-offset provisions were commonly used, with 38% of OECD countries introducing new or enhanced loss carry-back rules during 2020 (Figure 2.3). In a few countries, accelerated refunds were made available in relation to these loss carry-backs. Increased use of carry-forward provisions was seen in a few OECD countries, notably Portugal and the Slovak Republic.
- Tax measures to support investment were provided in many countries, including immediate expensing of larger investments (e.g. Australia, the Czech Republic and Norway), accelerated tax depreciation schemes and enhanced deductions for investment in new machinery and equipment. Incentives were often targeted by sector, region, or by environmental impact, or designed to promote research and development (R&D) or foreign direct investment (FDI).

Similarly, deferrals of value-added tax (VAT) liabilities were introduced in almost all OECD countries, often combined with the suspension or reduction of interest and penalties; targeted to particular sectors, SMEs or the self-employed. VAT refunds were accelerated in 15 OECD countries to further enhance cash flow and relief for bad debts was often expanded. Finally, a range of administrative simplifications and tax filing extensions were introduced in a number of countries to reduce compliance costs (OECD, 2021[8]).

Temporary changes to VAT rates were also widely seen across the OECD, either targeted toward the hospitality industry, restaurant services and cultural and sports sectors, or applying more generally. Many reductions were initially limited to a period of three to six months. Germany and Ireland reduced their standard VAT rates for six months: from 19% to 16% until the end of 2020 in Germany and from 23% to 21% until the end of February 2021 in Ireland. In both countries, this contributed to a fall in VAT revenues in nominal terms and a share of GDP. In Germany, reduced VAT rates were also lowered. Similarly, Norway also lowered their reduced VAT rates in response to the crisis. Over half of all OECD countries introduced temporary zero or reduced rates for medical equipment and personal protective equipment.[3] No OECD countries increased their standard VAT rate in 2020 (OECD, 2021[8]; OECD, 2020[11]).

In addition, all OECD countries have now adopted the rules and mechanisms recommended by the OECD's International VAT/GST Guidelines to ensure the effective taxation of cross-border supplies of services and intangibles. These rules and mechanisms are particularly relevant given the large increase in the volume of online sales by offshore vendors, made directly to consumers or through the intervention of digital platforms that was seen in 2020. The trend towards levying VAT on imports of low-value goods has continued and a growing number of countries are removing their VAT relief regimes for imports of low-value goods in light of the rapid growth in the volume of such imports (OECD, 2021[8]).

Figure 2.3. Main PIT, SSC, CIT and VAT/GST measures in response to COVID-19

Number of OECD countries reporting each type of measure

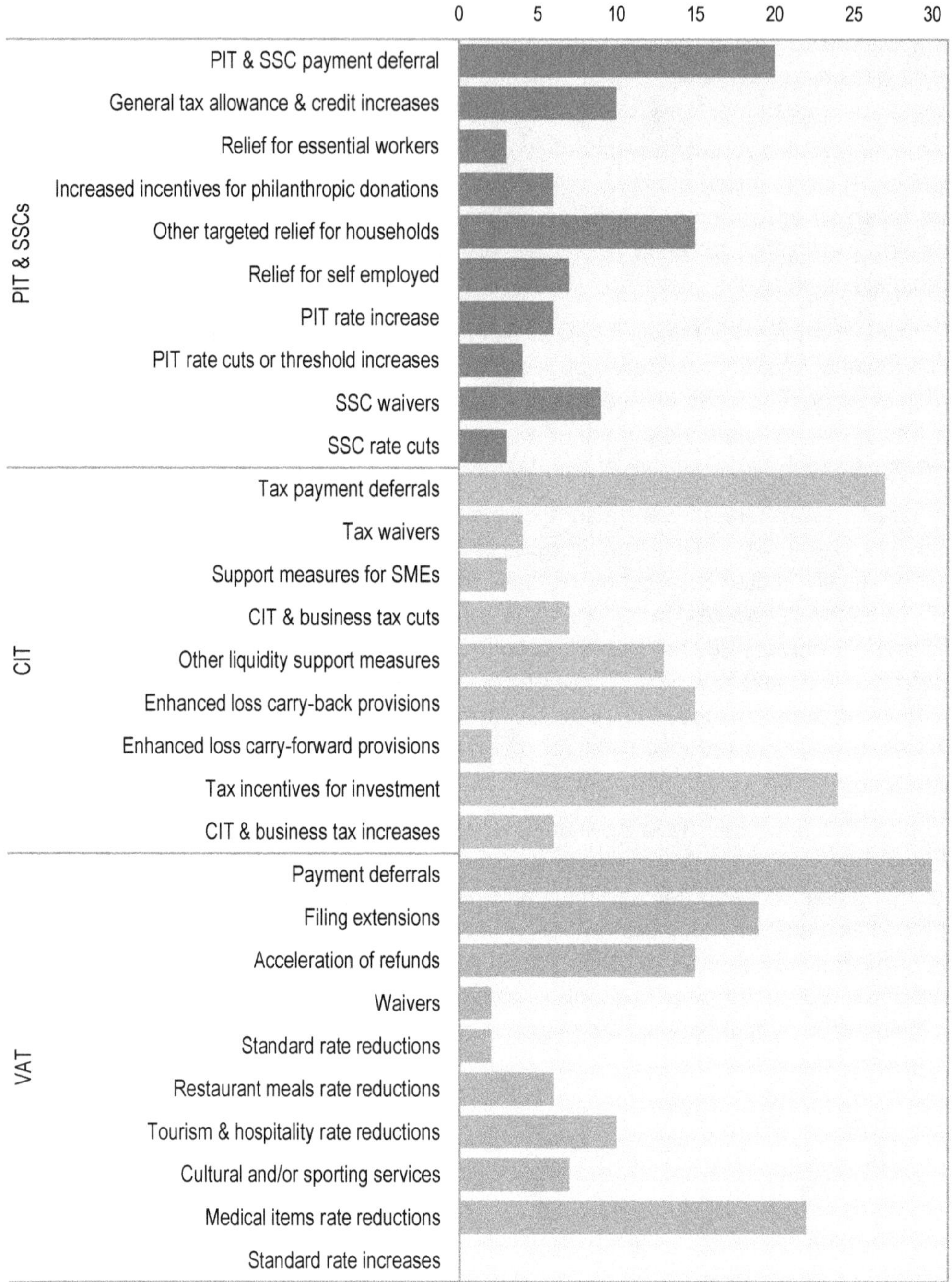

Note: Figure includes 37 OECD countries.
Source: OECD Tax Policy Reforms (OECD, 2021) and authors' calculations.

StatLink https://stat.link/oq07nd

COVID-19 also had a dramatic impact on the level and composition of consumption in the economy:

- Household consumption, particularly of luxury goods, was dramatically affected by the lockdowns and other restrictions designed to curb the spread of COVID-19, with sharp downturns in quarter two of 2020 in almost all OECD economies. Total final consumption fell by an average of 1.9% in nominal terms across the 33 countries for which these data are available, although this was lower than the unweighted average fall in nominal GDP across this group (2.3%), resulting in a slight increase in consumption as a share of GDP. However, the fall in the final consumption of households was considerably more steep (4.8%), offset by an increase in government consumption of 6.1%. These changes were more pronounced than those seen in the GFC, where total consumption fell by an average of 0.1% (compared to a nominal (unweighted) GDP decrease of 3.3%), with a fall in household consumption of 1.6% and a smaller rise in government consumption, of 4.3%.
- The composition of household consumption changed markedly in 2020. In the ten countries for which data are available, the share of household consumption expenditure on necessity goods[4] increased by 0.7 p.p. in 2020, from 8.5% to 9.2%, while the share of consumption on luxury goods[5] fell by 3.1 p.p. from 63.0% to 59.9%. In 2009,[6] the share of necessities barely changed (10.5%) and the share of luxury goods decreasing by 1.0 p.p. (63.7% to 62.7%).
- Household savings rates saw a sharp increase across OECD countries in 2020, which was considerably more pronounced than that of the GFC (OECD, 2020[12]). This put downward pressure on household consumption in most countries and contributed to falls in GDP.

The COVID-19 crisis led to a shift in the composition of GDP in 2020. Measured under the expenditure approach, the OECD average shares of household expenditure and investment in GDP fell between 2019 and 2020, while the shares of government expenditure and of net exports rose (Figure 2.4).[7]

Figure 2.4. Composition of GDP (expenditure approach), 2008-2009, 2019-2020

Average shares across OECD countries

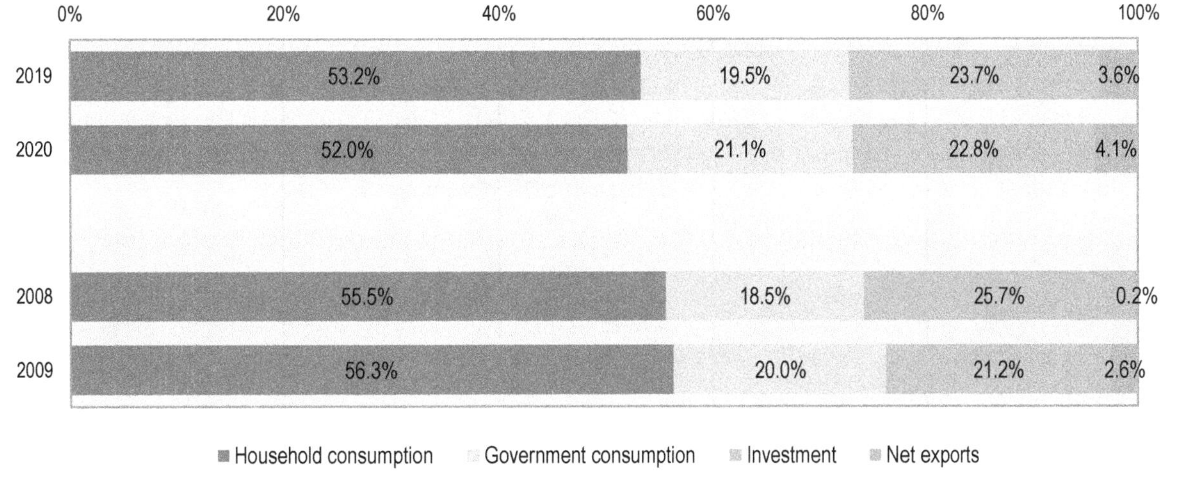

Note: Data for 2020 are the average of 33 OECD countries for which these data were available.
Source: OECD National Accounts and authors' calculations.

StatLink https://stat.link/z34n1h

Changes in revenues from different tax types, 2019-2020

This section provides an overview of revenue changes by tax type between 2019 and 2020, both as a share of GDP and in nominal terms. Box 2.2 provides more information on the tax types considered.

Changes in revenues by tax type as a share of GDP

Between 2019 and 2020, direct taxes on income were more strongly affected than indirect or property taxes. In 2020, the largest increases in revenues as a share of GDP were seen in PIT and SSCs, which both increased on average by 0.3 percentage points. The largest fall was seen in CIT, which decreased by 0.4 p.p., on average (Figure 2.5). No change was seen in property taxes or VAT as a share of GDP, on average, and a smaller decrease (of 0.1 p.p.) was seen for excise revenues.

For PIT and SSCs, the overall distribution of the increases was similar across OECD countries (Figure 2.5), with an average increase of 0.3 p.p. for both tax categories:

- Approximately one-quarter (9) of OECD countries saw decreases in PIT revenues as a share of GDP, half (18) of OECD countries saw increases of between 0 and 0.5 p.p. (PIT) and the remaining quarter (10 countries) had increases above this level. The country that saw the largest drop in PIT was Turkey, due to tax cuts and deferrals related to COVID-19,[8] as well as a decrease in employment and in total personal income. Decreases were also seen in Austria and Latvia (0.4 p.p. in both cases). In Austria, this was due to a combination of economic factors and a decrease in wage and capital incomes related to COVID-19, as well as the impact of several policy measures to support households in the pandemic. In Latvia, the change was due in part to lower wage growth and job losses (Central Statistical Bureau of Latvia, 2021[13]) as well as COVID-19 response measures. The country that saw the largest increase was Denmark, where the increase was largely due to the distribution of holiday pay accrued between 1 September 2019 and 31 August 2020, previously only accessible when leaving the Danish labour market (e.g. by retirement or leaving the country) (Lønmodtagernes Feriemidler, n.d.[14]). This distribution was implemented as a COVID-19 measure and was taxed as personal income when received. In addition, personal incomes in Denmark were heavily supported through a temporary wage compensation scheme.
- Seven OECD countries saw decreases in SSC revenues as a share of GDP, while 29 countries saw increases, 13 of which were greater than 0.5 p.p. The largest decrease in SSCs was of 0.7 p.p., in Hungary following a decrease in the employer social security rates in July 2020 as well as waivers of SSC rates related to COVID-19 (OECD, 2021[8]; OECD, 2021[9]).[9] The largest increase was seen in Spain (1.5 p.p.), although this was due to a much sharper fall in nominal GDP (9.9%, the largest contraction across the OECD) than in SSC revenues (4.8%).

Figure 2.5. Changes in tax revenues by category as a share of GDP, 2019-2020

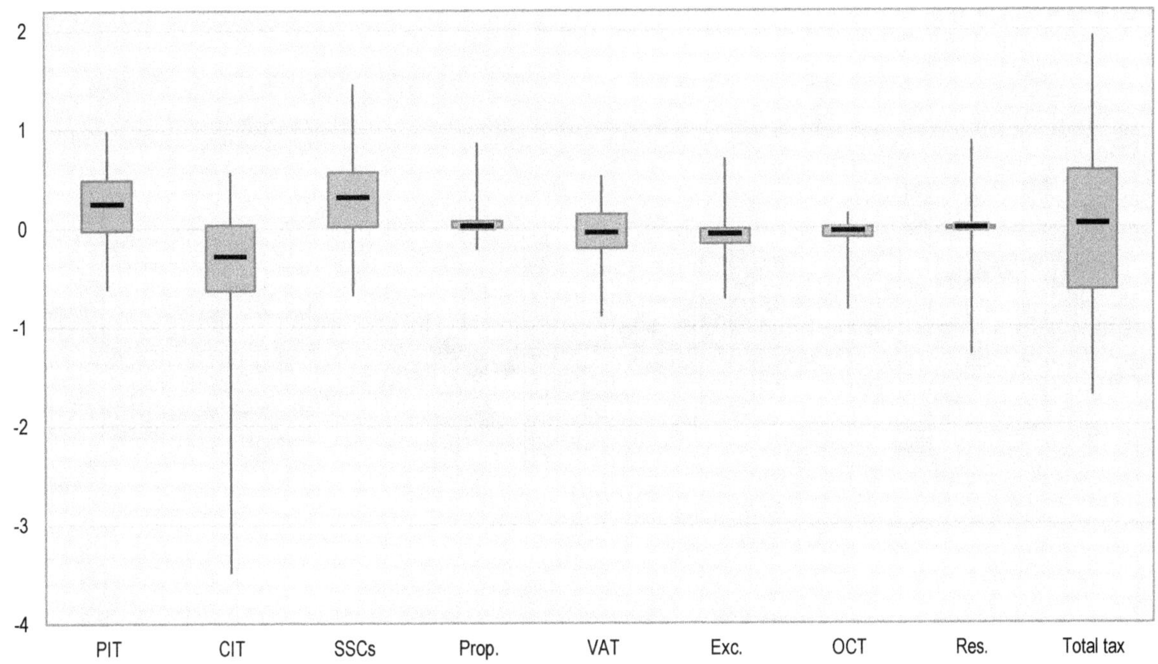

Note: Data for 2020 are preliminary and should be interpreted with caution; please see Box 2.1 for more details. In the figure, the lowest point represents the minimum country change for the tax type between 2019-2020; the box represents the changes for countries between the lower and upper quartiles (i.e. 50% of OECD countries had changes within the range shown by each box); and the upper point for each tax type represents the maximum country change. The line in each box represents the median country change (i.e. half of OECD countries were both above and below this line).
Source: *Revenue Statistics 2021* and authors' calculations.

StatLink https://stat.link/nsud9v

Corporate income taxes fell widely across the OECD countries in 2020, with an average fall of 0.37 p.p. and falls in 26 countries. The largest decrease was seen in Norway (3.5 p.p.), due to temporary changes in the petroleum tax act to help oil and gas companies execute planned investments as well as the opportunity to offset losses in 2020 against taxed surpluses from the previous two years. The Czech Republic also experienced a decrease of over 1 p.p. (1.3) due to COVID-19 and a range of business tax incentives including loss carry-back and accelerated depreciation of selected assets. Thirteen countries saw increases in CIT revenues in 2020 relative to 2019: the largest increase was seen in Latvia, due to tax revenues recovering after a high level of repayments of advance payments in 2019, following the introduction of the new corporate tax regime in 2018.

No change was observed in the average share of property tax revenues to GDP in 2020 relative to 2019 (a very small increase, of 0.05 p.p. of GDP). Twenty-nine OECD countries saw increases in the share of property tax revenues, with 18 of these between 0 and 0.7 p.p. The largest increase was seen in Korea (0.9 p.p.) due to higher revenues from security transaction taxes following an increase in transaction volumes. Of the nine OECD countries where property tax revenues fell as a share of GDP, the largest falls (0.2 p.p.) were seen in the Czech Republic and the United Kingdom, due to the abolition of the real property transfer tax from December 2019 in the Czech Republic and due to increases in the rate reliefs applied to non-domestic property taxes in the United Kingdom in response to COVID-19.

Figure 2.6. Decomposition of change in tax-to-GDP ratio by tax category, 2019-2020

Year-on-year change, p.p.

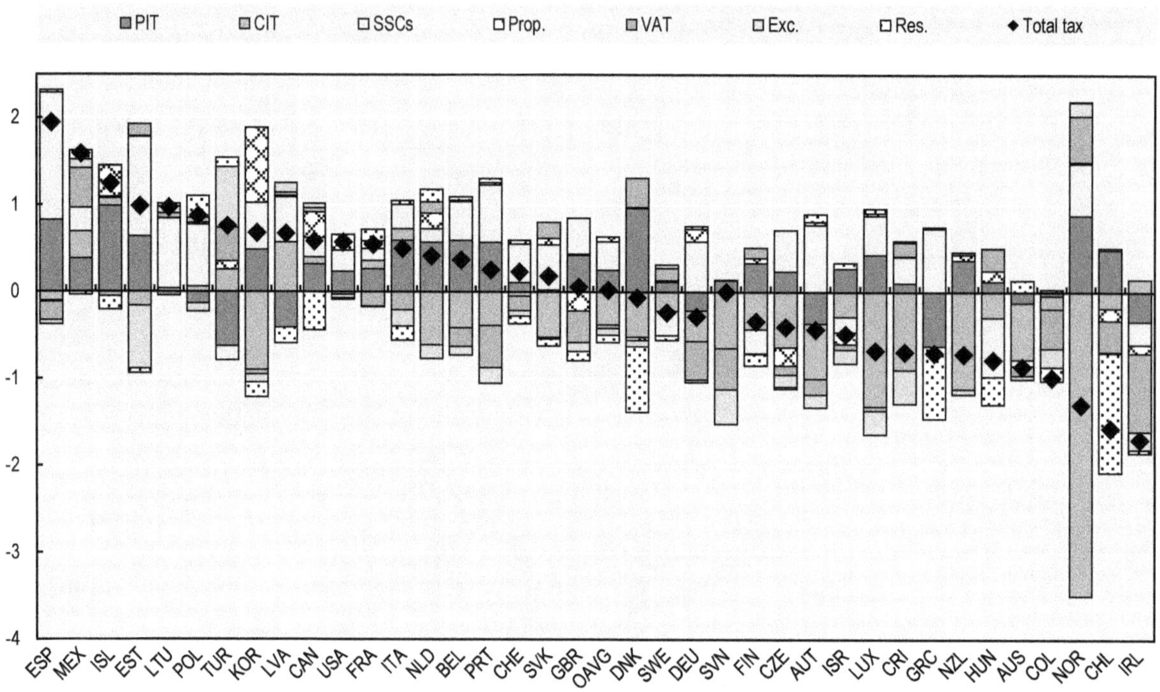

Note: Data for 2020 are preliminary and should be interpreted with caution; please see Box 2.1 for more details. This graph includes the change between years 2018 and 2019 for Australia and New Zealand, as both countries report tax revenues on a fiscal year basis that includes Q2 of 2020 in the 2019 fiscal year. Due to data availability, the average excludes Japan for SSCs (category 2000) and for total tax revenues; it also excludes Greece for PIT (category 1100), CIT (category 1200), VAT (category 5111) and excises (5111) due to disaggregated data for these categories not being available.
Source: *Revenue Statistics 2021* and authors' calculations.

StatLink https://stat.link/zegi46

Similarly, no change was observed in the average share of VAT to GDP in 2020 (a very small decrease of 0.04 p.p.). VAT revenues decreased as a share of GDP in 19 countries and increased in the other 17 countries that apply a VAT; with half of these changes situated between -0.2 and +0.1 p.p. of GDP. The largest fall was seen in Ireland (0.9 p.p.) due to the temporary VAT rate cut during the COVID-19 pandemic as well as a decrease in economic activity. The largest increase was seen in Norway, at 0.5 p.p. .

Revenues from excise taxes decreased slightly as a share of GDP on average, in 2020 and this tax category saw the most widespread falls in revenues of all tax types, with falls in 28 countries. Most decreases were caused by falls in fuel excises due to COVID-19-related mobility restrictions and lockdowns. The largest fall was seen in Estonia (-0.7 p.p.) in part due to the closure of the Latvian-Estonian border as well as a temporary reduction in the tax rate on natural gas used as propellant (OECD, 2021[8]) and the largest increase was seen in Turkey (0.7 p.p.), due to increases in the sales of motor vehicles and durable goods in the second half of 2020. Other than in Estonia and Turkey, the range of changes across countries was comparatively small, reflecting in part the smaller size of excises as a share of total tax revenues. No other changes in excise revenues exceeded 0.5 p.p. of GDP in 2020.

Box 2.2. Tax types considered and country assumptions

Tax types considered in the analysis

This chapter considers changes in both total tax revenues and several individual categories of tax revenues of particular size or policy significance. These taxes include:

Table 2.2. Individual tax types used in this chapter

Detailed tax types	Acronym	Corresponding *Revenue Statistics* codes
Personal income tax	PIT	1100 Personal income tax
Corporate income tax	CIT	1200 Corporate income tax
Social security contributions & payroll taxes	SSC	2000 Social security contributions; 3000 Payroll taxes
Property taxes	Prop.	4000 Taxes on property
Value-added taxes	VAT	5111 Value-added taxes
Excises	Exc.	5121 Excises
Other consumption taxes	OCT	All other taxes under 5000 (5112, 5113, 5122, 5123, 5124, 5125, 5126, 5127, 5128, 5200, 5300)
Residual	Res.	1300 Unallocable between 1100 and 1200; 6000 Other taxes

Information is presented for two different indicators: tax revenues in nominal currency and tax revenues as a share of GDP. The GDP data that is used for each country is the same as shown in Table 3.19 of the publication, except for adjustments related to the assumptions about fiscal years noted below. The years included in this chapter are from 1995-2020, which are available for all OECD countries.

The averages shown in this chapter are unweighted. For the reasons detailed below, they may differ from the other averages for 2020 presented elsewhere in the report.

Assumptions specific to individual countries

All OECD countries other than Australia, Japan and New Zealand provide data on a calendar year basis. In Australia and New Zealand, the fiscal year runs from 1 July of the current year to 30 June of the following year; whereas in Japan the fiscal year runs from 1 April in the current year to 31 March in the following year. The second quarter of 2020 occurred in fiscal year 2019 for Australia and New Zealand and in the year 2020 for all other countries, including Japan. In this chapter, the changes shown for Australia and New Zealand are from the 2018 to 2019 fiscal years.

In a few countries, preliminary data for the year 2020 was only partially available at the time this publication was prepared. These data include:

- Social security contributions in Japan: in this chapter, data is not presented for Japan for SSCs (category 2000) or for total tax revenues and Japan is not included in the averages for these two items. Data for Japan is included in the averages for all other tax types.
- A breakdown of income tax revenues (between PIT revenues (category 1100) and CIT revenues (category 1200) and of taxes on goods and services (including VAT (category 5111) and excises (category 5121)) in Greece: in this chapter, data is shown for all income taxes (category 1000) and all taxes on goods and services (category 5000). Greece is not included in the averages for PIT, CIT, VAT or excises.

Tax revenue data are available for most OECD countries on an accrual basis, except for Chile, Colombia, Costa Rica, Israel, Korea, Mexico and Turkey, which report on a cash basis. Personal income tax information in Canada is also reported on a cash basis. In addition, the preliminary 2020 data for Hungary are also on a cash basis while the final data for the years up to and including 2019 are on an accrual basis. More information is available in table 2A in the Annex to this chapter and in the detailed country tables in chapter 5 of the publication.

Changes in nominal tax revenues by tax type

In nominal terms, PIT and SSC revenues increased on average and country changes in these tax types were only weakly correlated with changes in nominal GDP (Table 2.3).[10] This suggests either that the tax base was relatively stable in light of broader GDP fluctuations, or that policy changes limited the impact of economic changes on revenues from these tax bases (e.g. by stabilising the base, or increasing the effective tax rate). Seventeen OECD countries saw increases in nominal PIT revenues and 20 saw increases in SSCs in nominal terms. Further, in many countries where these revenues fell in nominal terms, they did so more slowly than GDP.

Nominal revenues from VAT, which were relatively stable as a share of GDP, decreased slightly in nominal terms (2.6%) on average, lower than the average fall in nominal GDP. Twenty-four OECD countries saw decreases in nominal VAT revenues in 2020. Country changes in VAT revenues were more closely correlated to changes in GDP, contributing to their relative stability as a share of GDP on average; whereas changes in property taxes were very weakly correlated with GDP (Table 2.3).

Nominal revenues from excise taxes and CIT were the most affected on average and in terms of the number of countries affected. Nominal excise tax revenues fell by 5.4% on average, with 31 countries experiencing falls, whereas CIT revenues fell by 12.1%, with 30 countries experiencing falls. Changes in nominal excise tax revenues across OECD countries were the most closely correlated with GDP changes, primarily due to drops in fuel excise revenues due to COVID-19-related restrictions on mobility. By contrast, while CIT revenues faced the largest nominal falls across OECD countries, the changes in CIT revenues and in GDP in each country were not strongly correlated. All but two countries with falls in nominal GDP also saw falls in nominal CIT revenues that were generally larger than the fall in nominal GDP. Nominal CIT revenues also decreased in seven of the 11 OECD countries which saw increases in nominal GDP.

Table 2.3. Distribution of nominal revenue changes by tax category and of GDP

	2019-2020					2008-2009				
	Mean	Lower quartile	Median	Upper quartile	Correlation with GDP	Mean	Lower quartile	Median	Upper quartile	Correlation with GDP
PIT	1.4	-1.9	-0.4	3.5	29.0	-5.0	-7.9	-5.6	-0.6	66.6
CIT	-12.1	-20.0	-13.0	-2.5	44.5	-18.7	-30.1	-17.7	-8.1	54.0
SSC	2.0	-2.1	0.9	3.9	42.7	0.8	-3.6	0.9	5.1	41.3
Prop.	0.0	-4.1	-1.2	3.1	41.9	-3.0	-8.3	-1.8	0.5	5.5
VAT	-2.6	-8.3	-2.0	0.2	71.6	-6.1	-10.8	-4.3	0.7	45.3
Exc.	-5.4	-9.8	-5.9	-1.3	73.9	1.6	-4.0	0.3	4.1	-0.2
Total Tax	-2.1	-4.6	-2.1	-0.4	78.4	-5.3	-7.2	-4.4	-2.4	64.3
GDP	-2.1	-4.7	-2.7	0.3	-	-2.7	-4.3	-2.4	-0.1	-

Note: Data for 2020 are preliminary and should be interpreted with caution; please see Box 2.1 for more details.
The correlation for CIT revenues and GDP in 2020 excludes Latvia, which saw a significant increase in CIT revenues in nominal terms (346.4%) due to the correction following abnormally high repayments in 2019, see the discussion above for more information) and the relatively low share of CIT to GDP in Latvia (0.2% in 2019 and 0.7% in 2020). If Latvia were included in the correlation for nominal CIT revenues in 2020, it would be 4.7%.
Source: *Revenue Statistics 2021* and authors' calculations.

Although this edition does not calculate estimates of tax buoyancy, the changes in tax revenues between 2019 and 2020 are prima facie consistent with findings in the tax buoyancy literature that CIT revenues are the most responsive to economic change (see Box 2.3), while PIT, SSCs and property taxes are less buoyant. However, the results for 2020 are less consistent with the finding in several studies that tax responses to changes in GDP are more pronounced in times of economic contraction.

Box 2.3. Tax buoyancy and the relationship between changes in taxes and GDP during crises

Tax buoyancy measures the overall changes in tax revenues with respect to changes in GDP: $Tax\ Buoyancy = \%\Delta Tax\ Revenue\ \div \%\Delta GDP$. A tax buoyancy of one implies that a one percent change in GDP (would lead to a tax revenue change of one percent, resulting in an unchanged tax-to-GDP ratio, while a buoyancy larger than one would imply a larger change in tax revenue and a buoyancy smaller than one would imply a smaller change in tax revenue. The measure includes changes in tax revenue levels driven both by changes in the economy and by policy decisions.[11] Long-run buoyancy is important to understand the impact of economic growth on long-term fiscal sustainability, whereas short-run buoyancy indicates the cyclical variability of tax revenue and is closely related to the stabilisation function of fiscal policy (Belinga et al., 2014).

Many studies have estimated short-run and long-run tax buoyancies in advanced and developing economies, both for total tax revenues and for different tax types:

- (Belinga et al., 2014[16]) develops an error correction model to estimate jointly the short-run and long-run tax buoyancies in 34 OECD countries between 1965 and 2012. The model includes lags of the dependent variable (tax revenue) and of the independent variable (GDP). The study finds that short-run tax buoyancy does not significantly differ from one in most of these countries, while long-run buoyancy exceeds one in about half of the OECD countries. Corporate taxes (CIT) are the most buoyant and thus the most responsive to changes in GDP, while excises and property taxes are the least buoyant. Tax buoyancies for personal income taxes (PIT) and social security contributions (SSC) were found to have declined over time and become less than one. Finally, the paper finds that short-run buoyancy for total tax revenue is larger during economic contractions than during growth. This result suggests that tax systems in average OECD countries seem to work better as automatic stabilizer during recessions.
- (Dudine and Jalles, 2017[17]) uses an unrestricted error correction ARDL model with a lag of one year for both tax revenues and GDP and examines data from 107 countries, including 31 advanced economies, 38 emerging market economies and 38 low income countries, between 1980 and 2014. This study finds that short-run buoyancy is not statistically different from one in advanced economies, while it is generally larger than one in emerging markets and low income countries. On average, the study finds that long-run buoyancy of total tax revenue is not different from one across all country groups. By type of tax, the study notes that long-run buoyancy exceeds one for CIT in advanced economies, for PIT and SSC in emerging markets and for taxes on goods and services in low income countries. Contrary to the previous finding, this paper concludes that short-run buoyancy is generally smaller during economic contractions than economic expansions and only CIT (for all groups) and taxes on goods and services (for emerging markets) show larger buoyancy during contractions.
- (Deli et al., 2018[18]) uses an error correction ARDL model to estimate short-run and long-run tax buoyancies for a panel of 25 advanced OECD countries between 1965 and 2015. This study finds that both short-run and long-run tax buoyancies do not differ from one for total tax revenue, exceed one for CIT and are less than one for PIT. The study finds that short-run buoyancies for total tax, PIT and CIT are larger than one during economic contractions. In addition, all short-run buoyancies are larger during economic contractions than during economic expansions.

- A more recent study from (Lagravinese, Liberati and Sacchi, 2020[19]) looks at data from 35 OECD countries over the period 1995-2016 and estimates short-run and long-run tax buoyancies through a one-stage Error Correction Model. This paper used a different methodology from earlier studies and finds that both short-run and long-run tax buoyancies are consistently lower than one, a result which differs from the others.

This paper does not estimate tax buoyancies across OECD countries, although this could be a useful direction for future research once more final data for 2020 is available (see Box 2.1). However, it presents simple correlations of annual changes in nominal tax revenues and in nominal GDP across OECD countries to provide insights into the changes observed in the OECD average tax-to-GDP ratio for total tax revenues and different tax types in between 2019-2020 and between 2008-2009.

Comparison with changes in tax types during the global financial crisis

Difference in nominal changes and in tax types as a share of GDP

The two crises had very different initial impacts on the revenues of different tax types. Between 2008 and 2009, the average changes in nominal tax revenues from each tax type were considerably greater than in 2020 (Table 2.3). Nominal CIT and VAT revenues fell in both crises, although more significantly in the GFC; PIT and property tax revenues fell in 2009 but increased on average in 2020; SSCs increased in both crises, although by less on average in 2009 than in 2020; and excise revenues rose in 2009 but fell in 2020. Taken together, the more limited scale of the falls in CIT and VAT and the increases in PIT, SSCs and property taxes, meant that total nominal tax revenues between 2019 and 2020 fell by less than half of what was experienced between 2008 and 2009.

The correlation between GDP and revenues from the different tax types also differed in the two periods (Table 2.3). Changes in income taxes (both personal and corporate) were much less closely correlated with changes in GDP in 2020 than in 2009, suggesting that the income tax base was more stable during the COVID-19 crisis than the GFC. By contrast, changes in indirect taxes were much more closely correlated with GDP in 2020 than in 2009. In the GFC, VAT fell by more in nominal terms, often exceeding falls in GDP, whereas in 2020, VAT changes were broadly similar to changes in GDP. In 2009, changes in excises were not correlated with GDP changes, reflecting the inelastic nature of many goods subject to excises (notably fuel and tobacco), whereas they were the most closely correlated tax type in 2020, reflecting the specificities of the COVID-19 crisis and its limits on mobility. Changes in SSCs were roughly as equally correlated with GDP changes in both periods. The marked differences in the correlation of PIT, VAT, excises and property taxes has implications for tax policymakers' understanding of how these taxes behave in economic downturns, as well as the impact of support measures in stabilising revenues.

As a result, changes in each tax type as a share of GDP differed substantially between 2020 and 2009 (Figure 2.7). Personal income taxes rose in three-quarters of OECD countries in 2020, whereas the opposite occurred in 2009. Excises similarly reversed their trend in 2020, when they fell in most countries, compared to a general increase in 2009. Changes in VAT revenues also differed: while they declined in most countries in 2009, there was no change on average in 2020, with a roughly equal distribution of increases and decreases. Corporate income tax and SSC revenues experienced a similar scale of change in both crises, with the former falling and the latter rising.

Figure 2.7. Distribution of changes in tax types

Changes as p.p. of GDP, from lowest to highest: minimum, lower quartile, median, upper quartile, maximum

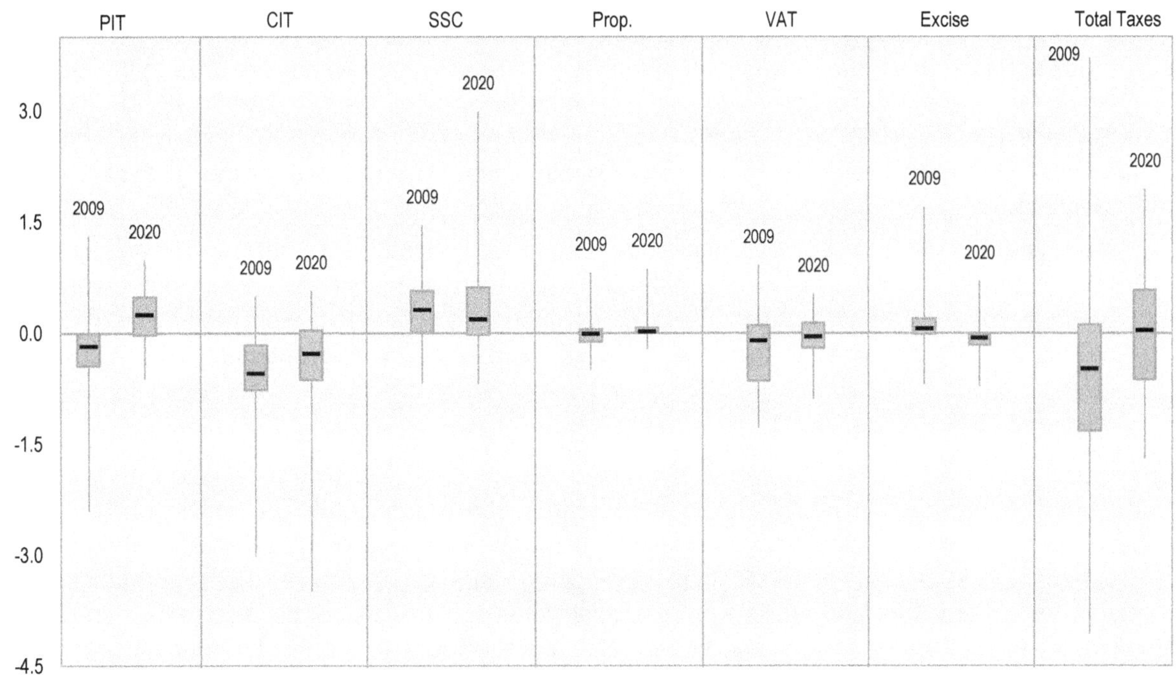

Note: Data for 2020 are preliminary and should be interpreted with caution; please see Box 2.1 for more details. In the figure, the lowest point represents the minimum country change for the tax type between 2019-2020; the box represents the changes for countries between the lower and upper quartiles (i.e. 50% of OECD countries had changes within the range shown by each box); and the upper point for each tax type represents the maximum country change. The line in each box represents the median country change (i.e. half of OECD countries were both above and below this line).
Source: *Revenue Statistics 2021* and authors' calculations.

StatLink https://stat.link/3ohky6

Discussion on differences between the COVID-19 crisis and the GFC

The differences between the tax revenue changes in the GFC and the COVID-19 crisis arise from the differences noted earlier between the nature of the two crises, including the shorter and sharper nature of the COVID-19 shock, its more strongly sectoral nature and its relatively disproportionate impact on households at lower income levels.

As noted, PIT and SSC revenues rose in 2020 in the majority of OECD countries as a share of GDP (28 and 29 countries respectively). This differs from the GFC, where PIT revenues fell as a share of GDP in 28 OECD countries. This may be due to a number of key differences between the two crises:

- **More restricted falls in employment in 2020 relative to 2009**: although employment rates dropped sharply in the second quarter of 2020, the overall loss of employment was greater in 2009 (relative to 2008) than in 2020 (relative to 2019). This is likely linked to the shorter nature of the initial shock in 2020, as discussed above, and to the impact of the use of job retention schemes, which were found to be effective in protecting employment. Job retention support was used in respect of around 20% of employment across the OECD in April 2020, supporting approximately 60 million jobs, more than ten times as many as during the GFC.[12] In 2020, the OECD average unemployment rate fell quickly after reaching a peak of 8.6% in the second quarter and was below

7.0% by the end of the year. By contrast, unemployment was more persistent during the GFC and remained above 8.0% throughout most of 2009 and all of 2010 (OECD, 2021[20]).

- **Difference in composition of job losses**: Employment reductions in 2020 were concentrated at the lower end of the income distribution, as were falls in working hours. As taxpayers at lower levels of income pay a lower level of taxation in almost all OECD countries due to the progressive nature of tax systems, this limited the impact of the COVID-19 crisis on revenues relative to the GFC, in which job losses and reductions in working hours were more evenly spread (OECD, 2021[10]). Similarly, job losses in 2020 were more concentrated by sector than in 2009. Finally, increases in tax rates on higher income earners in some countries may have reduced the overall decline in PIT revenues.
- **More limited falls in labour compensation**: Labour compensation (i.e. total wages and salaries) fell in both crises, but did so by more in the GFC. On average, labour compensation decreased by 3.14% in 2009 and 0.54% in 2020. In both crises, labour compensation decreased by less than the decline in GDP leading to an increase in the share of labour compensation to GDP, which was more pronounced in 2020 than in 2009 (+1.3 p.p. compared to +0.9 p.p.), increasing the tax base relative to GDP (OECD, 2021).

Corporate income tax revenues decreased in both crises, although to a slightly greater extent in 2009 than in 2020. Although many of the support measures (described above) reduced tax revenues, CIT revenues may have been partially protected by a lower level of corporate bankruptcies. (OECD, 2021[2]) notes that corporate bankruptcies were lower in 2020 than in preceding years, in part as a result of support measures and restrictions on creditors and banks from enforcing foreclosures, as well as the sharper and more sectoral nature of the declines in economic activity. Net operating surplus, a proxy for business profit, was more negatively affected in the GFC than in 2020. For the 19 OECD countries where 2020 data are available, the nominal growth rate of net operating surplus and mixed income was -7.8% in 2009 and -5.5% in 2020 (OECD, 2021). Finally, while the GDP impacts of the GFC were seen in 2009, the downturn in the economy and in revenues had already started in the fourth quarter of 2008, which meant that tax returns for 2009 may have already incorporated losses from the year before, further reducing profits. By comparison, the impacts of the COVID-19 crisis were felt initially in most countries in quarter two of 2020, which may have reduced losses in the first calendar year of the crisis.

The differences between the changes in VAT revenues in both crises are less easily understood than those seen for PIT. Despite the common use of VAT support measures and the changes in private consumption, which exceeded those of 2008-2009 (Simon and Harding, 2020[21]), VAT revenues did not see widespread declines in 2020. In nominal terms, VAT revenues decreased by an average of 2.3%, with falls seen in 24 OECD countries. As a share of GDP, they decreased by an average of 0.03 p.p., with falls in 19 OECD countries. Changes in VAT revenues were relatively correlated with changes in GDP in 2020, resulting in a relatively small and even spread of changes around zero as a share of GDP. The limited nature of the changes in VAT as a share of GDP in 2020 differ markedly from the changes in the GFC (Figure 2.7), where VAT declined in 23 countries, with an average decrease of 0.2 p.p. Nominal changes in VAT revenues were also much more strongly correlated with changes in GDP in 2020, leading to a more neutral impact on VAT revenues as a share of GDP. In 2020, VAT changes had a correlation ratio of 71.6%, compared to 45.3% in 2009.

Possible contributing factors to the limited falls in VAT include:

- **Lower levels of corporate bankruptcies:** As VAT is collected and remitted by businesses, the impact of the crisis on business solvency can have a significant effect on VAT revenues. VAT revenue losses from bankruptcy and business insolvencies can represent an important share of a country's VAT gap. A study by the European Commission noted that in the United Kingdom, payment difficulties arising from bankruptcy and financial insolvency accounted for one-fifth of the total compliance gap in 2010 and that in Australia, up to one-third of the compliance gap between

2009-10 was attributable to debt, compared to 15% in earlier years (European Commission, 2012[22]). The lower level of corporate bankruptcies in 2020 than in the GFC, as discussed earlier, is likely to have reduced losses from unremitted VAT due to business bankruptcies.

- **Increase in government consumption:** Although the overall share of consumption in GDP rose in 2020, it did so by less than it did in 2009; and the increase was primarily due to a larger rise in government consumption that offset a fall in household consumption. While government expenditure is exempt from VAT in all but one OECD country (New Zealand), governments effectively pay input VAT on most of their purchases. If government consumption increased more via the purchases of inputs subject to full VAT rates, rather than on government wages or on services or goods taxed at zero or reduced rates, the increase in government expenditure could lead to a rise in VAT revenue relative to GDP. An increase in intermediate consumption by VAT exempt entities, including in the healthcare sector, would have the same effect.
- **Onset of crisis part-way through the year:** The COVID-19 crisis may not have as dramatically affected annual revenues in 2020 as the GFC did in 2009, given that it primarily affected consumption in quarter two, with more limited impacts in quarters three and four. This differs from the GFC, where GDP falls were consistent in each quarter of the year, leading to larger overall changes in business profits and VAT receipts.
- **Nature of reporting**: Where data are reported on an accrual basis rather than on the basis of cash receipts of VAT due, early accrual-based reports may include a possibly significant amount of VAT that will not be remitted by businesses to the tax authorities. The deferrals of VAT payments adopted by many countries in the crisis may conceal some VAT revenues that will not be remitted in the future, with the impact in 2020 being more pronounced given the greater use of deferrals relative to the GFC. Similarly, few countries have relaxed their "bad debt relief" regimes to allow businesses to write off the output-VAT due on invoices that remain unpaid during the crisis. This means that businesses may have declared VAT on unpaid invoices in their VAT return that they will subsequently claim back upon completion of the normal bad debt relief regime. This may also contribute to artificially increasing reported VAT revenues in the short-term.

Finally, another key difference between the GFC and the current crisis are the changes seen in excise duties, which increased slightly in most countries in 2009, but decreased in most in 2020. The changes in excises were predominantly related to the unprecedented restrictions in mobility during the lockdowns associated with the COVID-19 pandemic, resulting in lower revenues from road and aviation excise taxes. Border closures also reduced trade in some countries.

References

Belinga, V. et al. (2014), "Tax Buoyancy in OECD Countries", *IMF Working Papers*, No. 14/110, IMF, Washington DC, https://www.imf.org/en/Publications/WP/Issues/2016/12/31/Tax-Buoyancy-in-OECD-Countries-41661 (accessed on 19 October 2021). [16]

BPS (2014), *Village Potential Statistics of Indonesia*, Statistics Indonesia, Jakarta, https://microdata.bps.go.id/mikrodata/index.php/citations/228. [25]

Central Statistical Bureau of Latvia (2021), *Changes of wages and salaries in 2020*, https://www.csb.gov.lv/en/statistics/statistics-by-theme/social-conditions/wages/search-in-theme/2944-changes-wages-and-salaries-2020 (accessed on 19 October 2021). [13]

Deli, Y. et al. (2018), “Dynamic tax revenue buoyancy estimates for a panel of OECD countries Dynamic tax revenue buoyancy estimates for a panel of OECD countries”, *ESRI Working Paper*, No. 592, http://hdl.handle.net/10419/193929www.econstor.eu (accessed on 19 October 2021). [18]

Dudine, P. and J. Jalles (2017), “How Buoyant is the Tax System? New Evidence from a Large Heterogeneous Panel”, *IMF Working Papers*, No. 17/4, IMF, Washington DC, https://www.imf.org/en/Publications/WP/Issues/2017/01/20/How-Buoyant-is-the-Tax-System-New-Evidence-from-a-Large-Heterogeneous-Panel-44551 (accessed on 19 October 2021). [17]

European Commission (2012), *Study to quantify and analyse the VAT Gap in the EU-27 Member States*, European Commission, http://gesd.free.fr/vatgap12.pdf. [22]

IMF (2021), *Fiscal Monitor Database of Country Fiscal Measures in Response to the COVID-19 Pandemic*, https://www.imf.org/en/Topics/imf-and-covid19/Fiscal-Policies-Database-in-Response-to-COVID-19 (accessed on 19 October 2021). [5]

IMF (2021), *World Economic Outlook: Managing Divergent Recoveries*, IMF, Washington DC, https://www.imf.org/en/Publications/WEO/Issues/2021/03/23/world-economic-outlook-april-2021 (accessed on 19 October 2021). [3]

IMF (2009), *IMF Update on Fiscal Stimulus and Financial Sector Measures*, https://www.imf.org/external/np/fad/2009/042609.htm (accessed on 19 October 2021). [6]

Kose, M., N. Sugawara and M. Terrones (2020), “Global Recessions”, No. 9172, World Bank Group, https://documents1.worldbank.org/curated/en/185391583249079464/pdf/Global-Recessions.pdf (accessed on 19 October 2021). [4]

Lagravinese, R., P. Liberati and A. Sacchi (2020), “Tax buoyancy in OECD countries: New empirical evidence”, *Journal of Macroeconomics*, Vol. 63, p. 103189, http://dx.doi.org/10.1016/J.JMACRO.2020.103189. [19]

Lønmodtagernes Feriemidler (n.d.), *Frozen holiday funds*, https://lifeindenmark.borger.dk/working/holiday-allowance-ny/frozen-holiday-funds---loenmodtagernes-feriemidler (accessed on 15 November 2021). [14]

OECD (2021), *Key Short-Term Economic Indicators*, https://stats.oecd.org/index.aspx?DatasetCode=KEI (accessed on 19 October 2021). [20]

OECD (2021), *OECD Economic Outlook, Volume 2021 Issue 1*, OECD Publishing, Paris, https://dx.doi.org/10.1787/edfbca02-en. [2]

OECD (2021), *OECD Employment Outlook 2021: Navigating the COVID-19 Crisis and Recovery*, OECD Publishing, Paris, https://dx.doi.org/10.1787/5a700c4b-en. [10]

OECD (2021), *OECD Sovereign Borrowing Outlook 2021*, OECD Publishing, Paris, https://dx.doi.org/10.1787/48828791-en. [1]

OECD (2021), *Tax Policy Reforms 2021: Special Edition on Tax Policy during the COVID-19 Pandemic | en | OECD | OCDE*, OECD Publishing, Paris, https://www.oecd.org/fr/fiscalite/tax-policy-reforms-26173433.htm (accessed on 11 October 2021). [8]

OECD (2021), *Taxing Wages 2021*, OECD Publishing, Paris, https://dx.doi.org/10.1787/83a87978-en. [9]

OECD (2021), "The territorial impact of COVID-19: Managing the crisis and recovery across levels of government", OECD Publishing, Paris, https://www.oecd-ilibrary.org/social-issues-migration-health/the-territorial-impact-of-covid-19-managing-the-crisis-and-recovery-across-levels-of-government_a2c6abaf-en (accessed on 19 October 2021). [7]

OECD (2020), *Consumption Tax Trends 2020: VAT/GST and Excise Rates, Trends and Policy Issues*, OECD Publishing, Paris, https://dx.doi.org/10.1787/152def2d-en. [11]

OECD (2020), *Statistical Insights: How did the first wave of the COVID-19 pandemic affect the household sector and public finances?*, https://www.oecd.org/fr/sdd/cn/statistical-insights-how-did-the-first-wave-of-the-covid-19-pandemic-affect-the-household-sector-and-public-finances.htm (accessed on 11 October 2021). [12]

OECD/UCLG (2016), *Subnational governments around the world: Structure and finance*, OECD Publishing, Paris, http://www.oecd.org/regional/regional-policy/Subnational-Governments-Around-the-World- Part-I.pdf. [23]

Simon, H. and M. Harding (2020), "What drives consumption tax revenues?: Disentangling policy and macroeconomic drivers", *OECD Taxation Working Papers*, No. 47, OECD, Paris, https://www.oecd-ilibrary.org/taxation/what-drives-consumption-tax-revenues_94ed8187-en (accessed on 19 October 2021). [21]

Trading Economics (2021), *Denmark - Labour costs: Wages and salaries (total)*, https://tradingeconomics.com/denmark/labour-costs-wages-salaries-total-eurostat-data.html (accessed on 19 October 2021). [15]

White, H. and D. Raitzer (2017), *Impact Evaluation of Development Interventions: A Practical Guide*, Asian Development Bank, Manila, https://www.adb.org/sites/default/files/publication/392376/impact-evaluation-development-interventions-guide.pdf. [24]

Annex 2.A. Changes in tax-to-GDP ratios by country and tax type

Annex Table 2.A.1. Changes in tax-to-GDP ratios, 2019-2020, by tax type

Year-on-year change, percentage points

	PIT	CIT	SSCs	Prop.	VAT	Excises	OCT	Res.	Total Taxes	Basis of reporting*
Australia	-0.1	-0.7	0.0	0.0	-0.1	0.0	0.1	-0.1	-0.9	Accrual (1998)
Austria	-0.4	-0.6	0.7	0.0	-0.2	-0.1	0.1	0.0	-0.4	Accrual
Belgium	0.6	-0.4	0.5	0.0	-0.2	-0.1	0.0	0.0	0.4	Accrual
Canada	0.3	0.1	0.2	0.3	0.0	0.1	-0.4	0.0	0.6	Accrual (1999)*
Chile	0.5	-0.2	0.0	-0.1	-0.4	0.0	-0.1	-1.3	-1.6	Cash
Colombia	0.0	-0.1	0.0	0.0	-0.5	-0.2	0.0	-0.1	-1.0	Cash
Costa Rica	0.1	-0.9	0.2	0.0	0.2	-0.4	-0.3	0.5	-0.7	Cash
Czech Republic	0.2	-0.6	0.5	-0.2	-0.1	-0.1	0.0	0.0	-0.4	Accrual
Denmark	1.0	-0.5	0.0	0.0	0.3	-0.1	-0.1	-0.7	-0.1	Accrual
Estonia	0.6	-0.2	1.1	0.0	0.1	-0.7	-0.1	0.0	1.0	Accrual
Finland	0.3	-0.4	-0.3	0.1	0.1	0.0	-0.1	0.0	-0.3	Accrual
France	0.3	0.1	0.0	0.1	-0.2	0.0	0.1	0.2	0.5	Accrual
Germany	-0.2	-0.3	0.6	0.1	-0.4	0.0	0.0	0.0	-0.3	Accrual (2002)
Greece	-0.6		0.7	0.0			-0.8	0.0	-0.7	Accrual (1998)
Hungary	0.1	-0.3	-0.6	0.1	0.3	0.0	-0.4	0.0	-0.8	Accrual (2002)*
Iceland	1.0	0.1	0.0	0.4	0.0	0.0	0.0	-0.1	1.2	Accrual (1998)
Ireland	-0.3	0.2	-0.2	-0.1	-0.9	-0.2	0.0	0.0	-1.7	Accrual (1998)
Israel	0.3	-0.3	-0.2	-0.1	-0.1	-0.2	0.0	0.1	-0.5	Cash
Italy	0.6	0.1	0.3	0.0	-0.2	-0.2	-0.1	-0.1	0.5	Accrual (2000)
Japan	0.1	-0.6		0.1	0.4	-0.1	0.0	0.0		Accrual
Korea	0.5	-0.9	0.5	0.9	0.0	-0.1	-0.1	-0.1	0.7	Cash
Latvia	-0.4	0.6	0.5	0.0	0.0	0.1	-0.2	0.0	0.7	Accrual
Lithuania	0.0	0.0	0.8	0.0	0.1	0.1	0.0	0.0	1.0	Accrual
Luxembourg	0.4	-1.3	0.4	0.0	0.0	-0.3	0.1	0.0	-0.7	Accrual
Mexico	0.4	0.3	0.3	0.0	0.5	0.1	0.0	0.1	1.6	Cash
Netherlands	0.6	-0.6	0.2	0.2	0.1	-0.2	0.0	0.1	0.4	Accrual (1999)
New Zealand	0.4	-1.1	0.0	0.1	0.0	-0.1	0.0	0.0	-0.7	Accrual
Norway	0.9	-3.5	0.6	0.0	0.5	0.2	0.0	0.0	-1.3	Accrual (2000)
Poland	-0.1	0.1	0.6	0.0	0.1	-0.1	-0.6	1.0	0.9	Accrual (2002)
Portugal	0.6	-0.4	0.7	0.0	-0.5	-0.2	0.0	0.1	0.3	Accrual
Slovak Republic	0.0	-0.5	0.5	0.1	0.2	0.0	-0.1	0.0	0.2	Accrual
Slovenia	0.1	-0.6	1.2	0.0	-0.5	-0.4	-0.1	0.0	-0.3	Accrual
Spain	0.8	-0.1	1.5	0.0	-0.2	0.0	0.0	0.0	1.9	Accrual (2000)
Sweden	0.1	-0.2	0.0	0.0	0.1	0.0	-0.1	-0.2	-0.2	Accrual (2000)
Switzerland	0.1	0.0	0.4	0.0	-0.2	-0.1	0.0	-0.1	0.2	Accrual
Turkey	-0.6	0.3	-0.2	0.1	0.4	0.7	0.2	0.0	0.8	Cash*
United Kingdom	0.4	0.0	0.4	-0.2	-0.4	-0.1	-0.1	0.0	0.1	Accrual
United States	0.2	0.0	0.2	0.2	0.0	0.0	0.0	0.0	0.6	Accrual
Average	**0.3**	**-0.4**	**0.3**	**0.1**	**0.0**	**-0.1**	**-0.1**	**0.0**	**0.1**	

Note: Data for 2020 are preliminary and should be interpreted with caution; please see Box 2.1 for more details. This graph includes the change between years 2018 and 2019 for Australia and New Zealand, as both countries report tax revenues on a fiscal year basis that includes Q2 of 2020 in the 2019 fiscal year. Due to data availability, the average excludes Japan for SSCs (category 2000) and for total tax revenues; it also excludes Greece for PIT (category 1100), CIT (category 1200), VAT (category 5111) and excises (5111) due to disaggregated data for these categories not being available.

* The basis of reporting reported here is as indicated in chapter 5 under each country table. The year indicated in brackets is the year from data on an accrual basis are available if this was later than 1995. Please also note: CAN: data are on accrual basis except that personal income taxes are on a modified cash basis; HUN: preliminary data for 2020 are on a cash basis; TUR: SSCs are reported on an assessment basis.

Source: Revenue Statistics 2021 and authors' calculations.

Annex Figure 2.A.1. Changes in tax-to-GDP ratios, 2019-2020, by tax type

Year-on-year percentage change

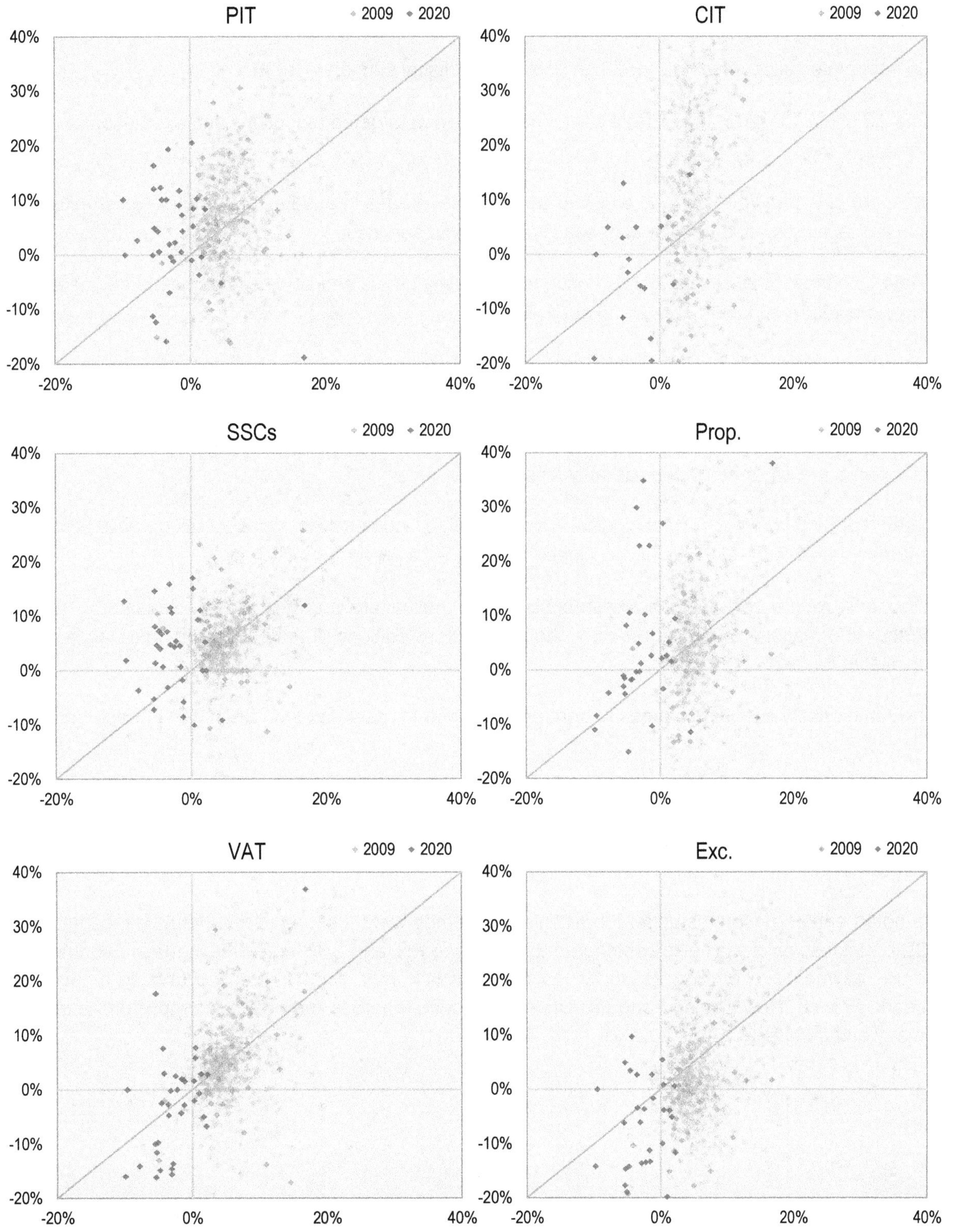

Note: Data for 2020 are preliminary and should be interpreted with caution; please see Box 2.1 for more details.
Source: Revenue Statistics 2021 and authors' calculations.

Notes

[1] The average is a weighted average of real GDP growth figures, based on the *OECD Economic Outlook*.

[2] G20 economies accounted for more than 95% of total fiscal support in 2020.

[3] Table 2.2 of (OECD, 2021) provides a complete overview of targeted reductions and exemptions in OECD countries.

[4] The share of expenditure on food and non-alcoholic beverages in private consumption expenditure has been used as a proxy of the share of necessity goods and services.

[5] Private consumption excluding consumption on necessity goods and services has been used as a proxy for the expenditure on luxury goods and services.

[6] Data were available for 36 OECD countries over 2008-09.

[7] The increase in net exports was due to slightly lower average falls in exports than in imports, although imports fell by considerably less on average in 2020 than they did in 2009, meaning that the average share of net exports in GDP rose by considerably less in 2020.

[8] Turkey reports revenues on a cash basis, which is likely to increase the impact of tax deferrals and other measures relative to an accruals basis. Please see Table 2A for further information.

[9] As Hungary reports revenues on a cash basis for the preliminary year (i.e. 2020 – please see Table 2A for further information), these figures may change in future editions of the publication once accrual data are available for 2020.

[10] The Annex show detailed changes in nominal revenues for each tax type and GDP in each country in 2020.

[11] A similar concept to tax buoyancy is called tax elasticity, which specifically measures the automatic response of tax revenue to economic changes, excluding the effects of discretionary policy changes such as legal changes in tax rates or tax base, the introduction of new taxes and administrative reforms (Mansfield, 1972).

[12] As noted earlier, payments under job retention schemes were also taxable in many, although not all, OECD countries, which has also contributed to protecting PIT and SSC revenues in these countries. For example, payments to employees under job retention schemes were treated as taxable in Australia, Denmark, France, New Zealand and the United Kingdom, whereas they were exempt from taxation in Germany and Sweden (OECD, 2021[9]).

3 Tax Levels and Tax Structures, 1965-2020

Chapter 3 provides an overview of tax levels and tax structures in OECD countries.

In all of the following tables the symbol (..) indicates not available/or not applicable. The main series in this chapter cover a selection of years between 1990 and 2019. A complete series is, however, available on line. Data for 1955 and 1960 (for nineteen OECD countries) are provided in part V of the 1998 edition of this Report.

The Gross Domestic Product (GDP) figures are based on the 2008 System of National Accounts (SNA) for all OECD countries.

Box 3.1. Treatment of capital transfers

Footnotes to Tables 3.1 to 3.18 refer to the treatment of the capital transfers that some countries make to account for taxes that have been assessed but not collected. The capital transfer has been subtracted from the total tax revenue for France, Luxembourg and Poland and this reduction has been allocated between tax headings in proportion to their tax revenues at the level of government against which these transfers were recorded. In the case of Austria, Belgium, Denmark, Lithuania and Switzerland the capital transfers were instead subtracted directly from the specific taxes to which they relate.

Countries reporting capital transfers include:

- Austria in 2020.
- Belgium from 1995.
- Denmark from 1971.
- France from 1992.
- Lithuania from 1999.
- Luxembourg from 2013.
- Poland from 1995 to 2019.
- Switzerland from 1990.

Table 3.1. Total tax revenue as % of GDP

	1965	1990	2000	2007	2010	2013	2015	2018	2019	2020p
Australia	20.6	28.1	30.5	29.5	25.2	27.0	27.7	28.5	27.7	..
Austria[1]	33.5	39.3	42.3	40.5	41.0	42.6	43.1	42.3	42.6	42.1
Belgium[1]	30.8	41.4	43.8	42.9	42.9	45.0	44.1	43.9	42.7	43.1
Canada	25.0	35.1	34.7	32.5	31.0	31.1	32.8	33.5	33.8	34.4
Chile	..	16.9	18.8	22.7	19.6	19.9	20.4	21.1	20.9	19.3
Colombia	..	11.3	15.7	19.3	18.1	20.0	19.9	19.3	19.7	18.7
Costa Rica	..	22.4	21.1	23.1	22.1	23.0	22.9	23.2	23.6	22.9
Czech Republic	..	..	32.3	34.1	32.2	33.7	33.1	35.0	34.8	34.4
Denmark[1]	29.1	44.4	46.9	46.4	44.8	45.9	46.1	44.2	46.6	46.5
Estonia	..	..	31.1	31.0	33.2	31.7	33.3	33.0	33.5	34.5
Finland	30.0	42.9	45.8	41.4	40.6	43.4	43.5	42.4	42.3	41.9
France[1]	33.7	41.2	43.4	42.5	42.1	45.4	45.3	45.9	44.9	45.4
Germany	31.7	34.8	36.4	35.4	35.5	37.0	37.3	38.4	38.6	38.3
Greece	17.1	25.2	33.4	31.8	32.3	35.9	36.6	40.0	39.5	38.8
Hungary	..	..	38.5	39.3	36.9	38.5	38.7	36.8	36.5	35.7
Iceland	25.7	30.5	35.9	38.3	32.1	34.3	35.1	36.4	34.8	36.1
Ireland	24.5	32.4	30.8	30.8	27.7	28.7	23.2	22.4	21.9	20.2
Israel	..	..	34.8	34.1	30.6	30.6	31.2	30.8	30.2	29.7
Italy	24.6	36.3	40.5	41.6	41.7	43.8	43.0	41.7	42.4	42.9
Japan	17.3	27.7	25.3	27.2	26.2	28.6	30.2	31.6	31.4	..
Korea	..	18.6	20.9	23.7	22.4	23.1	23.7	26.7	27.3	28.0
Latvia	..	..	29.1	28.2	28.6	29.2	29.9	31.1	31.2	31.9
Lithuania[1]	..	..	30.8	30.1	28.3	26.7	28.7	30.2	30.3	31.2
Luxembourg[1]	26.4	33.5	36.9	36.2	37.6	38.2	36.2	39.5	38.9	38.3
Mexico	..	12.1	11.5	12.0	12.8	13.3	15.9	16.1	16.3	17.9
Netherlands	30.5	39.7	36.9	35.7	35.7	36.1	37.0	38.8	39.3	39.7
New Zealand	24.5	36.2	32.5	33.9	30.3	30.5	31.5	32.2	31.5	32.2
Norway	29.4	40.2	41.7	42.0	41.8	39.8	38.4	39.4	39.9	38.6
Poland[1]	..	..	32.9	34.6	31.3	32.1	32.4	35.1	35.1	36.0
Portugal	15.7	26.5	30.9	31.8	30.4	34.0	34.4	34.7	34.5	34.8
Slovak Republic	..	..	33.6	29.2	28.1	31.0	32.7	34.2	34.6	34.8
Slovenia	..	..	37.7	38.1	37.8	37.2	37.3	37.3	37.2	36.9
Spain	14.3	31.5	33.0	36.4	31.3	33.1	33.8	34.7	34.7	36.6
Sweden	30.9	48.8	50.0	44.9	42.9	42.5	42.6	43.8	42.8	42.6
Switzerland[1]	16.0	23.1	27.0	25.4	25.6	26.0	26.6	26.8	27.4	27.6
Turkey	10.6	14.5	23.5	22.9	24.7	25.2	25.0	24.0	23.1	23.9
United Kingdom	30.1	32.9	32.8	32.9	32.1	31.9	31.8	32.9	32.7	32.8
United States	23.6	26.0	28.3	26.7	23.4	25.5	26.2	24.9	25.0	25.5
Unweighted average										
OECD Average[2]	**24.8**	**30.8**	**32.9**	**32.9**	**31.6**	**32.7**	**32.9**	**33.5**	**33.4**	**33.5**

.. Not available

Note: Full time series can be accessed at http://oe.cd/full-time-series.

1. The capital transfers were subtracted directly from the specific taxes to which they relate, except for France, Luxembourg and Poland, where the capital transfers have been allocated between tax headings in proportion to the reported tax revenue.
2. 2020: calculated by applying the unweighted average percentage change for 2020 in the 36 countries providing data for that year to the overall average tax to GDP ratio in 2019.

StatLink https://stat.link/1fnurv

Table 3.2. Total tax revenue in billions of US dollars at market exchange rates

	1965	1990	2000	2007	2010	2013	2015	2018	2019	2020p
Australia	5.6	90.8	117.3	289.9	346.5	401.9	344.3	401.2	380.0	..
Austria[1]	..	68.6	83.2	157.6	160.5	183.3	164.7	192.2	189.4	181.1
Belgium[1]	..	89.4	103.6	201.9	206.2	234.9	204.0	238.3	227.7	221.4
Canada	14.2	210.1	260.0	477.2	501.4	574.9	511.1	576.8	588.7	565.3
Chile	..	5.8	14.6	39.4	42.8	55.3	49.7	62.8	58.3	48.9
Colombia	..	5.1	14.7	39.8	51.9	76.5	58.4	64.4	63.7	50.8
Costa Rica	..	1.3	3.2	6.2	8.3	11.7	13.0	14.5	15.1	14.1
Czech Republic	..	..	20.0	64.9	67.4	71.4	62.3	87.1	87.8	84.3
Denmark[1]	3.0	61.4	76.9	148.3	144.2	157.6	139.5	157.7	162.0	165.7
Estonia	..	..	1.8	7.0	6.5	7.9	7.6	10.1	10.4	10.6
Finland	..	49.6	57.5	106.0	101.1	117.7	102.1	116.8	113.6	113.4
France[1]	..	550.7	591.8	1 130.7	1 113.7	1 275.1	1 104.3	1 279.6	1 224.8	1 192.1
Germany	..	577.4	706.9	1 210.4	1 206.8	1 379.1	1 250.9	1 527.5	1 501.4	1 471.1
Greece	..	14.6	43.5	101.3	95.9	85.7	71.6	84.8	81.1	73.3
Hungary	..	..	18.2	55.0	48.7	52.2	48.4	59.1	59.6	55.3
Iceland	0.1	2.0	3.2	8.3	4.4	5.5	6.2	9.6	8.7	7.8
Ireland	0.7	15.6	30.7	83.2	61.5	68.3	67.5	86.0	87.4	85.8
Israel	..	..	46.2	61.1	71.9	90.1	93.7	114.9	120.2	121.1
Italy	..	336.6	463.6	918.8	889.9	938.3	788.9	872.4	850.3	807.6
Japan	17.1	920.0	1 224.6	1 281.0	1 545.1	1 469.0	1 386.4	1 594.7	1 616.8	..
Korea	..	52.6	120.5	278.2	256.2	317.2	347.9	460.4	449.7	456.3
Latvia	..	..	1.8	8.8	6.8	8.9	8.1	10.7	10.6	10.7
Lithuania[1]	..	..	3.8	11.9	10.5	12.4	11.9	16.2	16.5	17.4
Luxembourg[1]	..	4.7	7.8	18.4	20.0	23.6	20.9	28.0	27.7	28.0
Mexico	..	35.9	81.2	126.5	135.9	169.6	186.1	198.0	207.9	193.7
Netherlands	..	132.6	153.7	302.5	301.9	316.6	283.3	354.4	357.3	361.7
New Zealand	1.4	16.1	17.3	46.0	47.0	59.5	56.8	67.4	65.2	71.0
Norway	2.4	48.2	71.4	168.5	179.3	208.1	148.2	172.0	161.9	140.0
Poland[1]	..	..	56.6	148.7	150.4	167.1	154.9	206.5	209.7	214.4
Portugal	..	18.8	36.6	76.5	72.2	76.9	68.5	83.9	82.6	80.2
Slovak Republic	..	..	9.8	25.3	25.4	30.6	28.9	36.1	36.3	36.3
Slovenia	..	..	6.6	18.3	18.2	18.0	16.1	20.2	20.1	19.7
Spain	..	131.6	197.3	536.1	444.4	448.5	404.6	492.2	483.1	468.1
Sweden	7.8	127.7	131.5	220.7	212.7	249.4	215.5	243.2	228.7	230.5
Switzerland[1]	2.6	61.6	75.5	125.4	154.6	185.3	187.1	197.2	200.2	207.5
Turkey	1.3	30.2	64.5	156.2	192.0	240.8	215.5	186.3	175.7	171.6
United Kingdom	30.6	359.4	544.0	1 018.0	795.1	889.1	933.8	939.5	926.0	887.8
United States	167.0	1 552.4	2 900.5	3 868.6	3 517.1	4 291.8	4 773.7	5 110.0	5 336.5	5 336.0
Unweighted average										
OECD Average	**19.5**	**192.1**	**220.1**	**356.4**	**347.8**	**394.0**	**382.5**	**430.9**	**432.7**	..

.. Not available

Note: Full time series can be accessed at http://oe.cd/full-time-series.

1. The capital transfers were subtracted directly from the specific taxes to which they relate, except for France, Luxembourg and Poland, where the capital transfers have been allocated between tax headings in proportion to the reported tax revenue.

StatLink https://stat.link/reyzs7

Table 3.3. Tax revenue of main headings as % of GDP, 2019

	1000 Income & profits	2000 Social security	3000 Payroll	4000 Property	5000 Goods and services[2]	6000 Others	Memorandum item: supranational revenues
Australia	16.4	0.0	1.3	2.7	7.3	0.0	..
Austria	12.5	14.9	2.7	0.5	11.7	0.2	0.2
Belgium[1]	15.1	13.2	0.0	3.4	11.0	0.0	0.4
Canada	16.8	4.7	0.7	3.9	7.7	0.0	..
Chile	7.3	1.5	0.0	1.1	11.1	-0.1	..
Colombia	6.4	1.9	0.3	1.8	8.5	0.9	..
Costa Rica	4.9	8.1	1.4	0.4	8.2	0.5	..
Czech Republic	7.9	15.4	0.0	0.4	11.1	0.0	0.2
Denmark[1]	30.1	0.0	0.3	2.0	14.1	0.0	0.1
Estonia	7.4	11.7	0.0	0.2	14.2	0.0	0.2
Finland	14.8	11.8	0.0	1.4	14.2	0.0	0.2
France[1]	11.5	14.8	1.8	3.9	12.4	0.5	0.2
Germany	12.6	14.6	0.0	1.1	10.3	0.0	0.2
Greece	8.5	12.2	0.0	3.1	15.7	0.0	0.2
Hungary	6.5	11.7	1.0	0.9	16.3	0.1	0.1
Iceland	17.4	3.2	0.3	2.1	11.3	0.6	..
Ireland	10.0	3.7	0.2	1.2	6.8	0.0	0.1
Israel	9.9	5.2	1.1	3.1	10.8	0.0	..
Italy	13.4	13.3	0.0	2.4	12.0	1.4	0.2
Japan	9.7	12.9	0.0	2.6	6.2	0.1	..
Korea	9.1	7.3	0.1	3.1	7.0	0.7	..
Latvia	6.7	9.6	0.0	0.9	14.1	0.0	0.2
Lithuania[1]	8.8	9.6	0.0	0.3	11.6	0.0	0.3
Luxembourg[1]	15.2	10.8	0.0	3.8	9.1	0.0	0.3
Mexico	6.9	2.3	0.4	0.3	6.2	0.3	..
Netherlands	12.2	13.4	0.0	1.5	12.1	0.1	0.4
New Zealand	17.3	0.0	0.0	1.9	12.2	0.0	..
Norway	16.3	10.6	0.1	1.3	11.7	0.0	..
Poland[1]	7.5	13.2	0.3	1.3	12.8	0.0	0.2
Portugal	9.5	9.6	0.0	1.4	13.7	0.3	0.2
Slovak Republic	7.1	15.0	0.0	0.4	12.1	0.0	0.2
Slovenia	7.2	15.7	0.0	0.6	13.6	0.0	0.1
Spain	9.9	12.3	0.0	2.5	10.0	0.0	0.2
Sweden	15.3	9.2	5.3	0.9	12.1	0.0	0.1
Switzerland[1]	13.2	6.5	0.0	2.1	5.4	0.1	..
Turkey	5.6	7.2	0.0	1.0	9.0	0.3	..
United Kingdom	11.3	6.5	0.1	4.1	10.7	0.0	0.2
United States	11.6	6.1	0.0	2.9	4.4	0.0	..
Unweighted average							
OECD Average	**11.3**	**8.9**	**0.5**	**1.8**	**10.8**	**0.2**	**0.2**

.. Not available

1. The capital transfers were subtracted directly from the specific taxes to which they relate, except for France, Luxembourg and Poland, where the capital transfers have been allocated between tax headings in proportion to the reported tax revenue.
2. The figures in category 5000 include supranational revenues, which are also presented separately under the Supranational heading.

StatLink https://stat.link/6epit3

Table 3.4. Tax revenue of main headings as % of total tax revenue, 2019

	1000 Income & profits	2000 Social security	3000 Payroll	4000 Property	5000 Goods and services[2]	6000 Others	Memorandum item: supranational revenues
Australia	59.2	0.0	4.7	9.8	26.3	0.0	..
Austria	29.5	34.9	6.4	1.3	27.5	0.5	0.4
Belgium[1]	35.3	31.0	0.0	8.0	25.6	0.0	1.0
Canada	49.6	13.9	2.2	11.4	22.8	0.1	..
Chile	34.8	7.3	0.0	5.5	53.0	-0.6	..
Colombia	32.3	9.5	1.7	9.1	43.0	4.4	..
Costa Rica	20.9	34.2	5.9	1.9	34.8	2.3	..
Czech Republic	22.8	44.2	0.0	1.2	31.9	0.0	0.4
Denmark[1]	64.7	0.1	0.6	4.3	30.3	0.0	0.3
Estonia	21.9	35.0	0.0	0.6	42.4	0.0	0.6
Finland	35.0	27.9	0.0	3.4	33.7	0.1	0.4
France[1]	25.7	33.0	4.0	8.7	27.6	1.1	0.4
Germany	32.6	37.9	0.0	2.9	26.6	0.0	0.5
Greece	21.6	30.8	0.0	7.7	39.9	0.0	0.5
Hungary	17.7	32.0	2.9	2.6	44.7	0.2	0.4
Iceland	49.9	9.2	0.9	6.0	32.3	1.8	..
Ireland	45.6	16.8	1.0	5.7	30.8	0.0	0.6
Israel	32.8	17.4	3.8	10.2	35.9	0.0	..
Italy	31.6	31.2	0.0	5.7	28.3	3.2	0.4
Japan	30.8	41.1	0.0	8.2	19.7	0.3	..
Korea	33.2	26.7	0.3	11.4	25.8	2.5	..
Latvia	21.3	30.6	0.0	3.0	45.0	0.0	0.5
Lithuania[1]	29.0	31.8	0.0	1.0	38.2	0.0	0.9
Luxembourg[1]	39.1	27.7	0.0	9.8	23.3	0.1	0.7
Mexico	42.4	13.8	2.5	2.0	37.6	1.6	..
Netherlands	31.0	34.2	0.0	3.8	30.7	0.2	1.1
New Zealand	55.1	0.0	0.0	6.2	38.7	0.0	..
Norway	40.7	26.5	0.1	3.2	29.4	0.0	..
Poland[1]	21.4	37.6	0.7	3.6	36.5	0.1	0.6
Portugal	27.4	27.8	0.0	4.1	39.8	0.8	0.5
Slovak Republic	20.4	43.4	0.0	1.2	35.0	0.0	0.4
Slovenia	19.5	42.2	0.1	1.7	36.6	0.0	0.4
Spain	28.7	35.3	0.0	7.1	28.9	0.0	0.6
Sweden	35.7	21.4	12.4	2.2	28.2	0.1	0.3
Switzerland[1]	48.2	23.7	0.0	7.7	19.9	0.5	..
Turkey	24.2	31.4	0.0	4.2	39.0	1.2	..
United Kingdom	34.7	19.7	0.4	12.4	32.8	0.0	0.5
United States	46.4	24.5	0.1	11.5	17.5	0.0	..
Unweighted average							
OECD Average	**34.0**	**25.9**	**1.3**	**5.5**	**32.6**	**0.5**	**0.5**

.. Not available

1. The capital transfers were subtracted directly from the specific taxes to which they relate, except for France, Luxembourg and Poland, where the capital transfers have been allocated between tax headings in proportion to the reported tax revenue.
2. The figures in category 5000 include supranational revenues, which are also presented separately under the Supranational heading.

StatLink https://stat.link/1qzecl

Table 3.5. Tax revenue of main headings as % of GDP, 2020p

	1000 Income & profits	2000 Social security	3000 Payroll	4000 Property	5000 Goods and services[2]	6000 Others	Memorandum item: supranational revenues
Australia	..	..	..	..	..	..	..
Austria[1]	11.6	15.6	2.7	0.6	11.5	0.2	0.2
Belgium[1]	15.2	13.7	0.0	3.4	10.7	0.0	0.4
Canada	17.1	4.9	0.8	4.2	7.4	0.0	..
Chile	6.3	1.5	0.0	1.0	10.6	-0.1	..
Colombia	6.2	1.9	0.4	1.8	7.8	0.8	..
Costa Rica	4.6	8.3	1.5	0.5	7.6	0.5	..
Czech Republic	7.5	15.8	0.0	0.2	10.8	0.0	0.1
Denmark[1]	29.9	0.1	0.3	2.0	14.3	0.0	0.1
Estonia	7.8	12.9	0.0	0.2	13.6	0.0	0.2
Finland	14.7	11.5	0.0	1.5	14.2	0.0	0.2
France[1]	11.9	14.8	1.9	4.0	12.3	0.5	0.2
Germany	12.0	15.2	0.0	1.3	9.8	0.0	0.2
Greece	7.9	12.9	0.0	3.1	14.9	0.0	0.2
Hungary	6.3	11.1	1.0	1.1	16.2	0.1	0.1
Iceland	18.3	3.2	0.3	2.4	11.2	0.7	..
Ireland	9.8	3.4	0.2	1.1	5.6	0.0	0.1
Israel	10.0	5.1	1.2	2.9	10.6	0.0	..
Italy	14.2	13.5	0.0	2.5	11.5	1.2	0.2
Japan	9.2	..	0.0	2.6	6.6	0.1	..
Korea	8.7	7.8	0.1	4.0	6.8	0.6	..
Latvia	6.8	10.1	0.0	0.9	14.0	0.0	0.1
Lithuania[1]	8.8	10.4	0.0	0.3	11.7	0.0	0.3
Luxembourg[1]	14.4	11.2	0.0	3.8	8.8	0.0	0.3
Mexico	7.6	2.5	0.5	0.3	6.7	0.4	..
Netherlands	12.1	13.6	0.0	1.7	12.0	0.2	0.4
New Zealand	17.8	0.0	0.0	1.9	12.5	0.0	..
Norway	13.6	11.2	0.1	1.3	12.4	0.0	..
Poland	7.5	13.8	0.3	1.3	12.2	0.9	0.2
Portugal	9.6	10.3	0.0	1.5	13.0	0.3	0.2
Slovak Republic	6.6	15.5	0.0	0.5	12.2	0.0	0.1
Slovenia	6.7	16.8	0.0	0.6	12.6	0.0	0.2
Spain	10.7	13.7	0.0	2.4	9.8	0.0	0.2
Sweden	15.2	9.1	5.1	1.0	12.2	0.0	0.1
Switzerland[1]	13.2	6.9	0.0	2.2	5.2	0.1	..
Turkey	5.2	7.1	0.0	1.1	10.2	0.2	..
United Kingdom	11.8	6.9	0.1	3.9	10.1	0.0	0.2
United States	11.8	6.3	0.0	3.0	4.3	0.0	..

.. Not available

1. The capital transfers were subtracted directly from the specific taxes to which they relate, except for France and Luxembourg, where the capital transfers have been allocated between tax headings in proportion to the reported tax revenue.
2. The figures in category 5000 include supranational revenues, which are also presented separately under the Supranational heading.

StatLink https://stat.link/e47prb

Table 3.6. Tax revenue of main headings as % of total tax revenue, 2020p

	1000 Income & profits	2000 Social security	3000 Payroll	4000 Property	5000 Goods and services[2]	6000 Others	Memorandum item: supranational revenues
Australia	..	..	..	..	..	..	..
Austria[1]	27.4	37.0	6.5	1.4	27.2	0.4	0.4
Belgium[1]	35.4	31.8	0.0	8.0	24.8	0.0	0.9
Canada	49.7	14.2	2.2	12.1	21.6	0.1	..
Chile	32.4	8.0	0.0	5.2	54.9	-0.5	..
Colombia	32.9	9.9	2.0	9.7	41.4	4.1	..
Costa Rica	20.1	36.1	6.5	2.0	33.3	2.0	..
Czech Republic	21.9	46.1	0.0	0.6	31.5	0.0	0.4
Denmark[1]	64.3	0.1	0.6	4.2	30.7	0.0	0.3
Estonia	22.7	37.3	0.0	0.6	39.3	0.0	0.5
Finland	35.0	27.5	0.0	3.6	33.9	0.1	0.4
France[1]	26.2	32.7	4.2	8.8	27.0	1.2	0.5
Germany	31.3	39.7	0.0	3.3	25.7	0.0	0.5
Greece	20.4	33.2	0.0	7.9	38.5	0.0	0.5
Hungary	17.7	31.0	2.7	3.0	45.4	0.3	0.4
Iceland	50.7	8.9	0.9	6.8	31.0	1.8	..
Ireland	48.6	17.0	1.0	5.7	27.8	0.0	0.5
Israel	33.5	17.0	3.9	9.9	35.7	0.0	..
Italy	33.0	31.5	0.0	5.7	26.9	2.9	0.4
Japan	..	..	..	..	..	..	..
Korea	30.9	28.0	0.3	14.2	24.4	2.1	..
Latvia	21.4	31.6	0.0	3.0	44.0	0.0	0.5
Lithuania[1]	28.1	33.4	0.0	1.0	37.5	0.0	0.9
Luxembourg[1]	37.5	29.3	0.0	10.0	23.0	0.1	0.9
Mexico	42.7	13.9	2.5	1.6	37.2	2.1	..
Netherlands	30.6	34.3	0.0	4.2	30.3	0.6	1.1
New Zealand	55.2	0.0	0.0	5.9	38.8	0.0	..
Norway	35.3	28.9	0.2	3.4	32.2	0.0	..
Poland	20.7	38.4	0.9	3.6	33.8	2.6	0.4
Portugal	27.8	29.5	0.0	4.2	37.5	1.0	0.5
Slovak Republic	18.9	44.6	0.0	1.4	35.1	0.0	0.4
Slovenia	18.3	45.7	0.1	1.7	34.2	0.0	0.4
Spain	29.1	37.5	0.0	6.7	26.7	0.0	0.6
Sweden	35.7	21.5	11.9	2.2	28.6	0.1	0.3
Switzerland[1]	47.8	25.1	0.0	7.8	18.8	0.5	..
Turkey	21.9	29.7	0.0	4.4	43.0	1.0	..
United Kingdom	35.9	20.9	0.4	11.8	31.0	0.0	0.5
United States	46.2	24.8	0.1	11.9	16.9	0.0	..

.. Not available

1. The capital transfers were subtracted directly from the specific taxes to which they relate, except for France and Luxembourg, where the capital transfers have been allocated between tax headings in proportion to the reported tax revenue.
2. The figures in category 5000 include supranational revenues, which are also presented separately under the Supranational heading.

StatLink https://stat.link/ho5dpm

Table 3.7. Taxes on income and profits (1000) as % of GDP and as % of total tax revenue

	% of GDP					% of total tax revenue				
	1990	2000	2010	2018	2019	1990	2000	2010	2018	2019
Australia	16.1	17.6	14.3	17.1	16.4	57.1	57.9	56.7	60.1	59.2
Austria	10.0	12.0	11.5	12.4	12.5	25.5	28.3	28.1	29.3	29.5
Belgium[1]	15.3	16.9	14.7	16.1	15.1	36.9	38.6	34.2	36.8	35.3
Canada	17.0	17.4	14.5	16.5	16.8	48.6	50.1	46.6	49.2	49.6
Chile	3.9	4.4	7.5	7.6	7.3	23.2	23.3	38.1	35.8	34.8
Colombia	3.4	3.6	4.8	6.5	6.4	29.9	23.2	26.6	33.7	32.3
Costa Rica	2.3	2.8	3.8	4.7	4.9	10.0	13.2	17.1	20.4	20.9
Czech Republic	..	7.4	6.5	7.9	7.9	..	22.8	20.2	22.6	22.8
Denmark[1]	27.2	28.8	27.5	27.4	30.1	61.2	61.4	61.5	62.1	64.7
Estonia	..	7.7	6.6	7.5	7.4	..	24.8	19.8	22.6	21.9
Finland	16.8	19.7	14.4	14.8	14.8	39.2	43.1	35.5	34.9	35.0
France[1]	6.6	10.8	9.5	11.5	11.5	16.1	24.8	22.6	25.1	25.7
Germany	11.3	11.0	10.1	12.6	12.6	32.4	30.1	28.3	32.7	32.6
Greece	5.0	9.0	7.1	9.2	8.5	19.9	26.8	22.0	22.9	21.6
Hungary	..	9.4	7.6	6.7	6.5	..	24.3	20.7	18.2	17.7
Iceland	9.0	14.3	14.3	18.0	17.4	29.7	39.9	44.4	49.4	49.9
Ireland	12.3	13.4	11.1	10.2	10.0	38.0	43.6	40.1	45.7	45.6
Israel	..	13.8	8.9	10.1	9.9	..	39.6	29.2	32.7	32.8
Italy	13.2	13.4	13.6	13.0	13.4	36.5	33.2	32.7	31.0	31.6
Japan	13.9	8.8	7.9	10.1	9.7	50.2	34.8	30.2	31.9	30.8
Korea	6.1	6.0	6.3	9.1	9.1	32.8	28.8	28.0	34.1	33.2
Latvia	..	7.0	7.2	7.0	6.7	..	24.1	25.0	22.6	21.3
Lithuania[1]	..	8.3	4.6	5.8	8.8	..	27.0	16.2	19.1	29.0
Luxembourg[1]	13.5	13.5	13.6	15.6	15.2	40.2	36.5	36.2	39.6	39.1
Mexico	4.1	4.1	5.1	7.1	6.9	34.0	36.0	39.8	44.0	42.4
Netherlands	12.8	9.6	9.9	11.5	12.2	32.3	25.9	27.9	29.6	31.0
New Zealand	21.6	19.5	16.3	18.1	17.3	59.6	60.0	53.8	56.3	55.1
Norway	14.2	18.9	19.8	16.4	16.3	35.2	45.3	47.3	41.8	40.7
Poland[1]	..	6.7	6.3	7.4	7.5	..	20.4	20.1	21.1	21.4
Portugal	6.8	9.1	8.1	9.8	9.5	25.7	29.4	26.7	28.3	27.4
Slovak Republic	..	6.9	5.3	7.1	7.1	..	20.5	18.8	20.8	20.4
Slovenia	..	6.8	7.4	7.3	7.2	..	18.0	19.6	19.6	19.5
Spain	9.7	9.3	8.7	10.1	9.9	30.6	28.1	28.0	29.3	28.7
Sweden	20.3	21.4	15.3	15.8	15.3	41.6	42.7	35.7	36.0	35.7
Switzerland[1]	10.8	11.8	11.7	12.8	13.2	46.8	43.8	45.7	47.6	48.2
Turkey	4.9	6.9	5.3	5.8	5.6	33.5	29.5	21.3	24.1	24.2
United Kingdom	12.9	13.0	12.0	11.6	11.3	39.3	39.6	37.4	35.2	34.7
United States	11.8	14.2	9.9	11.4	11.6	45.2	50.1	42.3	45.9	46.4
Unweighted average										
OECD Average	**11.5**	**11.5**	**10.2**	**11.3**	**11.3**	**36.2**	**33.9**	**32.2**	**34.0**	**34.0**

.. Not available

Note: Full time series can be accessed at http://oe.cd/full-time-series.

1. The capital transfers were subtracted directly from the specific taxes to which they relate, except for France, Luxembourg and Poland, where the capital transfers have been allocated between tax headings in proportion to the reported tax revenue.

StatLink https://stat.link/tr6zas

Table 3.8. Taxes on personal income (1100) as % of GDP and as % of total tax revenue

	% of GDP					% of total tax revenue				
	1990	2000	2010	2018	2019	1990	2000	2010	2018	2019
Australia	12.1	11.5	9.8	11.7	11.6	43.0	37.7	38.7	41.2	42.0
Austria	8.2	9.3	9.2	9.4	9.6	21.0	22.0	22.4	22.2	22.6
Belgium[1]	13.2	13.8	12.1	11.8	11.3	32.0	31.4	28.2	26.9	26.5
Canada	14.3	12.8	10.9	12.0	12.2	40.8	36.8	35.0	35.7	36.0
Chile	0.9	1.4	1.3	1.4	1.5	5.6	7.6	6.8	6.7	7.2
Colombia	0.2	0.8	1.0	1.2	1.3	1.8	4.9	5.3	6.4	6.8
Costa Rica	0.0	0.0	1.0	1.3	1.4	0.0	0.0	4.6	5.8	6.1
Czech Republic	..	4.2	3.3	4.3	4.4	..	12.9	10.2	12.2	12.7
Denmark[1]	24.0	24.7	23.3	24.1	24.3	54.0	52.6	52.0	54.5	52.1
Estonia	..	6.8	5.3	5.5	5.5	..	22.0	15.9	16.5	16.5
Finland	14.9	14.0	12.0	12.2	12.2	34.7	30.6	29.5	28.9	29.0
France[1]	4.4	7.8	7.2	9.4	9.3	10.7	17.9	17.0	20.5	20.7
Germany	9.6	9.2	8.6	10.5	10.6	27.6	25.3	24.1	27.2	27.4
Greece	3.6	4.3	4.0	6.4	6.0	14.1	13.0	12.4	16.1	15.2
Hungary	..	7.2	6.4	5.4	5.2	..	18.6	17.4	14.7	14.2
Iceland	8.2	12.5	11.7	14.5	14.3	26.9	34.8	36.5	39.8	41.0
Ireland	10.7	9.8	8.8	7.0	6.9	33.1	31.9	31.6	31.4	31.7
Israel	..	10.1	5.5	6.3	6.3	..	29.1	18.0	20.6	20.9
Italy	9.5	10.1	11.2	10.7	11.0	26.3	24.8	26.9	25.7	25.8
Japan	7.7	5.3	4.9	6.0	5.9	27.8	21.0	18.6	19.1	18.8
Korea	3.7	3.1	3.2	4.9	4.8	20.0	14.6	14.2	18.4	17.5
Latvia	..	5.5	6.2	6.0	6.5	..	18.8	21.6	19.2	20.8
Lithuania[1]	..	7.6	3.6	4.3	7.2	..	24.8	12.7	14.1	23.9
Luxembourg[1]	8.1	6.8	7.9	9.3	9.3	24.1	18.5	20.9	23.6	23.9
Mexico	..	..	2.3	3.4	3.4	..	..	18.3	21.2	20.8
Netherlands	9.8	5.6	7.7	8.0	8.5	24.7	15.1	21.5	20.5	21.6
New Zealand	17.4	14.0	11.4	12.1	12.4	48.0	43.1	37.7	37.5	39.5
Norway	10.5	10.1	9.9	10.0	10.4	26.2	24.2	23.7	25.4	26.0
Poland[1]	..	4.3	4.3	5.3	5.3	..	13.2	13.9	15.1	15.1
Portugal	4.2	5.3	5.4	6.5	6.3	15.9	17.0	17.7	18.7	18.4
Slovak Republic	..	3.3	2.6	3.6	3.8	..	9.9	9.3	10.5	10.9
Slovenia	..	5.5	5.6	5.4	5.3	..	14.6	14.7	14.4	14.2
Spain	6.9	6.4	6.9	7.7	7.9	21.7	19.3	22.1	22.1	22.7
Sweden	18.8	17.7	12.1	12.9	12.3	38.5	35.4	28.1	29.5	28.7
Switzerland[1]	7.5	7.9	8.1	8.2	8.4	32.3	29.4	31.8	30.7	30.6
Turkey	3.9	5.2	3.5	3.7	3.8	26.8	22.2	14.0	15.4	16.3
United Kingdom	9.7	9.5	9.2	9.0	9.0	29.4	29.0	28.6	27.4	27.6
United States	9.8	11.9	8.1	10.1	10.3	37.7	42.2	34.8	40.6	41.1
Unweighted average										
OECD Average	**9.0**	**8.3**	**7.2**	**7.9**	**8.0**	**26.6**	**23.4**	**22.0**	**23.1**	**23.5**

.. Not available

Note: Full time series can be accessed at http://oe.cd/full-time-series.

1. The capital transfers were subtracted directly from the specific taxes to which they relate, except for France, Luxembourg and Poland, where the capital transfers have been allocated between tax headings in proportion to the reported tax revenue.

StatLink https://stat.link/jwvq9b

Table 3.9. Taxes on corporate income (1200) as % of GDP and as % of total tax revenue

	% of GDP					% of total tax revenue				
	1990	2000	2010	2018	2019	1990	2000	2010	2018	2019
Australia	4.0	6.2	4.5	5.4	4.7	14.1	20.2	17.9	18.9	17.1
Austria	1.4	1.9	1.9	2.7	2.7	3.6	4.6	4.6	6.4	6.4
Belgium[1]	2.0	3.1	2.5	4.3	3.7	4.8	7.2	5.9	9.8	8.7
Canada	2.5	4.2	3.2	4.1	4.2	7.0	12.2	10.5	12.2	12.3
Chile	2.1	2.1	4.0	4.7	4.9	12.4	11.2	20.4	22.1	23.4
Colombia	1.6	2.6	3.8	4.9	4.7	13.9	16.7	20.7	25.6	24.0
Costa Rica	0.0	0.0	2.3	2.5	2.8	0.0	0.0	10.3	11.0	11.9
Czech Republic	..	3.2	3.2	3.6	3.5	..	9.9	10.0	10.4	10.1
Denmark[1]	1.7	3.2	2.3	2.8	3.1	3.9	6.8	5.1	6.2	6.7
Estonia	..	0.9	1.3	2.0	1.8	..	2.8	4.0	6.1	5.5
Finland	1.9	5.7	2.4	2.5	2.5	4.5	12.5	6.0	6.0	6.0
France[1]	2.2	3.0	2.3	2.1	2.2	5.3	6.9	5.5	4.6	4.9
Germany	1.7	1.8	1.5	2.1	2.0	4.8	4.8	4.2	5.6	5.2
Greece	1.4	4.0	2.6	2.2	2.2	5.5	11.9	7.9	5.6	5.6
Hungary	..	2.2	1.2	1.3	1.3	..	5.7	3.3	3.6	3.5
Iceland	0.8	1.2	0.9	2.4	2.1	2.8	3.3	2.7	6.5	5.9
Ireland	1.6	3.6	2.4	3.2	3.1	4.9	11.7	8.5	14.3	14.0
Israel	..	3.3	2.6	3.2	3.1	..	9.6	8.6	10.4	10.1
Italy	3.6	2.8	2.3	1.9	2.0	10.0	6.9	5.5	4.4	4.6
Japan	6.2	3.5	3.0	4.1	3.8	22.4	13.7	11.6	12.9	12.0
Korea	2.4	3.0	3.1	4.2	4.3	12.8	14.1	13.8	15.7	15.7
Latvia	..	1.5	1.0	1.1	0.2	..	5.3	3.4	3.4	0.5
Lithuania[1]	..	0.7	1.0	1.5	1.6	..	2.2	3.5	5.0	5.1
Luxembourg[1]	5.4	6.6	5.8	6.3	5.9	16.1	18.0	15.3	16.0	15.2
Mexico	..	..	1.8	3.4	3.3	..	..	14.4	21.3	20.1
Netherlands	3.0	4.0	2.3	3.5	3.7	7.5	10.9	6.4	9.0	9.4
New Zealand	2.3	4.0	3.7	5.0	3.9	6.5	12.4	12.2	15.6	12.4
Norway	3.6	8.8	9.9	6.5	5.9	9.0	21.0	23.6	16.4	14.7
Poland[1]	..	2.4	1.9	2.1	2.2	..	7.3	6.2	5.9	6.3
Portugal	2.1	3.7	2.7	3.3	3.1	8.0	11.9	9.0	9.6	9.0
Slovak Republic	..	2.6	2.4	3.3	3.0	..	7.6	8.7	9.6	8.8
Slovenia	..	1.1	1.8	1.9	2.0	..	3.0	4.9	5.2	5.3
Spain	2.8	2.9	1.8	2.5	2.1	8.8	8.8	5.9	7.1	6.0
Sweden	1.5	3.6	3.2	2.8	3.0	3.1	7.3	7.6	6.5	7.0
Switzerland[1]	1.7	2.4	2.6	3.0	3.1	7.3	8.8	10.1	11.4	11.4
Turkey	1.0	1.7	1.8	2.1	1.8	6.7	7.3	7.3	8.7	7.9
United Kingdom	3.3	3.5	2.8	2.6	2.3	9.9	10.6	8.9	7.8	7.0
United States	2.0	2.2	1.8	1.3	1.3	7.5	7.9	7.5	5.3	5.4
Unweighted average										
OECD Average	**2.3**	**3.1**	**2.7**	**3.1**	**3.0**	**8.0**	**9.3**	**9.0**	**10.1**	**9.6**

.. Not available

Note: Full time series can be accessed at http://oe.cd/full-time-series.

1. The capital transfers were subtracted directly from the specific taxes to which they relate, except for France, Luxembourg and Poland, where the capital transfers have been allocated between tax headings in proportion to the reported tax revenue.

StatLink https://stat.link/npf3sj

Table 3.10. Social security contributions (2000) as % of GDP and as % of total tax revenue

	% of GDP					% of total tax revenue				
	1990	2000	2010	2018	2019	1990	2000	2010	2018	2019
Australia	0.0	0.0	0.0	0.0	0.0	0.0	0.0	0.0	0.0	0.0
Austria	12.9	14.3	14.0	14.7	14.9	32.9	33.8	34.2	34.8	34.9
Belgium[1]	13.7	13.5	13.9	13.3	13.2	33.2	30.8	32.4	30.2	31.0
Canada	4.3	4.7	4.6	4.6	4.7	12.1	13.6	14.9	13.8	13.9
Chile	1.5	1.4	1.3	1.5	1.5	9.0	7.3	6.8	6.9	7.3
Colombia	0.9	2.6	2.1	1.8	1.9	7.9	16.3	11.7	9.6	9.5
Costa Rica	6.5	6.4	7.3	8.0	8.1	28.9	30.4	33.1	34.3	34.2
Czech Republic	..	14.3	14.4	15.3	15.4	..	44.3	44.8	43.8	44.2
Denmark[1]	0.0	0.6	0.1	0.0	0.0	0.0	1.4	0.2	0.1	0.1
Estonia	..	10.9	12.7	11.5	11.7	..	35.1	38.4	34.9	35.0
Finland	11.0	11.5	12.0	11.8	11.8	25.6	25.2	29.7	27.9	27.9
France[1]	18.1	15.6	16.1	16.0	14.8	44.1	35.8	38.2	34.9	33.0
Germany	13.0	14.2	13.8	14.5	14.6	37.5	39.0	38.9	37.7	37.9
Greece	7.6	10.1	11.0	11.9	12.2	30.2	30.3	34.2	29.9	30.8
Hungary	..	11.3	11.6	11.6	11.7	..	29.4	31.4	31.6	32.0
Iceland	1.0	2.8	3.8	3.5	3.2	3.1	7.7	11.8	9.5	9.2
Ireland	4.6	3.7	5.1	3.7	3.7	14.1	11.9	18.2	16.6	16.8
Israel	..	5.1	5.2	5.3	5.2	..	14.6	16.9	17.1	17.4
Italy	11.9	11.6	13.0	13.0	13.3	32.9	28.5	31.1	31.1	31.2
Japan	7.3	8.9	10.8	12.7	12.9	26.5	35.2	41.1	40.2	41.1
Korea	1.9	3.5	5.2	6.8	7.3	10.1	16.7	23.3	25.4	26.7
Latvia	..	9.8	8.6	9.1	9.6	..	33.5	30.1	29.3	30.6
Lithuania[1]	..	9.9	11.6	12.6	9.6	..	32.2	41.1	41.8	31.8
Luxembourg[1]	9.2	9.6	10.9	10.8	10.8	27.5	26.1	29.0	27.3	27.7
Mexico	2.0	2.1	2.1	2.2	2.3	16.8	18.0	16.2	13.4	13.8
Netherlands	14.9	14.3	12.9	14.0	13.4	37.4	38.7	36.3	36.0	34.2
New Zealand	0.0	0.0	0.0	0.0	0.0	0.0	0.0	0.0	0.0	0.0
Norway	10.6	8.8	9.4	10.1	10.6	26.3	21.0	22.4	25.5	26.5
Poland[1]	..	12.9	10.8	13.1	13.2	..	39.2	34.4	37.2	37.6
Portugal	7.2	7.9	8.6	9.3	9.6	27.2	25.6	28.4	26.9	27.8
Slovak Republic	..	13.9	12.0	14.7	15.0	..	41.4	42.6	43.0	43.4
Slovenia	..	15.0	15.8	15.4	15.7	..	39.7	41.9	41.4	42.2
Spain	11.2	11.5	11.9	11.7	12.3	35.4	34.9	37.9	33.9	35.3
Sweden	13.3	12.7	10.8	9.6	9.2	27.2	25.5	25.1	21.9	21.4
Switzerland[1]	5.4	6.5	6.1	6.4	6.5	23.3	24.2	23.7	23.8	23.7
Turkey	2.9	4.4	6.1	7.2	7.2	19.7	18.7	24.9	29.9	31.4
United Kingdom	5.6	5.5	6.1	6.3	6.5	17.0	16.8	18.9	19.2	19.7
United States	6.7	6.7	6.1	6.1	6.1	25.6	23.6	26.1	24.5	24.5
Unweighted average										
OECD Average	**7.1**	**8.4**	**8.6**	**9.0**	**8.9**	**21.8**	**24.9**	**26.6**	**25.9**	**25.9**

.. Not available

Note: Full time series can be accessed at http://oe.cd/full-time-series.

1. The capital transfers were subtracted directly from the specific taxes to which they relate, except for France, Luxembourg and Poland, where the capital transfers have been allocated between tax headings in proportion to the reported tax revenue.

StatLink https://stat.link/354lo2

Table 3.11. Taxes on payroll and workforce (3000) as % of GDP and as % of total tax revenue

	% of GDP					% of total tax revenue				
	1990	2000	2010	2018	2019	1990	2000	2010	2018	2019
Australia	1.7	1.4	1.3	1.4	1.3	6.1	4.5	5.2	4.8	4.7
Austria	2.4	2.7	2.8	2.7	2.7	6.0	6.4	6.9	6.4	6.4
Belgium[1]	0.0	0.0	0.0	0.0	0.0	0.0	0.0	0.0	0.0	0.0
Canada	0.8	0.7	0.6	0.7	0.7	2.3	2.1	2.1	2.0	2.2
Chile	0.0	0.0	0.0	0.0	0.0	0.0	0.0	0.0	0.0	0.0
Colombia	0.0	0.7	0.7	0.4	0.3	0.0	4.2	4.1	1.8	1.7
Costa Rica	1.4	1.3	1.3	1.4	1.4	6.4	6.3	5.9	6.0	5.9
Czech Republic	..	0.0	0.0	0.0	0.0	..	0.0	0.0	0.0	0.0
Denmark[1]	0.3	0.2	0.2	0.3	0.3	0.7	0.4	0.5	0.6	0.6
Estonia	..	0.0	0.0	0.0	0.0	..	0.0	0.0	0.0	0.0
Finland	0.0	0.0	0.0	0.0	0.0	0.0	0.0	0.0	0.0	0.0
France[1]	0.8	1.0	1.3	1.5	1.8	1.9	2.3	3.2	3.3	4.0
Germany	0.0	0.0	0.0	0.0	0.0	0.0	0.0	0.0	0.0	0.0
Greece	0.2	0.0	0.0	0.0	0.0	0.7	0.0	0.0	0.0	0.0
Hungary	..	1.4	0.4	0.9	1.0	..	3.6	1.1	2.6	2.9
Iceland	1.1	0.0	0.2	0.3	0.3	3.5	0.1	0.5	0.8	0.9
Ireland	0.4	0.0	0.2	0.2	0.2	1.3	0.0	0.7	0.8	1.0
Israel	..	1.3	1.2	1.2	1.1	..	3.6	3.8	3.8	3.8
Italy	0.1	0.0	0.0	0.0	0.0	0.3	0.0	0.0	0.0	0.0
Japan	0.0	0.0	0.0	0.0	0.0	0.0	0.0	0.0	0.0	0.0
Korea	0.1	0.0	0.1	0.1	0.1	0.4	0.2	0.2	0.3	0.3
Latvia	..	0.0	0.0	0.0	0.0	..	0.0	0.1	0.0	0.0
Lithuania[1]	..	0.0	0.0	0.0	0.0	..	0.0	0.0	0.0	0.0
Luxembourg[1]	0.0	0.0	0.0	0.0	0.0	0.0	0.0	0.0	0.0	0.0
Mexico	0.2	0.2	0.3	0.4	0.4	1.8	1.5	2.2	2.5	2.5
Netherlands	0.0	0.0	0.0	0.0	0.0	0.0	0.0	0.0	0.0	0.0
New Zealand	0.0	0.0	0.0	0.0	0.0	0.0	0.0	0.0	0.0	0.0
Norway	0.0	0.0	0.0	0.1	0.1	0.0	0.0	0.0	0.1	0.1
Poland[1]	..	0.2	0.3	0.2	0.3	..	0.7	0.8	0.6	0.7
Portugal	0.0	0.0	0.0	0.0	0.0	0.0	0.0	0.0	0.0	0.0
Slovak Republic	..	0.0	0.0	0.0	0.0	..	0.0	0.0	0.0	0.0
Slovenia	..	1.5	0.1	0.0	0.0	..	4.1	0.2	0.1	0.1
Spain	0.0	0.0	0.0	0.0	0.0	0.0	0.0	0.0	0.0	0.0
Sweden	1.2	2.1	3.0	5.1	5.3	2.5	4.2	7.0	11.6	12.4
Switzerland[1]	0.0	0.0	0.0	0.0	0.0	0.0	0.0	0.0	0.0	0.0
Turkey	0.0	0.0	0.0	0.0	0.0	0.0	0.0	0.0	0.0	0.0
United Kingdom	0.0	0.0	0.0	0.1	0.1	0.0	0.0	0.0	0.4	0.4
United States	0.0	0.0	0.0	0.0	0.0	0.0	0.0	0.1	0.0	0.1
Unweighted average										
OECD Average	**0.4**	**0.4**	**0.4**	**0.4**	**0.5**	**1.2**	**1.2**	**1.2**	**1.3**	**1.3**

.. Not available

Note: Full time series can be accessed at http://oe.cd/full-time-series.

1. The capital transfers were subtracted directly from the specific taxes to which they relate, except for France, Luxembourg and Poland, where the capital transfers have been allocated between tax headings in proportion to the reported tax revenue.

StatLink https://stat.link/h1xpoj

Table 3.12. Taxes on property (4000) as % of GDP and as % of total tax revenue

	% of GDP					% of total tax revenue				
	1990	2000	2010	2018	2019	1990	2000	2010	2018	2019
Australia	2.5	2.7	2.4	2.7	2.7	9.0	8.8	9.4	9.5	9.8
Austria	1.1	0.6	0.5	0.5	0.5	2.7	1.3	1.3	1.3	1.3
Belgium[1]	1.6	2.1	3.1	3.4	3.4	3.8	4.7	7.2	7.8	8.0
Canada	3.5	3.3	3.8	3.9	3.9	10.0	9.5	12.3	11.5	11.4
Chile	1.0	1.3	0.8	1.1	1.1	6.2	7.0	4.1	5.2	5.5
Colombia	0.2	1.0	1.6	1.5	1.8	2.2	6.6	8.7	8.0	9.1
Costa Rica	0.3	0.2	0.3	0.4	0.4	1.3	0.9	1.5	1.8	1.9
Czech Republic	..	0.5	0.4	0.5	0.4	..	1.4	1.3	1.3	1.2
Denmark[1]	1.9	1.6	1.9	1.8	2.0	4.3	3.3	4.1	4.1	4.3
Estonia	..	0.4	0.3	0.2	0.2	..	1.2	1.0	0.7	0.6
Finland	1.1	1.1	1.1	1.4	1.4	2.4	2.4	2.7	3.4	3.4
France[1]	2.6	3.0	3.5	4.0	3.9	6.3	6.9	8.4	8.7	8.7
Germany	1.2	0.8	0.8	1.1	1.1	3.4	2.3	2.3	2.8	2.9
Greece	1.2	2.6	1.7	3.1	3.1	4.6	7.7	5.2	7.7	7.7
Hungary	..	0.7	1.1	1.0	0.9	..	1.7	3.1	2.6	2.6
Iceland	2.6	2.8	2.3	2.0	2.1	8.4	7.9	7.0	5.5	6.0
Ireland	1.5	1.8	1.4	1.3	1.2	4.6	5.7	5.1	5.9	5.7
Israel	..	3.1	3.3	3.2	3.1	..	9.0	10.7	10.2	10.2
Italy	0.8	1.9	2.0	2.5	2.4	2.3	4.6	4.8	6.0	5.7
Japan	2.6	2.7	2.6	2.6	2.6	9.4	10.5	9.7	8.1	8.2
Korea	2.2	2.6	2.5	3.1	3.1	11.8	12.4	11.3	11.6	11.4
Latvia	..	1.1	0.9	0.9	0.9	..	3.8	3.0	3.0	3.0
Lithuania[1]	..	0.5	0.4	0.3	0.3	..	1.5	1.3	1.0	1.0
Luxembourg[1]	2.8	3.9	2.6	3.9	3.8	8.4	10.7	7.0	9.8	9.8
Mexico	0.2	0.2	0.3	0.3	0.3	1.9	1.8	2.3	2.0	2.0
Netherlands	1.5	1.9	1.4	1.6	1.5	3.7	5.3	3.8	4.0	3.8
New Zealand	2.5	1.7	2.0	1.9	1.9	6.8	5.3	6.6	5.8	6.2
Norway	1.2	1.0	1.1	1.2	1.3	2.9	2.3	2.6	3.1	3.2
Poland[1]	..	1.4	1.3	1.3	1.3	..	4.3	4.2	3.7	3.6
Portugal	0.7	1.1	1.1	1.4	1.4	2.7	3.7	3.7	4.2	4.1
Slovak Republic	..	0.6	0.4	0.4	0.4	..	1.8	1.4	1.2	1.2
Slovenia	..	0.6	0.6	0.6	0.6	..	1.7	1.6	1.6	1.7
Spain	1.7	2.1	2.1	2.5	2.5	5.5	6.5	6.6	7.3	7.1
Sweden	1.7	1.7	1.0	0.9	0.9	3.5	3.3	2.4	2.2	2.2
Switzerland[1]	2.1	2.6	2.0	2.0	2.1	8.9	9.7	7.7	7.5	7.7
Turkey	0.3	0.7	1.0	1.0	1.0	2.3	3.2	4.1	4.3	4.2
United Kingdom	2.7	3.8	3.8	4.1	4.1	8.2	11.4	12.0	12.6	12.4
United States	3.1	2.9	3.1	2.9	2.9	11.7	10.3	13.5	11.8	11.5
Unweighted average										
OECD Average	**1.7**	**1.7**	**1.6**	**1.8**	**1.8**	**5.5**	**5.3**	**5.4**	**5.5**	**5.5**

.. Not available

Note: Full time series can be accessed at http://oe.cd/full-time-series.

1. The capital transfers were subtracted directly from the specific taxes to which they relate, except for France, Luxembourg and Poland, where the capital transfers have been allocated between tax headings in proportion to the reported tax revenue.

StatLink https://stat.link/8t7sra

Table 3.13. Taxes on goods and services (5000) as % of GDP and as % of total tax revenue

	% of GDP					% of total tax revenue				
	1990	2000	2010	2018	2019	1990	2000	2010	2018	2019
Australia	7.8	8.8	7.2	7.3	7.3	27.8	28.8	28.8	25.5	26.3
Austria	12.4	12.4	11.7	11.7	11.7	31.5	29.3	28.7	27.7	27.5
Belgium[1]	10.8	11.3	11.2	11.1	11.0	26.1	25.9	26.1	25.2	25.6
Canada	9.1	8.4	7.4	7.8	7.7	25.8	24.2	24.0	23.4	22.8
Chile	10.6	12.0	10.0	11.3	11.1	62.9	63.8	51.2	53.3	53.0
Colombia	6.1	7.3	8.2	8.2	8.5	53.8	46.3	45.1	42.8	43.0
Costa Rica	10.2	9.9	8.9	8.1	8.2	45.5	46.7	40.3	35.0	34.8
Czech Republic	..	10.2	10.9	11.3	11.1	..	31.5	33.8	32.3	31.9
Denmark[1]	15.0	15.7	15.0	14.6	14.1	33.9	33.5	33.6	33.0	30.3
Estonia	..	12.1	13.5	13.8	14.2	..	38.8	40.7	41.8	42.4
Finland	14.0	13.4	13.0	14.3	14.2	32.5	29.2	32.0	33.8	33.7
France[1]	11.7	11.5	11.2	12.3	12.4	28.4	26.4	26.6	26.9	27.6
Germany	9.3	10.4	10.8	10.3	10.3	26.7	28.5	30.5	26.7	26.6
Greece	11.2	11.8	12.5	15.8	15.7	44.5	35.2	38.6	39.5	39.9
Hungary	..	15.6	16.0	16.5	16.3	..	40.6	43.3	44.8	44.7
Iceland	15.6	15.8	11.3	12.1	11.3	51.3	44.1	35.2	33.2	32.3
Ireland	13.6	11.9	9.9	6.9	6.8	41.9	38.8	35.8	31.0	30.8
Israel	..	11.5	12.0	11.1	10.8	..	33.1	39.4	36.2	35.9
Italy	10.2	11.4	11.1	12.0	12.0	28.0	28.2	26.6	28.7	28.3
Japan	3.8	4.9	4.9	6.2	6.2	13.7	19.3	18.7	19.5	19.7
Korea	8.2	8.0	7.5	7.0	7.0	44.3	38.4	33.7	26.3	25.8
Latvia	..	11.2	12.0	14.0	14.1	..	38.6	41.8	45.1	45.0
Lithuania[1]	..	12.1	11.7	11.5	11.6	..	39.4	41.4	38.1	38.2
Luxembourg[1]	7.9	9.8	10.4	9.1	9.1	23.6	26.6	27.6	23.2	23.3
Mexico	5.3	4.8	4.9	5.9	6.2	44.0	41.7	38.0	36.4	37.6
Netherlands	10.5	10.9	11.2	11.7	12.1	26.4	29.7	31.5	30.1	30.7
New Zealand	12.1	11.3	12.0	12.2	12.2	33.6	34.7	39.6	37.9	38.7
Norway	14.3	13.1	11.6	11.6	11.7	35.5	31.4	27.7	29.4	29.4
Poland[1]	..	11.6	12.6	13.1	12.8	..	35.3	40.3	37.2	36.5
Portugal	11.7	12.6	12.3	13.8	13.7	44.2	40.7	40.4	39.7	39.8
Slovak Republic	..	12.2	10.5	11.9	12.1	..	36.3	37.2	34.9	35.0
Slovenia	..	13.8	13.9	13.9	13.6	..	36.6	36.7	37.2	36.6
Spain	9.0	10.1	8.6	10.2	10.0	28.4	30.6	27.5	29.5	28.9
Sweden	12.2	12.1	12.7	12.4	12.1	25.0	24.2	29.7	28.2	28.2
Switzerland[1]	4.8	6.0	5.8	5.5	5.4	20.9	22.2	22.5	20.5	19.9
Turkey	4.1	9.9	11.8	9.7	9.0	27.9	42.0	47.7	40.5	39.0
United Kingdom	10.2	10.6	10.1	10.7	10.7	31.0	32.2	31.6	32.7	32.8
United States	4.5	4.5	4.2	4.4	4.4	17.5	16.0	18.1	17.7	17.5
Unweighted average										
OECD Average	**9.9**	**10.8**	**10.5**	**10.8**	**10.8**	**33.7**	**33.9**	**34.0**	**32.8**	**32.6**

.. Not available

Note: Full time series can be accessed at http://oe.cd/full-time-series.

1. The capital transfers were subtracted directly from the specific taxes to which they relate, except for France, Luxembourg and Poland, where the capital transfers have been allocated between tax headings in proportion to the reported tax revenue.

StatLink https://stat.link/l4d1wg

Table 3.14. Value added taxes (5111) as % of GDP and as % of total tax revenue

	% of GDP					% of total tax revenue				
	1990	2000	2010	2018	2019	1990	2000	2010	2018	2019
Australia	0.0	3.4	3.3	3.3	3.2	0.0	11.1	13.1	11.7	11.7
Austria	8.2	7.9	7.7	7.6	7.7	20.8	18.7	18.7	18.0	18.0
Belgium[1]	6.8	7.1	7.0	6.7	6.7	16.4	16.1	16.2	15.4	15.6
Canada	0.0	3.2	4.2	4.5	4.5	0.0	9.2	13.7	13.6	13.3
Chile	6.3	7.9	7.5	8.5	8.3	37.4	41.8	38.5	40.2	39.9
Colombia	2.6	4.3	5.3	5.7	5.8	22.6	27.6	29.3	29.4	29.6
Costa Rica	4.1	4.8	4.6	4.1	4.4	18.1	22.8	21.0	17.8	18.5
Czech Republic	..	5.9	6.6	7.6	7.5	..	18.3	20.5	21.6	21.6
Denmark[1]	8.3	9.1	9.4	9.5	9.3	18.7	19.5	20.9	21.5	20.1
Estonia	..	8.4	8.5	9.0	9.0	..	27.1	25.7	27.3	26.7
Finland	8.3	8.0	8.3	9.2	9.2	19.3	17.4	20.4	21.6	21.7
France[1]	7.6	7.2	6.8	7.1	7.1	18.4	16.7	16.1	15.4	15.9
Germany	5.8	6.7	7.0	7.0	7.0	16.6	18.4	19.8	18.2	18.2
Greece	6.2	6.3	7.1	8.5	8.4	24.6	18.9	22.0	21.3	21.3
Hungary	..	8.7	8.5	9.5	9.5	..	22.5	23.0	25.9	26.1
Iceland	8.7	10.2	7.3	8.6	8.0	28.4	28.5	22.7	23.6	22.9
Ireland	6.6	7.0	6.0	4.3	4.3	20.4	22.9	21.7	19.4	19.6
Israel	..	7.4	7.5	7.4	7.2	..	21.2	24.4	24.1	23.9
Italy	5.3	6.2	6.1	6.2	6.2	14.7	15.4	14.5	14.8	14.7
Japan	1.2	2.3	2.5	4.0	4.1	4.4	9.1	9.6	12.8	13.2
Korea	3.5	3.6	3.9	4.1	4.3	18.7	17.0	17.5	15.3	15.7
Latvia	..	6.9	6.7	8.4	8.7	..	23.9	23.3	27.0	27.7
Lithuania[1]	..	7.5	7.8	7.7	7.9	..	24.4	27.5	25.6	26.1
Luxembourg[1]	4.0	4.9	6.5	5.8	5.8	12.1	13.2	17.3	14.8	15.0
Mexico	3.2	2.8	3.8	3.9	3.8	26.1	24.7	29.4	24.3	23.4
Netherlands	6.5	6.4	6.7	6.8	7.1	16.5	17.3	18.7	17.6	18.2
New Zealand	8.1	8.1	9.3	9.5	9.5	22.4	24.9	30.7	29.6	30.3
Norway	7.6	8.2	7.8	8.4	8.6	18.8	19.8	18.6	21.2	21.6
Poland[1]	..	6.9	7.6	8.1	7.9	..	21.0	24.2	23.1	22.6
Portugal	5.2	7.6	7.5	8.7	8.8	19.6	24.5	24.8	25.1	25.4
Slovak Republic	..	6.8	6.1	7.1	7.3	..	20.4	21.8	20.7	21.0
Slovenia	..	8.5	8.1	8.2	8.0	..	22.6	21.3	22.0	21.6
Spain	5.0	5.8	5.2	6.6	6.5	15.7	17.6	16.5	19.0	18.7
Sweden	7.3	8.2	9.0	9.2	9.1	14.9	16.4	21.1	21.1	21.3
Switzerland[1]	2.7	3.5	3.3	3.1	3.1	11.5	13.0	12.7	11.7	11.2
Turkey	2.7	5.7	5.4	4.8	4.2	18.3	24.2	21.7	19.8	18.1
United Kingdom	5.5	5.9	6.1	7.0	7.0	16.9	18.1	19.0	21.2	21.3
United States	0.0	0.0	0.0	0.0	0.0	0.0	0.0	0.0	0.0	0.0
Unweighted average										
OECD Average	**5.1**	**6.3**	**6.4**	**6.7**	**6.7**	**17.0**	**19.6**	**20.5**	**20.3**	**20.3**

.. Not available

Note: Full time series can be accessed at http://oe.cd/full-time-series.

1. The capital transfers were subtracted directly from the specific taxes to which they relate, except for France, Luxembourg and Poland, where the capital transfers have been allocated between tax headings in proportion to the reported tax revenue.

StatLink https://stat.link/cdj3wz

Table 3.15. Tax revenues of sub-sectors of general government as % of GDP

	Supranational			Central government			State or Regional government			Local government			Social Security Funds		
	1975	1995	2019	1975	1995	2019	1975	1995	2019	1975	1995	2019	1975	1995	2019
Federal countries															
Australia	..	..	..	20.3	21.9	22.4	4.0	5.4	4.3	1.1	1.0	1.0	0.0	0.0	0.0
Austria	..	0.2	0.2	18.8	26.7	27.6	3.9	0.7	0.9	4.5	1.7	1.3	9.2	12.0	12.5
Belgium[1]	0.6	0.4	0.4	25.4	25.8	21.7	..	0.8	4.5	1.7	2.0	2.1	11.2	13.8	14.0
Canada	..	..	..	14.8	13.5	14.1	10.1	12.8	13.4	3.1	3.4	3.3	3.1	4.8	3.0
Germany	0.4	0.2	0.2	11.5	11.4	11.3	7.6	7.9	9.2	3.1	2.7	3.3	11.7	14.1	14.6
Mexico	..	..	..	..	7.5	13.1	..	0.3	0.7	..	0.2	0.3	..	2.2	2.3
Switzerland[1]	..	..	..	6.7	7.9	9.8	5.9	6.0	6.8	4.4	4.4	4.3	4.8	6.7	6.5
United States	..	..	..	11.2	11.0	10.0	4.8	5.3	5.2	3.6	3.5	3.7	5.0	6.7	6.1
Unweighted average	0.5	0.3	0.3	15.5	15.7	16.3	6.0	4.9	5.6	3.1	2.4	2.4	6.4	7.5	7.4
Regional countries															
Colombia[2]	..	..	..	..	10.1	14.4	..	0.9	1.0	..	1.4	2.5	..	3.6	1.9
Spain[2]	..	0.2	0.2	8.6	16.0	14.0	..	1.6	5.4	0.8	2.7	3.2	8.5	10.8	12.0
Unitary countries															
Chile	..	..	..	..	16.5	17.9	..	..	..	..	1.2	1.7	..	0.7	1.3
Costa Rica	..	..	..	..	12.4	13.6	..	..	..	..	0.3	0.7	..	6.2	9.2
Czech Republic	..	..	0.2	..	19.9	18.9	..	..	..	..	0.3	0.3	..	14.3	15.4
Denmark[1]	0.4	0.2	0.1	25.6	31.7	34.5	..	..	..	11.0	14.6	12.0	0.0	0.0	0.0
Estonia	..	..	0.2	..	29.5	27.5	..	..	..	..	0.3	0.3	..	5.2	5.6
Finland	..	0.2	0.2	20.3	20.7	20.6	..	..	..	8.5	9.9	9.6	7.4	13.7	11.8
France[1]	0.2	0.3	0.2	17.9	18.0	14.6	..	..	..	2.6	4.7	6.1	14.2	19.4	24.0
Greece	..	0.2	0.2	12.5	18.8	26.1	..	..	..	0.6	0.6	1.0	5.5	8.8	12.2
Hungary	..	..	0.1	..	26.0	22.9	..	..	..	..	1.0	2.1	..	13.7	11.4
Iceland	..	..	..	24.0	24.3	25.0	..	..	..	5.5	6.4	9.9	0.0	0.0	0.0
Ireland	0.6	0.5	0.1	21.6	26.4	18.1	..	..	..	2.0	0.8	0.4	3.6	4.0	3.3
Israel	..	..	..	..	28.1	22.6	..	..	..	..	2.2	2.4	..	4.9	5.2
Italy	..	0.1	0.2	13.0	24.1	24.2	..	..	..	0.2	2.1	4.8	11.2	12.1	13.3
Japan	..	..	..	9.0	10.5	11.1	..	..	..	5.1	6.4	7.4	5.7	8.5	12.9
Korea	..	..	..	13.2	13.0	15.3	..	..	..	1.5	3.5	4.7	0.1	2.3	7.3
Latvia	..	..	0.2	..	12.9	15.8	..	..	..	..	5.8	6.0	..	11.0	9.3
Lithuania[1]	..	..	0.3	..	19.8	20.0	..	..	..	..	0.6	0.3	..	7.2	9.6
Luxembourg[1]	0.2	0.2	0.3	20.0	23.1	26.3	..	..	..	2.1	2.3	1.9	9.1	9.3	10.5
Netherlands	0.6	0.5	0.4	22.2	20.9	24.0	..	..	..	0.4	1.2	1.3	14.5	14.7	13.4
New Zealand	..	..	..	27.7	33.7	29.3	..	..	..	2.3	1.9	2.2	0.0	0.0	0.0
Norway	..	..	..	19.7	22.7	33.7	..	..	..	8.7	7.9	6.2	10.5	8.8	0.0
Poland[1]	..	..	0.2	..	22.4	17.3	..	..	..	..	3.1	4.4	..	11.1	13.2
Portugal	..	0.2	0.2	12.3	21.2	22.7	..	..	..	0.0	1.6	2.5	6.5	6.3	9.2
Slovak Republic	..	..	0.2	..	24.7	19.2	..	..	..	..	0.5	0.6	..	14.2	14.6
Slovenia	..	..	0.1	..	19.8	18.2	..	..	..	..	2.4	3.3	..	17.0	15.5
Sweden	..	0.2	0.1	19.7	21.1	22.2	..	..	..	11.2	13.9	15.2	7.5	9.8	5.3
Turkey	..	..	..	..	12.3	13.7	..	..	..	..	2.1	2.1	..	2.0	7.2
United Kingdom	0.3	0.3	0.2	24.1	22.7	24.4	..	..	..	3.8	1.1	1.7	6.0	5.2	6.5
Unweighted average	0.4	0.3	0.2	18.9	21.3	21.4	..	..	..	4.1	3.5	4.0	6.4	8.2	8.8

.. Not available

1. The capital transfers were subtracted directly from the specific taxes to which they relate, except for France, Luxembourg and Poland, where the capital transfers have been allocated between tax headings in proportion to the reported tax revenue.
2. Colombia and Spain are not constitutionally federal countries, but both have a highly decentralised political structure, with high autonomy of their territorial entities.

StatLink https://stat.link/xstprk

Table 3.16. Main central government taxes as % of total tax revenues of central government, 2019

	1000 Income & profits	2000 Social security[3]	3000 Payroll	4000 Property	5000 Goods and services	6000 Others
Federal countries						
Australia	73.2	0.0	0.2	0.0	26.6	0.0
Austria	44.2	7.8	5.3	1.3	40.9	0.5
Belgium[1]	55.2	0.1	0.0	2.2	42.6	0.0
Canada	73.4	7.2	0.0	0.0	19.4	0.0
Germany	45.6	0.0	0.0	0.4	54.0	0.0
Mexico	52.7	0.0	0.0	0.0	46.0	1.3
Switzerland[1]	46.8	0.0	0.0	2.0	51.1	0.1
United States	91.2	0.0	0.0	0.8	8.1	0.0
Unweighted average	60.3	1.9	0.7	0.8	36.1	0.2
Regional countries						
Colombia[2]	44.2	0.0	2.4	6.7	46.3	0.4
Spain[2]	40.1	2.0	0.0	0.2	57.7	0.1
Unitary countries						
Chile	40.7	1.4	0.0	2.2	56.5	-0.7
Costa Rica	36.2	1.5	0.0	0.9	57.4	3.9
Czech Republic	41.8	0.0	0.0	1.2	57.0	0.0
Denmark[1]	56.5	0.1	0.8	2.0	40.6	0.0
Estonia	26.8	22.5	0.0	0.0	50.8	0.0
Finland	28.6	0.0	0.0	3.2	68.1	0.1
France[1]	40.3	2.3	3.1	5.7	48.2	0.3
Greece	32.6	0.1	0.0	8.3	59.0	0.0
Hungary	28.2	2.6	4.5	2.6	61.9	0.2
Iceland	37.9	12.8	1.2	1.5	44.1	2.4
Ireland	55.4	2.1	1.2	4.6	36.7	0.0
Israel	43.9	0.0	5.0	3.6	47.5	0.0
Italy	51.5	0.0	0.0	5.7	42.8	0.0
Japan	53.1	0.0	0.0	5.3	41.6	0.0
Korea	53.3	0.0	0.0	6.6	38.1	2.0
Latvia	9.1	2.1	0.1	1.0	87.7	0.0
Lithuania[1]	43.9	0.0	0.0	0.0	56.1	0.0
Luxembourg[1]	51.2	1.1	0.0	14.1	33.5	0.2
Netherlands	50.6	0.0	0.0	3.3	45.6	0.4
New Zealand	59.2	0.0	0.0	0.1	40.7	0.0
Norway	32.3	31.4	0.2	1.5	34.7	0.0
Poland[1]	26.5	0.0	1.5	0.0	72.0	0.0
Portugal	38.9	4.2	0.0	1.0	54.7	1.2
Slovak Republic	36.8	2.0	0.0	0.0	61.2	0.0
Slovenia	26.1	0.9	0.3	0.0	72.7	0.0
Sweden	2.1	17.5	23.9	2.6	53.7	0.1
Turkey	35.8	0.0	0.0	4.8	58.4	1.1
United Kingdom	46.5	0.0	0.5	9.7	43.3	0.0
Unweighted average	38.8	3.7	1.5	3.3	52.3	0.4

Note: Excluding social security contributions accruing to social security funds.

1. The capital transfers were subtracted directly from the specific taxes to which they relate, except for France, Luxembourg and Poland, where the capital transfers have been allocated between tax headings in proportion to the reported tax revenue.
2. Colombia and Spain are not constitutionally federal countries, but both have a highly decentralised political structure, with high autonomy of their territorial entities.
3. These comprise only social security contributions accruing to central government.

StatLink https://stat.link/olpk6e

Table 3.17. Main state government taxes as % of total tax revenues of state government, 2019

	1000 Income & profits	2000 Social security	3000 Payroll	4000 Property	5000 Goods and services	6000 Others
Federal countries						
Australia	0.0	0.0	29.1	40.1	30.8	0.0
Austria[1]	36.7	13.5	32.0	1.5	13.5	2.9
Belgium[1, 2]	46.5	1.2	0.0	37.6	14.7	0.0
Canada	48.1	4.7	5.6	4.9	36.8	0.0
Germany[1]	52.2	0.0	0.0	7.6	40.1	0.0
Mexico	0.0	0.0	61.9	17.8	15.4	4.9
Switzerland[2]	75.8	0.0	0.0	17.4	6.0	0.7
United States	43.2	0.0	0.3	3.3	53.3	0.0
Unweighted average	37.8	2.4	16.1	16.3	26.3	1.1
Regional countries						
Colombia[3]	0.0	0.0	0.0	0.0	71.6	28.4
Spain[1, 3]	70.5	0.0	0.0	19.2	10.3	0.0
Unitary countries						
Chile	..	..	..	..	..	..
Costa Rica	..	..	..	..	..	..
Czech Republic	..	..	..	..	..	..
Denmark	..	..	..	..	..	..
Estonia	..	..	..	..	..	..
Finland	..	..	..	..	..	..
France	..	..	..	..	..	..
Greece	..	..	..	..	..	..
Hungary	..	..	..	..	..	..
Iceland	..	..	..	..	..	..
Ireland	..	..	..	..	..	..
Israel	..	..	..	..	..	..
Italy	..	..	..	..	..	..
Japan	..	..	..	..	..	..
Korea	..	..	..	..	..	..
Latvia	..	..	..	..	..	..
Lithuania	..	..	..	..	..	..
Luxembourg	..	..	..	..	..	..
Netherlands	..	..	..	..	..	..
New Zealand	..	..	..	..	..	..
Norway	..	..	..	..	..	..
Poland	..	..	..	..	..	..
Portugal	..	..	..	..	..	..
Slovak Republic	..	..	..	..	..	..
Slovenia	..	..	..	..	..	..
Sweden	..	..	..	..	..	..
Turkey	..	..	..	..	..	..
United Kingdom	..	..	..	..	..	..
Unweighted average	..	..	..	..	..	..

.. Not available

1. Payments to the European Union are excluded from these comparisons.
2. The capital transfer has been allocated between tax headings in proportion to the reported tax revenue, except for Belgium, where the capital transfers were subtracted directly from the specific taxes to which they relate.
3. Colombia and Spain are not constitutionally federal countries, but both have a highly decentralised political structure, with high autonomy of their territorial entities.

StatLink https://stat.link/ernh2p

Table 3.18. Main local government taxes as % of total tax revenues of local government, 2019

	1000 Income & profits	2000 Social security	3000 Payroll	4000 Property	5000 Goods and services	6000 Others
Federal countries						
Australia	0.0	0.0	0.0	100.0	0.0	0.0
Austria[1]	0.0	4.6	71.7	13.5	7.3	2.9
Belgium[1, 2]	35.2	0.2	0.0	57.2	7.4	0.0
Canada	0.0	0.0	0.0	97.0	1.8	1.2
Germany[1]	79.8	0.0	0.0	11.4	8.6	0.3
Mexico	0.0	0.0	0.0	75.1	1.8	23.2
Switzerland[2]	80.5	0.0	0.0	16.8	0.7	2.0
United States	5.7	0.0	0.0	71.8	22.5	0.0
Unweighted average	25.1	0.6	9.0	55.4	6.3	3.7
Regional countries						
Colombia[3]	0.0	0.0	0.0	33.5	44.7	21.8
Spain[1, 3]	17.9	0.0	0.0	44.1	37.9	0.1
Unitary countries						
Chile	0.0	0.0	0.0	43.6	56.4	0.0
Costa Rica	0.0	0.0	0.0	46.0	54.0	0.0
Czech Republic[1]	0.0	0.0	0.0	56.0	44.0	0.0
Denmark[1, 2]	89.0	0.0	0.0	11.0	0.0	0.0
Estonia[1]	0.0	0.0	0.0	82.2	17.8	0.0
Finland[1]	91.9	0.0	0.0	8.1	0.0	0.0
France[1, 2]	0.0	0.0	7.5	50.1	35.4	7.1
Greece[1]	0.0	0.0	0.0	93.2	6.8	0.0
Hungary[1]	0.0	0.0	0.0	16.6	83.4	0.0
Iceland	80.2	0.0	0.0	17.4	2.4	0.0
Ireland[1]	0.0	5.3	0.0	94.7	0.0	0.0
Israel	0.0	0.0	0.0	95.3	4.7	0.0
Italy[1]	19.5	0.0	0.0	21.7	30.7	28.1
Japan	50.9	0.0	0.0	26.7	21.3	1.1
Korea	19.6	0.0	1.8	44.6	25.9	8.2
Latvia[1]	86.4	0.0	0.0	12.3	1.2	0.0
Lithuania[2]	0.0	0.0	0.0	84.2	15.8	0.0
Luxembourg[1, 2]	93.5	0.0	0.0	5.5	0.9	0.1
Netherlands[1]	0.0	0.0	0.0	52.4	47.6	0.0
New Zealand	0.0	0.0	0.0	87.7	12.3	0.0
Norway	86.6	0.0	0.0	12.7	0.8	0.0
Poland[1, 2]	66.4	0.0	0.0	28.6	3.9	1.1
Portugal[1]	25.3	0.0	0.0	47.7	26.7	0.2
Slovak Republic[1]	0.0	0.0	0.0	63.7	36.3	0.0
Slovenia[1]	75.0	0.0	0.0	18.5	6.5	0.0
Sweden[1]	97.6	0.0	0.0	2.4	0.0	0.0
Turkey	31.9	0.0	0.0	14.7	46.9	6.6
United Kingdom[1]	0.0	0.0	0.0	100.0	0.0	0.0
Unweighted average	32.6	0.2	0.3	44.2	20.8	1.9

1. Payments to the European Union are excluded from these comparisons.
2. The capital transfers were subtracted directly from the specific taxes to which they relate, except for France, Luxembourg and Poland, where the capital transfers have been allocated between tax headings in proportion to the reported tax revenue.
3. Colombia and Spain are not constitutionally federal countries, but both have a highly decentralised political structure, with high autonomy of their territorial entities.

StatLink https://stat.link/ayr3ke

Table 3.19. Gross domestic product for tax reporting years at market prices, in billions of national currency

		1965	1990	2000	2007	2010	2013	2015	2018	2019	2020p
Australia[1]	AUD	24.3	414.5	705.1	1 177.3	1 416.6	1 598.5	1 660.7	1 952.7	1 985.8	2 068.1
Austria	EUR	18.5	137.5	213.6	284.0	295.9	323.9	344.3	385.4	397.6	377.3
Belgium	EUR	20.9	170.1	256.4	343.6	363.1	392.9	416.7	460.4	476.3	451.2
Canada	CAD	61.3	696.1	1 125.5	1 577.7	1 666.0	1 902.2	1 990.4	2 231.2	2 310.7	2 204.9
Chile	CLP	..	10 522.7	42 005.2	90 702.9	111 508.6	137 876.2	159 553.3	190 825.8	196 379.3	200 512.4
Colombia	COP	..	22 731.4	195 108.6	428 506.0	544 060.0	714 093.0	804 692.0	987 791.0	1 061 119.0	1 002 587.2
Costa Rica[2]	CRC	..	525.3	4 627.1	13 889.1	19 802.0	25 463.0	30 171.9	35 966.1	37 558.1	35 983.5
Czech Republic	CZK	..	731.2	2 386.3	3 859.5	3 992.9	4 142.8	4 625.4	5 409.7	5 790.3	5 694.6
Denmark	DKK	71.5	855.6	1 326.9	1 738.8	1 810.9	1 929.7	2 036.4	2 253.3	2 318.0	2 329.6
Estonia	EUR	..	..	6.2	16.4	14.7	18.9	20.6	25.8	27.7	26.8
Finland	EUR	4.5	91.0	136.4	187.1	188.1	204.3	211.4	233.5	240.1	237.5
France	EUR	76.4	1 053.5	1 478.6	1 941.4	1 995.3	2 117.2	2 198.4	2 363.3	2 437.6	2 302.9
Germany	EUR	234.8	1 306.7	2 109.1	2 499.6	2 564.4	2 811.4	3 026.2	3 367.9	3 473.4	3 367.6
Greece	EUR	0.7	45.5	141.2	232.7	224.1	179.6	176.1	179.7	183.4	165.8
Hungary	HUF	..	..	13 324.1	25 701.4	27 431.3	30 290.9	34 937.3	43 350.4	47 524.0	47 743.5
Iceland	ISK	0.2	377.0	709.6	1 387.0	1 681.0	1 970.1	2 310.8	2 844.7	3 047.7	2 941.1
Ireland	EUR	1.3	37.9	108.5	197.1	167.4	179.4	262.8	326.0	356.5	372.9
Israel	ILS	..	119.2	540.1	736.0	877.4	1 062.2	1 166.4	1 341.6	1 418.4	1 401.4
Italy	EUR	22.4	730.9	1 241.5	1 614.8	1 611.3	1 612.8	1 655.4	1 771.6	1 790.9	1 651.6
Japan[1]	JPY	35 750.7	472 519.8	537 616.3	538 483.9	504 872.1	512 685.7	540 739.3	556 419.0	558 313.1	536 637.9
Korea[3]	KRW	831.4	200 556.2	651 634.4	1 089 660.2	1 322 611.2	1 500 819.1	1 658 020.4	1 898 192.6	1 919 039.9	1 924 453.0
Latvia	EUR	..	..	6.9	22.7	18.0	22.9	24.6	29.1	30.4	29.3
Lithuania	EUR	..	..	13.4	29.0	28.0	35.0	37.3	45.5	48.8	48.9
Luxembourg	EUR	1.0	11.0	23.1	37.2	40.2	46.5	52.1	60.1	63.5	64.1
Mexico	MXN	..	843.6	6 693.7	11 504.1	13 366.4	16 277.2	18 572.1	23 523.2	24 443.0	23 122.0
Netherlands	EUR	35.6	263.0	452.0	619.2	639.2	660.5	690.0	774.0	813.1	800.1
New Zealand[1]	NZD	4.1	75.9	122.2	188.8	205.7	237.0	258.7	310.3	317.2	339.9
Norway	NOK	57.2	749.9	1 507.3	2 350.2	2 591.5	3 071.2	3 111.2	3 553.9	3 568.5	3 413.5
Poland	PLN	..	62.7	748.5	1 187.5	1 446.8	1 646.7	1 801.1	2 121.6	2 293.2	2 323.9
Portugal	EUR	0.6	56.0	128.4	175.5	179.6	170.5	179.7	205.2	213.9	202.4
Slovak Republic	EUR	..	10.0	31.7	63.2	68.2	74.4	79.8	89.4	93.9	91.6
Slovenia	EUR	..	0.9	18.9	35.1	36.4	36.5	38.9	45.9	48.4	46.9
Spain	EUR	8.7	328.7	647.9	1 075.5	1 072.7	1 020.3	1 077.6	1 203.3	1 244.4	1 121.7
Sweden	SEK	129.3	1 549.8	2 408.2	3 320.3	3 573.6	3 822.7	4 260.5	4 828.3	5 049.6	4 983.4
Switzerland	CHF	70.1	369.5	472.6	592.4	629.3	660.6	675.7	719.3	727.2	706.2
Turkey	TRY	0.0	0.5	171.5	887.7	1 167.7	1 823.4	2 350.9	3 758.8	4 317.8	5 046.9
United Kingdom	GBP	36.4	615.7	1 095.9	1 546.1	1 606.0	1 780.3	1 919.6	2 141.8	2 217.8	2 112.0
United States	USD	709.0	5 963.1	10 251.0	14 474.2	15 049.0	16 843.2	18 206.0	20 527.2	21 372.6	20 893.7

.. Not available

1. GDP is fiscal year. The year Y is calculated (at annual rate) as the average of: Q2(Y) to Q1(Y+1) for Japan; and Q3(Y) to Q2(Y+1) for Australia and New Zealand.
2. The GDP shown for 1990 in Costa Rica is taken from the IMF (World Economic Outlook Database, accessed in October 2021). The GDP for all other years is taken from the OECD National Accounts.
3. The GDP shown for 2020 in Korea is taken from the OECD National Accounts, accessed in September 2021, and is an estimated value.

Source: OECD National Accounts.

StatLink https://stat.link/7zy435

Table 3.20. Exchange rates used, national currency per US dollar at market exchange rates

		1965	1990	2000	2007	2010	2013	2015	2018	2019	2020p
Australia	AUD	0.9	1.3	1.8	1.2	1.0	1.1	1.3	1.4	1.4	1.5
Austria	EUR	..	0.8	1.1	0.7	0.8	0.8	0.9	0.8	0.9	0.9
Belgium	EUR	..	0.8	1.1	0.7	0.8	0.8	0.9	0.8	0.9	0.9
Canada	CAD	1.1	1.2	1.5	1.1	1.0	1.0	1.3	1.3	1.3	1.3
Chile	CLP	0.0	304.9	539.4	522.2	510.0	495.3	654.3	641.9	703.3	791.7
Colombia	COP	10.5	502.3	2 087.9	2 078.3	1 898.6	1 868.8	2 741.9	2 955.7	3 280.8	3 694.9
Costa Rica	CRC	6.6	91.6	308.2	516.6	525.8	499.8	534.6	577.0	587.3	584.9
Czech Republic	CZK	..	..	38.6	20.3	19.1	19.6	24.6	21.7	22.9	23.2
Denmark	DKK	6.9	6.2	8.1	5.4	5.6	5.6	6.7	6.3	6.7	6.5
Estonia	EUR	..	0.8	1.1	0.7	0.8	0.8	0.9	0.8	0.9	0.9
Finland	EUR	..	0.8	1.1	0.7	0.8	0.8	0.9	0.8	0.9	0.9
France	EUR	..	0.8	1.1	0.7	0.8	0.8	0.9	0.8	0.9	0.9
Germany	EUR	..	0.8	1.1	0.7	0.8	0.8	0.9	0.8	0.9	0.9
Greece	EUR	..	0.8	1.1	0.7	0.8	0.8	0.9	0.8	0.9	0.9
Hungary	HUF	..	63.2	282.3	183.6	207.8	223.6	279.2	270.2	290.6	308.0
Iceland	ISK	0.4	58.4	78.8	64.1	122.2	122.2	131.9	108.3	122.6	135.4
Ireland	EUR	0.5	0.8	1.1	0.7	0.8	0.8	0.9	0.8	0.9	0.9
Israel	ILS	0.0	2.0	4.1	4.1	3.7	3.6	3.9	3.6	3.6	3.4
Italy	EUR	..	0.8	1.1	0.7	0.8	0.8	0.9	0.8	0.9	0.9
Japan	JPY	361.7	142.2	111.2	114.2	85.7	99.7	118.0	110.1	108.5	106.8
Korea	KRW	266.3	708.0	1 130.6	929.5	1 155.4	1 094.9	1 131.3	1 100.2	1 165.3	1 180.1
Latvia	EUR	..	0.8	1.1	0.7	0.8	0.8	0.9	0.8	0.9	0.9
Lithuania	EUR	..	0.8	1.1	0.7	0.8	0.8	0.9	0.8	0.9	0.9
Luxembourg	EUR	..	0.8	1.1	0.7	0.8	0.8	0.9	0.8	0.9	0.9
Mexico	MXN	0.0	2.8	9.5	10.9	12.6	12.8	15.9	19.2	19.2	21.4
Netherlands	EUR	..	0.8	1.1	0.7	0.8	0.8	0.9	0.8	0.9	0.9
New Zealand	NZD	0.7	1.7	2.3	1.4	1.3	1.2	1.4	1.5	1.5	1.5
Norway	NOK	7.2	6.3	8.8	5.9	6.0	5.9	8.1	8.1	8.8	9.4
Poland	PLN	0.0	1.0	4.3	2.8	3.0	3.2	3.8	3.6	3.8	3.9
Portugal	EUR	..	0.8	1.1	0.7	0.8	0.8	0.9	0.8	0.9	0.9
Slovak Republic	EUR	..	0.8	1.1	0.7	0.8	0.8	0.9	0.8	0.9	0.9
Slovenia	EUR	..	0.8	1.1	0.7	0.8	0.8	0.9	0.8	0.9	0.9
Spain	EUR	..	0.8	1.1	0.7	0.8	0.8	0.9	0.8	0.9	0.9
Sweden	SEK	5.2	5.9	9.2	6.8	7.2	6.5	8.4	8.7	9.5	9.2
Switzerland	CHF	4.3	1.4	1.7	1.2	1.0	0.9	1.0	1.0	1.0	0.9
Turkey	TRY	0.0	0.0	0.6	1.3	1.5	1.9	2.7	4.8	5.7	7.0
United Kingdom	GBP	0.4	0.6	0.7	0.5	0.6	0.6	0.7	0.7	0.8	0.8
United States	USD	1.0	1.0	1.0	1.0	1.0	1.0	1.0	1.0	1.0	1.0

.. Not available
Source: OECD Financial indicators data.

StatLink https://stat.link/lwpmaz

4 Country tables, 1990-2019

Chapter 4 provides a summary of tax revenues by category and by level of government for each OECD country.

4.1. Tax revenue and % of GDP by selected tax category and by level of government

In all of the following tables the symbol (..) indicates not available/or not applicable. The main series in this chapter cover a selection of years between 1990 and 2019. A complete series is, however, available on line. Data for 1955 and 1960 (for nineteen OECD countries) are provided in part V of the 1998 edition of this Report.

The Gross Domestic Product (GDP) figures are based on the 2008 System of National Accounts (SNA) for all OECD countries.

Box 4.1. Treatment of capital transfers

Some tables refer to the treatment of the capital transfers that some countries make to account for taxes that have been assessed but not collected. The capital transfer has been subtracted from the total tax revenue for France, Luxembourg and Poland and this reduction has been allocated between tax headings in proportion to their tax revenues at the level of government against which these transfers were recorded. In the case of Austria, Belgium, Denmark, Lithuania and Switzerland the capital transfers were instead subtracted directly from the specific taxes to which they relate.

Countries reporting capital transfers include:

- Austria in 2020.
- Belgium from 1995.
- Denmark from 1971.
- France from 1992.
- Lithuania from 1999.
- Luxembourg from 2013.
- Poland from 1995 to 2019.
- Switzerland from 1990.

Table 4.1. Australia, tax revenue and % of GDP by selected tax category

	Billion AUD					% of GDP				
	1990	2000	2010	2018	2019	1990	2000	2010	2018	2019
Total tax revenue	**116.5**	**214.8**	**356.7**	**557.2**	**549.5**	**28.1**	**30.5**	**25.2**	**28.5**	**27.7**
1000 Taxes on income, profits and capital gains	**66.5**	**124.4**	**202.2**	**334.9**	**325.1**	**16.1**	**17.6**	**14.3**	**17.1**	**16.4**
1100 Of individuals	50.1	81.0	138.2	229.4	230.9	12.1	11.5	9.8	11.7	11.6
1200 Corporate	16.5	43.4	64.0	105.4	94.2	4.0	6.2	4.5	5.4	4.7
1300 Unallocable between 1100 and 1200	0.0	0.0	0.0	0.0	0.0	0.0	0.0	0.0	0.0	0.0
2000 Social security contributions	**0.0**	**0.0**	**0.0**	**0.0**	**0.0**	**0.0**	**0.0**	**0.0**	**0.0**	**0.0**
2100 Employees	0.0	0.0	0.0	0.0	0.0	0.0	0.0	0.0	0.0	0.0
2200 Employers	0.0	0.0	0.0	0.0	0.0	0.0	0.0	0.0	0.0	0.0
2300 Self-employed or non-employed	0.0	0.0	0.0	0.0	0.0	0.0	0.0	0.0	0.0	0.0
2400 Unallocable between 2100, 2200 and 2300	0.0	0.0	0.0	0.0	0.0	0.0	0.0	0.0	0.0	0.0
3000 Taxes on payroll and workforce	**7.1**	**9.6**	**18.5**	**26.9**	**26.0**	**1.7**	**1.4**	**1.3**	**1.4**	**1.3**
4000 Taxes on property	**10.4**	**18.8**	**33.5**	**53.1**	**54.0**	**2.5**	**2.7**	**2.4**	**2.7**	**2.7**
4100 Recurrent taxes on immovable property	6.1	9.1	19.9	32.7	33.8	1.5	1.3	1.4	1.7	1.7
4200 Recurrent taxes on net wealth	0.0	0.0	0.0	0.0	0.0	0.0	0.0	0.0	0.0	0.0
4300 Estate, inheritance and gift taxes	0.0	0.0	0.0	0.0	0.0	0.0	0.0	0.0	0.0	0.0
4400 Taxes on financial and capital transactions	4.3	9.8	13.6	20.4	20.2	1.0	1.4	1.0	1.0	1.0
4500 Non-recurrent taxes	0.0	0.0	0.0	0.0	0.0	0.0	0.0	0.0	0.0	0.0
4600 Other recurrent taxes on property	0.0	0.0	0.0	0.0	0.0	0.0	0.0	0.0	0.0	0.0
5000 Taxes on goods and services	**32.4**	**61.9**	**102.6**	**142.3**	**144.4**	**7.8**	**8.8**	**7.2**	**7.3**	**7.3**
5100 Taxes on production, sale, transfer, etc	27.2	56.2	90.8	122.1	123.6	6.6	8.0	6.4	6.3	6.2
5110 General taxes	9.4	25.8	48.1	66.8	65.7	2.3	3.7	3.4	3.4	3.3
5111 Value added taxes	0.0	23.9	46.9	65.1	64.0	0.0	3.4	3.3	3.3	3.2
5120 Taxes on specific goods and services	17.8	30.3	42.7	55.2	57.9	4.3	4.3	3.0	2.8	2.9
5121 Excises	12.0	19.8	26.7	24.5	24.1	2.9	2.8	1.9	1.3	1.2
5200 Taxes on use of goods and perform activities	5.2	5.7	11.7	20.2	20.8	1.3	0.8	0.8	1.0	1.0
5300 Unallocable between 5100 and 5200	0.0	0.0	0.0	0.0	0.0	0.0	0.0	0.0	0.0	0.0
6000 Other taxes	**0.0**	**0.0**	**0.0**	**0.0**	**0.0**	**0.0**	**0.0**	**0.0**	**0.0**	**0.0**
Non-wastable tax credits										
Non-wastable tax credits against 1000	..	0.2	6.7	10.4	10.0	..	0.0	0.5	0.5	0.5
Transfer component	..	0.0	4.4	6.6	6.6	..	0.0	0.3	0.3	0.3
Tax expenditure component	..	0.2	2.4	3.8	3.5	..	0.0	0.2	0.2	0.2

.. Not available

Note: More detailed country data and country notes are available in online chapter 5 "Detailed country tables": https://doi.org/10.1787/0bbc27da-en. Full time series can be accessed at http://oe.cd/full-time-series.

Source: Australian Bureau of Statistics.

StatLink https://stat.link/g8bqnx

Table 4.2. Australia, tax revenue and % of GDP by level of government and main taxes

	Billion AUD					% of GDP				
	1990	2000	2010	2018	2019	1990	2000	2010	2018	2019
Federal or Central government										
Total tax revenue	**92.6**	**175.7**	**285.9**	**452.0**	**444.1**	**22.3**	**24.9**	**20.2**	**23.1**	**22.4**
1000 Taxes on income, profits and capital gains	66.5	124.4	202.2	334.9	325.1	16.1	17.6	14.3	17.1	16.4
2000 Social security contributions	0.0	0.0	0.0	0.0	0.0	0.0	0.0	0.0	0.0	0.0
3000 Taxes on payroll and workforce	1.3	0.1	0.5	1.1	1.0	0.3	0.0	0.0	0.1	0.1
4000 Taxes on property	0.2	0.0	0.0	0.0	0.0	0.1	0.0	0.0	0.0	0.0
5000 Taxes on goods and services	24.5	51.1	83.2	116.0	118.0	5.9	7.2	5.9	5.9	5.9
6000 Other taxes	0.0	0.0	0.0	0.0	0.0	0.0	0.0	0.0	0.0	0.0
State/Regional										
Total tax revenue	**19.7**	**32.7**	**58.4**	**86.3**	**85.8**	**4.7**	**4.6**	**4.1**	**4.4**	**4.3**
1000 Taxes on income, profits and capital gains	0.0	0.0	0.0	0.0	0.0	0.0	0.0	0.0	0.0	0.0
2000 Social security contributions	0.0	0.0	0.0	0.0	0.0	0.0	0.0	0.0	0.0	0.0
3000 Taxes on payroll and workforce	5.8	9.5	18.0	25.9	25.0	1.4	1.3	1.3	1.3	1.3
4000 Taxes on property	6.0	12.4	21.0	34.2	34.4	1.4	1.8	1.5	1.8	1.7
5000 Taxes on goods and services	7.9	10.8	19.3	26.3	26.4	1.9	1.5	1.4	1.3	1.3
6000 Other taxes	0.0	0.0	0.0	0.0	0.0	0.0	0.0	0.0	0.0	0.0
Local government										
Total tax revenue	**4.2**	**6.4**	**12.4**	**18.9**	**19.6**	**1.0**	**0.9**	**0.9**	**1.0**	**1.0**
1000 Taxes on income, profits and capital gains	0.0	0.0	0.0	0.0	0.0	0.0	0.0	0.0	0.0	0.0
2000 Social security contributions	0.0	0.0	0.0	0.0	0.0	0.0	0.0	0.0	0.0	0.0
3000 Taxes on payroll and workforce	0.0	0.0	0.0	0.0	0.0	0.0	0.0	0.0	0.0	0.0
4000 Taxes on property	4.2	6.4	12.4	18.9	19.6	1.0	0.9	0.9	1.0	1.0
5000 Taxes on goods and services	0.0	0.0	0.0	0.0	0.0	0.0	0.0	0.0	0.0	0.0
6000 Other taxes	0.0	0.0	0.0	0.0	0.0	0.0	0.0	0.0	0.0	0.0
Social Security Funds										
Total tax revenue	**0.0**	**0.0**	**0.0**	**0.0**	**0.0**	**0.0**	**0.0**	**0.0**	**0.0**	**0.0**
1000 Taxes on income, profits and capital gains	0.0	0.0	0.0	0.0	0.0	0.0	0.0	0.0	0.0	0.0
2000 Social security contributions	0.0	0.0	0.0	0.0	0.0	0.0	0.0	0.0	0.0	0.0
3000 Taxes on payroll and workforce	0.0	0.0	0.0	0.0	0.0	0.0	0.0	0.0	0.0	0.0
4000 Taxes on property	0.0	0.0	0.0	0.0	0.0	0.0	0.0	0.0	0.0	0.0
5000 Taxes on goods and services	0.0	0.0	0.0	0.0	0.0	0.0	0.0	0.0	0.0	0.0
6000 Other taxes	0.0	0.0	0.0	0.0	0.0	0.0	0.0	0.0	0.0	0.0

Note: More detailed country data and country notes are available in online chapter 6 "Tax revenues by sub-sectors of general government": https://doi.org/10.1787/0bbc27da-en. Full time series can be accessed at http://oe.cd/full-time-series.

Source: Australian Bureau of Statistics.

StatLink https://stat.link/3trdgq

Table 4.3. Austria, tax revenue and % of GDP by selected tax category

	Billion EUR					% of GDP				
	1990	2000	2010	2018	2019	1990	2000	2010	2018	2019
Total tax revenue	**54.0**	**90.3**	**121.2**	**162.8**	**169.2**	**39.3**	**42.3**	**41.0**	**42.3**	**42.6**
1000 Taxes on income, profits and capital gains	**13.8**	**25.6**	**34.0**	**47.8**	**49.9**	**10.0**	**12.0**	**11.5**	**12.4**	**12.5**
1100 Of individuals	11.3	19.9	27.1	36.2	38.2	8.2	9.3	9.2	9.4	9.6
1200 Corporate	1.9	4.2	5.5	10.4	10.8	1.4	1.9	1.9	2.7	2.7
1300 Unallocable between 1100 and 1200	0.5	1.5	1.4	1.1	0.8	0.4	0.7	0.5	0.3	0.2
2000 Social security contributions	**17.8**	**30.5**	**41.4**	**56.7**	**59.1**	**12.9**	**14.3**	**14.0**	**14.7**	**14.9**
2100 Employees	7.5	12.5	16.8	22.8	23.8	5.5	5.8	5.7	5.9	6.0
2200 Employers	8.8	14.7	19.4	26.7	27.8	6.4	6.9	6.6	6.9	7.0
2300 Self-employed or non-employed	1.5	3.4	5.2	7.2	7.5	1.1	1.6	1.7	1.9	1.9
2400 Unallocable between 2100, 2200 and 2300	0.0	0.0	0.0	0.0	0.0	0.0	0.0	0.0	0.0	0.0
3000 Taxes on payroll and workforce	**3.3**	**5.8**	**8.4**	**10.4**	**10.8**	**2.4**	**2.7**	**2.8**	**2.7**	**2.7**
4000 Taxes on property	**1.5**	**1.2**	**1.6**	**2.1**	**2.2**	**1.1**	**0.6**	**0.5**	**0.5**	**0.5**
4100 Recurrent taxes on immovable property	0.4	0.5	0.7	0.8	0.8	0.3	0.2	0.2	0.2	0.2
4200 Recurrent taxes on net wealth	0.6	0.0	0.0	0.0	0.0	0.5	0.0	0.0	0.0	0.0
4300 Estate, inheritance and gift taxes	0.1	0.1	0.0	0.0	0.0	0.1	0.1	0.0	0.0	0.0
4400 Taxes on financial and capital transactions	0.4	0.6	0.8	1.2	1.3	0.3	0.3	0.3	0.3	0.3
4500 Non-recurrent taxes	0.0	0.0	0.0	0.1	0.0	0.0	0.0	0.0	0.0	0.0
4600 Other recurrent taxes on property	0.0	0.0	0.0	0.0	0.0	0.0	0.0	0.0	0.0	0.0
5000 Taxes on goods and services	**17.0**	**26.5**	**34.7**	**45.1**	**46.5**	**12.4**	**12.4**	**11.7**	**11.7**	**11.7**
5100 Taxes on production, sale, transfer, etc	16.2	24.6	32.1	41.3	42.5	11.8	11.5	10.9	10.7	10.7
5110 General taxes	11.2	16.9	22.7	29.3	30.4	8.2	7.9	7.7	7.6	7.7
5111 Value added taxes	11.2	16.9	22.7	29.3	30.4	8.2	7.9	7.7	7.6	7.7
5120 Taxes on specific goods and services	4.9	7.7	9.4	12.0	12.0	3.5	3.6	3.2	3.1	3.0
5121 Excises	3.3	5.5	6.9	8.2	8.2	2.4	2.6	2.3	2.1	2.1
5200 Taxes on use of goods and perform activities	0.9	1.9	2.6	3.8	4.1	0.6	0.9	0.9	1.0	1.0
5300 Unallocable between 5100 and 5200	0.0	0.0	0.0	0.0	0.0	0.0	0.0	0.0	0.0	0.0
6000 Other taxes	**0.7**	**0.8**	**1.1**	**0.8**	**0.8**	**0.5**	**0.4**	**0.4**	**0.2**	**0.2**
Non-wastable tax credits										
Non-wastable tax credits against 1000	..	0.7	0.7	0.3	0.3	..	0.3	0.2	0.1	0.1
Transfer component	..	0.1	0.2	0.1	0.1	..	0.0	0.1	0.0	0.0
Tax expenditure component	..	0.6	0.4	0.2	0.2	..	0.3	0.1	0.1	0.1
Revenues collected on behalf of the EU										
Revenues collected on behalf of the EU, total	..	0.4	0.3	0.7	0.7	..	0.2	0.1	0.2	0.2
Customs duties	..	0.4	0.3	0.5	0.5	..	0.2	0.1	0.1	0.1
SRF contributions	..	..	..	0.2	0.2	..	..	..	0.1	0.0

.. Not available

Note: More detailed country data and country notes are available in online chapter 5 "Detailed country tables": https://doi.org/10.1787/0bbc27da-en. Full time series can be accessed at http://oe.cd/full-time-series.

Source: Statistics Austria.

StatLink https://stat.link/ce8n9p

Table 4.4. Austria, tax revenue and % of GDP by level of government and main taxes

	Billion EUR					% of GDP				
	1990	2000	2010	2018	2019	1990	2000	2010	2018	2019
Federal or Central government										
Total tax revenue	**27.2**	**60.5**	**80.7**	**106.0**	**109.9**	**19.8**	**28.3**	**27.3**	**27.5**	**27.6**
1000 Taxes on income, profits and capital gains	8.6	24.9	33.1	46.5	48.6	6.2	11.7	11.2	12.1	12.2
2000 Social security contributions	2.4	5.1	6.3	8.3	8.5	1.7	2.4	2.1	2.2	2.1
3000 Taxes on payroll and workforce	2.6	3.9	5.8	5.7	5.8	1.9	1.8	1.9	1.5	1.5
4000 Taxes on property	0.9	0.7	0.9	1.3	1.4	0.6	0.3	0.3	0.3	0.3
5000 Taxes on goods and services	12.3	25.3	33.7	43.6	45.0	8.9	11.8	11.4	11.3	11.3
6000 Other taxes	0.5	0.6	0.9	0.5	0.6	0.4	0.3	0.3	0.1	0.1
State/Regional										
Total tax revenue	**5.8**	**1.4**	**2.0**	**3.4**	**3.4**	**4.2**	**0.7**	**0.7**	**0.9**	**0.9**
1000 Taxes on income, profits and capital gains	2.8	0.6	0.9	1.2	1.3	2.0	0.3	0.3	0.3	0.3
2000 Social security contributions	0.2	0.4	0.5	0.5	0.5	0.2	0.2	0.2	0.1	0.1
3000 Taxes on payroll and workforce	0.0	0.1	0.2	1.1	1.1	0.0	0.1	0.1	0.3	0.3
4000 Taxes on property	0.1	0.0	0.0	0.0	0.1	0.0	0.0	0.0	0.0	0.0
5000 Taxes on goods and services	2.7	0.2	0.3	0.4	0.5	2.0	0.1	0.1	0.1	0.1
6000 Other taxes	0.0	0.1	0.1	0.1	0.1	0.0	0.0	0.0	0.0	0.0
Local government										
Total tax revenue	**6.1**	**3.2**	**3.8**	**5.1**	**5.3**	**4.4**	**1.5**	**1.3**	**1.3**	**1.3**
1000 Taxes on income, profits and capital gains	2.4	0.0	0.0	0.0	0.0	1.8	0.0	0.0	0.0	0.0
2000 Social security contributions	0.2	0.3	0.3	0.3	0.2	0.1	0.1	0.1	0.1	0.1
3000 Taxes on payroll and workforce	0.7	1.8	2.4	3.6	3.8	0.5	0.8	0.8	0.9	1.0
4000 Taxes on property	0.5	0.5	0.6	0.7	0.7	0.4	0.2	0.2	0.2	0.2
5000 Taxes on goods and services	2.1	0.6	0.4	0.4	0.4	1.5	0.3	0.1	0.1	0.1
6000 Other taxes	0.2	0.1	0.1	0.1	0.2	0.1	0.0	0.0	0.0	0.0
Social Security Funds										
Total tax revenue	**15.0**	**24.8**	**34.4**	**47.6**	**49.8**	**10.9**	**11.6**	**11.6**	**12.4**	**12.5**
1000 Taxes on income, profits and capital gains	0.0	0.0	0.0	0.0	0.0	0.0	0.0	0.0	0.0	0.0
2000 Social security contributions	15.0	24.8	34.4	47.6	49.8	10.9	11.6	11.6	12.4	12.5
3000 Taxes on payroll and workforce	0.0	0.0	0.0	0.0	0.0	0.0	0.0	0.0	0.0	0.0
4000 Taxes on property	0.0	0.0	0.0	0.0	0.0	0.0	0.0	0.0	0.0	0.0
5000 Taxes on goods and services	0.0	0.0	0.0	0.0	0.0	0.0	0.0	0.0	0.0	0.0
6000 Other taxes	0.0	0.0	0.0	0.0	0.0	0.0	0.0	0.0	0.0	0.0

Note: More detailed country data and country notes are available in online chapter 6 "Tax revenues by sub-sectors of general government": https://doi.org/10.1787/0bbc27da-en. Full time series can be accessed at http://oe.cd/full-time-series.

Source: Statistics Austria.

StatLink https://stat.link/af38ds

Table 4.5. Belgium, tax revenue and % of GDP by selected tax category

	Billion EUR					% of GDP				
	1990	2000	2010	2018	2019	1990	2000	2010	2018	2019
Total tax revenue	**70.4**	**112.4**	**155.7**	**202.0**	**203.4**	**41.4**	**43.8**	**42.9**	**43.9**	**42.7**
1000 Taxes on income, profits and capital gains	**26.0**	**43.4**	**53.2**	**74.2**	**71.8**	**15.3**	**16.9**	**14.7**	**16.1**	**15.1**
1100 Of individuals	22.5	35.3	44.0	54.4	54.0	13.2	13.8	12.1	11.8	11.3
1200 Corporate	3.4	8.1	9.2	19.8	17.7	2.0	3.1	2.5	4.3	3.7
1300 Unallocable between 1100 and 1200	0.0	0.1	0.0	0.1	0.1	0.0	0.0	0.0	0.0	0.0
2000 Social security contributions	**23.4**	**34.6**	**50.5**	**61.0**	**63.1**	**13.7**	**13.5**	**13.9**	**13.3**	**13.2**
2100 Employees	7.2	10.9	15.0	18.4	19.1	4.2	4.3	4.1	4.0	4.0
2200 Employers	14.7	20.8	30.9	36.5	37.8	8.6	8.1	8.5	7.9	7.9
2300 Self-employed or non-employed	1.5	2.9	4.6	6.1	6.2	0.9	1.1	1.3	1.3	1.3
2400 Unallocable between 2100, 2200 and 2300	0.0	0.0	0.0	0.0	0.0	0.0	0.0	0.0	0.0	0.0
3000 Taxes on payroll and workforce	**0.0**	**0.0**	**0.0**	**0.0**	**0.0**	**0.0**	**0.0**	**0.0**	**0.0**	**0.0**
4000 Taxes on property	**2.7**	**5.3**	**11.3**	**15.8**	**16.4**	**1.6**	**2.1**	**3.1**	**3.4**	**3.4**
4100 Recurrent taxes on immovable property	0.6	1.2	4.6	5.7	6.1	0.4	0.5	1.3	1.2	1.3
4200 Recurrent taxes on net wealth	0.0	0.1	0.2	1.0	0.9	0.0	0.0	0.1	0.2	0.2
4300 Estate, inheritance and gift taxes	0.5	1.1	2.3	3.2	2.9	0.3	0.4	0.6	0.7	0.6
4400 Taxes on financial and capital transactions	1.5	2.7	3.5	4.9	5.4	0.9	1.0	1.0	1.1	1.1
4500 Non-recurrent taxes	0.0	0.1	0.3	0.6	0.5	0.0	0.0	0.1	0.1	0.1
4600 Other recurrent taxes on property	0.1	0.2	0.3	0.5	0.5	0.1	0.1	0.1	0.1	0.1
5000 Taxes on goods and services	**18.4**	**29.1**	**40.7**	**50.9**	**52.2**	**10.8**	**11.3**	**11.2**	**11.1**	**11.0**
5100 Taxes on production, sale, transfer, etc	17.4	27.0	38.3	48.2	49.3	10.2	10.5	10.5	10.5	10.3
5110 General taxes	11.6	18.2	25.5	31.3	32.1	6.8	7.1	7.0	6.8	6.7
5111 Value added taxes	11.5	18.1	25.3	31.1	31.7	6.8	7.1	7.0	6.7	6.7
5120 Taxes on specific goods and services	5.8	8.7	12.8	17.0	17.2	3.4	3.4	3.5	3.7	3.6
5121 Excises	3.5	5.7	7.8	10.1	10.0	2.0	2.2	2.1	2.2	2.1
5200 Taxes on use of goods and perform activities	1.0	2.1	2.4	2.6	2.9	0.6	0.8	0.7	0.6	0.6
5300 Unallocable between 5100 and 5200	0.0	0.0	0.0	0.0	0.0	0.0	0.0	0.0	0.0	0.0
6000 Other taxes	**0.0**	**0.0**	**0.0**	**0.0**	**0.0**	**0.0**	**0.0**	**0.0**	**0.0**	**0.0**
Non-wastable tax credits										
Non-wastable tax credits against 1000	..	..	1.0	1.0	1.1	..	..	0.3	0.2	0.2
Transfer component	..	..	0.4	0.2	0.2	..	..	0.1	0.0	0.0
Tax expenditure component	..	..	0.6	0.8	0.9	..	..	0.2	0.2	0.2
Revenues collected on behalf of the EU										
Revenues collected on behalf of the EU, total	0.9	1.0	1.3	1.9	1.9	0.6	0.4	0.4	0.4	0.4
Customs duties	..	1.0	1.2	1.6	1.7	..	0.4	0.3	0.4	0.4
SRF contributions	..	..	..	0.3	0.3	..	..	..	0.1	0.1

.. Not available

Note: The total tax revenue has been reduced by the amount of any capital transfer that represents uncollected taxes. The capital transfers were subtracted directly from the specific taxes to which they relate. Therefore, the tax revenue amounts are different to those reported in the detailed country data available in online chapter 5 "Detailed country tables".

More detailed country data and country notes are available in online chapter 5 "Detailed country tables": https://doi.org/10.1787/0bbc27da-en. Full time series can be accessed at http://oe.cd/full-time-series.

Source: Federal Ministry of Finance.

StatLink https://stat.link/8gawc9

Table 4.6. Belgium, tax revenue and % of GDP by level of government and main taxes

	Billion EUR					% of GDP				
	1990	2000	2010	2018	2019	1990	2000	2010	2018	2019
Federal or Central government										
Total tax revenue	**42.5**	**69.4**	**87.8**	**106.0**	**103.3**	**25.0**	**27.1**	**24.2**	**23.0**	**21.7**
1000 Taxes on income, profits and capital gains	23.9	39.6	49.3	60.3	57.0	14.0	15.4	13.6	13.1	12.0
2000 Social security contributions	0.9	1.3	2.5	0.1	0.1	0.5	0.5	0.7	0.0	0.0
3000 Taxes on payroll and workforce	0.0	0.0	0.0	0.0	0.0	0.0	0.0	0.0	0.0	0.0
4000 Taxes on property	1.1	2.3	0.9	2.3	2.2	0.6	0.9	0.3	0.5	0.5
5000 Taxes on goods and services	16.7	26.3	35.0	43.3	44.0	9.8	10.2	9.7	9.4	9.2
6000 Other taxes	0.0	0.0	0.0	0.0	0.0	0.0	0.0	0.0	0.0	0.0
State/Regional										
Total tax revenue	**1.2**	**2.4**	**8.1**	**20.7**	**21.5**	**0.7**	**1.0**	**2.2**	**4.5**	**4.5**
1000 Taxes on income, profits and capital gains	0.0	0.1	0.0	9.5	10.0	0.0	0.0	0.0	2.1	2.1
2000 Social security contributions	0.0	0.0	0.0	0.3	0.3	0.0	0.0	0.0	0.1	0.1
3000 Taxes on payroll and workforce	0.0	0.0	0.0	0.0	0.0	0.0	0.0	0.0	0.0	0.0
4000 Taxes on property	0.9	1.9	5.6	7.9	8.1	0.5	0.7	1.5	1.7	1.7
5000 Taxes on goods and services	0.2	0.5	2.4	3.0	3.2	0.1	0.2	0.7	0.7	0.7
6000 Other taxes	0.0	0.0	0.0	0.0	0.0	0.0	0.0	0.0	0.0	0.0
Local government										
Total tax revenue	**3.1**	**4.6**	**7.9**	**9.2**	**10.0**	**1.8**	**1.8**	**2.2**	**2.0**	**2.1**
1000 Taxes on income, profits and capital gains	2.1	3.1	2.9	3.2	3.5	1.2	1.2	0.8	0.7	0.7
2000 Social security contributions	0.1	0.0	0.0	0.0	0.0	0.1	0.0	0.0	0.0	0.0
3000 Taxes on payroll and workforce	0.0	0.0	0.0	0.0	0.0	0.0	0.0	0.0	0.0	0.0
4000 Taxes on property	0.6	1.0	4.4	5.3	5.7	0.3	0.4	1.2	1.1	1.2
5000 Taxes on goods and services	0.3	0.4	0.6	0.7	0.7	0.2	0.2	0.2	0.2	0.2
6000 Other taxes	0.0	0.0	0.0	0.0	0.0	0.0	0.0	0.0	0.0	0.0
Social Security Funds										
Total tax revenue	**22.7**	**34.9**	**50.7**	**64.2**	**66.7**	**13.4**	**13.6**	**14.0**	**13.9**	**14.0**
1000 Taxes on income, profits and capital gains	0.0	0.6	1.0	1.3	1.3	0.0	0.2	0.3	0.3	0.3
2000 Social security contributions	22.4	33.3	48.0	60.7	62.8	13.2	13.0	13.2	13.2	13.2
3000 Taxes on payroll and workforce	0.0	0.0	0.0	0.0	0.0	0.0	0.0	0.0	0.0	0.0
4000 Taxes on property	0.1	0.2	0.3	0.3	0.3	0.1	0.1	0.1	0.1	0.1
5000 Taxes on goods and services	0.2	0.8	1.3	1.9	2.3	0.1	0.3	0.4	0.4	0.5
6000 Other taxes	0.0	0.0	0.0	0.0	0.0	0.0	0.0	0.0	0.0	0.0

Note: The total tax revenue has been reduced by the amount of any capital transfer that represents uncollected taxes. The capital transfers were subtracted directly from the specific taxes to which they relate. Therefore, the tax revenue amounts are different to those reported in the detailed country data available in online chapter 6 "Tax revenues by sub-sectors of general government".

More detailed country data and country notes are available in online chapter 6 "Tax revenues by sub-sectors of general government": https://doi.org/10.1787/0bbc27da-en. Full time series can be accessed at http://oe.cd/full-time-series.

Source: Federal Ministry of Finance.

StatLink https://stat.link/7x9j1t

Table 4.7. Canada, tax revenue and % of GDP by selected tax category

	Billion CAD					% of GDP				
	1990	2000	2010	2018	2019	1990	2000	2010	2018	2019
Total tax revenue	**244.2**	**390.2**	**516.6**	**747.6**	**781.2**	**35.1**	**34.7**	**31.0**	**33.5**	**33.8**
1000 Taxes on income, profits and capital gains	**118.6**	**195.3**	**241.0**	**367.5**	**387.6**	**17.0**	**17.4**	**14.5**	**16.5**	**16.8**
1100 Of individuals	99.7	143.7	180.9	267.2	281.4	14.3	12.8	10.9	12.0	12.2
1200 Corporate	17.2	47.6	54.1	91.4	96.2	2.5	4.2	3.2	4.1	4.2
1300 Unallocable between 1100 and 1200	1.7	4.0	6.0	8.9	10.0	0.2	0.4	0.4	0.4	0.4
2000 Social security contributions	**29.7**	**53.1**	**76.8**	**103.5**	**108.4**	**4.3**	**4.7**	**4.6**	**4.6**	**4.7**
2100 Employees	10.6	21.4	30.6	41.6	44.3	1.5	1.9	1.8	1.9	1.9
2200 Employers	18.4	30.3	43.5	58.2	60.2	2.7	2.7	2.6	2.6	2.6
2300 Self-employed or non-employed	0.6	1.4	2.6	3.7	3.9	0.1	0.1	0.2	0.2	0.2
2400 Unallocable between 2100, 2200 and 2300	0.0	0.0	0.0	0.0	0.0	0.0	0.0	0.0	0.0	0.0
3000 Taxes on payroll and workforce	**5.5**	**8.0**	**10.8**	**14.9**	**17.2**	**0.8**	**0.7**	**0.6**	**0.7**	**0.7**
4000 Taxes on property	**24.5**	**37.2**	**63.7**	**86.2**	**89.1**	**3.5**	**3.3**	**3.8**	**3.9**	**3.9**
4100 Recurrent taxes on immovable property	20.2	30.2	51.7	68.8	70.4	2.9	2.7	3.1	3.1	3.0
4200 Recurrent taxes on net wealth	1.9	4.2	1.5	0.5	0.4	0.3	0.4	0.1	0.0	0.0
4300 Estate, inheritance and gift taxes	0.0	0.0	0.2	0.3	0.3	0.0	0.0	0.0	0.0	0.0
4400 Taxes on financial and capital transactions	0.0	0.0	3.1	6.5	6.8	0.0	0.0	0.2	0.3	0.3
4500 Non-recurrent taxes	2.4	2.7	7.3	10.1	11.1	0.3	0.2	0.4	0.5	0.5
4600 Other recurrent taxes on property	0.0	0.0	0.0	0.0	0.0	0.0	0.0	0.0	0.0	0.0
5000 Taxes on goods and services	**63.1**	**94.5**	**123.8**	**174.7**	**178.0**	**9.1**	**8.4**	**7.4**	**7.8**	**7.7**
5100 Taxes on production, sale, transfer, etc	59.6	88.9	116.2	162.7	166.9	8.6	7.9	7.0	7.3	7.2
5110 General taxes	34.5	55.3	72.1	106.1	109.7	5.0	4.9	4.3	4.8	4.7
5111 Value added taxes	0.0	35.9	70.7	101.4	103.5	0.0	3.2	4.2	4.5	4.5
5120 Taxes on specific goods and services	25.2	33.6	44.0	56.5	57.2	3.6	3.0	2.6	2.5	2.5
5121 Excises	14.5	18.4	23.3	27.8	28.7	2.1	1.6	1.4	1.2	1.2
5200 Taxes on use of goods and perform activities	3.5	5.6	7.6	12.0	11.1	0.5	0.5	0.5	0.5	0.5
5300 Unallocable between 5100 and 5200	0.0	0.0	0.0	0.0	0.0	0.0	0.0	0.0	0.0	0.0
6000 Other taxes	**2.9**	**2.2**	**0.6**	**0.9**	**0.9**	**0.4**	**0.2**	**0.0**	**0.0**	**0.0**
Non-wastable tax credits										
Non-wastable tax credits against 1000	..	3.4	11.1	14.5	18.2	..	0.3	0.7	0.7	0.8
Transfer component	..	3.1	10.2	12.1	14.2	..	0.3	0.6	0.5	0.6
Tax expenditure component	..	0.3	0.9	2.4	4.0	..	0.0	0.1	0.1	0.2

.. Not available

Note: More detailed country data and country notes are available in online chapter 5 "Detailed country tables": https://doi.org/10.1787/0bbc27da-en. Full time series can be accessed at http://oe.cd/full-time-series.

Source: Statistics Canada.

StatLink https://stat.link/fpg3e1

Table 4.8. Canada, tax revenue and % of GDP by level of government and main taxes

	Billion CAD					% of GDP				
	1990	2000	2010	2018	2019	1990	2000	2010	2018	2019
Federal or Central government										
Total tax revenue	**101.7**	**184.4**	**212.8**	**311.8**	**325.7**	**14.6**	**16.4**	**12.8**	**14.0**	**14.1**
1000 Taxes on income, profits and capital gains	73.6	126.3	148.7	227.3	239.1	10.6	11.2	8.9	10.2	10.3
2000 Social security contributions	0.0	18.8	17.9	22.4	23.4	0.0	1.7	1.1	1.0	1.0
3000 Taxes on payroll and workforce	0.0	0.0	0.0	0.0	0.0	0.0	0.0	0.0	0.0	0.0
4000 Taxes on property	0.0	0.0	0.0	0.0	0.0	0.0	0.0	0.0	0.0	0.0
5000 Taxes on goods and services	28.1	39.4	46.2	62.1	63.1	4.0	3.5	2.8	2.8	2.7
6000 Other taxes	0.0	0.0	0.0	0.0	0.0	0.0	0.0	0.0	0.0	0.0
State/Regional										
Total tax revenue	**89.3**	**148.2**	**201.1**	**295.6**	**308.8**	**12.8**	**13.2**	**12.1**	**13.2**	**13.4**
1000 Taxes on income, profits and capital gains	44.9	69.0	92.2	140.1	148.5	6.5	6.1	5.5	6.3	6.4
2000 Social security contributions	0.0	8.3	11.7	15.3	14.6	0.0	0.7	0.7	0.7	0.6
3000 Taxes on payroll and workforce	5.5	8.0	10.8	14.9	17.2	0.8	0.7	0.6	0.7	0.7
4000 Taxes on property	4.2	8.4	9.8	14.0	15.0	0.6	0.7	0.6	0.6	0.6
5000 Taxes on goods and services	34.6	54.5	76.7	111.3	113.5	5.0	4.8	4.6	5.0	4.9
6000 Other taxes	0.0	0.0	0.0	0.0	0.0	0.0	0.0	0.0	0.0	0.0
Local government										
Total tax revenue	**23.5**	**31.5**	**55.4**	**74.4**	**76.4**	**3.4**	**2.8**	**3.3**	**3.3**	**3.3**
1000 Taxes on income, profits and capital gains	0.0	0.0	0.0	0.0	0.0	0.0	0.0	0.0	0.0	0.0
2000 Social security contributions	0.0	0.0	0.0	0.0	0.0	0.0	0.0	0.0	0.0	0.0
3000 Taxes on payroll and workforce	0.0	0.0	0.0	0.0	0.0	0.0	0.0	0.0	0.0	0.0
4000 Taxes on property	20.3	28.8	53.9	72.2	74.1	2.9	2.6	3.2	3.2	3.2
5000 Taxes on goods and services	0.4	0.6	0.9	1.3	1.4	0.1	0.1	0.1	0.1	0.1
6000 Other taxes	2.9	2.2	0.6	0.9	0.9	0.4	0.2	0.0	0.0	0.0
Social Security Funds										
Total tax revenue	**29.7**	**26.0**	**47.2**	**65.8**	**70.4**	**4.3**	**2.3**	**2.8**	**2.9**	**3.0**
1000 Taxes on income, profits and capital gains	0.0	0.0	0.0	0.0	0.0	0.0	0.0	0.0	0.0	0.0
2000 Social security contributions	29.7	26.0	47.2	65.8	70.4	4.3	2.3	2.8	2.9	3.0
3000 Taxes on payroll and workforce	0.0	0.0	0.0	0.0	0.0	0.0	0.0	0.0	0.0	0.0
4000 Taxes on property	0.0	0.0	0.0	0.0	0.0	0.0	0.0	0.0	0.0	0.0
5000 Taxes on goods and services	0.0	0.0	0.0	0.0	0.0	0.0	0.0	0.0	0.0	0.0
6000 Other taxes	0.0	0.0	0.0	0.0	0.0	0.0	0.0	0.0	0.0	0.0

Note: More detailed country data and country notes are available in online chapter 6 "Tax revenues by sub-sectors of general government": https://doi.org/10.1787/0bbc27da-en. Full time series can be accessed at http://oe.cd/full-time-series.
Source: Statistics Canada.

StatLink https://stat.link/ptjyvi

Table 4.9. Chile, tax revenue and % of GDP by selected tax category

	Billion CLP					% of GDP				
	1990	2000	2010	2018	2019	1990	2000	2010	2018	2019
Total tax revenue	**1 777.2**	**7 902.0**	**21 845.7**	**40 314.7**	**41 025.5**	**16.9**	**18.8**	**19.6**	**21.1**	**20.9**
1000 Taxes on income, profits and capital gains	**413.0**	**1 841.6**	**8 329.1**	**14 418.9**	**14 283.2**	**3.9**	**4.4**	**7.5**	**7.6**	**7.3**
1100 Of individuals	99.2	604.1	1 492.8	2 701.4	2 937.5	0.9	1.4	1.3	1.4	1.5
1200 Corporate	219.6	882.9	4 448.7	8 920.5	9 597.5	2.1	2.1	4.0	4.7	4.9
1300 Unallocable between 1100 and 1200	94.2	354.6	2 387.5	2 796.9	1 748.2	0.9	0.8	2.1	1.5	0.9
2000 Social security contributions	**159.6**	**576.8**	**1 494.0**	**2 786.2**	**2 994.9**	**1.5**	**1.4**	**1.3**	**1.5**	**1.5**
2100 Employees	154.0	553.9	1 433.2	2 703.3	2 894.7	1.5	1.3	1.3	1.4	1.5
2200 Employers	5.5	22.8	60.8	82.9	100.2	0.1	0.1	0.1	0.0	0.1
2300 Self-employed or non-employed	0.0	0.0	0.0	0.0	0.0	0.0	0.0	0.0	0.0	0.0
2400 Unallocable between 2100, 2200 and 2300	0.0	0.0	0.0	0.0	0.0	0.0	0.0	0.0	0.0	0.0
3000 Taxes on payroll and workforce	**0.0**	**0.0**	**0.0**	**0.0**	**0.0**	**0.0**	**0.0**	**0.0**	**0.0**	**0.0**
4000 Taxes on property	**109.3**	**554.0**	**898.6**	**2 086.9**	**2 242.6**	**1.0**	**1.3**	**0.8**	**1.1**	**1.1**
4100 Recurrent taxes on immovable property	60.0	302.2	662.4	1 373.5	1 507.2	0.6	0.7	0.6	0.7	0.8
4200 Recurrent taxes on net wealth	0.0	0.0	0.0	0.0	0.0	0.0	0.0	0.0	0.0	0.0
4300 Estate, inheritance and gift taxes	3.4	10.9	39.3	125.6	62.8	0.0	0.0	0.0	0.1	0.0
4400 Taxes on financial and capital transactions	45.9	240.9	196.9	587.7	672.6	0.4	0.6	0.2	0.3	0.3
4500 Non-recurrent taxes	0.0	0.0	0.0	0.0	0.0	0.0	0.0	0.0	0.0	0.0
4600 Other recurrent taxes on property	0.0	0.0	0.0	0.0	0.0	0.0	0.0	0.0	0.0	0.0
5000 Taxes on goods and services	**1 118.7**	**5 041.8**	**11 185.2**	**21 470.5**	**21 755.4**	**10.6**	**12.0**	**10.0**	**11.3**	**11.1**
5100 Taxes on production, sale, transfer, etc	1 074.0	4 789.8	10 532.9	19 953.0	20 167.0	10.2	11.4	9.4	10.5	10.3
5110 General taxes	664.4	3 306.4	8 399.9	16 211.6	16 348.9	6.3	7.9	7.5	8.5	8.3
5111 Value added taxes	664.4	3 306.4	8 399.9	16 211.6	16 348.9	6.3	7.9	7.5	8.5	8.3
5120 Taxes on specific goods and services	409.6	1 483.5	2 133.0	3 741.4	3 818.1	3.9	3.5	1.9	2.0	1.9
5121 Excises	166.0	816.2	1 561.2	2 796.0	2 862.3	1.6	1.9	1.4	1.5	1.5
5200 Taxes on use of goods and perform activities	44.7	251.9	652.3	1 517.5	1 588.4	0.4	0.6	0.6	0.8	0.8
5300 Unallocable between 5100 and 5200	0.0	0.0	0.0	0.0	0.0	0.0	0.0	0.0	0.0	0.0
6000 Other taxes	**-23.4**	**-112.2**	**-61.1**	**-447.7**	**-250.5**	**-0.2**	**-0.3**	**-0.1**	**-0.2**	**-0.1**
Non-wastable tax credits										
Non-wastable tax credits against 1000	0.0	0.0	0.0	251.6	278.8	0.0	0.0	0.0	0.1	0.1
Transfer component	..	..	..	186.8	200.6	..	..	..	0.1	0.1
Tax expenditure component	..	..	..	64.8	78.2	..	..	..	0.0	0.0

.. Not available

Note: More detailed country data and country notes are available in online chapter 5 "Detailed country tables": https://doi.org/10.1787/0bbc27da-en. Full time series can be accessed at http://oe.cd/full-time-series.

Source: Servicio de Impuestos internos (Chile's Tax Service).

StatLink https://stat.link/nk3otf

Table 4.10. Chile, tax revenue and % of GDP by level of government and main taxes

	Billion CLP					% of GDP				
	1990	2000	2010	2018	2019	1990	2000	2010	2018	2019
Federal or Central government										
Total tax revenue	**1 579.7**	**6 936.8**	**19 214.8**	**34 816.0**	**35 124.7**	**15.0**	**16.5**	**17.2**	**18.2**	**17.9**
1000 Taxes on income, profits and capital gains	413.0	1 841.6	8 329.1	14 418.9	14 283.2	3.9	4.4	7.5	7.6	7.3
2000 Social security contributions	66.7	232.7	371.4	474.0	495.1	0.6	0.6	0.3	0.2	0.3
3000 Taxes on payroll and workforce	0.0	0.0	0.0	0.0	0.0	0.0	0.0	0.0	0.0	0.0
4000 Taxes on property	59.7	255.4	245.0	736.3	759.3	0.6	0.6	0.2	0.4	0.4
5000 Taxes on goods and services	1 063.7	4 719.3	10 330.4	19 634.6	19 837.6	10.1	11.2	9.3	10.3	10.1
6000 Other taxes	-23.4	-112.2	-61.1	-447.7	-250.5	-0.2	-0.3	-0.1	-0.2	-0.1
State/Regional										
Total tax revenue	..	..	..	..	..	..	..	..	..	..
1000 Taxes on income, profits and capital gains	..	..	..	..	..	..	..	..	..	..
2000 Social security contributions	..	..	..	..	..	..	..	..	..	..
3000 Taxes on payroll and workforce	..	..	..	..	..	..	..	..	..	..
4000 Taxes on property	..	..	..	..	..	..	..	..	..	..
5000 Taxes on goods and services	..	..	..	..	..	..	..	..	..	..
6000 Other taxes	..	..	..	..	..	..	..	..	..	..
Local government										
Total tax revenue	**104.7**	**621.2**	**1 508.3**	**3 186.5**	**3 401.0**	**1.0**	**1.5**	**1.4**	**1.7**	**1.7**
1000 Taxes on income, profits and capital gains	0.0	0.0	0.0	0.0	0.0	0.0	0.0	0.0	0.0	0.0
2000 Social security contributions	0.0	0.0	0.0	0.0	0.0	0.0	0.0	0.0	0.0	0.0
3000 Taxes on payroll and workforce	0.0	0.0	0.0	0.0	0.0	0.0	0.0	0.0	0.0	0.0
4000 Taxes on property	49.6	298.7	653.6	1 350.5	1 483.3	0.5	0.7	0.6	0.7	0.8
5000 Taxes on goods and services	55.0	322.5	854.8	1 835.9	1 917.8	0.5	0.8	0.8	1.0	1.0
6000 Other taxes	0.0	0.0	0.0	0.0	0.0	0.0	0.0	0.0	0.0	0.0
Social Security Funds										
Total tax revenue	**92.8**	**344.0**	**1 122.6**	**2 312.2**	**2 499.8**	**0.9**	**0.8**	**1.0**	**1.2**	**1.3**
1000 Taxes on income, profits and capital gains	0.0	0.0	0.0	0.0	0.0	0.0	0.0	0.0	0.0	0.0
2000 Social security contributions	92.8	344.0	1 122.6	2 312.2	2 499.8	0.9	0.8	1.0	1.2	1.3
3000 Taxes on payroll and workforce	0.0	0.0	0.0	0.0	0.0	0.0	0.0	0.0	0.0	0.0
4000 Taxes on property	0.0	0.0	0.0	0.0	0.0	0.0	0.0	0.0	0.0	0.0
5000 Taxes on goods and services	0.0	0.0	0.0	0.0	0.0	0.0	0.0	0.0	0.0	0.0
6000 Other taxes	0.0	0.0	0.0	0.0	0.0	0.0	0.0	0.0	0.0	0.0

.. Not available

Note: More detailed country data and country notes are available in online chapter 6 "Tax revenues by sub-sectors of general government": https://doi.org/10.1787/0bbc27da-en. Full time series can be accessed at http://oe.cd/full-time-series.

Source: Servicio de Impuestos internos (Chile's Tax Service).

StatLink https://stat.link/s0lmx3

Table 4.11. Colombia, tax revenue and % of GDP by selected tax category

	Billion COP					% of GDP				
	1990	2000	2010	2018	2019	1990	2000	2010	2018	2019
Total tax revenue	**2 579.4**	**30 598.6**	**98 455.3**	**190 299.9**	**209 071.3**	**11.3**	**15.7**	**18.1**	**19.3**	**19.7**
1000 Taxes on income, profits and capital gains	**771.7**	**7 103.5**	**26 218.9**	**64 043.9**	**67 519.6**	**3.4**	**3.6**	**4.8**	**6.5**	**6.4**
1100 Of individuals	47.2	1 499.3	5 192.4	12 235.3	14 155.1	0.2	0.8	1.0	1.2	1.3
1200 Corporate	359.8	5 119.8	20 405.2	48 628.6	50 242.5	1.6	2.6	3.8	4.9	4.7
1300 Unallocable between 1100 and 1200	364.7	484.4	621.3	3 180.0	3 122.0	1.6	0.2	0.1	0.3	0.3
2000 Social security contributions	**203.6**	**4 989.0**	**11 478.1**	**18 192.0**	**19 875.4**	**0.9**	**2.6**	**2.1**	**1.8**	**1.9**
2100 Employees	..	..	..	..	..	..	..	..	..	..
2200 Employers	..	..	..	..	..	..	..	..	..	..
2300 Self-employed or non-employed	..	..	..	..	..	..	..	..	..	..
2400 Unallocable between 2100, 2200 and 2300	203.6	4 989.0	11 478.1	18 192.0	19 875.4	0.9	2.6	2.1	1.8	1.9
3000 Taxes on payroll and workforce	**0.0**	**1 286.8**	**4 022.5**	**3 461.4**	**3 604.1**	**0.0**	**0.7**	**0.7**	**0.4**	**0.3**
4000 Taxes on property	**56.2**	**2 027.7**	**8 535.2**	**15 265.5**	**18 984.4**	**0.2**	**1.0**	**1.6**	**1.5**	**1.8**
4100 Recurrent taxes on immovable property	56.2	991.1	3 338.9	7 982.0	8 743.1	0.2	0.5	0.6	0.8	0.8
4200 Recurrent taxes on net wealth	0.0	0.0	1 970.5	467.9	923.3	0.0	0.0	0.4	0.0	0.1
4300 Estate, inheritance and gift taxes	0.0	0.0	0.0	0.0	0.0	0.0	0.0	0.0	0.0	0.0
4400 Taxes on financial and capital transactions	0.0	1 036.6	3 225.8	6 815.6	8 190.5	0.0	0.5	0.6	0.7	0.8
4500 Non-recurrent taxes	0.0	0.0	0.0	0.0	1 127.5	0.0	0.0	0.0	0.0	0.1
4600 Other recurrent taxes on property	0.0	0.0	0.0	0.0	0.0	0.0	0.0	0.0	0.0	0.0
5000 Taxes on goods and services	**1 388.7**	**14 180.5**	**44 411.6**	**81 408.8**	**89 797.9**	**6.1**	**7.3**	**8.2**	**8.2**	**8.5**
5100 Taxes on production, sale, transfer, etc	1 388.7	14 048.7	44 038.1	79 935.3	88 064.1	6.1	7.2	8.1	8.1	8.3
5110 General taxes	672.4	9 585.9	33 333.8	64 316.0	71 235.1	3.0	4.9	6.1	6.5	6.7
5111 Value added taxes	583.1	8 445.8	28 811.7	55 879.1	61 936.3	2.6	4.3	5.3	5.7	5.8
5120 Taxes on specific goods and services	716.3	4 462.8	10 704.3	15 619.3	16 828.9	3.2	2.3	2.0	1.6	1.6
5121 Excises	404.7	2 718.7	6 052.3	12 061.1	12 996.0	1.8	1.4	1.1	1.2	1.2
5200 Taxes on use of goods and perform activities	0.0	131.8	373.6	1 473.5	1 733.8	0.0	0.1	0.1	0.1	0.2
5300 Unallocable between 5100 and 5200	0.0	0.0	0.0	0.0	0.0	0.0	0.0	0.0	0.0	0.0
6000 Other taxes	**159.3**	**1 011.2**	**3 789.0**	**7 928.3**	**9 289.9**	**0.7**	**0.5**	**0.7**	**0.8**	**0.9**
Non-wastable tax credits										
Non-wastable tax credits against 1000	..	..	..	..	..	..	..	..	..	..
Transfer component	..	..	..	..	..	..	..	..	..	..
Tax expenditure component	..	..	..	..	..	..	..	..	..	..

.. Not available

Note: More detailed country data and country notes are available in online chapter 5 "Detailed country tables": https://doi.org/10.1787/0bbc27da-en. Full time series can be accessed at http://oe.cd/full-time-series.

Source: Dirección de Impuestos y Aduanas Nacionales de Colombia, Ministerio de Hacienda y Crédito Público y Banco Central de Colombia. (National Tax and Customs Administration, Ministry of Finance and Public Credit and Central Bank of Colombia).

StatLink https://stat.link/ftjx51

Table 4.12. Colombia, tax revenue and % of GDP by level of government and main taxes

	Billion COP					% of GDP				
	1990	2000	2010	2018	2019	1990	2000	2010	2018	2019
Federal or Central government										
Total tax revenue	**1 885.9**	**21 016.3**	**71 304.3**	**139 228.1**	**152 621.7**	**8.3**	**10.8**	**13.1**	**14.1**	**14.4**
1000 Taxes on income, profits and capital gains	771.7	7 103.5	26 218.9	64 043.9	67 519.6	3.4	3.6	4.8	6.5	6.4
2000 Social security contributions	0.0	0.0	0.0	0.0	0.0	0.0	0.0	0.0	0.0	0.0
3000 Taxes on payroll and workforce	0.0	1 286.8	4 022.5	3 461.4	3 604.1	0.0	0.7	0.7	0.4	0.3
4000 Taxes on property	0.0	1 036.6	5 196.3	7 283.5	10 241.3	0.0	0.5	1.0	0.7	1.0
5000 Taxes on goods and services	1 035.9	11 108.6	35 382.9	63 898.3	70 637.1	4.6	5.7	6.5	6.5	6.7
6000 Other taxes	78.3	480.8	483.8	541.0	619.7	0.3	0.2	0.1	0.1	0.1
State/Regional										
Total tax revenue	**263.4**	**1 723.2**	**4 781.3**	**9 419.1**	**10 472.5**	**1.2**	**0.9**	**0.9**	**1.0**	**1.0**
1000 Taxes on income, profits and capital gains	0.0	0.0	0.0	0.0	0.0	0.0	0.0	0.0	0.0	0.0
2000 Social security contributions	0.0	0.0	0.0	0.0	0.0	0.0	0.0	0.0	0.0	0.0
3000 Taxes on payroll and workforce	0.0	0.0	0.0	0.0	0.0	0.0	0.0	0.0	0.0	0.0
4000 Taxes on property	0.0	0.0	0.0	0.0	0.0	0.0	0.0	0.0	0.0	0.0
5000 Taxes on goods and services	263.4	1 481.7	3 406.3	6 812.7	7 496.6	1.2	0.8	0.6	0.7	0.7
6000 Other taxes	0.0	241.5	1 375.0	2 606.4	2 975.9	0.0	0.1	0.3	0.3	0.3
Local government										
Total tax revenue	**226.5**	**2 870.1**	**10 891.7**	**23 460.7**	**26 101.8**	**1.0**	**1.5**	**2.0**	**2.4**	**2.5**
1000 Taxes on income, profits and capital gains	0.0	0.0	0.0	0.0	0.0	0.0	0.0	0.0	0.0	0.0
2000 Social security contributions	0.0	0.0	0.0	0.0	0.0	0.0	0.0	0.0	0.0	0.0
3000 Taxes on payroll and workforce	0.0	0.0	0.0	0.0	0.0	0.0	0.0	0.0	0.0	0.0
4000 Taxes on property	56.2	991.1	3 338.9	7 982.0	8 743.1	0.2	0.5	0.6	0.8	0.8
5000 Taxes on goods and services	89.3	1 590.1	5 622.5	10 697.8	11 664.3	0.4	0.8	1.0	1.1	1.1
6000 Other taxes	81.0	288.9	1 930.3	4 780.9	5 694.4	0.4	0.1	0.4	0.5	0.5
Social Security Funds										
Total tax revenue	**203.6**	**4 989.0**	**11 478.1**	**18 192.0**	**19 875.4**	**0.9**	**2.6**	**2.1**	**1.8**	**1.9**
1000 Taxes on income, profits and capital gains	0.0	0.0	0.0	0.0	0.0	0.0	0.0	0.0	0.0	0.0
2000 Social security contributions	203.6	4 989.0	11 478.1	18 192.0	19 875.4	0.9	2.6	2.1	1.8	1.9
3000 Taxes on payroll and workforce	0.0	0.0	0.0	0.0	0.0	0.0	0.0	0.0	0.0	0.0
4000 Taxes on property	0.0	0.0	0.0	0.0	0.0	0.0	0.0	0.0	0.0	0.0
5000 Taxes on goods and services	0.0	0.0	0.0	0.0	0.0	0.0	0.0	0.0	0.0	0.0
6000 Other taxes	0.0	0.0	0.0	0.0	0.0	0.0	0.0	0.0	0.0	0.0

Note: More detailed country data and country notes are available in online chapter 6 "Tax revenues by sub-sectors of general government": https://doi.org/10.1787/0bbc27da-en. Full time series can be accessed at http://oe.cd/full-time-series.

Source: Dirección de Impuestos y Aduanas Nacionales de Colombia, Ministerio de Hacienda y Crédito Público y Banco Central de Colombia. (National Tax and Customs Administration, Ministry of Finance and Public Credit and Central Bank of Colombia).

StatLink https://stat.link/2utwfs

Table 4.13. Costa Rica, tax revenue and % of GDP by selected tax category

	Billion CRC					% of GDP				
	1990	2000	2010	2018	2019	1990	2000	2010	2018	2019
Total tax revenue	**117.7**	**978.1**	**4 382.4**	**8 340.0**	**8 855.9**	**22.4**	**21.1**	**22.1**	**23.2**	**23.6**
1000 Taxes on income, profits and capital gains	**11.8**	**128.8**	**748.1**	**1 699.3**	**1 854.9**	**2.3**	**2.8**	**3.8**	**4.7**	**4.9**
1100 Of individuals	0.0	0.0	202.8	483.6	541.0	0.0	0.0	1.0	1.3	1.4
1200 Corporate	0.0	0.0	450.3	915.3	1 058.1	0.0	0.0	2.3	2.5	2.8
1300 Unallocable between 1100 and 1200	11.8	128.8	94.9	300.3	255.8	2.3	2.8	0.5	0.8	0.7
2000 Social security contributions	**34.0**	**297.1**	**1 450.5**	**2 859.5**	**3 026.7**	**6.5**	**6.4**	**7.3**	**8.0**	**8.1**
2100 Employees	0.0	0.0	0.0	0.0	0.0	0.0	0.0	0.0	0.0	0.0
2200 Employers	3.4	37.3	207.2	368.9	381.9	0.7	0.8	1.0	1.0	1.0
2300 Self-employed or non-employed	0.0	0.0	0.0	0.0	0.0	0.0	0.0	0.0	0.0	0.0
2400 Unallocable between 2100, 2200 and 2300	30.5	259.8	1 243.3	2 490.6	2 644.8	5.8	5.6	6.3	6.9	7.0
3000 Taxes on payroll and workforce	**7.6**	**61.8**	**260.7**	**498.6**	**522.5**	**1.4**	**1.3**	**1.3**	**1.4**	**1.4**
4000 Taxes on property	**1.6**	**8.4**	**63.7**	**149.3**	**168.0**	**0.3**	**0.2**	**0.3**	**0.4**	**0.4**
4100 Recurrent taxes on immovable property	1.2	5.4	49.0	113.6	125.4	0.2	0.1	0.2	0.3	0.3
4200 Recurrent taxes on net wealth	0.0	0.0	0.0	0.0	0.0	0.0	0.0	0.0	0.0	0.0
4300 Estate, inheritance and gift taxes	0.0	0.0	0.0	0.0	0.0	0.0	0.0	0.0	0.0	0.0
4400 Taxes on financial and capital transactions	0.4	3.0	14.7	35.7	42.6	0.1	0.1	0.1	0.1	0.1
4500 Non-recurrent taxes	0.0	0.0	0.0	0.0	0.0	0.0	0.0	0.0	0.0	0.0
4600 Other recurrent taxes on property	0.0	0.0	0.0	0.0	0.0	0.0	0.0	0.0	0.0	0.0
5000 Taxes on goods and services	**53.5**	**456.9**	**1 766.9**	**2 918.5**	**3 081.9**	**10.2**	**9.9**	**8.9**	**8.1**	**8.2**
5100 Taxes on production, sale, transfer, etc	49.9	425.7	1 600.3	2 608.9	2 756.8	9.5	9.2	8.1	7.3	7.3
5110 General taxes	21.3	222.8	920.3	1 513.7	1 662.5	4.1	4.8	4.6	4.2	4.4
5111 Value added taxes	21.3	222.8	920.3	1 487.6	1 635.0	4.1	4.8	4.6	4.1	4.4
5120 Taxes on specific goods and services	28.5	202.9	680.0	1 095.2	1 094.3	5.4	4.4	3.4	3.0	2.9
5121 Excises	11.1	157.2	523.6	858.4	865.0	2.1	3.4	2.6	2.4	2.3
5200 Taxes on use of goods and perform activities	3.6	31.1	166.6	309.6	325.2	0.7	0.7	0.8	0.9	0.9
5300 Unallocable between 5100 and 5200	0.0	0.0	0.0	0.0	0.0	0.0	0.0	0.0	0.0	0.0
6000 Other taxes	**9.3**	**25.2**	**92.5**	**214.9**	**201.9**	**1.8**	**0.5**	**0.5**	**0.6**	**0.5**
Non-wastable tax credits										
Non-wastable tax credits against 1000	..	..	..	..	..	..	..	..	..	..
Transfer component	..	..	..	..	..	..	..	..	..	..
Tax expenditure component	..	..	..	..	..	..	..	..	..	..

.. Not available

Note: More detailed country data and country notes are available in online chapter 5 "Detailed country tables": https://doi.org/10.1787/0bbc27da-en. Full time series can be accessed at http://oe.cd/full-time-series.

Source: Secretaría Técnica de la Autoridad Presupuestaria, Ministerio de Finanzas y Contraloría General de la República (Technical Secretary of the Budgeting Authority, Ministry of Finance and National General Comptroller).

StatLink https://stat.link/2n36ls

Table 4.14. Costa Rica, tax revenue and % of GDP by level of government and main taxes

	Billion CRC					% of GDP				
	1990	2000	2010	2018	2019	1990	2000	2010	2018	2019
Federal or Central government										
Total tax revenue	**75.0**	**619.3**	**2 616.6**	**4 821.9**	**5 121.6**	**14.3**	**13.4**	**13.2**	**13.4**	**13.6**
1000 Taxes on income, profits and capital gains	11.8	128.8	748.1	1 699.3	1 854.9	2.3	2.8	3.8	4.7	4.9
2000 Social security contributions	1.3	18.7	61.2	85.4	77.5	0.3	0.4	0.3	0.2	0.2
3000 Taxes on payroll and workforce	0.0	0.0	0.0	0.0	0.0	0.0	0.0	0.0	0.0	0.0
4000 Taxes on property	0.4	3.0	18.3	40.2	47.3	0.1	0.1	0.1	0.1	0.1
5000 Taxes on goods and services	52.2	444.9	1 696.6	2 782.2	2 940.1	9.9	9.6	8.6	7.7	7.8
6000 Other taxes	9.3	24.0	92.5	214.9	201.8	1.8	0.5	0.5	0.6	0.5
State/Regional										
Total tax revenue	..	..	..	..	..	..	..	..	..	..
1000 Taxes on income, profits and capital gains	..	..	..	..	..	..	..	..	..	..
2000 Social security contributions	..	..	..	..	..	..	..	..	..	..
3000 Taxes on payroll and workforce	..	..	..	..	..	..	..	..	..	..
4000 Taxes on property	..	..	..	..	..	..	..	..	..	..
5000 Taxes on goods and services	..	..	..	..	..	..	..	..	..	..
6000 Other taxes	..	..	..	..	..	..	..	..	..	..
Local government										
Total tax revenue	**2.5**	**18.6**	**115.8**	**245.5**	**262.6**	**0.5**	**0.4**	**0.6**	**0.7**	**0.7**
1000 Taxes on income, profits and capital gains	0.0	0.0	0.0	0.0	0.0	0.0	0.0	0.0	0.0	0.0
2000 Social security contributions	0.0	0.0	0.0	0.0	0.0	0.0	0.0	0.0	0.0	0.0
3000 Taxes on payroll and workforce	0.0	0.0	0.0	0.0	0.0	0.0	0.0	0.0	0.0	0.0
4000 Taxes on property	1.2	5.4	45.4	109.1	120.7	0.2	0.1	0.2	0.3	0.3
5000 Taxes on goods and services	1.3	12.0	70.3	136.3	141.8	0.2	0.3	0.4	0.4	0.4
6000 Other taxes	0.0	1.2	0.0	0.0	0.1	0.0	0.0	0.0	0.0	0.0
Social Security Funds										
Total tax revenue	**40.2**	**340.2**	**1 650.0**	**3 272.6**	**3 471.7**	**7.7**	**7.4**	**8.3**	**9.1**	**9.2**
1000 Taxes on income, profits and capital gains	0.0	0.0	0.0	0.0	0.0	0.0	0.0	0.0	0.0	0.0
2000 Social security contributions	32.6	278.4	1 389.3	2 774.1	2 949.2	6.2	6.0	7.0	7.7	7.9
3000 Taxes on payroll and workforce	7.6	61.8	260.7	498.6	522.5	1.4	1.3	1.3	1.4	1.4
4000 Taxes on property	0.0	0.0	0.0	0.0	0.0	0.0	0.0	0.0	0.0	0.0
5000 Taxes on goods and services	0.0	0.0	0.0	0.0	0.0	0.0	0.0	0.0	0.0	0.0
6000 Other taxes	0.0	0.0	0.0	0.0	0.0	0.0	0.0	0.0	0.0	0.0

.. Not available

Note: More detailed country data and country notes are available in online chapter 6 "Tax revenues by sub-sectors of general government": https://doi.org/10.1787/0bbc27da-en. Full time series can be accessed at http://oe.cd/full-time-series.

Source: Secretaría Técnica de la Autoridad Presupuestaria, Ministerio de Finanzas y Contraloría General de la República (Technical Secretary of the Budgeting Authority, Ministry of Finance and National General Comptroller).

StatLink https://stat.link/iskcmy

Table 4.15. Czech Republic, tax revenue and % of GDP by selected tax category

	Billion CZK					% of GDP				
	1990	2000	2010	2018	2019	1990	2000	2010	2018	2019
Total tax revenue	..	**771.6**	**1 286.9**	**1 892.4**	**2 013.9**	..	**32.3**	**32.2**	**35.0**	**34.8**
1000 Taxes on income, profits and capital gains	..	**175.8**	**259.9**	**427.0**	**458.5**	..	**7.4**	**6.5**	**7.9**	**7.9**
1100 Of individuals	..	99.7	131.7	231.0	255.4	..	4.2	3.3	4.3	4.4
1200 Corporate	..	76.2	128.2	196.0	203.1	..	3.2	3.2	3.6	3.5
1300 Unallocable between 1100 and 1200	..	0.0	0.0	0.0	0.0	..	0.0	0.0	0.0	0.0
2000 Social security contributions	..	**341.5**	**576.0**	**829.7**	**889.2**	..	**14.3**	**14.4**	**15.3**	**15.4**
2100 Employees	..	77.3	116.8	171.8	184.6	..	3.2	2.9	3.2	3.2
2200 Employers	..	220.2	363.1	531.6	569.5	..	9.2	9.1	9.8	9.8
2300 Self-employed or non-employed	..	44.1	96.1	126.2	135.2	..	1.8	2.4	2.3	2.3
2400 Unallocable between 2100, 2200 and 2300	..	0.0	0.0	0.0	0.0	..	0.0	0.0	0.0	0.0
3000 Taxes on payroll and workforce	..	**0.0**	**0.0**	**0.0**	**0.0**	..	**0.0**	**0.0**	**0.0**	**0.0**
4000 Taxes on property	..	**10.9**	**16.4**	**24.6**	**24.1**	..	**0.5**	**0.4**	**0.5**	**0.4**
4100 Recurrent taxes on immovable property	..	4.5	8.8	10.9	11.0	..	0.2	0.2	0.2	0.2
4200 Recurrent taxes on net wealth	..	0.0	0.0	0.0	0.0	..	0.0	0.0	0.0	0.0
4300 Estate, inheritance and gift taxes	..	0.6	0.2	0.0	0.0	..	0.0	0.0	0.0	0.0
4400 Taxes on financial and capital transactions	..	5.8	7.4	13.8	13.1	..	0.2	0.2	0.3	0.2
4500 Non-recurrent taxes	..	0.0	0.0	0.0	0.0	..	0.0	0.0	0.0	0.0
4600 Other recurrent taxes on property	..	0.0	0.0	0.0	0.0	..	0.0	0.0	0.0	0.0
5000 Taxes on goods and services	..	**243.0**	**434.4**	**610.8**	**641.9**	..	**10.2**	**10.9**	**11.3**	**11.1**
5100 Taxes on production, sale, transfer, etc	..	226.4	408.6	582.8	613.0	..	9.5	10.2	10.8	10.6
5110 General taxes	..	141.2	263.5	408.5	435.5	..	5.9	6.6	7.6	7.5
5111 Value added taxes	..	141.2	263.5	408.5	435.5	..	5.9	6.6	7.6	7.5
5120 Taxes on specific goods and services	..	85.1	145.2	174.2	177.5	..	3.6	3.6	3.2	3.1
5121 Excises	..	71.4	138.4	165.4	168.2	..	3.0	3.5	3.1	2.9
5200 Taxes on use of goods and perform activities	..	16.6	25.7	28.1	28.9	..	0.7	0.6	0.5	0.5
5300 Unallocable between 5100 and 5200	..	0.0	0.0	0.0	0.0	..	0.0	0.0	0.0	0.0
6000 Other taxes	..	**0.4**	**0.1**	**0.3**	**0.2**	..	**0.0**	**0.0**	**0.0**	**0.0**
Non-wastable tax credits										
Non-wastable tax credits against 1000	..	0.0	25.7	39.1	39.9	..	0.0	0.6	0.7	0.7
Transfer component	..	..	7.8	8.8	7.8	..	..	0.2	0.2	0.1
Tax expenditure component	..	..	17.9	30.3	32.1	..	..	0.4	0.6	0.6
Revenues collected on behalf of the EU										
Revenues collected on behalf of the EU, total	..	..	6.6	8.3	8.8	..	..	0.2	0.2	0.2
Customs duties	..	..	6.6	8.3	8.8	..	..	0.2	0.2	0.2

.. Not available

Note: More detailed country data and country notes are available in online chapter 5 "Detailed country tables": https://doi.org/10.1787/0bbc27da-en. Full time series can be accessed at http://oe.cd/full-time-series.

Source: Ministry of Finance, Economic Department.

StatLink https://stat.link/6arlv0

Table 4.16. Czech Republic, tax revenue and % of GDP by level of government and main taxes

	Billion CZK					% of GDP				
	1990	2000	2010	2018	2019	1990	2000	2010	2018	2019
Federal or Central government										
Total tax revenue	..	**423.4**	**687.3**	**1 035.4**	**1 096.4**	..	**17.7**	**17.2**	**19.1**	**18.9**
1000 Taxes on income, profits and capital gains	..	175.8	259.9	427.0	458.5	..	7.4	6.5	7.9	7.9
2000 Social security contributions	..	0.0	0.0	0.0	0.0	..	0.0	0.0	0.0	0.0
3000 Taxes on payroll and workforce	..	0.0	0.0	0.0	0.0	..	0.0	0.0	0.0	0.0
4000 Taxes on property	..	6.4	7.6	13.8	13.1	..	0.3	0.2	0.3	0.2
5000 Taxes on goods and services	..	241.0	419.6	594.3	624.5	..	10.1	10.5	11.0	10.8
6000 Other taxes	..	0.1	0.1	0.3	0.2	..	0.0	0.0	0.0	0.0
State/Regional										
Total tax revenue	..	..	..	..	..	..	..	..	..	..
1000 Taxes on income, profits and capital gains	..	..	..	..	..	..	..	..	..	..
2000 Social security contributions	..	..	..	..	..	..	..	..	..	..
3000 Taxes on payroll and workforce	..	..	..	..	..	..	..	..	..	..
4000 Taxes on property	..	..	..	..	..	..	..	..	..	..
5000 Taxes on goods and services	..	..	..	..	..	..	..	..	..	..
6000 Other taxes	..	..	..	..	..	..	..	..	..	..
Local government										
Total tax revenue	..	**6.7**	**17.0**	**19.0**	**19.5**	..	**0.3**	**0.4**	**0.4**	**0.3**
1000 Taxes on income, profits and capital gains	..	0.0	0.0	0.0	0.0	..	0.0	0.0	0.0	0.0
2000 Social security contributions	..	0.0	0.0	0.0	0.0	..	0.0	0.0	0.0	0.0
3000 Taxes on payroll and workforce	..	0.0	0.0	0.0	0.0	..	0.0	0.0	0.0	0.0
4000 Taxes on property	..	4.5	8.7	10.8	10.9	..	0.2	0.2	0.2	0.2
5000 Taxes on goods and services	..	2.0	8.2	8.2	8.6	..	0.1	0.2	0.2	0.1
6000 Other taxes	..	0.3	0.0	0.0	0.0	..	0.0	0.0	0.0	0.0
Social Security Funds										
Total tax revenue	..	**341.5**	**576.0**	**829.7**	**889.2**	..	**14.3**	**14.4**	**15.3**	**15.4**
1000 Taxes on income, profits and capital gains	..	0.0	0.0	0.0	0.0	..	0.0	0.0	0.0	0.0
2000 Social security contributions	..	341.5	576.0	829.7	889.2	..	14.3	14.4	15.3	15.4
3000 Taxes on payroll and workforce	..	0.0	0.0	0.0	0.0	..	0.0	0.0	0.0	0.0
4000 Taxes on property	..	0.0	0.0	0.0	0.0	..	0.0	0.0	0.0	0.0
5000 Taxes on goods and services	..	0.0	0.0	0.0	0.0	..	0.0	0.0	0.0	0.0
6000 Other taxes	..	0.0	0.0	0.0	0.0	..	0.0	0.0	0.0	0.0

.. Not available

Note: More detailed country data and country notes are available in online chapter 6 "Tax revenues by sub-sectors of general government": https://doi.org/10.1787/0bbc27da-en. Full time series can be accessed at http://oe.cd/full-time-series.

Source: Ministry of Finance, Economic Department.

StatLink https://stat.link/34en9x

Table 4.17. Denmark, tax revenue and % of GDP by selected tax category

	Billion DKK					% of GDP				
	1990	2000	2010	2018	2019	1990	2000	2010	2018	2019
Total tax revenue	**379.8**	**622.0**	**810.5**	**995.4**	**1 080.3**	**44.4**	**46.9**	**44.8**	**44.2**	**46.6**
1000 Taxes on income, profits and capital gains	**232.3**	**382.0**	**498.8**	**617.9**	**698.8**	**27.2**	**28.8**	**27.5**	**27.4**	**30.1**
1100 Of individuals	205.1	327.3	421.3	542.4	562.7	24.0	24.7	23.3	24.1	24.3
1200 Corporate	14.7	42.3	41.1	62.1	72.7	1.7	3.2	2.3	2.8	3.1
1300 Unallocable between 1100 and 1200	12.6	12.4	36.5	13.3	63.4	1.5	0.9	2.0	0.6	2.7
2000 Social security contributions	**0.1**	**8.5**	**1.8**	**1.1**	**1.0**	**0.0**	**0.6**	**0.1**	**0.0**	**0.0**
2100 Employees	0.1	8.2	0.9	0.8	0.7	0.0	0.6	0.0	0.0	0.0
2200 Employers	0.0	0.2	0.9	0.3	0.3	0.0	0.0	0.1	0.0	0.0
2300 Self-employed or non-employed	0.0	0.0	0.0	0.0	0.0	0.0	0.0	0.0	0.0	0.0
2400 Unallocable between 2100, 2200 and 2300	0.0	0.0	0.0	0.0	0.0	0.0	0.0	0.0	0.0	0.0
3000 Taxes on payroll and workforce	**2.5**	**2.3**	**4.2**	**6.3**	**6.5**	**0.3**	**0.2**	**0.2**	**0.3**	**0.3**
4000 Taxes on property	**16.3**	**20.7**	**33.5**	**41.2**	**46.3**	**1.9**	**1.6**	**1.9**	**1.8**	**2.0**
4100 Recurrent taxes on immovable property	8.9	13.6	24.2	29.6	30.6	1.0	1.0	1.3	1.3	1.3
4200 Recurrent taxes on net wealth	0.9	0.0	0.0	0.0	0.0	0.1	0.0	0.0	0.0	0.0
4300 Estate, inheritance and gift taxes	2.2	2.9	3.6	4.8	8.5	0.3	0.2	0.2	0.2	0.4
4400 Taxes on financial and capital transactions	4.2	4.2	5.7	6.8	7.2	0.5	0.3	0.3	0.3	0.3
4500 Non-recurrent taxes	0.1	0.1	0.0	0.0	0.0	0.0	0.0	0.0	0.0	0.0
4600 Other recurrent taxes on property	0.0	0.0	0.0	0.0	0.0	0.0	0.0	0.0	0.0	0.0
5000 Taxes on goods and services	**128.7**	**208.1**	**271.9**	**328.7**	**327.3**	**15.0**	**15.7**	**15.0**	**14.6**	**14.1**
5100 Taxes on production, sale, transfer, etc	122.7	197.3	252.3	303.6	301.9	14.3	14.9	13.9	13.5	13.0
5110 General taxes	79.7	121.2	169.6	214.4	216.7	9.3	9.1	9.4	9.5	9.3
5111 Value added taxes	71.2	121.2	169.6	214.4	216.7	8.3	9.1	9.4	9.5	9.3
5120 Taxes on specific goods and services	43.0	76.0	82.7	89.1	85.2	5.0	5.7	4.6	4.0	3.7
5121 Excises	38.3	69.0	74.0	81.0	76.8	4.5	5.2	4.1	3.6	3.3
5200 Taxes on use of goods and perform activities	4.4	7.5	14.7	16.3	16.2	0.5	0.6	0.8	0.7	0.7
5300 Unallocable between 5100 and 5200	1.6	3.4	4.9	8.9	9.3	0.2	0.3	0.3	0.4	0.4
6000 Other taxes	**0.0**	**0.4**	**0.2**	**0.3**	**0.3**	**0.0**	**0.0**	**0.0**	**0.0**	**0.0**
Non-wastable tax credits										
Non-wastable tax credits against 1000	..	..	5.0	3.8	3.1	..	..	0.3	0.2	0.1
Transfer component	..	..	0.2	0.2	0.2	..	..	0.0	0.0	0.0
Tax expenditure component	..	..	4.7	3.6	2.9	..	..	0.3	0.2	0.1
Revenues collected on behalf of the EU										
Revenues collected on behalf of the EU, total	2.7	2.6	3.3	3.2	3.1	0.3	0.2	0.2	0.1	0.1
Customs duties	1.8	2.3	3.2	3.2	3.1	0.2	0.2	0.2	0.1	0.1

.. Not available

Note: More detailed country data and country notes are available in online chapter 5 "Detailed country tables": https://doi.org/10.1787/0bbc27da-en. Full time series can be accessed at http://oe.cd/full-time-series.

The total tax revenue has been reduced by the amount of any capital transfer that represents uncollected taxes. The capital transfers were subtracted directly from the specific taxes to which they relate. Therefore, the tax revenue amounts are different to those reported in the detailed country data available in online chapter 5 "Detailed country tables".

Source: Danmarks Statistik.

StatLink https://stat.link/aiph89

Table 4.18. Denmark, tax revenue and % of GDP by level of government and main taxes

	Billion DKK					% of GDP				
	1990	2000	2010	2018	2019	1990	2000	2010	2018	2019
Federal or Central government										
Total tax revenue	**259.5**	**420.6**	**589.0**	**722.9**	**798.7**	**30.3**	**31.7**	**32.5**	**32.1**	**34.5**
1000 Taxes on income, profits and capital gains	123.4	203.9	305.7	378.4	451.2	14.4	15.4	16.9	16.8	19.5
2000 Social security contributions	0.1	1.4	0.9	0.8	0.7	0.0	0.1	0.1	0.0	0.0
3000 Taxes on payroll and workforce	2.5	2.3	4.2	6.3	6.5	0.3	0.2	0.2	0.3	0.3
4000 Taxes on property	7.6	7.2	9.4	11.6	15.7	0.9	0.5	0.5	0.5	0.7
5000 Taxes on goods and services	126.0	205.5	268.7	325.5	324.2	14.7	15.5	14.8	14.4	14.0
6000 Other taxes	0.0	0.4	0.2	0.3	0.3	0.0	0.0	0.0	0.0	0.0
State/Regional										
Total tax revenue	..	..	..	..	..	..	..	..	..	..
1000 Taxes on income, profits and capital gains	..	..	..	..	..	..	..	..	..	..
2000 Social security contributions	..	..	..	..	..	..	..	..	..	..
3000 Taxes on payroll and workforce	..	..	..	..	..	..	..	..	..	..
4000 Taxes on property	..	..	..	..	..	..	..	..	..	..
5000 Taxes on goods and services	..	..	..	..	..	..	..	..	..	..
6000 Other taxes	..	..	..	..	..	..	..	..	..	..
Local government										
Total tax revenue	**117.6**	**191.7**	**217.3**	**269.0**	**278.2**	**13.8**	**14.4**	**12.0**	**11.9**	**12.0**
1000 Taxes on income, profits and capital gains	108.9	178.1	193.1	239.4	247.6	12.7	13.4	10.7	10.6	10.7
2000 Social security contributions	0.0	0.0	0.0	0.0	0.0	0.0	0.0	0.0	0.0	0.0
3000 Taxes on payroll and workforce	0.0	0.0	0.0	0.0	0.0	0.0	0.0	0.0	0.0	0.0
4000 Taxes on property	8.7	13.6	24.2	29.6	30.6	1.0	1.0	1.3	1.3	1.3
5000 Taxes on goods and services	0.0	0.0	0.0	0.0	0.0	0.0	0.0	0.0	0.0	0.0
6000 Other taxes	0.0	0.0	0.0	0.0	0.0	0.0	0.0	0.0	0.0	0.0
Social Security Funds										
Total tax revenue	**0.0**	**7.1**	**0.9**	**0.3**	**0.3**	**0.0**	**0.5**	**0.1**	**0.0**	**0.0**
1000 Taxes on income, profits and capital gains	0.0	0.0	0.0	0.0	0.0	0.0	0.0	0.0	0.0	0.0
2000 Social security contributions	0.0	7.1	0.9	0.3	0.3	0.0	0.5	0.1	0.0	0.0
3000 Taxes on payroll and workforce	0.0	0.0	0.0	0.0	0.0	0.0	0.0	0.0	0.0	0.0
4000 Taxes on property	0.0	0.0	0.0	0.0	0.0	0.0	0.0	0.0	0.0	0.0
5000 Taxes on goods and services	0.0	0.0	0.0	0.0	0.0	0.0	0.0	0.0	0.0	0.0
6000 Other taxes	0.0	0.0	0.0	0.0	0.0	0.0	0.0	0.0	0.0	0.0

.. Not available

Note: More detailed country data and country notes are available in online chapter 6 "Tax revenues by sub-sectors of general government": https://doi.org/10.1787/0bbc27da-en. Full time series can be accessed at http://oe.cd/full-time-series.

The total tax revenue has been reduced by the amount of any capital transfer that represents uncollected taxes. The capital transfers were subtracted directly from the specific taxes to which they relate. Therefore, the tax revenue amounts are different to those reported in the detailed country data available in online chapter 6 "Tax revenues by sub-sectors of general government".

Source: Danmarks Statistik.

StatLink https://stat.link/d9oaeg

Table 4.19. Estonia, tax revenue and % of GDP by selected tax category

	Billion EUR					% of GDP				
	1990	2000	2010	2018	2019	1990	2000	2010	2018	2019
Total tax revenue	..	**1.9**	**4.9**	**8.5**	**9.3**	..	**31.1**	**33.2**	**33.0**	**33.5**
1000 Taxes on income, profits and capital gains	..	**0.5**	**1.0**	**1.9**	**2.0**	..	**7.7**	**6.6**	**7.5**	**7.4**
1100 Of individuals	..	0.4	0.8	1.4	1.5	..	6.8	5.3	5.5	5.5
1200 Corporate	..	0.1	0.2	0.5	0.5	..	0.9	1.3	2.0	1.8
1300 Unallocable between 1100 and 1200	..	0.0	0.0	0.0	0.0	..	0.0	0.0	0.0	0.0
2000 Social security contributions	..	**0.7**	**1.9**	**3.0**	**3.3**	..	**10.9**	**12.7**	**11.5**	**11.7**
2100 Employees	..	0.0	0.1	0.1	0.1	..	0.0	0.8	0.5	0.5
2200 Employers	..	0.7	1.7	2.8	3.1	..	10.7	11.8	11.0	11.2
2300 Self-employed or non-employed	..	0.0	0.0	0.0	0.0	..	0.2	0.1	0.1	0.1
2400 Unallocable between 2100, 2200 and 2300	..	0.0	0.0	0.0	0.0	..	0.0	0.0	0.0	0.0
3000 Taxes on payroll and workforce	..	**0.0**	**0.0**	**0.0**	**0.0**	..	**0.0**	**0.0**	**0.0**	**0.0**
4000 Taxes on property	..	**0.0**	**0.1**	**0.1**	**0.1**	..	**0.4**	**0.3**	**0.2**	**0.2**
4100 Recurrent taxes on immovable property	..	0.0	0.1	0.1	0.1	..	0.4	0.3	0.2	0.2
4200 Recurrent taxes on net wealth	..	0.0	0.0	0.0	0.0	..	0.0	0.0	0.0	0.0
4300 Estate, inheritance and gift taxes	..	0.0	0.0	0.0	0.0	..	0.0	0.0	0.0	0.0
4400 Taxes on financial and capital transactions	..	0.0	0.0	0.0	0.0	..	0.0	0.0	0.0	0.0
4500 Non-recurrent taxes	..	0.0	0.0	0.0	0.0	..	0.0	0.0	0.0	0.0
4600 Other recurrent taxes on property	..	0.0	0.0	0.0	0.0	..	0.0	0.0	0.0	0.0
5000 Taxes on goods and services	..	**0.7**	**2.0**	**3.6**	**3.9**	..	**12.1**	**13.5**	**13.8**	**14.2**
5100 Taxes on production, sale, transfer, etc	..	0.7	1.9	3.4	3.7	..	11.7	13.1	13.3	13.4
5110 General taxes	..	0.5	1.3	2.3	2.5	..	8.4	8.6	9.0	9.0
5111 Value added taxes	..	0.5	1.3	2.3	2.5	..	8.4	8.5	9.0	9.0
5120 Taxes on specific goods and services	..	0.2	0.7	1.1	1.2	..	3.3	4.6	4.3	4.5
5121 Excises	..	0.2	0.6	1.0	1.1	..	3.0	4.2	3.9	4.1
5200 Taxes on use of goods and perform activities	..	0.0	0.1	0.1	0.2	..	0.4	0.4	0.5	0.8
5300 Unallocable between 5100 and 5200	..	0.0	0.0	0.0	0.0	..	0.0	0.0	0.0	0.0
6000 Other taxes	..	**0.0**	**0.0**	**0.0**	**0.0**	..	**0.0**	**0.0**	**0.0**	**0.0**
Non-wastable tax credits										
Non-wastable tax credits against 1000	..	..	..	..	..	..	..	..	..	..
Transfer component	..	..	..	..	..	..	..	..	..	..
Tax expenditure component	..	..	..	..	..	..	..	..	..	..
Revenues collected on behalf of the EU										
Revenues collected on behalf of the EU, total	..	..	0.0	0.0	0.1	..	..	0.2	0.2	0.2
Customs duties	..	..	0.0	0.0	0.1	..	..	0.2	0.2	0.2
SRF contributions	..	..	..	0.0	0.0	..	..	..	0.0	0.0

.. Not available

Note: More detailed country data and country notes are available in online chapter 5 "Detailed country tables": https://doi.org/10.1787/0bbc27da-en. Full time series can be accessed at http://oe.cd/full-time-series.

Source: Statistics Estonia.

StatLink https://stat.link/ctjlvw

Table 4.20. Estonia, tax revenue and % of GDP by level of government and main taxes

	Billion EUR					% of GDP				
	1990	2000	2010	2018	2019	1990	2000	2010	2018	2019
Federal or Central government										
Total tax revenue	**..**	**1.6**	**3.9**	**7.0**	**7.6**	**..**	**26.3**	**26.7**	**27.1**	**27.5**
1000 Taxes on income, profits and capital gains	..	0.5	1.0	1.9	2.0	..	7.7	6.6	7.5	7.4
2000 Social security contributions	..	0.4	1.0	1.6	1.7	..	6.6	6.8	6.1	6.2
3000 Taxes on payroll and workforce	..	0.0	0.0	0.0	0.0	..	0.0	0.0	0.0	0.0
4000 Taxes on property	..	0.0	0.0	0.0	0.0	..	0.0	0.0	0.0	0.0
5000 Taxes on goods and services	..	0.7	2.0	3.5	3.9	..	12.0	13.2	13.6	14.0
6000 Other taxes	..	0.0	0.0	0.0	0.0	..	0.0	0.0	0.0	0.0
State/Regional										
Total tax revenue	**..**	**..**	**..**	**..**	**..**	**..**	**..**	**..**	**..**	**..**
1000 Taxes on income, profits and capital gains	..	..	..	..	..	..	..	..	..	..
2000 Social security contributions	..	..	..	..	..	..	..	..	..	..
3000 Taxes on payroll and workforce	..	..	..	..	..	..	..	..	..	..
4000 Taxes on property	..	..	..	..	..	..	..	..	..	..
5000 Taxes on goods and services	..	..	..	..	..	..	..	..	..	..
6000 Other taxes	..	..	..	..	..	..	..	..	..	..
Local government										
Total tax revenue	**..**	**0.0**	**0.1**	**0.1**	**0.1**	**..**	**0.5**	**0.5**	**0.3**	**0.3**
1000 Taxes on income, profits and capital gains	..	0.0	0.0	0.0	0.0	..	0.0	0.0	0.0	0.0
2000 Social security contributions	..	0.0	0.0	0.0	0.0	..	0.0	0.0	0.0	0.0
3000 Taxes on payroll and workforce	..	0.0	0.0	0.0	0.0	..	0.0	0.0	0.0	0.0
4000 Taxes on property	..	0.0	0.1	0.1	0.1	..	0.4	0.3	0.2	0.2
5000 Taxes on goods and services	..	0.0	0.0	0.0	0.0	..	0.1	0.1	0.0	0.0
6000 Other taxes	..	0.0	0.0	0.0	0.0	..	0.0	0.0	0.0	0.0
Social Security Funds										
Total tax revenue	**..**	**0.3**	**0.9**	**1.4**	**1.5**	**..**	**4.3**	**5.9**	**5.5**	**5.6**
1000 Taxes on income, profits and capital gains	..	0.0	0.0	0.0	0.0	..	0.0	0.0	0.0	0.0
2000 Social security contributions	..	0.3	0.9	1.4	1.5	..	4.3	5.9	5.5	5.6
3000 Taxes on payroll and workforce	..	0.0	0.0	0.0	0.0	..	0.0	0.0	0.0	0.0
4000 Taxes on property	..	0.0	0.0	0.0	0.0	..	0.0	0.0	0.0	0.0
5000 Taxes on goods and services	..	0.0	0.0	0.0	0.0	..	0.0	0.0	0.0	0.0
6000 Other taxes	..	0.0	0.0	0.0	0.0	..	0.0	0.0	0.0	0.0

.. Not available

Note: More detailed country data and country notes are available in online chapter 6 "Tax revenues by sub-sectors of general government": https://doi.org/10.1787/0bbc27da-en. Full time series can be accessed at http://oe.cd/full-time-series.

Source: Statistics Estonia.

StatLink https://stat.link/zjq5f0

Table 4.21. Finland, tax revenue and % of GDP by selected tax category

	Billion EUR					% of GDP				
	1990	2000	2010	2018	2019	1990	2000	2010	2018	2019
Total tax revenue	**39.1**	**62.4**	**76.3**	**99.0**	**101.4**	**42.9**	**45.8**	**40.6**	**42.4**	**42.3**
1000 Taxes on income, profits and capital gains	**15.3**	**26.9**	**27.1**	**34.5**	**35.5**	**16.8**	**19.7**	**14.4**	**14.8**	**14.8**
1100 Of individuals	13.6	19.1	22.5	28.6	29.4	14.9	14.0	12.0	12.2	12.2
1200 Corporate	1.8	7.8	4.6	5.9	6.1	1.9	5.7	2.4	2.5	2.5
1300 Unallocable between 1100 and 1200	0.0	0.0	0.0	0.0	0.0	0.0	0.0	0.0	0.0	0.0
2000 Social security contributions	**10.0**	**15.8**	**22.6**	**27.6**	**28.3**	**11.0**	**11.5**	**12.0**	**11.8**	**11.8**
2100 Employees	1.2	2.9	4.7	8.1	8.5	1.3	2.1	2.5	3.5	3.6
2200 Employers	8.1	11.6	16.0	17.6	17.8	8.9	8.5	8.5	7.6	7.4
2300 Self-employed or non-employed	0.7	1.3	1.9	1.9	2.0	0.8	0.9	1.0	0.8	0.8
2400 Unallocable between 2100, 2200 and 2300	0.0	0.0	0.0	0.0	0.0	0.0	0.0	0.0	0.0	0.0
3000 Taxes on payroll and workforce	**0.0**	**0.0**	**0.0**	**0.0**	**0.0**	**0.0**	**0.0**	**0.0**	**0.0**	**0.0**
4000 Taxes on property	**1.0**	**1.5**	**2.1**	**3.3**	**3.5**	**1.1**	**1.1**	**1.1**	**1.4**	**1.4**
4100 Recurrent taxes on immovable property	0.1	0.6	1.2	1.8	1.9	0.1	0.4	0.6	0.8	0.8
4200 Recurrent taxes on net wealth	0.0	0.2	0.0	0.0	0.0	0.0	0.1	0.0	0.0	0.0
4300 Estate, inheritance and gift taxes	0.1	0.4	0.4	0.7	0.7	0.2	0.3	0.2	0.3	0.3
4400 Taxes on financial and capital transactions	0.7	0.4	0.5	0.8	0.9	0.8	0.3	0.3	0.4	0.4
4500 Non-recurrent taxes	0.0	0.0	0.0	0.0	0.0	0.0	0.0	0.0	0.0	0.0
4600 Other recurrent taxes on property	0.0	0.0	0.0	0.0	0.0	0.0	0.0	0.0	0.0	0.0
5000 Taxes on goods and services	**12.7**	**18.2**	**24.4**	**33.4**	**34.2**	**14.0**	**13.4**	**13.0**	**14.3**	**14.2**
5100 Taxes on production, sale, transfer, etc	12.6	17.8	23.6	32.0	32.7	13.8	13.0	12.6	13.7	13.6
5110 General taxes	7.5	10.9	15.5	21.4	22.0	8.3	8.0	8.3	9.2	9.2
5111 Value added taxes	7.5	10.9	15.5	21.4	22.0	8.3	8.0	8.3	9.2	9.2
5120 Taxes on specific goods and services	5.0	6.9	8.1	10.7	10.7	5.5	5.1	4.3	4.6	4.5
5121 Excises	3.8	5.6	6.3	8.3	8.1	4.2	4.1	3.3	3.6	3.4
5200 Taxes on use of goods and perform activities	0.2	0.4	0.8	1.4	1.5	0.2	0.3	0.4	0.6	0.6
5300 Unallocable between 5100 and 5200	0.0	0.0	0.0	0.0	0.0	0.0	0.0	0.0	0.0	0.0
6000 Other taxes	**0.1**	**0.0**	**0.1**	**0.0**	**0.1**	**0.1**	**0.0**	**0.0**	**0.0**	**0.0**
Non-wastable tax credits										
Non-wastable tax credits against 1000	..	..	..	..	..	..	..	..	..	..
Transfer component	..	..	..	..	..	..	..	..	..	..
Tax expenditure component	..	..	..	..	..	..	..	..	..	..
Revenues collected on behalf of the EU										
Revenues collected on behalf of the EU, total	..	0.1	0.2	0.2	0.4	..	0.1	0.1	0.1	0.2
Customs duties	..	0.1	0.2	0.2	0.2	..	0.1	0.1	0.1	0.1
SRF contributions	..	..	..	0.1	0.2	..	..	..	0.0	0.1

.. Not available

Note: More detailed country data and country notes are available in online chapter 5 "Detailed country tables": https://doi.org/10.1787/0bbc27da-en. Full time series can be accessed at http://oe.cd/full-time-series.

Source: Bulletin of Statistics; Central Statistical Office (for Central Government revenues); the Annual report of the National Pension Institute and Official Statistics of Finland Series XXIIA published by the Ministry and Social Affairs (for the Social Security and private pension respectively); supplementary information from unpublished sources.

StatLink https://stat.link/348chp

Table 4.22. Finland, tax revenue and % of GDP by level of government and main taxes

	Billion EUR					% of GDP				
	1990	2000	2010	2018	2019	1990	2000	2010	2018	2019
Federal or Central government										
Total tax revenue	**20.7**	**33.1**	**35.0**	**48.6**	**49.6**	**22.7**	**24.2**	**18.6**	**20.8**	**20.6**
1000 Taxes on income, profits and capital gains	7.0	14.0	9.8	13.9	14.2	7.7	10.3	5.2	5.9	5.9
2000 Social security contributions	0.0	0.0	0.0	0.0	0.0	0.0	0.0	0.0	0.0	0.0
3000 Taxes on payroll and workforce	0.0	0.0	0.0	0.0	0.0	0.0	0.0	0.0	0.0	0.0
4000 Taxes on property	0.9	0.9	0.9	1.5	1.6	1.0	0.7	0.5	0.7	0.7
5000 Taxes on goods and services	12.7	18.1	24.3	33.2	33.7	14.0	13.2	12.9	14.2	14.1
6000 Other taxes	0.1	0.0	0.1	0.0	0.1	0.1	0.0	0.0	0.0	0.0
State/Regional										
Total tax revenue	..	..	..	..	..	..	..	..	..	..
1000 Taxes on income, profits and capital gains	..	..	..	..	..	..	..	..	..	..
2000 Social security contributions	..	..	..	..	..	..	..	..	..	..
3000 Taxes on payroll and workforce	..	..	..	..	..	..	..	..	..	..
4000 Taxes on property	..	..	..	..	..	..	..	..	..	..
5000 Taxes on goods and services	..	..	..	..	..	..	..	..	..	..
6000 Other taxes	..	..	..	..	..	..	..	..	..	..
Local government										
Total tax revenue	**8.4**	**13.5**	**18.5**	**22.5**	**23.2**	**9.2**	**9.9**	**9.8**	**9.6**	**9.6**
1000 Taxes on income, profits and capital gains	8.3	12.9	17.3	20.7	21.3	9.1	9.4	9.2	8.8	8.9
2000 Social security contributions	0.0	0.0	0.0	0.0	0.0	0.0	0.0	0.0	0.0	0.0
3000 Taxes on payroll and workforce	0.0	0.0	0.0	0.0	0.0	0.0	0.0	0.0	0.0	0.0
4000 Taxes on property	0.1	0.6	1.2	1.8	1.9	0.1	0.4	0.6	0.8	0.8
5000 Taxes on goods and services	0.0	0.0	0.0	0.0	0.0	0.0	0.0	0.0	0.0	0.0
6000 Other taxes	0.0	0.0	0.0	0.0	0.0	0.0	0.0	0.0	0.0	0.0
Social Security Funds										
Total tax revenue	**10.0**	**15.8**	**22.6**	**27.6**	**28.3**	**11.0**	**11.5**	**12.0**	**11.8**	**11.8**
1000 Taxes on income, profits and capital gains	0.0	0.0	0.0	0.0	0.0	0.0	0.0	0.0	0.0	0.0
2000 Social security contributions	10.0	15.8	22.6	27.6	28.3	11.0	11.5	12.0	11.8	11.8
3000 Taxes on payroll and workforce	0.0	0.0	0.0	0.0	0.0	0.0	0.0	0.0	0.0	0.0
4000 Taxes on property	0.0	0.0	0.0	0.0	0.0	0.0	0.0	0.0	0.0	0.0
5000 Taxes on goods and services	0.0	0.0	0.0	0.0	0.0	0.0	0.0	0.0	0.0	0.0
6000 Other taxes	0.0	0.0	0.0	0.0	0.0	0.0	0.0	0.0	0.0	0.0

.. Not available

Note: More detailed country data and country notes are available in online chapter 6 "Tax revenues by sub-sectors of general government": https://doi.org/10.1787/0bbc27da-en. Full time series can be accessed at http://oe.cd/full-time-series.

Source: Bulletin of Statistics; Central Statistical Office (for Central Government revenues); the Annual report of the National Pension Institute and Official Statistics of Finland Series XXIIA published by the Ministry and Social Affairs (for the Social Security and private pension respectively); supplementary information from unpublished sources.

StatLink https://stat.link/ywrc8u

Table 4.23. France, tax revenue and % of GDP by selected tax category

	Billion EUR					% of GDP				
	1990	2000	2010	2018	2019	1990	2000	2010	2018	2019
Total tax revenue	**433.8**	**642.2**	**840.9**	**1 084.2**	**1 094.1**	**41.2**	**43.4**	**42.1**	**45.9**	**44.9**
1000 Taxes on income, profits and capital gains	**69.6**	**159.5**	**189.7**	**272.2**	**280.8**	**6.6**	**10.8**	**9.5**	**11.5**	**11.5**
1100 Of individuals	46.3	115.2	143.1	222.6	226.7	4.4	7.8	7.2	9.4	9.3
1200 Corporate	23.1	44.3	46.6	49.6	54.2	2.2	3.0	2.3	2.1	2.2
1300 Unallocable between 1100 and 1200	0.3	0.0	0.0	0.0	0.0	0.0	0.0	0.0	0.0	0.0
2000 Social security contributions	**191.1**	**230.2**	**321.3**	**378.6**	**361.4**	**18.1**	**15.6**	**16.1**	**16.0**	**14.8**
2100 Employees	57.3	57.3	77.7	88.6	87.4	5.4	3.9	3.9	3.7	3.6
2200 Employers	118.1	158.3	218.0	263.6	245.8	11.2	10.7	10.9	11.2	10.1
2300 Self-employed or non-employed	15.7	14.6	25.7	26.4	28.3	1.5	1.0	1.3	1.1	1.2
2400 Unallocable between 2100, 2200 and 2300	0.0	0.0	0.0	0.0	0.0	0.0	0.0	0.0	0.0	0.0
3000 Taxes on payroll and workforce	**8.3**	**14.9**	**26.8**	**35.7**	**43.4**	**0.8**	**1.0**	**1.3**	**1.5**	**1.8**
4000 Taxes on property	**27.4**	**44.0**	**70.5**	**94.3**	**94.8**	**2.6**	**3.0**	**3.5**	**4.0**	**3.9**
4100 Recurrent taxes on immovable property	14.8	27.3	47.6	59.6	57.6	1.4	1.8	2.4	2.5	2.4
4200 Recurrent taxes on net wealth	2.6	2.4	4.4	1.8	2.0	0.2	0.2	0.2	0.1	0.1
4300 Estate, inheritance and gift taxes	4.1	6.9	7.7	14.3	15.2	0.4	0.5	0.4	0.6	0.6
4400 Taxes on financial and capital transactions	5.9	7.4	10.8	18.6	19.9	0.6	0.5	0.5	0.8	0.8
4500 Non-recurrent taxes	0.0	0.0	0.0	0.0	0.0	0.0	0.0	0.0	0.0	0.0
4600 Other recurrent taxes on property	0.0	0.0	0.0	0.0	0.0	0.0	0.0	0.0	0.0	0.0
5000 Taxes on goods and services	**123.2**	**169.5**	**223.3**	**291.8**	**301.5**	**11.7**	**11.5**	**11.2**	**12.3**	**12.4**
5100 Taxes on production, sale, transfer, etc	119.2	162.8	214.6	280.1	289.6	11.3	11.0	10.8	11.9	11.9
5110 General taxes	81.3	109.8	150.6	185.4	193.6	7.7	7.4	7.5	7.8	7.9
5111 Value added taxes	80.0	107.1	135.2	167.5	174.3	7.6	7.2	6.8	7.1	7.1
5120 Taxes on specific goods and services	37.9	53.0	64.0	94.7	96.0	3.6	3.6	3.2	4.0	3.9
5121 Excises	26.8	39.7	45.6	64.6	64.6	2.5	2.7	2.3	2.7	2.7
5200 Taxes on use of goods and perform activities	4.0	6.7	8.8	11.7	11.9	0.4	0.5	0.4	0.5	0.5
5300 Unallocable between 5100 and 5200	0.0	0.0	0.0	0.0	0.0	0.0	0.0	0.0	0.0	0.0
6000 Other taxes	**14.1**	**24.1**	**9.2**	**11.8**	**12.2**	**1.3**	**1.6**	**0.5**	**0.5**	**0.5**
Non-wastable tax credits										
Non-wastable tax credits against 1000	..	0.5	17.4	35.9	35.4	0.0	0.0	0.9	1.5	1.5
Transfer component	0.0	0.0	7.9	19.7	18.5	0.0	0.0	0.4	0.8	0.8
Tax expenditure component	0.0	0.0	9.5	16.2	16.9	0.0	0.0	0.5	0.7	0.7
Revenues collected on behalf of the EU										
Revenues collected on behalf of the EU, total	2.6	1.9	2.0	4.6	4.6	0.2	0.1	0.1	0.2	0.2
Customs duties	..	1.5	1.8	2.1	2.0	..	0.1	0.1	0.1	0.1
SRF contributions	..	..	..	2.3	2.4	..	..	..	0.1	0.1

.. Not available

Note: More detailed country data and country notes are available in online chapter 5 "Detailed country tables": https://doi.org/10.1787/0bbc27da-en. Full time series can be accessed at http://oe.cd/full-time-series.

The total tax revenue has been reduced by the amount of any capital transfer that represents uncollected taxes. The capital transfer has been allocated between tax headings in proportion to the reported tax revenue. Therefore, the tax revenue amounts are different to those reported in the detailed country data available in online chapter 5 "Detailed country tables".

Source: General Account of the Administration of finances for the figures of fiscal receipts. OSCE for the figures of Social Security from 1965 to 1969, and ESA for the following years.

StatLink https://stat.link/1xrejo

Table 4.24. France, tax revenue and % of GDP by level of government and main taxes

	Billion EUR					% of GDP				
	1990	2000	2010	2018	2019	1990	2000	2010	2018	2019
Federal or Central government										
Total tax revenue	**200.1**	**270.3**	**299.6**	**364.1**	**356.6**	**19.0**	**18.3**	**15.0**	**15.4**	**14.6**
1000 Taxes on income, profits and capital gains	69.6	94.4	97.0	130.6	143.7	6.6	6.4	4.9	5.5	5.9
2000 Social security contributions	3.2	5.4	7.6	8.2	8.1	0.3	0.4	0.4	0.3	0.3
3000 Taxes on payroll and workforce	6.2	10.6	4.2	3.8	11.2	0.6	0.7	0.2	0.2	0.5
4000 Taxes on property	8.6	11.4	13.4	19.5	20.5	0.8	0.8	0.7	0.8	0.8
5000 Taxes on goods and services	112.1	145.5	170.0	200.8	172.0	10.6	9.8	8.5	8.5	7.1
6000 Other taxes	0.4	3.1	7.4	1.3	1.1	0.0	0.2	0.4	0.1	0.0
State/Regional										
Total tax revenue	**..**	**..**	**..**	**..**	**..**	**..**	**..**	**..**	**..**	**..**
1000 Taxes on income, profits and capital gains	..	..	..	..	..	..	..	..	..	..
2000 Social security contributions	..	..	..	..	..	..	..	..	..	..
3000 Taxes on payroll and workforce	..	..	..	..	..	..	..	..	..	..
4000 Taxes on property	..	..	..	..	..	..	..	..	..	..
5000 Taxes on goods and services	..	..	..	..	..	..	..	..	..	..
6000 Other taxes	..	..	..	..	..	..	..	..	..	..
Local government										
Total tax revenue	**40.2**	**64.7**	**89.3**	**146.9**	**148.4**	**3.8**	**4.4**	**4.5**	**6.2**	**6.1**
1000 Taxes on income, profits and capital gains	0.0	0.0	0.1	0.0	0.0	0.0	0.0	0.0	0.0	0.0
2000 Social security contributions	0.0	0.0	0.0	0.0	0.0	0.0	0.0	0.0	0.0	0.0
3000 Taxes on payroll and workforce	1.7	3.9	7.5	10.6	11.1	0.2	0.3	0.4	0.5	0.5
4000 Taxes on property	18.8	32.7	57.1	74.8	74.3	1.8	2.2	2.9	3.2	3.0
5000 Taxes on goods and services	6.0	7.3	23.0	51.3	52.5	0.6	0.5	1.2	2.2	2.2
6000 Other taxes	13.7	20.9	1.6	10.1	10.5	1.3	1.4	0.1	0.4	0.4
Social Security Funds										
Total tax revenue	**190.9**	**305.3**	**450.1**	**568.7**	**584.5**	**18.1**	**20.6**	**22.6**	**24.1**	**24.0**
1000 Taxes on income, profits and capital gains	0.0	65.0	92.7	141.6	137.1	0.0	4.4	4.6	6.0	5.6
2000 Social security contributions	187.9	224.8	313.7	370.3	353.4	17.8	15.2	15.7	15.7	14.5
3000 Taxes on payroll and workforce	0.4	0.4	15.1	21.3	21.0	0.0	0.0	0.8	0.9	0.9
4000 Taxes on property	0.0	0.0	0.0	0.0	0.0	0.0	0.0	0.0	0.0	0.0
5000 Taxes on goods and services	2.5	14.9	28.4	35.1	72.4	0.2	1.0	1.4	1.5	3.0
6000 Other taxes	0.0	0.1	0.2	0.4	0.6	0.0	0.0	0.0	0.0	0.0

.. Not available

Note: More detailed country data and country notes are available in online chapter 6 "Tax revenues by sub-sectors of general government": https://doi.org/10.1787/0bbc27da-en. Full time series can be accessed at http://oe.cd/full-time-series.

The total tax revenue has been reduced by the amount of any capital transfer that represents uncollected taxes. The capital transfer has been allocated between tax headings in proportion to the reported tax revenue. Therefore, the tax revenue amounts are different to those reported in the detailed country data available in online chapter 6 "Tax revenues by sub-sectors of general government".

Source: General Account of the Administration of finances for the figures of fiscal receipts. OSCE for the figures of Social Security from 1965 to 1969, and ESA for the following years.

StatLink https://stat.link/rqby6e

Table 4.25. Germany, tax revenue and % of GDP by selected tax category

	Billion EUR					% of GDP				
	1990	2000	2010	2018	2019	1990	2000	2010	2018	2019
Total tax revenue	**454.8**	**767.0**	**911.2**	**1 294.3**	**1 341.3**	**34.8**	**36.4**	**35.5**	**38.4**	**38.6**
1000 Taxes on income, profits and capital gains	**147.3**	**231.2**	**257.8**	**423.9**	**436.8**	**11.3**	**11.0**	**10.1**	**12.6**	**12.6**
1100 Of individuals	125.3	194.2	219.4	352.0	367.3	9.6	9.2	8.6	10.5	10.6
1200 Corporate	22.0	37.1	38.4	71.9	69.4	1.7	1.8	1.5	2.1	2.0
1300 Unallocable between 1100 and 1200	0.0	0.0	0.0	0.0	0.0	0.0	0.0	0.0	0.0	0.0
2000 Social security contributions	**170.4**	**299.4**	**354.3**	**487.7**	**508.1**	**13.0**	**14.2**	**13.8**	**14.5**	**14.6**
2100 Employees	73.6	131.6	152.8	216.8	220.2	5.6	6.2	6.0	6.4	6.3
2200 Employers	86.7	147.4	165.5	223.5	238.4	6.6	7.0	6.5	6.6	6.9
2300 Self-employed or non-employed	10.2	20.4	36.0	47.4	49.6	0.8	1.0	1.4	1.4	1.4
2400 Unallocable between 2100, 2200 and 2300	0.0	0.0	0.0	0.0	0.0	0.0	0.0	0.0	0.0	0.0
3000 Taxes on payroll and workforce	**0.0**	**0.0**	**0.0**	**0.0**	**0.0**	**0.0**	**0.0**	**0.0**	**0.0**	**0.0**
4000 Taxes on property	**15.3**	**17.5**	**21.0**	**36.3**	**38.7**	**1.2**	**0.8**	**0.8**	**1.1**	**1.1**
4100 Recurrent taxes on immovable property	4.5	8.8	11.3	14.2	14.4	0.3	0.4	0.4	0.4	0.4
4200 Recurrent taxes on net wealth	6.2	0.4	0.0	1.2	1.5	0.5	0.0	0.0	0.0	0.0
4300 Estate, inheritance and gift taxes	1.5	3.0	4.4	6.8	7.0	0.1	0.1	0.2	0.2	0.2
4400 Taxes on financial and capital transactions	3.1	5.2	5.3	14.1	15.8	0.2	0.2	0.2	0.4	0.5
4500 Non-recurrent taxes	0.0	0.0	0.0	0.0	0.0	0.0	0.0	0.0	0.0	0.0
4600 Other recurrent taxes on property	0.0	0.0	0.0	0.0	0.0	0.0	0.0	0.0	0.0	0.0
5000 Taxes on goods and services	**121.6**	**218.7**	**277.9**	**346.2**	**357.4**	**9.3**	**10.4**	**10.8**	**10.3**	**10.3**
5100 Taxes on production, sale, transfer, etc	117.2	211.4	261.2	327.5	337.1	9.0	10.0	10.2	9.7	9.7
5110 General taxes	75.5	140.9	180.5	235.4	244.4	5.8	6.7	7.0	7.0	7.0
5111 Value added taxes	75.5	140.9	180.5	235.4	244.4	5.8	6.7	7.0	7.0	7.0
5120 Taxes on specific goods and services	41.7	70.6	80.3	91.7	92.3	3.2	3.3	3.1	2.7	2.7
5121 Excises	31.2	57.2	63.4	66.1	66.2	2.4	2.7	2.5	2.0	1.9
5200 Taxes on use of goods and perform activities	4.4	7.2	16.8	18.7	20.3	0.3	0.3	0.7	0.6	0.6
5300 Unallocable between 5100 and 5200	0.0	0.0	0.0	0.0	0.0	0.0	0.0	0.0	0.0	0.0
6000 Other taxes	**0.2**	**0.2**	**0.1**	**0.3**	**0.3**	**0.0**	**0.0**	**0.0**	**0.0**	**0.0**
Non-wastable tax credits										
Non-wastable tax credits against 1000	..	39.3	46.3	43.9	45.2	..	1.9	1.8	1.3	1.3
Transfer component	..	..	17.7	14.9	15.9	..	..	0.7	0.4	0.5
Tax expenditure component	..	..	28.6	29.0	29.3	..	..	1.1	0.9	0.8
Revenues collected on behalf of the EU										
Revenues collected on behalf of the EU, total	4.1	3.7	4.3	7.0	7.1	0.3	0.2	0.2	0.2	0.2
Customs duties	3.7	3.4	4.2	5.0	5.1	0.3	0.2	0.2	0.1	0.1
SRF contributions	..	..	..	2.0	2.0	..	..	..	0.1	0.1

.. Not available

Note: More detailed country data and country notes are available in online chapter 5 "Detailed country tables": https://doi.org/10.1787/0bbc27da-en. Full time series can be accessed at http://oe.cd/full-time-series.

Source: Finanzbericht, Bonn; Tax Statistics. Unpublished estimates by the Ministry of Finance.

StatLink https://stat.link/va7emk

Table 4.26. Germany, tax revenue and % of GDP by level of government and main taxes

	Billion EUR					% of GDP				
	1990	2000	2010	2018	2019	1990	2000	2010	2018	2019
Federal or Central government										
Total tax revenue	**143.9**	**234.8**	**283.2**	**382.9**	**393.6**	**11.0**	**11.1**	**11.0**	**11.4**	**11.3**
1000 Taxes on income, profits and capital gains	58.2	97.9	104.5	173.8	179.6	4.5	4.6	4.1	5.2	5.2
2000 Social security contributions	0.0	0.0	0.0	0.0	0.0	0.0	0.0	0.0	0.0	0.0
3000 Taxes on payroll and workforce	0.0	0.0	0.0	0.0	0.0	0.0	0.0	0.0	0.0	0.0
4000 Taxes on property	1.2	0.0	0.0	1.2	1.5	0.1	0.0	0.0	0.0	0.0
5000 Taxes on goods and services	84.6	136.9	178.6	207.9	212.5	6.5	6.5	7.0	6.2	6.1
6000 Other taxes	0.0	0.0	0.0	0.0	0.0	0.0	0.0	0.0	0.0	0.0
State/Regional										
Total tax revenue	**97.8**	**172.1**	**198.1**	**306.9**	**319.1**	**7.5**	**8.2**	**7.7**	**9.1**	**9.2**
1000 Taxes on income, profits and capital gains	58.2	88.9	97.6	162.2	166.7	4.5	4.2	3.8	4.8	4.8
2000 Social security contributions	0.0	0.0	0.0	0.0	0.0	0.0	0.0	0.0	0.0	0.0
3000 Taxes on payroll and workforce	0.0	0.0	0.0	0.0	0.0	0.0	0.0	0.0	0.0	0.0
4000 Taxes on property	7.0	8.5	9.7	22.4	24.3	0.5	0.4	0.4	0.7	0.7
5000 Taxes on goods and services	32.6	74.6	90.8	122.4	128.1	2.5	3.5	3.5	3.6	3.7
6000 Other taxes	0.0	0.0	0.0	0.0	0.0	0.0	0.0	0.0	0.0	0.0
Local government										
Total tax revenue	**38.4**	**57.0**	**71.4**	**109.8**	**113.4**	**2.9**	**2.7**	**2.8**	**3.3**	**3.3**
1000 Taxes on income, profits and capital gains	30.9	44.4	55.7	87.9	90.5	2.4	2.1	2.2	2.6	2.6
2000 Social security contributions	0.0	0.0	0.0	0.0	0.0	0.0	0.0	0.0	0.0	0.0
3000 Taxes on payroll and workforce	0.0	0.0	0.0	0.0	0.0	0.0	0.0	0.0	0.0	0.0
4000 Taxes on property	7.2	9.0	11.3	12.7	12.9	0.5	0.4	0.4	0.4	0.4
5000 Taxes on goods and services	0.3	3.4	4.3	9.0	9.7	0.0	0.2	0.2	0.3	0.3
6000 Other taxes	0.2	0.1	0.1	0.3	0.3	0.0	0.0	0.0	0.0	0.0
Social Security Funds										
Total tax revenue	**170.4**	**299.4**	**354.3**	**487.7**	**508.1**	**13.0**	**14.2**	**13.8**	**14.5**	**14.6**
1000 Taxes on income, profits and capital gains	0.0	0.0	0.0	0.0	0.0	0.0	0.0	0.0	0.0	0.0
2000 Social security contributions	170.4	299.4	354.3	487.7	508.1	13.0	14.2	13.8	14.5	14.6
3000 Taxes on payroll and workforce	0.0	0.0	0.0	0.0	0.0	0.0	0.0	0.0	0.0	0.0
4000 Taxes on property	0.0	0.0	0.0	0.0	0.0	0.0	0.0	0.0	0.0	0.0
5000 Taxes on goods and services	0.0	0.0	0.0	0.0	0.0	0.0	0.0	0.0	0.0	0.0
6000 Other taxes	0.0	0.0	0.0	0.0	0.0	0.0	0.0	0.0	0.0	0.0

Note: More detailed country data and country notes are available in online chapter 6 "Tax revenues by sub-sectors of general government": https://doi.org/10.1787/0bbc27da-en. Full time series can be accessed at http://oe.cd/full-time-series.
Source: Finanzbericht, Bonn; Tax Statistics. Unpublished estimates by the Ministry of Finance.

StatLink https://stat.link/bdt5gk

Table 4.27. Greece, tax revenue and % of GDP by selected tax category

	Billion EUR					% of GDP				
	1990	2000	2010	2018	2019	1990	2000	2010	2018	2019
Total tax revenue	**11.5**	**47.2**	**72.4**	**71.9**	**72.4**	**25.2**	**33.4**	**32.3**	**40.0**	**39.5**
1000 Taxes on income, profits and capital gains	**2.3**	**12.7**	**16.0**	**16.5**	**15.6**	**5.0**	**9.0**	**7.1**	**9.2**	**8.5**
1100 Of individuals	1.6	6.1	9.0	11.6	11.0	3.6	4.3	4.0	6.4	6.0
1200 Corporate	0.6	5.6	5.7	4.0	4.1	1.4	4.0	2.6	2.2	2.2
1300 Unallocable between 1100 and 1200	0.0	0.9	1.2	0.9	0.6	0.1	0.6	0.5	0.5	0.3
2000 Social security contributions	**3.5**	**14.3**	**24.7**	**21.5**	**22.3**	**7.6**	**10.1**	**11.0**	**11.9**	**12.2**
2100 Employees	1.7	7.6	13.3	11.9	12.1	3.8	5.4	5.9	6.6	6.6
2200 Employers	1.7	6.7	11.5	9.6	10.2	3.8	4.7	5.1	5.3	5.6
2300 Self-employed or non-employed	0.0	0.0	0.0	0.0	0.0	0.0	0.0	0.0	0.0	0.0
2400 Unallocable between 2100, 2200 and 2300	0.0	0.0	0.0	0.0	0.0	0.0	0.0	0.0	0.0	0.0
3000 Taxes on payroll and workforce	**0.1**	**0.0**	**0.0**	**0.0**	**0.0**	**0.2**	**0.0**	**0.0**	**0.0**	**0.0**
4000 Taxes on property	**0.5**	**3.6**	**3.7**	**5.6**	**5.6**	**1.2**	**2.6**	**1.7**	**3.1**	**3.1**
4100 Recurrent taxes on immovable property	0.0	0.4	0.6	3.6	3.3	0.0	0.3	0.2	2.0	1.8
4200 Recurrent taxes on net wealth	0.0	0.7	1.3	1.2	1.2	0.0	0.5	0.6	0.7	0.7
4300 Estate, inheritance and gift taxes	0.1	0.4	0.2	0.1	0.2	0.3	0.3	0.1	0.1	0.1
4400 Taxes on financial and capital transactions	0.4	2.0	1.1	0.6	0.9	0.8	1.4	0.5	0.4	0.5
4500 Non-recurrent taxes	0.0	0.0	0.0	0.0	0.0	0.0	0.0	0.0	0.0	0.0
4600 Other recurrent taxes on property	0.0	0.1	0.6	0.0	0.0	0.0	0.1	0.3	0.0	0.0
5000 Taxes on goods and services	**5.1**	**16.6**	**28.0**	**28.4**	**28.9**	**11.2**	**11.8**	**12.5**	**15.8**	**15.7**
5100 Taxes on production, sale, transfer, etc	4.9	14.8	25.5	24.7	24.9	10.7	10.5	11.4	13.7	13.6
5110 General taxes	3.0	9.2	16.5	15.4	15.5	6.7	6.5	7.4	8.6	8.4
5111 Value added taxes	2.8	8.9	16.0	15.3	15.4	6.2	6.3	7.1	8.5	8.4
5120 Taxes on specific goods and services	1.8	5.5	8.9	9.1	9.4	3.9	3.9	4.0	5.1	5.1
5121 Excises	1.4	4.1	7.6	7.1	7.2	3.0	2.9	3.4	4.0	3.9
5200 Taxes on use of goods and perform activities	0.2	1.3	1.7	3.1	3.3	0.5	0.9	0.8	1.7	1.8
5300 Unallocable between 5100 and 5200	0.0	0.5	0.8	0.6	0.7	0.0	0.4	0.4	0.4	0.4
6000 Other taxes	**0.0**	**0.0**	**0.0**	**0.0**	**0.0**	**0.0**	**0.0**	**0.0**	**0.0**	**0.0**
Non-wastable tax credits										
Non-wastable tax credits against 1000	..	..	..	..	..	..	..	..	..	..
Transfer component	..	..	..	..	..	..	..	..	..	..
Tax expenditure component	..	..	..	..	..	..	..	..	..	..
Revenues collected on behalf of the EU										
Revenues collected on behalf of the EU, total	0.1	0.2	0.3	0.3	0.4	0.2	0.2	0.1	0.2	0.2
Customs duties	0.1	0.2	0.3	0.2	0.3	0.2	0.1	0.1	0.1	0.2
SRF contributions	..	..	..	0.1	0.1	..	..	..	0.1	0.0

.. Not available

Note: More detailed country data and country notes are available in online chapter 5 "Detailed country tables": https://doi.org/10.1787/0bbc27da-en. Full time series can be accessed at http://oe.cd/full-time-series.

Source: Ministry of Finance, General accounting Office, 20th Directorate of Budget except the heading 2000 provided by the National Statistics Bureau.

StatLink https://stat.link/dzi6yc

Table 4.28. Greece, tax revenue and % of GDP by level of government and main taxes

	Billion EUR					% of GDP				
	1990	2000	2010	2018	2019	1990	2000	2010	2018	2019
Federal or Central government										
Total tax revenue	**7.8**	**31.9**	**46.5**	**48.3**	**47.9**	**17.1**	**22.6**	**20.7**	**26.9**	**26.1**
1000 Taxes on income, profits and capital gains	2.3	12.7	15.9	16.5	15.6	5.0	9.0	7.1	9.2	8.5
2000 Social security contributions	0.0	0.7	1.3	0.1	0.1	0.1	0.5	0.6	0.0	0.0
3000 Taxes on payroll and workforce	0.0	0.0	0.0	0.0	0.0	0.0	0.0	0.0	0.0	0.0
4000 Taxes on property	0.5	2.6	2.1	4.0	4.0	1.2	1.8	0.9	2.2	2.2
5000 Taxes on goods and services	4.9	16.0	27.1	27.8	28.3	10.9	11.3	12.1	15.5	15.4
6000 Other taxes	0.0	0.0	0.0	0.0	0.0	0.0	0.0	0.0	0.0	0.0
State/Regional										
Total tax revenue	..	..	..	..	..	..	..	..	..	..
1000 Taxes on income, profits and capital gains	..	..	..	..	..	..	..	..	..	..
2000 Social security contributions	..	..	..	..	..	..	..	..	..	..
3000 Taxes on payroll and workforce	..	..	..	..	..	..	..	..	..	..
4000 Taxes on property	..	..	..	..	..	..	..	..	..	..
5000 Taxes on goods and services	..	..	..	..	..	..	..	..	..	..
6000 Other taxes	..	..	..	..	..	..	..	..	..	..
Local government										
Total tax revenue	**0.1**	**1.0**	**1.7**	**1.7**	**1.7**	**0.3**	**0.7**	**0.8**	**1.0**	**1.0**
1000 Taxes on income, profits and capital gains	0.0	0.0	0.0	0.0	0.0	0.0	0.0	0.0	0.0	0.0
2000 Social security contributions	0.0	0.0	0.0	0.0	0.0	0.0	0.0	0.0	0.0	0.0
3000 Taxes on payroll and workforce	0.1	0.0	0.0	0.0	0.0	0.2	0.0	0.0	0.0	0.0
4000 Taxes on property	0.0	0.8	1.5	1.6	1.6	0.0	0.6	0.7	0.9	0.9
5000 Taxes on goods and services	0.1	0.2	0.2	0.1	0.1	0.1	0.1	0.1	0.1	0.1
6000 Other taxes	0.0	0.0	0.0	0.0	0.0	0.0	0.0	0.0	0.0	0.0
Social Security Funds										
Total tax revenue	**3.4**	**14.1**	**24.0**	**21.5**	**22.4**	**7.5**	**10.0**	**10.7**	**12.0**	**12.2**
1000 Taxes on income, profits and capital gains	0.0	0.0	0.0	0.0	0.0	0.0	0.0	0.0	0.0	0.0
2000 Social security contributions	3.4	13.6	23.4	21.4	22.2	7.5	9.6	10.5	11.9	12.1
3000 Taxes on payroll and workforce	0.0	0.0	0.0	0.0	0.0	0.0	0.0	0.0	0.0	0.0
4000 Taxes on property	0.0	0.2	0.1	0.0	0.0	0.0	0.1	0.1	0.0	0.0
5000 Taxes on goods and services	0.0	0.3	0.4	0.1	0.1	0.0	0.2	0.2	0.1	0.1
6000 Other taxes	0.0	0.0	0.0	0.0	0.0	0.0	0.0	0.0	0.0	0.0

.. Not available

Note: More detailed country data and country notes are available in online chapter 6 "Tax revenues by sub-sectors of general government": https://doi.org/10.1787/0bbc27da-en. Full time series can be accessed at http://oe.cd/full-time-series.

Source: Ministry of Finance, General accounting Office, 20th Directorate of Budget except the heading 2000 provided by the National Statistics Bureau.

StatLink https://stat.link/5gcrzf

Table 4.29. Hungary, tax revenue and % of GDP by selected tax category

	Billion HUF					% of GDP				
	1990	2000	2010	2018	2019	1990	2000	2010	2018	2019
Total tax revenue	..	**5 132.6**	**10 121.7**	**15 961.8**	**17 329.5**	..	**38.5**	**36.9**	**36.8**	**36.5**
1000 Taxes on income, profits and capital gains	..	**1 247.4**	**2 093.8**	**2 912.2**	**3 071.4**	..	**9.4**	**7.6**	**6.7**	**6.5**
1100 Of individuals	..	954.7	1 764.1	2 340.3	2 457.6	..	7.2	6.4	5.4	5.2
1200 Corporate	..	292.7	329.7	571.9	613.8	..	2.2	1.2	1.3	1.3
1300 Unallocable between 1100 and 1200	..	0.0	0.0	0.0	0.0	..	0.0	0.0	0.0	0.0
2000 Social security contributions	..	**1 506.8**	**3 179.5**	**5 049.8**	**5 544.8**	..	**11.3**	**11.6**	**11.6**	**11.7**
2100 Employees	..	275.3	1 112.6	2 432.7	2 771.0	..	2.1	4.1	5.6	5.8
2200 Employers	..	1 213.2	2 043.8	2 590.3	2 745.8	..	9.1	7.5	6.0	5.8
2300 Self-employed or non-employed	..	0.9	0.0	0.0	0.0	..	0.0	0.0	0.0	0.0
2400 Unallocable between 2100, 2200 and 2300	..	17.4	23.2	26.8	28.0	..	0.1	0.1	0.1	0.1
3000 Taxes on payroll and workforce	..	**183.4**	**113.7**	**410.2**	**495.0**	..	**1.4**	**0.4**	**0.9**	**1.0**
4000 Taxes on property	..	**89.0**	**312.1**	**417.8**	**446.5**	..	**0.7**	**1.1**	**1.0**	**0.9**
4100 Recurrent taxes on immovable property	..	30.8	92.5	219.1	221.4	..	0.2	0.3	0.5	0.5
4200 Recurrent taxes on net wealth	..	0.0	135.7	42.6	44.9	..	0.0	0.5	0.1	0.1
4300 Estate, inheritance and gift taxes	..	5.5	6.3	8.5	11.4	..	0.0	0.0	0.0	0.0
4400 Taxes on financial and capital transactions	..	52.8	77.6	147.6	168.7	..	0.4	0.3	0.3	0.4
4500 Non-recurrent taxes	..	0.0	0.0	0.0	0.0	..	0.0	0.0	0.0	0.0
4600 Other recurrent taxes on property	..	0.0	0.0	0.0	0.0	..	0.0	0.0	0.0	0.0
5000 Taxes on goods and services	..	**2 081.4**	**4 383.9**	**7 148.8**	**7 737.9**	..	**15.6**	**16.0**	**16.5**	**16.3**
5100 Taxes on production, sale, transfer, etc	..	2 052.7	4 272.3	6 987.0	7 523.5	..	15.4	15.6	16.1	15.8
5110 General taxes	..	1 340.6	3 010.8	5 042.4	5 526.3	..	10.1	11.0	11.6	11.6
5111 Value added taxes	..	1 153.7	2 325.6	4 129.5	4 526.8	..	8.7	8.5	9.5	9.5
5120 Taxes on specific goods and services	..	712.1	1 261.5	1 944.6	1 997.3	..	5.3	4.6	4.5	4.2
5121 Excises	..	533.5	929.9	1 270.1	1 303.9	..	4.0	3.4	2.9	2.7
5200 Taxes on use of goods and perform activities	..	28.7	111.6	161.8	214.4	..	0.2	0.4	0.4	0.5
5300 Unallocable between 5100 and 5200	..	0.0	0.0	0.0	0.0	..	0.0	0.0	0.0	0.0
6000 Other taxes	..	**24.5**	**38.7**	**23.0**	**33.9**	..	**0.2**	**0.1**	**0.1**	**0.1**
Non-wastable tax credits										
Non-wastable tax credits against 1000	..	..	..	..	..	..	..	..	..	..
Transfer component	..	..	..	..	..	..	..	..	..	..
Tax expenditure component	..	..	..	..	..	..	..	..	..	..
Revenues collected on behalf of the EU										
Revenues collected on behalf of the EU, total	..	..	25.7	63.4	64.3	..	..	0.1	0.1	0.1
Customs duties	..	..	25.0	63.4	64.3	..	..	0.1	0.1	0.1

.. Not available

Note: More detailed country data and country notes are available in online chapter 5 "Detailed country tables": https://doi.org/10.1787/0bbc27da-en. Full time series can be accessed at http://oe.cd/full-time-series.

Source: Ministry of Finance, Economic Department.

StatLink https://stat.link/hgxnol

Table 4.30. Hungary, tax revenue and % of GDP by level of government and main taxes

	Billion HUF					% of GDP				
	1990	2000	2010	2018	2019	1990	2000	2010	2018	2019
Federal or Central government										
Total tax revenue	..	**3 308.0**	**6 379.4**	**9 834.6**	**10 859.5**	..	**24.8**	**23.3**	**22.7**	**22.9**
1000 Taxes on income, profits and capital gains	..	1 230.8	2 064.3	2 773.4	3 059.4	..	9.2	7.5	6.4	6.4
2000 Social security contributions	..	136.6	182.0	199.7	286.9	..	1.0	0.7	0.5	0.6
3000 Taxes on payroll and workforce	..	15.4	103.1	399.1	484.8	..	0.1	0.4	0.9	1.0
4000 Taxes on property	..	29.1	182.8	252.9	279.5	..	0.2	0.7	0.6	0.6
5000 Taxes on goods and services	..	1 878.6	3 808.5	6 193.2	6 723.0	..	14.1	13.9	14.3	14.1
6000 Other taxes	..	17.5	38.7	16.3	25.8	..	0.1	0.1	0.0	0.1
State/Regional										
Total tax revenue	..	..	..	..	..	..	..	..	..	..
1000 Taxes on income, profits and capital gains	..	..	..	..	..	..	..	..	..	..
2000 Social security contributions	..	..	..	..	..	..	..	..	..	..
3000 Taxes on payroll and workforce	..	..	..	..	..	..	..	..	..	..
4000 Taxes on property	..	..	..	..	..	..	..	..	..	..
5000 Taxes on goods and services	..	..	..	..	..	..	..	..	..	..
6000 Other taxes	..	..	..	..	..	..	..	..	..	..
Local government										
Total tax revenue	..	**266.0**	**652.2**	**923.8**	**1 006.2**	..	**2.0**	**2.4**	**2.1**	**2.1**
1000 Taxes on income, profits and capital gains	..	2.2	0.1	0.0	0.0	..	0.0	0.0	0.0	0.0
2000 Social security contributions	..	0.0	0.0	0.0	0.0	..	0.0	0.0	0.0	0.0
3000 Taxes on payroll and workforce	..	1.2	1.2	0.0	0.0	..	0.0	0.0	0.0	0.0
4000 Taxes on property	..	59.9	129.3	164.9	166.9	..	0.4	0.5	0.4	0.4
5000 Taxes on goods and services	..	202.8	521.6	758.9	839.2	..	1.5	1.9	1.8	1.8
6000 Other taxes	..	0.0	0.0	0.0	0.0	..	0.0	0.0	0.0	0.0
Social Security Funds										
Total tax revenue	..	**1 558.6**	**3 064.5**	**5 139.9**	**5 399.6**	..	**11.7**	**11.2**	**11.9**	**11.4**
1000 Taxes on income, profits and capital gains	..	14.5	29.4	138.7	12.0	..	0.1	0.1	0.3	0.0
2000 Social security contributions	..	1 370.2	2 997.5	4 850.1	5 257.9	..	10.3	10.9	11.2	11.1
3000 Taxes on payroll and workforce	..	166.9	9.4	11.1	10.2	..	1.3	0.0	0.0	0.0
4000 Taxes on property	..	0.0	0.0	0.0	0.0	..	0.0	0.0	0.0	0.0
5000 Taxes on goods and services	..	0.0	28.1	133.2	111.4	..	0.0	0.1	0.3	0.2
6000 Other taxes	..	7.0	0.0	6.8	8.1	..	0.1	0.0	0.0	0.0

.. Not available

Note: More detailed country data and country notes are available in online chapter 6 "Tax revenues by sub-sectors of general government": https://doi.org/10.1787/0bbc27da-en. Full time series can be accessed at http://oe.cd/full-time-series.

Source: Ministry of Finance, Economic Department.

StatLink https://stat.link/x07lvp

Table 4.31. Iceland, tax revenue and % of GDP by selected tax category

	Billion ISK					% of GDP				
	1990	2000	2010	2018	2019	1990	2000	2010	2018	2019
Total tax revenue	**114.9**	**254.6**	**540.3**	**1 036.8**	**1 061.9**	**30.5**	**35.9**	**32.1**	**36.4**	**34.8**
1000 Taxes on income, profits and capital gains	**34.1**	**101.5**	**239.7**	**511.7**	**530.2**	**9.0**	**14.3**	**14.3**	**18.0**	**17.4**
1100 Of individuals	30.9	88.5	197.3	412.4	435.3	8.2	12.5	11.7	14.5	14.3
1200 Corporate	3.2	8.4	14.6	67.7	63.0	0.8	1.2	0.9	2.4	2.1
1300 Unallocable between 1100 and 1200	0.0	4.6	27.7	31.6	31.9	0.0	0.7	1.7	1.1	1.0
2000 Social security contributions	**3.6**	**19.7**	**63.6**	**98.2**	**97.4**	**1.0**	**2.8**	**3.8**	**3.5**	**3.2**
2100 Employees	0.3	..	..	..	..	0.1	..	..	..	..
2200 Employers	3.3	..	..	..	..	0.9	..	..	..	..
2300 Self-employed or non-employed	0.0	..	..	..	..	0.0	..	..	..	..
2400 Unallocable between 2100, 2200 and 2300	0.0	19.7	63.6	98.2	97.4	0.0	2.8	3.8	3.5	3.2
3000 Taxes on payroll and workforce	**4.1**	**0.2**	**2.8**	**8.5**	**9.1**	**1.1**	**0.0**	**0.2**	**0.3**	**0.3**
4000 Taxes on property	**9.7**	**20.0**	**38.1**	**56.8**	**63.6**	**2.6**	**2.8**	**2.3**	**2.0**	**2.1**
4100 Recurrent taxes on immovable property	4.1	10.1	28.5	46.5	52.5	1.1	1.4	1.7	1.6	1.7
4200 Recurrent taxes on net wealth	2.4	5.2	3.8	0.1	0.0	0.6	0.7	0.2	0.0	0.0
4300 Estate, inheritance and gift taxes	0.2	0.8	2.6	4.7	4.7	0.1	0.1	0.2	0.2	0.2
4400 Taxes on financial and capital transactions	2.9	3.1	2.7	5.0	5.3	0.8	0.4	0.2	0.2	0.2
4500 Non-recurrent taxes	0.0	0.1	0.1	0.5	0.6	0.0	0.0	0.0	0.0	0.0
4600 Other recurrent taxes on property	0.0	0.7	0.3	0.1	0.5	0.0	0.1	0.0	0.0	0.0
5000 Taxes on goods and services	**58.9**	**112.2**	**190.1**	**344.5**	**343.0**	**15.6**	**15.8**	**11.3**	**12.1**	**11.3**
5100 Taxes on production, sale, transfer, etc	56.6	100.7	179.0	324.8	320.5	15.0	14.2	10.6	11.4	10.5
5110 General taxes	37.1	72.7	122.4	244.6	243.3	9.8	10.2	7.3	8.6	8.0
5111 Value added taxes	32.7	72.7	122.4	244.6	243.3	8.7	10.2	7.3	8.6	8.0
5120 Taxes on specific goods and services	19.5	28.0	56.6	80.1	77.2	5.2	3.9	3.4	2.8	2.5
5121 Excises	2.3	23.6	46.7	69.5	66.8	0.6	3.3	2.8	2.4	2.2
5200 Taxes on use of goods and perform activities	2.4	11.6	11.1	19.8	22.5	0.6	1.6	0.7	0.7	0.7
5300 Unallocable between 5100 and 5200	0.0	0.0	0.0	0.0	0.0	0.0	0.0	0.0	0.0	0.0
6000 Other taxes	**4.5**	**1.0**	**6.0**	**17.0**	**18.6**	**1.2**	**0.1**	**0.4**	**0.6**	**0.6**
Non-wastable tax credits										
Non-wastable tax credits against 1000	..	..	..	3.1	3.6	..	..	..	0.1	0.1
Transfer component	..	..	..	2.5	3.0	..	..	..	0.1	0.1
Tax expenditure component	..	..	..	0.6	0.6	..	..	..	0.0	0.0

.. Not available

Note: More detailed country data and country notes are available in online chapter 5 "Detailed country tables": https://doi.org/10.1787/0bbc27da-en. Full time series can be accessed at http://oe.cd/full-time-series.

Source: Ministry of Finance, Economic Department.

StatLink https://stat.link/0jqals

Table 4.32. Iceland, tax revenue and % of GDP by level of government and main taxes

	Billion ISK					% of GDP				
	1990	2000	2010	2018	2019	1990	2000	2010	2018	2019
Federal or Central government										
Total tax revenue	**91.6**	**195.1**	**402.3**	**751.7**	**761.1**	**24.3**	**27.5**	**23.9**	**26.4**	**25.0**
1000 Taxes on income, profits and capital gains	19.9	55.5	132.9	281.0	288.8	5.3	7.8	7.9	9.9	9.5
2000 Social security contributions	3.6	19.7	63.6	98.2	97.4	1.0	2.8	3.8	3.5	3.2
3000 Taxes on payroll and workforce	4.1	0.2	2.8	8.5	9.1	1.1	0.0	0.2	0.3	0.3
4000 Taxes on property	6.0	9.9	9.7	10.5	11.4	1.6	1.4	0.6	0.4	0.4
5000 Taxes on goods and services	57.7	108.9	187.4	336.5	335.8	15.3	15.3	11.1	11.8	11.0
6000 Other taxes	0.4	1.0	6.0	17.0	18.6	0.1	0.1	0.4	0.6	0.6
State/Regional										
Total tax revenue	..	..	..	..	..	..	..	..	..	..
1000 Taxes on income, profits and capital gains	..	..	..	..	..	..	..	..	..	..
2000 Social security contributions	..	..	..	..	..	..	..	..	..	..
3000 Taxes on payroll and workforce	..	..	..	..	..	..	..	..	..	..
4000 Taxes on property	..	..	..	..	..	..	..	..	..	..
5000 Taxes on goods and services	..	..	..	..	..	..	..	..	..	..
6000 Other taxes	..	..	..	..	..	..	..	..	..	..
Local government										
Total tax revenue	**23.3**	**59.4**	**138.0**	**285.1**	**300.8**	**6.2**	**8.4**	**8.2**	**10.0**	**9.9**
1000 Taxes on income, profits and capital gains	14.2	46.0	106.8	230.8	241.4	3.8	6.5	6.4	8.1	7.9
2000 Social security contributions	0.0	0.0	0.0	0.0	0.0	0.0	0.0	0.0	0.0	0.0
3000 Taxes on payroll and workforce	0.0	0.0	0.0	0.0	0.0	0.0	0.0	0.0	0.0	0.0
4000 Taxes on property	3.7	10.1	28.4	46.3	52.3	1.0	1.4	1.7	1.6	1.7
5000 Taxes on goods and services	1.2	3.3	2.8	8.1	7.2	0.3	0.5	0.2	0.3	0.2
6000 Other taxes	4.1	0.0	0.0	0.0	0.0	1.1	0.0	0.0	0.0	0.0
Social Security Funds										
Total tax revenue	**0.0**	**0.0**	**0.0**	**0.0**	**0.0**	**0.0**	**0.0**	**0.0**	**0.0**	**0.0**
1000 Taxes on income, profits and capital gains	0.0	0.0	0.0	0.0	0.0	0.0	0.0	0.0	0.0	0.0
2000 Social security contributions	0.0	0.0	0.0	0.0	0.0	0.0	0.0	0.0	0.0	0.0
3000 Taxes on payroll and workforce	0.0	0.0	0.0	0.0	0.0	0.0	0.0	0.0	0.0	0.0
4000 Taxes on property	0.0	0.0	0.0	0.0	0.0	0.0	0.0	0.0	0.0	0.0
5000 Taxes on goods and services	0.0	0.0	0.0	0.0	0.0	0.0	0.0	0.0	0.0	0.0
6000 Other taxes	0.0	0.0	0.0	0.0	0.0	0.0	0.0	0.0	0.0	0.0

.. Not available

Note: More detailed country data and country notes are available in online chapter 5 "Detailed country tables": https://doi.org/10.1787/0bbc27da-en. Full time series can be accessed at http://oe.cd/full-time-series.

Source: Ministry of Finance, Economic Department.

StatLink https://stat.link/ajp6qe

Table 4.33. Ireland, tax revenue and % of GDP by selected tax category

	Billion EUR					% of GDP				
	1990	2000	2010	2018	2019	1990	2000	2010	2018	2019
Total tax revenue	**12.3**	**33.4**	**46.4**	**72.9**	**78.1**	**32.4**	**30.8**	**27.7**	**22.4**	**21.9**
1000 Taxes on income, profits and capital gains	**4.7**	**14.6**	**18.6**	**33.3**	**35.6**	**12.3**	**13.4**	**11.1**	**10.2**	**10.0**
1100 Of individuals	4.1	10.6	14.7	22.9	24.8	10.7	9.8	8.8	7.0	6.9
1200 Corporate	0.6	3.9	3.9	10.4	10.9	1.6	3.6	2.4	3.2	3.1
1300 Unallocable between 1100 and 1200	0.0	0.0	0.0	0.0	0.0	0.0	0.0	0.0	0.0	0.0
2000 Social security contributions	**1.7**	**4.0**	**8.5**	**12.1**	**13.1**	**4.6**	**3.7**	**5.1**	**3.7**	**3.7**
2100 Employees	0.6	1.0	3.2	3.7	4.0	1.5	0.9	1.9	1.1	1.1
2200 Employers	1.1	2.8	4.9	7.7	8.5	2.9	2.6	2.9	2.4	2.4
2300 Self-employed or non-employed	0.1	0.2	0.3	0.6	0.6	0.2	0.2	0.2	0.2	0.2
2400 Unallocable between 2100, 2200 and 2300	0.0	0.0	0.0	0.0	0.0	0.0	0.0	0.0	0.0	0.0
3000 Taxes on payroll and workforce	**0.2**	**0.0**	**0.3**	**0.6**	**0.8**	**0.4**	**0.0**	**0.2**	**0.2**	**0.2**
4000 Taxes on property	**0.6**	**1.9**	**2.4**	**4.3**	**4.4**	**1.5**	**1.8**	**1.4**	**1.3**	**1.2**
4100 Recurrent taxes on immovable property	0.3	0.6	1.3	1.9	1.9	0.8	0.5	0.8	0.6	0.5
4200 Recurrent taxes on net wealth	0.0	0.0	0.0	0.0	0.0	0.0	0.0	0.0	0.0	0.0
4300 Estate, inheritance and gift taxes	0.0	0.2	0.2	0.5	0.5	0.1	0.2	0.1	0.2	0.1
4400 Taxes on financial and capital transactions	0.2	1.1	0.8	1.9	2.0	0.6	1.0	0.5	0.6	0.6
4500 Non-recurrent taxes	0.0	0.0	0.0	0.0	0.0	0.0	0.0	0.0	0.0	0.0
4600 Other recurrent taxes on property	0.0	0.0	0.0	0.0	0.0	0.0	0.0	0.0	0.0	0.0
5000 Taxes on goods and services	**5.1**	**12.9**	**16.6**	**22.6**	**24.1**	**13.6**	**11.9**	**9.9**	**6.9**	**6.8**
5100 Taxes on production, sale, transfer, etc	4.9	12.4	15.3	20.6	22.3	13.0	11.4	9.2	6.3	6.2
5110 General taxes	2.5	7.6	10.1	14.2	15.3	6.6	7.0	6.0	4.3	4.3
5111 Value added taxes	2.5	7.6	10.1	14.2	15.3	6.6	7.0	6.0	4.3	4.3
5120 Taxes on specific goods and services	2.4	4.7	5.3	6.5	7.0	6.4	4.4	3.1	2.0	2.0
5121 Excises	2.1	4.4	4.9	5.5	6.0	5.5	4.1	2.9	1.7	1.7
5200 Taxes on use of goods and perform activities	0.2	0.6	1.3	2.0	1.8	0.5	0.5	0.8	0.6	0.5
5300 Unallocable between 5100 and 5200	0.0	0.0	0.0	0.0	0.0	0.0	0.0	0.0	0.0	0.0
6000 Other taxes	**0.0**	**0.0**	**0.0**	**0.0**	**0.0**	**0.0**	**0.0**	**0.0**	**0.0**	**0.0**
Non-wastable tax credits										
Non-wastable tax credits against 1000	..	..	1.1	0.5	0.4	..	..	0.6	0.1	0.1
Transfer component	0.0	0.0	0.0	0.0	0.0	0.0	0.0	0.0	0.0	0.0
Tax expenditure component	0.0	0.0	1.1	0.5	0.4	0.0	0.0	0.6	0.1	0.1
Revenues collected on behalf of the EU										
Revenues collected on behalf of the EU, total	0.2	0.2	0.2	0.4	0.5	0.5	0.2	0.1	0.1	0.1
Customs duties	0.1	0.2	0.2	0.3	0.3	0.4	0.2	0.1	0.1	0.1
SRF contributions	..	..	..	0.1	0.1	..	..	..	0.0	0.0

.. Not available

Note: More detailed country data and country notes are available in online chapter 5 "Detailed country tables": https://doi.org/10.1787/0bbc27da-en. Full time series can be accessed at http://oe.cd/full-time-series.

Source: Annual Report of the Revenue Commissioners, Financial Accounts and National Income and Expenditure Accounts.

StatLink https://stat.link/qyex5o

Table 4.34. Ireland, tax revenue and % of GDP by level of government and main taxes

	Billion EUR					% of GDP				
	1990	2000	2010	2018	2019	1990	2000	2010	2018	2019
Federal or Central government										
Total tax revenue	**10.1**	**28.7**	**37.9**	**60.2**	**64.4**	**26.7**	**26.5**	**22.7**	**18.5**	**18.1**
1000 Taxes on income, profits and capital gains	4.7	14.6	18.6	33.3	35.6	12.3	13.4	11.1	10.2	10.0
2000 Social security contributions	0.1	0.1	1.5	1.3	1.4	0.2	0.1	0.9	0.4	0.4
3000 Taxes on payroll and workforce	0.2	0.0	0.3	0.6	0.8	0.4	0.0	0.2	0.2	0.2
4000 Taxes on property	0.3	1.3	1.1	2.9	3.0	0.7	1.2	0.6	0.9	0.8
5000 Taxes on goods and services	5.0	12.7	16.4	22.2	23.6	13.1	11.7	9.8	6.8	6.6
6000 Other taxes	0.0	0.0	0.0	0.0	0.0	0.0	0.0	0.0	0.0	0.0
State/Regional										
Total tax revenue	..	..	..	..	..	..	..	..	..	..
1000 Taxes on income, profits and capital gains	..	..	..	..	..	..	..	..	..	..
2000 Social security contributions	..	..	..	..	..	..	..	..	..	..
3000 Taxes on payroll and workforce	..	..	..	..	..	..	..	..	..	..
4000 Taxes on property	..	..	..	..	..	..	..	..	..	..
5000 Taxes on goods and services	..	..	..	..	..	..	..	..	..	..
6000 Other taxes	..	..	..	..	..	..	..	..	..	..
Local government										
Total tax revenue	**0.3**	**0.7**	**1.5**	**1.6**	**1.5**	**0.9**	**0.6**	**0.9**	**0.5**	**0.4**
1000 Taxes on income, profits and capital gains	0.0	0.0	0.0	0.0	0.0	0.0	0.0	0.0	0.0	0.0
2000 Social security contributions	0.0	0.1	0.2	0.1	0.1	0.1	0.1	0.1	0.0	0.0
3000 Taxes on payroll and workforce	0.0	0.0	0.0	0.0	0.0	0.0	0.0	0.0	0.0	0.0
4000 Taxes on property	0.3	0.6	1.3	1.4	1.5	0.8	0.5	0.8	0.4	0.4
5000 Taxes on goods and services	0.0	0.0	0.0	0.0	0.0	0.0	0.0	0.0	0.0	0.0
6000 Other taxes	0.0	0.0	0.0	0.0	0.0	0.0	0.0	0.0	0.0	0.0
Social Security Funds										
Total tax revenue	**1.6**	**3.8**	**6.7**	**10.6**	**11.7**	**4.3**	**3.5**	**4.0**	**3.3**	**3.3**
1000 Taxes on income, profits and capital gains	0.0	0.0	0.0	0.0	0.0	0.0	0.0	0.0	0.0	0.0
2000 Social security contributions	1.6	3.8	6.7	10.6	11.7	4.3	3.5	4.0	3.3	3.3
3000 Taxes on payroll and workforce	0.0	0.0	0.0	0.0	0.0	0.0	0.0	0.0	0.0	0.0
4000 Taxes on property	0.0	0.0	0.0	0.0	0.0	0.0	0.0	0.0	0.0	0.0
5000 Taxes on goods and services	0.0	0.0	0.0	0.0	0.0	0.0	0.0	0.0	0.0	0.0
6000 Other taxes	0.0	0.0	0.0	0.0	0.0	0.0	0.0	0.0	0.0	0.0

.. Not available

Note: More detailed country data and country notes are available in online chapter 6 "Tax revenues by sub-sectors of general government": https://doi.org/10.1787/0bbc27da-en. Full time series can be accessed at http://oe.cd/full-time-series.

Source: Annual Report of the Revenue Commissioners, Financial Accounts and National Income and Expenditure Accounts.

StatLink https://stat.link/42helm

Table 4.35. Israel, tax revenue and % of GDP by selected tax category

	Billion ILS					% of GDP				
	1990	2000	2010	2018	2019	1990	2000	2010	2018	2019
Total tax revenue	..	**188.2**	**268.4**	**413.2**	**428.5**	..	**34.8**	**30.6**	**30.8**	**30.2**
1000 Taxes on income, profits and capital gains	..	**74.6**	**78.3**	**135.0**	**140.5**	..	**13.8**	**8.9**	**10.1**	**9.9**
1100 Of individuals	..	54.8	48.2	84.9	89.5	..	10.1	5.5	6.3	6.3
1200 Corporate	..	18.0	23.1	42.9	43.3	..	3.3	2.6	3.2	3.1
1300 Unallocable between 1100 and 1200	..	1.8	6.9	7.1	7.7	..	0.3	0.8	0.5	0.5
2000 Social security contributions	..	**27.6**	**45.3**	**70.6**	**74.4**	..	**5.1**	**5.2**	**5.3**	**5.2**
2100 Employees	..	15.8	27.8	40.0	41.9	..	2.9	3.2	3.0	3.0
2200 Employers	..	8.2	11.4	21.8	23.1	..	1.5	1.3	1.6	1.6
2300 Self-employed or non-employed	..	3.6	6.1	8.9	9.5	..	0.7	0.7	0.7	0.7
2400 Unallocable between 2100, 2200 and 2300	..	0.0	0.0	0.0	0.0	..	0.0	0.0	0.0	0.0
3000 Taxes on payroll and workforce	..	**6.8**	**10.3**	**15.8**	**16.2**	..	**1.3**	**1.2**	**1.2**	**1.1**
4000 Taxes on property	..	**16.9**	**28.8**	**42.3**	**43.8**	..	**3.1**	**3.3**	**3.2**	**3.1**
4100 Recurrent taxes on immovable property	..	11.3	18.8	26.1	27.1	..	2.1	2.1	1.9	1.9
4200 Recurrent taxes on net wealth	..	0.0	0.0	0.0	0.0	..	0.0	0.0	0.0	0.0
4300 Estate, inheritance and gift taxes	..	0.0	0.0	0.0	0.0	..	0.0	0.0	0.0	0.0
4400 Taxes on financial and capital transactions	..	3.2	4.1	6.7	6.9	..	0.6	0.5	0.5	0.5
4500 Non-recurrent taxes	..	2.4	6.0	9.5	9.7	..	0.5	0.7	0.7	0.7
4600 Other recurrent taxes on property	..	0.0	0.0	0.0	0.0	..	0.0	0.0	0.0	0.0
5000 Taxes on goods and services	..	**62.3**	**105.7**	**149.4**	**153.7**	..	**11.5**	**12.0**	**11.1**	**10.8**
5100 Taxes on production, sale, transfer, etc	..	57.9	98.1	138.9	143.1	..	10.7	11.2	10.4	10.1
5110 General taxes	..	49.9	79.9	117.3	120.5	..	9.2	9.1	8.7	8.5
5111 Value added taxes	..	39.8	65.5	99.4	102.5	..	7.4	7.5	7.4	7.2
5120 Taxes on specific goods and services	..	8.0	18.1	21.7	22.5	..	1.5	2.1	1.6	1.6
5121 Excises	..	6.6	15.5	18.9	19.5	..	1.2	1.8	1.4	1.4
5200 Taxes on use of goods and perform activities	..	4.4	7.6	10.5	10.7	..	0.8	0.9	0.8	0.8
5300 Unallocable between 5100 and 5200	..	0.0	0.0	0.0	0.0	..	0.0	0.0	0.0	0.0
6000 Other taxes	..	**0.0**	**0.0**	**0.0**	**0.0**	..	**0.0**	**0.0**	**0.0**	**0.0**
Non-wastable tax credits										
Non-wastable tax credits against 1000	..	..	0.1	0.8	1.3	..	..	0.0	0.1	0.1
Transfer component	..	..	0.0	0.0	0.0	..	..	0.0	0.0	0.0
Tax expenditure component	..	..	0.1	0.8	1.3	..	..	0.0	0.1	0.1

.. Not available

Note: More detailed country data and country notes are available in online chapter 5 "Detailed country tables": https://doi.org/10.1787/0bbc27da-en. Full time series can be accessed at http://oe.cd/full-time-series.

Source: Israel Central Bureau of Statistics and Israel Ministry of Finance.

StatLink https://stat.link/v1n9gp

Table 4.36. Israel, tax revenue and % of GDP by level of government and main taxes

	Billion ILS					% of GDP				
	1990	2000	2010	2018	2019	1990	2000	2010	2018	2019
Federal or Central government										
Total tax revenue	..	**148.0**	**199.9**	**310.1**	**320.2**	..	**27.4**	**22.8**	**23.1**	**22.6**
1000 Taxes on income, profits and capital gains	..	74.6	78.3	135.0	140.5	..	13.8	8.9	10.1	9.9
2000 Social security contributions	..	0.0	0.0	0.0	0.0	..	0.0	0.0	0.0	0.0
3000 Taxes on payroll and workforce	..	6.8	10.3	15.8	16.2	..	1.3	1.2	1.2	1.1
4000 Taxes on property	..	4.8	6.6	11.3	11.4	..	0.9	0.7	0.8	0.8
5000 Taxes on goods and services	..	61.8	104.7	147.9	152.1	..	11.4	11.9	11.0	10.7
6000 Other taxes	..	0.0	0.0	0.0	0.0	..	0.0	0.0	0.0	0.0
State/Regional										
Total tax revenue	..	..	..	..	..	..	..	..	..	..
1000 Taxes on income, profits and capital gains	..	..	..	..	..	..	..	..	..	..
2000 Social security contributions	..	..	..	..	..	..	..	..	..	..
3000 Taxes on payroll and workforce	..	..	..	..	..	..	..	..	..	..
4000 Taxes on property	..	..	..	..	..	..	..	..	..	..
5000 Taxes on goods and services	..	..	..	..	..	..	..	..	..	..
6000 Other taxes	..	..	..	..	..	..	..	..	..	..
Local government										
Total tax revenue	..	**12.6**	**23.2**	**32.5**	**33.9**	..	**2.3**	**2.6**	**2.4**	**2.4**
1000 Taxes on income, profits and capital gains	..	0.0	0.0	0.0	0.0	..	0.0	0.0	0.0	0.0
2000 Social security contributions	..	0.0	0.0	0.0	0.0	..	0.0	0.0	0.0	0.0
3000 Taxes on payroll and workforce	..	0.0	0.0	0.0	0.0	..	0.0	0.0	0.0	0.0
4000 Taxes on property	..	12.1	22.2	31.0	32.3	..	2.2	2.5	2.3	2.3
5000 Taxes on goods and services	..	0.5	1.0	1.5	1.6	..	0.1	0.1	0.1	0.1
6000 Other taxes	..	0.0	0.0	0.0	0.0	..	0.0	0.0	0.0	0.0
Social Security Funds										
Total tax revenue	..	**27.6**	**45.3**	**70.6**	**74.4**	..	**5.1**	**5.2**	**5.3**	**5.2**
1000 Taxes on income, profits and capital gains	..	0.0	0.0	0.0	0.0	..	0.0	0.0	0.0	0.0
2000 Social security contributions	..	27.6	45.3	70.6	74.4	..	5.1	5.2	5.3	5.2
3000 Taxes on payroll and workforce	..	0.0	0.0	0.0	0.0	..	0.0	0.0	0.0	0.0
4000 Taxes on property	..	0.0	0.0	0.0	0.0	..	0.0	0.0	0.0	0.0
5000 Taxes on goods and services	..	0.0	0.0	0.0	0.0	..	0.0	0.0	0.0	0.0
6000 Other taxes	..	0.0	0.0	0.0	0.0	..	0.0	0.0	0.0	0.0

.. Not available

Note: More detailed country data and country notes are available in online chapter 6 "Tax revenues by sub-sectors of general government": https://doi.org/10.1787/0bbc27da-en. Full time series can be accessed at http://oe.cd/full-time-series.

Source: Israel Central Bureau of Statistics and Israel Ministry of Finance.

StatLink https://stat.link/wcjry0

Table 4.37. Italy, tax revenue and % of GDP by selected tax category

	Billion EUR					% of GDP				
	1990	2000	2010	2018	2019	1990	2000	2010	2018	2019
Total tax revenue	**265.1**	**503.1**	**671.9**	**739.2**	**759.6**	**36.3**	**40.5**	**41.7**	**41.7**	**42.4**
1000 Taxes on income, profits and capital gains	**96.7**	**166.9**	**219.5**	**229.5**	**239.8**	**13.2**	**13.4**	**13.6**	**13.0**	**13.4**
1100 Of individuals	69.7	124.9	180.5	189.9	196.1	9.5	10.1	11.2	10.7	11.0
1200 Corporate	26.6	34.7	36.7	32.9	35.3	3.6	2.8	2.3	1.9	2.0
1300 Unallocable between 1100 and 1200	0.4	7.3	2.3	6.7	8.4	0.1	0.6	0.1	0.4	0.5
2000 Social security contributions	**87.3**	**143.6**	**209.1**	**229.6**	**237.3**	**11.9**	**11.6**	**13.0**	**13.0**	**13.3**
2100 Employees	16.8	27.3	37.6	42.7	44.5	2.3	2.2	2.3	2.4	2.5
2200 Employers	62.5	99.9	144.3	153.9	158.6	8.6	8.0	9.0	8.7	8.9
2300 Self-employed or non-employed	8.0	16.4	27.2	33.0	34.2	1.1	1.3	1.7	1.9	1.9
2400 Unallocable between 2100, 2200 and 2300	0.0	0.0	0.0	0.0	0.0	0.0	0.0	0.0	0.0	0.0
3000 Taxes on payroll and workforce	**0.9**	**0.0**	**0.0**	**0.0**	**0.0**	**0.1**	**0.0**	**0.0**	**0.0**	**0.0**
4000 Taxes on property	**6.0**	**23.4**	**32.4**	**44.1**	**43.2**	**0.8**	**1.9**	**2.0**	**2.5**	**2.4**
4100 Recurrent taxes on immovable property	0.0	9.4	9.7	22.0	22.0	0.0	0.8	0.6	1.2	1.2
4200 Recurrent taxes on net wealth	0.0	0.0	2.1	0.3	0.2	0.0	0.0	0.1	0.0	0.0
4300 Estate, inheritance and gift taxes	0.4	1.0	0.5	0.8	0.8	0.1	0.1	0.0	0.0	0.0
4400 Taxes on financial and capital transactions	5.6	12.3	17.4	18.8	18.8	0.8	1.0	1.1	1.1	1.0
4500 Non-recurrent taxes	0.0	0.1	0.9	0.4	0.2	0.0	0.0	0.1	0.0	0.0
4600 Other recurrent taxes on property	0.0	0.6	1.9	1.7	1.2	0.0	0.0	0.1	0.1	0.1
5000 Taxes on goods and services	**74.3**	**141.9**	**178.9**	**212.1**	**215.0**	**10.2**	**11.4**	**11.1**	**12.0**	**12.0**
5100 Taxes on production, sale, transfer, etc	67.1	127.3	160.8	184.7	187.7	9.2	10.3	10.0	10.4	10.5
5110 General taxes	38.9	77.5	97.6	109.3	111.5	5.3	6.2	6.1	6.2	6.2
5111 Value added taxes	38.9	77.5	97.6	109.3	111.5	5.3	6.2	6.1	6.2	6.2
5120 Taxes on specific goods and services	28.0	49.8	63.2	75.4	76.2	3.8	4.0	3.9	4.3	4.3
5121 Excises	20.3	31.5	36.4	47.1	47.1	2.8	2.5	2.3	2.7	2.6
5200 Taxes on use of goods and perform activities	4.5	8.5	10.5	14.5	14.1	0.6	0.7	0.7	0.8	0.8
5300 Unallocable between 5100 and 5200	2.7	6.1	7.6	12.8	13.2	0.4	0.5	0.5	0.7	0.7
6000 Other taxes	**0.0**	**27.3**	**31.9**	**23.9**	**24.3**	**0.0**	**2.2**	**2.0**	**1.4**	**1.4**
Non-wastable tax credits										
Non-wastable tax credits against 1000	..	..	0.0	11.8	10.4	..	..	0.0	0.7	0.6
Transfer component	..	..	0.1	2.6	1.4	..	..	0.0	0.1	0.1
Tax expenditure component	..	..	-0.1	9.1	8.9	..	..	0.0	0.5	0.5
Revenues collected on behalf of the EU										
Revenues collected on behalf of the EU, total	1.3	1.5	2.2	3.4	3.2	0.2	0.1	0.1	0.2	0.2
Customs duties	0.8	1.5	2.2	2.3	2.3	0.1	0.1	0.1	0.1	0.1
SRF contributions	..	..	..	1.1	0.8	..	..	..	0.1	0.0

.. Not available

Note: More detailed country data and country notes are available in online chapter 5 "Detailed country tables": https://doi.org/10.1787/0bbc27da-en. Full time series can be accessed at http://oe.cd/full-time-series.

Source: Ministero dell'economia e delle finanze; Istituto nazionale di statistica.

StatLink https://stat.link/13tgui

Table 4.38. Italy, tax revenue and % of GDP by level of government and main taxes

	Billion EUR					% of GDP				
	1990	2000	2010	2018	2019	1990	2000	2010	2018	2019
Federal or Central government										
Total tax revenue	**168.9**	**280.8**	**357.3**	**420.2**	**432.8**	**23.1**	**22.6**	**22.2**	**23.7**	**24.2**
1000 Taxes on income, profits and capital gains	92.7	154.2	193.9	213.1	223.0	12.7	12.4	12.0	12.0	12.4
2000 Social security contributions	0.0	0.0	0.0	0.0	0.0	0.0	0.0	0.0	0.0	0.0
3000 Taxes on payroll and workforce	0.9	0.0	0.0	0.0	0.0	0.1	0.0	0.0	0.0	0.0
4000 Taxes on property	6.0	12.9	21.0	24.9	24.5	0.8	1.0	1.3	1.4	1.4
5000 Taxes on goods and services	69.3	113.6	142.5	182.2	185.3	9.5	9.2	8.8	10.3	10.3
6000 Other taxes	0.0	0.0	0.0	0.0	0.0	0.0	0.0	0.0	0.0	0.0
State/Regional										
Total tax revenue	..	..	..	..	..	..	..	..	..	..
1000 Taxes on income, profits and capital gains	..	..	..	..	..	..	..	..	..	..
2000 Social security contributions	..	..	..	..	..	..	..	..	..	..
3000 Taxes on payroll and workforce	..	..	..	..	..	..	..	..	..	..
4000 Taxes on property	..	..	..	..	..	..	..	..	..	..
5000 Taxes on goods and services	..	..	..	..	..	..	..	..	..	..
6000 Other taxes	..	..	..	..	..	..	..	..	..	..
Local government										
Total tax revenue	**7.7**	**77.2**	**103.2**	**85.9**	**86.4**	**1.1**	**6.2**	**6.4**	**4.9**	**4.8**
1000 Taxes on income, profits and capital gains	4.0	12.7	25.6	16.3	16.8	0.6	1.0	1.6	0.9	0.9
2000 Social security contributions	0.0	0.0	0.0	0.0	0.0	0.0	0.0	0.0	0.0	0.0
3000 Taxes on payroll and workforce	0.0	0.0	0.0	0.0	0.0	0.0	0.0	0.0	0.0	0.0
4000 Taxes on property	0.0	10.5	11.5	19.2	18.7	0.0	0.8	0.7	1.1	1.0
5000 Taxes on goods and services	3.7	26.7	34.2	26.5	26.5	0.5	2.1	2.1	1.5	1.5
6000 Other taxes	0.0	27.3	31.9	23.9	24.3	0.0	2.2	2.0	1.4	1.4
Social Security Funds										
Total tax revenue	**87.3**	**143.6**	**209.1**	**229.6**	**237.3**	**11.9**	**11.6**	**13.0**	**13.0**	**13.3**
1000 Taxes on income, profits and capital gains	0.0	0.0	0.0	0.0	0.0	0.0	0.0	0.0	0.0	0.0
2000 Social security contributions	87.3	143.6	209.1	229.6	237.3	11.9	11.6	13.0	13.0	13.3
3000 Taxes on payroll and workforce	0.0	0.0	0.0	0.0	0.0	0.0	0.0	0.0	0.0	0.0
4000 Taxes on property	0.0	0.0	0.0	0.0	0.0	0.0	0.0	0.0	0.0	0.0
5000 Taxes on goods and services	0.0	0.0	0.0	0.0	0.0	0.0	0.0	0.0	0.0	0.0
6000 Other taxes	0.0	0.0	0.0	0.0	0.0	0.0	0.0	0.0	0.0	0.0

.. Not available

Note: More detailed country data and country notes are available in online chapter 6 "Tax revenues by sub-sectors of general government": https://doi.org/10.1787/0bbc27da-en. Full time series can be accessed at http://oe.cd/full-time-series.

Source: Ministero dell'economia e delle finanze; Istituto nazionale di statistica.

StatLink https://stat.link/3jlan9

Table 4.39. Japan, tax revenue and % of GDP by selected tax category

	Billion JPY					% of GDP				
	1990	2000	2010	2018	2019	1990	2000	2010	2018	2019
Total tax revenue	**130 842.7**	**136 235.8**	**132 484.3**	**175 563.5**	**175 379.7**	**27.7**	**25.3**	**26.2**	**31.6**	**31.4**
1000 Taxes on income, profits and capital gains	**65 681.6**	**47 398.2**	**40 034.3**	**56 083.2**	**53 993.6**	**13.9**	**8.8**	**7.9**	**10.1**	**9.7**
1100 Of individuals	36 393.6	28 677.3	24 662.7	33 491.8	32 947.2	7.7	5.3	4.9	6.0	5.9
1200 Corporate	29 288.0	18 720.9	15 371.6	22 591.4	21 046.4	6.2	3.5	3.0	4.1	3.8
1300 Unallocable between 1100 and 1200	0.0	0.0	0.0	0.0	0.0	0.0	0.0	0.0	0.0	0.0
2000 Social security contributions	**34 612.6**	**47 968.3**	**54 460.6**	**70 588.1**	**71 993.4**	**7.3**	**8.9**	**10.8**	**12.7**	**12.9**
2100 Employees	13 895.0	19 829.9	23 592.6	31 243.4	31 954.0	2.9	3.7	4.7	5.6	5.7
2200 Employers	16 648.8	22 455.5	24 674.2	32 663.5	33 487.9	3.5	4.2	4.9	5.9	6.0
2300 Self-employed or non-employed	4 068.8	5 682.9	6 193.8	6 681.2	6 551.5	0.9	1.1	1.2	1.2	1.2
2400 Unallocable between 2100, 2200 and 2300	0.0	0.0	0.0	0.0	0.0	0.0	0.0	0.0	0.0	0.0
3000 Taxes on payroll and workforce	**0.0**	**0.0**	**0.0**	**0.0**	**0.0**	**0.0**	**0.0**	**0.0**	**0.0**	**0.0**
4000 Taxes on property	**12 296.3**	**14 294.4**	**12 878.3**	**14 195.5**	**14 339.8**	**2.6**	**2.7**	**2.6**	**2.6**	**2.6**
4100 Recurrent taxes on immovable property	7 098.5	10 413.7	10 225.0	10 385.7	10 611.9	1.5	1.9	2.0	1.9	1.9
4200 Recurrent taxes on net wealth	0.0	0.0	0.0	0.0	0.0	0.0	0.0	0.0	0.0	0.0
4300 Estate, inheritance and gift taxes	1 918.0	1 782.2	1 250.4	2 333.3	2 300.5	0.4	0.3	0.2	0.4	0.4
4400 Taxes on financial and capital transactions	3 279.8	2 098.5	1 402.9	1 476.5	1 427.4	0.7	0.4	0.3	0.3	0.3
4500 Non-recurrent taxes	0.0	0.0	0.0	0.0	0.0	0.0	0.0	0.0	0.0	0.0
4600 Other recurrent taxes on property	0.0	0.0	0.0	0.0	0.0	0.0	0.0	0.0	0.0	0.0
5000 Taxes on goods and services	**17 916.8**	**26 227.2**	**24 730.2**	**34 251.8**	**34 598.6**	**3.8**	**4.9**	**4.9**	**6.2**	**6.2**
5100 Taxes on production, sale, transfer, etc	15 646.5	23 180.2	22 160.4	31 754.0	32 045.9	3.3	4.3	4.4	5.7	5.7
5110 General taxes	5 778.3	12 350.3	12 675.2	22 496.4	23 148.2	1.2	2.3	2.5	4.0	4.1
5111 Value added taxes	5 778.3	12 350.3	12 675.2	22 496.4	23 148.2	1.2	2.3	2.5	4.0	4.1
5120 Taxes on specific goods and services	9 868.2	10 829.9	9 485.2	9 257.6	8 897.7	2.1	2.0	1.9	1.7	1.6
5121 Excises	8 637.2	9 837.0	8 622.4	8 120.8	7 890.9	1.8	1.8	1.7	1.5	1.4
5200 Taxes on use of goods and perform activities	2 270.3	3 047.0	2 569.8	2 497.8	2 552.7	0.5	0.6	0.5	0.4	0.5
5300 Unallocable between 5100 and 5200	0.0	0.0	0.0	0.0	0.0	0.0	0.0	0.0	0.0	0.0
6000 Other taxes	**335.4**	**347.7**	**381.1**	**444.9**	**454.3**	**0.1**	**0.1**	**0.1**	**0.1**	**0.1**
Non-wastable tax credits										
Non-wastable tax credits against 1000	..	..	..	..	..	..	..	..	..	..
Transfer component	..	..	..	..	..	..	..	..	..	..
Tax expenditure component	..	..	..	..	..	..	..	..	..	..

.. Not available

Note: More detailed country data and country notes are available in online chapter 5 "Detailed country tables": https://doi.org/10.1787/0bbc27da-en. Full time series can be accessed at http://oe.cd/full-time-series.

Source: Tax Bureau, Ministry of Finance.

StatLink https://stat.link/zjmo4k

Table 4.40. Japan, tax revenue and % of GDP by level of government and main taxes

	Billion JPY					% of GDP				
	1990	2000	2010	2018	2019	1990	2000	2010	2018	2019
Federal or Central government										
Total tax revenue	**62 779.7**	**52 720.8**	**43 707.4**	**64 224.1**	**62 175.1**	**13.3**	**9.8**	**8.7**	**11.5**	**11.1**
1000 Taxes on income, profits and capital gains	44 379.1	30 536.2	23 372.1	35 402.6	33 015.7	9.4	5.7	4.6	6.4	5.9
2000 Social security contributions	0.0	0.0	0.0	0.0	0.0	0.0	0.0	0.0	0.0	0.0
3000 Taxes on payroll and workforce	0.0	0.0	0.0	0.0	0.0	0.0	0.0	0.0	0.0	0.0
4000 Taxes on property	4 601.6	3 314.9	2 274.5	3 406.2	3 323.7	1.0	0.6	0.5	0.6	0.6
5000 Taxes on goods and services	13 799.0	18 869.7	18 060.9	25 413.7	25 835.1	2.9	3.5	3.6	4.6	4.6
6000 Other taxes	0.0	0.0	0.0	1.6	0.6	0.0	0.0	0.0	0.0	0.0
State/Regional										
Total tax revenue	..	..	..	..	..	..	..	..	..	..
1000 Taxes on income, profits and capital gains	..	..	..	..	..	..	..	..	..	..
2000 Social security contributions	..	..	..	..	..	..	..	..	..	..
3000 Taxes on payroll and workforce	..	..	..	..	..	..	..	..	..	..
4000 Taxes on property	..	..	..	..	..	..	..	..	..	..
5000 Taxes on goods and services	..	..	..	..	..	..	..	..	..	..
6000 Other taxes	..	..	..	..	..	..	..	..	..	..
Local government										
Total tax revenue	**33 450.4**	**35 546.7**	**34 316.3**	**40 751.3**	**41 211.2**	**7.1**	**6.6**	**6.8**	**7.3**	**7.4**
1000 Taxes on income, profits and capital gains	21 302.5	16 862.0	16 662.2	20 680.6	20 977.9	4.5	3.1	3.3	3.7	3.8
2000 Social security contributions	0.0	0.0	0.0	0.0	0.0	0.0	0.0	0.0	0.0	0.0
3000 Taxes on payroll and workforce	0.0	0.0	0.0	0.0	0.0	0.0	0.0	0.0	0.0	0.0
4000 Taxes on property	7 694.7	10 979.5	10 603.8	10 789.3	11 016.1	1.6	2.0	2.1	1.9	2.0
5000 Taxes on goods and services	4 117.8	7 357.5	6 669.3	8 838.1	8 763.5	0.9	1.4	1.3	1.6	1.6
6000 Other taxes	335.4	347.7	381.1	443.3	453.7	0.1	0.1	0.1	0.1	0.1
Social Security Funds										
Total tax revenue	**34 612.6**	**47 968.3**	**54 460.6**	**70 588.1**	**71 993.4**	**7.3**	**8.9**	**10.8**	**12.7**	**12.9**
1000 Taxes on income, profits and capital gains	0.0	0.0	0.0	0.0	0.0	0.0	0.0	0.0	0.0	0.0
2000 Social security contributions	34 612.6	47 968.3	54 460.6	70 588.1	71 993.4	7.3	8.9	10.8	12.7	12.9
3000 Taxes on payroll and workforce	0.0	0.0	0.0	0.0	0.0	0.0	0.0	0.0	0.0	0.0
4000 Taxes on property	0.0	0.0	0.0	0.0	0.0	0.0	0.0	0.0	0.0	0.0
5000 Taxes on goods and services	0.0	0.0	0.0	0.0	0.0	0.0	0.0	0.0	0.0	0.0
6000 Other taxes	0.0	0.0	0.0	0.0	0.0	0.0	0.0	0.0	0.0	0.0

.. Not available

Note: More detailed country data and country notes are available in online chapter 6 "Tax revenues by sub-sectors of general government": https://doi.org/10.1787/0bbc27da-en. Full time series can be accessed at http://oe.cd/full-time-series.

Source: Tax Bureau, Ministry of Finance.

StatLink https://stat.link/aowklf

Table 4.41. Korea, tax revenue and % of GDP by selected tax category

	Billion KRW					% of GDP				
	1990	2000	2010	2018	2019	1990	2000	2010	2018	2019
Total tax revenue	**37 261.7**	**136 295.0**	**295 968.0**	**506 548.0**	**523 985.0**	**18.6**	**20.9**	**22.4**	**26.7**	**27.3**
1000 Taxes on income, profits and capital gains	**12 203.5**	**39 254.0**	**82 905.0**	**172 976.0**	**174 040.0**	**6.1**	**6.0**	**6.3**	**9.1**	**9.1**
1100 Of individuals	7 440.4	19 950.0	42 098.0	93 274.0	91 714.0	3.7	3.1	3.2	4.9	4.8
1200 Corporate	4 756.6	19 271.0	40 807.0	79 702.0	82 326.0	2.4	3.0	3.1	4.2	4.3
1300 Unallocable between 1100 and 1200	6.5	33.0	0.0	0.0	0.0	0.0	0.0	0.0	0.0	0.0
2000 Social security contributions	**3 760.0**	**22 759.0**	**69 090.0**	**128 660.0**	**140 071.0**	**1.9**	**3.5**	**5.2**	**6.8**	**7.3**
2100 Employees	1 464.0	8 578.0	28 213.0	55 257.0	60 682.0	0.7	1.3	2.1	2.9	3.2
2200 Employers	1 694.0	9 409.0	30 856.0	58 712.0	63 780.0	0.8	1.4	2.3	3.1	3.3
2300 Self-employed or non-employed	602.0	4 772.0	10 021.0	14 691.0	15 609.0	0.3	0.7	0.8	0.8	0.8
2400 Unallocable between 2100, 2200 and 2300	0.0	0.0	0.0	0.0	0.0	0.0	0.0	0.0	0.0	0.0
3000 Taxes on payroll and workforce	**152.8**	**258.0**	**714.0**	**1 492.0**	**1 597.0**	**0.1**	**0.0**	**0.1**	**0.1**	**0.1**
4000 Taxes on property	**4 388.9**	**16 846.0**	**33 516.0**	**58 811.0**	**59 732.0**	**2.2**	**2.6**	**2.5**	**3.1**	**3.1**
4100 Recurrent taxes on immovable property	980.0	3 385.0	9 270.0	15 589.0	17 750.0	0.5	0.5	0.7	0.8	0.9
4200 Recurrent taxes on net wealth	0.0	0.0	0.0	0.0	0.0	0.0	0.0	0.0	0.0	0.0
4300 Estate, inheritance and gift taxes	353.9	989.0	3 076.0	7 359.0	8 329.0	0.2	0.2	0.2	0.4	0.4
4400 Taxes on financial and capital transactions	2 959.7	11 935.0	21 170.0	35 863.0	33 653.0	1.5	1.8	1.6	1.9	1.8
4500 Non-recurrent taxes	95.3	537.0	0.0	0.0	0.0	0.0	0.1	0.0	0.0	0.0
4600 Other recurrent taxes on property	0.0	0.0	0.0	0.0	0.0	0.0	0.0	0.0	0.0	0.0
5000 Taxes on goods and services	**16 497.5**	**52 271.0**	**99 769.0**	**133 095.0**	**135 276.0**	**8.2**	**8.0**	**7.5**	**7.0**	**7.0**
5100 Taxes on production, sale, transfer, etc	16 023.5	50 023.0	96 573.0	125 207.0	127 551.0	8.0	7.7	7.3	6.6	6.6
5110 General taxes	6 964.4	23 212.0	51 800.0	77 471.0	82 174.0	3.5	3.6	3.9	4.1	4.3
5111 Value added taxes	6 964.4	23 212.0	51 800.0	77 471.0	82 174.0	3.5	3.6	3.9	4.1	4.3
5120 Taxes on specific goods and services	9 059.1	26 811.0	44 773.0	47 736.0	45 377.0	4.5	4.1	3.4	2.5	2.4
5121 Excises	4 923.7	18 155.0	31 340.0	36 218.0	34 691.0	2.5	2.8	2.4	1.9	1.8
5200 Taxes on use of goods and perform activities	473.9	2 248.0	3 196.0	7 888.0	7 725.0	0.2	0.3	0.2	0.4	0.4
5300 Unallocable between 5100 and 5200	0.0	0.0	0.0	0.0	0.0	0.0	0.0	0.0	0.0	0.0
6000 Other taxes	**259.1**	**4 907.0**	**9 974.0**	**11 514.0**	**13 269.0**	**0.1**	**0.8**	**0.8**	**0.6**	**0.7**
Non-wastable tax credits										
Non-wastable tax credits against 1000	..	..	..	..	..	..	..	..	..	..
Transfer component	..	..	..	..	..	..	..	..	..	..
Tax expenditure component	..	..	..	..	..	..	..	..	..	..

.. Not available

Note: More detailed country data and country notes are available in online chapter 5 "Detailed country tables": https://doi.org/10.1787/0bbc27da-en. Full time series can be accessed at http://oe.cd/full-time-series.

Source: Ministry of Finance and Economy, Ministry of Home Affairs.

StatLink https://stat.link/lw50is

Table 4.42. Korea, tax revenue and % of GDP by level of government and main taxes

	Billion KRW					% of GDP				
	1990	2000	2010	2018	2019	1990	2000	2010	2018	2019
Federal or Central government										
Total tax revenue	**27 140.8**	**92 935.0**	**177 718.0**	**293 570.0**	**293 454.0**	**13.5**	**14.3**	**13.4**	**15.5**	**15.3**
1000 Taxes on income, profits and capital gains	11 655.2	35 824.0	75 352.0	155 969.0	156 298.0	5.8	5.5	5.7	8.2	8.1
2000 Social security contributions	0.0	0.0	0.0	0.0	0.0	0.0	0.0	0.0	0.0	0.0
3000 Taxes on payroll and workforce	29.3	0.0	0.0	0.0	0.0	0.0	0.0	0.0	0.0	0.0
4000 Taxes on property	866.3	5 866.0	11 288.0	19 920.0	19 406.0	0.4	0.9	0.9	1.0	1.0
5000 Taxes on goods and services	14 377.5	46 812.0	86 629.0	113 251.0	111 877.0	7.2	7.2	6.5	6.0	5.8
6000 Other taxes	212.5	4 433.0	4 449.0	4 430.0	5 873.0	0.1	0.7	0.3	0.2	0.3
State/Regional										
Total tax revenue	**..**	**..**	**..**	**..**	**..**	**..**	**..**	**..**	**..**	**..**
1000 Taxes on income, profits and capital gains	..	..	..	..	..	..	..	..	..	..
2000 Social security contributions	..	..	..	..	..	..	..	..	..	..
3000 Taxes on payroll and workforce	..	..	..	..	..	..	..	..	..	..
4000 Taxes on property	..	..	..	..	..	..	..	..	..	..
5000 Taxes on goods and services	..	..	..	..	..	..	..	..	..	..
6000 Other taxes	..	..	..	..	..	..	..	..	..	..
Local government										
Total tax revenue	**6 360.9**	**20 601.0**	**49 160.0**	**84 318.0**	**90 460.0**	**3.2**	**3.2**	**3.7**	**4.4**	**4.7**
1000 Taxes on income, profits and capital gains	548.3	3 430.0	7 553.0	17 007.0	17 742.0	0.3	0.5	0.6	0.9	0.9
2000 Social security contributions	0.0	0.0	0.0	0.0	0.0	0.0	0.0	0.0	0.0	0.0
3000 Taxes on payroll and workforce	123.5	258.0	714.0	1 492.0	1 597.0	0.1	0.0	0.1	0.1	0.1
4000 Taxes on property	3 522.6	10 980.0	22 228.0	38 891.0	40 326.0	1.8	1.7	1.7	2.0	2.1
5000 Taxes on goods and services	2 120.0	5 459.0	13 140.0	19 844.0	23 399.0	1.1	0.8	1.0	1.0	1.2
6000 Other taxes	46.6	474.0	5 525.0	7 084.0	7 396.0	0.0	0.1	0.4	0.4	0.4
Social Security Funds										
Total tax revenue	**3 760.0**	**22 759.0**	**69 090.0**	**128 660.0**	**140 071.0**	**1.9**	**3.5**	**5.2**	**6.8**	**7.3**
1000 Taxes on income, profits and capital gains	0.0	0.0	0.0	0.0	0.0	0.0	0.0	0.0	0.0	0.0
2000 Social security contributions	3 760.0	22 759.0	69 090.0	128 660.0	140 071.0	1.9	3.5	5.2	6.8	7.3
3000 Taxes on payroll and workforce	0.0	0.0	0.0	0.0	0.0	0.0	0.0	0.0	0.0	0.0
4000 Taxes on property	0.0	0.0	0.0	0.0	0.0	0.0	0.0	0.0	0.0	0.0
5000 Taxes on goods and services	0.0	0.0	0.0	0.0	0.0	0.0	0.0	0.0	0.0	0.0
6000 Other taxes	0.0	0.0	0.0	0.0	0.0	0.0	0.0	0.0	0.0	0.0

.. Not available

Note: More detailed country data and country notes are available in online chapter 6 "Tax revenues by sub-sectors of general government": https://doi.org/10.1787/0bbc27da-en. Full time series can be accessed at http://oe.cd/full-time-series.

Source: Ministry of Finance and Economy, Ministry of Home Affairs.

StatLink https://stat.link/blujn1

Table 4.43. Latvia, tax revenue and % of GDP by selected tax category

	Billion EUR					% of GDP				
	1990	2000	2010	2018	2019	1990	2000	2010	2018	2019
Total tax revenue	..	**2.0**	**5.2**	**9.1**	**9.5**	..	**29.1**	**28.6**	**31.1**	**31.2**
1000 Taxes on income, profits and capital gains	..	**0.5**	**1.3**	**2.0**	**2.0**	..	**7.0**	**7.2**	**7.0**	**6.7**
1100 Of individuals	..	0.4	1.1	1.7	2.0	..	5.5	6.2	6.0	6.5
1200 Corporate	..	0.1	0.2	0.3	0.0	..	1.5	1.0	1.1	0.2
1300 Unallocable between 1100 and 1200	..	0.0	0.0	0.0	0.0	..	0.0	0.0	0.0	0.0
2000 Social security contributions	..	**0.7**	**1.6**	**2.7**	**2.9**	..	**9.8**	**8.6**	**9.1**	**9.6**
2100 Employees	..	0.2	0.4	0.8	0.8	..	2.4	2.2	2.7	2.8
2200 Employers	..	0.5	1.2	1.9	2.0	..	7.3	6.4	6.4	6.7
2300 Self-employed or non-employed	..	0.0	0.0	0.0	0.0	..	0.0	0.1	0.1	0.1
2400 Unallocable between 2100, 2200 and 2300	..	0.0	0.0	0.0	0.0	..	0.0	0.0	0.0	0.0
3000 Taxes on payroll and workforce	..	**0.0**	**0.0**	**0.0**	**0.0**	..	**0.0**	**0.0**	**0.0**	**0.0**
4000 Taxes on property	..	**0.1**	**0.2**	**0.3**	**0.3**	..	**1.1**	**0.9**	**0.9**	**0.9**
4100 Recurrent taxes on immovable property	..	0.1	0.1	0.2	0.2	..	0.9	0.7	0.8	0.7
4200 Recurrent taxes on net wealth	..	0.0	0.0	0.0	0.0	..	0.0	0.0	0.0	0.0
4300 Estate, inheritance and gift taxes	..	0.0	0.0	0.0	0.0	..	0.0	0.0	0.0	0.0
4400 Taxes on financial and capital transactions	..	0.0	0.0	0.0	0.0	..	0.2	0.1	0.1	0.1
4500 Non-recurrent taxes	..	0.0	0.0	0.0	0.0	..	0.0	0.0	0.0	0.0
4600 Other recurrent taxes on property	..	0.0	0.0	0.0	0.0	..	0.0	0.0	0.0	0.0
5000 Taxes on goods and services	..	**0.8**	**2.2**	**4.1**	**4.3**	..	**11.2**	**12.0**	**14.0**	**14.1**
5100 Taxes on production, sale, transfer, etc	..	0.7	2.0	3.9	4.0	..	10.8	11.3	13.3	13.1
5110 General taxes	..	0.5	1.3	2.7	2.8	..	6.9	7.2	9.3	9.1
5111 Value added taxes	..	0.5	1.2	2.4	2.6	..	6.9	6.7	8.4	8.7
5120 Taxes on specific goods and services	..	0.3	0.7	1.2	1.2	..	3.8	4.1	4.0	3.9
5121 Excises	..	0.2	0.6	1.0	1.1	..	3.4	3.6	3.6	3.5
5200 Taxes on use of goods and perform activities	..	0.0	0.1	0.2	0.3	..	0.5	0.7	0.7	1.0
5300 Unallocable between 5100 and 5200	..	0.0	0.0	0.0	0.0	..	0.0	0.0	0.0	0.0
6000 Other taxes	..	**0.0**	**0.0**	**0.0**	**0.0**	..	**0.0**	**0.0**	**0.0**	**0.0**
Non-wastable tax credits										
Non-wastable tax credits against 1000	..	..	..	..	..	..	..	..	..	..
Transfer component	..	..	..	..	..	..	..	..	..	..
Tax expenditure component	..	..	..	..	..	..	..	..	..	..
Revenues collected on behalf of the EU										
Revenues collected on behalf of the EU, total	..	..	0.0	0.1	0.0	..	..	0.1	0.2	0.2
Customs duties	..	..	0.0	0.1	0.0	..	..	0.1	0.2	0.1
SRF contributions	..	..	..	0.0	0.0	..	..	..	0.0	0.0

.. Not available

Note: More detailed country data and country notes are available in online chapter 5 "Detailed country tables": https://doi.org/10.1787/0bbc27da-en. Full time series can be accessed at http://oe.cd/full-time-series.

Source: Ministry of Finance.

StatLink https://stat.link/nhk8gj

Table 4.44. Latvia, tax revenue and % of GDP by level of government and main taxes

	Billion EUR					% of GDP				
	1990	2000	2010	2018	2019	1990	2000	2010	2018	2019
Federal or Central government										
Total tax revenue	..	**1.0**	**2.5**	**4.8**	**4.8**	..	**14.4**	**14.1**	**16.4**	**15.8**
1000 Taxes on income, profits and capital gains	..	0.2	0.4	0.6	0.4	..	3.1	2.2	2.2	1.4
2000 Social security contributions	..	0.0	0.0	0.1	0.1	..	0.0	0.0	0.3	0.3
3000 Taxes on payroll and workforce	..	0.0	0.0	0.0	0.0	..	0.0	0.0	0.0	0.0
4000 Taxes on property	..	0.0	0.0	0.0	0.0	..	0.2	0.2	0.2	0.2
5000 Taxes on goods and services	..	0.8	2.1	4.0	4.2	..	11.2	11.8	13.8	13.8
6000 Other taxes	..	0.0	0.0	0.0	0.0	..	0.0	0.0	0.0	0.0
State/Regional										
Total tax revenue	..	..	..	..	..	..	..	..	..	..
1000 Taxes on income, profits and capital gains	..	..	..	..	..	..	..	..	..	..
2000 Social security contributions	..	..	..	..	..	..	..	..	..	..
3000 Taxes on payroll and workforce	..	..	..	..	..	..	..	..	..	..
4000 Taxes on property	..	..	..	..	..	..	..	..	..	..
5000 Taxes on goods and services	..	..	..	..	..	..	..	..	..	..
6000 Other taxes	..	..	..	..	..	..	..	..	..	..
Local government										
Total tax revenue	..	**0.3**	**1.0**	**1.6**	**1.8**	..	**4.9**	**5.7**	**5.6**	**6.0**
1000 Taxes on income, profits and capital gains	..	0.3	0.9	1.4	1.6	..	3.9	5.0	4.8	5.2
2000 Social security contributions	..	0.0	0.0	0.0	0.0	..	0.0	0.0	0.0	0.0
3000 Taxes on payroll and workforce	..	0.0	0.0	0.0	0.0	..	0.0	0.0	0.0	0.0
4000 Taxes on property	..	0.1	0.1	0.2	0.2	..	0.9	0.7	0.8	0.7
5000 Taxes on goods and services	..	0.0	0.0	0.0	0.0	..	0.1	0.1	0.1	0.1
6000 Other taxes	..	0.0	0.0	0.0	0.0	..	0.0	0.0	0.0	0.0
Social Security Funds										
Total tax revenue	..	**0.7**	**1.6**	**2.6**	**2.8**	..	**9.8**	**8.6**	**8.9**	**9.3**
1000 Taxes on income, profits and capital gains	..	0.0	0.0	0.0	0.0	..	0.0	0.0	0.0	0.0
2000 Social security contributions	..	0.7	1.6	2.6	2.8	..	9.8	8.6	8.8	9.2
3000 Taxes on payroll and workforce	..	0.0	0.0	0.0	0.0	..	0.0	0.0	0.0	0.0
4000 Taxes on property	..	0.0	0.0	0.0	0.0	..	0.0	0.0	0.0	0.0
5000 Taxes on goods and services	..	0.0	0.0	0.0	0.0	..	0.0	0.0	0.0	0.0
6000 Other taxes	..	0.0	0.0	0.0	0.0	..	0.0	0.0	0.0	0.0

.. Not available

Note: More detailed country data and country notes are available in online chapter 6 "Tax revenues by sub-sectors of general government": https://doi.org/10.1787/0bbc27da-en. Full time series can be accessed at http://oe.cd/full-time-series.

Source: Ministry of Finance.

StatLink https://stat.link/hsek59

Table 4.45. Lithuania, tax revenue and % of GDP by selected tax category

	Billion EUR					% of GDP				
	1990	2000	2010	2018	2019	1990	2000	2010	2018	2019
Total tax revenue	..	**4.1**	**7.9**	**13.8**	**14.8**	..	**30.8**	**28.3**	**30.2**	**30.3**
1000 Taxes on income, profits and capital gains	..	**1.1**	**1.3**	**2.6**	**4.3**	..	**8.3**	**4.6**	**5.8**	**8.8**
1100 Of individuals	..	1.0	1.0	1.9	3.5	..	7.6	3.6	4.3	7.2
1200 Corporate	..	0.1	0.3	0.7	0.8	..	0.7	1.0	1.5	1.6
1300 Unallocable between 1100 and 1200	..	0.0	0.0	0.0	0.0	..	0.0	0.0	0.0	0.0
2000 Social security contributions	..	**1.3**	**3.3**	**5.7**	**4.7**	..	**9.9**	**11.6**	**12.6**	**9.6**
2100 Employees	..	0.1	0.6	1.2	3.6	..	0.8	2.2	2.5	7.3
2200 Employers	..	1.1	2.1	3.9	0.4	..	8.1	7.4	8.5	0.7
2300 Self-employed or non-employed	..	0.1	0.5	0.7	0.8	..	1.0	1.9	1.5	1.6
2400 Unallocable between 2100, 2200 and 2300	..	0.0	0.0	0.0	0.0	..	0.0	0.0	0.0	0.0
3000 Taxes on payroll and workforce	..	**0.0**	**0.0**	**0.0**	**0.0**	..	**0.0**	**0.0**	**0.0**	**0.0**
4000 Taxes on property	..	**0.1**	**0.1**	**0.1**	**0.1**	..	**0.5**	**0.4**	**0.3**	**0.3**
4100 Recurrent taxes on immovable property	..	0.1	0.1	0.1	0.1	..	0.5	0.4	0.3	0.3
4200 Recurrent taxes on net wealth	..	0.0	0.0	0.0	0.0	..	0.0	0.0	0.0	0.0
4300 Estate, inheritance and gift taxes	..	0.0	0.0	0.0	0.0	..	0.0	0.0	0.0	0.0
4400 Taxes on financial and capital transactions	..	0.0	0.0	0.0	0.0	..	0.0	0.0	0.0	0.0
4500 Non-recurrent taxes	..	0.0	0.0	0.0	0.0	..	0.0	0.0	0.0	0.0
4600 Other recurrent taxes on property	..	0.0	0.0	0.0	0.0	..	0.0	0.0	0.0	0.0
5000 Taxes on goods and services	..	**1.6**	**3.3**	**5.2**	**5.6**	..	**12.1**	**11.7**	**11.5**	**11.6**
5100 Taxes on production, sale, transfer, etc	..	1.6	3.2	5.2	5.5	..	11.7	11.4	11.3	11.4
5110 General taxes	..	1.1	2.2	3.6	3.9	..	8.1	7.8	7.8	7.9
5111 Value added taxes	..	1.0	2.2	3.5	3.9	..	7.5	7.8	7.7	7.9
5120 Taxes on specific goods and services	..	0.5	1.0	1.6	1.7	..	3.5	3.6	3.5	3.4
5121 Excises	..	0.4	0.9	1.4	1.5	..	3.2	3.2	3.2	3.1
5200 Taxes on use of goods and perform activities	..	0.1	0.1	0.1	0.1	..	0.5	0.3	0.2	0.2
5300 Unallocable between 5100 and 5200	..	0.0	0.0	0.0	0.0	..	0.0	0.0	0.0	0.0
6000 Other taxes	..	**0.0**	**0.0**	**0.0**	**0.0**	..	**0.0**	**0.0**	**0.0**	**0.0**
Non-wastable tax credits										
Non-wastable tax credits against 1000	..	..	..	..	..	..	..	..	..	..
Transfer component	..	..	..	..	..	..	..	..	..	..
Tax expenditure component	..	..	..	..	..	..	..	..	..	..
Revenues collected on behalf of the EU										
Revenues collected on behalf of the EU, total	..	..	0.1	0.1	0.1	..	..	0.2	0.3	0.3
Customs duties	..	..	0.1	0.1	0.1	..	..	0.2	0.3	0.3
SRF contributions	..	..	..	0.0	0.0	..	..	..	0.0	0.0

.. Not available

Note: More detailed country data and country notes are available in online chapter 5 "Detailed country tables": https://doi.org/10.1787/0bbc27da-en. Full time series can be accessed at http://oe.cd/full-time-series.

The total tax revenue has been reduced by the amount of any capital transfer that represents uncollected taxes. The capital transfers were subtracted directly from the specific taxes to which they relate. Therefore, the tax revenue amounts are different to those reported in the detailed country data available in online chapter 5 "Detailed country tables".

Source: Ministry of Finance.

StatLink https://stat.link/lmijcx

Table 4.46. Lithuania, tax revenue and % of GDP by level of government and main taxes

	Billion EUR					% of GDP				
	1990	2000	2010	2018	2019	1990	2000	2010	2018	2019
Federal or Central government										
Total tax revenue	..	**2.7**	**4.5**	**7.7**	**9.8**	..	**20.3**	**16.0**	**17.0**	**20.0**
1000 Taxes on income, profits and capital gains	..	1.1	1.3	2.6	4.3	..	8.3	4.6	5.8	8.8
2000 Social security contributions	..	0.0	0.0	0.0	0.0	..	0.0	0.0	0.0	0.0
3000 Taxes on payroll and workforce	..	0.0	0.0	0.0	0.0	..	0.0	0.0	0.0	0.0
4000 Taxes on property	..	0.0	0.0	0.0	0.0	..	0.0	0.0	0.0	0.0
5000 Taxes on goods and services	..	1.6	3.2	5.1	5.5	..	12.0	11.4	11.2	11.2
6000 Other taxes	..	0.0	0.0	0.0	0.0	..	0.0	0.0	0.0	0.0
State/Regional										
Total tax revenue	..	..	..	..	..	..	..	..	..	..
1000 Taxes on income, profits and capital gains	..	..	..	..	..	..	..	..	..	..
2000 Social security contributions	..	..	..	..	..	..	..	..	..	..
3000 Taxes on payroll and workforce	..	..	..	..	..	..	..	..	..	..
4000 Taxes on property	..	..	..	..	..	..	..	..	..	..
5000 Taxes on goods and services	..	..	..	..	..	..	..	..	..	..
6000 Other taxes	..	..	..	..	..	..	..	..	..	..
Local government										
Total tax revenue	..	**0.1**	**0.1**	**0.2**	**0.2**	..	**0.6**	**0.5**	**0.3**	**0.3**
1000 Taxes on income, profits and capital gains	..	0.0	0.0	0.0	0.0	..	0.0	0.0	0.0	0.0
2000 Social security contributions	..	0.0	0.0	0.0	0.0	..	0.0	0.0	0.0	0.0
3000 Taxes on payroll and workforce	..	0.0	0.0	0.0	0.0	..	0.0	0.0	0.0	0.0
4000 Taxes on property	..	0.1	0.1	0.1	0.1	..	0.5	0.4	0.3	0.3
5000 Taxes on goods and services	..	0.0	0.0	0.0	0.0	..	0.1	0.1	0.1	0.1
6000 Other taxes	..	0.0	0.0	0.0	0.0	..	0.0	0.0	0.0	0.0
Social Security Funds										
Total tax revenue	..	**1.3**	**3.3**	**5.7**	**4.7**	..	**9.9**	**11.6**	**12.6**	**9.6**
1000 Taxes on income, profits and capital gains	..	0.0	0.0	0.0	0.0	..	0.0	0.0	0.0	0.0
2000 Social security contributions	..	1.3	3.3	5.7	4.7	..	9.9	11.6	12.6	9.6
3000 Taxes on payroll and workforce	..	0.0	0.0	0.0	0.0	..	0.0	0.0	0.0	0.0
4000 Taxes on property	..	0.0	0.0	0.0	0.0	..	0.0	0.0	0.0	0.0
5000 Taxes on goods and services	..	0.0	0.0	0.0	0.0	..	0.0	0.0	0.0	0.0
6000 Other taxes	..	0.0	0.0	0.0	0.0	..	0.0	0.0	0.0	0.0

.. Not available

Note: More detailed country data and country notes are available in online chapter 6 "Tax revenues by sub-sectors of general government": https://doi.org/10.1787/0bbc27da-en. Full time series can be accessed at http://oe.cd/full-time-series.

The total tax revenue has been reduced by the amount of any capital transfer that represents uncollected taxes. The capital transfers were subtracted directly from the specific taxes to which they relate. Therefore, the tax revenue amounts are different to those reported in the detailed country data available in online chapter 6 "Tax revenues by sub-sectors of general government".

Source: Ministry of Finance.

StatLink https://stat.link/wpa37u

Table 4.47. Luxembourg, tax revenue and % of GDP by selected tax category

	Billion EUR					% of GDP				
	1990	2000	2010	2018	2019	1990	2000	2010	2018	2019
Total tax revenue	**3.7**	**8.5**	**15.1**	**23.7**	**24.7**	**33.5**	**36.9**	**37.6**	**39.5**	**38.9**
1000 Taxes on income, profits and capital gains	**1.5**	**3.1**	**5.5**	**9.4**	**9.7**	**13.5**	**13.5**	**13.6**	**15.6**	**15.2**
1100 Of individuals	0.9	1.6	3.2	5.6	5.9	8.1	6.8	7.9	9.3	9.3
1200 Corporate	0.6	1.5	2.3	3.8	3.8	5.4	6.6	5.8	6.3	5.9
1300 Unallocable between 1100 and 1200	0.0	0.0	0.0	0.0	0.0	0.0	0.0	0.0	0.0	0.0
2000 Social security contributions	**1.0**	**2.2**	**4.4**	**6.5**	**6.8**	**9.2**	**9.6**	**10.9**	**10.8**	**10.8**
2100 Employees	0.4	1.0	2.0	3.0	3.2	3.5	4.3	5.0	4.9	5.0
2200 Employers	0.5	1.0	1.9	2.7	2.8	4.5	4.2	4.7	4.5	4.5
2300 Self-employed or non-employed	0.1	0.3	0.5	0.8	0.8	1.2	1.2	1.2	1.3	1.3
2400 Unallocable between 2100, 2200 and 2300	0.0	0.0	0.0	0.0	0.0	0.0	0.0	0.0	0.0	0.0
3000 Taxes on payroll and workforce	**0.0**	**0.0**	**0.0**	**0.0**	**0.0**	**0.0**	**0.0**	**0.0**	**0.0**	**0.0**
4000 Taxes on property	**0.3**	**0.9**	**1.1**	**2.3**	**2.4**	**2.8**	**3.9**	**2.6**	**3.9**	**3.8**
4100 Recurrent taxes on immovable property	0.0	0.0	0.0	0.0	0.0	0.1	0.1	0.1	0.1	0.1
4200 Recurrent taxes on net wealth	0.2	0.6	0.8	1.7	1.8	1.6	2.7	2.1	2.8	2.9
4300 Estate, inheritance and gift taxes	0.0	0.0	0.1	0.1	0.1	0.1	0.1	0.1	0.2	0.2
4400 Taxes on financial and capital transactions	0.1	0.2	0.2	0.5	0.4	1.0	1.0	0.4	0.8	0.7
4500 Non-recurrent taxes	0.0	0.0	0.0	0.0	0.0	0.0	0.0	0.0	0.0	0.0
4600 Other recurrent taxes on property	0.0	0.0	0.0	0.0	0.0	0.0	0.0	0.0	0.0	0.0
5000 Taxes on goods and services	**0.9**	**2.3**	**4.2**	**5.5**	**5.8**	**7.9**	**9.8**	**10.4**	**9.1**	**9.1**
5100 Taxes on production, sale, transfer, etc	0.8	2.2	4.1	5.4	5.7	7.7	9.7	10.2	9.0	8.9
5110 General taxes	0.4	1.1	2.6	3.5	3.7	4.0	4.9	6.5	5.8	5.8
5111 Value added taxes	0.4	1.1	2.6	3.5	3.7	4.0	4.9	6.5	5.8	5.8
5120 Taxes on specific goods and services	0.4	1.1	1.5	1.9	2.0	3.7	4.8	3.7	3.1	3.1
5121 Excises	0.4	1.0	1.4	1.6	1.7	3.3	4.5	3.5	2.6	2.6
5200 Taxes on use of goods and perform activities	0.0	0.0	0.1	0.1	0.1	0.2	0.1	0.2	0.2	0.2
5300 Unallocable between 5100 and 5200	0.0	0.0	0.0	0.0	0.0	0.0	0.0	0.0	0.0	0.0
6000 Other taxes	**0.0**	**0.0**	**0.0**	**0.0**	**0.0**	**0.1**	**0.0**	**0.1**	**0.0**	**0.0**
Non-wastable tax credits										
Non-wastable tax credits against 1000	..	..	..	0.2	0.2	..	..	..	0.3	0.3
Transfer component	..	..	..	..	..	..	..	..	..	..
Tax expenditure component	..	..	..	..	..	..	..	..	..	..
Revenues collected on behalf of the EU										
Revenues collected on behalf of the EU, total	0.0	0.0	0.0	0.2	0.2	0.2	0.1	0.0	0.3	0.3
Customs duties	0.0	0.0	0.0	0.0	0.0	0.1	0.1	0.0	0.0	0.0
SRF contributions	..	..	..	0.1	0.1	..	..	..	0.2	0.2

.. Not available

Note: The total tax revenue has been reduced by the amount of any capital transfer that represents uncollected taxes. The capital transfer has been allocated between tax headings in proportion to the reported tax revenue. Therefore, the tax revenue amounts are different to those reported in the detailed country data available in online chapter 5 "Detailed country tables".

More detailed country data and country notes are available in online chapter 5 "Detailed country tables": https://doi.org/10.1787/0bbc27da-en. Full time series can be accessed at http://oe.cd/full-time-series.

Source: General account of the State.

StatLink https://stat.link/t43r0x

Table 4.48. Luxembourg, tax revenue and % of GDP by level of government and main taxes

	Billion EUR					% of GDP				
	1990	2000	2010	2018	2019	1990	2000	2010	2018	2019
Federal or Central government										
Total tax revenue	**2.4**	**5.8**	**10.2**	**16.2**	**16.7**	**22.1**	**25.3**	**25.3**	**26.9**	**26.3**
1000 Taxes on income, profits and capital gains	1.3	2.6	4.9	8.4	8.6	11.6	11.5	12.1	14.0	13.5
2000 Social security contributions	0.0	0.1	0.1	0.2	0.2	0.1	0.3	0.3	0.3	0.3
3000 Taxes on payroll and workforce	0.0	0.0	0.0	0.0	0.0	0.0	0.0	0.0	0.0	0.0
4000 Taxes on property	0.3	0.9	1.0	2.2	2.4	2.6	3.8	2.5	3.7	3.7
5000 Taxes on goods and services	0.8	2.2	4.2	5.3	5.6	7.7	9.6	10.3	8.9	8.8
6000 Other taxes	0.0	0.0	0.0	0.0	0.0	0.1	0.0	0.0	0.0	0.0
State/Regional										
Total tax revenue	**..**	**..**	**..**	**..**	**..**	**..**	**..**	**..**	**..**	**..**
1000 Taxes on income, profits and capital gains	..	..	..	..	..	..	..	..	..	..
2000 Social security contributions	..	..	..	..	..	..	..	..	..	..
3000 Taxes on payroll and workforce	..	..	..	..	..	..	..	..	..	..
4000 Taxes on property	..	..	..	..	..	..	..	..	..	..
5000 Taxes on goods and services	..	..	..	..	..	..	..	..	..	..
6000 Other taxes	..	..	..	..	..	..	..	..	..	..
Local government										
Total tax revenue	**0.2**	**0.5**	**0.7**	**1.1**	**1.2**	**2.1**	**2.1**	**1.6**	**1.8**	**1.9**
1000 Taxes on income, profits and capital gains	0.2	0.5	0.6	1.0	1.1	1.9	2.0	1.5	1.7	1.7
2000 Social security contributions	0.0	0.0	0.0	0.0	0.0	0.0	0.0	0.0	0.0	0.0
3000 Taxes on payroll and workforce	0.0	0.0	0.0	0.0	0.0	0.0	0.0	0.0	0.0	0.0
4000 Taxes on property	0.0	0.0	0.0	0.1	0.1	0.2	0.1	0.1	0.1	0.1
5000 Taxes on goods and services	0.0	0.0	0.0	0.0	0.0	0.0	0.0	0.0	0.0	0.0
6000 Other taxes	0.0	0.0	0.0	0.0	0.0	0.0	0.0	0.0	0.0	0.0
Social Security Funds										
Total tax revenue	**1.0**	**2.2**	**4.3**	**6.3**	**6.7**	**9.1**	**9.4**	**10.6**	**10.5**	**10.5**
1000 Taxes on income, profits and capital gains	0.0	0.0	0.0	0.0	0.0	0.0	0.0	0.0	0.0	0.0
2000 Social security contributions	1.0	2.2	4.3	6.3	6.7	9.1	9.4	10.6	10.5	10.5
3000 Taxes on payroll and workforce	0.0	0.0	0.0	0.0	0.0	0.0	0.0	0.0	0.0	0.0
4000 Taxes on property	0.0	0.0	0.0	0.0	0.0	0.0	0.0	0.0	0.0	0.0
5000 Taxes on goods and services	0.0	0.0	0.0	0.0	0.0	0.0	0.0	0.0	0.0	0.0
6000 Other taxes	0.0	0.0	0.0	0.0	0.0	0.0	0.0	0.0	0.0	0.0

.. Not available

Note: The total tax revenue has been reduced by the amount of any capital transfer that represents uncollected taxes. The capital transfer has been allocated between tax headings in proportion to the reported tax revenue. Therefore, the tax revenue amounts are different to those reported in the detailed country data available in online chapter 6 "Tax revenues by sub-sectors of general government".

More detailed country data and country notes are available in online chapter 6 "Tax revenues by sub-sectors of general government": https://doi.org/10.1787/0bbc27da-en. Full time series can be accessed at http://oe.cd/full-time-series.

Source: General account of the State.

StatLink https://stat.link/rusypm

Table 4.49. Mexico, tax revenue and % of GDP by selected tax category

	Billion MXN					% of GDP				
	1990	2000	2010	2018	2019	1990	2000	2010	2018	2019
Total tax revenue	**102.0**	**767.2**	**1 716.2**	**3 797.9**	**3 995.7**	**12.1**	**11.5**	**12.8**	**16.1**	**16.3**
1000 Taxes on income, profits and capital gains	**34.7**	**276.5**	**683.6**	**1 671.5**	**1 694.1**	**4.1**	**4.1**	**5.1**	**7.1**	**6.9**
1100 Of individuals	..	..	313.5	804.2	829.5	..	..	2.3	3.4	3.4
1200 Corporate	..	..	246.7	809.8	803.6	..	..	1.8	3.4	3.3
1300 Unallocable between 1100 and 1200	34.7	276.5	123.4	57.4	61.0	4.1	4.1	0.9	0.2	0.2
2000 Social security contributions	**17.2**	**138.2**	**277.5**	**509.1**	**552.1**	**2.0**	**2.1**	**2.1**	**2.2**	**2.3**
2100 Employees	..	..	..	..	..	..	..	..	..	..
2200 Employers	..	..	..	..	..	..	..	..	..	..
2300 Self-employed or non-employed	..	..	..	..	..	..	..	..	..	..
2400 Unallocable between 2100, 2200 and 2300	17.2	138.2	277.5	509.1	552.1	2.0	2.1	2.1	2.2	2.3
3000 Taxes on payroll and workforce	**1.8**	**11.2**	**36.9**	**93.3**	**101.3**	**0.2**	**0.2**	**0.3**	**0.4**	**0.4**
4000 Taxes on property	**1.9**	**14.0**	**39.0**	**77.1**	**79.3**	**0.2**	**0.2**	**0.3**	**0.3**	**0.3**
4100 Recurrent taxes on immovable property	1.0	9.9	25.7	49.4	50.5	0.1	0.1	0.2	0.2	0.2
4200 Recurrent taxes on net wealth	0.0	0.0	0.0	0.0	0.0	0.0	0.0	0.0	0.0	0.0
4300 Estate, inheritance and gift taxes	0.0	0.0	0.0	0.0	0.0	0.0	0.0	0.0	0.0	0.0
4400 Taxes on financial and capital transactions	0.9	4.0	13.2	27.7	28.7	0.1	0.1	0.1	0.1	0.1
4500 Non-recurrent taxes	0.0	0.0	0.0	0.0	0.0	0.0	0.0	0.0	0.0	0.0
4600 Other recurrent taxes on property	0.0	0.0	0.0	0.0	0.0	0.0	0.0	0.0	0.0	0.0
5000 Taxes on goods and services	**44.8**	**319.6**	**651.9**	**1 381.7**	**1 504.3**	**5.3**	**4.8**	**4.9**	**5.9**	**6.2**
5100 Taxes on production, sale, transfer, etc	44.2	310.3	630.1	1 364.2	1 486.8	5.2	4.6	4.7	5.8	6.1
5110 General taxes	26.6	189.6	504.5	922.2	933.3	3.2	2.8	3.8	3.9	3.8
5111 Value added taxes	26.6	189.6	504.5	922.2	933.3	3.2	2.8	3.8	3.9	3.8
5120 Taxes on specific goods and services	17.5	120.7	125.6	442.0	553.4	2.1	1.8	0.9	1.9	2.3
5121 Excises	10.1	86.2	86.1	358.6	471.0	1.2	1.3	0.6	1.5	1.9
5200 Taxes on use of goods and perform activities	0.7	9.3	21.8	17.5	17.5	0.1	0.1	0.2	0.1	0.1
5300 Unallocable between 5100 and 5200	0.0	0.0	0.0	0.0	0.0	0.0	0.0	0.0	0.0	0.0
6000 Other taxes	**1.6**	**7.7**	**27.4**	**65.2**	**64.7**	**0.2**	**0.1**	**0.2**	**0.3**	**0.3**
Non-wastable tax credits										
Non-wastable tax credits against 1000	..	..	40.3	49.1	50.6	..	..	0.3	0.2	0.2
Transfer component	..	..	9.7	1.2	1.3	..	..	0.1	0.0	0.0
Tax expenditure component	..	..	30.6	47.9	49.4	..	..	0.2	0.2	0.2

.. Not available

Note: More detailed country data and country notes are available in online chapter 5 "Detailed country tables": https://doi.org/10.1787/0bbc27da-en. Full time series can be accessed at http://oe.cd/full-time-series.

Source: Ministry of Finance, Economic Department.

StatLink https://stat.link/vcro0h

Table 4.50. Mexico, tax revenue and % of GDP by level of government and main taxes

	Billion MXN					% of GDP				
	1990	2000	2010	2018	2019	1990	2000	2010	2018	2019
Federal or Central government										
Total tax revenue	**81.4**	**600.5**	**1 351.5**	**3 073.4**	**3 213.2**	**9.7**	**9.0**	**10.1**	**13.1**	**13.1**
1000 Taxes on income, profits and capital gains	34.7	276.5	683.6	1 671.5	1 694.1	4.1	4.1	5.1	7.1	6.9
2000 Social security contributions	0.0	0.0	0.0	0.0	0.0	0.0	0.0	0.0	0.0	0.0
3000 Taxes on payroll and workforce	0.8	0.0	0.0	0.0	0.0	0.1	0.0	0.0	0.0	0.0
4000 Taxes on property	0.0	0.0	0.0	0.0	0.0	0.0	0.0	0.0	0.0	0.0
5000 Taxes on goods and services	44.6	318.1	645.6	1 355.6	1 477.9	5.3	4.8	4.8	5.8	6.0
6000 Other taxes	1.3	5.9	22.2	46.3	41.1	0.2	0.1	0.2	0.2	0.2
State/Regional										
Total tax revenue	**2.2**	**20.5**	**58.3**	**153.7**	**163.7**	**0.3**	**0.3**	**0.4**	**0.7**	**0.7**
1000 Taxes on income, profits and capital gains	0.0	0.0	0.0	0.0	0.0	0.0	0.0	0.0	0.0	0.0
2000 Social security contributions	0.0	0.0	0.0	0.0	0.0	0.0	0.0	0.0	0.0	0.0
3000 Taxes on payroll and workforce	1.0	11.2	36.8	93.3	101.3	0.1	0.2	0.3	0.4	0.4
4000 Taxes on property	0.9	7.0	13.1	28.7	29.2	0.1	0.1	0.1	0.1	0.1
5000 Taxes on goods and services	0.1	1.3	5.8	24.3	25.2	0.0	0.0	0.0	0.1	0.1
6000 Other taxes	0.2	0.9	2.5	7.4	8.1	0.0	0.0	0.0	0.0	0.0
Local government										
Total tax revenue	**1.3**	**8.0**	**29.0**	**61.7**	**66.7**	**0.1**	**0.1**	**0.2**	**0.3**	**0.3**
1000 Taxes on income, profits and capital gains	0.0	0.0	0.0	0.0	0.0	0.0	0.0	0.0	0.0	0.0
2000 Social security contributions	0.0	0.0	0.0	0.0	0.0	0.0	0.0	0.0	0.0	0.0
3000 Taxes on payroll and workforce	0.0	0.0	0.1	0.0	0.0	0.0	0.0	0.0	0.0	0.0
4000 Taxes on property	1.0	6.9	25.8	48.4	50.1	0.1	0.1	0.2	0.2	0.2
5000 Taxes on goods and services	0.1	0.2	0.5	1.7	1.2	0.0	0.0	0.0	0.0	0.0
6000 Other taxes	0.1	0.9	2.6	11.5	15.5	0.0	0.0	0.0	0.0	0.1
Social Security Funds										
Total tax revenue	**17.2**	**138.2**	**277.5**	**509.1**	**552.1**	**2.0**	**2.1**	**2.1**	**2.2**	**2.3**
1000 Taxes on income, profits and capital gains	0.0	0.0	0.0	0.0	0.0	0.0	0.0	0.0	0.0	0.0
2000 Social security contributions	17.2	138.2	277.5	509.1	552.1	2.0	2.1	2.1	2.2	2.3
3000 Taxes on payroll and workforce	0.0	0.0	0.0	0.0	0.0	0.0	0.0	0.0	0.0	0.0
4000 Taxes on property	0.0	0.0	0.0	0.0	0.0	0.0	0.0	0.0	0.0	0.0
5000 Taxes on goods and services	0.0	0.0	0.0	0.0	0.0	0.0	0.0	0.0	0.0	0.0
6000 Other taxes	0.0	0.0	0.0	0.0	0.0	0.0	0.0	0.0	0.0	0.0

Note: More detailed country data and country notes are available in online chapter 6 "Tax revenues by sub-sectors of general government": https://doi.org/10.1787/0bbc27da-en. Full time series can be accessed at http://oe.cd/full-time-series.
Source: Ministry of Finance, Economic Department.

StatLink https://stat.link/4hvjyi

Table 4.51. Netherlands, tax revenue and % of GDP by selected tax category

	Billion EUR					% of GDP				
	1990	2000	2010	2018	2019	1990	2000	2010	2018	2019
Total tax revenue	**104.4**	**166.8**	**227.9**	**300.3**	**319.2**	**39.7**	**36.9**	**35.7**	**38.8**	**39.3**
1000 Taxes on income, profits and capital gains	**33.7**	**43.3**	**63.6**	**88.8**	**99.0**	**12.8**	**9.6**	**9.9**	**11.5**	**12.2**
1100 Of individuals	25.8	25.1	49.0	61.7	69.0	9.8	5.6	7.7	8.0	8.5
1200 Corporate	7.9	18.1	14.6	27.1	30.0	3.0	4.0	2.3	3.5	3.7
1300 Unallocable between 1100 and 1200	0.0	0.0	0.0	0.0	0.0	0.0	0.0	0.0	0.0	0.0
2000 Social security contributions	**39.1**	**64.5**	**82.7**	**108.0**	**109.3**	**14.9**	**14.3**	**12.9**	**14.0**	**13.4**
2100 Employees	24.1	35.3	41.6	41.8	40.7	9.2	7.8	6.5	5.4	5.0
2200 Employers	7.8	18.7	29.4	40.7	43.7	3.0	4.1	4.6	5.3	5.4
2300 Self-employed or non-employed	7.1	10.5	11.7	25.6	24.9	2.7	2.3	1.8	3.3	3.1
2400 Unallocable between 2100, 2200 and 2300	0.0	0.0	0.0	0.0	0.0	0.0	0.0	0.0	0.0	0.0
3000 Taxes on payroll and workforce	**0.0**	**0.0**	**0.0**	**0.0**	**0.0**	**0.0**	**0.0**	**0.0**	**0.0**	**0.0**
4000 Taxes on property	**3.8**	**8.8**	**8.8**	**12.1**	**12.2**	**1.5**	**1.9**	**1.4**	**1.6**	**1.5**
4100 Recurrent taxes on immovable property	1.7	3.1	4.2	7.4	7.4	0.7	0.7	0.7	1.0	0.9
4200 Recurrent taxes on net wealth	0.6	0.8	0.0	0.0	0.0	0.2	0.2	0.0	0.0	0.0
4300 Estate, inheritance and gift taxes	0.5	1.5	1.7	1.7	1.8	0.2	0.3	0.3	0.2	0.2
4400 Taxes on financial and capital transactions	1.0	3.4	2.8	3.0	3.0	0.4	0.8	0.4	0.4	0.4
4500 Non-recurrent taxes	0.0	0.0	0.0	0.0	0.0	0.0	0.0	0.0	0.0	0.0
4600 Other recurrent taxes on property	0.0	0.0	0.0	0.0	0.0	0.0	0.0	0.0	0.0	0.0
5000 Taxes on goods and services	**27.6**	**49.5**	**71.9**	**90.5**	**98.0**	**10.5**	**10.9**	**11.2**	**11.7**	**12.1**
5100 Taxes on production, sale, transfer, etc	25.1	44.9	64.2	81.5	88.5	9.5	9.9	10.1	10.5	10.9
5110 General taxes	17.2	28.9	42.7	52.8	58.2	6.5	6.4	6.7	6.8	7.2
5111 Value added taxes	17.2	28.8	42.7	52.7	58.1	6.5	6.4	6.7	6.8	7.1
5120 Taxes on specific goods and services	7.9	16.0	21.6	28.7	30.3	3.0	3.5	3.4	3.7	3.7
5121 Excises	6.0	13.8	18.4	21.0	22.0	2.3	3.0	2.9	2.7	2.7
5200 Taxes on use of goods and perform activities	2.5	4.6	7.6	9.1	9.5	1.0	1.0	1.2	1.2	1.2
5300 Unallocable between 5100 and 5200	0.0	0.0	0.0	0.0	0.0	0.0	0.0	0.0	0.0	0.0
6000 Other taxes	**0.3**	**0.8**	**1.0**	**0.8**	**0.8**	**0.1**	**0.2**	**0.2**	**0.1**	**0.1**
Non-wastable tax credits										
Non-wastable tax credits against 1000	..	..	..	..	..	..	..	..	..	..
Transfer component	..	..	..	..	..	..	..	..	..	..
Tax expenditure component	..	..	..	..	..	..	..	..	..	..
Revenues collected on behalf of the EU										
Revenues collected on behalf of the EU, total	1.5	1.6	2.0	3.4	3.6	0.6	0.4	0.3	0.4	0.4
Customs duties	..	1.3	1.7	2.5	2.7	..	0.3	0.3	0.3	0.3
SRF contributions	..	..	..	0.6	0.6	..	..	..	0.1	0.1

.. Not available

Note: More detailed country data and country notes are available in online chapter 5 "Detailed country tables": https://doi.org/10.1787/0bbc27da-en. Full time series can be accessed at http://oe.cd/full-time-series.

Source: Social security contributions and local taxes: Central Bureau of Statistics. Other taxes: Ministry of Finance.

StatLink https://stat.link/lzmw19

Table 4.52. Netherlands, tax revenue and % of GDP by level of government and main taxes

	Billion EUR					% of GDP				
	1990	2000	2010	2018	2019	1990	2000	2010	2018	2019
Federal or Central government										
Total tax revenue	**61.4**	**95.1**	**135.1**	**178.4**	**195.5**	**23.3**	**21.0**	**21.1**	**23.1**	**24.0**
1000 Taxes on income, profits and capital gains	33.7	43.3	63.6	88.8	99.0	12.8	9.6	9.9	11.5	12.2
2000 Social security contributions	0.0	0.0	0.0	0.0	0.0	0.0	0.0	0.0	0.0	0.0
3000 Taxes on payroll and workforce	0.0	0.0	0.0	0.0	0.0	0.0	0.0	0.0	0.0	0.0
4000 Taxes on property	2.1	5.7	4.6	6.7	6.5	0.8	1.3	0.7	0.9	0.8
5000 Taxes on goods and services	25.3	45.4	66.2	82.2	89.2	9.6	10.0	10.3	10.6	11.0
6000 Other taxes	0.3	0.8	0.8	0.8	0.8	0.1	0.2	0.1	0.1	0.1
State/Regional										
Total tax revenue	..	..	..	..	..	..	..	..	..	..
1000 Taxes on income, profits and capital gains	..	..	..	..	..	..	..	..	..	..
2000 Social security contributions	..	..	..	..	..	..	..	..	..	..
3000 Taxes on payroll and workforce	..	..	..	..	..	..	..	..	..	..
4000 Taxes on property	..	..	..	..	..	..	..	..	..	..
5000 Taxes on goods and services	..	..	..	..	..	..	..	..	..	..
6000 Other taxes	..	..	..	..	..	..	..	..	..	..
Local government										
Total tax revenue	**2.5**	**5.6**	**8.1**	**10.5**	**10.9**	**0.9**	**1.2**	**1.3**	**1.4**	**1.3**
1000 Taxes on income, profits and capital gains	0.0	0.0	0.0	0.0	0.0	0.0	0.0	0.0	0.0	0.0
2000 Social security contributions	0.0	0.0	0.0	0.0	0.0	0.0	0.0	0.0	0.0	0.0
3000 Taxes on payroll and workforce	0.0	0.0	0.0	0.0	0.0	0.0	0.0	0.0	0.0	0.0
4000 Taxes on property	1.7	3.1	4.2	5.5	5.7	0.7	0.7	0.7	0.7	0.7
5000 Taxes on goods and services	0.8	2.5	3.7	5.0	5.2	0.3	0.6	0.6	0.6	0.6
6000 Other taxes	0.0	0.0	0.2	0.0	0.0	0.0	0.0	0.0	0.0	0.0
Social Security Funds										
Total tax revenue	**39.1**	**64.5**	**82.7**	**108.0**	**109.3**	**14.9**	**14.3**	**12.9**	**14.0**	**13.4**
1000 Taxes on income, profits and capital gains	0.0	0.0	0.0	0.0	0.0	0.0	0.0	0.0	0.0	0.0
2000 Social security contributions	39.1	64.5	82.7	108.0	109.3	14.9	14.3	12.9	14.0	13.4
3000 Taxes on payroll and workforce	0.0	0.0	0.0	0.0	0.0	0.0	0.0	0.0	0.0	0.0
4000 Taxes on property	0.0	0.0	0.0	0.0	0.0	0.0	0.0	0.0	0.0	0.0
5000 Taxes on goods and services	0.0	0.0	0.0	0.0	0.0	0.0	0.0	0.0	0.0	0.0
6000 Other taxes	0.0	0.0	0.0	0.0	0.0	0.0	0.0	0.0	0.0	0.0

.. Not available

Note: More detailed country data and country notes are available in online chapter 6 "Tax revenues by sub-sectors of general government": https://doi.org/10.1787/0bbc27da-en. Full time series can be accessed at http://oe.cd/full-time-series.

Source: Social security contributions and local taxes: Central Bureau of Statistics. Other taxes: Ministry of Finance.

StatLink https://stat.link/h4zlvb

Table 4.53. New Zealand, tax revenue and % of GDP by selected tax category

	Billion NZD					% of GDP				
	1990	2000	2010	2018	2019	1990	2000	2010	2018	2019
Total tax revenue	**27.5**	**39.8**	**62.3**	**99.8**	**99.8**	**36.2**	**32.5**	**30.3**	**32.2**	**31.5**
1000 Taxes on income, profits and capital gains	**16.4**	**23.9**	**33.5**	**56.2**	**55.0**	**21.6**	**19.5**	**16.3**	**18.1**	**17.3**
1100 Of individuals	13.2	17.1	23.5	37.5	39.5	17.4	14.0	11.4	12.1	12.4
1200 Corporate	1.8	4.9	7.6	15.6	12.4	2.3	4.0	3.7	5.0	3.9
1300 Unallocable between 1100 and 1200	1.4	1.8	2.4	3.1	2.9	1.9	1.5	1.2	1.0	0.9
2000 Social security contributions	**0.0**	**0.0**	**0.0**	**0.0**	**0.0**	**0.0**	**0.0**	**0.0**	**0.0**	**0.0**
2100 Employees	0.0	0.0	0.0	0.0	0.0	0.0	0.0	0.0	0.0	0.0
2200 Employers	0.0	0.0	0.0	0.0	0.0	0.0	0.0	0.0	0.0	0.0
2300 Self-employed or non-employed	0.0	0.0	0.0	0.0	0.0	0.0	0.0	0.0	0.0	0.0
2400 Unallocable between 2100, 2200 and 2300	0.0	0.0	0.0	0.0	0.0	0.0	0.0	0.0	0.0	0.0
3000 Taxes on payroll and workforce	**0.0**	**0.0**	**0.0**	**0.0**	**0.0**	**0.0**	**0.0**	**0.0**	**0.0**	**0.0**
4000 Taxes on property	**1.9**	**2.1**	**4.1**	**5.8**	**6.2**	**2.5**	**1.7**	**2.0**	**1.9**	**1.9**
4100 Recurrent taxes on immovable property	1.7	2.0	4.0	5.7	6.1	2.3	1.7	2.0	1.8	1.9
4200 Recurrent taxes on net wealth	0.0	0.0	0.0	0.0	0.0	0.0	0.0	0.0	0.0	0.0
4300 Estate, inheritance and gift taxes	0.1	0.0	0.0	0.0	0.0	0.1	0.0	0.0	0.0	0.0
4400 Taxes on financial and capital transactions	0.1	0.1	0.1	0.1	0.1	0.1	0.0	0.0	0.0	0.0
4500 Non-recurrent taxes	0.0	0.0	0.0	0.0	..	0.0	0.0	0.0	0.0	..
4600 Other recurrent taxes on property	0.0	0.0	0.0	0.0	0.0	0.0	0.0	0.0	0.0	0.0
5000 Taxes on goods and services	**9.2**	**13.8**	**24.7**	**37.8**	**38.6**	**12.1**	**11.3**	**12.0**	**12.2**	**12.2**
5100 Taxes on production, sale, transfer, etc	8.7	12.9	23.1	35.3	36.0	11.4	10.5	11.2	11.4	11.4
5110 General taxes	6.2	9.9	19.1	29.5	30.3	8.1	8.1	9.3	9.5	9.5
5111 Value added taxes	6.2	9.9	19.1	29.5	30.3	8.1	8.1	9.3	9.5	9.5
5120 Taxes on specific goods and services	2.5	3.0	4.0	5.8	5.8	3.3	2.5	1.9	1.9	1.8
5121 Excises	1.9	2.1	1.8	2.6	2.5	2.5	1.8	0.9	0.8	0.8
5200 Taxes on use of goods and perform activities	0.5	0.9	1.6	2.6	2.7	0.7	0.7	0.8	0.8	0.8
5300 Unallocable between 5100 and 5200	0.0	0.0	0.0	0.0	0.0	0.0	0.0	0.0	0.0	0.0
6000 Other taxes	**0.0**	**0.0**	**0.0**	**0.0**	**0.0**	**0.0**	**0.0**	**0.0**	**0.0**	**0.0**
Non-wastable tax credits										
Non-wastable tax credits against 1000	..	1.1	2.8	2.8	2.8	..	0.9	1.4	0.9	0.9
Transfer component	..	0.7	1.8	1.2	1.4	..	0.6	0.9	0.4	0.4
Tax expenditure component	..	0.3	1.0	1.5	1.4	..	0.3	0.5	0.5	0.5

.. Not available

Note: More detailed country data and country notes are available in online chapter 5 "Detailed country tables": https://doi.org/10.1787/0bbc27da-en. Full time series can be accessed at http://oe.cd/full-time-series.

Source: Local Authorities Statistics, Department of Statistics, Wellington.

StatLink https://stat.link/whn9jq

Table 4.54. New Zealand, tax revenue and % of GDP by level of government and main taxes

	Billion NZD					% of GDP				
	1990	2000	2010	2018	2019	1990	2000	2010	2018	2019
Federal or Central government										
Total tax revenue	**25.8**	**37.5**	**57.9**	**93.3**	**92.9**	**34.0**	**30.7**	**28.1**	**30.1**	**29.3**
1000 Taxes on income, profits and capital gains	16.4	23.9	33.5	56.2	55.0	21.6	19.5	16.3	18.1	17.3
2000 Social security contributions	0.0	0.0	0.0	0.0	0.0	0.0	0.0	0.0	0.0	0.0
3000 Taxes on payroll and workforce	0.0	0.0	0.0	0.0	0.0	0.0	0.0	0.0	0.0	0.0
4000 Taxes on property	0.3	0.1	0.1	0.1	0.1	0.4	0.1	0.0	0.0	0.0
5000 Taxes on goods and services	9.1	13.6	24.3	37.0	37.8	12.0	11.1	11.8	11.9	11.9
6000 Other taxes	0.0	0.0	0.0	0.0	0.0	0.0	0.0	0.0	0.0	0.0
State/Regional										
Total tax revenue	..	..	..	..	..	..	..	..	..	..
1000 Taxes on income, profits and capital gains	..	..	..	..	..	..	..	..	..	..
2000 Social security contributions	..	..	..	..	..	..	..	..	..	..
3000 Taxes on payroll and workforce	..	..	..	..	..	..	..	..	..	..
4000 Taxes on property	..	..	..	..	..	..	..	..	..	..
5000 Taxes on goods and services	..	..	..	..	..	..	..	..	..	..
6000 Other taxes	..	..	..	..	..	..	..	..	..	..
Local government										
Total tax revenue	**1.7**	**2.3**	**4.5**	**6.6**	**6.9**	**2.2**	**1.9**	**2.2**	**2.1**	**2.2**
1000 Taxes on income, profits and capital gains	0.0	0.0	0.0	0.0	0.0	0.0	0.0	0.0	0.0	0.0
2000 Social security contributions	0.0	0.0	0.0	0.0	0.0	0.0	0.0	0.0	0.0	0.0
3000 Taxes on payroll and workforce	0.0	0.0	0.0	0.0	0.0	0.0	0.0	0.0	0.0	0.0
4000 Taxes on property	1.6	2.0	4.0	5.7	6.1	2.0	1.7	2.0	1.8	1.9
5000 Taxes on goods and services	0.1	0.2	0.4	0.9	0.8	0.2	0.2	0.2	0.3	0.3
6000 Other taxes	0.0	0.0	0.0	0.0	0.0	0.0	0.0	0.0	0.0	0.0
Social Security Funds										
Total tax revenue	**0.0**	**0.0**	**0.0**	**0.0**	**0.0**	**0.0**	**0.0**	**0.0**	**0.0**	**0.0**
1000 Taxes on income, profits and capital gains	0.0	0.0	0.0	0.0	0.0	0.0	0.0	0.0	0.0	0.0
2000 Social security contributions	0.0	0.0	0.0	0.0	0.0	0.0	0.0	0.0	0.0	0.0
3000 Taxes on payroll and workforce	0.0	0.0	0.0	0.0	0.0	0.0	0.0	0.0	0.0	0.0
4000 Taxes on property	0.0	0.0	0.0	0.0	0.0	0.0	0.0	0.0	0.0	0.0
5000 Taxes on goods and services	0.0	0.0	0.0	0.0	0.0	0.0	0.0	0.0	0.0	0.0
6000 Other taxes	0.0	0.0	0.0	0.0	0.0	0.0	0.0	0.0	0.0	0.0

.. Not available

Note: More detailed country data and country notes are available in online chapter 6 "Tax revenues by sub-sectors of general government": https://doi.org/10.1787/0bbc27da-en. Full time series can be accessed at http://oe.cd/full-time-series.

Source: Local Authorities Statistics, Department of Statistics, Wellington.

StatLink https://stat.link/z9hj6i

Table 4.55. Norway, tax revenue and % of GDP by selected tax category

	Billion NOK					% of GDP				
	1990	2000	2010	2018	2019	1990	2000	2010	2018	2019
Total tax revenue	**301.8**	**628.0**	**1 083.3**	**1 399.1**	**1 424.1**	**40.2**	**41.7**	**41.8**	**39.4**	**39.9**
1000 Taxes on income, profits and capital gains	**106.3**	**284.2**	**512.2**	**584.3**	**580.1**	**14.2**	**18.9**	**19.8**	**16.4**	**16.3**
1100 Of individuals	79.1	152.0	256.5	354.7	370.4	10.5	10.1	9.9	10.0	10.4
1200 Corporate	27.2	132.2	255.7	229.6	209.7	3.6	8.8	9.9	6.5	5.9
1300 Unallocable between 1100 and 1200	0.0	0.0	0.0	0.0	0.0	0.0	0.0	0.0	0.0	0.0
2000 Social security contributions	**79.4**	**132.2**	**243.0**	**357.3**	**377.4**	**10.6**	**8.8**	**9.4**	**10.1**	**10.6**
2100 Employees	25.3	45.2	81.0	124.5	131.0	3.4	3.0	3.1	3.5	3.7
2200 Employers	50.1	79.2	148.0	208.8	221.2	6.7	5.3	5.7	5.9	6.2
2300 Self-employed or non-employed	3.9	7.8	13.9	24.0	25.2	0.5	0.5	0.5	0.7	0.7
2400 Unallocable between 2100, 2200 and 2300	0.0	0.0	0.0	0.0	0.0	0.0	0.0	0.0	0.0	0.0
3000 Taxes on payroll and workforce	**0.0**	**0.0**	**0.0**	**2.0**	**2.0**	**0.0**	**0.0**	**0.0**	**0.1**	**0.1**
4000 Taxes on property	**8.9**	**14.4**	**28.5**	**43.7**	**45.7**	**1.2**	**1.0**	**1.1**	**1.2**	**1.3**
4100 Recurrent taxes on immovable property	2.2	2.7	7.1	14.2	14.7	0.3	0.2	0.3	0.4	0.4
4200 Recurrent taxes on net wealth	5.1	7.7	13.2	19.9	20.5	0.7	0.5	0.5	0.6	0.6
4300 Estate, inheritance and gift taxes	0.4	1.3	2.4	0.1	0.0	0.1	0.1	0.1	0.0	0.0
4400 Taxes on financial and capital transactions	1.1	2.7	5.9	9.6	10.3	0.1	0.2	0.2	0.3	0.3
4500 Non-recurrent taxes	0.0	0.0	0.0	0.0	0.0	0.0	0.0	0.0	0.0	0.0
4600 Other recurrent taxes on property	0.0	0.0	0.0	0.0	0.0	0.0	0.0	0.0	0.0	0.0
5000 Taxes on goods and services	**107.3**	**197.2**	**299.5**	**411.8**	**418.9**	**14.3**	**13.1**	**11.6**	**11.6**	**11.7**
5100 Taxes on production, sale, transfer, etc	102.9	185.9	284.6	392.8	399.0	13.7	12.3	11.0	11.1	11.2
5110 General taxes	56.7	125.0	201.8	297.9	308.3	7.6	8.3	7.8	8.4	8.6
5111 Value added taxes	56.7	124.2	201.2	296.9	307.0	7.6	8.2	7.8	8.4	8.6
5120 Taxes on specific goods and services	46.2	60.9	82.8	94.9	90.7	6.2	4.0	3.2	2.7	2.5
5121 Excises	37.5	54.9	76.3	84.0	79.7	5.0	3.6	2.9	2.4	2.2
5200 Taxes on use of goods and perform activities	4.4	11.3	14.9	19.0	19.9	0.6	0.7	0.6	0.5	0.6
5300 Unallocable between 5100 and 5200	0.0	0.0	0.0	0.0	0.0	0.0	0.0	0.0	0.0	0.0
6000 Other taxes	**0.0**	**0.0**	**0.0**	**0.0**	**0.0**	**0.0**	**0.0**	**0.0**	**0.0**	**0.0**
Non-wastable tax credits										
Non-wastable tax credits against 1000	..	..	1.2	4.0	4.2	..	..	0.0	0.1	0.1
Transfer component	..	..	1.2	3.2	3.4	..	..	0.0	0.1	0.1
Tax expenditure component	..	..	0.1	0.8	0.8	..	..	0.0	0.0	0.0

.. Not available

Note: More detailed country data and country notes are available in online chapter 5 "Detailed country tables": https://doi.org/10.1787/0bbc27da-en. Full time series can be accessed at http://oe.cd/full-time-series.

Source: Statistics Norway; National Accounts.

StatLink https://stat.link/v98jwe

Table 4.56. Norway, tax revenue and % of GDP by level of government and main taxes

	Billion NOK					% of GDP				
	1990	2000	2010	2018	2019	1990	2000	2010	2018	2019
Federal or Central government										
Total tax revenue	**165.4**	**532.5**	**935.7**	**1 185.5**	**1 203.5**	**22.1**	**35.3**	**36.1**	**33.4**	**33.7**
1000 Taxes on income, profits and capital gains	50.6	198.4	381.0	399.5	389.1	6.8	13.2	14.7	11.2	10.9
2000 Social security contributions	4.7	132.2	243.0	357.3	377.4	0.6	8.8	9.4	10.1	10.6
3000 Taxes on payroll and workforce	0.0	0.0	0.0	2.0	2.0	0.0	0.0	0.0	0.1	0.1
4000 Taxes on property	3.4	6.8	13.7	16.6	17.7	0.5	0.5	0.5	0.5	0.5
5000 Taxes on goods and services	106.7	195.1	298.0	410.1	417.2	14.2	12.9	11.5	11.5	11.7
6000 Other taxes	0.0	0.0	0.0	0.0	0.0	0.0	0.0	0.0	0.0	0.0
State/Regional										
Total tax revenue	..	..	..	..	..	..	..	..	..	..
1000 Taxes on income, profits and capital gains	..	..	..	..	..	..	..	..	..	..
2000 Social security contributions	..	..	..	..	..	..	..	..	..	..
3000 Taxes on payroll and workforce	..	..	..	..	..	..	..	..	..	..
4000 Taxes on property	..	..	..	..	..	..	..	..	..	..
5000 Taxes on goods and services	..	..	..	..	..	..	..	..	..	..
6000 Other taxes	..	..	..	..	..	..	..	..	..	..
Local government										
Total tax revenue	**61.6**	**95.5**	**147.7**	**213.6**	**220.5**	**8.2**	**6.3**	**5.7**	**6.0**	**6.2**
1000 Taxes on income, profits and capital gains	55.7	85.8	131.2	184.8	190.9	7.4	5.7	5.1	5.2	5.4
2000 Social security contributions	0.0	0.0	0.0	0.0	0.0	0.0	0.0	0.0	0.0	0.0
3000 Taxes on payroll and workforce	0.0	0.0	0.0	0.0	0.0	0.0	0.0	0.0	0.0	0.0
4000 Taxes on property	5.5	7.6	14.9	27.1	27.9	0.7	0.5	0.6	0.8	0.8
5000 Taxes on goods and services	0.4	2.1	1.6	1.7	1.7	0.1	0.1	0.1	0.0	0.0
6000 Other taxes	0.0	0.0	0.0	0.0	0.0	0.0	0.0	0.0	0.0	0.0
Social Security Funds										
Total tax revenue	**74.8**	**0.0**	**0.0**	**0.0**	**0.0**	**10.0**	**0.0**	**0.0**	**0.0**	**0.0**
1000 Taxes on income, profits and capital gains	0.0	0.0	0.0	0.0	0.0	0.0	0.0	0.0	0.0	0.0
2000 Social security contributions	74.6	0.0	0.0	0.0	0.0	10.0	0.0	0.0	0.0	0.0
3000 Taxes on payroll and workforce	0.0	0.0	0.0	0.0	0.0	0.0	0.0	0.0	0.0	0.0
4000 Taxes on property	0.0	0.0	0.0	0.0	0.0	0.0	0.0	0.0	0.0	0.0
5000 Taxes on goods and services	0.2	0.0	0.0	0.0	0.0	0.0	0.0	0.0	0.0	0.0
6000 Other taxes	0.0	0.0	0.0	0.0	0.0	0.0	0.0	0.0	0.0	0.0

.. Not available

Note: More detailed country data and country notes are available in online chapter 6 "Tax revenues by sub-sectors of general government": https://doi.org/10.1787/0bbc27da-en. Full time series can be accessed at http://oe.cd/full-time-series.

Source: Statistics Norway; National Accounts.

StatLink https://stat.link/n3rbtv

Table 4.57. Poland, tax revenue and % of GDP by selected tax category

	Billion PLN					% of GDP				
	1990	2000	2010	2018	2019	1990	2000	2010	2018	2019
Total tax revenue	..	**246.0**	**453.3**	**745.6**	**805.0**	..	**32.9**	**31.3**	**35.1**	**35.1**
1000 Taxes on income, profits and capital gains	..	**50.3**	**91.0**	**157.0**	**172.5**	..	**6.7**	**6.3**	**7.4**	**7.5**
1100 Of individuals	..	32.4	62.9	112.7	121.9	..	4.3	4.3	5.3	5.3
1200 Corporate	..	17.9	28.1	44.3	50.6	..	2.4	1.9	2.1	2.2
1300 Unallocable between 1100 and 1200	..	0.0	0.0	0.0	0.0	..	0.0	0.0	0.0	0.0
2000 Social security contributions	..	**96.4**	**156.0**	**277.7**	**302.3**	..	**12.9**	**10.8**	**13.1**	**13.2**
2100 Employees	..	42.4	60.2	115.8	126.1	..	5.7	4.2	5.5	5.5
2200 Employers	..	41.1	65.4	108.7	117.4	..	5.5	4.5	5.1	5.1
2300 Self-employed or non-employed	..	12.9	30.4	53.2	58.8	..	1.7	2.1	2.5	2.6
2400 Unallocable between 2100, 2200 and 2300	..	0.0	0.0	0.0	0.0	..	0.0	0.0	0.0	0.0
3000 Taxes on payroll and workforce	..	**1.6**	**3.7**	**4.7**	**5.9**	..	**0.2**	**0.3**	**0.2**	**0.3**
4000 Taxes on property	..	**10.6**	**19.1**	**27.9**	**29.0**	..	**1.4**	**1.3**	**1.3**	**1.3**
4100 Recurrent taxes on immovable property	..	8.4	16.4	24.3	25.2	..	1.1	1.1	1.1	1.1
4200 Recurrent taxes on net wealth	..	0.0	0.0	0.0	0.0	..	0.0	0.0	0.0	0.0
4300 Estate, inheritance and gift taxes	..	0.2	0.3	0.3	0.3	..	0.0	0.0	0.0	0.0
4400 Taxes on financial and capital transactions	..	2.0	2.4	3.2	3.5	..	0.3	0.2	0.2	0.2
4500 Non-recurrent taxes	..	0.0	0.0	0.0	0.0	..	0.0	0.0	0.0	0.0
4600 Other recurrent taxes on property	..	0.0	0.0	0.0	0.0	..	0.0	0.0	0.0	0.0
5000 Taxes on goods and services	..	**86.9**	**182.8**	**277.3**	**294.1**	..	**11.6**	**12.6**	**13.1**	**12.8**
5100 Taxes on production, sale, transfer, etc	..	84.9	176.0	268.3	281.8	..	11.3	12.2	12.6	12.3
5110 General taxes	..	51.6	109.7	172.3	182.1	..	6.9	7.6	8.1	7.9
5111 Value added taxes	..	51.6	109.7	172.3	182.1	..	6.9	7.6	8.1	7.9
5120 Taxes on specific goods and services	..	33.3	66.3	96.0	99.6	..	4.4	4.6	4.5	4.3
5121 Excises	..	27.2	62.0	82.1	83.9	..	3.6	4.3	3.9	3.7
5200 Taxes on use of goods and perform activities	..	2.0	6.8	9.0	12.4	..	0.3	0.5	0.4	0.5
5300 Unallocable between 5100 and 5200	..	0.0	0.0	0.0	0.0	..	0.0	0.0	0.0	0.0
6000 Other taxes	..	**0.3**	**0.6**	**1.1**	**1.1**	..	**0.0**	**0.0**	**0.1**	**0.0**
Non-wastable tax credits										
Non-wastable tax credits against 1000	..	..	..	..	..	..	..	..	..	..
Transfer component	..	..	..	..	..	..	..	..	..	..
Tax expenditure component	..	..	..	..	..	..	..	..	..	..
Revenues collected on behalf of the EU										
Revenues collected on behalf of the EU, total	..	..	1.7	3.9	4.5	..	..	0.1	0.2	0.2
Customs duties	..	..	1.6	3.9	4.5	..	..	0.1	0.2	0.2

.. Not available

Note: More detailed country data and country notes are available in online chapter 5 "Detailed country tables": https://doi.org/10.1787/0bbc27da-en. Full time series can be accessed at http://oe.cd/full-time-series.

The total tax revenue has been reduced by the amount of any capital transfer that represents uncollected taxes. The capital transfer has been allocated between tax headings in proportion to the reported tax revenue. Therefore, the tax revenue amounts are different to those reported in the detailed country data available in online chapter 5 "Detailed country tables".

Source: Ministry of Finance, Economic Department.

StatLink https://stat.link/xfzqy8

Table 4.58. Poland, tax revenue and % of GDP by level of government and main taxes

	Billion PLN					% of GDP				
	1990	2000	2010	2018	2019	1990	2000	2010	2018	2019
Federal or Central government										
Total tax revenue	**..**	**126.9**	**238.4**	**369.1**	**396.7**	**..**	**17.0**	**16.5**	**17.4**	**17.3**
1000 Taxes on income, profits and capital gains	..	40.0	57.7	95.2	105.1	..	5.3	4.0	4.5	4.6
2000 Social security contributions	..	0.0	0.0	0.0	0.0	..	0.0	0.0	0.0	0.0
3000 Taxes on payroll and workforce	..	1.6	3.7	4.7	5.9	..	0.2	0.3	0.2	0.3
4000 Taxes on property	..	0.0	0.0	0.0	0.0	..	0.0	0.0	0.0	0.0
5000 Taxes on goods and services	..	85.3	177.0	269.2	285.7	..	11.4	12.2	12.7	12.5
6000 Other taxes	..	0.0	0.0	0.0	0.0	..	0.0	0.0	0.0	0.0
State/Regional										
Total tax revenue	**..**	**..**	**..**	**..**	**..**	**..**	**..**	**..**	**..**	**..**
1000 Taxes on income, profits and capital gains	..	..	..	..	..	..	..	..	..	..
2000 Social security contributions	..	..	..	..	..	..	..	..	..	..
3000 Taxes on payroll and workforce	..	..	..	..	..	..	..	..	..	..
4000 Taxes on property	..	..	..	..	..	..	..	..	..	..
5000 Taxes on goods and services	..	..	..	..	..	..	..	..	..	..
6000 Other taxes	..	..	..	..	..	..	..	..	..	..
Local government										
Total tax revenue	**..**	**22.7**	**57.1**	**94.9**	**101.5**	**..**	**3.0**	**3.9**	**4.5**	**4.4**
1000 Taxes on income, profits and capital gains	..	10.3	33.3	61.8	67.4	..	1.4	2.3	2.9	2.9
2000 Social security contributions	..	0.0	0.0	0.0	0.0	..	0.0	0.0	0.0	0.0
3000 Taxes on payroll and workforce	..	0.0	0.0	0.0	0.0	..	0.0	0.0	0.0	0.0
4000 Taxes on property	..	10.6	19.1	27.9	29.0	..	1.4	1.3	1.3	1.3
5000 Taxes on goods and services	..	1.5	4.1	4.2	4.0	..	0.2	0.3	0.2	0.2
6000 Other taxes	..	0.3	0.6	1.1	1.1	..	0.0	0.0	0.1	0.0
Social Security Funds										
Total tax revenue	**..**	**96.4**	**156.0**	**277.7**	**302.3**	**..**	**12.9**	**10.8**	**13.1**	**13.2**
1000 Taxes on income, profits and capital gains	..	0.0	0.0	0.0	0.0	..	0.0	0.0	0.0	0.0
2000 Social security contributions	..	96.4	156.0	277.7	302.3	..	12.9	10.8	13.1	13.2
3000 Taxes on payroll and workforce	..	0.0	0.0	0.0	0.0	..	0.0	0.0	0.0	0.0
4000 Taxes on property	..	0.0	0.0	0.0	0.0	..	0.0	0.0	0.0	0.0
5000 Taxes on goods and services	..	0.0	0.0	0.0	0.0	..	0.0	0.0	0.0	0.0
6000 Other taxes	..	0.0	0.0	0.0	0.0	..	0.0	0.0	0.0	0.0

.. Not available

Note: More detailed country data and country notes are available in online chapter 6 "Tax revenues by sub-sectors of general government": https://doi.org/10.1787/0bbc27da-en. Full time series can be accessed at http://oe.cd/full-time-series.

The total tax revenue has been reduced by the amount of any capital transfer that represents uncollected taxes. The capital transfer has been allocated between tax headings in proportion to the reported tax revenue. Therefore, the tax revenue amounts are different to those reported in the detailed country data available in online chapter 6 "Tax revenues by sub-sectors of general government".

Source: Ministry of Finance, Economic Department.

StatLink https://stat.link/fhk706

Table 4.59. Portugal, tax revenue and % of GDP by selected tax category

	Billion EUR					% of GDP				
	1990	2000	2010	2018	2019	1990	2000	2010	2018	2019
Total tax revenue	**14.8**	**39.7**	**54.5**	**71.1**	**73.8**	**26.5**	**30.9**	**30.4**	**34.7**	**34.5**
1000 Taxes on income, profits and capital gains	**3.8**	**11.7**	**14.6**	**20.1**	**20.2**	**6.8**	**9.1**	**8.1**	**9.8**	**9.5**
1100 Of individuals	2.4	6.8	9.6	13.3	13.6	4.2	5.3	5.4	6.5	6.3
1200 Corporate	1.2	4.7	4.9	6.8	6.7	2.1	3.7	2.7	3.3	3.1
1300 Unallocable between 1100 and 1200	0.3	0.2	0.0	0.0	0.0	0.5	0.1	0.0	0.0	0.0
2000 Social security contributions	**4.0**	**10.2**	**15.5**	**19.1**	**20.5**	**7.2**	**7.9**	**8.6**	**9.3**	**9.6**
2100 Employees	1.5	4.3	6.7	7.7	8.2	2.6	3.3	3.7	3.7	3.8
2200 Employers	2.4	5.9	8.8	11.4	12.4	4.3	4.6	4.9	5.6	5.8
2300 Self-employed or non-employed	0.1	0.0	0.0	0.0	0.0	0.3	0.0	0.0	0.0	0.0
2400 Unallocable between 2100, 2200 and 2300	0.0	0.0	0.0	0.0	0.0	0.0	0.0	0.0	0.0	0.0
3000 Taxes on payroll and workforce	**0.0**	**0.0**	**0.0**	**0.0**	**0.0**	**0.0**	**0.0**	**0.0**	**0.0**	**0.0**
4000 Taxes on property	**0.4**	**1.5**	**2.0**	**3.0**	**3.0**	**0.7**	**1.1**	**1.1**	**1.4**	**1.4**
4100 Recurrent taxes on immovable property	0.1	0.5	1.1	1.6	1.7	0.2	0.4	0.6	0.8	0.8
4200 Recurrent taxes on net wealth	0.0	0.0	0.0	0.0	0.0	0.0	0.0	0.0	0.0	0.0
4300 Estate, inheritance and gift taxes	0.1	0.1	0.1	0.0	0.0	0.1	0.1	0.0	0.0	0.0
4400 Taxes on financial and capital transactions	0.2	0.9	0.8	1.3	1.4	0.3	0.7	0.5	0.6	0.6
4500 Non-recurrent taxes	0.0	0.0	0.0	0.0	0.0	0.0	0.0	0.0	0.0	0.0
4600 Other recurrent taxes on property	0.0	0.0	0.0	0.0	0.0	0.0	0.0	0.0	0.0	0.0
5000 Taxes on goods and services	**6.6**	**16.2**	**22.0**	**28.2**	**29.4**	**11.7**	**12.6**	**12.3**	**13.8**	**13.7**
5100 Taxes on production, sale, transfer, etc	6.4	15.8	21.4	27.0	28.1	11.5	12.3	11.9	13.2	13.1
5110 General taxes	2.9	9.7	13.5	17.9	18.8	5.2	7.6	7.5	8.7	8.8
5111 Value added taxes	2.9	9.7	13.5	17.9	18.8	5.2	7.6	7.5	8.7	8.8
5120 Taxes on specific goods and services	3.5	6.1	7.9	9.2	9.3	6.3	4.8	4.4	4.5	4.3
5121 Excises	2.1	4.5	5.7	6.2	6.2	3.7	3.5	3.1	3.0	2.9
5200 Taxes on use of goods and perform activities	0.1	0.3	0.6	1.2	1.3	0.2	0.2	0.3	0.6	0.6
5300 Unallocable between 5100 and 5200	0.0	0.0	0.0	0.0	0.0	0.0	0.0	0.0	0.0	0.0
6000 Other taxes	**0.0**	**0.2**	**0.4**	**0.7**	**0.6**	**0.1**	**0.2**	**0.2**	**0.3**	**0.3**
Non-wastable tax credits										
Non-wastable tax credits against 1000	..	..	..	..	..	..	..	..	..	..
Transfer component	..	..	..	..	..	..	..	..	..	..
Tax expenditure component	..	..	..	..	..	..	..	..	..	..
Revenues collected on behalf of the EU										
Revenues collected on behalf of the EU, total	0.2	0.2	0.2	0.4	0.4	0.3	0.2	0.1	0.2	0.2
Customs duties	..	0.2	0.2	0.2	0.2	..	0.1	0.1	0.1	0.1
SRF contributions	..	..	..	0.1	0.1	..	..	..	0.1	0.1

.. Not available

Note: More detailed country data and country notes are available in online chapter 5 "Detailed country tables": https://doi.org/10.1787/0bbc27da-en. Full time series can be accessed at http://oe.cd/full-time-series.

Source: Instituto Nacionale de Estatistica; Conta do Estado, Contas de Gerência dos Fundos e Serviços Autonomos da Administraçao Central; Estatisticas das Financas publicas; Relatorio do Instituto de Gestao Financeira da Seguranta Social, Contas de Gerência das Regioes Autonomas da Madeira e dos Atores.

StatLink https://stat.link/9gjvey

Table 4.60. Portugal, tax revenue and % of GDP by level of government and main taxes

	Billion EUR					% of GDP				
	1990	2000	2010	2018	2019	1990	2000	2010	2018	2019
Federal or Central government										
Total tax revenue	**9.8**	**27.6**	**36.4**	**47.5**	**48.5**	**17.6**	**21.5**	**20.2**	**23.2**	**22.7**
1000 Taxes on income, profits and capital gains	3.6	11.1	13.5	18.8	18.9	6.4	8.7	7.5	9.2	8.8
2000 Social security contributions	0.0	1.3	1.9	2.1	2.1	0.0	1.0	1.1	1.0	1.0
3000 Taxes on payroll and workforce	0.0	0.0	0.0	0.0	0.0	0.0	0.0	0.0	0.0	0.0
4000 Taxes on property	0.1	0.3	0.3	0.5	0.5	0.1	0.2	0.2	0.2	0.2
5000 Taxes on goods and services	6.1	14.7	20.2	25.4	26.5	10.9	11.4	11.2	12.4	12.4
6000 Other taxes	0.0	0.2	0.4	0.7	0.6	0.1	0.2	0.2	0.3	0.3
State/Regional										
Total tax revenue	..	..	..	..	..	..	..	..	..	..
1000 Taxes on income, profits and capital gains	..	..	..	..	..	..	..	..	..	..
2000 Social security contributions	..	..	..	..	..	..	..	..	..	..
3000 Taxes on payroll and workforce	..	..	..	..	..	..	..	..	..	..
4000 Taxes on property	..	..	..	..	..	..	..	..	..	..
5000 Taxes on goods and services	..	..	..	..	..	..	..	..	..	..
6000 Other taxes	..	..	..	..	..	..	..	..	..	..
Local government										
Total tax revenue	**0.8**	**2.5**	**3.6**	**5.1**	**5.3**	**1.5**	**2.0**	**2.0**	**2.5**	**2.5**
1000 Taxes on income, profits and capital gains	0.2	0.6	1.1	1.3	1.3	0.4	0.4	0.6	0.6	0.6
2000 Social security contributions	0.0	0.0	0.0	0.0	0.0	0.0	0.0	0.0	0.0	0.0
3000 Taxes on payroll and workforce	0.0	0.0	0.0	0.0	0.0	0.0	0.0	0.0	0.0	0.0
4000 Taxes on property	0.3	1.2	1.7	2.5	2.5	0.6	0.9	1.0	1.2	1.2
5000 Taxes on goods and services	0.3	0.7	0.8	1.4	1.4	0.5	0.6	0.4	0.7	0.7
6000 Other taxes	0.0	0.0	0.0	0.0	0.0	0.0	0.0	0.0	0.0	0.0
Social Security Funds										
Total tax revenue	**4.0**	**9.4**	**14.4**	**18.1**	**19.6**	**7.2**	**7.3**	**8.0**	**8.8**	**9.2**
1000 Taxes on income, profits and capital gains	0.0	0.0	0.0	0.0	0.0	0.0	0.0	0.0	0.0	0.0
2000 Social security contributions	4.0	8.8	13.5	17.0	18.5	7.2	6.9	7.5	8.3	8.6
3000 Taxes on payroll and workforce	0.0	0.0	0.0	0.0	0.0	0.0	0.0	0.0	0.0	0.0
4000 Taxes on property	0.0	0.0	0.0	0.0	0.0	0.0	0.0	0.0	0.0	0.0
5000 Taxes on goods and services	0.0	0.5	0.8	1.1	1.1	0.0	0.4	0.5	0.5	0.5
6000 Other taxes	0.0	0.0	0.0	0.0	0.0	0.0	0.0	0.0	0.0	0.0

.. Not available

Note: More detailed country data and country notes are available in online chapter 6 "Tax revenues by sub-sectors of general government": https://doi.org/10.1787/0bbc27da-en. Full time series can be accessed at http://oe.cd/full-time-series.

Source: Instituto Nacionale de Estatistica; Conta do Estado, Contas de Gerência dos Fundos e Serviços Autonomos da Administraçao Central; Estatisticas das Financas publicas; Relatorio do Instituto de Gestao Financeira da Seguranta Social, Contas de Gerência das Regioes Autonomas da Madeira e dos Atores.

StatLink https://stat.link/rfhiwv

Table 4.61. Slovak Republic, tax revenue and % of GDP by selected tax category

	Billion EUR					% of GDP				
	1990	2000	2010	2018	2019	1990	2000	2010	2018	2019
Total tax revenue	..	**10.6**	**19.2**	**30.6**	**32.5**	..	**33.6**	**28.1**	**34.2**	**34.6**
1000 Taxes on income, profits and capital gains	..	**2.2**	**3.6**	**6.4**	**6.6**	..	**6.9**	**5.3**	**7.1**	**7.1**
1100 Of individuals	..	1.1	1.8	3.2	3.5	..	3.3	2.6	3.6	3.8
1200 Corporate	..	0.8	1.7	2.9	2.8	..	2.6	2.4	3.3	3.0
1300 Unallocable between 1100 and 1200	..	0.3	0.2	0.2	0.2	..	1.0	0.2	0.2	0.3
2000 Social security contributions	..	**4.4**	**8.2**	**13.1**	**14.1**	..	**13.9**	**12.0**	**14.7**	**15.0**
2100 Employees	..	0.9	2.1	3.3	3.4	..	2.8	3.0	3.7	3.7
2200 Employers	..	2.9	4.6	7.8	8.5	..	9.0	6.7	8.7	9.1
2300 Self-employed or non-employed	..	0.7	1.5	2.1	2.1	..	2.1	2.2	2.4	2.2
2400 Unallocable between 2100, 2200 and 2300	..	0.0	0.0	0.0	0.0	..	0.0	0.0	0.0	0.0
3000 Taxes on payroll and workforce	..	**0.0**	**0.0**	**0.0**	**0.0**	..	**0.0**	**0.0**	**0.0**	**0.0**
4000 Taxes on property	..	**0.2**	**0.3**	**0.4**	**0.4**	..	**0.6**	**0.4**	**0.4**	**0.4**
4100 Recurrent taxes on immovable property	..	0.1	0.3	0.4	0.4	..	0.5	0.4	0.4	0.4
4200 Recurrent taxes on net wealth	..	0.0	0.0	0.0	0.0	..	0.0	0.0	0.0	0.0
4300 Estate, inheritance and gift taxes	..	0.0	0.0	0.0	0.0	..	0.0	0.0	0.0	0.0
4400 Taxes on financial and capital transactions	..	0.0	0.0	0.0	0.0	..	0.1	0.0	0.0	0.0
4500 Non-recurrent taxes	..	0.0	0.0	0.0	0.0	..	0.0	0.0	0.0	0.0
4600 Other recurrent taxes on property	..	0.0	0.0	0.0	0.0	..	0.0	0.0	0.0	0.0
5000 Taxes on goods and services	..	**3.9**	**7.1**	**10.7**	**11.4**	..	**12.2**	**10.5**	**11.9**	**12.1**
5100 Taxes on production, sale, transfer, etc	..	3.6	6.6	9.9	10.5	..	11.5	9.6	11.1	11.2
5110 General taxes	..	2.2	4.2	6.3	6.8	..	6.8	6.1	7.1	7.3
5111 Value added taxes	..	2.2	4.2	6.3	6.8	..	6.8	6.1	7.1	7.3
5120 Taxes on specific goods and services	..	1.5	2.4	3.6	3.7	..	4.6	3.5	4.0	3.9
5121 Excises	..	1.0	2.1	2.8	2.8	..	3.1	3.1	3.1	3.0
5200 Taxes on use of goods and perform activities	..	0.2	0.4	0.6	0.7	..	0.7	0.6	0.7	0.7
5300 Unallocable between 5100 and 5200	..	0.0	0.1	0.2	0.2	..	0.0	0.2	0.2	0.2
6000 Other taxes	..	**0.0**	**0.0**	**0.0**	**0.0**	..	**0.0**	**0.0**	**0.0**	**0.0**
Non-wastable tax credits										
Non-wastable tax credits against 1000	..	..	0.3	0.3	0.3	..	..	0.4	0.3	0.4
Transfer component	..	..	..	..	..	..	..	..	..	..
Tax expenditure component	..	..	..	..	..	..	..	..	..	..
Revenues collected on behalf of the EU										
Revenues collected on behalf of the EU, total	..	..	0.1	0.2	0.1	..	..	0.2	0.2	0.2
Customs duties	..	..	0.1	0.1	0.1	..	..	0.2	0.2	0.1
SRF contributions	..	..	..	0.0	0.0	..	..	..	0.0	0.0

.. Not available

Note: More detailed country data and country notes are available in online chapter 5 "Detailed country tables": https://doi.org/10.1787/0bbc27da-en. Full time series can be accessed at http://oe.cd/full-time-series.

Source: Ministry of Finance.

StatLink https://stat.link/1gwrs3

Table 4.62. Slovak Republic, tax revenue and % of GDP by level of government and main taxes

	Billion EUR					% of GDP				
	1990	2000	2010	2018	2019	1990	2000	2010	2018	2019
Federal or Central government										
Total tax revenue	..	**6.2**	**10.5**	**17.0**	**18.0**	..	**19.5**	**15.5**	**19.0**	**19.2**
1000 Taxes on income, profits and capital gains	..	2.2	3.6	6.4	6.6	..	6.9	5.3	7.1	7.1
2000 Social security contributions	..	0.1	0.2	0.3	0.4	..	0.3	0.3	0.4	0.4
3000 Taxes on payroll and workforce	..	0.0	0.0	0.0	0.0	..	0.0	0.0	0.0	0.0
4000 Taxes on property	..	0.1	0.0	0.0	0.0	..	0.2	0.0	0.0	0.0
5000 Taxes on goods and services	..	3.9	6.7	10.3	11.0	..	12.2	9.8	11.6	11.7
6000 Other taxes	..	0.0	0.0	0.0	0.0	..	0.0	0.0	0.0	0.0
State/Regional										
Total tax revenue	..	..	..	..	..	..	..	..	..	..
1000 Taxes on income, profits and capital gains	..	..	..	..	..	..	..	..	..	..
2000 Social security contributions	..	..	..	..	..	..	..	..	..	..
3000 Taxes on payroll and workforce	..	..	..	..	..	..	..	..	..	..
4000 Taxes on property	..	..	..	..	..	..	..	..	..	..
5000 Taxes on goods and services	..	..	..	..	..	..	..	..	..	..
6000 Other taxes	..	..	..	..	..	..	..	..	..	..
Local government										
Total tax revenue	..	**0.1**	**0.5**	**0.6**	**0.6**	..	**0.5**	**0.8**	**0.6**	**0.6**
1000 Taxes on income, profits and capital gains	..	0.0	0.0	0.0	0.0	..	0.0	0.0	0.0	0.0
2000 Social security contributions	..	0.0	0.0	0.0	0.0	..	0.0	0.0	0.0	0.0
3000 Taxes on payroll and workforce	..	0.0	0.0	0.0	0.0	..	0.0	0.0	0.0	0.0
4000 Taxes on property	..	0.1	0.3	0.4	0.4	..	0.4	0.4	0.4	0.4
5000 Taxes on goods and services	..	0.0	0.3	0.2	0.2	..	0.0	0.4	0.2	0.2
6000 Other taxes	..	0.0	0.0	0.0	0.0	..	0.0	0.0	0.0	0.0
Social Security Funds										
Total tax revenue	..	**4.3**	**7.9**	**12.8**	**13.7**	..	**13.6**	**11.6**	**14.4**	**14.6**
1000 Taxes on income, profits and capital gains	..	0.0	0.0	0.0	0.0	..	0.0	0.0	0.0	0.0
2000 Social security contributions	..	4.3	7.9	12.8	13.7	..	13.6	11.6	14.4	14.6
3000 Taxes on payroll and workforce	..	0.0	0.0	0.0	0.0	..	0.0	0.0	0.0	0.0
4000 Taxes on property	..	0.0	0.0	0.0	0.0	..	0.0	0.0	0.0	0.0
5000 Taxes on goods and services	..	0.0	0.0	0.0	0.0	..	0.0	0.0	0.0	0.0
6000 Other taxes	..	0.0	0.0	0.0	0.0	..	0.0	0.0	0.0	0.0

.. Not available

Note: More detailed country data and country notes are available in online chapter 6 "Tax revenues by sub-sectors of general government": https://doi.org/10.1787/0bbc27da-en. Full time series can be accessed at http://oe.cd/full-time-series.

Source: Ministry of Finance.

StatLink https://stat.link/zb93wx

Table 4.63. Slovenia, tax revenue and % of GDP by selected tax category

	Billion EUR					% of GDP				
	1990	2000	2010	2018	2019	1990	2000	2010	2018	2019
Total tax revenue	**..**	**7.1**	**13.8**	**17.1**	**18.0**	**..**	**37.7**	**37.8**	**37.3**	**37.2**
1000 Taxes on income, profits and capital gains	**..**	**1.3**	**2.7**	**3.3**	**3.5**	**..**	**6.8**	**7.4**	**7.3**	**7.2**
1100 Of individuals	..	1.0	2.0	2.5	2.5	..	5.5	5.6	5.4	5.3
1200 Corporate	..	0.2	0.7	0.9	1.0	..	1.1	1.8	1.9	2.0
1300 Unallocable between 1100 and 1200	..	0.0	0.0	0.0	0.0	..	0.1	0.0	0.0	0.0
2000 Social security contributions	**..**	**2.8**	**5.8**	**7.1**	**7.6**	**..**	**15.0**	**15.8**	**15.4**	**15.7**
2100 Employees	..	1.4	2.8	3.5	3.8	..	7.7	7.7	7.6	7.7
2200 Employers	..	1.0	2.1	2.6	2.8	..	5.4	5.7	5.6	5.7
2300 Self-employed or non-employed	..	0.4	0.9	1.0	1.1	..	1.9	2.5	2.2	2.2
2400 Unallocable between 2100, 2200 and 2300	..	0.0	0.0	0.0	0.0	..	0.0	0.0	0.0	0.0
3000 Taxes on payroll and workforce	**..**	**0.3**	**0.0**	**0.0**	**0.0**	**..**	**1.5**	**0.1**	**0.0**	**0.0**
4000 Taxes on property	**..**	**0.1**	**0.2**	**0.3**	**0.3**	**..**	**0.6**	**0.6**	**0.6**	**0.6**
4100 Recurrent taxes on immovable property	..	0.1	0.2	0.2	0.2	..	0.4	0.5	0.5	0.5
4200 Recurrent taxes on net wealth	..	0.0	0.0	0.0	0.0	..	0.0	0.0	0.0	0.0
4300 Estate, inheritance and gift taxes	..	0.0	0.0	0.0	0.0	..	0.0	0.0	0.0	0.0
4400 Taxes on financial and capital transactions	..	0.0	0.0	0.0	0.0	..	0.1	0.1	0.1	0.1
4500 Non-recurrent taxes	..	0.0	0.0	0.0	0.0	..	0.1	0.0	0.0	0.0
4600 Other recurrent taxes on property	..	0.0	0.0	0.0	0.0	..	0.0	0.0	0.0	0.0
5000 Taxes on goods and services	**..**	**2.6**	**5.1**	**6.4**	**6.6**	**..**	**13.8**	**13.9**	**13.9**	**13.6**
5100 Taxes on production, sale, transfer, etc	..	2.5	4.8	6.0	6.1	..	13.2	13.3	13.0	12.6
5110 General taxes	..	1.6	2.9	3.8	3.9	..	8.7	8.1	8.2	8.0
5111 Value added taxes	..	1.6	2.9	3.8	3.9	..	8.5	8.1	8.2	8.0
5120 Taxes on specific goods and services	..	0.8	1.9	2.2	2.2	..	4.5	5.3	4.8	4.6
5121 Excises	..	0.6	1.6	1.7	1.7	..	3.1	4.3	3.7	3.5
5200 Taxes on use of goods and perform activities	..	0.1	0.2	0.4	0.5	..	0.6	0.6	0.9	1.0
5300 Unallocable between 5100 and 5200	..	0.0	0.0	0.0	0.0	..	0.0	0.0	0.0	0.0
6000 Other taxes	**..**	**0.0**	**0.0**	**0.0**	**0.0**	**..**	**0.0**	**0.0**	**0.0**	**0.0**
Non-wastable tax credits										
Non-wastable tax credits against 1000	..	..	..	..	..	..	..	..	..	..
Transfer component	..	..	..	..	..	..	..	..	..	..
Tax expenditure component	..	..	..	..	..	..	..	..	..	..
Revenues collected on behalf of the EU										
Revenues collected on behalf of the EU, total	..	..	0.1	0.1	0.1	..	..	0.2	0.1	0.1
Customs duties	..	..	0.1	0.1	0.1	..	..	0.2	0.1	0.1
SRF contributions	..	..	..	0.0	0.0	..	..	..	0.0	0.0

.. Not available

Note: More detailed country data and country notes are available in online chapter 5 "Detailed country tables": https://doi.org/10.1787/0bbc27da-en. Full time series can be accessed at http://oe.cd/full-time-series.

Source: Statistical Office of the Republic of Slovenia.

StatLink https://stat.link/aqh7eu

Table 4.64. Slovenia, tax revenue and % of GDP by level of government and main taxes

	Billion EUR					% of GDP				
	1990	2000	2010	2018	2019	1990	2000	2010	2018	2019
Federal or Central government										
Total tax revenue	..	**3.8**	**6.5**	**8.5**	**8.8**	..	**20.2**	**18.0**	**18.5**	**18.2**
1000 Taxes on income, profits and capital gains	..	0.9	1.6	2.2	2.3	..	4.8	4.3	4.7	4.8
2000 Social security contributions	..	0.0	0.1	0.1	0.1	..	0.1	0.2	0.2	0.2
3000 Taxes on payroll and workforce	..	0.3	0.0	0.0	0.0	..	1.5	0.1	0.0	0.0
4000 Taxes on property	..	0.0	0.0	0.0	0.0	..	0.1	0.0	0.0	0.0
5000 Taxes on goods and services	..	2.6	4.9	6.2	6.4	..	13.7	13.5	13.5	13.2
6000 Other taxes	..	0.0	0.0	0.0	0.0	..	0.0	0.0	0.0	0.0
State/Regional										
Total tax revenue	..	..	..	..	..	..	..	..	..	..
1000 Taxes on income, profits and capital gains	..	..	..	..	..	..	..	..	..	..
2000 Social security contributions	..	..	..	..	..	..	..	..	..	..
3000 Taxes on payroll and workforce	..	..	..	..	..	..	..	..	..	..
4000 Taxes on property	..	..	..	..	..	..	..	..	..	..
5000 Taxes on goods and services	..	..	..	..	..	..	..	..	..	..
6000 Other taxes	..	..	..	..	..	..	..	..	..	..
Local government										
Total tax revenue	..	**0.5**	**1.5**	**1.5**	**1.6**	..	**2.7**	**4.0**	**3.4**	**3.3**
1000 Taxes on income, profits and capital gains	..	0.4	1.1	1.2	1.2	..	2.0	3.1	2.6	2.5
2000 Social security contributions	..	0.0	0.0	0.0	0.0	..	0.0	0.0	0.0	0.0
3000 Taxes on payroll and workforce	..	0.0	0.0	0.0	0.0	..	0.0	0.0	0.0	0.0
4000 Taxes on property	..	0.1	0.2	0.3	0.3	..	0.6	0.6	0.6	0.6
5000 Taxes on goods and services	..	0.0	0.1	0.1	0.1	..	0.1	0.3	0.2	0.2
6000 Other taxes	..	0.0	0.0	0.0	0.0	..	0.0	0.0	0.0	0.0
Social Security Funds										
Total tax revenue	..	**2.8**	**5.7**	**7.0**	**7.5**	..	**14.8**	**15.7**	**15.3**	**15.5**
1000 Taxes on income, profits and capital gains	..	0.0	0.0	0.0	0.0	..	0.0	0.0	0.0	0.0
2000 Social security contributions	..	2.8	5.7	7.0	7.5	..	14.8	15.7	15.3	15.5
3000 Taxes on payroll and workforce	..	0.0	0.0	0.0	0.0	..	0.0	0.0	0.0	0.0
4000 Taxes on property	..	0.0	0.0	0.0	0.0	..	0.0	0.0	0.0	0.0
5000 Taxes on goods and services	..	0.0	0.0	0.0	0.0	..	0.0	0.0	0.0	0.0
6000 Other taxes	..	0.0	0.0	0.0	0.0	..	0.0	0.0	0.0	0.0

.. Not available

Note: More detailed country data and country notes are available in online chapter 6 "Tax revenues by sub-sectors of general government": https://doi.org/10.1787/0bbc27da-en. Full time series can be accessed at http://oe.cd/full-time-series.

Source: Statistical Office of the Republic of Slovenia.

StatLink https://stat.link/qnkus2

Table 4.65. Spain, tax revenue and % of GDP by selected tax category

	Billion EUR					% of GDP				
	1990	2000	2010	2018	2019	1990	2000	2010	2018	2019
Total tax revenue	**103.7**	**214.1**	**335.6**	**417.1**	**431.6**	**31.5**	**33.0**	**31.3**	**34.7**	**34.7**
1000 Taxes on income, profits and capital gains	**31.8**	**60.1**	**93.8**	**122.0**	**123.7**	**9.7**	**9.3**	**8.7**	**10.1**	**9.9**
1100 Of individuals	22.5	41.2	74.1	92.4	98.0	6.9	6.4	6.9	7.7	7.9
1200 Corporate	9.1	18.9	19.7	29.7	25.7	2.8	2.9	1.8	2.5	2.1
1300 Unallocable between 1100 and 1200	0.1	0.0	0.0	0.0	0.0	0.0	0.0	0.0	0.0	0.0
2000 Social security contributions	**36.7**	**74.7**	**127.2**	**141.3**	**152.5**	**11.2**	**11.5**	**11.9**	**11.7**	**12.3**
2100 Employees	6.0	11.7	19.4	21.6	23.3	1.8	1.8	1.8	1.8	1.9
2200 Employers	26.4	54.2	89.7	103.4	112.3	8.0	8.4	8.4	8.6	9.0
2300 Self-employed or non-employed	4.4	8.7	18.1	16.3	17.0	1.3	1.4	1.7	1.4	1.4
2400 Unallocable between 2100, 2200 and 2300	0.0	0.0	0.0	0.0	0.0	0.0	0.0	0.0	0.0	0.0
3000 Taxes on payroll and workforce	**0.0**	**0.0**	**0.0**	**0.0**	**0.0**	**0.0**	**0.0**	**0.0**	**0.0**	**0.0**
4000 Taxes on property	**5.7**	**13.8**	**22.2**	**30.5**	**30.5**	**1.7**	**2.1**	**2.1**	**2.5**	**2.5**
4100 Recurrent taxes on immovable property	1.5	4.0	9.7	13.4	13.4	0.4	0.6	0.9	1.1	1.1
4200 Recurrent taxes on net wealth	0.6	1.4	0.7	2.2	2.2	0.2	0.2	0.1	0.2	0.2
4300 Estate, inheritance and gift taxes	0.4	1.4	2.4	2.7	2.5	0.1	0.2	0.2	0.2	0.2
4400 Taxes on financial and capital transactions	2.5	5.9	7.6	9.3	9.3	0.8	0.9	0.7	0.8	0.7
4500 Non-recurrent taxes	0.6	1.1	1.8	2.9	3.0	0.2	0.2	0.2	0.2	0.2
4600 Other recurrent taxes on property	0.0	0.0	0.0	0.0	0.0	0.0	0.0	0.0	0.0	0.0
5000 Taxes on goods and services	**29.4**	**65.5**	**92.3**	**123.0**	**124.7**	**9.0**	**10.1**	**8.6**	**10.2**	**10.0**
5100 Taxes on production, sale, transfer, etc	26.7	59.4	85.0	113.8	115.0	8.1	9.2	7.9	9.5	9.2
5110 General taxes	16.6	37.8	55.6	79.4	81.1	5.1	5.8	5.2	6.6	6.5
5111 Value added taxes	16.3	37.8	55.3	79.2	80.9	5.0	5.8	5.2	6.6	6.5
5120 Taxes on specific goods and services	10.1	21.6	29.4	34.4	34.0	3.1	3.3	2.7	2.9	2.7
5121 Excises	6.0	18.0	24.4	26.8	26.2	1.8	2.8	2.3	2.2	2.1
5200 Taxes on use of goods and perform activities	2.6	6.1	7.4	9.2	9.7	0.8	0.9	0.7	0.8	0.8
5300 Unallocable between 5100 and 5200	0.1	0.0	0.0	0.0	0.0	0.0	0.0	0.0	0.0	0.0
6000 Other taxes	**0.0**	**0.0**	**0.0**	**0.2**	**0.2**	**0.0**	**0.0**	**0.0**	**0.0**	**0.0**
Non-wastable tax credits										
Non-wastable tax credits against 1000	..	..	1.9	3.1	2.6	..	..	0.2	0.3	0.2
Transfer component	..	..	1.2	2.2	1.4	..	..	0.1	0.2	0.1
Tax expenditure component	..	..	0.7	0.9	1.1	..	..	0.1	0.1	0.1
Revenues collected on behalf of the EU										
Revenues collected on behalf of the EU, total	0.5	1.0	1.5	2.7	2.7	0.2	0.2	0.1	0.2	0.2
Customs duties	..	1.0	1.5	1.9	2.0	..	0.1	0.1	0.2	0.2
SRF contributions	..	..	..	0.7	0.7	..	..	..	0.1	0.1

.. Not available

Note: More detailed country data and country notes are available in online chapter 5 "Detailed country tables": https://doi.org/10.1787/0bbc27da-en. Full time series can be accessed at http://oe.cd/full-time-series.

Source: Información Estadística del Ministerio de Hacienda (for national taxes). Cuentas de las Administraciones Públicas (for local taxes and social security) both published by Secretaría General Técnica del Ministerio de Hacienda.

StatLink https://stat.link/yfztnk

Table 4.66. Spain, tax revenue and % of GDP by level of government and main taxes

	Billion EUR					% of GDP				
	1990	2000	2010	2018	2019	1990	2000	2010	2018	2019
Federal or Central government										
Total tax revenue	**53.7**	**104.7**	**135.9**	**173.8**	**173.6**	**16.3**	**16.2**	**12.7**	**14.4**	**14.0**
1000 Taxes on income, profits and capital gains	29.5	51.0	60.6	71.7	69.6	9.0	7.9	5.6	6.0	5.6
2000 Social security contributions	0.4	2.3	3.5	3.5	3.5	0.1	0.4	0.3	0.3	0.3
3000 Taxes on payroll and workforce	0.0	0.0	0.0	0.0	0.0	0.0	0.0	0.0	0.0	0.0
4000 Taxes on property	0.4	0.4	0.1	0.4	0.3	0.1	0.1	0.0	0.0	0.0
5000 Taxes on goods and services	23.4	51.1	71.7	98.0	100.2	7.1	7.9	6.7	8.1	8.0
6000 Other taxes	0.0	0.0	0.0	0.2	0.1	0.0	0.0	0.0	0.0	0.0
State/Regional										
Total tax revenue	**5.0**	**16.9**	**44.1**	**63.8**	**66.7**	**1.5**	**2.6**	**4.1**	**5.3**	**5.4**
1000 Taxes on income, profits and capital gains	0.4	5.6	28.1	43.4	47.0	0.1	0.9	2.6	3.6	3.8
2000 Social security contributions	0.0	0.0	0.0	0.0	0.0	0.0	0.0	0.0	0.0	0.0
3000 Taxes on payroll and workforce	0.0	0.0	0.0	0.0	0.0	0.0	0.0	0.0	0.0	0.0
4000 Taxes on property	3.0	7.7	9.7	12.7	12.8	0.9	1.2	0.9	1.1	1.0
5000 Taxes on goods and services	1.6	3.6	6.3	7.7	6.9	0.5	0.6	0.6	0.6	0.6
6000 Other taxes	0.0	0.0	0.0	0.0	0.0	0.0	0.0	0.0	0.0	0.0
Local government										
Total tax revenue	**8.1**	**19.0**	**30.3**	**39.0**	**39.5**	**2.5**	**2.9**	**2.8**	**3.2**	**3.2**
1000 Taxes on income, profits and capital gains	1.9	3.5	5.2	6.9	7.1	0.6	0.5	0.5	0.6	0.6
2000 Social security contributions	0.0	0.0	0.0	0.0	0.0	0.0	0.0	0.0	0.0	0.0
3000 Taxes on payroll and workforce	0.0	0.0	0.0	0.0	0.0	0.0	0.0	0.0	0.0	0.0
4000 Taxes on property	2.3	5.8	12.4	17.4	17.4	0.7	0.9	1.2	1.4	1.4
5000 Taxes on goods and services	3.9	9.7	12.8	14.6	15.0	1.2	1.5	1.2	1.2	1.2
6000 Other taxes	0.0	0.0	0.0	0.0	0.0	0.0	0.0	0.0	0.0	0.0
Social Security Funds										
Total tax revenue	**36.4**	**72.4**	**123.7**	**137.8**	**149.0**	**11.1**	**11.2**	**11.5**	**11.5**	**12.0**
1000 Taxes on income, profits and capital gains	0.0	0.0	0.0	0.0	0.0	0.0	0.0	0.0	0.0	0.0
2000 Social security contributions	36.4	72.4	123.7	137.8	149.0	11.1	11.2	11.5	11.5	12.0
3000 Taxes on payroll and workforce	0.0	0.0	0.0	0.0	0.0	0.0	0.0	0.0	0.0	0.0
4000 Taxes on property	0.0	0.0	0.0	0.0	0.0	0.0	0.0	0.0	0.0	0.0
5000 Taxes on goods and services	0.0	0.0	0.0	0.0	0.0	0.0	0.0	0.0	0.0	0.0
6000 Other taxes	0.0	0.0	0.0	0.0	0.0	0.0	0.0	0.0	0.0	0.0

Note: More detailed country data and country notes are available in online chapter 6 "Tax revenues by sub-sectors of general government": https://doi.org/10.1787/0bbc27da-en. Full time series can be accessed at http://oe.cd/full-time-series.

Source: Información Estadística del Ministerio de Hacienda (for national taxes). Cuentas de las Administraciones Públicas (for local taxes and social security) both published by Secretaría General Técnica del Ministerio de Hacienda.

StatLink https://stat.link/udqxse

Table 4.67. Sweden, tax revenue and % of GDP by selected tax category

	Billion SEK					% of GDP				
	1990	2000	2010	2018	2019	1990	2000	2010	2018	2019
Total tax revenue	**756.0**	**1 204.8**	**1 532.3**	**2 113.5**	**2 162.9**	**48.8**	**50.0**	**42.9**	**43.8**	**42.8**
1000 Taxes on income, profits and capital gains	**314.8**	**514.7**	**546.7**	**761.0**	**772.1**	**20.3**	**21.4**	**15.3**	**15.8**	**15.3**
1100 Of individuals	291.1	427.0	430.9	623.6	620.2	18.8	17.7	12.1	12.9	12.3
1200 Corporate	23.7	87.8	115.8	137.4	152.0	1.5	3.6	3.2	2.8	3.0
1300 Unallocable between 1100 and 1200	0.0	0.0	0.0	0.0	0.0	0.0	0.0	0.0	0.0	0.0
2000 Social security contributions	**205.9**	**307.0**	**384.7**	**463.3**	**462.9**	**13.3**	**12.7**	**10.8**	**9.6**	**9.2**
2100 Employees	0.8	63.1	89.2	123.7	128.2	0.1	2.6	2.5	2.6	2.5
2200 Employers	196.9	237.6	288.3	335.4	331.1	12.7	9.9	8.1	6.9	6.6
2300 Self-employed or non-employed	8.1	5.6	7.6	4.8	4.3	0.5	0.2	0.2	0.1	0.1
2400 Unallocable between 2100, 2200 and 2300	0.0	0.8	-0.4	-0.5	-0.7	0.0	0.0	0.0	0.0	0.0
3000 Taxes on payroll and workforce	**18.7**	**50.1**	**107.5**	**245.0**	**268.8**	**1.2**	**2.1**	**3.0**	**5.1**	**5.3**
4000 Taxes on property	**26.6**	**39.9**	**36.5**	**45.8**	**47.3**	**1.7**	**1.7**	**1.0**	**0.9**	**0.9**
4100 Recurrent taxes on immovable property	8.9	23.3	26.4	33.2	34.4	0.6	1.0	0.7	0.7	0.7
4200 Recurrent taxes on net wealth	3.2	8.2	0.0	0.0	0.0	0.2	0.3	0.0	0.0	0.0
4300 Estate, inheritance and gift taxes	1.4	2.5	0.0	0.0	0.0	0.1	0.1	0.0	0.0	0.0
4400 Taxes on financial and capital transactions	13.1	5.8	10.1	12.6	12.9	0.8	0.2	0.3	0.3	0.3
4500 Non-recurrent taxes	0.0	0.0	0.0	0.0	0.0	0.0	0.0	0.0	0.0	0.0
4600 Other recurrent taxes on property	0.0	0.0	0.0	0.0	0.0	0.0	0.0	0.0	0.0	0.0
5000 Taxes on goods and services	**188.7**	**291.6**	**455.4**	**596.4**	**610.2**	**12.2**	**12.1**	**12.7**	**12.4**	**12.1**
5100 Taxes on production, sale, transfer, etc	181.6	284.2	439.1	576.5	589.5	11.7	11.8	12.3	11.9	11.7
5110 General taxes	112.4	199.6	326.7	445.5	459.8	7.3	8.3	9.1	9.2	9.1
5111 Value added taxes	112.4	197.5	322.6	445.4	459.7	7.3	8.2	9.0	9.2	9.1
5120 Taxes on specific goods and services	69.2	84.6	112.4	131.0	129.7	4.5	3.5	3.1	2.7	2.6
5121 Excises	55.3	70.3	91.5	102.1	104.5	3.6	2.9	2.6	2.1	2.1
5200 Taxes on use of goods and perform activities	7.1	7.4	16.4	19.8	20.7	0.5	0.3	0.5	0.4	0.4
5300 Unallocable between 5100 and 5200	0.0	0.0	0.0	0.0	0.0	0.0	0.0	0.0	0.0	0.0
6000 Other taxes	**1.3**	**1.5**	**1.4**	**1.9**	**1.7**	**0.1**	**0.1**	**0.0**	**0.0**	**0.0**
Non-wastable tax credits										
Non-wastable tax credits against 1000	..	..	..	..	..	..	..	..	..	..
Transfer component	..	..	..	..	..	..	..	..	..	..
Tax expenditure component	..	..	..	..	..	..	..	..	..	..
Revenues collected on behalf of the EU										
Revenues collected on behalf of the EU, total	..	3.8	5.7	6.5	6.9	..	0.2	0.2	0.1	0.1
Customs duties	..	3.4	5.4	6.5	6.9	..	0.1	0.2	0.1	0.1

.. Not available

Note: More detailed country data and country notes are available in online chapter 5 "Detailed country tables": https://doi.org/10.1787/0bbc27da-en. Full time series can be accessed at http://oe.cd/full-time-series.

Source: Monthly reports of central Government Revenues (unpublished) National Audit Bureau, Stockholm. Local Government Finance (SOS), Tax assessment statistics (SOS), National Central Bureau of Statistics, Stockholm. National Accounts (Statistical Reports), National Bureau of Statistics, Stockholm.

StatLink https://stat.link/f5bze1

Table 4.68. Sweden, tax revenue and % of GDP by level of government and main taxes

	Billion SEK					% of GDP				
	1990	2000	2010	2018	2019	1990	2000	2010	2018	2019
Federal or Central government										
Total tax revenue	**383.9**	**737.9**	**806.2**	**1 106.0**	**1 122.7**	**24.8**	**30.6**	**22.6**	**22.9**	**22.2**
1000 Taxes on income, profits and capital gains	94.7	178.4	23.8	34.8	23.9	6.1	7.4	0.7	0.7	0.5
2000 Social security contributions	54.8	180.2	201.2	206.6	196.3	3.5	7.5	5.6	4.3	3.9
3000 Taxes on payroll and workforce	18.7	50.1	107.5	245.0	268.8	1.2	2.1	3.0	5.1	5.3
4000 Taxes on property	26.6	39.9	22.5	27.8	28.6	1.7	1.7	0.6	0.6	0.6
5000 Taxes on goods and services	187.8	287.8	449.8	589.9	603.3	12.1	12.0	12.6	12.2	11.9
6000 Other taxes	1.3	1.5	1.4	1.9	1.7	0.1	0.1	0.0	0.0	0.0
State/Regional										
Total tax revenue	..	..	..	..	..	..	..	..	..	..
1000 Taxes on income, profits and capital gains	..	..	..	..	..	..	..	..	..	..
2000 Social security contributions	..	..	..	..	..	..	..	..	..	..
3000 Taxes on payroll and workforce	..	..	..	..	..	..	..	..	..	..
4000 Taxes on property	..	..	..	..	..	..	..	..	..	..
5000 Taxes on goods and services	..	..	..	..	..	..	..	..	..	..
6000 Other taxes	..	..	..	..	..	..	..	..	..	..
Local government										
Total tax revenue	**221.0**	**336.3**	**536.9**	**744.3**	**766.8**	**14.3**	**14.0**	**15.0**	**15.4**	**15.2**
1000 Taxes on income, profits and capital gains	220.1	336.3	522.9	726.2	748.2	14.2	14.0	14.6	15.0	14.8
2000 Social security contributions	0.0	0.0	0.0	0.0	0.0	0.0	0.0	0.0	0.0	0.0
3000 Taxes on payroll and workforce	0.0	0.0	0.0	0.0	0.0	0.0	0.0	0.0	0.0	0.0
4000 Taxes on property	0.0	0.0	14.0	18.1	18.6	0.0	0.0	0.4	0.4	0.4
5000 Taxes on goods and services	0.9	0.0	0.0	0.0	0.0	0.1	0.0	0.0	0.0	0.0
6000 Other taxes	0.0	0.0	0.0	0.0	0.0	0.0	0.0	0.0	0.0	0.0
Social Security Funds										
Total tax revenue	**151.1**	**126.8**	**183.5**	**256.7**	**266.5**	**9.7**	**5.3**	**5.1**	**5.3**	**5.3**
1000 Taxes on income, profits and capital gains	0.0	0.0	0.0	0.0	0.0	0.0	0.0	0.0	0.0	0.0
2000 Social security contributions	151.1	126.8	183.5	256.7	266.5	9.7	5.3	5.1	5.3	5.3
3000 Taxes on payroll and workforce	0.0	0.0	0.0	0.0	0.0	0.0	0.0	0.0	0.0	0.0
4000 Taxes on property	0.0	0.0	0.0	0.0	0.0	0.0	0.0	0.0	0.0	0.0
5000 Taxes on goods and services	0.0	0.0	0.0	0.0	0.0	0.0	0.0	0.0	0.0	0.0
6000 Other taxes	0.0	0.0	0.0	0.0	0.0	0.0	0.0	0.0	0.0	0.0

.. Not available

Note: More detailed country data and country notes are available in online chapter 6 "Tax revenues by sub-sectors of general government": https://doi.org/10.1787/0bbc27da-en. Full time series can be accessed at http://oe.cd/full-time-series.

Source: Monthly reports of central Government Revenues (unpublished) National Audit Bureau, Stockholm. Local Government Finance (SOS), Tax assessment statistics (SOS), National Central Bureau of Statistics, Stockholm. National Accounts (Statistical Reports), National Bureau of Statistics, Stockholm.

StatLink https://stat.link/sb2l6i

Table 4.69. Switzerland, tax revenue and % of GDP by selected tax category

	Billion CHF					% of GDP				
	1990	2000	2010	2018	2019	1990	2000	2010	2018	2019
Total tax revenue	**85.5**	**127.5**	**161.2**	**192.8**	**198.9**	**23.1**	**27.0**	**25.6**	**26.8**	**27.4**
1000 Taxes on income, profits and capital gains	**40.0**	**55.8**	**73.6**	**91.9**	**96.0**	**10.8**	**11.8**	**11.7**	**12.8**	**13.2**
1100 Of individuals	27.7	37.5	51.2	59.2	60.8	7.5	7.9	8.1	8.2	8.4
1200 Corporate	6.3	11.2	16.2	21.9	22.6	1.7	2.4	2.6	3.0	3.1
1300 Unallocable between 1100 and 1200	6.1	7.1	6.2	10.8	12.6	1.6	1.5	1.0	1.5	1.7
2000 Social security contributions	**19.9**	**30.8**	**38.3**	**45.9**	**47.1**	**5.4**	**6.5**	**6.1**	**6.4**	**6.5**
2100 Employees	9.3	14.5	17.5	21.3	21.8	2.5	3.1	2.8	3.0	3.0
2200 Employers	9.3	14.5	17.6	21.6	22.1	2.5	3.1	2.8	3.0	3.0
2300 Self-employed or non-employed	1.2	1.9	3.2	3.1	3.1	0.3	0.4	0.5	0.4	0.4
2400 Unallocable between 2100, 2200 and 2300	0.0	0.0	0.0	0.0	0.0	0.0	0.0	0.0	0.0	0.0
3000 Taxes on payroll and workforce	**0.0**	**0.0**	**0.0**	**0.0**	**0.0**	**0.0**	**0.0**	**0.0**	**0.0**	**0.0**
4000 Taxes on property	**7.6**	**12.3**	**12.4**	**14.5**	**15.3**	**2.1**	**2.6**	**2.0**	**2.0**	**2.1**
4100 Recurrent taxes on immovable property	0.4	0.7	1.0	1.2	1.3	0.1	0.2	0.2	0.2	0.2
4200 Recurrent taxes on net wealth	3.4	5.3	7.1	9.3	10.0	0.9	1.1	1.1	1.3	1.4
4300 Estate, inheritance and gift taxes	0.9	1.2	1.0	1.2	1.2	0.2	0.3	0.2	0.2	0.2
4400 Taxes on financial and capital transactions	2.2	4.3	2.4	1.7	1.7	0.6	0.9	0.4	0.2	0.2
4500 Non-recurrent taxes	0.0	0.0	0.0	0.0	0.0	0.0	0.0	0.0	0.0	0.0
4600 Other recurrent taxes on property	0.6	0.8	0.9	1.1	1.1	0.2	0.2	0.1	0.2	0.1
5000 Taxes on goods and services	**17.9**	**28.3**	**36.4**	**39.5**	**39.5**	**4.8**	**6.0**	**5.8**	**5.5**	**5.4**
5100 Taxes on production, sale, transfer, etc	16.0	25.3	32.1	34.3	34.2	4.3	5.4	5.1	4.8	4.7
5110 General taxes	9.9	16.9	20.9	22.9	22.7	2.7	3.6	3.3	3.2	3.1
5111 Value added taxes	9.9	16.6	20.5	22.5	22.3	2.7	3.5	3.3	3.1	3.1
5120 Taxes on specific goods and services	6.1	8.3	11.2	11.3	11.3	1.6	1.8	1.8	1.6	1.6
5121 Excises	4.6	6.8	8.3	8.5	8.4	1.2	1.4	1.3	1.2	1.1
5200 Taxes on use of goods and perform activities	1.9	3.0	4.2	5.2	5.4	0.5	0.6	0.7	0.7	0.7
5300 Unallocable between 5100 and 5200	0.0	0.0	0.0	0.0	0.0	0.0	0.0	0.0	0.0	0.0
6000 Other taxes	**0.1**	**0.2**	**0.6**	**1.0**	**1.0**	**0.0**	**0.0**	**0.1**	**0.1**	**0.1**
Non-wastable tax credits										
Non-wastable tax credits against 1000	..	..	..	..	..	..	..	..	..	..
Transfer component	..	..	..	..	..	..	..	..	..	..
Tax expenditure component	..	..	..	..	..	..	..	..	..	..

.. Not available

Note: More detailed country data and country notes are available in online chapter 5 "Detailed country tables": https://doi.org/10.1787/0bbc27da-en. Full time series can be accessed at http://oe.cd/full-time-series.

The total tax revenue has been reduced by the amount of any capital transfer that represents uncollected taxes. The capital transfers were subtracted directly from the specific taxes to which they relate. Therefore, the tax revenue amounts are different to those reported in the detailed country data available in online chapter 5 "Detailed country tables".

Source: Financial Statistics, Federal Finance Administration.

StatLink https://stat.link/ypnf1q

Table 4.70. Switzerland, tax revenue and % of GDP by level of government and main taxes

	Billion CHF					% of GDP				
	1990	2000	2010	2018	2019	1990	2000	2010	2018	2019
Federal or Central government										
Total tax revenue	**29.4**	**47.3**	**58.5**	**68.8**	**71.1**	**7.9**	**10.0**	**9.3**	**9.6**	**9.8**
1000 Taxes on income, profits and capital gains	10.9	17.0	22.7	30.9	33.3	2.9	3.6	3.6	4.3	4.6
2000 Social security contributions	0.0	0.0	0.0	0.0	0.0	0.0	0.0	0.0	0.0	0.0
3000 Taxes on payroll and workforce	0.0	0.0	0.0	0.0	0.0	0.0	0.0	0.0	0.0	0.0
4000 Taxes on property	2.1	4.1	2.2	1.4	1.4	0.6	0.9	0.3	0.2	0.2
5000 Taxes on goods and services	16.4	26.1	33.5	36.3	36.3	4.4	5.5	5.3	5.1	5.0
6000 Other taxes	0.0	0.0	0.0	0.1	0.1	0.0	0.0	0.0	0.0	0.0
State/Regional										
Total tax revenue	**21.3**	**28.9**	**39.9**	**48.2**	**49.6**	**5.8**	**6.1**	**6.3**	**6.7**	**6.8**
1000 Taxes on income, profits and capital gains	16.4	21.7	30.8	36.6	37.6	4.4	4.6	4.9	5.1	5.2
2000 Social security contributions	0.0	0.0	0.0	0.0	0.0	0.0	0.0	0.0	0.0	0.0
3000 Taxes on payroll and workforce	0.0	0.0	0.0	0.0	0.0	0.0	0.0	0.0	0.0	0.0
4000 Taxes on property	3.5	5.1	6.4	8.2	8.7	0.9	1.1	1.0	1.1	1.2
5000 Taxes on goods and services	1.4	2.1	2.7	3.0	3.0	0.4	0.4	0.4	0.4	0.4
6000 Other taxes	0.0	0.0	0.0	0.4	0.3	0.0	0.0	0.0	0.0	0.0
Local government										
Total tax revenue	**14.9**	**20.5**	**24.6**	**30.0**	**31.2**	**4.0**	**4.3**	**3.9**	**4.2**	**4.3**
1000 Taxes on income, profits and capital gains	12.7	17.1	20.1	24.3	25.1	3.4	3.6	3.2	3.4	3.4
2000 Social security contributions	0.0	0.0	0.0	0.0	0.0	0.0	0.0	0.0	0.0	0.0
3000 Taxes on payroll and workforce	0.0	0.0	0.0	0.0	0.0	0.0	0.0	0.0	0.0	0.0
4000 Taxes on property	2.0	3.1	3.8	4.9	5.2	0.5	0.7	0.6	0.7	0.7
5000 Taxes on goods and services	0.1	0.1	0.1	0.2	0.2	0.0	0.0	0.0	0.0	0.0
6000 Other taxes	0.1	0.2	0.6	0.6	0.6	0.0	0.0	0.1	0.1	0.1
Social Security Funds										
Total tax revenue	**19.9**	**30.8**	**38.3**	**45.9**	**47.1**	**5.4**	**6.5**	**6.1**	**6.4**	**6.5**
1000 Taxes on income, profits and capital gains	0.0	0.0	0.0	0.0	0.0	0.0	0.0	0.0	0.0	0.0
2000 Social security contributions	19.9	30.8	38.3	45.9	47.1	5.4	6.5	6.1	6.4	6.5
3000 Taxes on payroll and workforce	0.0	0.0	0.0	0.0	0.0	0.0	0.0	0.0	0.0	0.0
4000 Taxes on property	0.0	0.0	0.0	0.0	0.0	0.0	0.0	0.0	0.0	0.0
5000 Taxes on goods and services	0.0	0.0	0.0	0.0	0.0	0.0	0.0	0.0	0.0	0.0
6000 Other taxes	0.0	0.0	0.0	0.0	0.0	0.0	0.0	0.0	0.0	0.0

Note: More detailed country data and country notes are available in online chapter 6 "Tax revenues by sub-sectors of general government": https://doi.org/10.1787/0bbc27da-en. Full time series can be accessed at http://oe.cd/full-time-series.

The total tax revenue has been reduced by the amount of any capital transfer that represents uncollected taxes. The capital transfers were subtracted directly from the specific taxes to which they relate. Therefore, the tax revenue amounts are different to those reported in the detailed country data available in online chapter 6 "Tax revenues by sub-sectors of general government".

Source: Financial Statistics, Federal Finance Administration.

StatLink https://stat.link/9wuof0

Table 4.71. Turkey, tax revenue and % of GDP by selected tax category

	Billion TRY					% of GDP				
	1990	2000	2010	2018	2019	1990	2000	2010	2018	2019
Total tax revenue	**0.1**	**40.3**	**287.9**	**901.5**	**997.6**	**14.5**	**23.5**	**24.7**	**24.0**	**23.1**
1000 Taxes on income, profits and capital gains	**0.0**	**11.9**	**61.3**	**217.7**	**241.5**	**4.9**	**6.9**	**5.3**	**5.8**	**5.6**
1100 Of individuals	0.0	9.0	40.4	139.0	162.7	3.9	5.2	3.5	3.7	3.8
1200 Corporate	0.0	2.9	20.9	78.7	78.8	1.0	1.7	1.8	2.1	1.8
1300 Unallocable between 1100 and 1200	0.0	0.0	0.0	0.0	0.0	0.0	0.0	0.0	0.0	0.0
2000 Social security contributions	**0.0**	**7.5**	**71.7**	**269.9**	**312.8**	**2.9**	**4.4**	**6.1**	**7.2**	**7.2**
2100 Employees	0.0	2.7	26.9	101.7	120.1	1.1	1.6	2.3	2.7	2.8
2200 Employers	0.0	3.6	39.4	151.4	178.3	1.6	2.1	3.4	4.0	4.1
2300 Self-employed or non-employed	0.0	1.2	5.4	16.9	14.4	0.2	0.7	0.5	0.4	0.3
2400 Unallocable between 2100, 2200 and 2300	0.0	0.0	0.0	0.0	0.0	0.0	0.0	0.0	0.0	0.0
3000 Taxes on payroll and workforce	**0.0**	**0.0**	**0.0**	**0.0**	**0.0**	**0.0**	**0.0**	**0.0**	**0.0**	**0.0**
4000 Taxes on property	**0.0**	**1.3**	**11.7**	**38.9**	**41.7**	**0.3**	**0.7**	**1.0**	**1.0**	**1.0**
4100 Recurrent taxes on immovable property	0.0	0.2	2.7	8.7	9.7	0.0	0.1	0.2	0.2	0.2
4200 Recurrent taxes on net wealth	0.0	0.0	0.0	0.0	0.0	0.0	0.0	0.0	0.0	0.0
4300 Estate, inheritance and gift taxes	0.0	0.0	0.2	0.9	1.1	0.0	0.0	0.0	0.0	0.0
4400 Taxes on financial and capital transactions	0.0	1.1	8.8	29.3	30.9	0.3	0.6	0.8	0.8	0.7
4500 Non-recurrent taxes	0.0	0.0	0.0	0.0	0.0	0.0	0.0	0.0	0.0	0.0
4600 Other recurrent taxes on property	0.0	0.0	0.0	0.0	0.0	0.0	0.0	0.0	0.0	0.0
5000 Taxes on goods and services	**0.0**	**16.9**	**137.3**	**365.0**	**389.1**	**4.1**	**9.9**	**11.8**	**9.7**	**9.0**
5100 Taxes on production, sale, transfer, etc	0.0	16.3	131.9	351.5	373.7	4.0	9.5	11.3	9.4	8.7
5110 General taxes	0.0	9.7	62.5	178.6	180.7	2.9	5.7	5.4	4.8	4.2
5111 Value added taxes	0.0	9.7	62.5	178.6	180.7	2.7	5.7	5.4	4.8	4.2
5120 Taxes on specific goods and services	0.0	6.6	69.3	172.8	193.0	1.1	3.8	5.9	4.6	4.5
5121 Excises	0.0	4.7	57.3	133.9	147.1	0.1	2.8	4.9	3.6	3.4
5200 Taxes on use of goods and perform activities	0.0	0.6	5.4	13.5	15.4	0.1	0.3	0.5	0.4	0.4
5300 Unallocable between 5100 and 5200	0.0	0.0	0.0	0.0	0.0	0.0	0.0	0.0	0.0	0.0
6000 Other taxes	**0.0**	**2.7**	**5.9**	**10.0**	**12.4**	**2.4**	**1.6**	**0.5**	**0.3**	**0.3**
Non-wastable tax credits										
Non-wastable tax credits against 1000	..	..	..	..	..	..	..	..	..	..
Transfer component	..	..	..	..	..	..	..	..	..	..
Tax expenditure component	..	..	..	..	..	..	..	..	..	..

.. Not available

Note: More detailed country data and country notes are available in online chapter 5 "Detailed country tables": https://doi.org/10.1787/0bbc27da-en. Full time series can be accessed at http://oe.cd/full-time-series.

Source: Bulletin of national accounts and the Budget revenue Bulletin.

StatLink https://stat.link/wb9s7u

Table 4.72. Turkey, tax revenue and % of GDP by level of government and main taxes

	Billion TRY					% of GDP				
	1990	2000	2010	2018	2019	1990	2000	2010	2018	2019
Federal or Central government										
Total tax revenue	**0.1**	**29.1**	**189.4**	**545.0**	**593.1**	**10.4**	**17.0**	**16.2**	**14.5**	**13.7**
1000 Taxes on income, profits and capital gains	0.0	10.5	54.6	191.7	212.3	4.3	6.1	4.7	5.1	4.9
2000 Social security contributions	0.0	0.0	0.0	0.0	0.0	0.0	0.0	0.0	0.0	0.0
3000 Taxes on payroll and workforce	0.0	0.0	0.0	0.0	0.0	0.0	0.0	0.0	0.0	0.0
4000 Taxes on property	0.0	0.9	8.1	26.5	28.3	0.3	0.5	0.7	0.7	0.7
5000 Taxes on goods and services	0.0	15.2	124.0	322.7	346.1	3.6	8.9	10.6	8.6	8.0
6000 Other taxes	0.0	2.5	2.7	4.2	6.4	2.2	1.4	0.2	0.1	0.1
State/Regional										
Total tax revenue	..	..	..	..	..	..	..	..	..	..
1000 Taxes on income, profits and capital gains	..	..	..	..	..	..	..	..	..	..
2000 Social security contributions	..	..	..	..	..	..	..	..	..	..
3000 Taxes on payroll and workforce	..	..	..	..	..	..	..	..	..	..
4000 Taxes on property	..	..	..	..	..	..	..	..	..	..
5000 Taxes on goods and services	..	..	..	..	..	..	..	..	..	..
6000 Other taxes	..	..	..	..	..	..	..	..	..	..
Local government										
Total tax revenue	**0.0**	**3.6**	**26.8**	**86.5**	**91.7**	**1.3**	**2.1**	**2.3**	**2.3**	**2.1**
1000 Taxes on income, profits and capital gains	0.0	1.4	6.7	26.0	29.2	0.6	0.8	0.6	0.7	0.7
2000 Social security contributions	0.0	0.0	0.0	0.0	0.0	0.0	0.0	0.0	0.0	0.0
3000 Taxes on payroll and workforce	0.0	0.0	0.0	0.0	0.0	0.0	0.0	0.0	0.0	0.0
4000 Taxes on property	0.0	0.3	3.6	12.5	13.4	0.0	0.2	0.3	0.3	0.3
5000 Taxes on goods and services	0.0	1.7	13.3	42.3	43.0	0.5	1.0	1.1	1.1	1.0
6000 Other taxes	0.0	0.2	3.2	5.8	6.0	0.2	0.1	0.3	0.2	0.1
Social Security Funds										
Total tax revenue	**0.0**	**7.5**	**71.7**	**269.9**	**312.8**	**2.9**	**4.4**	**6.1**	**7.2**	**7.2**
1000 Taxes on income, profits and capital gains	0.0	0.0	0.0	0.0	0.0	0.0	0.0	0.0	0.0	0.0
2000 Social security contributions	0.0	7.5	71.7	269.9	312.8	2.9	4.4	6.1	7.2	7.2
3000 Taxes on payroll and workforce	0.0	0.0	0.0	0.0	0.0	0.0	0.0	0.0	0.0	0.0
4000 Taxes on property	0.0	0.0	0.0	0.0	0.0	0.0	0.0	0.0	0.0	0.0
5000 Taxes on goods and services	0.0	0.0	0.0	0.0	0.0	0.0	0.0	0.0	0.0	0.0
6000 Other taxes	0.0	0.0	0.0	0.0	0.0	0.0	0.0	0.0	0.0	0.0

.. Not available

Note: More detailed country data and country notes are available in online chapter 6 "Tax revenues by sub-sectors of general government": https://doi.org/10.1787/0bbc27da-en. Full time series can be accessed at http://oe.cd/full-time-series.

Source: Bulletin of national accounts and the Budget revenue Bulletin.

StatLink https://stat.link/9i7pbd

Table 4.73. United Kingdom, tax revenue and % of GDP by selected tax category

	Billion GBP					% of GDP				
	1990	2000	2010	2018	2019	1990	2000	2010	2018	2019
Total tax revenue	**202.4**	**359.4**	**514.8**	**704.4**	**725.6**	**32.9**	**32.8**	**32.1**	**32.9**	**32.7**
1000 Taxes on income, profits and capital gains	**79.6**	**142.2**	**192.8**	**247.8**	**251.5**	**12.9**	**13.0**	**12.0**	**11.6**	**11.3**
1100 Of individuals	59.5	104.1	147.0	192.8	200.5	9.7	9.5	9.2	9.0	9.0
1200 Corporate	20.1	38.1	45.8	55.0	51.0	3.3	3.5	2.8	2.6	2.3
1300 Unallocable between 1100 and 1200	0.0	0.0	0.0	0.0	0.0	0.0	0.0	0.0	0.0	0.0
2000 Social security contributions	**34.5**	**60.3**	**97.3**	**135.2**	**143.3**	**5.6**	**5.5**	**6.1**	**6.3**	**6.5**
2100 Employees	13.3	24.2	38.7	52.1	56.2	2.2	2.2	2.4	2.4	2.5
2200 Employers	20.0	34.0	55.9	79.2	82.7	3.2	3.1	3.5	3.7	3.7
2300 Self-employed or non-employed	1.2	2.0	2.8	3.8	4.4	0.2	0.2	0.2	0.2	0.2
2400 Unallocable between 2100, 2200 and 2300	0.0	0.0	0.0	0.0	0.0	0.0	0.0	0.0	0.0	0.0
3000 Taxes on payroll and workforce	**0.0**	**0.0**	**0.0**	**2.6**	**2.8**	**0.0**	**0.0**	**0.0**	**0.1**	**0.1**
4000 Taxes on property	**16.5**	**41.1**	**61.8**	**88.7**	**90.3**	**2.7**	**3.8**	**3.8**	**4.1**	**4.1**
4100 Recurrent taxes on immovable property	13.5	30.6	50.0	66.4	68.7	2.2	2.8	3.1	3.1	3.1
4200 Recurrent taxes on net wealth	0.0	0.0	0.0	0.0	0.0	0.0	0.0	0.0	0.0	0.0
4300 Estate, inheritance and gift taxes	1.3	2.2	2.6	5.3	5.2	0.2	0.2	0.2	0.2	0.2
4400 Taxes on financial and capital transactions	1.8	8.4	9.1	16.7	16.0	0.3	0.8	0.6	0.8	0.7
4500 Non-recurrent taxes	0.0	0.0	0.0	0.3	0.4	0.0	0.0	0.0	0.0	0.0
4600 Other recurrent taxes on property	0.0	0.0	0.0	0.0	0.0	0.0	0.0	0.0	0.0	0.0
5000 Taxes on goods and services	**62.8**	**115.8**	**162.9**	**230.1**	**237.8**	**10.2**	**10.6**	**10.1**	**10.7**	**10.7**
5100 Taxes on production, sale, transfer, etc	59.4	110.8	155.5	222.1	229.3	9.6	10.1	9.7	10.4	10.3
5110 General taxes	34.1	65.0	97.6	149.1	154.8	5.5	5.9	6.1	7.0	7.0
5111 Value added taxes	34.1	65.0	97.6	149.1	154.8	5.5	5.9	6.1	7.0	7.0
5120 Taxes on specific goods and services	25.2	45.8	57.8	73.0	74.6	4.1	4.2	3.6	3.4	3.4
5121 Excises	19.7	37.3	45.5	49.1	49.3	3.2	3.4	2.8	2.3	2.2
5200 Taxes on use of goods and perform activities	3.4	5.0	7.4	8.0	8.5	0.6	0.5	0.5	0.4	0.4
5300 Unallocable between 5100 and 5200	0.0	0.0	0.0	0.0	0.0	0.0	0.0	0.0	0.0	0.0
6000 Other taxes	**9.0**	**0.0**	**0.0**	**0.0**	**0.0**	**1.5**	**0.0**	**0.0**	**0.0**	**0.0**
Non-wastable tax credits										
Non-wastable tax credits against 1000	7.5	4.7	30.2	29.1	25.3	1.2	0.4	1.9	1.4	1.1
Transfer component	0.5	3.4	23.7	25.1	21.4	0.1	0.3	1.5	1.2	1.0
Tax expenditure component	7.0	1.2	6.5	4.1	3.9	1.1	0.1	0.4	0.2	0.2
Revenues collected on behalf of the EU										
Revenues collected on behalf of the EU, total	1.8	2.1	2.9	3.6	3.7	0.3	0.2	0.2	0.2	0.2
Customs duties	..	1.8	2.9	3.3	3.3	..	0.2	0.2	0.2	0.2

.. Not available

Note: Please note that the non-wastable tax credit data for the United Kingdom is on a cash basis and includes estimates in some years. Please see the footnotes in the table for the United Kingdom in chapter 5 for more information.

Note: More detailed country data and country notes are available in online chapter 5 "Detailed country tables": https://doi.org/10.1787/0bbc27da-en. Full time series can be accessed at http://oe.cd/full-time-series.

Source: National Income and Expenditure; Central Statistical Office; Annual reports of Her Majesty's Revenue and Customs.

StatLink https://stat.link/d5h6sm

Table 4.74. United Kingdom, tax revenue and % of GDP by level of government and main taxes

	Billion GBP					% of GDP				
	1990	2000	2010	2018	2019	1990	2000	2010	2018	2019
Federal or Central government										
Total tax revenue	**151.9**	**282.8**	**388.3**	**529.9**	**541.1**	**24.7**	**25.8**	**24.2**	**24.7**	**24.4**
1000 Taxes on income, profits and capital gains	79.6	142.2	192.8	247.8	251.5	12.9	13.0	12.0	11.6	11.3
2000 Social security contributions	0.0	0.0	0.0	0.0	0.0	0.0	0.0	0.0	0.0	0.0
3000 Taxes on payroll and workforce	0.0	0.0	0.0	2.6	2.8	0.0	0.0	0.0	0.1	0.1
4000 Taxes on property	11.4	26.9	35.5	53.0	52.7	1.9	2.5	2.2	2.5	2.4
5000 Taxes on goods and services	60.9	113.7	160.0	226.5	234.2	9.9	10.4	10.0	10.6	10.6
6000 Other taxes	0.0	0.0	0.0	0.0	0.0	0.0	0.0	0.0	0.0	0.0
State/Regional										
Total tax revenue	..	..	..	..	..	..	..	..	..	..
1000 Taxes on income, profits and capital gains	..	..	..	..	..	..	..	..	..	..
2000 Social security contributions	..	..	..	..	..	..	..	..	..	..
3000 Taxes on payroll and workforce	..	..	..	..	..	..	..	..	..	..
4000 Taxes on property	..	..	..	..	..	..	..	..	..	..
5000 Taxes on goods and services	..	..	..	..	..	..	..	..	..	..
6000 Other taxes	..	..	..	..	..	..	..	..	..	..
Local government										
Total tax revenue	**14.1**	**14.2**	**26.2**	**35.7**	**37.5**	**2.3**	**1.3**	**1.6**	**1.7**	**1.7**
1000 Taxes on income, profits and capital gains	0.0	0.0	0.0	0.0	0.0	0.0	0.0	0.0	0.0	0.0
2000 Social security contributions	0.0	0.0	0.0	0.0	0.0	0.0	0.0	0.0	0.0	0.0
3000 Taxes on payroll and workforce	0.0	0.0	0.0	0.0	0.0	0.0	0.0	0.0	0.0	0.0
4000 Taxes on property	5.1	14.2	26.2	35.7	37.5	0.8	1.3	1.6	1.7	1.7
5000 Taxes on goods and services	0.0	0.0	0.0	0.0	0.0	0.0	0.0	0.0	0.0	0.0
6000 Other taxes	9.0	0.0	0.0	0.0	0.0	1.5	0.0	0.0	0.0	0.0
Social Security Funds										
Total tax revenue	**34.5**	**60.3**	**97.3**	**135.2**	**143.3**	**5.6**	**5.5**	**6.1**	**6.3**	**6.5**
1000 Taxes on income, profits and capital gains	0.0	0.0	0.0	0.0	0.0	0.0	0.0	0.0	0.0	0.0
2000 Social security contributions	34.5	60.3	97.3	135.2	143.3	5.6	5.5	6.1	6.3	6.5
3000 Taxes on payroll and workforce	0.0	0.0	0.0	0.0	0.0	0.0	0.0	0.0	0.0	0.0
4000 Taxes on property	0.0	0.0	0.0	0.0	0.0	0.0	0.0	0.0	0.0	0.0
5000 Taxes on goods and services	0.0	0.0	0.0	0.0	0.0	0.0	0.0	0.0	0.0	0.0
6000 Other taxes	0.0	0.0	0.0	0.0	0.0	0.0	0.0	0.0	0.0	0.0

.. Not available

Note: More detailed country data and country notes are available in online chapter 5 "Detailed country tables": https://doi.org/10.1787/0bbc27da-en. Full time series can be accessed at http://oe.cd/full-time-series.

Source: National Income and Expenditure; Central Statistical Office; Annual reports of Her Majesty's Revenue and Customs.

StatLink https://stat.link/gdx8cy

Table 4.75. United States, tax revenue and % of GDP by selected tax category

	Billion USD					% of GDP				
	1990	2000	2010	2018	2019	1990	2000	2010	2018	2019
Total tax revenue	**1 552.4**	**2 900.5**	**3 517.1**	**5 110.0**	**5 336.5**	**26.0**	**28.3**	**23.4**	**24.9**	**25.0**
1000 Taxes on income, profits and capital gains	**701.7**	**1 453.9**	**1 488.7**	**2 344.7**	**2 478.5**	**11.8**	**14.2**	**9.9**	**11.4**	**11.6**
1100 Of individuals	584.7	1 224.5	1 223.2	2 073.7	2 191.7	9.8	11.9	8.1	10.1	10.3
1200 Corporate	117.0	229.3	265.5	271.0	286.8	2.0	2.2	1.8	1.3	1.3
1300 Unallocable between 1100 and 1200	0.0	0.0	0.0	0.0	0.0	0.0	0.0	0.0	0.0	0.0
2000 Social security contributions	**397.0**	**683.1**	**917.4**	**1 254.4**	**1 306.0**	**6.7**	**6.7**	**6.1**	**6.1**	**6.1**
2100 Employees	173.9	305.6	406.4	570.1	595.6	2.9	3.0	2.7	2.8	2.8
2200 Employers	204.1	343.2	461.7	618.5	642.2	3.4	3.3	3.1	3.0	3.0
2300 Self-employed or non-employed	19.0	34.4	49.3	65.8	68.2	0.3	0.3	0.3	0.3	0.3
2400 Unallocable between 2100, 2200 and 2300	0.0	0.0	0.0	0.0	0.0	0.0	0.0	0.0	0.0	0.0
3000 Taxes on payroll and workforce	**0.0**	**0.0**	**2.3**	**2.2**	**2.8**	**0.0**	**0.0**	**0.0**	**0.0**	**0.0**
4000 Taxes on property	**182.4**	**299.5**	**473.4**	**603.8**	**612.9**	**3.1**	**2.9**	**3.1**	**2.9**	**2.9**
4100 Recurrent taxes on immovable property	161.5	254.7	438.6	549.2	564.0	2.7	2.5	2.9	2.7	2.6
4200 Recurrent taxes on net wealth	0.0	0.0	0.0	0.0	0.0	0.0	0.0	0.0	0.0	0.0
4300 Estate, inheritance and gift taxes	15.8	35.6	19.7	28.3	21.7	0.3	0.3	0.1	0.1	0.1
4400 Taxes on financial and capital transactions	2.1	4.4	7.5	16.4	16.9	0.0	0.0	0.0	0.1	0.1
4500 Non-recurrent taxes	0.0	0.0	0.0	0.0	0.0	0.0	0.0	0.0	0.0	0.0
4600 Other recurrent taxes on property	3.0	4.8	7.7	10.0	10.2	0.0	0.0	0.1	0.0	0.0
5000 Taxes on goods and services	**271.3**	**464.0**	**635.3**	**905.0**	**936.4**	**4.5**	**4.5**	**4.2**	**4.4**	**4.4**
5100 Taxes on production, sale, transfer, etc	235.2	404.1	546.7	789.0	816.9	3.9	3.9	3.6	3.8	3.8
5110 General taxes	125.6	221.4	295.1	421.2	434.8	2.1	2.2	2.0	2.1	2.0
5111 Value added taxes	0.0	0.0	0.0	0.0	0.0	0.0	0.0	0.0	0.0	0.0
5120 Taxes on specific goods and services	109.7	182.7	251.6	367.9	382.1	1.8	1.8	1.7	1.8	1.8
5121 Excises	65.0	108.6	146.6	164.2	163.6	1.1	1.1	1.0	0.8	0.8
5200 Taxes on use of goods and perform activities	36.1	59.9	88.6	115.9	119.4	0.6	0.6	0.6	0.6	0.6
5300 Unallocable between 5100 and 5200	0.0	0.0	0.0	0.0	0.0	0.0	0.0	0.0	0.0	0.0
6000 Other taxes	**0.0**	**0.0**	**0.0**	**0.0**	**0.0**	**0.0**	**0.0**	**0.0**	**0.0**	**0.0**
Non-wastable tax credits										
Non-wastable tax credits against 1000	6.2	36.5	171.9	194.7	256.0	0.1	0.4	1.1	0.9	1.2
Transfer component	4.4	26.9	101.8	137.0	153.0	0.1	0.3	0.7	0.7	0.7
Tax expenditure component	1.8	9.6	70.1	57.7	103.0	0.0	0.1	0.5	0.3	0.5

Note: More detailed country data and country notes are available in online chapter 5 "Detailed country tables": https://doi.org/10.1787/0bbc27da-en. Full time series can be accessed at http://oe.cd/full-time-series.

Source: Federal estimates are derived from the US Budget, the Final Monthly Treasury Statement and the Annual Report of the US Treasury Department. The State and Local estimates are derived from Government Finances, published by the Bureau of the Census.

StatLink https://stat.link/q6ixte

Table 4.76. United States, tax revenue and % of GDP by level of government and main taxes

	Billion USD					% of GDP				
	1990	2000	2010	2018	2019	1990	2000	2010	2018	2019
Federal or Central government										
Total tax revenue	**632.2**	**1 316.6**	**1 288.7**	**2 039.7**	**2 147.8**	**10.6**	**12.8**	**8.6**	**9.9**	**10.0**
1000 Taxes on income, profits and capital gains	569.7	1 201.3	1 176.8	1 854.3	1 958.0	9.6	11.7	7.8	9.0	9.2
2000 Social security contributions	0.0	0.0	0.0	0.0	0.0	0.0	0.0	0.0	0.0	0.0
3000 Taxes on payroll and workforce	0.0	0.0	0.0	0.0	0.0	0.0	0.0	0.0	0.0	0.0
4000 Taxes on property	11.6	28.1	15.1	22.7	16.2	0.2	0.3	0.1	0.1	0.1
5000 Taxes on goods and services	50.9	87.3	96.8	162.8	173.7	0.9	0.9	0.6	0.8	0.8
6000 Other taxes	0.0	0.0	0.0	0.0	0.0	0.0	0.0	0.0	0.0	0.0
State/Regional										
Total tax revenue	**309.7**	**547.6**	**723.9**	**1 055.6**	**1 101.6**	**5.2**	**5.3**	**4.8**	**5.1**	**5.2**
1000 Taxes on income, profits and capital gains	120.2	231.0	279.4	446.8	476.0	2.0	2.3	1.9	2.2	2.2
2000 Social security contributions	0.0	0.0	0.0	0.0	0.0	0.0	0.0	0.0	0.0	0.0
3000 Taxes on payroll and workforce	0.0	0.0	2.3	2.2	2.8	0.0	0.0	0.0	0.0	0.0
4000 Taxes on property	12.2	21.9	23.1	35.3	36.0	0.2	0.2	0.2	0.2	0.2
5000 Taxes on goods and services	177.3	294.7	419.1	571.4	586.8	3.0	2.9	2.8	2.8	2.7
6000 Other taxes	0.0	0.0	0.0	0.0	0.0	0.0	0.0	0.0	0.0	0.0
Local government										
Total tax revenue	**213.6**	**353.2**	**587.2**	**760.2**	**781.1**	**3.6**	**3.4**	**3.9**	**3.7**	**3.7**
1000 Taxes on income, profits and capital gains	11.9	21.6	32.5	43.6	44.5	0.2	0.2	0.2	0.2	0.2
2000 Social security contributions	0.0	0.0	0.0	0.0	0.0	0.0	0.0	0.0	0.0	0.0
3000 Taxes on payroll and workforce	0.0	0.0	0.0	0.0	0.0	0.0	0.0	0.0	0.0	0.0
4000 Taxes on property	158.6	249.5	435.3	545.9	560.7	2.7	2.4	2.9	2.7	2.6
5000 Taxes on goods and services	43.1	82.0	119.4	170.8	175.9	0.7	0.8	0.8	0.8	0.8
6000 Other taxes	0.0	0.0	0.0	0.0	0.0	0.0	0.0	0.0	0.0	0.0
Social Security Funds										
Total tax revenue	**397.0**	**683.1**	**917.4**	**1 254.4**	**1 306.0**	**6.7**	**6.7**	**6.1**	**6.1**	**6.1**
1000 Taxes on income, profits and capital gains	0.0	0.0	0.0	0.0	0.0	0.0	0.0	0.0	0.0	0.0
2000 Social security contributions	397.0	683.1	917.4	1 254.4	1 306.0	6.7	6.7	6.1	6.1	6.1
3000 Taxes on payroll and workforce	0.0	0.0	0.0	0.0	0.0	0.0	0.0	0.0	0.0	0.0
4000 Taxes on property	0.0	0.0	0.0	0.0	0.0	0.0	0.0	0.0	0.0	0.0
5000 Taxes on goods and services	0.0	0.0	0.0	0.0	0.0	0.0	0.0	0.0	0.0	0.0
6000 Other taxes	0.0	0.0	0.0	0.0	0.0	0.0	0.0	0.0	0.0	0.0

Note: More detailed country data and country notes are available in online chapter 6 "Tax revenues by sub-sectors of general government": https://doi.org/10.1787/0bbc27da-en. Full time series can be accessed at http://oe.cd/full-time-series.

Source: Federal estimates are derived from the US Budget, the Final Monthly Treasury Statement and the Annual Report of the US Treasury Department. The State and Local estimates are derived from Government Finances, published by the Bureau of the Census.

StatLink https://stat.link/j2m6vz

4.2. Memorandum tables

Table 4.77 shows different sources for financing social benefits, beyond compulsory social security contributions reported in section 4.1. In addition, this table shows also data on other taxes, on voluntary contributions to government and on compulsory contributions to private sector.

Table 4.78 shows social security contributions and payroll taxes paid by government. During the revision of the Interpretative Guide in 1984, the question arose of how to treat taxes paid by government. The two most prominent examples of such taxes are social security contributions and payroll taxes paid by government in respect of its employees. After a long discussion it was decided that the data shown in this publication should continue to include taxes paid by government (see §7 of the Interpretative Guide in annex A).

Whilst it was recognised that for certain purposes (e.g. to show the cash flow to the government sector from the private sector) it would be appropriate to eliminate taxes paid by one sector of government to another or tax payments between different units of the same sector of government, the view was taken that to record tax flows in the context of the economy as a whole required that taxes paid by government should be included in the data. This treatment ensures that the different resource flows of an economy, including the calculation of the output of government, are measured consistently in after-tax units. Nevertheless, it was decided that data on identifiable taxes paid by government should be separately identified in a memorandum item and this is the purpose of the country tables which follow.

The data that are reproduced in the following tables refer to actual compulsory payments made by general government in respect of their employees. Fictive, voluntary and imputed contributions are excluded from these data. The definitions of social security contributions, payroll taxes and general government are those set out in §40 to §46, §47 and §3 to §4 of the Interpretative Guide. Information on the other taxes paid by government (namely property taxes and consumption taxes) is not available in most countries, although it is believed that in all countries taxes based upon payroll are the most important taxes paid by government. In many cases, the data are estimates and are not always constructed on a basis consistent with that used in the main tables.

Table 4.77. Financing of social security benefits

As % of GDP

	Total					2019				
	1990	2000	2010	2018	2019	Social security contributions	Other taxes	Voluntary contributions to government	Compulsory contributions to private sector	Total
Australia	0.0	0.0	0.0	0.0	0.0	..	..	..	..	0.0
Austria	13.0	14.4	14.1	14.8	14.9	14.9	0.0	0.1	0.0	14.9
Belgium	14.2	15.7	18.6	17.3	17.4	13.3	4.1	0.0	0.0	17.4
Canada	4.3	4.7	4.6	4.6	4.7	4.7	0.0	0.0	0.0	4.7
Chile	4.6	6.2	6.2	7.3	7.6	1.5	0.0	0.0	6.1	7.6
Colombia	0.9	2.6	7.1	5.9	6.0	1.9	0.0	0.0	4.1	6.0
Costa Rica	6.5	6.4	7.3	8.0	8.1	8.1	..	..	..	8.1
Czech Republic	..	14.5	14.6	15.5	15.5	15.4	0.0	0.0	0.2	15.5
Denmark	1.1	2.0	1.3	0.8	0.8	0.0	0.0	0.6	0.1	0.8
Estonia	..	10.9	13.0	13.1	12.8	11.7	0.0	0.0	1.1	12.8
Finland	12.2	12.4	12.5	12.2	12.2	11.8	0.0	0.1	0.3	12.2
France	18.4	21.2	23.1	24.6	24.5	14.9	9.5	0.0	0.0	24.5
Germany	14.2	15.6	14.4	15.1	15.2	14.6	0.0	0.2	0.4	15.2
Greece	7.6	10.1	11.0	11.9	12.2	12.2	0.0	0.0	0.0	12.2
Hungary	..	13.2	12.9	12.4	12.0	11.7	0.3	0.0	0.0	12.0
Iceland	10.0	13.4	14.1	16.0	15.5	3.2	6.2	0.0	6.1	15.5
Ireland	4.6	3.7	5.1	3.7	3.7	3.7	0.0	0.0	0.0	3.7
Israel	..	5.1	6.2	7.9	7.9	5.2	0.0	0.0	2.7	7.9
Italy	11.9	11.6	13.0	13.0	13.3	13.3	0.0	0.0	0.0	13.3
Japan	7.3	8.9	10.8	12.7	12.9	12.9	0.0	0.0	0.0	12.9
Korea	1.9	3.5	5.2	6.8	7.3	7.3	0.0	0.0	0.0	7.3
Latvia	..	9.9	8.8	9.5	10.1	9.6	0.5	0.0	0.0	10.1
Lithuania	..	10.2	12.1	13.1	9.7	9.6	0.0	0.0	0.0	9.7
Luxembourg	9.3	9.7	11.0	10.9	10.9	10.8	0.0	0.1	0.0	10.9
Mexico	2.5	3.1	3.2	3.3	3.5	2.3	0.0	0.0	1.2	3.5
Netherlands	17.1	22.5	12.9	14.0	13.4	13.4	0.0	0.0	..	13.4
New Zealand	0.0	0.0	0.0	0.0	0.0	..	..	..	..	0.0
Norway	10.6	8.8	9.4	10.1	10.6	10.6	0.0	0.0	0.0	10.6
Poland	..	13.0	10.9	13.2	13.3	13.3	0.0	0.0	0.0	13.3
Portugal	7.2	8.3	9.0	9.7	10.0	9.6	0.4	0.0	0.0	10.0
Slovak Republic	..	13.9	13.1	15.4	15.8	15.0	0.0	0.0	0.8	15.8
Slovenia	..	15.0	15.8	15.4	15.7	15.7	0.0	0.0	0.0	15.7
Spain	11.2	11.6	12.0	11.8	12.3	12.3	0.0	0.1	0.0	12.3
Sweden	13.3	13.1	11.1	10.1	9.7	9.2	0.0	0.5	0.0	9.7
Switzerland	11.3	13.8	14.5	15.5	15.5	6.5	0.9	0.0	8.2	15.5
Turkey	2.9	4.4	6.1	7.2	7.2	7.2	0.0	0.0	0.0	7.2
United Kingdom	7.4	7.0	8.0	7.6	7.7	6.5	0.0	1.5	0.0	7.7
United States	6.9	6.9	6.5	6.6	6.6	6.1	0.0	0.5	0.0	6.6

.. Not available

StatLink https://stat.link/k5mvx7

Table 4.78. Social security contributions and payroll taxes paid by government, totals

As % of GDP

	Total					2019				
	1990	2000	2010	2018	2019	Federal or Central government	State/Regional	Local government	Social security Funds	Total
Australia[1]	0.0	0.0	0.0	0.0	0.0	0.0	0.0	0.0	0.0	0.0
Austria	1.0	1.4	1.9	1.9	1.9	0.7	0.6	0.6	0.1	1.9
Belgium	1.0	1.2	1.5	1.8	1.8	0.2	0.6	0.9	0.1	1.8
Canada	..	0.6	0.6	0.6	0.6	0.1	0.3	0.2	0.0	0.6
Chile	..	0.1	0.2	0.2	0.2	0.1	..	0.1	0.0	0.2
Colombia	..	..	..	0.2	0.2	0.1	0.0	0.0	0.2	0.2
Costa Rica	0.7	0.9	1.1	1.1	1.1	1.0	0.0	0.1	0.0	1.1
Czech Republic	..	1.4	1.4	1.9	2.0	0.9	..	1.1	0.0	2.0
Denmark	0.0	0.0	0.0	0.0	0.0	..	..	..	..	0.0
Estonia	..	2.9	3.6	3.5	3.6	2.1	..	1.2	0.3	3.6
Finland	2.1	2.8	3.0	2.3	2.3	0.5	..	1.8	0.0	2.3
France	2.2	2.5	2.7	2.6	2.6	0.7	..	0.9	1.0	2.6
Germany	1.0	0.8	0.8	0.8	0.8	0.1	0.3	0.4	0.1	0.8
Greece	0.3	1.2	1.6	1.0	1.2	1.0	..	0.0	0.2	1.2
Hungary	..	2.8	2.4	1.6	1.5	1.2	..	0.3	0.0	1.5
Iceland	..	..	..	..	..	..	..	..	..	..
Ireland	0.4	0.4	0.7	0.5	0.5	0.2	..	0.4	0.0	0.5
Israel	..	0.8	0.8	0.8	0.8	0.7	..	0.2	0.0	0.8
Italy	..	3.0	3.1	2.9	2.9	0.0	..	0.0	2.9	2.9
Japan	0.4	0.5	0.6	0.6	0.6	0.2	..	0.5	0.0	0.6
Korea	..	..	..	..	..	..	..	..	..	..
Latvia	..	0.6	1.0	1.2	1.2	..	..	..	..	1.2
Lithuania	..	2.7	2.5	2.2	0.2	0.1	..	0.1	0.0	0.2
Luxembourg	2.4	1.2	1.3	1.3	1.3	1.2	..	0.0	0.0	1.3
Mexico	0.3	0.7	0.8	0.7	0.8	0.8	0.0	0.0	0.0	0.8
Netherlands	0.1	0.4	0.0	0.0	0.0	..	..	..	..	0.0
New Zealand	0.0	0.0	0.0	0.0	0.0	..	..	..	..	0.0
Norway	2.4	2.4	2.9	3.3	3.5	1.5	..	2.0	0.0	3.5
Poland	..	1.5	1.3	1.4	1.4	0.5	..	0.8	0.0	1.4
Portugal	0.1	0.2	0.0	0.0	0.0	..	..	..	..	0.0
Slovak Republic	..	2.0	2.0	2.2	2.5	1.4	..	1.0	0.1	2.5
Slovenia	..	1.9	1.7	1.5	1.6	1.0	..	0.5	0.0	1.6
Spain	1.2	1.5	1.7	1.8	1.8	0.2	1.1	0.4	0.0	1.8
Sweden	4.5	4.2	3.8	4.0	4.0	0.9	..	3.1	0.0	4.0
Switzerland	0.4	0.4	0.4	0.5	0.5	0.1	0.3	0.1	0.0	0.5
Turkey	1.6	2.1	3.4	4.0	4.1	4.1	..	0.0	0.0	4.1
United Kingdom	0.7	0.6	0.7	0.7	0.7	0.5	..	0.2	0.0	0.7
United States	0.5	0.4	0.5	0.4	0.4	0.1	0.3	0.0	0.0	0.4

.. Not available

1. For Australia, the total differs from the sum of the four levels of government. The difference is due to a multi-jurisdictional (University) sector specific to this country. This sector contains units where jurisdiction is shared between two or more governments, or where classification of a unit to a jurisdiction is otherwise unclear. The main type of units currently falling into this category is public universities.

StatLink https://stat.link/wif7m2

5 Detailed country tables, 1965-2019

Chapter 5 provides detailed country information on tax revenues for each OECD country.

5.1. Tax revenues

In all of the following tables the symbol (..) indicates not available/or not applicable. The main series in this chapter cover a selection of years between 1965 and 2019. A complete series is available on line. Data for 1955 and 1960 (for nineteen OECD countries) are provided in part V of the 1998 edition of this Report.

Table 5.1. Australia: Details of tax revenue, 1965-2019

Million AUD

	1965	1980	1990	2000	2007	2010	2013	2015	2018	2019
Total tax revenue	**5 024**	**39 878**	**116 500**	**214 753**	**346 772**	**356 747**	**431 200**	**460 729**	**557 175**	**549 536**
1000 Taxes on income, profits and capital gains	**2 547**	**22 383**	**66 542**	**124 427**	**206 134**	**202 184**	**246 073**	**261 345**	**334 856**	**325 116**
1100 Of individuals	1 729	17 532	50 062	80 991	127 587	138 163	169 972	191 720	229 439	230 932
1110 On income and profits	1 729	17 532	49 888	80 991	127 587	138 163	169 972	191 720	229 439	230 932
1120 On capital gains	0	0	174	0	0	0	0	0	0	0
1200 Corporate	818	4 851	16 480	43 436	78 547	64 021	76 101	69 625	105 417	94 184
1210 On profits	818	4 851	16 315	43 436	78 547	64 021	76 101	69 625	105 417	94 184
Income tax on companies	791	4 574	15 220	42 221	76 655	62 549	74 535	67 794	103 318	92 191
Dividend and interest taxes	17	161	899	846	1 892	1 472	1 566	1 831	2 099	1 993
Other withholding taxes	0	116	196	369	0	0	0	0	0	0
1220 On capital gains	0	0	165	0	0	0	0	0	0	0
1300 Unallocable between 1100 and 1200	0	0	0	0	0	0	0	0	0	0
2000 Social security contributions	**0**	**0**	**0**	**0**	**0**	**0**	**0**	**0**	**0**	**0**
2100 Employees	0	0	0	0	0	0	0	0	0	0
2110 On a payroll basis	..	..	..	..	..	..	..	..	..	..
2120 On an income tax basis	..	..	..	..	..	..	..	..	..	..
2200 Employers	0	0	0	0	0	0	0	0	0	0
2210 On a payroll basis	..	..	..	..	..	..	..	..	..	..
2220 On an income tax basis	..	..	..	..	..	..	..	..	..	..
2300 Self-employed or non-employed	0	0	0	0	0	0	0	0	0	0
2310 On a payroll basis	..	..	..	..	..	..	..	..	..	..
2320 On an income tax basis	..	..	..	..	..	..	..	..	..	..
2400 Unallocable between 2100, 2200 and 2300	0	0	0	0	0	0	0	0	0	0
2410 On a payroll basis	..	..	..	..	..	..	..	..	..	..
2420 On an income tax basis	..	..	..	..	..	..	..	..	..	..
3000 Taxes on payroll and workforce	**157**	**1 988**	**7 115**	**9 624**	**16 407**	**18 492**	**22 210**	**23 354**	**26 923**	**26 027**
4000 Taxes on property	**576**	**3 105**	**10 427**	**18 825**	**31 130**	**33 498**	**40 929**	**49 168**	**53 114**	**53 982**
4100 Recurrent taxes on immovable property	341	1 886	6 148	9 067	15 615	19 907	23 603	26 649	32 694	33 803
4110 Households	..	..	..	..	..	..	..	..	..	..
4120 Others	..	..	..	..	..	..	..	..	..	..
4200 Recurrent taxes on net wealth	0	0	0	0	0	0	0	0	0	0
4210 Individual	..	..	..	..	..	..	..	..	..	..
4220 Corporate	..	..	..	..	..	..	..	..	..	..
4300 Estate, inheritance and gift taxes	137	175	0	0	0	0	0	0	0	0
4310 Estate and inheritance taxes	131	174	..	..	..	..	..	..	..	..
Estate duty central government	36	17	..	..	..	..	..	..	..	..
St. and loc. estate probate and succession	95	157	..	..	..	..	..	..	..	..
4320 Gift taxes	7	1	..	..	..	..	..	..	..	..
4400 Taxes on financial and capital transactions	98	1 044	4 279	9 758	15 515	13 591	17 326	22 519	20 420	20 179
4500 Non-recurrent taxes	0	0	0	0	0	0	0	0	0	0
4510 On net wealth	..	..	..	..	..	..	..	..	..	..
4520 Other non-recurrent taxes	..	..	..	..	..	..	..	..	..	..
4600 Other recurrent taxes on property	0	0	0	0	0	0	0	0	0	0
5000 Taxes on goods and services	**1 744**	**12 402**	**32 416**	**61 877**	**93 101**	**102 573**	**121 988**	**126 862**	**142 282**	**144 411**
5100 Taxes on production, sale, transfer, etc.	1 508	11 097	27 213	56 179	84 104	90 824	101 312	109 050	122 053	123 639
5110 General taxes	370	2 102	9 365	25 830	44 739	48 146	54 711	60 680	66 829	65 720
5111 Value added taxes	0	0	0	23 854	43 634	46 910	53 409	59 177	65 147	64 048
5112 Sales tax	370	2 102	9 365	1 976	1 105	1 236	1 302	1 503	1 682	1 672
5113 Other	0	0	0	0	0	0	0	0	0	0
5120 Taxes on specific goods and services	1 138	8 995	17 848	30 349	39 365	42 678	46 601	48 370	55 224	57 919
5121 Excise duties	781	6 183	11 975	19 768	24 357	26 689	26 472	22 541	24 486	24 065
Excises central government	752	5 834	10 359	19 019	23 526	25 803	25 648	21 625	23 488	23 116
Statutory corporate payments	0	83	378	295	231	452	343	405	435	480
Primary production charges	29	266	1 238	454	600	434	481	511	563	469
5122 Profits of fiscal monopolies	0	0	0	0	0	0	0	0	0	0
5123 Customs and import duties	271	1 799	3 319	4 606	6 070	5 828	9 280	14 046	15 944	19 507
Customs duties central government	271	1 799	3 319	4 606	6 070	5 828	9 280	14 046	15 944	19 507
5124 Taxes on exports	1	117	57	0	10	11	10	11	0	0
Customs duties on coal exports	0	85	54	..	0	0	0	0	..	..
Other	1	32	3	..	10	11	10	11	..	..
5125 Taxes on investment goods	0	0	0	0	0	0	0	0	0	0
5126 Taxes on specific services	85	896	2 497	5 975	8 928	10 150	10 839	11 772	14 794	14 347
Taxes race meetings	31	240	651	301	359	373	326	265	411	596
Poker machines	16	140	295	2 074	3 009	3 125	3 238	3 684	3 986	3 202
Lotteries	7	122	325	890	1 118	1 141	1 250	1 362	1 632	1 676
Levies on fire insurance companies	16	157	363	574	937	1 232	740	786	806	932
Other	15	237	863	2 136	3 505	4 279	5 285	5 675	7 959	7 941
5127 Other taxes on internat. trade and transactions	0	0	0	0	0	0	0	0	0	0
5128 Other taxes	0	0	0	0	0	0	0	0	0	0

	1965	1980	1990	2000	2007	2010	2013	2015	2018	2019
5130 Unallocable between 5110 and 5120	0	0	0	0	0	0	0	0	0	0
5200 Taxes on use of goods and perform activities	236	1 305	5 203	5 698	8 997	11 749	20 676	17 812	20 229	20 772
5210 Recurrent taxes	197	1 260	5 109	5 698	8 997	11 749	20 676	15 898	17 899	18 615
5211 Paid by households: motor vehicles	65	448	1 373	2 748	4 381	5 064	6 533	7 253	7 914	8 128
5212 Paid by others: motor vehicles	65	351	937	1 285	2 005	2 397	2 357	2 649	3 072	3 174
Fees on motor vehicle registry	46	312	794	778	1 165	1 499	1 338	1 530	1 864	1 975
Drivers licences	12	30	111	0	0	0	0	0	0	0
Stamp duty on vehicle registry	6	9	32	506	839	898	1 019	1 119	1 208	1 199
5213 Paid in respect of other goods	67	461	2 799	1 665	2 611	4 288	11 786	5 996	6 913	7 313
Broadcasting tv licences	37	21	125	210	288	150	157	128	52	37
Business franchise lic. tobac. fuel	0	221	2 016	227	0	0	2	1	0	0
Other taxes	2	12	33	1 129	2 321	4 136	11 603	5 846	6 816	7 271
Liquor taxes	28	206	603	97	2	1	24	22	45	5
Dog licenses	0	1	22	0	0	0	0	0	0	0
5220 Non-recurrent taxes	39	45	94	0	0	0	0	1 914	2 330	2 157
5300 Unallocable between 5100 and 5200	0	0	0	0	0	0	0	0	0	0
6000 Other taxes	**0**	**0**	**0**	**0**	**0**	**0**	**0**	**0**	**0**	**0**
6100 Paid solely by business	..	..	..	..	..	..	..	..	..	..
6200 Other	..	..	..	..	..	..	..	..	..	..
Non-wastable tax credits										
Non-wastable tax credits against 1110	..	..	..	195	2 585	991	323	460	437	378
Tax expenditure component	..	..	..	175	178	110	215	334	310	266
Transfer component	..	..	..	20	2 407	881	108	126	127	112
Non-wastable tax credits against 1210	..	..	..	0	4 564	5 726	7 914	8 951	9 963	9 642
Tax expenditure component	..	..	..	..	1 922	2 253	2 147	3 438	3 501	3 198
Transfer component	..	..	..	..	2 642	3 473	5 767	5 513	6 462	6 444
Total tax revenue on cash basis	**5 024**	**39 878**	**116 500**	**..**	**..**	**..**	**..**	**..**	**..**	**..**
Total tax revenue on accrual basis	**..**	**..**	**..**	**214 753**	**346 772**	**356 747**	**431 200**	**460 729**	**557 175**	**549 536**
Conciliation with National Accounts										
Additional taxes included in National Accounts	..	..	..	0	0	0	0	0	0	0
Taxes excluded from National Accounts	..	..	..	0	0	0	0	0	0	0
Difference in treatment of tax credits	..	..	..	175	2 100	2 363	2 362	3 772	3 811	3 464
Capital transfer for uncollected revenue	..	..	..	0	0	0	0	0	0	0
Voluntary social security contributions	..	..	..	0	0	0	0	0	0	0
Miscellaneous differences	..	..	..	0	0	0	0	0	0	0
National Accounts: Taxes and actual social contributions	..	..	..	214 928	348 872	359 110	433 562	464 501	560 986	553 000
Imputed social contributions	..	..	..	0	0	0	0	0	0	0
National Accounts: Taxes and all social contributions	..	..	..	214 928	348 872	359 110	433 562	464 501	560 986	553 000

.. Not available

Note: Data are on a fiscal year basis beginning 1st July.

From 1998 taxes are recorded on an accrual basis; prior to that they were on a cash basis.

Direct taxes paid by public trading enterprises are excluded from receipts.

The figures for total tax revenue do not match the published totals in Taxation Revenue Australia. The latter is based on an accrual IMF GFS methodology and there are some differences between that and the OECD equivalent.

Heading 5213 includes radio and television licenses fees, though these are usually not regarded as a tax revenue in the OECD list.

Headings for non-wastable tax credits 1110 and 1210 include the private health insurance tax offset, family benefit, baby bonus tax offsets (paid during the 2003-04 budget year), film tax offset, and research and development tax offsets. The estimation of non-wastable credits into the expenditure and transfer components is in accordance with the OECD guidelines on the treatment and the data for this memorandum item has been provided by the Australian Taxation Office.

Source: Australian Bureau of Statistics.

StatLink https://stat.link/zmd07q

Table 5.2. Austria: Details of tax revenue, 1965-2019

Million EUR

	1965	1980	1990	2000	2007	2010	2013	2015	2018	2019
Total tax revenue	**6 210**	**29 759**	**54 040**	**90 324**	**115 146**	**121 192**	**138 099**	**148 469**	**162 817**	**169 216**
Total tax revenue exclusive of taxes collected for the EU	..	..	**54 040**	**89 897**	**114 728**	**120 843**	**137 741**	**147 841**	**162 137**	**168 535**
1000 Taxes on income, profits and capital gains	**1 584**	**7 959**	**13 797**	**25 553**	**34 319**	**34 021**	**39 792**	**44 796**	**47 758**	**49 864**
1100 Of individuals	1 240	6 899	11 326	19 890	25 741	27 098	31 474	35 841	36 194	38 239
1110 On income and profits	1 240	6 899	11 326	19 890	25 741	27 098	31 474	35 841	36 194	38 239
Income tax	415	1 576	2 501	3 202	3 253	3 358	3 737	4 274	5 014	5 572
Special income tax	0	0	0	0	0	0	0	0	0	0
Wage tax	417	4 626	7 823	15 630	20 607	21 783	25 669	28 429	28 344	29 631
Tax on industry and trade	196	402	454	7	0	0	0	0	0	0
Tax on capital yields	2	14	46	354	970	938	981	1 979	1 533	1 683
Contribution to chambers	60	279	501	697	910	1 018	1 087	1 159	1 302	1 352
Water supply fund	151	0	0	0	0	0	0	0	0	0
Contribution emergency fund	0	0	0	0	0	0	0	0	0	0
1120 On capital gains	0	0	0	0	0	0	0	0	0	0
1200 Corporate	334	1 049	1 930	4 157	6 622	5 519	6 963	7 659	10 440	10 795
1210 On profits	334	1 049	1 930	4 157	6 622	5 519	6 963	7 659	10 440	10 795
Corporation tax	195	698	998	3 865	6 094	4 978	6 377	6 752	9 676	9 995
Tax on industry and trade	83	254	624	10	0	1	0	0	0	0
Special tax on income	0	0	0	0	0	0	0	0	0	0
Tax on capital yields	5	33	108	118	346	347	370	684	513	561
Water supply fund	35	0	0	0	0	0	0	0	0	0
Contribution emergency fund	0	0	0	0	0	0	0	0	0	0
Contribution to chambers	14	58	200	164	182	193	216	224	251	240
Directors tax	2	6	0	0	0	0	0	0	0	0
1220 On capital gains	0	0	0	0	0	0	0	0	0	0
1300 Unallocable between 1100 and 1200	10	12	540	1 506	1 956	1 405	1 354	1 295	1 125	830
Fines related to tax offences	10	12	18	33	77	99	73	70	96	85
Tax on interest	0	0	522	1 473	1 879	1 305	1 282	1 225	1 028	746
2000 Social security contributions	**1 548**	**9 200**	**17 763**	**30 510**	**38 453**	**41 423**	**46 845**	**49 867**	**56 671**	**59 077**
2100 Employees	686	3 792	7 512	12 477	15 612	16 846	18 931	20 115	22 806	23 772
2110 On a payroll basis	..	..	..	12 477	15 612	16 846	18 931	20 115	22 806	23 772
Health insurance contributions	..	..	..	2 606	3 326	3 675	4 082	4 347	4 989	5 206
Pension insurance contributions	..	..	..	6 410	8 274	8 986	10 183	10 896	12 568	13 211
Pension contributions, civil servants	..	..	..	1 489	1 579	1 625	1 672	1 629	1 570	1 553
Unemployment insurance contributions	..	..	..	1 854	2 284	2 385	2 803	3 040	3 453	3 567
Health insurance contributions, local government employees	..	..	..	100	130	156	169	181	199	206
Special unemployment insurance contributions	..	..	..	17	19	20	22	23	27	29
2120 On an income tax basis	..	..	..	0	0	0	0	0	0	0
2200 Employers	721	4 563	8 768	14 651	18 091	19 421	21 922	23 281	26 710	27 826
2210 On a payroll basis	..	..	..	14 651	18 091	19 421	21 922	23 281	26 710	27 826
Health insurance contributions	..	..	..	2 667	3 395	3 669	4 075	4 339	4 980	5 197
Pension insurance contributions	..	..	..	7 888	10 214	11 145	12 642	13 549	15 681	16 475
Pension contributions, civil servants	..	..	..	438	376	361	297	298	265	261
Accident insurance contributions	..	..	..	952	1 157	1 254	1 409	1 394	1 573	1 527
Unemployment insurance contributions	..	..	..	1 854	2 284	2 385	2 803	3 040	3 453	3 567
Health insurance contributions, local government employees	..	..	..	101	141	157	170	181	199	207
Contributions to sickness benefit fund	..	..	..	341	0	0	0	0	0	0
Special pension contributions, nightshift workers	..	..	..	11	18	15	31	38	42	44
Contributions to insolvency fund	..	..	..	381	488	416	473	419	374	394
Special unemployment insurance contributions construction workers	..	..	..	17	19	20	22	23	143	154
2220 On an income tax basis	..	..	..	0	0	0	0	0	0	0
2300 Self-employed or non-employed	141	845	1 482	3 382	4 750	5 155	5 993	6 470	7 156	7 479
2310 On a payroll basis	..	..	..	3 382	4 750	5 155	5 993	6 470	7 156	7 479
Health insurance contributions	..	..	..	1 971	2 724	3 090	3 441	3 664	3 987	4 142
Pension insurance contributions	..	..	..	1 117	1 527	1 524	1 973	2 210	2 562	2 712
Pension contributions, civil servants (retired)	..	..	..	116	274	297	315	317	309	308
Accident insurance contributions	..	..	..	77	85	88	95	98	98	110
Health insurance contributions, local government employees	..	..	..	101	140	156	169	181	199	206
2320 On an income tax basis	..	..	..	0	0	0	0	0	0	0
2400 Unallocable between 2100, 2200 and 2300	0	0	0	0	0	0	0	0	0	0
2410 On a payroll basis	..	..	..	..	..	..	..	..	..	..
2420 On an income tax basis	..	..	..	..	..	..	..	..	..	..

	1965	1980	1990	2000	2007	2010	2013	2015	2018	2019
3000 Taxes on payroll and workforce	**472**	**2 097**	**3 259**	**5 788**	**7 266**	**8 359**	**9 489**	**10 040**	**10 416**	**10 780**
Emplr. contr. equaliz. of family.burdens	318	1 397	2 147	3 140	3 915	4 762	5 319	5 623	5 399	5 548
Tax on sum of wages	82	375	669	1 735	2 238	2 402	2 742	2 911	3 300	3 471
Promotion residential buildings	44	217	389	595	754	811	915	965	1 125	1 162
Tax on employment (Vienna undergr.)	0	20	21	21	22	22	67	65	67	70
Special levy for households allowances	26	80	0	0	0	0	0	0	0	0
Disabled persons equalization levy	2	8	34	54	83	91	138	148	155	160
Contributions to chambers	0	0	0	242	253	271	308	327	369	369
4000 Taxes on property	**246**	**858**	**1 473**	**1 206**	**1 572**	**1 555**	**2 341**	**1 965**	**2 100**	**2 158**
4100 Recurrent taxes on immovable property	92	231	355	526	626	682	736	761	807	829
4110 Households	47	66	84	87	92	93	105	107	110	133
Duty on farms	9	15	20	20	20	20	29	30	30	40
Farm contr. equaliz. of family burdens	5	6	6	6	6	6	6	6	7	8
Farm contribution to chambers	14	23	32	32	39	40	43	44	46	51
Contr. residential buildings reconstruction	4	0	0	0	0	0	0	0	0	0
Land tax A	16	22	25	28	26	26	26	26	28	34
4120 Others	45	165	271	440	534	589	631	654	697	696
Tax on vacant plots	1	4	5	5	5	6	6	6	6	6
Land tax B	44	161	266	435	529	583	625	649	691	690
4200 Recurrent taxes on net wealth	103	401	642	1	0	0	0	0	0	0
4210 Individual	37	140	189	1	..	..	..	..	..	..
Capital tax	25	109	189	1	..	..	..	..	..	..
Contribution emergency fund	0	0	0	0	..	..	..	..	..	..
Tax on industry and trade	10	26	0	0	..	..	..	..	..	..
Contribution to chambers	2	6	0	0	..	..	..	..	..	..
4220 Corporate	66	260	453	0	..	..	..	..	..	..
Capital tax	24	139	322	0	..	..	..	..	..	..
Capital death duty	20	53	131	0	..	..	..	..	..	..
Contribution emergency fund	0	0	0	0	..	..	..	..	..	..
Tax on industry and trade	19	56	0	0	..	..	..	..	..	..
Contribution to chambers	3	13	0	0	..	..	..	..	..	..
4300 Estate, inheritance and gift taxes	16	50	77	111	155	35	19	12	9	1
4310 Estate and inheritance taxes	..	..	..	..	..	..	..	..	..	..
4320 Gift taxes	..	..	..	..	..	..	..	..	..	..
4400 Taxes on financial and capital transactions	35	176	399	568	791	828	858	1 116	1 210	1 318
Land transfer tax	30	150	251	452	644	727	790	1 014	1 208	1 317
Capital transfer tax	5	27	148	115	147	102	67	102	2	1
4500 Non-recurrent taxes	0	0	0	0	0	10	728	76	75	11
4510 On net wealth	..	..	..	..	..	0	717	4	-1	0
Withholding tax	..	..	..	..	..	..	717	4	-1	0
4520 Other non-recurrent taxes	..	..	..	..	..	10	11	72	75	11
Foundation tax	..	..	..	..	..	10	11	72	75	11
4600 Other recurrent taxes on property	0	0	0	0	0	0	0	0	0	0
5000 Taxes on goods and services	**2 321**	**9 379**	**17 034**	**26 497**	**32 609**	**34 740**	**38 701**	**41 064**	**45 096**	**46 529**
5100 Taxes on production, sale, transfer, etc.	2 275	9 006	16 169	24 616	30 180	32 114	35 721	37 633	41 293	42 476
5110 General taxes	1 160	5 984	11 229	16 857	20 941	22 711	24 920	26 282	29 324	30 426
5111 Value added taxes	0	5 984	11 229	16 857	20 941	22 711	24 920	26 282	29 324	30 426
5112 Sales tax	0	0	0	0	0	0	0	0	0	0
5113 Other	1 160	0	0	0	0	0	0	0	0	0
Turnover tax	664	..	..	..	..	..	..	..	..	..
Additional federal levy-turnover	332	..	..	..	..	..	..	..	..	..
Additional lieu invoice stp.	164	..	..	..	..	..	..	..	..	..
5120 Taxes on specific goods and services	1 115	2 996	4 873	7 721	9 236	9 400	10 800	11 348	11 967	12 046

	1965	1980	1990	2000	2007	2010	2013	2015	2018	2019
5121 Excise duties	610	2 219	3 290	5 484	6 760	6 921	7 598	7 749	8 196	8 217
Tax on beer	39	44	56	161	200	198	193	189	200	190
Tax on wine	7	0	0	0	0	0	0	0	0	0
Tax on sparkling wine	1	7	25	25	1	1	1	19	23	24
Tax on tobacco	188	519	820	1 197	1 446	1 502	1 664	1 782	1 919	1 891
Tax on mineral oils	50	136	1 426	2 726	3 689	3 854	4 173	4 218	4 363	4 480
Additional federal levy mineral oils	202	876	0	0	0	0	0	0	0	0
Special duty alcoholic drinks	0	142	193	0	0	0	0	0	0	0
Special duty vehicles	0	0	0	0	0	0	0	0	0	0
Duty on starch products	0	4	13	0	0	0	0	0	0	0
Beverage tax	46	216	364	178	3	-1	-1	0	0	0
Other receipts-Market Organisation Act	26	35	9	0	1	0	0	0	0	0
Transport equality levy	0	5	1	0	0	0	0	0	0	0
Market Organisation Act - milk	35	177	192	0	0	0	0	0	0	0
Market Organisation Act - livestock	0	0	0	0	0	0	0	0	0	0
Market Organisation Act - grain	16	23	142	0	0	0	0	0	0	0
Duty promotion milk distrib.	0	34	13	0	0	0	0	0	0	0
Special tax on mineral oils	0	0	37	0	0	0	0	0	0	0
Duty on vehicles (fuel consumption)	0	0	0	433	457	453	455	395	532	555
Agricultural fund	0	0	0	23	16	18	18	17	18	17
Tax on energy	0	0	0	562	764	726	886	931	943	866
Social contributions to the artists' fund	0	0	0	0	11	6	7	13	7	7
Duty on exceeding milk-quota	0	0	0	36	24	6	26	11	0	0
Car registration taxes	0	0	0	143	148	158	175	174	191	188
5122 Profits of fiscal monopolies	37	57	52	130	122	129	324	328	403	400
Duty on spirits	5	14	17	130	122	129	130	120	154	154
Federal monopolies salt	1	0	0	0	0	0	0	0	0	0
Federal monopolies spirits	30	43	35	0	0	0	0	0	0	0
Federal monopolies gambling	0	0	0	0	0	0	194	208	248	246
5123 Customs and import duties	332	354	677	351	390	340	328	415	484	483
Customs duties	310	237	418	352	390	339	328	415	484	483
Other import duties	0	21	61	0	0	0	0	0	0	0
Contribution promote foreign trade	10	63	171	0	0	0	0	0	0	0
Import equalization duties	12	33	27	0	0	0	0	0	0	0
5124 Taxes on exports	8	36	1	0	0	0	0	0	0	0
Contribution to promote foreign trade	8	36	1	..	..	..	..	..	..	..
5125 Taxes on investment goods	0	33	0	0	0	0	0	0	0	0
5126 Taxes on specific services	129	297	854	1 720	1 967	2 005	2 545	2 852	2 887	2 945
Insurance tax	25	135	384	745	993	1 017	1 056	1 122	1 179	1 215
Transport tax	63	0	0	0	0	0	0	0	0	0
Duty on casinos	2	28	64	105	71	55	45	70	105	114
Fire protection tax	5	24	50	45	54	56	57	61	63	66
Advertisement tax	7	31	65	62	0	0	0	0	0	0
Entertainment tax	2	2	2	5	8	9	21	18	1	0
Tax on tourism	8	43	71	103	142	171	182	186	239	255
Amusement tax	13	17	51	73	94	107	84	30	16	18
Announcement tax	3	18	40	81	0	1	0	0	0	0
Tax on interest yields	0	0	0	0	0	0	0	0	0	0
Tax on gambling stakes - licences	0	0	116	197	202	221	251	254	292	273
Tax on advertisement	0	0	0	33	108	110	110	107	108	106
Levy on dangerous waste	0	0	10	71	72	51	53	56	79	69
Duty for airways security	0	0	0	28	56	30	0	0	0	0
Tax on gambling stakes - gains	0	0	0	171	166	176	0	0	0	0
Flight Charge	0	0	0	0	0	0	98	109	71	72
Financial Institutions Stability Fees	0	0	0	0	0	0	588	640	534	558
SRF Contributions	..	..	..	..	..	..	..	198	199	198
5127 Other taxes on internat. trade and transactions	0	0	0	0	0	0	0	0	0	0
5128 Other taxes	0	0	0	34	-3	4	4	4	-3	0
Levy on sugar	..	..	..	34	-3	4	4	4	-3	..
5130 Unallocable between 5110 and 5120	0	26	66	38	3	4	2	4	3	5
Fines related to tax offenses	..	26	66	38	3	4	2	4	3	5
5200 Taxes on use of goods and perform activities	46	373	865	1 881	2 429	2 626	2 980	3 431	3 803	4 052
5210 Recurrent taxes	38	335	757	1 733	2 253	2 416	2 715	3 124	3 469	3 571
5211 Paid by households: motor vehicles	22	156	366	811	1 173	1 293	1 482	1 814	2 033	2 106
5212 Paid by others: motor vehicles	13	41	97	298	370	334	352	421	471	487
5213 Paid in respect of other goods	3	138	294	624	710	789	881	890	965	978
Hunting and fishing duties	1	4	7	10	10	10	19	22	22	24
Dog tax	1	4	6	8	10	11	17	18	20	21
Contribution to promotion of arts	1	3	8	71	120	132	147	143	167	170
Tax on radio and tv - licenses	0	15	46	450	571	636	698	708	756	763
Road transport duty	0	112	226	84	0	0	0	0	0	0

	1965	1980	1990	2000	2007	2010	2013	2015	2018	2019
5220 Non-recurrent taxes	8	38	108	147	175	210	265	307	334	481
Certain user fees; taxes on emission of noxious gases	8	38	108	147	175	210	265	307	334	481
5300 Unallocable between 5100 and 5200	0	0	0	0	0	0	0	0	0	0
6000 Other taxes	**38**	**266**	**714**	**770**	**928**	**1 095**	**931**	**737**	**776**	**808**
Tax on financial institutions	0	0	123	-3	0	0	0	0	0	0
Administration duties	4	17	32	278	366	521	517	302	331	338
Stamp fees	7	46	76	135	92	84	27	32	33	35
Contributions of interested persons	0	0	130	0	0	0	0	0	0	0
Parking duty	0	0	6	0	0	0	0	0	0	0
Contrbutions to students' associations	0	0	0	4	8	11	12	11	14	15
Duty on contribution to political parties	0	0	0	0	-1	1	0	0	0	0
Other fees, taxes on production n.e.c.	0	0	0	272	346	353	227	252	248	263
Embossing fee	0	0	0	0	1	1	1	1	1	1
Other taxes	28	202	347	82	115	124	145	137	146	151
Compensation levy according to the Vienna Tree Protection Act	..	..	0	1	1	2	1	2	3	5
6100 Paid solely by business	..	..	..	..	..	..	..	..	..	..
6200 Other	..	..	..	..	..	..	..	..	..	..
Memorandum items										
Customs duties collected on behalf of the EU	..	..	..	352	390	339	328	415	484	483
SRF contributions collected on behalf of the EU	..	..	..	..	..	..	..	198	199	198
Non-wastable tax credits										
Non-wastable tax credits against 1110	..	..	..	650	650	650	570	540	330	330
Tax expenditure component	..	..	..	590	450	422	341	295	230	230
Transfer component	..	..	..	60	200	228	229	245	100	100
Non-wastable tax credits against 1210	..	..	..	..	..	..	..	..	..	..
Tax expenditure component	..	..	..	..	..	..	..	..	..	..
Transfer component	..	..	..	..	..	..	..	..	..	..
Total tax revenue on cash basis	**6 210**	**29 759**	**54 040**	**90 299**	**115 045**	**120 735**	**137 970**	**148 036**	**162 777**	**168 647**
Total tax revenue on accrual basis	**..**	**..**	**..**	**90 324**	**115 146**	**121 192**	**138 099**	**148 469**	**162 817**	**169 216**
Conciliation with National Accounts										
Additional taxes included in National Accounts	..	..	..	..	..	..	..	..	..	..
Taxes excluded from National Accounts	..	..	..	..	..	..	..	..	..	..
Difference in treatment of tax credits	..	..	..	590	450	422	341	295	230	230
Capital transfer for uncollected revenue	..	..	..	..	..	..	..	..	..	..
Voluntary social security contributions	..	..	..	206	256	339	299	321	321	336
Miscellaneous differences	..	..	..	0	0	0	0	0	0	0
National Accounts: Taxes and actual social contributions	..	..	..	91 120	115 853	121 953	138 739	149 085	163 368	169 781
Imputed social contributions	..	..	..	2 485	2 177	2 106	1 972	1 925	1 757	1 703
National Accounts: Taxes and all social contributions	..	..	..	93 605	118 030	124 060	140 711	151 010	165 126	171 485

.. Not available

Note: Year ending 31st December.

From 1995 data are on accrual basis.

Following national practice, one-third of the revenues from stamp fees (heading 6000) and fifty percent of the revenues from administration duties (heading 6000) are treated as tax revenues, the remainder being treated as non-tax revenue.

From 1988 onwards promoting residential building is being mainly financed by capital transfers from the Federal Government to the Länder. For the years 1985 to 1987 legally fixed shares of some taxes have been transmitted automatically from Federal Government to the Länder for this purpose and these funds have been classified as tax receipts of the Länder in those years. From 1988, they are classified as Federal Government tax revenues. This break in the time series (1987/1988) affects only the shares of the different subsectors and not total tax revenues.

From 1998 contributions of interested persons and parking duties are classified as non-tax revenues (sales) and no longer reported under heading 6000.

Source: Statistics Austria.

StatLink https://stat.link/qlpahy

Table 5.3. Belgium: Details of tax revenue, 1965-2019

Million EUR

	1965	1980	1990	2000	2007	2010	2013	2015	2018	2019
Total tax revenue	**6 421**	**37 443**	**70 408**	**112 710**	**147 861**	**156 317**	**177 665**	**184 429**	**202 587**	**204 023**
Total tax revenue exclusive of taxes collected for the EU	..	..	..	**111 675**	**146 411**	**155 042**	**176 488**	**182 812**	**200 670**	**202 080**
1000 Taxes on income, profits and capital gains	**1 774**	**15 379**	**25 983**	**43 461**	**52 854**	**53 313**	**62 762**	**65 572**	**74 279**	**71 804**
1100 Of individuals	1 317	13 626	22 538	35 318	41 020	44 027	50 518	51 877	54 421	53 997
1110 On income and profits	1 317	13 626	22 538	35 318	41 020	44 027	50 518	51 877	54 421	53 997
Immovable income withholding tax	148	532	1 053	1 857	0	0	0	0	0	0
Movable income withholding tax	119	1 062	3 014	1 755	2 351	2 426	4 314	4 104	3 641	3 693
Earned income withholding tax	740	9 119	15 422	27 778	36 022	39 829	44 686	45 658	47 602	47 635
Advance payments PIT	125	1 776	2 144	1 959	1 747	1 611	1 508	1 547	1 664	1 586
Non residents tax	0	-2	4	585	792	810	841	926	1 080	1 133
Assessments PIT	183	1 128	878	774	-915	-1 697	-1 988	-1 512	-859	-1 360
Special social contributions	0	0	19	602	957	1 032	1 117	1 106	1 253	1 267
Other income taxes	0	12	2	8	65	17	41	48	39	42
1120 On capital gains	0	0	0	0	0	0	0	0	0	0
1200 Corporate	397	1 744	3 405	8 065	11 749	9 249	12 192	13 644	19 787	17 736
1210 On profits	397	1 744	3 405	8 065	11 749	9 249	12 192	13 644	19 787	17 736
Immovable income withholding tax (corporate)	33	0	0	0	0	0	0	0	0	0
Movable income withholding tax (corporate)	41	367	1 206	527	686	315	477	466	354	361
Advance payments (corporate)	262	1 273	2 735	7 112	9 733	7 691	7 930	8 539	13 965	14 621
Assessments (corporate)	60	79	-553	404	1 270	1 196	3 662	4 466	5 276	2 571
Non residents tax (corporate)	0	-6	18	17	41	43	113	154	194	191
Other income taxes (corporate)	0	32	-2	5	19	4	10	19	-2	-7
1220 On capital gains	0	0	0	0	0	0	0	0	0	0
1300 Unallocable between 1100 and 1200	61	9	40	77	85	38	52	51	72	71
Former income taxes	51	0	0	0	0	0	0	0	0	0
Penalties	3	0	0	0	0	0	0	0	0	0
Other	7	9	40	77	85	38	52	51	72	71
2000 Social security contributions	**2 018**	**10 798**	**23 386**	**34 865**	**45 929**	**50 674**	**56 527**	**58 812**	**61 105**	**63 203**
2100 Employees	569	3 130	7 152	10 932	13 847	14 996	16 476	17 036	18 418	19 071
2110 On a payroll basis	..	3 130	7 152	10 932	13 847	14 996	16 476	17 036	18 418	19 071
On gross wages	..	3 130	7 062	10 932	13 847	14 996	16 476	17 036	18 418	19 071
On social benefits	..	0	89	0	0	0	0	0	0	0
2120 On an income tax basis	..	0	0	0	0	0	0	0	0	0
2200 Employers	1 320	6 791	14 689	21 027	28 216	31 041	34 915	36 240	36 585	37 902
2210 On a payroll basis	..	6 791	14 689	21 027	28 216	31 041	34 915	36 240	36 585	37 902
Contributions by government	..	1 059	1 769	3 105	4 493	5 381	6 678	7 686	8 263	8 541
Contributions by other sectors	..	5 732	12 920	17 922	23 723	25 661	28 236	28 554	28 322	29 362
2220 On an income tax basis	..	0	0	0	0	0	0	0	0	0
2300 Self-employed or non-employed	129	877	1 546	2 906	3 866	4 637	5 136	5 537	6 102	6 230
Self-employed	..	803	1 230	2 053	2 678	3 342	3 703	3 975	4 238	4 327
Unemployed	..	0	0	0	0	0	0	0	0	0
Retired	..	29	198	709	1 012	1 134	1 324	1 449	1 744	1 778
Other	..	45	118	144	176	161	109	113	120	125
2310 On a payroll basis	..	877	1 546	2 906	3 866	4 637	5 136	5 537	6 102	6 230
2320 On an income tax basis	..	0	0	0	0	0	0	0	0	0
2400 Unallocable between 2100, 2200 and 2300	0	0	0	0	0	0	0	0	0	0
2410 On a payroll basis	..	..	..	..	..	..	..	..	..	..
2420 On an income tax basis	..	..	..	..	..	..	..	..	..	..
3000 Taxes on payroll and workforce	**0**	**0**	**0**	**0**	**6**	**7**	**8**	**8**	**7**	**9**
Levy on public mandates	..	..	..	..	6	7	8	8	7	9
4000 Taxes on property	**240**	**1 161**	**2 679**	**5 282**	**10 550**	**11 252**	**13 805**	**14 408**	**15 832**	**16 358**
4100 Recurrent taxes on immovable property	2	210	599	1 164	4 146	4 632	5 187	5 433	5 685	6 145
4110 Households	0	26	63	102	2 779	3 115	3 478	3 651	3 855	4 174
4120 Others	2	184	536	1 063	1 367	1 517	1 710	1 782	1 831	1 971
Tax on non profit institutions	2	7	17	41	32	33	38	41	47	47
Immovable income withholding tax (corporate)	0	177	519	929	1 269	1 416	1 584	1 651	1 686	1 830
Regional tax (Brussels)	0	0	0	94	66	68	88	90	98	94
4200 Recurrent taxes on net wealth	0	0	0	92	253	237	451	661	952	922
4210 Individual	..	..	..	0	0	0	0	0	0	0
4220 Corporate	..	..	..	92	253	237	451	661	952	922
4300 Estate, inheritance and gift taxes	75	309	504	1 101	2 053	2 269	3 096	2 996	3 196	2 936
4310 Estate and inheritance taxes	69	281	475	1 042	1 702	1 939	2 634	2 504	2 677	2 400
4320 Gift taxes	6	29	29	59	351	330	463	492	519	536

	1965	1980	1990	2000	2007	2010	2013	2015	2018	2019
4400 Taxes on financial and capital transactions	163	633	1 478	2 669	3 704	3 493	3 886	4 358	4 899	5 379
Registration duties	153	527	1 213	1 967	3 325	3 210	3 542	3 899	4 439	4 911
Mortgage duties	2	10	29	37	76	75	72	93	83	95
Court duties	2	8	29	38	31	34	37	41	31	32
Economic expansion fund	0	0	0	0	0	0	0	0	0	0
Tax on stock exchange transactions	4	31	92	386	234	134	193	287	307	298
Tax on stock exchange listings	2	4	21	0	0	0	0	0	0	0
Tax on bearer securities	0	0	0	79	3	0	6	0	0	0
Stamp duties	0	53	94	161	35	40	36	38	41	42
4500 Non-recurrent taxes	0	0	0	74	163	327	877	643	576	456
4510 On net wealth	..	..	..	0	0	0	0	0	0	0
4520 Other non-recurrent taxes	..	..	..	74	163	327	877	643	576	456
Tax on long term savings	..	..	..	74	163	194	207	413	361	342
Voluntary disclosure tax	..	..	..	0	0	0	0	0	0	0
Voluntary disclosure tax (Diamond)	..	..	..	0	0	0	0	0	0	0
Voluntary disclosure tax (bis)	..	..	..	0	0	133	614	152	66	28
Voluntary disclosure tax (ter)	..	..	..	0	0	0	54	78	148	85
Special contribution on credit associations	..	..	..	0	0	0	2	0	0	0
4600 Other recurrent taxes on property	0	8	99	182	232	294	309	318	524	522
Levy for fighting the non-use of an electric power production site by a producer	..	..	..	0	-16	0	0	0	0	0
Transfer to the Fund for Industrial Accidents of recognized private insurance corporations	..	..	..	182	249	294	309	318	297	305
Tax on securities accounts	..	..	..	0	0	0	0	0	226	217
5000 Taxes on goods and services	**2 386**	**10 105**	**18 360**	**29 103**	**38 462**	**41 035**	**44 517**	**45 589**	**51 364**	**52 649**
5100 Taxes on production, sale, transfer, etc.	2 187	9 606	17 387	27 000	36 091	38 646	42 087	43 098	48 731	49 760
5110 General taxes	1 355	6 321	11 570	18 258	24 411	25 882	27 979	28 170	31 775	32 563
5111 Value added taxes	0	6 321	11 547	18 132	24 140	25 628	27 738	27 952	31 545	32 181
VAT	..	6 293	11 491	18 132	24 140	25 628	27 738	27 952	31 545	32 181
Vehicle immatriculation tax	..	28	56	0	0	0	0	0	0	0
5112 Sales tax	0	0	23	126	271	253	241	219	230	381
5113 Other	1 355	0	0	0	0	0	0	0	0	0
Taxes assimilated to stamp duties	1 355	..	..	..	..	..	..	..	..	..
5120 Taxes on specific goods and services	832	3 285	5 818	8 742	11 680	12 764	14 109	14 927	16 955	17 197
5121 Excise duties	531	1 997	3 478	5 690	7 367	7 783	8 036	8 649	10 129	9 990
Mineral oil	278	1 109	2 017	3 392	3 891	4 148	4 072	4 556	5 545	5 426
Liquified gases and benzol	0	4	0	0	0	0	0	0	0	0
Tobacco	132	501	868	1 342	1 821	1 885	2 197	2 262	2 363	2 404
Spirits	23	123	191	206	225	235	272	318	314	311
Consumption tax on alcohol and spirits	26	54	0	0	0	0	0	0	0	0
Fermented sparkling beverages	1	7	11	24	39	57	77	92	102	104
Fermented fruit beverages	18	57	88	101	115	116	132	148	173	174
Beer	38	93	170	208	191	188	183	194	201	200
Non-alcoholic beverages	10	44	113	148	49	54	58	56	175	183
Coffee, sugar and syrup	5	5	22	13	12	13	15	14	14	15
Levy on energy	0	0	0	193	341	383	337	343	337	340
Intermediate alcoholic products	0	0	0	32	28	26	26	26	26	25
Inspection fee on domestic fuel oil	0	0	0	29	43	51	41	36	31	30
Ecotax	0	0	0	2	1	0	1	0	0	0
Levy on packaging	0	0	0	0	296	320	332	336	352	349
Federal contribution on electricity and natural gas	0	0	0	0	311	292	281	269	497	430
Environmental charge	0	0	0	0	5	15	14	1	0	0
5122 Profits of fiscal monopolies	0	0	0	0	0	0	0	0	0	0
5123 Customs and import duties	272	627	809	960	1 388	1 234	1 185	1 373	1 632	1 673
Import duties	206	0	0	0	0	0	0	0	0	0
Levies on agricultural products	63	0	0	0	0	0	0	0	0	0
ECSC levies	2	0	0	0	0	0	0	0	0	0
EU levies, import duties	0	383	716	932	1 365	1 210	1 149	1 368	1 632	1 673
EU levies on agricultural products	0	244	93	28	23	23	36	5	0	0
5124 Taxes on exports	0	1	0	0	0	0	0	0	0	0
5125 Taxes on investment goods	0	0	0	0	0	0	0	0	0	0
5126 Taxes on specific services	29	452	937	1 365	2 044	2 454	3 136	3 210	3 293	3 320
Gambling and betting tax	9	47	51	45	64	77	73	80	103	107
Insurance levy	19	404	885	1 282	1 930	2 123	2 285	2 307	2 470	2 512
Bill-posting tax	0	0	1	1	3	3	3	3	3	3
Deposit insurance	0	0	0	36	48	252	609	441	432	428
Resolution fund	..	..	..	..	..	..	167	380	285	270
5127 Other taxes on internat. trade and transactions	0	0	0	0	0	0	0	0	0	0
5128 Other taxes	0	208	593	726	881	1 294	1 751	1 695	1 901	2 214
5130 Unallocable between 5110 and 5120	0	0	0	0	0	0	0	0	0	0
5200 Taxes on use of goods and perform activities	199	496	966	2 096	2 363	2 384	2 420	2 482	2 622	2 877
5210 Recurrent taxes	199	496	966	1 887	2 032	2 005	2 023	2 032	1 955	1 973
Traffic tax	100	368	712	1 413	1 693	1 702	1 830	1 851	1 852	1 897

	1965	1980	1990	2000	2007	2010	2013	2015	2018	2019
5211 Paid by households: motor vehicles	0	204	458	889	1 051	1 054	1 148	1 163	1 240	1 270
5212 Paid by others: motor vehicles	0	164	254	525	642	648	683	689	612	626
5213 Paid in respect of other goods	99	127	254	474	338	303	193	181	104	76
Tax on entertainment devices	6	20	20	71	56	58	74	56	52	53
Tax on pubs	1	5	24	18	0	0	0	0	0	0
Hunting tax	2	0	0	0	0	0	0	0	0	0
Local taxes	90	15	19	38	99	112	10	22	23	23
Radio and television licence fees	0	87	191	347	184	133	108	103	29	0
5220 Non-recurrent taxes	0	0	0	209	332	379	397	451	667	904
Vehicle registration tax	..	..	..	209	332	379	360	349	473	497
Vehicle registration tax (households)	..	..	..	139	221	252	240	233	315	331
Vehicle registration tax (others)	..	..	..	70	111	126	120	116	158	166
Emission permits	..	..	..	0	0	0	36	101	193	407
5300 Unallocable between 5100 and 5200	0	3	7	7	7	6	10	9	11	13
6000 Other taxes	**2**	**0**	**0**	**0**	**61**	**36**	**46**	**40**	**0**	**0**
6100 Paid solely by business	0	..	..	..	0	0	0	0	..	..
6200 Other	2	..	..	..	61	36	46	40	..	..
Fines and interest	2	..	..	..	0	0	0	0	..	..
Memorandum items										
Customs duties collected on behalf of the EU	..	..	..	960	1 388	1 234	1 185	1 373	1 632	1 673
SRF contributions collected on behalf of the EU	..	..	..	..	..	..	167	380	285	270
Other taxes collected on behalf of the EU	..	..	..	75	62	42	-7	9	..	..
Taxes and compulsory social security contributions paid by EU civil servants	..	..	..	310	521	685	665	731	825	869
Taxes paid by EU civil servants: income taxes	..	..	..	174	270	345	336	370	421	444
Taxes paid by EU civil servants: compulsory social security contributions	..	..	..	136	250	340	330	360	404	425
Non-wastable tax credits										
Non-wastable tax credits against 1110	..	..	..	..	348	1 037	1 492	830	967	1 083
Tax expenditure component	..	..	..	..	78	588	1 077	537	769	855
Transfer component	..	..	..	..	270	449	415	293	197	228
Non-wastable tax credits against 1210	..	..	..	..	..	..	..	..	..	..
Tax expenditure component	..	..	..	..	..	..	..	..	..	..
Transfer component	..	..	..	..	..	..	..	..	..	..
Total tax revenue on cash basis	**6 421**	**37 438**	**70 268**	**..**	**..**	**..**	**..**	**..**	**..**	**..**
Total tax revenue on accrual basis	**..**	**37 443**	**70 408**	**112 710**	**147 861**	**156 317**	**177 665**	**184 429**	**202 587**	**204 023**
Conciliation with National Accounts										
Additional taxes included in National Accounts	..	107	447	1 300	1 740	2 458	3 354	3 616	4 105	4 267
National lottery profits	..	107	262	279	225	243	215	206	185	185
Water levies	..	0	66	378	119	137	122	104	140	142
Sanitel levy	..	0	0	14	13	15	14	6	14	8
Levy on industrial waste	..	0	27	74	68	54	46	55	88	81
Levy on manure	..	0	0	11	11	5	5	1	4	2
Levy on household waste	..	0	0	20	..	..	..	..	..	..
Earned income withholding tax (EU)	..	0	93	174	270	345	336	370	421	444
Social contributions (EU)	..	0	0	136	250	340	330	360	404	425
Imputed social contributions (EU)	..	0	0	213	431	508	511	554	631	660
Green certificates	..	..	..	..	354	812	1 777	1 959	2 219	2 320
Taxes excluded from National Accounts	..	0	0	0	0	0	0	0	0	0
Deposit insurance	..	..	..	..	..	..	..	..	..	..
Difference in treatment of tax credits	..	0	..	..	78	588	1 077	537	769	855
Capital transfer for uncollected revenue	..	0	0	-291	-381	-597	-730	-547	-629	-625
VAT on products assessed but unlikely to be collected	..	..	..	-18	-276	-367	-488	-357	-492	-479
Earned income withholding tax assessed but unlikely to be collected	..	..	..	-40	-53	-71	-47	-49	-47	-45
Employers' actual social contributions assessed but unlikely to be collected	..	..	..	-233	-52	-159	-194	-141	-90	-100
Voluntary social security contributions	..	41	52	58	57	59	77	70	85	84
Miscellaneous differences	..	0	0	0	0	0	0	0	0	0
Reallocation national levels of government	..	..	..	..	..	..	..	..	..	..
Reallocation EU	..	..	..	..	..	..	..	..	..	..
National Accounts: Taxes and actual social contributions	..	37 590	70 907	113 564	148 924	158 318	180 932	187 550	206 286	207 944
Imputed social contributions	..	1 497	2 886	5 377	7 568	8 713	10 071	9 812	10 817	11 056
National Accounts: Taxes and all social contributions	..	39 087	73 793	118 940	156 492	167 031	191 003	197 362	217 103	219 001

.. Not available

Note: Year ending 31st December. From 1970, data are on accrual basis

Source: Federal Ministry of Finance.

StatLink https://stat.link/q3j7xe

Table 5.4. Canada: Details of tax revenue, 1965-2019

Million CAD

	1965	1980	1990	2000	2007	2010	2013	2015	2018	2019
Total tax revenue	**15 318**	**101 015**	**244 152**	**390 234**	**512 663**	**516 591**	**592 206**	**653 269**	**747 568**	**781 201**
1000 Taxes on income, profits and capital gains	**5 910**	**47 064**	**118 566**	**195 320**	**251 198**	**240 961**	**281 787**	**314 841**	**367 456**	**387 568**
1100 Of individuals	3 464	34 451	99 722	143 652	190 025	180 894	214 054	240 304	267 173	281 374
1110 On income and profits	3 464	34 451	99 722	143 652	190 025	180 894	214 054	240 304	267 173	281 374
Taxes federal government	2 635	21 231	60 252	90 694	116 395	109 341	127 655	143 315	161 879	169 476
Taxes on individuals - province	829	13 220	39 470	52 958	73 630	71 553	86 399	96 989	105 294	111 898
1120 On capital gains	0	0	0	0	0	0	0	0	0	0
1200 Corporate	2 276	11 741	17 190	47 643	54 272	54 101	62 359	67 894	91 358	96 160
1210 On profits	2 276	11 741	17 190	47 643	54 272	54 101	62 359	67 894	91 358	96 160
Taxes federal government	1 752	8 110	11 726	31 570	37 093	33 419	38 142	41 726	56 505	59 605
Taxes on corporations - province	524	3 631	5 464	16 073	17 179	20 682	24 217	26 168	34 853	36 555
1220 On capital gains	0	0	0	0	0	0	0	0	0	0
1300 Unallocable between 1100 and 1200	170	872	1 654	4 025	6 901	5 966	5 374	6 643	8 925	10 034
Non-resident withhold taxes - federal	170	872	1 654	4 025	6 901	5 966	5 374	6 643	8 925	10 034
2000 Social security contributions	**854**	**10 649**	**29 653**	**53 109**	**73 722**	**76 787**	**90 394**	**96 371**	**103 502**	**108 364**
2100 Employees	318	3 756	10 634	21 361	29 361	30 626	36 057	38 685	41 643	44 258
Canada pension plan	47	1 265	3 745	9 401	16 194	16 852	20 021	21 491	23 645	25 257
Quebec pension plan	15	431	1 108	2 897	4 124	5 450	5 815	6 293	7 413	7 963
Employment insurance	164	1 393	5 284	7 782	7 084	7 388	9 198	9 772	9 255	9 680
Hospital insurance premiums	92	667	496	1 281	1 959	937	1 023	1 128	1 331	1 357
2110 On a payroll basis	..	..	10 634	20 976	28 654	29 689	35 034	37 557	40 312	42 901
2120 On an income tax basis	..	..	0	385	707	937	1 023	1 128	1 331	1 357
2200 Employers	536	6 697	18 449	30 307	41 922	43 525	51 261	54 380	58 180	60 173
Canada pension plan	48	1 266	3 745	9 401	16 194	16 852	20 021	21 491	23 645	25 257
Quebec pension plan	15	432	1 108	2 897	4 124	5 450	5 815	6 293	7 413	7 963
Employment insurance	164	2 006	7 398	10 894	9 917	10 343	12 877	13 681	12 956	13 553
Hospital insurance premiums	92	1 270	496	897	1 252	0	0	0	0	0
Social insurance levies	217	1 723	5 702	6 218	10 434	10 881	12 548	12 914	14 166	13 400
2210 On a payroll basis	..	..	18 449	30 307	41 922	43 525	51 261	54 380	58 180	60 173
2220 On an income tax basis	..	..	0	0	0	0	0	0	0	0
2300 Self-employed or non-employed	0	196	570	1 442	2 440	2 636	3 076	3 307	3 679	3 933
Canada pension plan	..	153	478	1 200	2 096	2 181	2 591	2 781	3 060	3 268
Quebec pension plan	..	43	92	242	344	455	486	525	619	665
2310 On a payroll basis	..	196	570	1 442	2 440	2 636	3 076	3 307	3 679	3 933
2320 On an income tax basis	..	0	0	0	0	0	0	0	0	0
2400 Unallocable between 2100, 2200 and 2300	0	0	0	0	0	0	0	0	0	0
2410 On a payroll basis	..	..	..	..	..	..	..	..	..	..
2420 On an income tax basis	..	..	..	..	..	..	..	..	..	..
3000 Taxes on payroll and workforce	**0**	**0**	**5 499**	**8 013**	**10 038**	**10 760**	**12 482**	**13 256**	**14 867**	**17 245**
4000 Taxes on property	**2 186**	**9 195**	**24 467**	**37 157**	**54 507**	**63 735**	**70 451**	**77 778**	**86 198**	**89 093**
4100 Recurrent taxes on immovable property	1 830	8 315	20 189	30 242	44 567	51 702	57 769	62 651	68 826	70 436
On property provincial government	11	133	1 645	3 078	3 164	4 476	4 946	5 410	6 825	7 050
Personal property local government	17	0	18 544	27 165	41 403	47 226	52 823	57 241	62 001	63 386
Real property local government	1 802	8 182	0	0	0	0	0	0	0	0
4110 Households	..	..	..	..	..	..	..	..	..	..
4120 Others	..	..	..	..	..	..	..	..	..	..
4200 Recurrent taxes on net wealth	25	512	1 911	4 171	2 970	1 523	414	372	456	441
4210 Individual	0	0	0	0	0	0	0	0	0	0
4220 Corporate	25	512	1 911	4 171	2 970	1 523	414	372	456	441
4300 Estate, inheritance and gift taxes	223	75	3	2	0	178	221	268	334	347
4310 Estate and inheritance taxes	216	75	3	2	..	178	221	268	334	347
On inheritances federal government	108	0	0	0	..	0	0	0	0	0
Succession duties provincial government	108	75	3	2	..	178	221	268	334	347
4320 Gift taxes	7	0	0	0	..	0	0	0	0	0
On gifts federal government	7	..	..	..	..	..	..	..	..	..
4400 Taxes on financial and capital transactions	0	0	0	0	2 868	3 077	3 646	4 975	6 462	6 789
4500 Non-recurrent taxes	108	293	2 365	2 742	4 102	7 254	8 401	9 512	10 120	11 080
4510 On net wealth	0	0	0	0	0	0	0	0	0	0
4520 Other non-recurrent taxes	108	293	2 365	2 742	4 102	7 254	8 401	9 512	10 120	11 080
Special assessments and charges local govt.	108	293	2 365	2 742	4 102	7 254	8 401	9 512	10 120	11 080
4600 Other recurrent taxes on property	0	0	0	0	0	0	0	0	0	0
5000 Taxes on goods and services	**6 202**	**32 909**	**63 092**	**94 468**	**122 855**	**123 752**	**136 396**	**150 275**	**174 660**	**178 036**
5100 Taxes on production, sale, transfer, etc.	5 310	24 808	59 627	88 879	114 701	116 160	128 554	140 750	162 662	166 932
5110 General taxes	2 730	11 658	34 475	55 313	71 242	72 130	81 452	90 598	106 140	109 700
5111 Value added taxes	0	0	0	35 884	46 072	70 712	78 292	86 694	101 401	103 539
5112 Sales tax	2 730	11 658	34 475	19 429	25 170	1 418	3 160	3 904	4 739	6 161
Sales taxes federal government	813	5 429	16 866	0	0	0	0	0	0	0
Sales taxes provincial, local govt.	1 917	6 229	17 609	19 429	25 170	1 418	3 160	3 904	4 739	6 161
5113 Other	0	0	0	0	0	0	0	0	0	0

	1965	1980	1990	2000	2007	2010	2013	2015	2018	2019
5120 Taxes on specific goods and services	2 580	13 150	25 153	33 565	43 459	44 030	47 102	50 152	56 522	57 233
5121 Excise duties	1 499	6 805	14 473	18 417	22 759	23 281	24 470	25 284	27 761	28 713
Excises federal government	740	3 850	6 405	8 377	9 249	10 244	10 261	10 372	11 378	12 948
Liquor	..	..	926	1 103	1 224	1 554	1 488	1 521	1 809	1 881
Tobacco	..	..	2 247	2 176	2 466	3 025	3 019	2 875	3 387	3 024
Gasoline and motive fuel	..	..	2 472	4 807	5 272	5 306	5 460	5 678	5 737	5 964
Remitted gaming profits	..	..	45	0	0	0	0	0	0	0
Miscellaneous consumption taxes	..	..	715	291	287	358	294	297	445	2 079
Excises provincial government	759	2 955	8 067	10 039	13 510	13 037	14 209	14 912	16 383	15 765
Motor fuel	680	1 863	4 674	7 031	8 065	8 198	9 094	9 727	10 072	10 219
Tobacco	53	772	2 776	2 279	4 181	4 620	4 879	5 108	4 965	4 709
Other	26	320	617	730	1 264	219	236	77	1 346	837
5122 Profits of fiscal monopolies	294	1 406	3 758	8 756	11 565	11 565	12 059	13 016	14 309	14 782
Own enterprises contributions	294	1 406	3 758	8 756	11 565	11 565	12 059	13 016	14 309	14 782
5123 Customs and import duties	686	3 199	4 021	2 824	3 829	3 441	4 193	5 181	6 642	5 493
Customs and import duties federal govt.	686	3 199	4 021	2 824	3 829	3 441	4 193	5 181	6 642	5 493
5124 Taxes on exports	0	842	0	0	0	0	0	0	0	0
5125 Taxes on investment goods	0	0	0	0	0	0	0	0	0	0
5126 Taxes on specific services	84	575	2 385	2 524	4 088	4 489	5 087	5 213	6 547	6 600
Tax on insurance premiums, provincial govt.	45	261	1 141	1 740	2 796	3 305	3 901	3 962	5 020	5 125
Tax on insurance premiums, federal govt.	0	1	1	1	11	28	13	10	0	9
Amusement and admission taxes	4	25	126	538	537	322	280	291	318	327
Air transportation taxes	0	166	488	0	403	600	662	722	872	800
Racetrack betting	35	122	155	55	36	36	32	33	25	23
Tax on meals and hotels	0	0	473	191	305	198	199	195	312	316
5127 Other taxes on internat. trade and transactions	0	0	0	0	0	0	0	0	0	0
5128 Other taxes	17	323	517	1 045	1 217	1 255	1 292	1 458	1 263	1 645
Other taxes federal government	0	98	272	758	762	557	439	544	474	499
Other taxes provincial government	17	225	245	287	455	698	853	914	789	1 146
5130 Unallocable between 5110 and 5120	0	0	0	0	0	0	0	0	0	0
5200 Taxes on use of goods and perform activities	892	8 101	3 465	5 589	8 154	7 592	7 842	9 525	11 998	11 104
5210 Recurrent taxes	306	1 500	2 393	3 644	4 368	4 452	5 017	5 589	6 242	6 312
5211 Paid by households: motor vehicles	103	666	1 056	1 696	2 241	1 986	2 237	2 478	2 927	2 995
5212 Paid by others: motor vehicles	141	509	697	1 039	1 242	1 153	1 343	1 552	1 717	1 747
5213 Paid in respect of other goods	62	325	640	909	885	1 313	1 437	1 559	1 598	1 570
5220 Non-recurrent taxes	586	6 601	1 072	1 945	3 786	3 140	2 825	3 936	5 756	4 792
Licences and permits local govt.	36	132	317	499	889	807	952	1 023	1 113	1 195
Licences and permits provincial govt.	550	6 469	755	1 446	2 897	2 333	1 873	2 913	4 643	3 597
5300 Unallocable between 5100 and 5200	0	0	0	0	0	0	0	0	0	0
6000 Other taxes	**166**	**1 198**	**2 875**	**2 167**	**342**	**596**	**696**	**748**	**886**	**894**
6100 Paid solely by business	139	943	2 386	1 280	0	0	0	0	0	0
6200 Other	27	255	489	887	342	596	696	748	886	894
Poll tax local government	5	0	0	0	0	0	0	0	0	0
Miscellaneous local government	11	358	489	887	342	596	696	748	886	894
Other federal government	11	-103	0	0	0	0	0	0	0	0
Non-wastable tax credits										
Non-wastable tax credits against 1110	..	..	..	1 633	5 550	6 415	7 326	7 510	10 681	13 949
Tax expenditure component	..	..	..	276	824	875	965	968	2 372	3 952
Transfer component	..	..	..	1 357	4 726	5 540	6 361	6 542	8 309	9 997
Non-wastable tax credits against 1210	..	..	..	1 758	3 445	4 726	3 754	3 768	3 828	4 250
Tax expenditure component	..	..	..	20	12	19	17	15	16	23
Transfer component	..	..	..	1 738	3 433	4 707	3 737	3 753	3 812	4 227
Total tax revenue on cash basis	**15 318**	**101 015**	**244 152**	**388 833**	**527 734**	**..**	**..**	**..**	**..**	**..**
Total tax revenue on accrual basis	**..**	**..**	**..**	**390 234**	**512 663**	**516 591**	**592 206**	**653 269**	**747 568**	**781 201**
Conciliation with National Accounts										
Additional taxes included in National Accounts	..	..	..	0	0	0	0	0	0	0
Taxes excluded from National Accounts	..	..	..	0	0	0	0	0	0	0
Difference in treatment of tax credits	..	..	..	296	836	894	982	983	2 388	3 976
Capital transfer for uncollected revenue	..	..	..	0	0	0	0	0	0	0
Voluntary social security contributions	..	..	..	0	0	0	0	0	0	0
Miscellaneous differences	..	..	..	0	0	0	0	0	0	0
National Accounts: Taxes and actual social contributions	..	..	..	390 234	513 499	517 485	593 188	654 252	749 956	785 176
Imputed social contributions	..	..	..	0	0	0	0	0	0	0
National Accounts: Taxes and all social contributions	..	..	..	390 234	513 499	517 485	593 188	654 252	749 956	785 176

.. Not available

Note: From 2001, all data are for the year ending 31st December. For 2000 and earlier years, data for the Federal, Provincial and Territorial governments and Social security funds are on a fiscal year basis commencing 1st April. Data for local government are on a fiscal year basis commencing 1st January. From 1999 data are on accrual basis except that personal income taxes are on a modified cash basis.

There are some minor differences between the data for the years 1965 to 1978 and those for subsequent years. These mostly relate to the inclusion of fines and penalities or late payment of taxes and deductions for the child tax credits in the data for the years 1979 to 1983.

Heading 1210 - Taxes federal government: Federal corporate taxes include capital taxes.

Heading 2000: Includes receipts from the Canadian Pension Plan, Quebec Pension Plan, Unemployement Insurance Fund and Provincial Health Insurance. Premiums, Medicare Premiums and Social Insurance levies but excludes that part of the taxes on income and sales taxes earmarked for old age security. The practice of earmarking these taxes was discontinued in June 1975.

Heading 4400: From 2002 onward includes land transfer taxes of the provincial, territorial and local governments. Prior to 2002 land transfer taxes of the local government were included in line 6000 and those provincial and territorial governments were included in line 4520.

Heading 5121: The large increase in this heading between 1980 and 1981 is due to the introduction of a 'special petroleum compensation charge', a 'Canadian ownership special charge' and to an increase in the natural gas tax of C$ 2399 millions.

Heading 5122: From 1988, profits on fiscal monopolies include lottery profits.

Heading 5128: From 1988, other taxes of Federal Government include the annual fees for managing the spectrum (airwaves) allocation to the cellular industry.

Heading 5211: Some Québec motor vehicle licence administrative fees are included in sales of goods and services for the period 1988-89 to 1997-98. From 1998-99 onward, these fees are included under other taxes - motor vehicle licences.

Source: Statistics Canada.

StatLink https://stat.link/n94z1h

Table 5.5. Chile: Details of tax revenue, 1965-2019

Million CLP

	1965	1980	1990	2000	2007	2010	2013	2015	2018	2019
Total tax revenue	..	..	**1 777 218**	**7 901 998**	**20 598 963**	**21 845 693**	**27 381 686**	**32 532 354**	**40 314 703**	**41 025 508**
1000 Taxes on income, profits and capital gains	..	..	**412 974**	**1 841 630**	**9 412 056**	**8 329 060**	**9 520 709**	**11 840 521**	**14 418 859**	**14 283 183**
1100 Of individuals	..	..	99 154	604 100	989 348	1 492 837	1 964 172	3 199 876	2 701 416	2 937 532
Second category tax	..	..	65 552	490 980	993 129	1 449 099	1 981 699	2 350 120	2 848 205	3 015 794
Global complementary tax	..	..	33 603	113 120	-3 781	43 738	-17 527	-36 757	-146 789	-78 261
Other	..	..	0	0	0	0	0	886 513	0	0
1110 On income and profits	..	..	..	..	..	..	..	..	..	..
1120 On capital gains	..	..	..	..	..	..	..	..	..	..
1200 Corporate	..	..	219 586	882 896	6 054 487	4 448 745	6 041 089	6 839 133	8 920 497	9 597 472
First category tax	..	..	200 891	815 747	5 084 996	3 913 870	5 473 355	6 183 830	7 836 379	8 880 080
Surtax on state owned enterprises	..	..	16 074	47 634	113 334	194 203	124 220	132 352	184 442	122 054
Mining tax	..	..	0	0	835 452	298 558	324 577	323 507	184 382	277 861
Other	..	..	2 621	19 516	20 705	42 114	118 937	199 444	715 293	317 477
1210 On profits	..	..	..	..	..	..	..	..	..	..
1220 On capital gains	..	..	..	..	..	..	..	..	..	..
1300 Unallocable between 1100 and 1200	..	..	94 233	354 634	2 368 221	2 387 478	1 515 449	1 801 512	2 796 947	1 748 179
Additional tax	..	..	59 082	350 301	1 462 715	1 414 057	1 337 721	1 429 758	2 127 948	1 902 585
Other	..	..	35 151	4 332	905 507	973 421	177 727	371 755	668 998	-154 406
2000 Social security contributions	..	..	**159 559**	**576 758**	**1 148 647**	**1 493 987**	**1 968 973**	**2 252 489**	**2 786 173**	**2 994 906**
2100 Employees	..	..	154 021	553 937	1 098 620	1 433 159	1 906 340	2 188 575	2 703 261	2 894 725
2110 On a payroll basis	..	..	154 021	553 937	1 098 620	1 433 159	1 906 340	2 188 575	2 703 261	2 894 725
2120 On an income tax basis	..	..	0	0	0	0	0	0	0	0
2200 Employers	..	..	5 538	22 821	50 027	60 828	62 633	63 914	82 912	100 181
2210 On a payroll basis	..	..	5 538	22 821	50 027	60 828	62 633	63 914	82 912	100 181
2220 On an income tax basis	..	..	0	0	0	0	0	0	0	0
2300 Self-employed or non-employed	..	..	0	0	0	0	0	0	0	0
2310 On a payroll basis	..	..	..	..	..	..	..	..	..	..
2320 On an income tax basis	..	..	..	..	..	..	..	..	..	..
2400 Unallocable between 2100, 2200 and 2300	..	..	0	0	0	0	0	0	0	0
2410 On a payroll basis	..	..	..	..	..	..	..	..	..	..
2420 On an income tax basis	..	..	..	..	..	..	..	..	..	..
3000 Taxes on payroll and workforce	..	..	**0**	**0**	**0**	**0**	**0**	**0**	**0**	**0**
4000 Taxes on property	..	..	**109 319**	**554 037**	**1 013 571**	**898 607**	**1 133 765**	**1 421 274**	**2 086 866**	**2 242 561**
4100 Recurrent taxes on immovable property	..	..	59 968	302 244	496 311	662 368	840 842	1 056 920	1 373 495	1 507 182
4110 Households	..	..	..	..	..	..	..	..	..	..
4120 Others	..	..	..	..	..	..	..	..	..	..
4200 Recurrent taxes on net wealth	..	..	0	0	0	0	0	0	0	0
4210 Individual	..	..	..	..	..	..	..	..	..	..
4220 Corporate	..	..	..	..	..	..	..	..	..	..
4300 Estate, inheritance and gift taxes	..	..	3 444	10 906	28 501	39 338	45 550	92 236	125 649	62 824
4310 Estate and inheritance taxes	..	..	..	..	..	..	..	..	..	..
4320 Gift taxes	..	..	..	..	..	..	..	..	..	..
4400 Taxes on financial and capital transactions	..	..	45 907	240 886	488 759	196 901	247 373	272 118	587 721	672 555
4500 Non-recurrent taxes	..	..	0	0	0	0	0	0	0	0
4510 On net wealth	..	..	..	..	..	..	..	..	..	..
4520 Other non-recurrent taxes	..	..	..	..	..	..	..	..	..	..
4600 Other recurrent taxes on property	..	..	0	0	0	0	0	0	0	0
5000 Taxes on goods and services	..	..	**1 118 722**	**5 041 769**	**9 023 666**	**11 185 156**	**14 779 915**	**17 597 378**	**21 470 498**	**21 755 381**
5100 Taxes on production, sale, transfer, etc.	..	..	1 074 009	4 789 827	8 578 636	10 532 904	13 869 529	16 515 485	19 953 036	20 167 012
5110 General taxes	..	..	664 421	3 306 350	6 781 501	8 399 926	11 170 794	13 273 958	16 211 646	16 348 944
5111 Value added taxes	..	..	664 421	3 306 350	6 781 501	8 399 926	11 170 794	13 273 958	16 211 646	16 348 944
5112 Sales tax	..	..	0	0	0	0	0	0	0	0
5113 Other	..	..	0	0	0	0	0	0	0	0
5120 Taxes on specific goods and services	..	..	409 588	1 483 477	1 797 135	2 132 978	2 698 735	3 241 527	3 741 389	3 818 068
5121 Excise duties	..	..	166 050	816 160	1 299 844	1 561 205	1 987 475	2 412 773	2 796 033	2 862 327
Cigarettes and tobacco	..	..	60 604	283 275	455 595	647 637	815 991	981 422	981 456	973 335
Gasolene and diesel	..	..	105 445	532 885	844 249	913 568	1 171 483	1 388 218	1 727 392	1 811 132
Oil stabilisation fund	..	..	0	0	0	0	0	0	0	0
Fisheries Law Extraction Rights	..	..	0	0	0	0	0	8 558	19 623	17 662
Additional tax on new motor vehicles	..	..	0	0	0	0	0	34 575	67 561	60 197
5122 Profits of fiscal monopolies	..	..	0	0	0	0	0	0	0	0
5123 Customs and import duties	..	..	222 486	548 571	300 416	267 331	303 393	343 491	347 555	331 846
5124 Taxes on exports	..	..	0	0	0	0	0	0	0	0
5125 Taxes on investment goods	..	..	0	0	0	0	0	0	0	0
5126 Taxes on specific services	..	..	21 052	118 746	196 875	304 442	407 867	485 263	597 802	623 895
5127 Other taxes on internat. trade and transactions	..	..	0	0	0	0	0	0	0	0
5128 Other taxes	..	..	0	0	0	0	0	0	0	0
5130 Unallocable between 5110 and 5120	..	..	0	0	0	0	0	0	0	0
5200 Taxes on use of goods and perform activities	..	..	44 714	251 942	445 030	652 252	910 386	1 081 893	1 517 462	1 588 369

	1965	1980	1990	2000	2007	2010	2013	2015	2018	2019
5210 Recurrent taxes	..	..	44 714	251 942	445 030	652 252	910 386	1 081 893	1 402 110	1 461 686
Motor vehicles	..	..	24 469	93 880	155 158	218 219	330 754	397 608	539 918	592 327
5211 Paid by households: motor vehicles	..	..	0	0	0	0	0	0	0	0
5212 Paid by others: motor vehicles	..	..	0	0	0	0	0	0	0	0
5213 Paid in respect of other goods	..	..	20 245	158 062	289 872	434 033	579 632	684 285	862 192	869 359
Municipal permits	..	..	18 401	136 138	263 996	396 944	527 955	630 943	806 734	813 159
Mining patents	..	..	3 374	34 730	25 184	36 213	50 094	51 767	53 854	54 696
Other	..	..	-1 530	-12 806	692	876	1 583	1 575	1 604	1 504
5220 Non-recurrent taxes	..	..	0	0	0	0	0	0	115 352	126 683
Tax on Polluting Fixed Sources	..	..	..	..	..	..	..	..	115 352	126 683
5300 Unallocable between 5100 and 5200	..	..	0	0	0	0	0	0	0	0
6000 Other taxes	**..**	**..**	**-23 356**	**-112 195**	**1 023**	**-61 117**	**-21 676**	**-579 308**	**-447 692**	**-250 523**
6100 Paid solely by business	..	..	0	0	0	0	0	0	0	0
6200 Other	..	..	-23 356	-112 195	1 023	-61 117	-21 676	-579 308	-447 692	-250 523
Non-wastable tax credits										
Non-wastable tax credits against 1110	..	..	0	0	0	0	0	0	0	0
Tax expenditure component	..	..	..	..	..	..	..	..	..	..
Transfer component	..	..	..	..	..	..	..	..	..	..
Non-wastable tax credits against 1210	..	..	0	0	0	0	0	175 468	251 606	278 792
Tax expenditure component	..	..	..	..	..	..	..	45 774	64 837	78 226
Transfer component	..	..	..	..	..	..	..	129 694	186 769	200 566
Total tax revenue on cash basis	**..**	**..**	**1 777 218**	**7 901 998**	**20 598 963**	**21 845 693**	**27 381 686**	**32 532 354**	**40 314 703**	**41 025 508**
Total tax revenue on accrual basis	**..**	**..**	**..**	**..**	**..**	**..**	**..**	**..**	**..**	**..**
Conciliation with National Accounts										
Additional taxes included in National Accounts	..	..	..	..	..	..	..	..	..	..
Taxes excluded from National Accounts	..	..	..	..	..	..	..	..	..	..
Difference in treatment of tax credits	..	..	..	..	..	..	..	..	..	..
Capital transfer for uncollected revenue	..	..	..	..	..	..	..	..	..	..
Voluntary social security contributions	..	..	..	..	..	..	..	..	..	..
Miscellaneous differences	..	..	..	..	..	..	..	..	..	..
National Accounts: Taxes and actual social contributions	..	..	..	..	..	..	..	..	..	..
Imputed social contributions	..	..	..	..	..	..	..	..	..	..
National Accounts: Taxes and all social contributions	..	..	..	..	..	..	..	..	..	..

.. Not available

Note: Year ending 31st December.

The data are on a cash basis.

Source: Servicio de Impuestos internos (Chile's Tax Service).

StatLink https://stat.link/t0am2e

Table 5.6. Colombia: Details of tax revenue, 1965-2019

Million COP

	1965	1980	1990	2000	2007	2010	2013	2015	2018	2019
Total tax revenue	..	..	**2 579 426**	**30 598 630**	**82 697 457**	**98 455 335**	**142 976 023**	**160 157 693**	**190 299 911**	**209 071 314**
1000 Taxes on income, profits and capital gains	..	..	**771 694**	**7 103 525**	**24 010 404**	**26 218 852**	**47 743 096**	**52 656 876**	**64 043 928**	**67 519 599**
1100 Of individuals	..	..	47 210	1 499 345	4 751 580	5 192 384	7 787 903	9 215 137	12 235 324	14 155 111
1110 On income and profits	..	..	47 210	1 499 345	4 751 580	5 192 384	7 787 903	9 215 137	12 235 324	14 155 111
Income tax	..	..	47 210	1 499 345	4 751 580	5 192 384	7 787 903	9 215 137	12 235 324	14 148 562
Simple tax regime	..	..	0	0	0	0	0	0	0	6 549
1120 On capital gains	..	..	..	..	..	..	..	..	..	..
1200 Corporate	..	..	359 758	5 119 828	18 427 899	20 405 209	38 788 220	41 401 857	48 628 587	50 242 515
1210 On profits	..	..	359 758	5 119 828	18 427 899	20 405 209	38 788 220	41 401 857	48 628 587	50 242 515
Income tax	..	..	359 758	5 119 828	18 427 899	20 405 209	35 848 641	27 475 688	48 495 864	50 126 648
Pro Equity Income Tax - CREE	..	..	0	0	0	0	2 939 579	13 926 169	132 723	99 798
Simple tax regime	..	..	0	0	0	0	0	0	0	16 068
1220 On capital gains	..	..	..	..	..	..	..	..	..	..
1300 Unallocable between 1100 and 1200	..	..	364 726	484 352	830 925	621 258	1 166 973	2 039 882	3 180 016	3 121 974
Income tax	..	..	364 726	484 352	830 925	621 258	1 166 973	2 039 882	3 180 016	3 121 974
Pro Equity Income Tax - CREE	..	..	0	0	0	0	0	0	0	0
2000 Social security contributions	..	..	**203 596**	**4 989 000**	**9 694 000**	**11 478 085**	**16 644 445**	**13 585 138**	**18 192 049**	**19 875 398**
2100 Employees	..	..	..	..	..	..	..	..	..	..
2110 On a payroll basis	..	..	..	..	..	..	..	..	..	..
2120 On an income tax basis	..	..	..	..	..	..	..	..	..	..
2200 Employers	..	..	..	..	..	..	..	..	..	..
2210 On a payroll basis	..	..	..	..	..	..	..	..	..	..
2220 On an income tax basis	..	..	..	..	..	..	..	..	..	..
2300 Self-employed or non-employed	..	..	..	..	..	..	..	..	..	..
2310 On a payroll basis	..	..	..	..	..	..	..	..	..	..
2320 On an income tax basis	..	..	..	..	..	..	..	..	..	..
2400 Unallocable between 2100, 2200 and 2300	..	..	203 596	4 989 000	9 694 000	11 478 085	16 644 445	13 585 138	18 192 049	19 875 398
2410 On a payroll basis	..	..	203 596	4 989 000	9 694 000	11 478 085	16 644 445	13 585 138	18 192 049	19 875 398
2420 On an income tax basis	..	..	0	0	0	0	0	0	0	0
3000 Taxes on payroll and workforce	..	..	**0**	**1 286 803**	**2 798 906**	**4 022 503**	**3 527 459**	**2 797 308**	**3 461 352**	**3 604 071**
4000 Taxes on property	..	..	**56 160**	**2 027 654**	**6 459 259**	**8 535 238**	**14 907 909**	**18 156 105**	**15 265 472**	**18 984 414**
4100 Recurrent taxes on immovable property	..	..	56 160	991 070	2 298 829	3 338 935	4 735 321	6 061 965	7 981 989	8 743 115
4110 Households	..	..	0	0	0	0	0	0	0	0
4120 Others	..	..	56 160	991 070	2 298 829	3 338 935	4 735 321	6 061 965	7 981 989	8 743 115
4200 Recurrent taxes on net wealth	..	..	0	0	1 170 908	1 970 530	4 274 832	5 352 940	467 925	923 255
4210 Individual	..	..	..	..	1 170 908	1 970 530	4 274 832	5 352 940	467 925	923 255
4220 Corporate	..	..	..	..	0	0	0	0	0	0
4300 Estate, inheritance and gift taxes	..	..	0	0	0	0	0	0	0	0
4310 Estate and inheritance taxes	..	..	..	..	..	..	..	..	..	..
4320 Gift taxes	..	..	..	..	..	..	..	..	..	..
4400 Taxes on financial and capital transactions	..	..	0	1 036 584	2 989 522	3 225 773	5 897 755	6 741 200	6 815 558	8 190 516
4500 Non-recurrent taxes	..	..	0	0	0	0	0	0	0	1 127 528
4510 On net wealth	..	..	..	..	..	..	..	..	..	0
4520 Other non-recurrent taxes	..	..	..	..	..	..	..	..	..	1 127 528
4600 Other recurrent taxes on property	..	..	0	0	0	0	0	0	0	0
5000 Taxes on goods and services	..	..	**1 388 653**	**14 180 450**	**36 766 741**	**44 411 642**	**55 285 569**	**65 716 566**	**81 408 789**	**89 797 927**
5100 Taxes on production, sale, transfer, etc.	..	..	1 388 653	14 048 655	36 447 297	44 038 074	54 326 006	64 688 081	79 935 336	88 064 087
5110 General taxes	..	..	672 368	9 585 866	26 910 512	33 333 802	40 479 366	48 684 900	64 316 019	71 235 138
5111 Value added taxes	..	..	583 078	8 445 776	23 377 821	28 811 682	34 642 822	41 659 696	55 879 110	61 936 282
5112 Sales tax	..	..	89 290	1 140 090	3 532 691	4 522 121	5 836 544	7 025 204	8 436 909	9 298 856
Industry and commerce tax (State)	..	..	89 290	1 140 090	3 532 691	4 522 121	5 836 544	7 025 204	8 436 909	9 298 856
5113 Other	..	..	0	0	0	0	0	0	0	0
5120 Taxes on specific goods and services	..	..	716 285	4 462 789	9 536 785	10 704 271	13 846 640	16 003 181	15 619 317	16 828 948
5121 Excise duties	..	..	404 699	2 718 692	5 276 999	6 052 273	9 949 457	11 412 250	12 061 132	12 995 955
Petrol	..	..	141 270	833 004	1 211 511	1 418 766	2 883 410	3 297 392	1 517 546	1 585 141
Tobacco (State)	..	..	52 898	213 412	330 016	390 472	496 513	524 357	1 145 879	1 278 561
Beer (State)	..	..	85 722	471 135	1 203 838	1 432 453	2 031 349	2 305 895	2 637 674	2 611 466
Liquors (State)	..	..	124 808	520 394	834 390	929 328	1 292 743	1 253 466	1 800 605	2 146 818
Restaurant service, vehicle sale and mobile telephone service	..	..	0	0	0	0	1 181 998	1 684 179	2 047 419	2 208 669
Carbon	..	..	0	0	0	0	0	0	288 373	436 914
Plastic bags	..	..	0	0	0	0	0	0	28 099	37 331
Medicinal cannabis	..	..	0	0	0	0	0	0	3	145
Diesel surcharge	..	..	0	85 716	388 091	500 405	572 022	598 993	579 613	599 600
Petrol surcharge	..	..	0	595 031	1 309 154	1 380 848	1 491 423	1 747 969	2 015 922	2 091 310
5122 Profits of fiscal monopolies	..	..	0	0	0	0	0	0	0	0
5123 Customs and import duties	..	..	311 586	1 744 097	4 259 786	4 651 999	3 897 184	4 590 931	3 558 185	3 832 994
Custom duties	..	..	180 989	1 744 097	4 259 786	4 651 999	3 897 184	4 590 931	3 558 185	3 832 994
Imports surcharge	..	..	130 597	0	0	0	0	0	0	0

	1965	1980	1990	2000	2007	2010	2013	2015	2018	2019
5124 Taxes on exports	..	..	0	0	0	0	0	0	0	0
5125 Taxes on investment goods	..	..	0	0	0	0	0	0	0	0
5126 Taxes on specific services	..	..	0	0	0	0	0	0	0	0
5127 Other taxes on internat. trade and transactions	..	..	0	0	0	0	0	0	0	0
5128 Other taxes	..	..	0	0	0	0	0	0	0	0
5130 Unallocable between 5110 and 5120	..	..	0	0	0	0	0	0	0	0
5200 Taxes on use of goods and perform activities	..	..	0	131 795	319 444	373 568	959 563	1 028 485	1 473 453	1 733 840
5210 Recurrent taxes	..	..	..	131 795	319 444	373 568	959 563	1 028 485	1 473 453	1 733 840
5211 Paid by households: motor vehicles	..	..	..	131 795	319 444	373 568	959 563	1 028 485	1 473 453	1 733 840
Tax on motor vehicle ownership	..	..	..	131 795	319 444	373 568	959 563	1 028 485	1 473 453	1 733 840
5212 Paid by others: motor vehicles	..	..	..	..	..	..	..	..	..	..
5213 Paid in respect of other goods	..	..	..	..	..	..	..	..	..	..
5220 Non-recurrent taxes	..	..	..	..	..	..	..	..	..	..
5300 Unallocable between 5100 and 5200	..	..	0	0	0	0	0	0	0	0
6000 Other taxes	**..**	**..**	**159 323**	**1 011 197**	**2 968 147**	**3 789 014**	**4 867 545**	**7 245 701**	**7 928 320**	**9 289 906**
6100 Paid solely by business	..	..	0	0	0	0	0	0	0	0
6200 Other	..	..	159 323	1 011 197	2 968 147	3 789 014	4 867 545	7 245 701	7 928 320	9 289 906
Stamp tax	..	..	0	401 497	759 787	357 160	58 378	101 668	79 868	85 799
Other	..	..	78 306	79 287	86 297	126 602	200 465	318 271	461 160	533 852
Other (sub-national)	..	..	81 017	530 413	2 122 062	3 305 252	4 608 702	6 825 762	7 387 293	8 670 255
Total tax revenue on cash basis	**..**	**..**	**2 579 426**	**30 598 630**	**82 697 457**	**98 455 335**	**142 976 023**	**160 157 693**	**190 299 911**	**209 071 314**
Total tax revenue on accrual basis	**..**	**..**	**..**	**..**	**..**	**..**	**..**	**..**	**..**	**..**
Conciliation with National Accounts										
Additional taxes included in National Accounts	..	..	..	..	..	..	..	..	..	..
Taxes excluded from National Accounts	..	..	..	..	..	..	..	..	..	..
Difference in treatment of tax credits	..	..	..	..	..	..	..	..	..	..
Capital transfer for uncollected revenue	..	..	..	..	..	..	..	..	..	..
Voluntary social security contributions	..	..	..	..	..	..	..	..	..	..
Miscellaneous differences	..	..	..	..	..	..	..	..	..	..
National Accounts: Taxes and actual social contributions	..	..	..	..	..	..	..	..	..	..
Imputed social contributions	..	..	..	..	..	..	..	..	..	..
National Accounts: Taxes and all social contributions	..	..	..	..	..	..	..	..	..	..

.. Not available

Note: Year ending 31st December.

Data on an cash basis.

Includes the reported consolidated revenues of the territorial entities (departments and municipalities).

Heading 2000: Before 2013, social security contributions did not include all the contributions entering FOSYGA (Solidarity and Guarantee Fund). Only the portion of the contributions used to finance the subsidised regime (up to 1.5 pp of the 12.5% of the monthly wage paid by employers and employees as an obligatory health contribution) was included. The part of the contributions entering FOSYGA to finance the contributory regime was classified in the social security sector as "other incomes".

From 2013 onwards, all of the health contributions entering FOSYGA are classified as social security contributions. The portion of the contributions not entering FOSYGA that is both collected and spent by the health insurers – EPS - is not part of the fiscal accounts.

Headings 1100 and 1200: The data are estimated.

Source: Dirección de Impuestos y Aduanas Nacionales de Colombia, Ministerio de Hacienda y Crédito Público y Banco Central de Colombia.
(National Tax and Customs Administration, Ministry of Finance and Public Credit and Central Bank of Colombia).

StatLink https://stat.link/v1gip7

Table 5.7. Costa Rica: Details of tax revenue, 1965-2019

Million CRC

	1965	1980	1990	2000	2007	2010	2013	2015	2018	2019
Total tax revenue	..	..	**117 711**	**978 114**	**3 213 401**	**4 382 367**	**5 851 096**	**6 923 575**	**8 339 991**	**8 855 885**
1000 Taxes on income, profits and capital gains	..	..	**11 820**	**128 805**	**531 552**	**748 093**	**1 014 440**	**1 247 308**	**1 699 258**	**1 854 866**
1100 Of individuals	..	..	..	..	123 194	202 849	316 894	386 241	483 645	540 954
1110 On income and profits	..	..	..	..	123 194	202 849	316 894	386 241	483 645	535 412
1120 On capital gains	..	..	..	..	0	0	0	0	0	5 542
1200 Corporate	..	..	..	..	348 826	450 312	545 183	659 951	915 284	1 058 086
1210 On profits	..	..	..	..	348 826	450 312	545 183	659 951	915 284	955 908
1220 On capital gains	..	..	..	..	0	0	0	0	0	102 177
1300 Unallocable between 1100 and 1200	..	..	11 820	128 805	59 531	94 932	152 363	201 116	300 330	255 827
2000 Social security contributions	..	..	**33 990**	**297 069**	**885 053**	**1 450 531**	**1 928 082**	**2 305 133**	**2 859 467**	**3 026 691**
2100 Employees	..	..	..	..	..	..	..	..	..	..
2110 On a payroll basis	..	..	..	..	..	..	..	..	..	..
2120 On an income tax basis	..	..	..	..	..	..	..	..	..	..
2200 Employers	..	..	3 447	37 313	107 398	207 206	272 706	318 652	368 865	381 940
Government contributions	..	..	3 447	37 313	107 398	207 206	272 706	318 652	368 865	381 940
2210 On a payroll basis	..	..	..	..	..	..	..	..	..	..
2220 On an income tax basis	..	..	..	..	..	..	..	..	..	..
2300 Self-employed or non-employed	..	..	..	..	..	..	..	..	..	..
2310 On a payroll basis	..	..	..	..	..	..	..	..	..	..
2320 On an income tax basis	..	..	..	..	..	..	..	..	..	..
2400 Unallocable between 2100, 2200 and 2300	..	..	30 543	259 756	777 654	1 243 325	1 655 376	1 986 481	2 490 602	2 644 751
Contributions by employees and non-government employers	..	..	30 543	249 182	727 844	1 139 265	1 511 383	1 785 522	2 157 256	2 274 644
Contributions for the special regimes	..	..	0	10 574	49 811	104 060	143 993	200 959	247 939	292 634
2410 On a payroll basis	..	..	..	..	..	..	..	..	..	..
2420 On an income tax basis	..	..	..	..	..	..	..	..	..	..
3000 Taxes on payroll and workforce	..	..	**7 575**	**61 796**	**170 996**	**260 664**	**352 755**	**423 616**	**498 577**	**522 529**
Contributions by non-government employers	..	..	7 484	59 129	165 677	248 259	337 696	406 296	478 523	501 734
Contributions by government employers	..	..	91	2 666	5 320	12 405	15 059	17 321	20 054	20 795
4000 Taxes on property	..	..	**1 566**	**8 396**	**42 658**	**63 706**	**99 030**	**123 261**	**149 310**	**167 952**
4100 Recurrent taxes on immovable property	..	..	1 200	5 390	23 293	48 963	70 785	90 003	113 586	125 398
Land tax	..	..	0	0	0	0	0	0	0	0
Additional land tax	..	..	0	0	0	0	0	0	0	0
Tax on sumptuary constructions	..	..	0	0	0	0	0	0	0	0
Immovable property tax	..	..	0	0	0	3 527	3 998	4 076	4 468	4 699
Municipal immovable property tax	..	..	1 200	5 390	23 293	45 436	66 787	85 927	109 119	120 698
4110 Households	..	..	..	..	..	..	..	..	..	..
4120 Others	..	..	..	..	..	..	..	..	..	..
4200 Recurrent taxes on net wealth	..	..	0	0	0	0	0	0	0	0
4210 Individual	..	..	..	..	..	..	..	..	..	..
4220 Corporate	..	..	..	..	..	..	..	..	..	..
4300 Estate, inheritance and gift taxes	..	..	0	0	0	0	0	0	0	0
4310 Estate and inheritance taxes	..	..	..	..	..	..	..	..	..	..
4320 Gift taxes	..	..	..	..	..	..	..	..	..	..
4400 Taxes on financial and capital transactions	..	..	366	3 007	19 366	14 743	28 246	33 258	35 724	42 554
4500 Non-recurrent taxes	..	..	0	0	0	0	0	0	0	0
4510 On net wealth	..	..	..	..	..	..	..	..	..	..
4520 Other non-recurrent taxes	..	..	..	..	..	..	..	..	..	..
4600 Other recurrent taxes on property	..	..	0	0	0	0	0	0	0	0
5000 Taxes on goods and services	..	..	**53 509**	**456 851**	**1 505 510**	**1 766 914**	**2 302 986**	**2 661 902**	**2 918 471**	**3 081 941**
5100 Taxes on production, sale, transfer, etc.	..	..	49 867	425 713	1 406 100	1 600 302	2 092 588	2 388 900	2 608 864	2 756 759
5110 General taxes	..	..	21 326	222 775	797 850	920 298	1 212 471	1 368 601	1 513 677	1 662 503
5111 Value added taxes	..	..	21 326	222 775	797 850	920 298	1 176 745	1 336 075	1 487 620	1 634 986
5112 Sales tax	..	..	0	0	0	0	0	0	0	0
5113 Other	..	..	0	0	0	0	35 726	32 526	26 057	27 517
5120 Taxes on specific goods and services	..	..	28 541	202 939	608 250	680 004	880 117	1 020 299	1 095 187	1 094 256
5121 Excise duties	..	..	11 096	157 204	447 168	523 617	689 528	798 412	858 424	864 985
Fuels and energy	..	..	0	0	250 577	320 638	404 210	457 827	517 666	552 017
Alcoholic beverages	..	..	0	8 229	23 802	28 035	35 254	43 095	45 610	43 849
Non alcoholic beverages	..	..	0	0	18 263	26 566	32 519	36 353	40 182	41 247
Soaps	..	..	0	0	883	1 317	1 989	2 562	2 712	3 020
Cement	..	..	0	0	0	227	291	304	289	216
Tobaco	..	..	0	0	0	0	38 860	33 681	30 766	27 185
Abolished specific taxes on production and consumption	..	..	0	0	0	0	0	0	0	0
Other specific taxes on consumption	..	..	11 096	148 975	153 643	146 834	176 405	224 590	221 200	197 452
5122 Profits of fiscal monopolies	..	..	0	0	0	0	0	0	0	0

	1965	1980	1990	2000	2007	2010	2013	2015	2018	2019
5123 Customs and import duties	..	..	15 052	40 485	134 576	126 134	154 576	174 568	175 368	164 224
Import duties	..	..	13 977	32 336	107 565	103 851	130 634	148 666	149 017	140 919
Custom duties	..	..	1 075	8 149	27 011	22 284	23 942	25 902	26 351	23 305
Import duties on animals	..	..	0	0	0	0	0	0	0	0
5124 Taxes on exports	..	..	2 113	2 238	2 432	3 973	4 877	4 468	5 468	5 412
Export duties	..	..	..	..	..	..	..	..	..	..
Export duties Law 133	..	..	..	..	..	..	..	..	..	..
Export duties Law 5519	..	..	..	..	..	..	..	..	..	..
Tax on banana exports	..	..	..	..	..	..	..	..	..	..
Export tax on ground transportation	..	..	..	..	..	..	..	..	..	..
5125 Taxes on investment goods	..	..	0	0	0	0	0	0	0	0
5126 Taxes on specific services	..	..	280	2 929	23 242	24 767	28 571	38 687	50 554	54 556
Casinos and gambling	..	..	0	225	442	445	1 019	1 455	1 060	1 241
Port cargo movements	..	..	0	6	0	0	0	0	0	0
Overseas departure tax	..	..	0	0	22 799	24 322	27 552	37 232	49 494	53 315
10% on public shows	..	..	0	0	0	0	0	0	0	0
Pro-national airports stamp tax	..	..	0	0	0	0	0	0	0	0
Stamp tax on the use of borders and ports	..	..	280	2 697	0	0	0	0	0	0
5127 Other taxes on internat. trade and transactions	..	..	0	83	832	1 513	2 565	3 093	3 785	3 841
5128 Other taxes	..	..	0	0	0	0	0	1 071	1 589	1 238
5130 Unallocable between 5110 and 5120	..	..	0	0	0	0	0	0	0	0
5200 Taxes on use of goods and perform activities	..	..	3 642	31 138	99 410	166 612	210 398	273 003	309 607	325 182
5210 Recurrent taxes	..	..	3 642	31 138	99 410	166 612	210 398	273 003	309 607	325 182
5211 Paid by households: motor vehicles	..	..	0	0	0	0	0	0	0	0
5212 Paid by others: motor vehicles	..	..	1 425	15 374	52 511	94 102	113 727	145 894	171 523	181 198
Property tax on vehicles, aircraft and boats	..	..	1 425	15 374	52 511	94 102	113 727	145 894	171 523	181 198
5213 Paid in respect of other goods	..	..	2 217	15 763	46 899	72 510	96 671	127 109	138 084	143 984
Local taxes	..	..	1 262	11 898	43 874	68 808	91 163	122 248	132 514	137 979
Hunting and fishing licences	..	..	0	0	0	0	0	0	0	0
Spirits license	..	..	0	0	0	0	0	0	0	0
Revenue stamps	..	..	955	3 866	3 025	3 702	5 508	4 861	5 571	6 004
Sport stamp tax	..	..	0	0	0	0	0	0	0	0
5220 Non-recurrent taxes	..	..	0	0	0	0	0	0	0	0
5300 Unallocable between 5100 and 5200	..	..	0	0	0	0	0	0	0	0
6000 Other taxes	**..**	**..**	**9 251**	**25 198**	**77 632**	**92 460**	**153 803**	**162 355**	**214 908**	**201 906**
6100 Paid solely by business	..	..	0	0	0	0	0	0	0	0
6200 Other	..	..	9 251	25 198	77 632	92 460	153 803	162 355	214 908	201 906
Transfers of vehicles, aircraft and boats	..	..	497	2 530	9 937	12 311	17 177	20 999	22 265	23 223
Tax revenue from decentralised units	..	..	2 764	15 048	22 257	29 969	45 700	49 334	63 329	67 968
Other taxes	..	..	5 990	7 620	45 438	50 180	90 926	92 022	129 268	110 654
Total tax revenue on cash basis	**..**	**..**	**..**	**..**	**..**	**..**	**..**	**..**	**..**	**..**
Total tax revenue on accrual basis	**..**	**..**	**..**	**..**	**..**	**..**	**..**	**..**	**..**	**..**
Conciliation with National Accounts										
Additional taxes included in National Accounts	..	..	..	..	..	..	..	..	..	..
Taxes excluded from National Accounts	..	..	..	..	..	..	..	..	..	..
Difference in treatment of tax credits	..	..	..	..	..	..	..	..	..	..
Capital transfer for uncollected revenue	..	..	..	..	..	..	..	..	..	..
Voluntary social security contributions	..	..	..	..	..	..	..	..	..	..
Miscellaneous differences	..	..	..	..	..	..	..	..	..	..
National Accounts: Taxes and actual social contributions	..	..	..	..	..	..	..	..	..	..
Imputed social contributions	..	..	..	..	..	..	..	..	..	..
National Accounts: Taxes and all social contributions	..	..	..	..	..	..	..	..	..	..

.. Not available

Note: Note: Year ending 31st December.

Data on an cash basis.

Heading 2000: The data include social security contributions paid by the governments for their employees as well as the contributions for special regimes (teachers and magistrates). In ECLAC data, social security contributions also include INA (National Institute of Apprenticeship), IMAS (Joint Social Aid Institute) and FODESAF (Social Development and Family Allowances Fund).

Heading 3000: In Costa Rica and for ECLAC, payments from decentralised institutions are classified under heading 2000.

Heading 5212: In ECLAC data, tax on ownership of vehicles, aircraft and boats is classified in category 4000.

In ECLAC data, the tax on the transfer of used vehicles Law No. 7088 of 30/11/87 is classified as a property tax.

Source: Secretaría Técnica de la Autoridad Presupuestaria, Ministerio de Finanzas y Contraloría General de la República.

(Technical Secretary of the Budgeting Authority, Ministry of Finance and National General Comptroller).

StatLink https://stat.link/6w1x2h

Table 5.8. Czech Republic: Details of tax revenue, 1965-2019

Million CZK

	1965	1980	1990	2000	2007	2010	2013	2015	2018	2019
Total tax revenue	..	..	..	**771 596**	**1 316 197**	**1 286 861**	**1 396 555**	**1 532 565**	**1 892 396**	**2 013 918**
Total tax revenue exclusive of taxes collected for the EU	..	..	..	**771 596**	**1 309 754**	**1 280 288**	**1 390 999**	**1 524 653**	**1 884 100**	**2 005 147**
1000 Taxes on income, profits and capital gains	..	..	..	**175 846**	**327 771**	**259 934**	**290 263**	**329 768**	**426 988**	**458 514**
1100 Of individuals	..	..	..	99 668	155 817	131 706	149 831	164 678	230 973	255 398
1110 On income and profits	..	..	..	99 668	155 817	131 706	149 831	164 678	230 973	255 398
Wages and salaries withholding	..	..	..	73 474	127 524	115 755	129 793	139 888	198 827	221 720
Of unincorporated individuals	..	..	..	17 254	19 568	5 747	7 437	9 100	13 632	12 988
Withheld on interest and dividends paid to individuals	..	..	..	8 940	8 725	10 204	12 602	15 691	18 513	20 690
1120 On capital gains	..	..	..	0	0	0	0	0	0	0
1200 Corporate	..	..	..	76 178	171 954	128 228	140 432	165 090	196 015	203 116
1210 On profits	..	..	..	76 178	171 954	128 228	140 432	165 090	196 015	203 116
Profit tax	..	..	..	68 945	164 016	118 248	124 820	147 157	179 022	184 705
Withheld on interest and dividends paid to corporations	..	..	..	7 233	7 162	9 156	7 736	9 415	7 892	7 708
Levy on lottery revenue	..	..	..	0	776	824	7 876	8 518	9 101	10 703
1220 On capital gains	..	..	..	0	0	0	0	0	0	0
1300 Unallocable between 1100 and 1200	..	..	..	0	0	0	0	0	0	0
2000 Social security contributions	..	..	..	**341 544**	**573 417**	**576 029**	**603 072**	**659 743**	**829 702**	**889 237**
2100 Employees	..	..	..	77 272	127 662	116 818	123 353	133 878	171 835	184 563
2110 On a payroll basis	..	..	..	77 272	127 662	116 818	123 353	133 878	171 835	184 563
Retirement	..	..	..	40 489	66 644	69 272	71 871	78 120	100 580	108 137
State employment policy	..	..	..	2 492	4 101	0	0	0	0	0
Sick leave	..	..	..	6 852	11 279	0	0	0	0	0
Health insurance	..	..	..	27 439	45 638	47 546	51 482	55 758	71 255	76 426
2120 On an income tax basis	..	..	..	0	0	0	0	0	0	0
2200 Employers	..	..	..	220 207	359 493	363 074	382 498	417 778	531 640	569 522
2210 On a payroll basis	..	..	..	220 207	359 493	363 074	382 498	417 778	531 640	569 522
Retirement	..	..	..	121 547	220 591	229 450	239 248	261 786	333 281	358 382
State employment policy	..	..	..	19 933	12 303	12 756	13 345	14 604	18 590	19 989
Sick leave	..	..	..	20 555	33 834	24 332	25 454	27 851	35 450	36 427
Health insurance	..	..	..	54 879	91 275	95 095	102 964	111 517	142 511	152 853
Penalties	..	..	..	3 293	1 490	1 441	1 487	2 020	1 808	1 871
2220 On an income tax basis	..	..	..	0	0	0	0	0	0	0
2300 Self-employed or non-employed	..	..	..	44 065	86 262	96 137	97 221	108 088	126 227	135 153
2310 On a payroll basis	..	..	..	44 065	86 262	96 137	97 221	108 088	126 227	135 153
Retirement	..	..	..	7 819	19 508	20 510	21 262	22 472	26 825	30 441
State employment policy	..	..	..	1 082	1 114	1 173	911	962	1 149	1 305
Sick leave	..	..	..	0	0	0	0	0	0	0
Health insurance	..	..	..	34 992	65 483	74 299	74 908	84 460	98 089	103 232
Self-employed	..	..	..	7 328	15 921	17 603	18 732	20 748	25 583	27 925
Non-employed	..	..	..	200	2 103	3 996	2 500	2 768	4 146	3 458
Government	..	..	..	27 464	47 459	52 700	53 676	60 944	68 360	71 849
Penalties	..	..	..	172	157	155	140	193	164	175
2320 On an income tax basis	..	..	..	0	0	0	0	0	0	0
2400 Unallocable between 2100, 2200 and 2300	..	..	..	0	0	0	0	0	0	0
2410 On a payroll basis	..	..	..	..	..	..	..	..	..	..
2420 On an income tax basis	..	..	..	..	..	..	..	..	..	..
3000 Taxes on payroll and workforce	..	..	..	**0**	**0**	**0**	**0**	**0**	**0**	**0**
4000 Taxes on property	..	..	..	**10 890**	**15 495**	**16 364**	**19 210**	**21 920**	**24 618**	**24 080**
4100 Recurrent taxes on immovable property	..	..	..	4 469	5 126	8 752	9 852	10 333	10 855	10 967
4110 Households	..	..	..	1 452	2 228	4 302	5 387	5 433	5 772	5 828
Real property tax	..	..	..	1 452	2 228	4 302	5 387	5 433	5 772	5 828
4120 Others	..	..	..	3 017	2 898	4 450	4 465	4 900	5 084	5 138
Levy collected by Winery Fund	..	..	..	0	2	5	5	20	26	32
Real property tax	..	..	..	3 017	2 895	4 445	4 461	4 880	5 057	5 106
4200 Recurrent taxes on net wealth	..	..	..	0	0	0	0	0	0	0
4210 Individual	..	..	..	..	..	..	..	..	..	..
4220 Corporate	..	..	..	..	..	..	..	..	..	..
4300 Estate, inheritance and gift taxes	..	..	..	587	460	218	215	20	3	1
4310 Estate and inheritance taxes	..	..	..	112	115	78	76	10	1	0
Inheritance tax	..	..	..	112	115	78	76	10	1	0
4320 Gift taxes	..	..	..	475	345	140	139	10	1	0
Gift tax	..	..	..	475	345	140	139	10	1	0
4400 Taxes on financial and capital transactions	..	..	..	5 834	9 909	7 394	9 143	11 566	13 760	13 113
Real property transfer tax	..	..	..	5 834	9 909	7 394	9 143	11 566	13 760	13 113
4500 Non-recurrent taxes	..	..	..	0	0	0	0	0	0	0
4510 On net wealth	..	..	..	..	..	..	..	..	..	..
4520 Other non-recurrent taxes	..	..	..	..	..	..	..	..	..	..

	1965	1980	1990	2000	2007	2010	2013	2015	2018	2019
4600 Other recurrent taxes on property	..	..	..	0	0	0	0	0	0	0
5000 Taxes on goods and services	**..**	**..**	**..**	**242 960**	**399 484**	**434 386**	**483 943**	**520 747**	**610 830**	**641 867**
5100 Taxes on production, sale, transfer, etc.	..	..	..	226 354	372 441	408 645	459 419	495 291	582 754	613 003
5110 General taxes	..	..	..	141 235	232 288	263 457	303 822	333 274	408 538	435 463
5111 Value added taxes	..	..	..	141 235	232 288	263 457	303 822	333 274	408 538	435 463
5112 Sales tax	..	..	..	0	0	0	0	0	0	0
5113 Other	..	..	..	0	0	0	0	0	0	0
Previous turnover tax	..	..	..	..	..	..	..	..	..	..
5120 Taxes on specific goods and services	..	..	..	85 119	140 153	145 188	155 597	162 017	174 216	177 540
5121 Excise duties	..	..	..	71 404	133 492	138 401	149 760	153 785	165 377	168 195
On mineral oils	..	..	..	46 998	81 661	80 508	77 160	83 460	89 990	92 194
On alcohol and liquor	..	..	..	5 629	7 201	5 820	6 658	7 203	8 075	9 388
On beer	..	..	..	3 410	3 564	4 396	4 545	4 648	4 756	4 782
On wine	..	..	..	350	342	317	288	332	423	407
On tobacco products	..	..	..	14 984	40 713	44 062	52 193	53 380	56 621	55 967
Duty on CFC	..	..	..	33	0	0	0	0	0	0
Levy collected by Winery Fund	..	..	..	0	11	24	21	0	5	5
On electricity	..	..	..	0	0	1 433	1 305	1 229	1 562	1 575
On natural gas	..	..	..	0	0	1 347	1 256	1 146	1 346	1 360
On solid fuels	..	..	..	0	0	495	469	415	401	353
Fee on electricity from solar radiation	..	..	..	0	0	0	5 866	1 972	2 198	2 166
5122 Profits of fiscal monopolies	..	..	..	0	0	0	0	0	0	0
5123 Customs and import duties	..	..	..	13 572	6 443	6 573	5 556	7 912	8 296	8 772
Customs duties	..	..	..	13 572	6 443	6 573	5 556	7 912	8 296	8 772
Previous import surcharge	..	..	..	0	0	0	0	0	0	0
5124 Taxes on exports	..	..	..	0	0	0	0	0	0	0
5125 Taxes on investment goods	..	..	..	0	0	0	0	0	0	0
5126 Taxes on specific services	..	..	..	143	218	214	281	320	543	573
Fees on entry tickets	..	..	..	65	61	53	56	53	70	82
Fees on recreational units (based on capacity)	..	..	..	69	144	147	213	240	288	297
Fees on advertising facilities	..	..	..	0	0	0	0	0	0	0
Restaurant sale alcoh. beverages and tobac. products	..	..	..	0	0	0	0	0	0	0
Fees collected by the cinematography EBF	..	..	..	9	13	14	12	27	0	0
Fees on advertisement	..	..	..	0	0	0	126	191	185	194
5127 Other taxes on internat. trade and transactions	..	..	..	0	0	0	0	0	0	0
5128 Other taxes	..	..	..	0	0	0	0	0	0	0
5130 Unallocable between 5110 and 5120	..	..	..	0	0	0	0	0	0	0
5200 Taxes on use of goods and perform activities	..	..	..	16 606	27 043	25 740	24 523	25 456	28 076	28 864
5210 Recurrent taxes	..	..	..	10 788	18 100	18 461	18 176	19 023	20 911	21 627
Highway fee	..	..	..	1 753	2 429	3 061	3 803	4 397	5 212	5 384
5211 Paid by households: motor vehicles	..	..	..	0	0	0	0	0	0	0
5212 Paid by others: motor vehicles	..	..	..	5 456	5 882	5 138	5 323	5 868	6 319	6 501
Road tax (commercial)	..	..	..	5 456	5 882	5 138	5 323	5 868	6 319	6 501
5213 Paid in respect of other goods	..	..	..	3 579	9 790	10 262	9 050	8 758	9 379	9 743
Resort and recreation fees on visitors	..	..	..	232	312	284	301	327	407	435
Dog fees	..	..	..	191	277	281	281	277	273	275
Motor vehicle entry fees	..	..	..	32	25	23	14	13	19	19
Water pollution fee	..	..	..	520	404	202	208	173	201	22
Air pollution fee	..	..	..	685	525	399	268	283	270	457
Waste deposit fee	..	..	..	454	5 728	5 948	6 162	6 218	6 443	6 723
Levy on temp. withdrawal of land from agriculture	..	..	..	94	40	34	52	39	86	88
Radioactive waste fee	..	..	..	642	1 310	1 430	1 563	1 393	1 646	1 692
Fees on operated gambling machines	..	..	..	722	1 145	927	131	0	0	0
Fees on registration and recording of packaging	..	..	..	0	17	17	16	18	17	17
Levy on temp. withdrawal of land from forestry	..	..	..	7	6	6	6	7	8	7
Other environmental fees	..	..	..	0	0	710	47	11	9	7
5220 Non-recurrent taxes	..	..	..	5 818	8 943	7 280	6 348	6 433	7 165	7 237
Levy on withdrawal of land from agriculture	..	..	..	532	361	306	469	348	776	791
Levy on withdrawal of land from forestry	..	..	..	40	57	57	55	59	72	63
Tax on use of public space	..	..	..	645	639	626	629	632	674	739
Misc. licence and permit fees	..	..	..	4 601	7 881	6 279	5 187	5 382	5 621	5 631
Land betterment fee	..	..	..	0	4	11	7	11	22	12
Licence for lorry transport	..	..	..	0	1	1	0	1	0	0
5300 Unallocable between 5100 and 5200	..	..	..	0	0	0	0	0	0	0
6000 Other taxes	**..**	**..**	**..**	**356**	**29**	**149**	**67**	**387**	**258**	**220**
Unallocated previous taxes and levies	..	..	..	0	0	0	0	0	0	0
6100 Paid solely by business	..	..	..	0	0	0	0	0	0	0
6200 Other	..	..	..	356	29	149	67	387	258	220
Other taxes, fees and related payments	..	..	..	356	29	149	67	387	258	220
Memorandum item										
Customs duties collected on behalf of the EU	..	..	..	..	6 443	6 573	5 556	7 912	8 296	8 772

	1965	1980	1990	2000	2007	2010	2013	2015	2018	2019
Non-wastable tax credits										
Non-wastable tax credits against 1110	..	..	..	0	13 093	25 727	28 696	31 415	39 083	39 854
Tax expenditure component	..	..	..	..	10 487	17 922	20 203	22 532	30 320	32 057
Transfer component	..	..	..	..	2 606	7 805	8 493	8 883	8 763	7 798
Total tax revenue on cash basis	**..**	**..**	**..**	**772 272**	**1 310 618**	**1 273 676**	**1 353 469**	**1 478 758**	**1 867 024**	**1 982 448**
Total tax revenue on accrual basis	**..**	**..**	**..**	**771 596**	**1 316 197**	**1 286 861**	**1 396 555**	**1 532 565**	**1 892 396**	**2 013 918**
Conciliation with National Accounts										
Additional taxes included in National Accounts	..	..	..	2 837	5 757	6 094	6 424	0	0	0
Compulsory injury insurance	..	..	..	2 837	5 757	6 094	6 424	0	0	0
Driving licence fees	..	..	..	0	0	0	0	0	0	0
Taxes excluded from National Accounts	..	..	..	-9 488	-17 797	-20 096	-18 893	-20 314	-22 904	-22 857
Tax on use of public space	..	..	..	-645	-639	-632	-629	-632	-674	-739
Waste deposit fee	..	..	..	-454	-5 728	-5 948	-6 162	-6 218	-6 443	-6 723
Misc. licence and permit fees	..	..	..	-2 301	-3 940	-3 139	-2 593	-2 691	-2 810	-2 816
Radioactive waste fee	..	..	..	-642	-1 310	-1 430	-1 563	-1 393	-1 646	-1 692
Health insurance: non-employed	..	..	..	-200	-2 103	-3 996	-2 500	-2 768	-4 146	-3 458
Health insurance: government	..	..	..	0	0	0	0	0	0	0
Soc. Security contr. employers: Penalties	..	..	..	-3 293	-1 490	-1 441	-1 487	-2 020	-1 808	-1 871
Soc. Security contr. Self-employed or non-employed: Penalties	..	..	..	-200	-157	-155	-140	-193	-164	-175
Licence for lorry transport	..	..	..	0	-1	-1	0	-1	0	0
Highway fee	..	..	..	-1 753	-2 429	-3 061	-3 803	-4 397	-5 212	-5 384
Other environmental fees	..	..	..	0	0	-105	-14	0	0	0
Levy on loterry revenue	..	..	..	0	0	-187	0	0	0	0
Value added taxes	..	..	..	0	0	0	0	0	0	0
Difference in treatment of tax credits	..	..	..	0	-127	451	-778	118	-2	-231
Capital transfer for uncollected revenue	..	..	..	0	0	0	0	0	0	0
Voluntary social security contributions	..	..	..	1 099	974	661	337	386	523	578
Miscellaneous differences	..	..	..	2 162	0	0	0	0	0	0
National Accounts: Taxes and actual social contributions	..	..	..	768 206	1 305 004	1 273 971	1 383 645	1 512 755	1 870 013	1 991 408
Imputed social contributions	..	..	..	423	299	600	934	1 027	1 426	1 867
National Accounts: Taxes and all social contributions	..	..	..	768 629	1 305 303	1 274 571	1 384 579	1 513 782	1 871 439	1 993 275

.. Not available

Note: Year ending 31st December.

From 1995 data are on accrual basis.

Source: Ministry of Finance, Economic Department.

StatLink https://stat.link/dubi4v

Table 5.9. Denmark: Details of tax revenue, 1965-2019

Million DKK

	1965	1980	1990	2000	2007	2010	2013	2015	2018	2019
Total tax revenue	**20 821**	**166 358**	**382 232**	**623 911**	**809 988**	**813 972**	**901 001**	**957 281**	**1 005 199**	**1 092 946**
Total tax revenue exclusive of taxes collected for the EU	..	..	**379 547**	**621 274**	**806 337**	**810 697**	**898 126**	**953 963**	**1 002 013**	**1 089 817**
1000 Taxes on income, profits and capital gains	**9 712**	**92 404**	**233 739**	**383 244**	**486 845**	**500 276**	**564 937**	**605 698**	**623 303**	**705 407**
1100 Of individuals	8 758	86 958	206 478	328 532	427 412	422 685	490 887	525 144	547 882	569 272
1110 On income and profits	8 758	86 909	206 335	328 305	427 070	422 364	490 627	524 856	547 612	569 048
Central government income tax	5 020	33 351	91 638	77 491	155 540	124 943	141 399	169 059	187 470	197 956
County income tax	0	10 742	31 361	56 135	0	0	0	0	0	0
Municipality income tax	2 948	33 555	77 571	121 975	173 114	193 111	209 303	220 815	239 416	247 583
Seaman's income tax	66	457	0	0	0	0	0	0	0	0
Old-age pension fund contributions	592	2 163	0	0	0	0	0	0	0	0
Social pension fund contributions	0	3 340	0	0	0	0	0	0	0	0
Sickness benefit fund contributions	0	1 804	0	0	0	0	0	0	0	0
Pension schemes and annuity insurance	22	355	2 627	6 923	8 948	9 842	42 974	22 842	5 559	5 555
Special income tax	101	1 054	2 810	0	0	0	0	0	0	0
Duty on canceled pension schemes	9	82	0	0	0	0	0	0	0	0
Duty on feed rent increases	0	8	5	0	0	0	0	0	0	0
Duty on employees' remuneration compens. fund releases	0	0	325	654	1 144	982	1 129	11 177	2 360	2 406
Duty on interest on consumer loans	0	0	0	0	0	0	0	0	0	0
Labour market contributions	0	0	0	56 729	76 609	80 863	82 599	87 359	98 325	100 780
Imputed income from owner-occupied dwelling	0	0	0	8 399	11 716	12 623	13 223	13 604	14 482	14 768
1120 On capital gains	0	49	144	226	343	321	260	289	270	224
Tax on winnings from lotteries, pools, etc.	..	49	144	226	343	321	260	289	270	224
1200 Corporate	954	5 446	14 660	42 279	54 871	41 057	54 066	57 723	62 074	72 724
1210 On profits	954	5 446	14 660	42 279	54 871	41 057	54 066	57 723	62 074	72 724
1220 On capital gains	0	0	0	0	0	0	0	0	0	0
1300 Unallocable between 1100 and 1200	0	0	12 601	12 434	4 562	36 535	19 984	22 832	13 347	63 411
2000 Social security contributions	**690**	**710**	**101**	**8 453**	**1 286**	**1 815**	**1 618**	**1 378**	**1 061**	**991**
2100 Employees	567	1	98	8 209	1 057	900	879	826	751	684
Sickness benefit fund contributions	30	0	0	0	0	0	0	0	0	0
Sickday benefit contributions, ordinary	534	0	0	0	0	0	0	0	0	0
Sickday benefit contributions, special	3	0	0	0	0	0	0	0	0	0
Contribution to merchant marine's welf. board	0	1	1	0	0	0	0	0	0	0
Special pension scheme savings	0	0	0	6 846	0	0	0	0	0	0
Contr. to pension funds from officials in companies	0	0	0	879	555	450	476	438	410	355
Contr. to pension funds from officials in non-profit institutions	0	0	96	485	502	450	403	388	341	328
2110 On a payroll basis	..	..	..	..	..	..	..	..	..	..
2120 On an income tax basis	..	..	..	..	..	..	..	..	..	..
2200 Employers	123	709	3	244	229	914	739	552	311	308
Unemployment insurance contributions	41	598	0	0	0	0	0	0	0	0
Disablement insurance contributions	21	58	0	0	0	0	0	0	0	0
Sickness benefit fund contributions	61	0	0	0	0	0	0	0	0	0
Contribution to employee's wage guarantee fund	0	50	0	241	227	908	731	542	299	305
Contribution to merchant marine's welf. board	0	1	1	0	0	0	0	0	0	0
Shipping owners contr. sickness assist. seamen	0	1	2	3	2	6	8	10	12	3
2210 On a payroll basis	..	..	..	..	..	..	..	..	..	..
2220 On an income tax basis	..	..	..	..	..	..	..	..	..	..
2300 Self-employed or non-employed	0	0	0	0	0	0	0	0	0	0
2310 On a payroll basis	..	..	..	..	..	..	..	..	..	..
2320 On an income tax basis	..	..	..	..	..	..	..	..	..	..
2400 Unallocable between 2100, 2200 and 2300	0	0	0	0	0	0	0	0	0	0
2410 On a payroll basis	..	..	..	..	..	..	..	..	..	..
2420 On an income tax basis	..	..	..	..	..	..	..	..	..	..
3000 Taxes on payroll and workforce	**0**	**0**	**2 494**	**2 258**	**3 975**	**4 160**	**6 130**	**5 894**	**6 314**	**6 534**
4000 Taxes on property	**1 691**	**9 806**	**16 269**	**20 738**	**31 556**	**33 533**	**34 995**	**39 169**	**41 215**	**46 352**
4100 Recurrent taxes on immovable property	1 029	5 676	8 891	13 565	18 996	24 161	26 370	28 085	29 578	30 567
Central government land tax	130	264	0	0	0	0	0	0	0	0
County land tax	169	2 315	2 915	4 070	0	0	0	0	0	0
Municipal land tax	408	2 257	4 123	7 049	15 601	19 645	22 580	24 707	26 394	27 433
Centr. Govt. fixed tax on real property	32	11	0	0	0	0	0	0	0	0
County fixed tax on real property	45	0	0	0	0	0	0	0	0	0
Municipal fixed tax on real property	190	91	0	0	0	0	0	0	0	0
County duty on land (public property)	4	22	22	25	0	0	0	0	0	0
County duty on buildings (public property)	0	53	88	97	0	0	0	0	0	0
Municipal duty on land (public property)	26	103	244	383	393	434	359	364	339	333
Municipal duty on buildings (residential)	0	195	335	381	757	814	641	599	554	556
Municipal duty on buildings (business)	25	366	1 165	1 560	2 244	3 269	2 789	2 416	2 291	2 245
4110 Households	..	..	..	..	..	..	..	..	..	..

	1965	1980	1990	2000	2007	2010	2013	2015	2018	2019
4120 Others	..	..	..	..	..	..	..	..	..	..
4200 Recurrent taxes on net wealth	306	963	934	0	0	0	0	0	0	0
4210 Individual	306	963	934	..	..	..	..	..	..	..
4220 Corporate	0	0	0	..	..	..	..	..	..	..
4300 Estate, inheritance and gift taxes	137	738	2 197	2 863	3 896	3 646	3 940	5 177	4 810	8 571
4310 Estate and inheritance taxes	..	..	..	..	..	..	..	..	..	..
4320 Gift taxes	..	..	..	..	..	..	..	..	..	..
4400 Taxes on financial and capital transactions	219	2 313	4 166	4 171	8 659	5 726	4 685	5 907	6 828	7 214
Stamp duties	214	2 243	2 829	4 125	8 574	5 695	4 664	5 879	6 786	7 165
Duty on share capital creation	0	32	500	0	0	0	0	0	0	0
Duty to land registry office	5	38	28	46	85	30	21	28	41	49
Duty on transfers of shares	0	0	809	0	0	0	0	0	0	0
4500 Non-recurrent taxes	0	116	81	140	6	0	0	0	0	0
4510 On net wealth	..	0	0	0	0	0	..	..	..	..
4520 Other non-recurrent taxes	..	116	81	140	6	0	..	..	..	..
4600 Other recurrent taxes on property	0	0	0	0	0	0	0	0	0	0
5000 Taxes on goods and services	**8 727**	**63 437**	**129 630**	**208 826**	**286 136**	**273 982**	**293 170**	**304 823**	**333 041**	**333 372**
5100 Taxes on production, sale, transfer, etc.	8 239	60 545	123 645	197 991	267 325	254 303	270 493	281 109	306 772	307 951
5110 General taxes	2 139	37 727	80 650	121 955	174 639	171 583	181 378	191 479	217 627	222 730
5111 Value added taxes	2 139	37 727	72 120	121 955	174 639	171 583	181 378	191 479	217 627	222 730
5112 Sales tax	0	0	0	0	0	0	0	0	0	0
5113 Other	0	0	8 530	0	0	0	0	0	0	0
Labour market contrib. concerning imports	..	..	4 903	..	..	..	..	..	..	..
Labour market contrib. concerning value added	..	..	3 627	..	..	..	..	..	..	..
5120 Taxes on specific goods and services	6 100	22 817	42 995	76 036	92 686	82 720	89 116	89 630	89 145	85 221
5121 Excise duties	5 466	20 473	38 339	68 977	82 861	74 032	81 894	81 893	81 020	76 758
Duty on petrol	1 016	3 713	5 637	10 005	9 154	8 029	7 286	7 348	7 521	7 658
Motor vehicle registration duty	818	2 989	7 917	13 858	24 289	13 586	15 218	17 988	20 602	20 307
Cigarettes and tobacco duties	1 469	4 472	6 516	7 489	7 201	8 283	8 417	7 658	7 045	7 830
Duties on cigars, cheroots and cigarillos	234	220	128	80	40	32	47	113	45	46
Sale of revenue labels	0	3	10	13	13	5	4	4	0	0
Sales duties on chocolate and sugar	254	331	801	1 205	1 289	1 470	2 020	2 156	2 168	2 191
Raw material duty on chocolate and sugar	11	14	54	60	93	144	180	187	132	94
Special tax on chocolate and sugar	0	2	13	76	46	51	68	103	104	93
Duty on ice-cream	33	58	135	168	180	201	297	297	354	356
Duty on coffee	5	249	224	266	250	243	271	280	280	277
Duty on mineral water	68	195	466	505	418	383	374	0	0	0
Duty on beer	622	1 983	3 100	1 510	1 080	895	977	916	943	810
Duty on wine	122	611	1 448	1 166	1 032	1 071	1 674	1 764	1 732	1 664
Duty on spirits	412	1 432	1 982	1 756	1 213	1 028	1 127	1 201	1 187	1 205
Duty on restaurant sales of alcoholic bev.	150	0	0	0	0	0	0	0	0	0
Duty on wireless sets	55	67	0	0	0	0	0	0	0	0
Duty on television sets	0	93	-18	0	0	0	0	0	0	0
Duty on video recorders	0	17	-15	0	0	0	0	0	0	0
Duty on major household appliances	0	199	-10	0	0	0	0	0	0	0
Duty on grammophone records	10	46	84	0	0	0	0	0	0	0
Duty on playing cards	1	2	0	0	0	0	0	0	0	0
Duty on matches	5	3	-1	0	0	0	0	0	0	0
Duty on lighters	1	8	-4	0	0	0	0	0	0	0
Duty on electric bulbs	36	67	152	176	211	117	95	86	54	42
Duty on perfumery and toilet articles	91	214	506	0	0	0	0	0	0	0
Duty on almanacs	3	0	0	0	0	0	0	0	0	0
Duty on salmon	0	1	0	0	0	0	0	0	0	0
Duty on paper and cardboard	45	0	0	0	0	0	0	0	0	0
Duty on sugar	0	174	-8	0	0	0	0	0	0	0
Duty on tea	0	12	10	8	8	8	8	8	0	0
Duty on electricity	0	1 222	4 317	7 430	8 665	10 195	10 013	11 501	12 119	11 178
Duty on certain oil products	0	1 719	2 938	6 757	8 549	8 623	9 306	9 347	10 012	9 971
Duty on certain retail containers	0	100	397	594	727	706	715	316	365	244
Duty on gas	0	56	47	0	0	0	0	0	0	0
Duty on extraction and import of raw materials	0	16	129	172	220	119	132	148	165	163
Duty on disposable tableware	0	0	72	65	126	120	121	138	148	140
Duty on insecticides, herbicides, etc.	0	0	13	366	449	466	656	598	568	590
Duty on videotapes	0	0	0	0	0	0	0	0	0	0
Duty on coal, etc.	0	0	849	1 217	1 450	2 587	2 991	2 255	1 852	1 766
Other duties on goods and services	5	186	20	53	147	189	-13	186	178	178
Duty on waste	0	0	404	1 025	1 225	51	167	130	154	120
Duty on CFC	0	0	27	0	53	56	82	65	55	45
Duty on CO2	0	0	0	4 883	5 108	5 822	5 762	3 652	3 627	3 565
Duty on cigarette paper	0	0	0	68	32	28	36	38	31	32
Duty on rechargeable Ni-Cd batteries	0	0	0	21	17	4	3	2	0	1
Duty on piped water	0	0	0	1 357	1 371	1 334	1 584	1 688	1 649	1 673

	1965	1980	1990	2000	2007	2010	2013	2015	2018	2019
Duty on carrier bags made of paper, plastic, etc.	0	0	0	178	210	201	186	208	178	166
Duty on tires	0	0	0	29	45	62	50	57	53	47
Duty on sulphur	0	0	0	165	108	48	51	42	39	33
Duty on chlorinated solvents	0	0	0	2	0	0	0	0	0	0
Duty on natural gas	0	0	0	2 532	3 375	4 524	5 255	3 160	3 325	2 781
Duty on nitrogen	0	0	0	30	27	26	21	17	13	14
Duty on specific growth stimulants	0	0	0	0	0	0	0	0	0	0
Duty on PVC-film	0	0	0	7	12	11	10	11	11	0
Duty on PVC and phathalates	0	0	0	31	42	23	18	19	16	0
Duty on lead accumulators	0	0	0	14	0	0	0	0	0	0
Duty on mineral phosphorus	0	0	0	0	51	51	49	52	53	25
Surcharge on alcoholic soft drinks	0	0	0	0	17	26	33	33	0	0
Duty on nitrogen oxides	0	0	0	0	0	212	870	820	183	152
Duty on saturated fat	0	0	0	0	0	0	0	0	0	0
Duty on PSO (Public Service Obligations)	0	0	0	3 641	4 319	3 004	5 734	7 302	4 060	1 301
5122 Profits of fiscal monopolies	16	183	404	1 402	1 648	1 481	1 339	1 230	1 535	1 989
5123 Customs and import duties	556	1 113	1 849	2 325	3 282	3 242	2 824	3 285	3 186	3 129
Customs duties	0	1 032	1 779	2 325	3 282	3 242	2 824	3 285	3 186	3 129
Temporary import surcharge	556	0	0	0	0	0	0	0	0	0
Import duties on agricultural produce	0	81	70	0	0	0	0	0	0	0
5124 Taxes on exports	0	0	0	0	0	0	0	0	0	0
5125 Taxes on investment goods	0	0	0	0	0	0	0	0	0	0
5126 Taxes on specific services	62	771	1 567	3 019	4 525	3 932	3 008	3 189	3 404	3 346
Sales tax on gambling stakes races	17	28	20	12	18	16	15	14	0	0
Tax on football pools	31	152	284	942	1 143	1 071	0	0	0	0
Tax on cinema tickets	14	0	0	0	0	0	0	0	0	0
Duty on motor vehicle compl. insurance	0	470	923	1 327	2 104	1 854	1 598	1 529	1 491	1 478
Duty on insurance on pleasure boats	0	13	57	66	100	122	127	126	119	93
Duty on charter flight	0	109	283	0	0	0	0	0	0	0
Turnover tax on 6-win horse race betting	0	0	0	0	0	0	0	0	0	0
Duty on casinos	0	0	0	180	261	173	192	200	202	198
Passenger duty	0	0	0	477	6	0	0	0	0	0
Duty on the Danish State Lottery	0	0	0	16	35	41	42	44	44	44
Duty on slot machines	0	0	0	0	858	656	545	618	592	569
Duty on gambling	0	0	0	0	0	0	288	397	511	490
Duty on online casinos	0	0	0	0	0	0	202	261	445	475
5127 Other taxes on internat. trade and transactions	0	0	0	0	0	0	0	0	0	0
5128 Other taxes	0	277	837	312	370	33	51	33	0	0
Duty paid to ECSC	..	4	5	0	0	0	0	0	..	..
Sugar storing duty	..	83	113	62	0	0	0	0	..	..
Duty on the production of sugar	..	81	145	249	-26	33	51	33	..	..
Duty on milk co-reponsibility levy	..	109	255	0	0	0	0	0	..	..
Grain co-reponsibility levy	..	0	319	0	0	0	0	0	..	..
Restructuring scheme for EU sugar system	..	0	0	0	397	0	0	0	..	..
5130 Unallocable between 5110 and 5120	0	0	0	0	0	0	0	0	0	0
5200 Taxes on use of goods and perform activities	488	2 893	4 410	7 468	14 088	14 731	16 180	16 537	17 383	16 099
5210 Recurrent taxes	488	2 893	4 410	7 468	14 088	14 731	15 966	16 171	15 968	14 859
5211 Paid by households: motor vehicles	199	1 874	2 922	5 485	7 105	7 614	8 094	8 136	7 531	7 411
Weight duty automobiles	199	1 874	2 922	5 318	6 954	7 467	7 936	7 859	7 283	7 161
Recycling fee on cars	0	0	0	167	151	147	158	277	247	251
5212 Paid by others: motor vehicles	287	1 014	1 441	1 919	3 125	2 980	3 336	3 483	3 848	3 822
Weight duty automobiles	287	1 014	1 441	1 612	2 652	2 611	2 952	3 088	3 359	3 303
Road charges	0	0	0	307	473	370	383	395	489	519
5213 Paid in respect of other goods	2	5	47	64	3 858	4 137	4 537	4 552	4 590	3 626
5220 Non-recurrent taxes	0	0	0	0	0	0	214	365	1 415	1 240
5300 Unallocable between 5100 and 5200	0	0	1 575	3 368	4 724	4 948	6 497	7 177	8 887	9 322
6000 Other taxes	**0**	**0**	**0**	**391**	**190**	**206**	**152**	**320**	**265**	**289**
6100 Paid solely by business	..	..	..	391	190	206	152	320	265	289
6200 Other	..	..	..	0	0	0	0	0	0	0
Memorandum item										
Customs duties collected on behalf of the EU	..	..	1 779	2 325	3 282	3 242	2 824	3 285	3 186	3 129
Non-wastable tax credits										
Non-wastable tax credits against 1110	..	..	..	..	..	4 960	5 515	4 228	3 765	3 096
Tax expenditure component	..	..	..	..	..	4 712	5 240	4 016	3 577	2 942
Transfer component	..	..	..	..	..	248	276	211	188	155
Non-wastable tax credits against 1210	..	..	..	..	..	0	0	0	0	0
Tax expenditure component	..	..	..	..	..	..	..	..	..	..
Transfer component	..	..	..	..	..	..	..	..	..	..
Total tax revenue on cash basis	**..**	**..**	**..**	**..**	**..**	**..**	**..**	**..**	**..**	**..**
Total tax revenue on accrual basis	**20 821**	**166 358**	**382 232**	**623 911**	**809 988**	**813 972**	**901 001**	**957 281**	**1 005 199**	**1 092 946**

	1965	1980	1990	2000	2007	2010	2013	2015	2018	2019
Conciliation with National Accounts										
Additional taxes included in National Accounts	0	0	..	..	..	..	..	..	..	..
Taxes excluded from National Accounts	0	0	..	..	..	..	..	..	..	..
Difference in treatment of tax credits	0	0	0	0	0	4 712	5 240	4 016	3 577	2 942
Capital transfer for uncollected revenue	0	-1 374	-2 387	-1 917	-2 726	-3 475	-15 512	-19 396	-9 791	-12 676
Voluntary social security contributions	0	1 673	8 087	16 633	17 061	17 192	14 655	14 721	14 751	14 792
Miscellaneous differences	0	0	..	..	..	..	..	..	..	..
National Accounts: Taxes and actual social contributions	20 821	166 657	387 932	638 626	824 323	832 401	905 384	956 623	1 013 736	1 098 003
Imputed social contributions	0	5 958	4 592	6 223	5 693	5 356	4 520	4 067	3 214	3 227
National Accounts: Taxes and all social contributions	20 821	172 615	392 525	644 849	830 017	837 758	909 904	960 690	1 016 949	1 101 231

.. Not available

Note: Year ending 31st December.

The figures are on an accrual basis.

Heading 2300 includes a small amount of voluntary contributions which cannot be isolated.

Source: Danmarks Statistik.

StatLink https://stat.link/qae1ng

Table 5.10. Estonia: Details of tax revenue, 1965-2019

Million EUR

	1965	1980	1990	2000	2007	2010	2013	2015	2018	2019
Total tax revenue	..	..	..	**1 919**	**5 082**	**4 894**	**5 988**	**6 874**	**8 532**	**9 298**
Total tax revenue exclusive of taxes collected for the EU	..	..	..	**1 919**	**5 047**	**4 870**	**5 960**	**6 840**	**8 484**	**9 239**
1000 Taxes on income, profits and capital gains	..	..	..	**476**	**1 197**	**970**	**1 357**	**1 607**	**1 929**	**2 041**
1100 Of individuals	..	..	..	421	936	776	1 031	1 182	1 411	1 532
1110 On income and profits	..	..	..	421	936	776	1 031	1 182	1 411	1 532
1120 On capital gains	..	..	..	0	0	0	0	0	0	0
1200 Corporate	..	..	..	55	261	194	327	424	518	509
1210 On profits	..	..	..	55	65	35	62	38	71	94
1220 On capital gains	..	..	..	0	196	159	265	386	447	416
1300 Unallocable between 1100 and 1200	..	..	..	0	0	0	0	0	0	0
2000 Social security contributions	..	..	..	**674**	**1 683**	**1 879**	**2 077**	**2 300**	**2 978**	**3 256**
2100 Employees	..	..	..	0	28	116	109	99	123	136
2110 On a payroll basis	..	..	..	..	28	116	109	99	123	136
2120 On an income tax basis	..	..	..	..	0	0	0	0	0	0
2200 Employers	..	..	..	662	1 635	1 742	1 949	2 181	2 835	3 101
2210 On a payroll basis	..	..	..	662	1 635	1 742	1 949	2 181	2 835	3 101
2220 On an income tax basis	..	..	..	0	0	0	0	0	0	0
2300 Self-employed or non-employed	..	..	..	12	21	21	19	20	21	20
2310 On a payroll basis	..	..	..	12	21	21	19	20	21	20
2320 On an income tax basis	..	..	..	0	0	0	0	0	0	0
2400 Unallocable between 2100, 2200 and 2300	..	..	..	0	0	0	0	0	0	0
2410 On a payroll basis	..	..	..	..	..	..	..	..	..	..
2420 On an income tax basis	..	..	..	..	..	..	..	..	..	..
3000 Taxes on payroll and workforce	..	..	..	**0**	**0**	**0**	**0**	**0**	**0**	**0**
4000 Taxes on property	..	..	..	**24**	**35**	**51**	**57**	**58**	**58**	**58**
4100 Recurrent taxes on immovable property	..	..	..	24	35	51	57	58	58	58
Land tax	..	..	..	24	35	51	57	58	58	58
4110 Households	..	..	..	..	..	..	..	..	..	..
4120 Others	..	..	..	..	..	..	..	..	..	..
4200 Recurrent taxes on net wealth	..	..	..	0	0	0	0	0	0	0
4210 Individual	..	..	..	..	..	..	..	..	..	..
4220 Corporate	..	..	..	..	..	..	..	..	..	..
4300 Estate, inheritance and gift taxes	..	..	..	0	0	0	0	0	0	0
4310 Estate and inheritance taxes	..	..	..	..	..	..	..	..	..	..
4320 Gift taxes	..	..	..	..	..	..	..	..	..	..
4400 Taxes on financial and capital transactions	..	..	..	0	0	0	0	0	0	0
4500 Non-recurrent taxes	..	..	..	0	0	0	0	0	0	0
4510 On net wealth	..	..	..	..	..	..	..	..	..	..
4520 Other non-recurrent taxes	..	..	..	..	..	..	..	..	..	..
4600 Other recurrent taxes on property	..	..	..	0	0	0	0	0	0	0
5000 Taxes on goods and services	..	..	..	**745**	**2 166**	**1 993**	**2 496**	**2 909**	**3 566**	**3 943**
5100 Taxes on production, sale, transfer, etc.	..	..	..	723	2 099	1 938	2 431	2 829	3 437	3 725
5110 General taxes	..	..	..	521	1 423	1 263	1 558	1 873	2 331	2 483
5111 Value added taxes	..	..	..	520	1 423	1 257	1 558	1 873	2 331	2 483
5112 Sales tax	..	..	..	0	0	6	0	0	0	0
5113 Other	..	..	..	0	0	0	0	0	0	0
5120 Taxes on specific goods and services	..	..	..	202	675	675	873	956	1 106	1 243
5121 Excise duties	..	..	..	183	577	619	796	869	1 012	1 128
Alcohol	..	..	..	62	153	154	212	207	232	225
Tobacco	..	..	..	36	134	91	169	183	200	231
Fuel	..	..	..	76	290	343	383	444	543	638
Motor vehicle	..	..	..	9	0	0	0	0	0	0
Package	..	..	..	0	0	0	0	1	0	0
Fur	..	..	..	0	0	0	0	0	0	0
Electricity	..	..	..	0	0	31	33	34	37	34
5122 Profits of fiscal monopolies	..	..	..	0	0	0	0	0	0	0
5123 Customs and import duties	..	..	..	2	35	24	29	34	43	52
5124 Taxes on exports	..	..	..	0	0	0	0	0	0	0
5125 Taxes on investment goods	..	..	..	0	0	0	0	0	0	0
5126 Taxes on specific services	..	..	..	17	64	33	48	53	52	62
Gambling tax	..	..	..	7	30	21	22	23	27	30
Advertising tax	..	..	..	1	3	2	4	4	6	6
Postal service payment	..	..	..	0	0	0	0	0	0	0
Liquid fuel stockpiling fee	..	..	..	0	2	5	6	5	4	5
Contributions to the Guarantee Fund	..	..	..	9	29	5	17	20	14	21
5127 Other taxes on internat. trade and transactions	..	..	..	0	0	0	0	0	0	0
5128 Other taxes	..	..	..	0	0	0	0	0	0	0
5130 Unallocable between 5110 and 5120	..	..	..	0	0	0	0	0	0	0

	1965	1980	1990	2000	2007	2010	2013	2015	2018	2019
5200 Taxes on use of goods and perform activities	..	..	..	22	68	55	65	80	129	217
5210 Recurrent taxes	..	..	..	22	68	55	65	73	90	77
Car registration fee	..	..	..	2	5	4	7	7	8	8
Heavy vehicle tax	..	..	..	0	4	4	4	5	5	5
5211 Paid by households: motor vehicles	..	..	..	..	..	..	..	..	..	..
5212 Paid by others: motor vehicles	..	..	..	..	..	..	..	..	..	..
5213 Paid in respect of other goods	..	..	..	20	58	47	55	61	77	64
Business and professional licenses	..	..	..	3	2	1	1	1	3	4
Pollution fee	..	..	..	10	44	31	37	44	54	44
Specific use of water	..	..	..	4	9	13	14	13	16	13
Fees for closure of roads, streets and squares	..	..	..	0	1	1	1	2	2	2
Fishing fees	..	..	..	1	1	1	2	2	2	2
Tax on motor vehicle	..	..	..	2	0	0	0	0	0	0
Boat tax	..	..	..	0	0	0	0	0	0	0
Animal tax	..	..	..	0	0	0	0	0	0	0
5220 Non-recurrent taxes	..	..	..	0	0	0	0	7	39	140
Revenue from the sale of emission permits	..	..	..	..	..	..	..	7	39	140
5300 Unallocable between 5100 and 5200	..	..	..	0	0	0	0	0	0	0
6000 Other taxes	**..**	**..**	**..**	**0**	**0**	**0**	**0**	**0**	**0**	**0**
6100 Paid solely by business	..	..	..	..	..	..	..	..	..	..
6200 Other	..	..	..	..	..	..	..	..	..	..
Other taxes	..	..	..	..	..	..	..	..	..	..
Memorandum item										
Customs duties collected on behalf of the EU	..	..	..	..	35	24	29	34	43	52
SRF contributions collected on behalf of the EU	..	..	..	..	..	..	..	..	5	7
Total tax revenue on cash basis	**..**	**..**	**..**	**1 907**	**5 003**	**4 921**	**5 964**	**6 848**	**8 528**	**9 195**
Total tax revenue on accrual basis	**..**	**..**	**..**	**1 919**	**5 082**	**4 894**	**5 988**	**6 874**	**8 532**	**9 298**
Conciliation with National Accounts										
Additional taxes included in National Accounts	..	..	..	0	0	0	0	0	0	0
Taxes excluded from National Accounts	..	..	..	0	0	0	0	0	0	0
Difference in treatment of tax credits	..	..	..	0	0	0	0	0	0	0
Capital transfer for uncollected revenue	..	..	..	0	0	0	0	0	0	0
Voluntary social security contributions	..	..	..	0	0	0	0	0	0	0
Miscellaneous differences	..	..	..	0	0	0	0	0	0	0
National Accounts: Taxes and actual social contributions	..	..	..	1 919	5 082	4 894	5 988	6 874	8 532	9 298
Imputed social contributions	..	..	..	4	20	30	38	49	66	73
National Accounts: Taxes and all social contributions	..	..	..	1 922	5 102	4 924	6 026	6 923	8 597	9 371

.. Not available

Note: Year ending 31st December.
Data on an accrual basis.

Source: Statistics Estonia.

StatLink https://stat.link/esvzr8

Table 5.11. Finland: Details of tax revenue, 1965-2019

Million EUR

	1965	1980	1990	2000	2007	2010	2013	2015	2018	2019
Total tax revenue	**1 362**	**11 895**	**39 052**	**62 435**	**77 447**	**76 315**	**88 688**	**92 003**	**98 958**	**101 443**
Total tax revenue exclusive of taxes collected for the EU	..	..	**39 052**	**62 296**	**77 247**	**76 163**	**88 521**	**91 760**	**98 728**	**101 040**
1000 Taxes on income, profits and capital gains	**564**	**4 654**	**15 323**	**26 910**	**30 358**	**27 104**	**30 797**	**32 371**	**34 505**	**35 470**
1100 Of individuals	453	4 248	13 562	19 118	23 396	22 545	25 998	27 824	28 569	29 401
1110 On income and profits	453	4 234	13 520	19 118	23 396	22 545	25 998	27 824	28 569	29 401
Tax on income	125	1 827	5 917	9 036	9 086	6 465	7 903	9 138	9 734	9 986
The final withdrawal tax on interest income	0	0	0	92	254	205	207	110	44	39
Communal tax	279	2 376	7 603	9 990	14 056	15 875	17 888	18 576	18 791	19 376
Seaman's tax	3	31	0	0	0	0	0	0	0	0
National pension contributions	32	0	0	0	0	0	0	0	0	0
National health insurance contributions	15	0	0	0	0	0	0	0	0	0
1120 On capital gains	0	14	42	0	0	0	0	0	0	0
Tax on lottery prizes	..	14	42	..	..	..	..	..	..	..
1200 Corporate	111	405	1 761	7 792	6 962	4 559	4 799	4 547	5 936	6 069
1210 On profits	111	405	1 761	7 792	6 962	4 559	4 799	4 547	5 936	6 069
Tax on income	72	202	1 001	4 758	5 298	2 972	3 227	2 761	4 077	4 151
Communal tax	36	187	699	2 900	1 541	1 471	1 456	1 668	1 859	1 918
Church tax	3	16	61	134	123	116	116	118	0	0
1220 On capital gains	0	0	0	0	0	0	0	0	0	0
1300 Unallocable between 1100 and 1200	0	0	0	0	0	0	0	0	0	0
2000 Social security contributions	**93**	**2 776**	**10 012**	**15 756**	**21 384**	**22 648**	**25 632**	**26 639**	**27 647**	**28 295**
2100 Employees	1	394	1 152	2 926	4 050	4 710	5 811	6 364	8 102	8 546
For employment pension schemes	1	10	23	2 120	2 950	3 386	4 235	4 714	5 567	6 078
For unemployment schemes	0	0	0	435	369	267	457	489	1 519	1 379
2110 On a payroll basis	..	10	23	2 565	3 319	3 653	4 692	5 203	7 086	7 457
2120 On an income tax basis	..	384	1 129	361	731	1 057	1 119	1 161	1 016	1 089
National pension contributions	..	251	502	2	0	0	0	0	0	0
National health insurance contributions	..	133	627	359	731	1 057	1 119	1 161	1 016	1 089
2200 Employers	93	2 230	8 127	11 571	15 715	16 041	17 888	18 232	17 631	17 778
For national pension schemes	29	685	1 502	1 566	1 331	0	0	0	0	0
For national health insurance	10	244	792	839	1 142	1 590	1 612	1 662	748	694
For unemployment schemes	3	106	206	1 143	1 346	1 377	1 775	1 676	1 493	1 260
For employment pension schemes	50	1 195	5 627	8 023	11 896	13 074	14 501	14 894	15 390	15 824
For accident and group life insurance premiums	0	0	0	0	0	0	0	0	0	0
2210 On a payroll basis	..	2 230	8 127	11 571	15 715	16 041	17 888	18 232	17 631	17 778
2220 On an income tax basis	..	0	0	0	0	0	0	0	0	0
2300 Self-employed or non-employed	0	152	733	1 259	1 619	1 897	1 933	2 043	1 914	1 971
For employment pension schemes	..	84	394	576	817	932	1 187	1 269	1 237	1 245
2310 On a payroll basis	..	84	394	576	817	932	1 187	1 269	1 237	1 245
2320 On an income tax basis	..	68	339	683	802	965	746	774	677	726
National pension contributions	..	43	151	5	0	0	0	0	0	0
National health insurance contributions	..	25	188	678	802	965	746	774	677	726
2400 Unallocable between 2100, 2200 and 2300	0	0	0	0	0	0	0	0	0	0
2410 On a payroll basis	..	..	..	..	..	..	..	..	..	..
2420 On an income tax basis	..	..	..	..	..	..	..	..	..	..
3000 Taxes on payroll and workforce	**70**	**22**	**0**	**0**	**0**	**0**	**0**	**0**	**0**	**0**
Soc. Sec. contr. for children allowance	70	22	..	..	..	..	..	..	..	..
4000 Taxes on property	**54**	**221**	**956**	**1 518**	**2 012**	**2 087**	**2 599**	**3 017**	**3 349**	**3 477**
4100 Recurrent taxes on immovable property	0	0	76	570	855	1 169	1 363	1 603	1 813	1 871
4110 Households	..	..	46	273	405	576	623	733	834	860
4120 Others	..	..	30	297	450	593	740	870	979	1 011
4200 Recurrent taxes on net wealth	24	24	27	179	0	0	0	0	0	0
4210 Individual	11	23	25	175	..	..	..	..	..	..
4220 Corporate	13	2	2	4	..	..	..	..	..	..
4300 Estate, inheritance and gift taxes	3	26	146	368	459	387	646	631	692	749
4310 Estate and inheritance taxes	3	21	121	307	384	324	541	528	579	612
4320 Gift taxes	1	5	25	61	75	63	105	103	113	137
4400 Taxes on financial and capital transactions	27	170	707	401	698	531	590	783	844	857
Stamp duty excluded entertainment	27	170	688	-20	0	0	0	0	0	0
Credit tax	0	0	19	0	0	0	0	0	0	0
Transfer tax	0	0	0	421	698	531	590	783	844	857
4500 Non-recurrent taxes	0	0	0	0	0	0	0	0	0	0
4510 On net wealth	..	..	..	..	..	..	..	..	..	..
4520 Other non-recurrent taxes	..	..	..	..	..	..	..	..	..	..
4600 Other recurrent taxes on property	0	0	0	0	0	0	0	0	0	0
5000 Taxes on goods and services	**578**	**4 202**	**12 711**	**18 221**	**23 624**	**24 407**	**29 596**	**29 895**	**33 413**	**34 150**
5100 Taxes on production, sale, transfer, etc.	570	4 158	12 555	17 781	22 953	23 642	28 662	28 836	32 040	32 671
5110 General taxes	251	2 062	7 519	10 869	15 207	15 533	18 888	18 974	21 364	21 974

	1965	1980	1990	2000	2007	2010	2013	2015	2018	2019
5111 Value added taxes	251	2 062	7 519	10 869	15 207	15 533	18 888	18 974	21 364	21 974
Value added taxes	251	2 062	7 519	9 616	13 657	13 691	16 561	16 680	18 487	18 929
VAT repayments of local government	0	0	0	849	1 550	1 842	2 327	2 294	2 877	3 045
Social Insur. Institutions' part of VAT revenue	0	0	0	404	0	0	0	0	0	0
5112 Sales tax	0	0	0	0	0	0	0	0	0	0
5113 Other	0	0	0	0	0	0	0	0	0	0
Suppl. sales tax on consumer durables	..	..	..	..	..	..	..	..	..	..
5120 Taxes on specific goods and services	319	2 096	5 036	6 912	7 746	8 109	9 774	9 862	10 676	10 697
5121 Excise duties	183	1 615	3 813	5 613	6 013	6 286	7 511	7 678	8 323	8 118
Excise on tobacco products	52	206	473	561	622	655	852	885	1 048	1 019
Excise on sweetments	6	23	26	0	0	0	0	0	0	0
Excise on medium, strong beer	3	109	419	0	0	0	0	0	0	0
Excise on non-alcoholic beverages	2	17	22	32	35	37	204	250	154	180
Excise on certain foodstuffs	3	218	36	0	0	0	0	0	0	0
Excise on liquid fuels	58	504	986	2 583	2 907	3 167	3 925	4 054	4 395	4 294
Excise on motor cars	28	238	697	1 059	1 217	941	931	882	995	886
Tax on alcoholic beverages	29	353	813	1 239	1 016	1 279	1 355	1 356	1 475	1 483
Levies on pharmacy	2	16	46	85	113	122	153	165	180	188
Levies for price reduction on butter	0	3	0	0	0	0	0	0	0	0
Levies for marketing of milk	0	12	58	0	0	0	0	0	0	0
Excise on margarines	0	18	55	0	0	0	0	0	0	0
Stock-building levies on liquid fuels	0	15	44	46	50	48	45	43	45	43
Excise on sugar products	0	18	34	0	0	0	0	0	0	0
Excise on feeding stuffs	0	0	0	0	0	0	0	0	0	0
Excise on fertilizers	0	21	21	0	0	0	0	0	0	0
Excise on oil-based concentrated feed	0	1	0	0	0	0	0	0	0	0
Excise on protein feed	0	0	0	0	0	0	0	0	0	0
Equalization fee agricultural products	0	8	29	0	0	0	0	0	0	0
Excise on albumen	0	0	30	0	0	0	0	0	0	0
Tax on electricity	0	65	0	0	0	0	0	0	0	0
Oil damage levy	0	0	7	5	8	20	27	24	12	7
Oil waste levy	0	0	4	3	4	4	4	4	4	4
Price difference compensations	0	-231	0	0	0	0	0	0	0	0
The milk quota charge	0	0	6	0	0	0	0	0	0	0
Levies for marketing of special agric. prod.	0	0	0	0	0	0	0	0	0	0
Excise on phosphorous fertilizers	0	0	7	0	0	0	0	0	0	0
Excise on certain beverage packages	0	0	0	0	41	13	15	15	15	14
5122 Profits of fiscal monopolies	38	86	202	0	0	0	0	0	0	0
Excess profits on alcohol	38	86	202	..	..	..	..	..	..	..
5123 Customs and import duties	88	235	423	130	199	151	166	166	174	187
Import duties	62	126	232	0	0	0	0	0	0	0
Import levies on agricultural products	26	6	12	0	0	0	0	0	0	0
Local import duties (Town dues)	1	0	0	0	0	0	0	0	0	0
Import levies price stabilisation fund	0	3	0	0	0	0	0	0	0	0
Agricultural levies	0	0	0	0	0	0	0	0	0	0
Equalization tax	0	100	179	0	0	0	0	0	0	0
Custom duties	..	..	..	130	199	151	166	166	174	187
5124 Taxes on exports	0	0	0	0	0	0	0	0	0	0
Export duties	..	..	..	..	..	..	..	..	..	..
Levies on export	..	..	..	..	..	..	..	..	..	..
Counter-cyclical tax exports	..	..	..	..	..	..	..	..	..	..
5125 Taxes on investment goods	0	0	0	0	0	0	0	0	0	0
Investment tax on buildings	..	..	..	..	..	..	..	..	..	..
5126 Taxes on specific services	9	161	598	1 160	1 533	1 671	2 096	2 017	2 178	2 392
Net revenue of betting	8	94	328	704	807	874	948	967	1 109	1 099
Tax on motion pictures	0	0	0	0	0	0	0	0	0	0
Stamp duties on entertainment	2	5	0	0	0	0	0	0	0	0
Fire protection levy	0	3	7	6	8	9	10	11	11	11
Tax on waste	0	0	0	33	56	42	56	32	7	3
Rail tax	0	0	0	0	18	18	19	6	2	0
Tax on insurance premiums	0	58	263	337	509	584	712	777	772	789
Tax on lottery prizes	0	0	0	80	135	144	217	222	226	221
Tax on telecommunications	0	0	0	0	0	0	0	0	0	0
Bank tax	0	0	0	0	0	0	134	-74	-4	-3
Contributions to the Resolution Fund	..	..	..	..	..	..	..	76	55	216
Contributions to the Deposit Guarantee Fund	..	..	0	0	0	0	0	0	0	56
5127 Other taxes on internat. trade and transactions	0	0	0	0	0	0	0	0	0	0
Tax on charter flights	..	..	..	..	..	..	..	..	..	..
5128 Other taxes	0	0	0	9	1	1	1	1	1	0
Sugar levy	..	..	..	9	1	1	1	1	1	..
Steel and coal levy	..	..	..	0	0	0	0	0	0	..
5130 Unallocable between 5110 and 5120	0	0	0	0	0	0	0	0	0	0

	1965	1980	1990	2000	2007	2010	2013	2015	2018	2019
5200 Taxes on use of goods and perform activities	8	44	156	440	671	765	934	1 059	1 373	1 479
5210 Recurrent taxes	8	44	156	423	637	725	897	960	1 233	1 189
5211 Paid by households: motor vehicles	0	2	5	165	486	541	696	748	979	949
5212 Paid by others: motor vehicles	7	32	135	235	126	150	170	182	215	201
5213 Paid in respect of other goods	1	10	16	23	25	34	31	30	39	39
Dog licenses	1	2	4	5	3	2	2	1	0	0
Hunting and fishing licenses	1	7	12	17	17	24	23	22	27	27
Seamens welfare and rescue levy	0	0	0	1	1	1	1	0	0	0
Nuclear energy research levy	0	0	0	0	4	7	5	7	12	12
5220 Non-recurrent taxes	0	0	0	17	34	40	37	99	140	290
Vehicle registration tax	..	..	..	17	34	40	37	36	27	27
Income from auction of emission allowances	..	..	..	0	0	0	0	63	113	263
5300 Unallocable between 5100 and 5200	0	0	0	0	0	0	0	0	0	0
6000 Other taxes	**2**	**21**	**50**	**30**	**69**	**69**	**64**	**81**	**44**	**51**
6100 Paid solely by business	0	0	0	0	0	0	0	0	0	0
6200 Other	2	21	50	30	69	69	64	81	44	51
Memorandum items										
Customs duties collected on behalf of the EU	..	..	..	130	199	151	166	166	174	187
SRF contributions collected on behalf of the EU	..	..	..	..	..	..	..	76	55	216
Total tax revenue on cash basis	**1 362**	**11 895**	**39 396**	**61 638**	**77 110**	**76 176**	**88 425**	**91 846**	**98 552**	**101 219**
Total tax revenue on accrual basis	**..**	**..**	**39 052**	**62 435**	**77 447**	**76 315**	**88 688**	**92 003**	**98 958**	**101 443**
Conciliation with National Accounts										
Additional taxes included in National Accounts	..	0	0	0	0	0	0	0	0	0
Taxes excluded from National Accounts	..	0	0	0	0	0	0	0	0	0
Difference in treatment of tax credits	..	0	0	0	0	0	0	0	0	0
Capital transfer for uncollected revenue	..	0	0	0	0	0	0	0	0	0
Voluntary social security contributions	..	262	632	236	228	254	270	303	269	246
Miscellaneous differences	..	0	0	0	0	0	0	0	0	0
National Accounts: Taxes and actual social contributions	..	12 157	39 684	62 671	77 675	76 569	88 958	92 306	99 227	101 689
Imputed social contributions	..	513	688	30	0	0	0	0	0	..
National Accounts: Taxes and all social contributions	..	12 670	40 372	62 701	77 675	76 569	88 958	92 306	99 227	101 689

.. Not available

Note: Year ending 31st December.

From 1988 data are on accrual basis.

Finland has an imputation system where the full credit is taken into account in shareholders taxation. According to estimates made by the National Board of Taxation, the credit given to shareholders was 193 millions euros in 1991; the effects on personal income taxation are estimated.

Headings 2120 and 2320: The breakdown of contributions paid by employees and self-employed or non-employed is estimated.

Heading 4200: All figures in this subheading are estimated.

Heading 4400: Stamp duties include payment for some government services where the levy can be regarded as requited (the levy is linked to the cost of providing the service). However they are classified as taxes and recorded under this subheading as taxes on financial and capital transactions because the amounts involved cannot be identified.

Heading 5121: The negative item under the title 'Price difference compensations' refers to the subsidies paid out on agricultural products under the price compensation scheme which can be offset against any positive tax liability which arising under the same scheme. From 1983 this item has been offset against revenues from excises on certain foodstuffs, on medium and stronger beer and on non-alcoholic beverages.

Heading 5126: Prior to 1979, no figures are available for amounts paid under the Fire protection levy .

Heading 5212: Prior to 1990, a part of the tax is paid by 'households'.

Source: Bulletin of Statistics; Central Statistical Office (for Central Government revenues); the Annual report of the National Pension Institute and Official Statistics of Finland Series XXIIA published by the Ministry and Social Affairs (for the Social Security and private pension respectively); supplementary information from unpublished sources.

StatLink https://stat.link/dk7h1i

Table 5.12. France: Details of tax revenue, 1965-2019

Million EUR

	1965	1980	1990	2000	2007	2010	2013	2015	2018	2019
Total tax revenue	**25 776**	**178 576**	**433 771**	**645 528**	**831 226**	**846 318**	**966 817**	**1 002 131**	**1 090 876**	**1 098 902**
Total tax revenue exclusive of taxes collected for the EU	..	..	..	**643 655**	**829 411**	**844 346**	**964 743**	**999 064**	**1 086 297**	**1 094 291**
1000 Taxes on income, profits and capital gains	**4 095**	**30 019**	**69 649**	**160 363**	**197 939**	**191 085**	**235 964**	**234 532**	**274 103**	**282 086**
1100 Of individuals	2 736	20 734	46 272	115 885	141 405	144 165	179 715	188 357	224 195	227 806
1110 On income and profits	2 723	20 674	46 252	115 884	141 405	144 165	179 715	188 357	224 195	227 806
Tax on individual income	..	18 207	39 237	49 548	48 597	49 575	70 098	72 750	77 572	77 681
Tax on non business profits	..	51	189	293	559	446	598	927	808	979
Tax on financial assets	..	2 333	3 971	0	0	0	0	0	0	0
CSG, CRDS, social security contributions for the benefit of the FSV, FNAL and / or the FS	..	0	0	65 953	92 204	93 972	108 247	113 065	140 372	135 098
Flat-rate tax on precious metals	..	70	58	47	37	52	69	71	78	104
Tax on multiple wages	..	7	20	38	0	0	0	0	0	0
Solidarity levy	..	0	2 207	5	0	82	381	0	2 746	10 537
Others	..	6	571	0	8	38	322	1 544	2 619	3 407
1120 On capital gains	14	59	20	1	0	0	0	0	0	0
On capital gains	..	0	0	0	..	..	..	..	..	..
Levies on construction profits	..	59	20	1	..	..	..	..	..	..
1200 Corporate	1 358	9 158	23 117	44 478	56 534	46 920	56 249	46 175	49 908	54 280
1210 On profits	1 358	9 158	23 117	44 478	56 534	46 920	56 249	46 175	49 908	54 280
Corporations' tax (excluding tax credits to reduce or remove the taxation)	..	8 524	20 804	39 755	51 063	39 095	46 474	39 579	44 835	48 670
3% tax on dividends	..	0	0	0	0	0	1 943	2 165	4	0
Tax on financial assets	..	487	1 333	1 460	3 492	5 952	5 894	3 325	3 814	4 339
Precount on distributed profits (exceptional levy of 25% since 2005)	..	36	247	1 135	88	28	-6	4	0	-131
Exceptional levies on temporary work corporations	..	0	0	0	0	0	0	0	0	0
Social contribution on corporation profits	..	0	0	589	158	842	1 160	971	1 119	1 240
Annual flat-rate tax	..	111	658	1 484	1 656	599	680	4	1	1
Exceptionnal levies on insurances	..	0	61	55	64	94	104	127	135	161
Other	..	0	14	0	13	310	0	0	0	0
1220 On capital gains	0	0	0	0	0	0	0	0	0	0
1300 Unallocable between 1100 and 1200	0	127	260	0	0	0	0	0	0	0
2000 Social security contributions	**8 804**	**76 235**	**191 141**	**231 875**	**307 663**	**323 816**	**356 934**	**370 375**	**381 230**	**363 817**
2100 Employees	1 701	19 851	57 347	57 686	76 815	78 268	88 097	93 767	89 240	87 940
Actual cotisations	0	19 851	57 347	57 686	76 815	78 268	88 097	93 767	89 240	87 940
2110 On a payroll basis	0	0	0	57 686	76 815	78 268	88 097	93 767	89 240	87 940
2120 On an income tax basis	0	0	0	0	0	0	0	0	0	0
2200 Employers	6 525	50 742	118 079	159 476	208 688	219 687	240 672	248 173	265 446	247 437
Actual cotisations	0	50 742	118 079	159 476	208 688	219 687	240 672	248 173	265 446	247 437
2210 On a payroll basis	0	0	0	159 476	208 688	219 687	240 672	248 173	265 446	247 437
2220 On an income tax basis	0	0	0	0	0	0	0	0	0	0
2300 Self-employed or non-employed	578	5 642	15 714	14 713	22 160	25 861	28 165	28 435	26 544	28 440
Actual cotisations	..	5 642	15 714	14 713	22 160	25 861	28 165	28 435	26 544	28 440
2310 On a payroll basis	0	0	0	14 713	22 160	25 861	28 165	28 435	26 544	28 440
2320 On an income tax basis	0	0	0	0	0	0	0	0	0	0
2400 Unallocable between 2100, 2200 and 2300	0	0	0	0	0	0	0	0	0	0
2410 On a payroll basis	0	0	0	..	..	..	..	..	..	..
2420 On an income tax basis	0	0	0	..	..	..	..	..	..	..
3000 Taxes on payroll and workforce	**1 189**	**3 935**	**8 254**	**14 916**	**22 874**	**26 926**	**33 595**	**34 574**	**35 852**	**43 522**
Tax on wages	0	2 413	5 208	7 583	10 272	11 440	13 127	13 165	13 321	13 533
Corporate social contributions	0	0	0	0	0	657	4 654	5 019	5 715	5 251
Apprenticeship tax	0	172	101	102	964	1 130	1 317	1 436	1 938	3 758
Tax benefitting the wage garantee scheme (AGS): royalties for concessions, patents, licenses, trademarks, processes, rights and similar values	0	263	379	551	736	1 759	1 435	1 479	810	841
Tax on vocational training	0	236	30	97	19	13	17	17	20	5 447
Tax benefitting the FNAL: ACOSS (employer contributions)	0	120	754	1 506	2 412	2 465	3 123	2 929	2 691	2 855
Tax benefitting the transports union	0	731	1 600	3 786	5 738	6 344	7 326	7 842	8 950	9 402
Payment benefitting the UNEDIC	0	0	23	24	0	0	0	0	0	0
Tax on re-employed pensioners income	0	0	0	0	0	0	0	0	0	0
Providence contribution	0	0	0	415	773	1 120	496	415	343	331
Others	0	0	159	851	100	81	49	27	18	26
Taxes benefitting the national solidarity fund for autonomy (CNSA)	0	0	0	0	1 860	1 917	2 051	1 891	2 033	2 049
Employers' contribution to the early retirement of asbestos workers regime (FCAATA)	0	0	0	0	0	0	0	0	0	0
Exceptional levy on high wages	0	0	0	0	0	0	0	354	13	29
4000 Taxes on property	**1 105**	**8 591**	**27 434**	**44 070**	**65 318**	**70 613**	**81 343**	**89 311**	**94 428**	**94 802**
4100 Recurrent taxes on immovable property	506	5 358	14 808	27 340	39 875	47 589	54 545	57 431	59 597	57 572

	1965	1980	1990	2000	2007	2010	2013	2015	2018	2019
4110 Households	198	4 454	11 493	20 186	30 584	36 480	41 818	43 861	44 602	42 235
Council tax	0	2 306	5 100	8 366	12 433	15 254	17 470	18 424	16 892	13 928
Tax on real-estate properties	0	1 034	4 040	8 460	11 983	14 403	16 539	17 557	19 484	19 936
Waste collection tax	0	534	1 219	3 103	5 117	5 699	6 552	6 567	6 942	7 027
Tax on non-developped land	0	506	979	172	851	919	955	980	977	998
Chamber of Agriculture tax	0	0	0	53	59	61	62	61	55	56
Street-cleaning tax	0	0	0	68	74	75	109	109	114	112
Other taxes	0	74	156	-36	67	69	131	163	138	178
4120 Others	308	904	3 315	7 154	9 291	11 109	12 727	13 570	14 995	15 337
Tax on real-estate properties	0	759	3 032	6 256	9 054	10 865	12 477	13 246	14 699	15 039
Tax on non-developped land	0	127	245	688	0	0	0	0	0	0
Chamber of Agriculture tax	0	18	39	210	237	244	250	242	221	222
Other taxes	0	0	0	0	0	0	0	82	75	76
4200 Recurrent taxes on net wealth	0	0	2 615	2 440	4 390	4 461	4 372	5 224	1 847	2 054
4210 Individual	..	..	938	2 440	4 390	4 461	4 372	5 224	1 847	2 054
4220 Corporate	..	..	1 677	0	0	0	0	0	0	0
4300 Estate, inheritance and gift taxes	145	1 010	4 124	6 907	8 910	7 738	10 456	12 317	14 399	15 252
4310 Estate and inheritance taxes	140	875	3 490	5 508	7 853	6 862	9 368	10 690	11 982	12 311
Inheritance taxes	0	861	3 453	5 428	7 794	6 806	8 433	10 540	11 895	12 208
Various receipts and tax fines	0	14	37	80	59	56	935	150	87	103
4320 Gift taxes	5	135	634	1 399	1 057	876	1 088	1 627	2 417	2 941
Donations	0	113	568	1 399	1 057	876	1 088	1 627	2 417	2 941
Various receipts and tax fines	0	0	0	0	0	0	0	0	0	0
Other taxes	0	22	66	0	0	0	0	0	0	0
4400 Taxes on financial and capital transactions	447	2 224	5 886	7 383	12 143	10 825	11 970	14 339	18 585	19 924
Debts, annuities, officies	0	30	209	279	443	279	359	335	514	428
Business assets	0	253	518	199	268	154	135	132	146	159
Tangible movable assets	0	14	18	0	0	1	0	1	1	0
Properties and real property rights	0	63	4	2	2	3	1	1	0	0
Agreements and civil acts between companies	0	95	218	4	5	8	6	7	1	0
Various receipts and tax fines	0	35	60	367	179	253	4	6	15	15
Judicial and extra-judicial documents	0	6	10	0	0	0	0	0	0	0
Land registration tax	0	781	38	68	130	140	703	770	960	1 034
Various stamps and fees	0	94	242	0	0	0	0	0	0	0
Taxes on stock exchange transactions	0	168	525	407	271	0	0	0	0	0
Tax on financial transactions	0	0	0	0	0	0	697	917	1 047	906
Additional registration taxes	0	679	4 002	5 339	10 396	9 567	9 538	11 618	15 309	16 844
Other taxes and receipts	0	5	44	718	449	420	527	552	592	538
4500 Non-recurrent taxes	8	0	0	0	0	0	0	0	0	0
4510 On net wealth	8	..	..	..	..	..	..	..	..	..
4520 Other non-recurrent taxes	0	..	..	..	..	..	..	..	..	..
4600 Other recurrent taxes on property	0	0	0	0	0	0	0	0	0	0
5000 Taxes on goods and services	**9 902**	**54 317**	**123 235**	**170 220**	**210 205**	**224 637**	**248 337**	**261 968**	**293 493**	**302 425**
5100 Taxes on production, sale, transfer, etc.	9 676	52 719	119 201	163 520	202 109	215 844	238 774	251 793	281 777	290 464
5110 General taxes	5 994	37 760	81 341	110 296	142 033	151 565	163 103	169 913	186 619	194 261
5111 Value added taxes	5 173	37 282	79 972	107 511	137 137	136 129	145 264	152 550	168 624	174 894
VAT (general budget)	0	36 895	78 902	103 054	136 927	135 578	144 490	151 680	167 720	173 953
VAT (BAPSA)	0	62	101	4 111	0	0	0	0	0	0
Other VAT	0	325	969	0	0	0	0	0	0	0
Sub-compensations of agricultural VAT	0	0	0	346	138	330	462	381	393	406
Value added taxes on subsidies	0	0	0	0	72	221	312	489	511	535
5112 Sales tax	822	0	0	0	0	0	0	0	0	0
5113 Other	0	477	1 369	2 784	4 896	15 436	17 839	17 363	17 995	19 367
Social solidarity contribution	..	477	1 369	2 784	4 896	5 090	5 671	4 390	3 769	3 899
Contributions on the value added of the corporations	..	..	..	0	0	10 346	12 168	12 973	14 226	15 191
Tax on digital services	..	..	..	0	0	0	0	0	0	277
5120 Taxes on specific goods and services	3 682	14 960	37 860	53 225	60 076	64 279	75 671	81 880	95 158	96 203
5121 Excise duties	2 775	11 013	26 834	39 850	44 013	45 770	52 343	56 660	64 891	64 796
Excise tax on energy products	0	7 136	17 476	23 493	24 318	23 577	23 693	26 238	31 898	31 438
Exceptional levies on oil product corporations	0	0	0	0	0	0	0	0	0	0
Taxes on wines, ciders and meads	0	97	174	0	121	121	486	501	534	572
Taxes on alcohol	0	1 238	1 593	3 025	484	2 482	2 950	2 956	2 945	2 900
Taxes on beer and mineral water	0	58	91	20	409	538	803	931	1 055	1 114
Other taxes and receipts	0	136	38	19	2 169	100	90	110	139	76
Taxes on tobaccos and matches	0	1 188	2 989	7 965	9 659	11 083	12 227	12 318	13 340	13 682
Fines and confiscations	0	2	1	0	0	0	0	0	0	0
Gold and silver warranty	0	6	19	29	2	0	0	0	0	0
ANDA taxes	0	84	147	89	0	0	0	0	0	0
Tax on health protection and the organisation of meat markets	0	0	0	48	46	43	41	43	43	41
Tax on cereals	0	147	275	19	19	24	18	14	8	4
Fees on tobacco stores	0	0	0	0	0	0	0	0	0	0
Fees on potash salt	0	0	0	0	0	0	0	0	0	0

	1965	1980	1990	2000	2007	2010	2013	2015	2018	2019
Tax on flour	0	0	0	38	0	0	0	0	0	0
Fees included in fuel price	0	36	32	453	485	495	499	493	555	558
National Book Fund tax	0	7	17	0	0	0	0	0	0	0
Tax on logging products	0	11	0	0	0	0	0	0	0	0
Mining fees	0	16	59	43	23	25	22	16	18	19
Tax on electricity and heating	0	426	1 340	1 061	2 990	3 717	7 253	8 703	9 843	9 955
Surtax on appetizers	0	12	17	0	0	0	0	0	0	0
Pharmaceutical taxes	0	4	559	0	0	0	0	0	0	0
Tax on beet, sugar and alcohol	0	22	400	0	0	0	0	0	0	0
Solidarity tax on oil seeds	0	8	41	0	0	0	0	0	0	0
Tax on food fats	0	32	89	99	0	0	0	0	0	0
National Literature Fund tax	0	23	0	0	0	0	0	0	0	0
Tax on water consumption	0	34	51	74	5	11	1	2	0	0
Tax on meat	0	25	36	0	19	1	1	0	0	0
Tax on pollution, distribution, collection and extraction of water	0	217	609	1 624	1 821	1 763	2 175	2 268	2 340	2 237
Sugar market fund tax	0	0	0	0	0	0	0	0	0	0
Exceptional contribution on pharmacies and laboratories	0	16	0	522	0	0	0	0	0	0
Local tax	0	5	8	241	247	325	127	126	66	64
Contribution of low voltage electric energy suppliers	0	0	0	183	322	324	374	375	377	378
ADEME tax	0	0	0	80	212	489	499	449	0	0
Dock dues	0	0	0	449	544	581	386	422	453	466
General tax on polluting activities	0	0	0	6	16	16	205	117	316	331
Tax on oil products	0	0	0	0	0	0	367	379	386	401
Other taxes	0	30	772	78	102	55	126	199	575	560
Tax benefitting the French petrol institute (IFP)	0	0	0	193	0	0	0	0	0	0
5122 Profits of fiscal monopolies	0	0	0	0	0	0	0	0	0	0
5123 Customs and import duties	471	966	1 669	1 810	2 043	2 180	2 605	2 665	2 858	2 848
Import duties (State)	0	0	0	0	0	0	0	0	0	0
Import duties (UE)	0	873	1 623	0	0	0	0	0	0	0
Dock dues	0	0	0	267	327	361	627	678	741	765
Other taxes	0	94	46	30	59	67	136	55	48	56
5124 Taxes on exports	0	75	15	0	0	0	0	0	0	0
Agricultural levies (State part)	..	0	0	..	..	..	..	..	..	..
Agricultural levies (EU part)	..	75	15	..	..	..	..	..	..	..
5125 Taxes on investment goods	0	0	0	0	0	0	0	0	0	0
5126 Taxes on specific services	431	2 690	8 373	11 204	14 007	16 274	20 656	22 501	27 355	28 559
Levies on horse-race bets	0	446	545	502	719	626	434	446	431	421
Levies on gambling casinos	0	0	0	727	1 022	748	708	691	746	803
Levies on the French national lottery	0	200	702	1 305	1 982	1 800	1 941	2 118	2 388	2 593
Exceptionnal levies on banks and lending institutions	0	0	0	0	0	0	0	0	0	0
Tax on insurance policies	0	1 292	4 782	5 097	6 571	7 099	9 973	10 386	11 003	11 407
Tax on leases	0	264	633	573	29	-5	-1	0	0	0
Taxes on funerals	0	11	32	14	11	12	12	12	13	13
Stamp taxes for transportation contracts	0	9	77	10	0	0	0	0	0	0
Tax on expertise and technical checks	0	0	0	0	0	0	0	0	0	0
ANAEM tax	0	0	0	33	58	129	145	146	115	115
Tax on the use of inland waterways	0	0	0	104	157	169	192	183	177	176
Other various taxes	0	98	272	273	449	1 007	547	798	2 484	2 686
Taxes on entertainment	0	75	195	274	372	425	799	785	1 086	1 238
Insurances contributions to the guarantee funds	0	32	135	223	274	323	387	450	757	766
Tax on automobile insurance	0	0	0	55	0	0	0	0	0	0
Additional contribution on insurance contracts to the FNGCA	0	0	0	261	96	101	120	125	60	60
National fund for housing improvement, 5% levy	0	114	258	678	604	604	726	932	977	992
Movie-making corporations contributions to the CNC	0	52	207	397	144	766	735	695	708	741
Agricultural insurances fund tax on food	0	0	0	0	0	0	0	0	0	0
National Sports Fund tax	0	3	0	0	0	0	0	0	0	0
Annuities and pensions upgrading fund tax	0	15	0	0	0	0	0	0	0	0
Annual tax on outstanding loans	0	0	0	0	0	0	0	0	0	0
Tax on advertisement	0	0	26	52	38	156	219	232	248	247
Levies on mortgage recording officers wages	0	67	188	0	0	0	0	0	0	0
Tax on safety and security	0	0	0	220	353	459	521	574	725	773
Tax on systemic risk	0	0	0	0	0	0	899	591	285	29
CMU tax on mutual insurances	0	0	0	247	560	1 637	1 851	1 909	2 305	2 430
Major natural disasters prevention fund (FPRNM) tax	0	0	0	0	0	0	197	205	129	137
SRF Contributions collected for the EU	..	..	..	..	..	..	..	916	2 291	2 419
Other taxes	0	10	320	159	568	218	251	307	427	513
5127 Other taxes on internat. trade and transactions	0	0	0	0	0	0	0	0	0	0
5128 Other taxes	5	215	970	360	13	55	67	54	54	0
Co-responsibility tax on milk	0	48	119	0	0	0	0	0	0	..
Co-responsibility tax on cereals	0	0	520	0	0	0	0	0	0	..

	1965	1980	1990	2000	2007	2010	2013	2015	2018	2019
European Coal and Steel Community levy	0	14	0	0	0	0	0	0	0	..
Collector of customs	0	9	24	0	0	0	0	0	0	..
Various taxes (local government)	0	0	0	0	0	0	0	0	0	..
Contributions on sugar	0	68	185	270	0	42	54	41	41	..
Sugar market fund tax	0	76	120	76	0	0	0	0	0	..
Other taxes	0	0	2	14	13	13	13	13	13	..
5130 Unallocable between 5110 and 5120	0	0	0	0	0	0	0	0	0	0
5200 Taxes on use of goods and perform activities	226	1 598	4 034	6 700	8 096	8 793	9 563	10 175	11 716	11 961
5210 Recurrent taxes	178	1 226	3 024	4 909	5 264	5 338	5 715	5 681	6 287	6 177
5211 Paid by households: motor vehicles	27	545	1 236	126	0	0	0	0	0	0
Tax differential (central and local government)	0	545	1 236	126	..	..	..	..	..	..
5212 Paid by others: motor vehicles	79	545	1 086	1 280	1 559	1 269	1 181	1 028	896	917
Tax on corporation vehicles	0	197	345	644	891	992	876	753	751	767
Tax on vehicles (central and local government)	0	348	741	636	668	277	305	275	145	150
5213 Paid in respect of other goods	72	136	702	3 503	3 705	4 069	4 534	4 653	5 391	5 260
Special tax on use of roads	0	0	0	420	526	539	573	574	618	640
Weighing tax	0	17	14	0	0	0	0	0	0	0
Various taxes (local government)	0	7	33	0	0	0	0	0	0	0
Tax on video recorders	0	0	0	0	0	0	0	0	0	0
Fee on nuclear power plants monitoring	0	8	41	0	0	0	0	0	0	0
Tax on use of slaughterhouses	0	19	13	0	0	0	0	0	0	0
Corporation contributions on medicines preparation	0	0	20	238	0	379	213	255	284	252
Tax on electric pylons	0	1	66	128	183	213	244	231	258	272
Beverage licences	0	8	22	23	0	0	0	0	0	0
Gallicisation and navigation annual right (DAFN)	0	0	0	0	0	39	37	37	38	38
Fees on radio frequencies use	0	0	0	191	280	275	262	187	301	270
Contribution to public broadcasting	..	..	..	2 099	2 255	2 472	2 866	3 012	3 215	3 147
Other taxes	0	75	493	404	461	152	339	357	677	641
5220 Non-recurrent taxes	47	372	1 010	1 791	2 832	3 455	3 848	4 494	5 429	5 784
Entry into service receipt	0	75	0	0	0	0	0	0	0	0
Carbon emission allowances	..	..	..	0	0	0	48	215	313	828
Beverage taxes and licences	0	0	0	3	0	0	0	0	0	0
Fee for the right to build	0	79	53	72	0	18	18	0	0	0
Building permit tax	0	146	263	305	848	1 252	1 381	1 839	2 231	2 164
Car registration tax	0	0	0	1 373	1 939	1 917	2 042	2 086	2 326	2 299
Tax on exceeding the density legal ceiling	0	38	270	38	45	82	82	52	0	0
Additional tax on car registration	0	0	0	0	0	186	277	302	559	493
Other taxes	0	35	423	0	0	0	0	0	0	0
5300 Unallocable between 5100 and 5200	0	0	0	0	0	0	0	0	0	0
6000 Other taxes	**681**	**5 480**	**14 060**	**24 084**	**27 227**	**9 241**	**10 644**	**11 371**	**11 770**	**12 250**
6100 Paid solely by business	678	5 480	14 060	22 398	27 219	9 235	10 638	11 365	11 764	12 227
National Institute of intellectual property (INPI) tax on services	0	43	67	115	156	165	180	193	225	231
Tax on general charges	0	0	0	0	0	0	0	0	0	0
Tax on the use of fixed assets	0	5 152	13 381	19 641	22 035	0	0	0	0	0
Tax on union benefits (local government)	0	36	197	293	0	0	0	0	0	0
Various taxes (central government)	0	0	0	61	236	255	478	649	722	813
Annual tax on outstanding loans	0	110	0	0	0	0	0	0	0	0
Exceptionnal levies on insurance corporations	0	0	0	0	0	0	0	0	0	0
Fees of the chambers of commerce and industry	0	36	125	155	203	275	233	253	196	200
Payments of industrial enterprises to the benefit of the FNE	0	4	240	204	33	10	3	0	0	0
Other taxes	0	98	50	1 127	3 721	1 078	727	1 269	986	1 046
(ANDA) and (ADAR) tax	0	0	0	32	0	0	0	0	0	0
Property contributions of the corporations	..	..	..	0	0	10 346	12 168	12 973	14 226	15 191
Flat-rate tax on network corporations	0	0	0	0	0	1 223	1 206	1 297	1 346	1 408
Exit tax on insurance	0	0	0	0	0	0	0	0	0	0
Fees of the chambers of commerce and industry	0	0	0	770	835	1 103	1 323	458	720	655
Employers' contribution on stock options	0	0	0	0	0	185	380	490	287	567
Tax on railway companies profit	0	0	0	0	0	0	200	400	453	226
6200 Other	3	0	0	1 686	8	6	6	6	6	23
Other taxes	0	..	..	1 686	8	6	6	6	6	23
Sectors accounts differential	0	..	..	0	0	0	0	0	0	0
Memorandum items										
Customs duties collected on behalf of the EU	..	..	..	1 513	1 657	1 752	1 842	1 932	2 069	2 027
SRF contributions collected on behalf of the EU	..	..	..	..	..	..	..	916	2 291	2 419

	1965	1980	1990	2000	2007	2010	2013	2015	2018	2019
Non-wastable tax credits										
Non-wastable tax credits against 1110	..	..	..	0	7 663	10 761	8 214	8 041	9 236	8 473
Tax component	..	..	..	..	..	8 234	6 755	5 669	5 448	6 245
Transfer component	..	..	..	..	..	2 527	1 459	2 372	3 788	2 228
Non-wastable tax credits against 1210	..	..	..	457	1 860	6 655	5 466	18 618	26 683	26 885
Tax component	..	..	..	..	..	1 277	3 572	10 560	10 773	10 661
Transfer component	..	..	..	..	..	5 378	1 894	8 058	15 910	16 224
Non-wastable tax credits against 3000	..	..	..	0	0	0	0	0	574	578
Tax expenditure component	..	..	..	0	0	0	0	0	574	578
Transfer component	..	..	..	0	0	0	0	0	0	0
Total tax revenue on cash basis	**25 776**	**178 576**	**433 771**	**642 156**	**825 954**	**840 905**	**960 513**	**995 462**	**1 084 237**	**1 100 141**
Total tax revenue on accrual basis	**..**	**..**	**..**	**645 528**	**831 226**	**846 318**	**966 817**	**1 002 131**	**1 090 876**	**1 098 902**
Conciliation with National Accounts										
Additional taxes included in national accounts	..	..	..	0	0	0	0	0	0	0
Tax excluded from national accounts	..	..	..	-3 171	-5 191	-5 774	-6 661	-6 676	-7 056	-7 139
Waste collection tax	..	..	..	-3 103	-5 117	-5 699	-6 552	-6 567	-6 942	-7 027
Tax on electric pylons	..	..	..	0	0	0	0	0	0	0
Street-cleaning tax	..	..	..	-68	-74	-75	-109	-109	-114	-112
Difference in treatment of tax credits	..	..	..	0	0	9 511	10 327	16 229	16 795	17 484
Capital transfer for uncollected revenue	..	..	..	-3 372	-5 272	-5 413	-6 304	-6 669	-6 639	-4 761
Voluntary social security contributions	..	..	..	0	0	0	0	0	0	0
Miscellaneous differences	..	..	..	0	0	0	0	0	0	0
National Accounts: taxes and actual social contributions	..	..	..	638 985	820 763	844 642	964 179	1 005 015	1 093 976	1 104 486
Imputed social contributions	..	..	..	25 875	33 510	38 028	41 947	42 655	43 659	43 965
National Accounts: taxes and all social contributions	..	..	..	664 860	854 273	882 670	1 006 126	1 047 670	1 137 635	1 148 451

.. Not available

Note: Calendar year ending on December 31st.

From 1992, the data are on an accrual basis.

From 1970, figures were calculated according to the new System of National Accounts and are not, therefore, comparable to those of the previous years.

The section 2000 includes certain voluntary contributions.

The section 4220 corresponds to the remuneration for the guarantee of the State given to savings banks.

Source: General Account of the Administration of finances for the figures of fiscal receipts. OSCE for the figures of Social Security from 1965 to 1969, and ESA for the following years.

StatLink https://stat.link/84hsik

Table 5.13. Germany: Details of tax revenue, 1965-2019

Million EUR

	1965	1980	1990	2000	2007	2010	2013	2015	2018	2019
Total tax revenue	**74 359**	**287 373**	**454 764**	**767 046**	**884 216**	**911 161**	**1 038 902**	**1 127 631**	**1 294 272**	**1 341 294**
Total tax revenue exclusive of taxes collected for the EU	..	..	**450 620**	**763 301**	**880 273**	**906 897**	**1 034 587**	**1 120 820**	**1 287 304**	**1 334 205**
1000 Taxes on income, profits and capital gains	**25 059**	**100 821**	**147 257**	**231 249**	**273 596**	**257 817**	**319 926**	**351 473**	**423 858**	**436 762**
1100 Of individuals	19 254	85 134	125 296	194 173	218 848	219 387	270 179	299 379	351 970	367 322
1110 On income and profits	19 254	85 134	125 296	194 173	218 848	219 387	270 179	299 379	351 970	367 322
Taxes on wages and salaries	8 558	57 039	90 801	135 733	146 365	145 202	174 512	194 116	224 270	236 355
Assessed income tax	7 567	18 813	18 672	12 225	25 341	31 346	42 586	48 902	60 927	63 781
Withholding tax on dividends	691	2 135	5 538	13 515	13 572	12 982	17 258	17 944	23 196	23 486
Supplementary tax	0	0	0	10 347	10 907	10 706	13 085	14 555	17 041	17 829
Enterprise tax	2 438	7 147	10 285	16 486	14 630	13 709	17 305	18 570	22 430	22 297
Stabilisation tax	0	0	0	0	0	0	0	0	0	0
Withholding tax on interest	0	0	0	5 867	8 033	5 442	5 433	5 292	4 106	3 574
1120 On capital gains	0	0	0	0	0	0	0	0	0	0
1200 Corporate	5 806	15 686	21 961	37 076	54 748	38 430	49 747	52 094	71 888	69 440
1210 On profits	5 806	15 686	21 961	37 076	54 748	38 430	49 747	52 094	71 888	69 440
Corporation tax	4 177	10 902	15 385	23 575	23 386	12 516	19 762	20 224	34 170	32 284
Supplementary tax	0	20	1	1 494	1 550	982	1 337	1 409	1 975	1 896
Sacrifice for Berlin	3	0	0	0	0	0	0	0	0	0
Enterprise tax	1 625	4 765	6 576	10 540	25 486	22 002	25 722	27 613	33 533	33 336
Stabilisation tax	0	0	0	0	0	0	0	0	0	0
Withholding tax on interest	0	0	0	1 467	4 326	2 930	2 926	2 848	2 210	1 924
1220 On capital gains	0	0	0	0	0	0	0	0	..	..
1300 Unallocable between 1100 and 1200	0	0	0	0	0	0	0	0	0	..
2000 Social security contributions	**19 876**	**98 659**	**170 449**	**299 440**	**320 750**	**354 320**	**392 378**	**424 841**	**487 654**	**508 124**
2100 Employees	8 723	43 833	73 580	131 610	139 927	152 843	171 657	186 305	216 757	220 204
Payments by employees total	8 723	43 833	73 580	131 610	139 927	152 843	171 657	186 305	216 757	220 204
2110 On a payroll basis	..	..	..	131 610	139 927	152 843	171 657	186 305	216 757	220 204
2120 On an income tax basis	..	..	..	0	0	0	0	0	0	0
2200 Employers	10 693	52 985	86 659	147 410	151 094	165 476	181 782	196 679	223 539	238 358
Payments by employers total	10 693	52 985	86 659	147 410	151 094	165 476	181 782	196 679	223 539	238 358
2210 On a payroll basis	..	..	..	147 410	151 094	165 476	181 782	196 679	223 539	238 358
2220 On an income tax basis	..	..	..	0	0	0	0	0	0	0
2300 Self-employed or non-employed	460	1 841	10 210	20 420	29 729	36 001	38 939	41 857	47 358	49 562
Payments total	460	1 841	10 210	20 420	29 729	36 001	38 939	41 857	47 358	49 562
2310 On a payroll basis	..	..	..	20 420	29 729	36 001	38 939	41 857	47 358	49 562
2320 On an income tax basis	..	..	..	0	0	0	0	0	0	0
2400 Unallocable between 2100, 2200 and 2300	0	0	0	0	0	0	0	0	0	0
2410 On a payroll basis	..	..	..	..	..	..	..	..	..	..
2420 On an income tax basis	..	..	..	..	..	..	..	..	..	..
3000 Taxes on payroll and workforce	**477**	**445**	**0**	**0**	**0**	**0**	**0**	**0**	**0**	**0**
Payroll tax	477	445	..	..	..	..	..	..	..	..
4000 Taxes on property	**4 313**	**9 414**	**15 321**	**17 505**	**21 873**	**21 012**	**26 104**	**31 076**	**36 307**	**38 680**
4100 Recurrent taxes on immovable property	1 079	2 968	4 461	8 849	10 713	11 315	12 377	13 215	14 203	14 439
4110 Households	644	1 187	1 784	3 540	4 285	4 526	4 951	5 286	5 681	5 776
4120 Others	435	1 780	2 676	5 309	6 428	6 789	7 426	7 929	8 522	8 663
4200 Recurrent taxes on net wealth	2 530	4 362	6 213	433	5	2	700	322	1 207	1 466
4210 Individual	973	977	1 425	191	2	1	0	-1	0	0
General wealth tax	471	954	1 425	191	2	1	0	-1	0	0
Equalization of war burden	502	23	0	0	0	0	..	0	..	..
4220 Corporate	1 557	3 385	4 788	242	3	1	700	323	1 207	1 466
General wealth tax	490	1 431	1 813	242	3	1	0	-1	0	0
Equalization of war burden	350	15	0	0	0	0	0	0	..	..
Enterprise tax	717	1 939	2 975	0	0	0	0	0	..	..
Bank levy	0	0	0	0	0	0	520	0	11	14
Contribution to Deposit Protection Fund	0	0	0	0	0	0	180	324	1 196	1 452
4300 Estate, inheritance and gift taxes	162	520	1 545	2 982	4 203	4 405	4 633	6 290	6 814	6 986
4310 Estate and inheritance taxes	134	416	1 359	2 624	3 699	3 876	4 077	5 535	5 996	6 148
4320 Gift taxes	28	104	186	358	504	529	556	755	818	838
4400 Taxes on financial and capital transactions	542	1 564	3 103	5 241	6 952	5 290	8 394	11 249	14 083	15 789
Real property transfer tax	150	521	1 999	5 081	6 952	5 290	8 394	11 249	14 083	15 789
Additional real property transfer	198	680	148	160	0	0	0	0	0	0
Capital transfer tax	111	200	807	0	0	0	0	0	..	..
Bill of exchange tax	83	163	149	0	0	0	0	0	..	..
4500 Non-recurrent taxes	0	0	0	0	0	0	0	0	0	0
4510 On net wealth	..	..	..	..	..	..	..	..	..	..
4520 Other non-recurrent taxes	..	..	..	..	..	..	..	..	..	..
4600 Other recurrent taxes on property	0	0	0	0	0	0	0	0	0	..
5000 Taxes on goods and services	**24 462**	**77 863**	**121 577**	**218 687**	**267 901**	**277 912**	**300 366**	**320 025**	**346 183**	**357 409**

	1965	1980	1990	2000	2007	2010	2013	2015	2018	2019
5100 Taxes on production, sale, transfer, etc.	23 079	74 406	117 209	211 445	251 558	261 160	281 995	301 099	327 461	337 061
5110 General taxes	12 235	47 779	75 459	140 872	170 387	180 533	197 326	211 936	235 449	244 433
5111 Value added taxes	0	47 779	75 459	140 872	170 387	180 533	197 326	211 936	235 449	244 433
5112 Sales tax	0	0	0	0	0	0	0	0	0	0
5113 Other	12 235	0	0	0	0	0	0	0	0	0
Turnover tax old	11 028	..	..	..	..	..	..	..	..	..
Old turnover tax on import	1 208	..	..	..	..	..	..	..	..	..
5120 Taxes on specific goods and services	10 844	26 627	41 750	70 573	80 819	80 287	84 381	88 871	91 724	92 340
5121 Excise duties	8 213	20 566	31 158	57 224	63 780	63 438	64 621	65 330	66 140	66 187
Duty on mineral oils	3 798	10 917	17 701	37 826	38 877	39 601	39 260	39 605	40 834	40 837
Duty on power	0	0	0	3 356	6 439	6 167	6 987	6 560	6 848	6 696
Duty on tobacco	2 402	5 771	8 898	11 443	14 108	13 453	14 131	14 963	14 254	14 469
Duty on alcohol	771	1 986	2 162	2 151	2 169	2 049	2 098	2 073	2 119	2 116
Duty on beer	501	645	693	843	750	708	675	679	663	604
Duty on coffee	488	756	986	1 087	985	998	1 030	1 034	1 030	1 069
Duty on sugar	59	72	79	0	0	0	0	0	0	0
Duty on tea	16	32	31	0	0	0	0	0	0	0
Duty on salt	20	20	23	0	0	0	0	0	0	0
Duty on electric lamps	34	63	83	0	0	0	0	0	0	0
Duty on playing cards	2	4	0	0	0	0	0	0	0	0
Duty on beverages	46	22	8	6	1	0	0	0	0	0
Duty on acetic acid	3	2	0	0	0	0	0	0	0	0
Duty on champagne	69	274	494	512	451	462	440	416	392	396
Duty on matches	5	2	0	0	0	0	0	0	0	0
Duty on ice cream	1	0	0	0	0	0	0	0	0	0
5122 Profits of fiscal monopolies	8	2	0	0	0	0	0	0	0	0
5123 Customs and import duties	1 658	3 125	3 847	3 394	3 972	4 234	4 251	5 195	5 018	5 092
Monetary compensation accounts	0	368	1	..	..	..	..	..	..	..
Customs (mainly EU)	1 294	2 353	3 662	3 394	3 972	4 234	4 251	5 195	5 018	5 092
Agricultural levies EU	364	404	184	..	..	..	..	..	..	..
5124 Taxes on exports	0	0	0	0	0	0	0	0	0	0
5125 Taxes on investment goods	0	0	0	0	0	0	0	0	0	..
5126 Taxes on specific services	942	2 689	6 443	9 599	13 095	12 583	15 443	18 306	20 600	21 059
Duty transport goods on residents	0	0	0	0	0	0	0	0	0	0
Transport tax	452	0	0	0	0	0	0	0	0	0
Insurance tax	198	910	2 266	7 243	10 410	10 261	11 588	12 445	13 747	14 179
Fire insurance tax	33	124	200	288	319	326	392	413	467	482
Entertainment tax	55	44	140	267	210	376	708	881	1 072	997
Taxes on betting and gambling	204	655	1 046	1 801	1 702	1 412	1 635	1 711	1 893	1 974
Tax on electricity bills	0	956	2 792	0	0	0	0	0	..	..
Aviation tax	0	0	0	0	0	0	955	1 027	1 203	1 168
Gaming casinos levy	0	0	0	0	454	208	165	251	232	262
SRF Contributions	..	..	..	..	..	..	..	1 578	1 986	1 997
5127 Other taxes on internat. trade and transactions	0	0	4	5	1	2	2	2	2	2
5128 Other taxes	24	244	298	351	-29	30	64	38	-36	0
Levies CECA	24	56	36	0	0	0	0	0	0	0
Cotisation sugar EU	0	112	224	351	-29	30	64	38	-36	0
Levy on milk	0	75	38	0	0	0	0	0	0	0
5130 Unallocable between 5110 and 5120	0	0	0	0	352	340	288	292	288	288
Contributions to the German National Petroleum Stockpiling Agency	..	..	..	..	352	340	288	292	288	288
5200 Taxes on use of goods and perform activities	1 383	3 457	4 368	7 242	16 343	16 752	18 371	18 926	18 722	20 348
5210 Recurrent taxes	1 369	3 454	4 368	7 239	16 343	16 189	17 699	18 171	17 218	17 597
5211 Paid by households: motor vehicles	614	1 892	2 950	5 177	6 823	6 447	6 393	6 992	7 102	7 338
5212 Paid by others: motor vehicles	728	1 475	1 300	1 838	2 075	2 041	2 097	1 812	1 945	2 034
5213 Paid in respect of other goods	27	87	118	224	7 445	7 701	9 209	9 367	8 171	8 225
Dog taxes	24	75	101	198	240	258	299	322	359	370
Hunting and fishing taxes	4	13	17	26	23	19	10	10	9	8
Nuclear fuel tax	0	0	0	0	0	0	1 285	1 018	0	0
Licence fee (private households)	0	0	0	0	6 464	6 681	6 914	7 280	7 085	7 125
Licence fee (companies)	0	0	0	0	718	743	701	737	718	722
5220 Non-recurrent taxes	14	3	1	3	0	563	672	755	1 504	2 751
Non-recurrent taxes	..	..	..	..	0	0	0	0	0	0
CO2 emission certificates	..	..	..	..	0	563	672	755	1 504	2 751
5300 Unallocable between 5100 and 5200	0	0	0	0	0	0	0	0	0	0
6000 Other taxes	**172**	**172**	**160**	**165**	**96**	**100**	**128**	**216**	**270**	**319**
6100 Paid solely by business	0	0	0	0	0	0	0	0	..	..
6200 Other	172	172	160	165	96	100	128	216	270	319
Memorandum items										
Customs duties collected on behalf of the EU	..	..	3 662	3 394	3 972	4 234	4 251	5 195	5 018	5 092
SRF contributions collected on behalf of the EU	..	..	..	..	..	..	..	1 578	1 986	1 997

	1965	1980	1990	2000	2007	2010	2013	2015	2018	2019
Non-wastable tax credits										
Non-wastable tax credits against 1110	..	..	..	38 355	43 602	45 475	41 890	41 951	43 913	45 148
Tax expenditure component	..	..	..	..	29 499	28 268	26 275	26 817	29 026	29 271
Transfer component	..	..	..	..	14 104	17 207	15 616	15 134	14 887	15 878
Non-wastable tax credits against 1210	..	..	..	962	804	802	426	200	12	44
Tax expenditure component	..	..	..	..	348	326	172	120	12	40
Transfer component	..	..	..	..	456	474	254	80	0	6
Total tax revenue on cash basis	**74 359**	**287 373**	**454 764**	**767 046**	**881 517**	**911 154**	**1 037 605**	**1 125 844**	**1 293 189**	**1 338 426**
Total tax revenue on accrual basis	**..**	**..**	**..**	**..**	**884 216**	**911 161**	**1 038 902**	**1 127 631**	**1 294 272**	**1 341 294**
Conciliation with National Accounts										
Additional taxes included in National Accounts	..	..	..	..	2 406	2 067	2 411	2 856	2 361	2 450
Several duties, administrative fees and other revenues	..	..	..	..	2 406	2 067	2 411	2 856	2 361	2 450
Taxes excluded from National Accounts	..	..	..	..	0	0	0	0	..	..
Difference in treatment of tax credits	..	..	..	..	12 623	9 230	6 358	5 619	6 355	5 720
Capital transfer for uncollected revenue	..	..	..	..	0	0	0	0	..	..
Voluntary social security contributions	..	..	..	..	21 409	5 102	5 352	6 068	7 490	7 262
Miscellaneous differences	..	..	..	..	33 134	34 234	34 083	35 690	39 161	42 948
National Accounts: Taxes and actual social contributions	..	..	..	..	953 788	961 794	1 087 106	1 177 864	1 349 639	1 399 674
Imputed social contributions	..	..	..	..	29 509	32 687	33 506	34 543	38 181	40 053
National Accounts: Taxes and all social contributions	..	..	..	..	983 297	994 481	1 120 612	1 212 407	1 387 820	1 439 727

.. Not available

Note: Year ending 31st December.

From 2002 data are on accrual basis.

The tax revenues for Germany refer to the old Länder until 1990 and to all Germany beginning in 1991.

Heading 1000: In the years up to 2000, the revenues shown take into account the whole amount of non-wastable tax credits including that part paid out by the tax authorities which should, under the OECD criteria, be treated as expenditure. From 2001, the data necessary to make the adjustment have become available and the revenue figures comply with the OECD criteria from that year. The impact of this change is shown in Table D in Part I of this Report.

Heading for non-wastable tax credits against 1110 comprise child tax credits (paid out of wage tax revenue), tax credits for owner occupied housing (paid out of assessed income tax revenue) and investment tax credits for unincorporated businesses (for investment in former East Germany; paid out of assessed income tax revenue).

Heading for non-wastable tax credits against 1210 are investment tax credits for incorporated businesses (for investment in former East Germany; paid out of corporate income tax revenue).

Source: Finanzbericht, Bonn; Tax Statistics. Unpublished estimates by the Ministry of Finance.

StatLink https://stat.link/7kc1dq

Table 5.14. Greece: Details of tax revenue, 1965-2019

Million EUR

	1965	1980	1990	2000	2007	2010	2013	2015	2018	2019
Total tax revenue	**116**	**1 475**	**11 472**	**47 211**	**73 990**	**72 414**	**64 560**	**64 510**	**71 891**	**72 419**
Total tax revenue exclusive of taxes collected for the EU	..	..	**11 361**	**46 990**	**73 683**	**72 134**	**64 410**	**64 235**	**71 564**	**72 036**
1000 Taxes on income, profits and capital gains	**11**	**286**	**2 283**	**12 662**	**17 176**	**15 953**	**14 015**	**14 586**	**16 468**	**15 642**
1100 Of individuals	8	220	1 619	6 127	10 554	9 015	10 780	10 155	11 550	11 001
1110 On income and profits	8	220	1 619	6 102	10 500	8 948	10 698	10 047	11 427	10 855
Personal income tax	..	..	1 414	..	..	..	..	..	..	..
Receipts from previous years	..	..	62	..	..	..	..	..	..	..
Agricultural social security fund	..	..	143	..	..	..	..	..	..	..
1120 On capital gains	0	0	0	25	54	67	82	108	123	146
1200 Corporate	2	56	631	5 625	5 304	5 717	2 071	3 800	3 998	4 071
1210 On profits	2	56	631	5 625	5 304	5 717	2 071	3 800	3 998	4 071
Corporation income tax	2	39	553	..	..	..	..	..	..	..
Receipts from previous years	0	8	33	..	..	..	..	..	..	..
Agricultural social security fund	0	9	46	..	..	..	..	..	..	..
1220 On capital gains	0	0	0	0	0	0	0	0	0	0
1300 Unallocable between 1100 and 1200	1	10	32	910	1 318	1 221	1 164	631	920	570
Extraordinary taxes	0	10	32	..	..	..	..	..	..	..
Other taxes on income and profits	1	0	0	..	..	..	..	..	..	..
2000 Social security contributions	**37**	**485**	**3 466**	**14 284**	**24 940**	**24 748**	**19 354**	**18 807**	**21 473**	**22 293**
2100 Employees	15	214	1 735	7 629	13 417	13 292	10 881	11 095	11 887	12 080
2110 On a payroll basis	..	..	..	..	..	..	..	..	..	..
2120 On an income tax basis	..	..	..	..	..	..	..	..	..	..
2200 Employers	14	213	1 728	6 655	11 523	11 456	8 473	7 712	9 586	10 213
2210 On a payroll basis	..	..	..	..	..	..	..	..	..	..
2220 On an income tax basis	..	..	..	..	..	..	..	..	..	..
2300 Self-employed or non-employed	0	0	3	0	0	0	0	0	0	0
2310 On a payroll basis	..	..	..	..	..	..	..	..	..	..
2320 On an income tax basis	..	..	..	..	..	..	..	..	..	..
2400 Unallocable between 2100, 2200 and 2300	7	58	0	0	0	0	0	0	0	0
2410 On a payroll basis	..	..	..	..	..	..	..	..	..	..
2420 On an income tax basis	..	..	..	..	..	..	..	..	..	..
3000 Taxes on payroll and workforce	**1**	**27**	**79**	**0**	**0**	**0**	**0**	**0**	**0**	**0**
4000 Taxes on property	**11**	**68**	**532**	**3 631**	**4 908**	**3 741**	**5 698**	**5 418**	**5 556**	**5 602**
4100 Recurrent taxes on immovable property	0	4	22	372	709	553	2 619	3 592	3 595	3 268
4110 Households	0	3	22	..	..	..	..	..	..	..
4120 Others	0	1	0	..	..	..	..	..	..	..
Taxes on immovable property	0	0	..	..	..	..	..	..	..	..
4200 Recurrent taxes on net wealth	0	0	0	714	1 208	1 272	1 084	1 083	1 176	1 193
4210 Individual	..	..	..	..	..	..	..	..	..	..
4220 Corporate	..	..	..	..	..	..	..	..	..	..
4300 Estate, inheritance and gift taxes	1	18	141	372	208	165	99	134	135	244
4310 Estate and inheritance taxes	1	13	85	..	..	..	..	..	..	..
4320 Gift taxes	0	4	55	..	..	..	..	..	..	..
4400 Taxes on financial and capital transactions	10	44	368	2 035	2 556	1 146	615	547	640	869
Stamp and transaction taxes	10	41	368	2 035	2 556	1 146	615	547	640	869
Receipts from previous years	0	3	0	0	0	0	0	0	0	0
4500 Non-recurrent taxes	0	2	1	27	0	1	0	0	0	0
4510 On net wealth	0	0	0	..	..	..	..	..	..	..
4520 Other non-recurrent taxes	0	2	1	..	..	..	..	..	..	..
4600 Other recurrent taxes on property	0	0	0	111	227	604	1 281	62	10	28
5000 Taxes on goods and services	**57**	**608**	**5 109**	**16 634**	**26 966**	**27 972**	**25 493**	**25 699**	**28 394**	**28 882**
5100 Taxes on production, sale, transfer, etc.	51	564	4 881	14 797	24 541	25 505	21 536	21 480	24 670	24 892
5110 General taxes	12	194	3 040	9 234	17 020	16 504	13 100	13 077	15 385	15 474
5111 Value added taxes	0	0	2 821	8 927	16 511	15 958	12 593	12 885	15 288	15 390
5112 Sales tax	9	185	123	0	0	0	0	0	0	0
5113 Other	2	9	96	307	509	546	507	192	97	84
Other taxes on goods and services	1	9	34	307	509	546	507	192	97	84
Receipts from previous years	1	0	62	0	0	0	0	0	0	0
5120 Taxes on specific goods and services	39	370	1 789	5 526	7 407	8 922	8 327	8 302	9 143	9 373
5121 Excise duties	20	165	1 372	4 069	5 876	7 567	6 997	6 929	7 134	7 215
Duty on tobacco products	8	45	357	1 769	2 657	2 712	2 506	2 365	2 244	2 207
Duty on alcohol and spirits	1	7	50	262	334	501	417	393	530	504
Duty on mineral oil	7	75	637	2 016	2 878	4 242	3 894	3 971	4 052	4 182
Duty on sugar	3	6	0	0	0	0	0	0	0	0
Duty on coton and other products	0	30	328	22	7	112	180	200	308	322
5122 Profits of fiscal monopolies	2	6	0	0	0	0	0	0	0	0

	1965	1980	1990	2000	2007	2010	2013	2015	2018	2019
5123 Customs and import duties	12	94	112	220	314	279	153	181	232	299
Import duties	11	90	111	220	314	279	153	181	232	299
Agricultural social security fund	1	5	1	0	0	0	0	0	0	0
5124 Taxes on exports	0	1	1	0	0	0	0	0	0	0
5125 Taxes on investment goods	0	0	0	0	0	0	0	0	0	0
5126 Taxes on specific services	2	47	293	1 237	1 217	1 076	1 177	1 192	1 777	1 859
5127 Other taxes on internat. trade and transactions	0	0	0	0	0	0	0	0	0	0
5128 Other taxes	4	58	10	0	0	0	0	0	0	0
Agricultural social security fund	2	..	0	..	..	..	..	..	..	..
Other taxes	2	..	0	..	..	..	..	..	..	..
5130 Unallocable between 5110 and 5120	0	0	52	37	114	79	109	101	142	45
5200 Taxes on use of goods and perform activities	6	44	228	1 320	2 169	1 682	2 954	3 217	3 091	3 257
5210 Recurrent taxes	5	24	219	1 320	2 169	1 682	2 954	3 217	3 091	3 257
Motor vehicle tax	5	0	0	0	0	0	0	0	0	0
5211 Paid by households: motor vehicles	..	23	210	281	598	825	781	780	804	819
5212 Paid by others: motor vehicles	..	0	8	735	1 182	272	120	207	272	301
5213 Paid in respect of other goods	0	1	1	304	389	585	2 053	2 230	2 015	2 137
Taxes on boats/ships	0	0	1	..	..	..	..	..	..	..
5220 Non-recurrent taxes	1	20	9	0	0	0	0	0	0	0
Exceptional tax on construction of buildings	0	..	9	..	..	..	..	..	..	..
Building permits	0	..	0	..	..	..	..	..	..	..
5300 Unallocable between 5100 and 5200	0	0	0	517	256	785	1 003	1 002	633	733
6000 Other taxes	**0**	**1**	**3**	**0**	**0**	**0**	**0**	**0**	**0**	**0**
6100 Paid solely by business	..	0	0	..	..	..	..	..	..	..
6200 Other	..	1	3	..	..	..	..	..	..	..
Memorandum items										
Customs duties collected on behalf of the EU	..	..	100	210	307	278	148	181	225	299
SRF contributions collected on behalf of the EU	..	..	..	..	..	..	..	92	102	84
Total tax revenue on cash basis	**116**	**1 475**	**11 472**	**45 979**	**72 429**	**73 083**	**62 632**	**63 210**	**70 110**	**71 559**
Total tax revenue on accrual basis	**..**	**..**	**..**	**47 211**	**73 990**	**72 414**	**64 560**	**64 510**	**71 891**	**72 419**
Conciliation with National Accounts										
Additional taxes included in National Accounts	..	..	..	0	0	0	0	0	0	0
Taxes excluded from National Accounts	..	..	..	0	0	0	0	0	0	0
Difference in treatment of tax credits	..	..	..	0	0	0	0	0	0	0
Capital transfer for uncollected revenue	..	..	..	0	0	0	0	0	0	0
Tax (Employer's actual social contributions)	..	..	..	..	..	..	..	..	..	..
Tax (Employee's actual social contributions)	..	..	..	..	..	..	..	..	..	..
Voluntary social security contributions	..	..	..	0	0	0	0	0	0	0
Miscellaneous differences	..	..	..	0	0	0	0	0	0	0
National Accounts: Taxes and actual social contributions	..	..	..	47 211	73 990	72 414	64 560	64 510	71 891	72 419
Imputed social contributions	..	..	..	2 055	3 952	4 952	5 101	5 615	4 826	4 394
National Accounts: Taxes and all social contributions	..	..	..	49 266	77 942	77 366	69 661	70 125	76 717	76 813

.. Not available

Note: Year ending 31st December.

From 1998 data are on accrual basis.

Source: Ministry of Finance, General accounting Office, 20th Directorate of Budget except the heading 2000 provided by the National Statistics Bureau.

StatLink https://stat.link/dh0em9

Table 5.15. Hungary: Details of tax revenue, 1965-2019

Million HUF

	1965	1980	1990	2000	2007	2010	2013	2015	2018	2019
Total tax revenue	..	..	..	**5 132 570**	**10 098 955**	**10 121 687**	**11 668 441**	**13 519 622**	**15 961 757**	**17 329 497**
Total tax revenue exclusive of taxes collected for the EU	..	..	..	**5 132 570**	**10 055 315**	**10 096 033**	**11 641 223**	**13 479 897**	**15 898 326**	**17 265 217**
1000 Taxes on income, profits and capital gains	..	..	..	**1 247 420**	**2 539 389**	**2 093 830**	**2 009 010**	**2 425 958**	**2 912 179**	**3 071 393**
1100 Of individuals	..	..	..	954 698	1 838 563	1 764 082	1 604 686	1 824 671	2 340 282	2 457 567
1110 On income and profits	..	..	..	954 698	1 838 563	1 764 082	1 604 686	1 824 671	2 340 282	2 457 567
1120 On capital gains	..	..	..	0	0	0	0	0	0	0
1200 Corporate	..	..	..	292 722	700 826	329 748	404 324	601 287	571 897	613 826
Corporate income tax	..	..	..	292 722	510 781	323 370	322 467	539 777	506 674	554 018
Research and development fund levy	..	..	..	0	0	0	0	0	0	0
Financial institutions' special tax	..	..	..	0	10 890	21 618	27 686	19 902	5 566	8 253
Separate tax for companies	..	..	..	0	178 598	-32 390	0	0	0	0
Medicine tax	..	..	..	0	558	163	111	0	0	0
Energy corporations' special tax	..	..	..	0	0	16 987	54 060	41 608	59 657	51 555
1210 On profits	..	..	..	..	..	..	..	..	..	..
1220 On capital gains	..	..	..	..	..	..	..	..	..	..
1300 Unallocable between 1100 and 1200	..	..	..	0	0	0	0	0	0	0
Interest withholding	..	..	..	..	..	..	..	..	..	..
2000 Social security contributions	..	..	..	**1 506 755**	**3 402 194**	**3 179 509**	**3 899 154**	**4 433 464**	**5 049 751**	**5 544 824**
2100 Employees	..	..	..	275 323	941 682	1 112 583	1 592 995	1 770 923	2 432 664	2 771 032
Pensions	..	..	..	150 585	336 855	537 556	875 371	969 908	1 335 868	1 481 874
Health	..	..	..	81 874	513 633	467 208	591 224	656 147	898 485	1 003 683
Unemployment	..	..	..	42 864	91 194	107 819	126 400	144 868	198 311	285 475
2110 On a payroll basis	..	..	..	..	..	..	..	..	..	..
2120 On an income tax basis	..	..	..	..	..	..	..	..	..	..
2200 Employers	..	..	..	1 213 190	2 402 941	2 043 771	2 280 505	2 637 330	2 590 306	2 745 827
Pensions	..	..	..	734 456	1 508 490	1 800 864	2 254 959	2 235 536	2 037 548	1 961 323
Health	..	..	..	385 019	693 705	169 202	25 546	398 618	551 406	783 069
Unemployment	..	..	..	93 715	200 746	73 705	0	3 176	1 352	1 435
2210 On a payroll basis	..	..	..	..	..	..	..	..	..	..
2220 On an income tax basis	..	..	..	..	..	..	..	..	..	..
2300 Self-employed or non-employed	..	..	..	873	2 534	0	0	0	0	0
Pensions: of which	..	..	..	0	0	..	..	..	..	..
Self-employed	..	..	..	0	0	..	..	..	..	..
Unemployed	..	..	..	0	0	..	..	..	..	..
Retired	..	..	..	0	0	..	..	..	..	..
Other	..	..	..	0	0	..	..	..	..	..
Health: of which	..	..	..	873	2 534	..	..	..	..	..
Self-employed	..	..	..	873	2 534	..	..	..	..	..
Unemployed	..	..	..	0	0	..	..	..	..	..
Retired	..	..	..	0	0	..	..	..	..	..
Other	..	..	..	0	0	..	..	..	..	..
2310 On a payroll basis	..	..	..	..	..	..	..	..	..	..
2320 On an income tax basis	..	..	..	..	..	..	..	..	..	..
2400 Unallocable between 2100, 2200 and 2300	..	..	..	17 368	55 037	23 155	25 654	25 211	26 781	27 965
2410 On a payroll basis	..	..	..	..	..	..	..	..	..	..
2420 On an income tax basis	..	..	..	..	..	..	..	..	..	..
3000 Taxes on payroll and workforce	..	..	..	**183 430**	**82 068**	**113 689**	**206 426**	**241 750**	**410 207**	**495 006**
Rehabilitation contribution	..	..	..	2 184	13 559	56 004	64 400	67 460	92 654	102 990
Training levy	..	..	..	13 186	36 612	47 083	89 348	96 427	133 618	145 380
Wage guarantee contribution	..	..	..	0	0	0	0	0	0	0
Communal tax on enterprises	..	..	..	1 192	1 261	1 170	2	0	0	0
Health contribution	..	..	..	166 869	20 427	0	0	0	0	0
Medicine tax	..	..	..	0	10 209	9 431	9 547	10 283	11 113	10 179
Tax on home-workers	..	..	..	0	0	1	23	29	24	24
Lump sum tax for small taxpayers	..	..	..	0	0	0	31 241	55 409	127 779	161 207
Small business tax	..	..	..	0	0	0	11 865	12 142	45 019	75 226
4000 Taxes on property	..	..	..	**89 024**	**202 711**	**312 059**	**388 824**	**437 329**	**417 804**	**446 471**
4100 Recurrent taxes on immovable property	..	..	..	30 810	72 071	92 525	190 249	200 906	219 132	221 441
Land tax	..	..	..	0	0	0	0	0	0	0
Building tax	..	..	..	22 262	54 556	71 025	102 719	111 963	126 277	127 594
Development land tax	..	..	..	3 099	6 900	9 861	19 395	19 102	23 165	24 095
Communal tax on recreational howes	..	..	..	893	1 412	1 515	21	26	0	0
Communal tax on households	..	..	..	4 557	9 069	10 124	13 175	13 451	14 621	14 566
Luxury tax	..	..	..	0	134	0	0	0	0	0
Public utility tax	..	..	..	0	0	0	54 939	55 906	54 254	54 509
Community tax	..	..	..	0	0	0	0	458	815	677
4110 Households	..	..	..	..	..	..	..	..	..	..
4120 Others	..	..	..	..	..	..	..	..	..	..

	1965	1980	1990	2000	2007	2010	2013	2015	2018	2019
4200 Recurrent taxes on net wealth	..	..	..	0	0	135 652	128 560	135 661	42 591	44 894
Surtax payable by financial institutions	..	..	..	..	..	135 652	128 560	135 661	42 591	44 894
4210 Individual	..	..	..	..	..	..	..	..	..	..
4220 Corporate	..	..	..	..	..	..	..	..	..	..
4300 Estate, inheritance and gift taxes	..	..	..	5 460	13 175	6 264	5 307	7 373	8 519	11 428
4310 Estate and inheritance taxes	..	..	..	4 020	10 775	4 243	4 097	6 230	7 313	9 758
Inheritance tax-local	..	..	..	2 010	4 658	1 858	0	0	0	0
Inheritance tax-central	..	..	..	2 010	6 117	2 385	4 097	6 230	7 313	9 758
4320 Gift taxes	..	..	..	1 440	2 400	2 021	1 210	1 143	1 206	1 670
Gift tax-local	..	..	..	720	1 038	885	0	0	0	0
Gift tax-central	..	..	..	720	1 363	1 136	1 210	1 143	1 206	1 670
4400 Taxes on financial and capital transactions	..	..	..	52 754	117 465	77 618	64 708	93 389	147 562	168 708
Property transfer tax-local	..	..	..	26 349	50 783	33 990	0	0	0	0
Property transfer tax-central	..	..	..	26 405	66 682	43 628	64 708	93 389	147 562	168 708
4500 Non-recurrent taxes	..	..	..	0	0	0	0	0	0	0
4510 On net wealth	..	..	..	..	..	..	..	..	..	..
4520 Other non-recurrent taxes	..	..	..	..	..	..	..	..	..	..
4600 Other recurrent taxes on property	..	..	..	0	0	0	0	0	0	0
5000 Taxes on goods and services	**..**	**..**	**..**	**2 081 439**	**3 832 361**	**4 383 865**	**5 127 520**	**5 936 435**	**7 148 810**	**7 737 909**
5100 Taxes on production, sale, transfer, etc.	..	..	..	2 052 712	3 751 218	4 272 312	5 002 824	5 798 298	6 986 981	7 523 531
5110 General taxes	..	..	..	1 340 572	2 622 027	3 010 781	3 414 342	4 099 741	5 042 361	5 526 275
5111 Value added taxes	..	..	..	1 153 750	2 013 271	2 325 608	2 693 555	3 309 540	4 129 537	4 526 757
5112 Sales tax	..	..	..	0	0	37 795	47 927	50 635	73 573	90 743
Public health product tax	..	..	..	..	..	0	19 090	29 882	40 727	54 912
Hydrocarbons stockholding fee	..	..	..	..	..	37 795	28 837	20 753	32 846	35 831
5113 Other	..	..	..	186 823	608 756	647 378	672 860	739 566	839 251	908 775
Local tax on company sales	..	..	..	186 823	427 134	443 093	500 868	584 380	711 276	788 308
Simplified business tax	..	..	..	0	152 812	181 880	110 021	89 406	54 117	43 364
Research and development contribution	..	..	..	0	28 810	22 405	61 971	65 780	73 858	77 103
5120 Taxes on specific goods and services	..	..	..	712 140	1 129 192	1 261 531	1 588 482	1 698 557	1 944 620	1 997 256
5121 Excise duties	..	..	..	533 502	969 730	929 881	992 269	1 119 189	1 270 129	1 303 858
Road fund petrol tax	..	..	..	0	0	0	0	0	0	0
Alcohol production duty	..	..	..	3 848	5 621	3 021	196	8 007	8 078	7 640
Water fund tax	..	..	..	6 017	13 171	14 444	13 164	12 305	12 701	12 513
Forestry fund tax	..	..	..	2 858	3 353	284	0	0	0	0
Environment petrol tax	..	..	..	14 837	19 447	17 274	46 711	65 534	77 023	80 511
Budget excises (central budget)	..	..	..	505 942	916 869	877 778	915 546	1 015 555	1 153 070	1 184 136
Coffee	..	..	..	3 200	0	0	0	0	0	0
Alcohol	..	..	..	53 500	88 600	83 078	85 487	87 369	104 113	90 126
Tobacco	..	..	..	107 000	252 400	251 778	312 509	321 922	349 483	369 155
Petrol	..	..	..	156 000	218 200	216 728	189 755	206 220	230 138	238 390
Diesel	..	..	..	157 000	256 600	293 588	308 736	375 026	441 366	459 013
Other oil	..	..	..	6 000	2 200	2 567	3 451	3 608	2 617	2 364
Other budget excises	..	..	..	30 343	93 442	30 039	15 608	21 410	25 353	25 088
Energy tax	..	..	..	0	11 269	17 080	16 652	17 788	19 257	19 058
5122 Profits of fiscal monopolies	..	..	..	0	0	0	0	0	0	0
5123 Customs and import duties	..	..	..	137 730	37 174	33 446	35 307	52 395	79 130	80 315
Customs duties	..	..	..	137 730	37 174	33 446	35 307	52 395	79 130	80 315
5124 Taxes on exports	..	..	..	0	0	0	0	0	0	0
5125 Taxes on investment goods	..	..	..	0	0	0	0	0	0	0
5126 Taxes on specific services	..	..	..	40 908	106 629	297 554	507 201	465 479	567 329	587 967
Gambling tax	..	..	..	27 935	71 804	62 718	41 316	44 972	39 265	39 656
Tourism tax	..	..	..	4 379	0	0	0	0	0	0
Communal tourism tax	..	..	..	2 943	4 935	5 798	8 411	10 475	14 863	16 249
Cultural contribution	..	..	..	4 387	8 432	1 096	105	127	152	0
Pork slaughterhouse tax	..	..	..	32	0	0	0	0	0	0
Breeding contribution	..	..	..	899	919	0	0	0	0	0
Medicine tax	..	..	..	0	19 789	28 104	40 496	45 529	48 676	51 318
Surtax payable by financial institutions	..	..	..	0	0	39 611	1 217	4 155	3 269	3 428
Specific sectors' surtax	..	..	..	0	0	151 693	9 815	285	669	94
Telecommunication services tax	..	..	..	0	0	0	50 176	54 516	53 732	53 412
Accident tax	..	..	..	0	0	0	23 313	27 694	43 801	5 125
Insurance tax	..	..	..	0	0	4 018	28 088	30 108	40 010	87 784
Financial transaction levy	..	..	..	0	0	0	289 321	205 616	234 364	245 548
Waste dumping contribution	..	..	..	0	0	0	6 639	11 123	14 648	16 177
Advertising tax	..	..	..	0	0	0	0	5 675	13 903	6 451
Protection Fund levies (BEVA)	..	..	..	0	0	1 036	1 000	2 600	7 545	7 328
Protection Fund levies (OBA)	..	..	..	0	0	2 435	7 299	14 391	15 347	10 041
Protection Fund levies (Resolution Fund)	..	..	..	0	0	0	0	7 290	10 553	12 114
Protection Fund levies (SZHTKA)	..	..	..	0	0	0	5	923	1 159	1 166
Protection Fund levies (KA)	..	..	..	0	0	0	0	0	4 285	4 765
Tourism development contribution	..	..	..	0	0	0	0	0	21 088	27 311

	1965	1980	1990	2000	2007	2010	2013	2015	2018	2019
Protection Fund Levies (PGA)	..	..	..	332	750	1 045	0	0	0	0
Retail tax	..	..	..	..	..	..	..	..	..	..
5127 Other taxes on internat. trade and transactions	..	..	..	0	0	0	0	0	0	0
Previous differential producer's turnover tax	..	..	..	..	..	..	..	..	..	..
5128 Other taxes	..	..	..	0	15 659	650	53 705	61 494	28 032	25 116
Sugar duty	..	..	..	..	15 659	650	881	765	0	0
Payments by companies in the energy sector (MAVIR)	..	..	..	..	0	0	52 824	60 729	28 032	25 116
5130 Unallocable between 5110 and 5120	..	..	..	0	0	0	0	0	0	0
5200 Taxes on use of goods and perform activities	..	..	..	28 727	81 143	111 553	124 696	138 137	161 829	214 378
5210 Recurrent taxes	..	..	..	25 454	74 268	106 903	121 126	130 238	149 641	201 235
Tax on domestically registered vehicles-local	..	..	..	12 622	62 432	71 112	69 248	73 248	79 811	84 095
Tax on domestically registered vehicles-extra budget	..	..	..	0	0	0	0	0	0	0
Tax on domestically registered vehicles-central	..	..	..	8 250	0	79	0	0	0	0
Tax on foreign registered vehicles extra budget fund	..	..	..	0	0	0	0	0	0	0
Tax on foreign registered vehicles-central	..	..	..	3 078	1 655	1 397	0	0	0	0
Company car tax	..	..	..	0	0	25 867	32 935	31 570	35 676	36 928
5211 Paid by households: motor vehicles	..	..	..	0	0	0	0	0	0	0
5212 Paid by others: motor vehicles	..	..	..	0	0	0	0	0	0	0
5213 Paid in respect of other goods	..	..	..	1 504	10 181	8 448	18 943	25 420	34 154	80 212
Environmental protection charge	..	..	..	5	13	27	0	0	0	0
Fishing development contribution	..	..	..	40	104	0	0	0	0	0
Environmental pollution charge	..	..	..	0	8 785	7 653	7 861	6 680	6 303	6 413
Air pollution levy	..	..	..	751	610	53	0	0	0	0
Water pollution levy	..	..	..	225	186	0	0	0	0	0
Toxic waste levy	..	..	..	65	42	130	0	0	0	0
Noise abatement levy	..	..	..	13	8	19	0	0	0	0
Unidentified environmental protection levies paid to local governments	..	..	..	404	433	566	521	265	193	144
Sale of emission allowances	..	..	..	0	0	0	10 561	17 479	26 411	72 223
Concession fees (tobacco shops)	..	..	..	0	0	0	0	996	1 247	1 432
5220 Non-recurrent taxes	..	..	..	3 273	6 875	4 650	3 570	7 899	12 188	13 143
Land protection levy	..	..	..	1 640	3 777	2 488	1 881	3 610	7 555	8 331
Vehicle weight fee	..	..	..	805	1 288	820	624	0	0	0
Game protection contribution	..	..	..	178	176	1	0	0	0	0
Casino license fee	..	..	..	650	1 635	1 341	1 065	4 289	4 633	4 812
5300 Unallocable between 5100 and 5200	..	..	..	0	0	0	0	0	0	0
6000 Other taxes	**..**	**..**	**..**	**24 503**	**40 232**	**38 735**	**37 507**	**44 686**	**23 006**	**33 894**
Unallocable tax penalties	..	..	..	23 546	33 321	36 250	37 507	35 530	15 565	25 751
6100 Paid solely by business	..	..	..	957	6 911	2 485	0	9 156	7 441	8 143
Nuclear contribution	..	..	..	957	6 711	2 485	..	9 156	7 441	8 143
Medicine tax	..	..	..	0	200	0	..	0	0	0
6200 Other	..	..	..	0	0	0	0	0	0	0
Memorandum item										
Customs duties collected on behalf of the EU	..	..	..	..	27 981	25 004	26 337	38 960	63 431	64 280
Total tax revenue on cash basis	**..**	**..**	**..**	**5 132 570**	**10 020 734**	**10 137 257**	**11 480 296**	**13 218 609**	**15 345 821**	**16 799 260**
Total tax revenue on accrual basis	**..**	**..**	**..**	**..**	**10 098 955**	**10 121 687**	**11 668 441**	**13 519 622**	**15 961 757**	**17 329 497**
Conciliation with National Accounts										
Additional taxes included in National Accounts	..	..	..	..	45 120	49 057	73 565	76 364	74 070	38 847
Social security contributions	..	..	..	..	0	11 675	36 063	40 688	39 096	3 386
Duty for state procedures	..	..	..	..	45 084	37 331	37 417	35 653	34 954	35 443
Other taxes	..	..	..	..	36	51	85	23	20	18
Taxes excluded from National Accounts	..	..	..	..	-49 439	-53 707	-51 838	-48 414	-28 483	-38 432
Water fund tax	..	..	..	..	-13 171	-14 444	-13 164	-12 305	-12 701	-12 513
Tax on foreign registered vehicles	..	..	..	..	-1 655	-1 397	0	0	0	0
Environmental protection fee	..	..	..	..	-446	-593	-520	-265	-193	-144
Air pollution levy	..	..	..	..	-610	-53	0	0	0	0
Water pollution levy	..	..	..	..	-186	0	0	0	0	0
Toxic waste levy	..	..	..	..	-42	-130	0	0	0	0
Noise abatement levy	..	..	..	..	-8	-19	0	0	0	0
Vehicle weight fee	..	..	..	..	0	-820	-624	0	0	0
Unallocable tax penalties	..	..	..	..	-33 320	-36 250	-37 507	-35 530	-15 565	-25 751
Tax on home-workers	..	..	..	..	0	-1	-23	-29	-24	-24
Specific sectors' surtax correction	..	..	..	..	0	0	0	-285	0	0
Difference in treatment of tax credits	..	..	..	..	0	0	0	0	0	0
Capital transfer for uncollected revenue	..	..	..	..	0	0	0	0	0	0
Voluntary social security contributions	..	..	..	..	1 762	1 693	1 523	1 229	1 090	983
Miscellaneous differences	..	..	..	..	-2 687	-28	2	-43	-866	191
Inheritance tax	..	..	..	..	0	0	0	0	0	0
Gift tax	..	..	..	..	0	0	0	0	0	0
Property transfer tax	..	..	..	..	0	0	0	0	0	0
Rounding	..	..	..	..	4	-2	2	0	0	0
Taxes on income and profits	..	..	..	..	-2 087	0	0	0	0	0

	1965	1980	1990	2000	2007	2010	2013	2015	2018	2019
Corporate income tax	..	..	..	..	0	0	0	0	0	0
Customs duties	..	..	..	..	-603	-26	0	-43	-866	191
Vehicle weight fee	..	..	..	..	0	0	0	0	0	0
Environment petrol tax	..	..	..	..	0	0	0	0	0	0
Social security contributions	..	..	..	..	0	0	0	0	0	0
Credit institutions' special tax	..	..	..	..	0	0	0	0	0	0
National Accounts: Taxes and actual social contributions	..	..	..	..	10 093 712	10 118 702	11 691 693	13 548 758	16 007 568	17 331 086
Imputed social contributions	..	..	..	..	21 113	24 841	21 669	28 783	22 650	21 799
National Accounts: Taxes and all social contributions	..	..	..	..	10 114 825	10 143 543	11 713 362	13 577 541	16 030 218	17 352 885

.. Not available

Note: Year ending 31st December.

From 2002 onwards, data are on accrual basis, except for the preliminary year, which is on a cash basis.

Heading 5121: the aggregate figure for excise tax revenues is on a cash basis. Revenue from specific excises is in several cases reported on an accrual basis.

Tax base for "Environment petrol tax" is broader than petrol only.

Heading 5123: part of environmentally related payments is attributable to Local government. It is not possible to present a more detailed breakdown of these figures.

Source: Ministry of Finance, Economic Department.

StatLink https://stat.link/5g3i12

Table 5.16. Iceland: Details of tax revenue, 1965-2019

Million ISK

	1965	1980	1990	2000	2007	2010	2013	2015	2018	2019
Total tax revenue	**60**	**4 731**	**114 932**	**254 556**	**531 760**	**540 276**	**676 142**	**812 002**	**1 036 846**	**1 061 948**
1000 Taxes on income, profits and capital gains	**13**	**1 211**	**34 106**	**101 473**	**241 378**	**239 664**	**315 577**	**380 979**	**511 724**	**530 162**
1100 Of individuals	12	1 092	30 908	88 492	180 070	197 318	258 623	297 979	412 430	435 321
1110 On income and profits	..	..	30 908	88 492	180 070	197 318	258 623	297 979	412 430	435 321
1120 On capital gains	..	..	..	0	0	0	0	0	0	0
1200 Corporate	1	119	3 198	8 356	32 555	14 609	40 479	52 544	67 724	62 972
1210 On profits	..	..	3 198	8 356	32 555	14 609	40 479	52 544	67 724	62 972
1220 On capital gains	..	..	..	0	0	0	0	0	0	0
1300 Unallocable between 1100 and 1200	0	0	0	4 625	28 754	27 737	16 475	30 457	31 569	31 868
2000 Social security contributions	**5**	**102**	**3 607**	**19 680**	**39 594**	**63 599**	**69 899**	**79 707**	**98 230**	**97 423**
2100 Employees	0	0	315	..	..	..	..	..	..	..
2110 On a payroll basis	..	..	..	..	..	..	..	..	..	..
2120 On an income tax basis	..	..	..	..	..	..	..	..	..	..
2200 Employers	5	102	3 292	..	..	..	..	..	..	..
2210 On a payroll basis	..	..	..	..	..	..	..	..	..	..
2220 On an income tax basis	..	..	..	..	..	..	..	..	..	..
2300 Self-employed or non-employed	0	0	0	..	..	..	..	..	..	..
2310 On a payroll basis	..	..	..	..	..	..	..	..	..	..
2320 On an income tax basis	..	..	..	..	..	..	..	..	..	..
2400 Unallocable between 2100, 2200 and 2300	0	0	0	19 680	39 594	63 599	69 899	79 707	98 230	97 423
2410 On a payroll basis	..	..	..	19 680	39 594	63 599	69 899	79 707	98 230	97 423
2420 On an income tax basis	..	..	..	0	0	0	0	0	0	0
3000 Taxes on payroll and workforce	**1**	**180**	**4 071**	**184**	**1 519**	**2 827**	**6 534**	**6 638**	**8 542**	**9 124**
4000 Taxes on property	**2**	**297**	**9 689**	**19 983**	**32 523**	**38 068**	**46 493**	**43 487**	**56 798**	**63 635**
4100 Recurrent taxes on immovable property	1	138	4 131	10 107	20 567	28 542	30 664	34 879	46 497	52 522
4110 Households	0	50	1 862	..	..	..	..	..	..	..
4120 Others	1	88	2 269	..	..	..	..	..	..	..
4200 Recurrent taxes on net wealth	0	69	2 402	5 173	-8	3 849	8 886	657	100	10
4210 Individual	..	29	1 476	..	..	..	..	..	..	..
4220 Corporate	..	40	926	..	..	..	..	..	..	..
4300 Estate, inheritance and gift taxes	0	6	235	765	1 663	2 613	2 437	2 919	4 703	4 668
4310 Estate and inheritance taxes	0	6	235	765	1 663	2 613	2 437	2 919	4 703	4 668
4320 Gift taxes	0	0	0	0	0	0	0	0	0	0
4400 Taxes on financial and capital transactions	1	84	2 921	3 143	9 484	2 656	3 973	4 327	4 962	5 269
4500 Non-recurrent taxes	0	0	0	113	460	146	233	362	470	623
4510 On net wealth	..	..	..	0	0	0	0	0	0	0
4520 Other non-recurrent taxes	..	..	..	113	460	146	233	362	470	623
4600 Other recurrent taxes on property	0	0	0	681	356	263	299	343	65	542
5000 Taxes on goods and services	**37**	**2 834**	**58 943**	**112 245**	**214 988**	**190 131**	**226 619**	**262 828**	**344 534**	**343 009**
5100 Taxes on production, sale, transfer, etc.	37	2 778	56 564	100 669	191 957	178 995	215 271	250 095	324 763	320 533
5110 General taxes	10	1 368	37 084	72 667	137 593	122 393	149 828	183 674	244 624	243 285
5111 Value added taxes	0	0	32 698	72 667	137 593	122 393	149 828	183 674	244 624	243 285
5112 Sales tax	10	1 368	4 386	0	0	0	0	0	0	0
5113 Other	0	0	0	0	0	0	0	0	0	0
5120 Taxes on specific goods and services	27	1 410	19 480	28 002	54 364	56 603	65 444	66 421	80 138	77 248
5121 Excise duties	1	311	2 346	23 585	45 891	46 711	55 171	56 909	69 524	66 833
5122 Profits of fiscal monopolies	5	263	5 986	0	0	0	0	0	0	0
5123 Customs and import duties	20	715	9 181	2 702	5 446	5 950	5 815	4 989	4 118	3 430
5124 Taxes on exports	1	2	0	1	0	2	0	0	0	0
5125 Taxes on investment goods	0	0	0	0	0	0	0	0	0	0
5126 Taxes on specific services	1	69	1 404	1 715	3 026	3 940	4 457	4 523	6 497	6 986
5127 Other taxes on internat. trade and transactions	0	50	563	0	0	0	0	0	0	0
5128 Other taxes	0	0	0	0	0	0	0	0	0	0
5130 Unallocable between 5110 and 5120	0	0	0	0	0	0	0	0	0	0
5200 Taxes on use of goods and perform activities	1	56	2 379	11 576	23 032	11 135	11 347	12 733	19 772	22 476
5210 Recurrent taxes	1	56	2 379	..	..	..	..	..	..	..
5211 Paid by households: motor vehicles	0	10	970	..	..	..	..	..	..	..
5212 Paid by others: motor vehicles	0	41	1 331	..	..	..	..	..	..	..
5213 Paid in respect of other goods	0	5	78	..	..	..	..	..	..	..
5220 Non-recurrent taxes	0	0	0	..	..	..	..	..	..	..
5300 Unallocable between 5100 and 5200	0	0	0	0	0	0	0	0	0	0
6000 Other taxes	**2**	**107**	**4 516**	**991**	**1 758**	**5 988**	**11 020**	**38 364**	**17 019**	**18 594**
6100 Paid solely by business	2	107	4 145	418	628	763	5 255	32 477	10 414	11 629
6200 Other	0	0	371	573	1 130	5 225	5 766	5 887	6 605	6 966

	1965	1980	1990	2000	2007	2010	2013	2015	2018	2019
Non-wastable tax credits										
Non-wastable tax credits against 1110	..	..	..	..	..	..	0	0	0	0
Tax expenditure component	..	..	..	..	..	..	0	0	0	0
Transfer component	..	..	..	..	..	..	0	0	0	0
Non-wastable tax credits against 1210	..	..	..	..	..	..	1 085	1 304	3 079	3 577
Tax expenditure component	..	..	..	..	..	..	148	176	572	608
Transfer component	..	..	..	..	..	..	937	1 128	2 507	2 969
Total tax revenue on cash basis	**60**	**4 731**	**114 932**	**..**	**..**	**..**	**..**	**..**	**..**	**..**
Total tax revenue on accrual basis	**..**	**..**	**..**	**254 556**	**531 760**	**540 276**	**676 142**	**812 002**	**1 036 846**	**1 061 948**
Conciliation with National Accounts										
Additional taxes included in National Accounts	..	..	..	0	0	0	0	0	0	0
Taxes excluded from National Accounts	..	..	..	-765	-1 663	-2 613	-2 437	-2 919	-4 703	-4 668
Estate and inheritance taxes (4310)	..	..	..	-765	-1 663	-2 613	-2 437	-2 919	-4 703	-4 668
Difference in treatment of tax credits	..	..	..	0	0	0	0	0	0	0
Capital transfer for uncollected revenue	..	..	..	0	0	0	0	0	0	0
Voluntary social security contributions	..	..	..	0	0	0	0	0	0	0
Miscellaneous differences	..	..	..	0	0	0	0	0	0	0
National Accounts: Taxes and actual social contributions	..	..	..	253 791	530 097	537 662	673 704	809 084	1 032 143	1 057 280
Imputed social contributions	..	..	..	0	0	0	0	0	0	0
National Accounts: Taxes and all social contributions	..	..	..	253 791	530 097	537 662	673 704	809 084	1 032 143	1 057 280

.. Not available

Note: Year ending 31st December.

From 1998 data are on accrual basis.

Source: Ministry of Finance, Economic Department.

StatLink https://stat.link/086lnh

Table 5.17. Ireland: Details of tax revenue, 1965-2019

Million EUR

	1965	1980	1990	2000	2007	2010	2013	2015	2018	2019
Total tax revenue	**317**	**4 046**	**12 260**	**33 363**	**60 790**	**46 399**	**51 442**	**60 892**	**72 884**	**78 088**
Total tax revenue exclusive of taxes collected for the EU	..	..	**12 075**	**33 155**	**60 517**	**46 170**	**51 195**	**60 565**	**72 451**	**77 632**
1000 Taxes on income, profits and capital gains	**82**	**1 478**	**4 662**	**14 551**	**25 364**	**18 617**	**21 298**	**26 599**	**33 291**	**35 646**
1100 Of individuals	53	1 294	4 059	10 650	18 970	14 665	17 020	19 722	22 889	24 753
1110 On income and profits	53	1 286	4 023	9 876	15 872	14 320	16 652	19 053	21 897	23 680
Income tax	66	1 286	4 023	9 876	15 872	14 320	16 652	19 053	21 897	23 680
Surtax	3	0	0	0	0	0	0	0	0	0
Income tax paid by corporations	-17	0	0	0	0	0	0	0	0	0
1120 On capital gains	0	8	36	774	3 097	345	369	669	992	1 072
1200 Corporate	29	184	603	3 900	6 395	3 945	4 273	6 873	10 402	10 894
1210 On profits	29	184	603	3 900	6 395	3 945	4 273	6 873	10 402	10 894
Corporation profits tax	12	2	0	0	0	0	0	0	0	0
Corporation tax	0	176	603	3 885	6 393	3 944	4 272	6 872	10 401	10 893
Income tax paid by corporation	17	0	0	0	0	0	0	0	0	0
Agricultural produce duty	0	6	0	14	1	1	1	1	1	1
1220 On capital gains	0	0	0	0	0	0	0	0	0	0
1300 Unallocable between 1100 and 1200	0	0	0	2	0	7	4	4	0	0
2000 Social security contributions	**21**	**578**	**1 729**	**3 966**	**8 143**	**8 458**	**8 854**	**9 992**	**12 085**	**13 140**
2100 Employees	10	190	570	962	1 926	3 195	3 125	3 321	3 746	4 012
2110 On a payroll basis	..	..	570	962	1 926	3 195	3 125	3 321	3 746	4 012
2120 On an income tax basis	..	..	0	0	0	0	0	0	0	0
2200 Employers	10	380	1 092	2 814	5 796	4 932	5 326	6 211	7 734	8 495
2210 On a payroll basis	..	..	1 092	2 814	5 796	4 932	5 326	6 211	7 734	8 495
2220 On an income tax basis	..	..	0	0	0	0	0	0	0	0
2300 Self-employed or non-employed	0	8	67	190	421	331	403	460	605	632
2310 On a payroll basis	..	..	67	190	421	331	403	460	605	632
2320 On an income tax basis	..	..	0	0	0	0	0	0	0	0
2400 Unallocable between 2100, 2200 and 2300	0	0	0	0	0	0	0	0	0	0
2410 On a payroll basis	..	..	..	..	..	..	..	..	..	..
2420 On an income tax basis	..	..	..	..	..	..	..	..	..	..
3000 Taxes on payroll and workforce	**0**	**9**	**159**	**15**	**411**	**310**	**314**	**357**	**565**	**774**
4000 Taxes on property	**48**	**213**	**569**	**1 902**	**4 789**	**2 389**	**3 632**	**3 918**	**4 317**	**4 435**
4100 Recurrent taxes on immovable property	39	139	312	587	1 233	1 322	1 724	1 864	1 918	1 933
4110 Households	..	..	..	..	..	..	..	..	..	..
4120 Others	..	..	..	..	..	..	..	..	..	..
4200 Recurrent taxes on net wealth	0	1	0	0	0	0	536	169	0	0
4210 Individual	..	..	..	..	..	..	0	0	0	0
4220 Corporate	..	..	..	..	..	..	536	169	0	0
4300 Estate, inheritance and gift taxes	6	14	48	225	405	235	278	401	518	531
4310 Estate and inheritance taxes	6	14	45	210	337	192	259	365	469	467
Estate duty	5	..	0	0	0	0	0	0	0	0
Legacy duty	1	..	0	0	0	0	0	0	0	0
Succession duty	0	..	0	0	0	0	0	0	0	0
4320 Gift taxes	0	0	3	15	68	43	20	36	50	64
4400 Taxes on financial and capital transactions	3	59	209	1 090	3 151	832	1 093	1 484	1 880	1 971
Stamp duty	3	59	209	1 090	3 151	832	1 093	1 484	1 880	1 971
4500 Non-recurrent taxes	0	0	0	0	0	0	0	0	0	0
4510 On net wealth	..	..	..	..	..	..	..	..	..	..
4520 Other non-recurrent taxes	..	..	..	..	..	..	..	..	..	..
4600 Other recurrent taxes on property	0	0	0	0	0	0	0	0	0	0
5000 Taxes on goods and services	**167**	**1 769**	**5 140**	**12 929**	**22 082**	**16 619**	**17 321**	**20 013**	**22 617**	**24 088**
5100 Taxes on production, sale, transfer, etc.	155	1 741	4 939	12 374	20 982	15 319	15 789	18 036	20 650	22 273
5110 General taxes	18	597	2 500	7 643	14 355	10 067	10 372	11 831	14 175	15 281
5111 Value added taxes	0	597	2 500	7 643	14 355	10 067	10 372	11 831	14 175	15 281
Value added tax	..	597	2 500	7 643	14 355	10 067	10 372	11 831	14 175	15 281
5112 Sales tax	18	0	0	0	0	0	0	0	0	0
Turnover tax	18	..	..	..	..	..	..	..	..	..
Wholesale tax	0	..	..	..	..	..	..	..	..	..
5113 Other	0	0	0	0	0	0	0	0	0	0
5120 Taxes on specific goods and services	137	1 143	2 439	4 731	6 627	5 252	5 417	6 205	6 475	6 992

	1965	1980	1990	2000	2007	2010	2013	2015	2018	2019
5121 Excise duties	124	1 045	2 084	4 402	6 125	4 859	5 013	5 474	5 487	5 974
Beer	19	192	356	475	459	316	363	418	433	421
Oils	31	330	745	1 491	2 204	2 099	2 035	2 120	2 154	2 165
Spirits	16	148	153	241	363	244	282	313	373	375
Table waters	0	11	23	0	0	0	0	0	0	0
Tobacco	50	187	419	1 035	1 192	1 160	1 064	1 055	748	1 137
Wine, cider, perry	1	18	46	154	297	266	354	414	431	433
Motor vehicle (incl. tyres)	7	148	331	985	1 554	395	459	702	872	950
Others	1	11	11	20	57	379	457	451	476	493
5122 Profits of fiscal monopolies	0	0	0	0	0	0	0	0	0	0
5123 Customs and import duties	10	62	147	208	273	229	247	327	325	342
5124 Taxes on exports	0	0	0	0	0	0	0	0	0	0
UE agriculture levies	..	..	0	..	..	..	..	..	..	..
5125 Taxes on investment goods	0	0	0	0	0	0	0	0	0	0
5126 Taxes on specific services	3	21	171	122	229	164	157	404	662	676
Duty on betting	2	19	37	59	36	30	26	37	51	110
Sweepstakes duty	1	1	0	0	0	0	0	0	0	0
Bank levy	0	0	46	61	66	-70	-23	190	422	398
Other	0	1	88	2	127	204	154	178	190	168
5127 Other taxes on internat. trade and transactions	0	0	0	0	0	0	0	0	0	0
5128 Other taxes	0	14	37	0	0	0	0	0	0	0
5130 Unallocable between 5110 and 5120	0	0	0	0	0	0	0	0	0	0
5200 Taxes on use of goods and perform activities	11	28	201	555	1 100	1 300	1 532	1 977	1 967	1 815
5210 Recurrent taxes	11	28	201	555	1 100	1 300	1 532	1 977	1 967	1 815
5211 Paid by households: motor vehicles	6	14	100	373	723	768	888	904	799	795
5212 Paid by others: motor vehicles	5	11	82	124	239	256	284	281	245	241
5213 Paid in respect of other goods	0	3	20	58	138	276	360	792	922	779
5220 Non-recurrent taxes	0	0	0	0	0	0	0	0	0	0
5300 Unallocable between 5100 and 5200	0	0	0	0	0	0	0	0	0	0
6000 Other taxes	**0**	**0**	**0**	**0**	**0**	**6**	**23**	**12**	**9**	**5**
6100 Paid solely by business	..	..	..	..	..	0	0	0	0	0
6200 Other	..	..	..	..	..	6	23	12	9	5
Memorandum items										
Customs duties collected on behalf of the EU	..	..	148	208	273	229	247	327	325	342
SRF contributions collected on behalf of the EU	..	..	..	..	..	..	..	..	107	114
Non-wastable tax credits										
Non-wastable tax credits against 1110	..	..	..	..	843	1 073	816	555	472	413
Tax expenditure component	..	..	..	..	843	1 073	816	555	472	413
Transfer component	..	..	..	..	0	0	0	0	0	0
Total tax revenue on cash basis	**317**	**4 046**	**12 260**	**32 997**	**60 836**	**46 609**	**51 474**	**60 861**	**72 882**	**77 926**
Total tax revenue on accrual basis	**..**	**..**	**..**	**33 363**	**60 790**	**46 399**	**51 442**	**60 892**	**72 884**	**78 088**
Conciliation with National Accounts										
Additional taxes included in National Accounts	..	..	..	0	0	178	178	177	182	185
Taxes excluded from National Accounts	..	..	..	0	0	0	0	0	0	0
Difference in treatment of tax credits	..	..	..	0	0	0	0	0	0	0
Capital transfer for uncollected revenue	..	..	..	0	0	0	0	0	0	0
Voluntary social security contributions	..	..	..	0	0	0	0	0	0	0
Miscellaneous differences	..	..	..	0	0	0	0	0	0	0
National Accounts: Taxes and actual social contributions	..	..	..	33 363	60 790	46 577	51 620	61 069	73 066	78 273
Imputed social contributions	..	..	..	1 366	2 579	1 053	1 986	2 142	2 541	2 694
National Accounts: Taxes and all social contributions	..	..	..	34 729	63 369	47 630	53 606	63 210	75 607	80 967

.. Not available

Note: The personal income tax data shown for the country table for Ireland is different to the ESA2010 presentation as the expenditure component of the payable tax credits are excluded in accordance with the OECD Interpretative Guide.

The data for years 1965 to 1973 are on fiscal year basis (commencing on 1st April) and are therefore not strictly comparable with the data for later years, which are on a calendar year basis.

From 1998, data are on accrual basis.

Heading 1200: Capital gains taxes paid by corporations are included in heading 1210.

Heading 2100: Includes contributions by self-employed and certain voluntary contributions.

Heading 2200: Since 1976 income tax paid by corporations and corporation profits tax have been replaced by corporation tax.

Heading 5111: Includes arrears of the wholesale and turnover taxes.

Tax receipts in 1988 were inflated by the success of the new arrangements for assessment and collection of tax.These arrangements included an amnesty for tax arrears paid by 30th September. This amnesty waived penalities and interest charge tax. It resulted in payments of 631 millons of euros spread across the main tax headings.

Source: Annual Report of he Revenue Commissioners, Financial Accounts and National Income and Expenditure Accounts.

StatLink https://stat.link/yu2q7d

Table 5.18. Israel: Details of tax revenue, 1965-2019

Million ILS

	1965	1980	1990	2000	2007	2010	2013	2015	2018	2019
Total tax revenue	..	..	..	**188 199**	**251 159**	**268 399**	**325 269**	**364 181**	**413 233**	**428 534**
1000 Taxes on income, profits and capital gains	..	..	..	**74 551**	**91 530**	**78 265**	**101 481**	**113 966**	**135 001**	**140 453**
1100 Of individuals	..	..	..	54 753	56 434	48 214	57 311	70 885	84 922	89 493
1110 On income and profits	..	..	..	53 698	55 213	47 550	55 831	68 455	81 642	86 463
On wages – deduction at source	..	..	..	45 278	45 515	40 159	46 458	54 087	65 249	68 041
On self employement income – deduction at source	..	..	..	573	0	853	1 051	0	47	83
On self employement income – other	..	..	..	7 847	9 698	6 538	8 322	14 368	16 346	18 339
1120 On capital gains	..	..	..	1 055	1 221	664	1 480	2 430	3 280	3 030
1200 Corporate	..	..	..	18 001	30 210	23 113	36 639	34 676	42 932	43 291
1210 On profits	..	..	..	16 109	27 582	22 291	33 959	33 446	41 382	41 861
Deduction at source	..	..	..	315	0	520	751	0	25	41
In lieu of VAT on the profits of Financial Institutions	..	..	..	1 290	2 200	1 920	2 560	1 910	2 300	2 400
Other	..	..	..	14 504	25 382	19 850	30 648	31 536	39 057	39 420
1220 On capital gains	..	..	..	1 892	2 628	822	2 680	1 230	1 550	1 430
1300 Unallocable between 1100 and 1200	..	..	..	1 797	4 886	6 938	7 531	8 405	7 147	7 669
Tax deducted at the source on the capital market	..	..	..	1 797	4 886	6 938	7 531	8 405	7 147	7 669
2000 Social security contributions	..	..	..	**27 565**	**37 909**	**45 343**	**53 364**	**59 561**	**70 635**	**74 420**
2100 Employees	..	..	..	15 771	23 093	27 788	31 537	34 692	39 963	41 852
2110 On a payroll basis	..	..	..	15 771	23 093	27 788	31 537	34 692	39 963	41 852
2120 On an income tax basis	..	..	..	0	0	0	0	0	0	0
2200 Employers	..	..	..	8 182	9 960	11 427	15 026	17 247	21 753	23 105
2210 On a payroll basis	..	..	..	8 182	9 960	11 427	15 026	17 247	21 753	23 105
2220 On an income tax basis	..	..	..	0	0	0	0	0	0	0
2300 Self-employed or non-employed	..	..	..	3 612	4 856	6 128	6 802	7 622	8 920	9 464
2310 On a payroll basis	..	..	..	3 612	4 856	6 128	6 802	7 622	8 920	9 464
2320 On an income tax basis	..	..	..	0	0	0	0	0	0	0
2400 Unallocable between 2100, 2200 and 2300	..	..	..	0	0	0	0	0	0	0
2410 On a payroll basis	..	..	..	..	..	..	..	..	..	..
2420 On an income tax basis	..	..	..	..	..	..	..	..	..	..
3000 Taxes on payroll and workforce	..	..	..	**6 850**	**9 920**	**10 280**	**12 780**	**13 770**	**15 828**	**16 168**
Employers tax on the the non-profit sector other than govt	..	..	..	1 250	1 500	320	390	410	502	555
In lieu of VAT on the wage-bill in the non-profit sector	..	..	..	4 260	6 580	7 650	9 540	10 320	11 948	12 521
In lieu VAT on the wage-bill in Financial Institutions	..	..	..	1 340	1 840	2 310	2 850	3 040	3 378	3 092
4000 Taxes on property	..	..	..	**16 935**	**24 282**	**28 817**	**32 637**	**38 741**	**42 330**	**43 773**
4100 Recurrent taxes on immovable property	..	..	..	11 311	16 156	18 768	21 499	23 702	26 142	27 105
Land tax	..	..	..	442	52	48	59	44	25	25
4110 Households	..	..	..	0	0	0	0	0	0	0
4120 Others	..	..	..	10 869	16 104	18 720	21 440	23 658	26 117	27 080
4200 Recurrent taxes on net wealth	..	..	..	0	0	0	0	0	0	0
4210 Individual	..	..	..	..	..	..	..	..	..	..
4220 Corporate	..	..	..	..	..	..	..	..	..	..
4300 Estate, inheritance and gift taxes	..	..	..	0	0	0	0	0	0	0
4310 Estate and inheritance taxes	..	..	..	..	..	..	..	..	..	..
4320 Gift taxes	..	..	..	..	..	..	..	..	..	..
4400 Taxes on financial and capital transactions	..	..	..	3 181	3 555	4 071	4 532	6 732	6 660	6 923
Transaction tax on the buyer of real estate	..	..	..	1 972	3 084	4 024	4 513	6 731	6 654	6 917
Transaction tax on the seller of real estate	..	..	..	206	404	27	19	1	6	6
Stamp tax	..	..	..	1 003	67	20	0	0	0	0
4500 Non-recurrent taxes	..	..	..	2 443	4 572	5 979	6 607	8 307	9 528	9 745
4510 On net wealth	..	..	..	0	0	0	0	0	0	0
4520 Other non-recurrent taxes	..	..	..	2 443	4 572	5 979	6 607	8 307	9 528	9 745
Capital gains tax on real estate	..	..	..	2 443	4 572	5 979	6 607	8 307	9 528	9 745
4600 Other recurrent taxes on property	..	..	..	0	0	0	0	0	0	0
5000 Taxes on goods and services	..	..	..	**62 298**	**87 518**	**105 694**	**125 007**	**138 143**	**149 438**	**153 719**
5100 Taxes on production, sale, transfer, etc.	..	..	..	57 887	81 107	98 092	116 335	128 277	138 931	143 066
5110 General taxes	..	..	..	49 876	67 569	79 945	97 357	107 765	117 251	120 541
5111 Value added taxes	..	..	..	39 805	53 982	65 508	81 524	90 824	99 442	102 463
5112 Sales tax	..	..	..	10 071	13 587	14 437	15 833	16 941	17 809	18 078
On domestic production	..	..	..	662	287	291	457	450	328	287
On imports	..	..	..	9 409	13 300	14 146	15 376	16 491	17 481	17 791
5113 Other	..	..	..	0	0	0	0	0	0	0
5120 Taxes on specific goods and services	..	..	..	8 012	13 538	18 147	18 978	20 512	21 680	22 525
5121 Excise duties	..	..	..	6 595	11 323	15 458	16 680	17 642	18 895	19 509
On domestically refined fuel	..	..	..	5 666	10 590	14 637	15 876	17 008	18 387	18 966
On domestically processed tobacco products	..	..	..	929	733	821	804	634	508	543
5122 Profits of fiscal monopolies	..	..	..	0	0	0	0	0	0	0
5123 Customs and import duties	..	..	..	1 417	2 215	2 689	2 298	2 870	2 785	3 016
5124 Taxes on exports	..	..	..	0	0	0	0	0	0	0

	1965	1980	1990	2000	2007	2010	2013	2015	2018	2019
5125 Taxes on investment goods	..	..	..	0	0	0	0	0	0	0
5126 Taxes on specific services	..	..	..	0	0	0	0	0	0	0
5127 Other taxes on internat. trade and transactions	..	..	..	0	0	0	0	0	0	0
5128 Other taxes	..	..	..	0	0	0	0	0	0	0
5130 Unallocable between 5110 and 5120	..	..	..	0	0	0	0	0	0	0
5200 Taxes on use of goods and perform activities	..	..	..	4 411	6 411	7 601	8 673	9 866	10 507	10 653
5210 Recurrent taxes	..	..	..	4 411	6 411	7 601	8 673	9 866	10 507	10 653
5211 Paid by households: motor vehicles	..	..	..	1 436	1 895	2 274	2 872	3 179	3 597	3 669
5212 Paid by others: motor vehicles	..	..	..	479	632	758	957	1 060	1 199	1 223
5213 Paid in respect of other goods	..	..	..	2 497	3 885	4 569	4 843	5 628	5 711	5 761
Licences collected by the Ministry of Transportation	..	..	..	257	535	350	132	196	128	165
Licences collected by the Ministry of Communication	..	..	..	151	0	274	299	338	338	371
Licences collected by other ministries	..	..	..	1 587	2 597	2 988	3 228	3 781	3 703	3 624
Business and professional licences paid locally	..	..	..	451	667	856	1 060	1 186	1 392	1 446
Other local authority fees	..	..	..	51	86	101	125	128	149	155
5220 Non-recurrent taxes	..	..	..	0	0	0	0	0	0	0
5300 Unallocable between 5100 and 5200	..	..	..	0	0	0	0	0	0	0
6000 Other taxes	**..**	**..**	**..**	**0**	**0**	**0**	**0**	**0**	**0**	**0**
6100 Paid solely by business	..	..	..	..	..	..	..	..	..	..
6200 Other	..	..	..	..	..	..	..	..	..	..
Non-wastable tax credits										
Non-wastable tax credits against 1110	..	..	..	..	..	87	911	1 415	807	1 327
Tax expenditure component	..	..	..	..	..	84	879	1 348	807	1 327
Transfer component	..	..	..	..	..	3	32	67	0	0
Non-wastable tax credits against 1210	..	..	..	..	..	0	0	0	0	0
Tax expenditure component	..	..	..	..	..	0	0	0	0	0
Transfer component	..	..	..	..	..	0	0	0	0	0
Total tax revenue on cash basis	**..**	**..**	**..**	**188 199**	**251 159**	**268 399**	**325 269**	**364 181**	**413 233**	**428 534**
Total tax revenue on accrual basis	**..**	**..**	**..**	**..**	**..**	**..**	**..**	**..**	**..**	**..**
Conciliation with National Accounts										
Additional taxes included in National Accounts	..	..	..	0	0	0	0	0	0	0
Taxes excluded from National Accounts	..	..	..	..	..	..	..	..	..	..
Difference in treatment of tax credits	..	..	..	..	..	..	..	..	..	..
Capital transfer for uncollected revenue	..	..	..	..	..	..	..	..	..	..
Voluntary social security contributions	..	..	..	..	..	..	..	..	..	..
Miscellaneous differences	..	..	..	..	..	..	..	..	..	..
National Accounts: Taxes and actual social contributions	..	..	..	188 199	251 159	268 399	325 269	364 181	413 233	428 534
Imputed social contributions	..	..	..	6 172	7 131	8 203	9 084	9 186	9 145	9 067
National Accounts: Taxes and all social contributions	..	..	..	194 371	258 290	276 601	334 354	373 367	422 377	437 601

.. Not available

Note: Year ending 31st December.

Data are on a cash basis.

Source: Israel Central Bureau of Statistics and Israel Ministry of Finance.

StatLink https://stat.link/8q75yk

Table 5.19. Italy: Details of tax revenue, 1965-2019

Million EUR

	1965	1980	1990	2000	2007	2010	2013	2015	2018	2019
Total tax revenue	**5 505**	**60 422**	**265 116**	**503 096**	**671 189**	**671 912**	**706 829**	**711 114**	**739 193**	**759 633**
Total tax revenue exclusive of taxes collected for the EU	..	..	**263 829**	**501 560**	**668 928**	**669 687**	**704 939**	**706 522**	**735 761**	**756 473**
1000 Taxes on income, profits and capital gains	**982**	**18 821**	**96 707**	**166 912**	**226 498**	**219 547**	**233 294**	**225 934**	**229 458**	**239 799**
1100 Of individuals	603	13 940	69 654	124 918	172 136	180 512	185 996	184 622	189 917	196 135
1110 On income and profits	603	13 796	68 786	124 233	172 122	180 505	185 991	184 619	189 917	196 135
Personal income tax	0	11 538	57 318	121 211	162 644	173 991	175 921	173 007	180 403	185 705
Local income tax paid by households	0	829	4 492	67	0	0	0	0	0	0
Tax on income from investiments (60%)	319	55	15	0	0	0	11	80	52	47
10% Surcharge on income	94	37	5	0	0	0	0	0	0	0
10% proportional surcharge	1	0	0	0	0	0	0	0	0	0
Withholding tax on company dividends paid by households	23	51	496	110	542	393	564	875	1 158	1 751
Law 1177 proportional surcharge (60%)	39	0	1	0	0	0	0	0	0	0
Direct taxes 5% proportional surcharge (60%)	0	8	72	0	0	0	0	0	0	0
Additional Treasury increase (60%)	23	6	1	0	0	0	0	0	0	0
Decree 1132 revenues (60%)	0	0	0	0	0	0	0	0	0	0
Tax on households	65	7	0	0	0	0	0	0	0	0
Rental value tax	2	0	0	0	0	0	0	0	0	0
Driving licence tax	1	0	0	0	0	0	0	0	0	0
Municipal surcharge on buildings (40%)	37	5	0	22	0	0	0	0	0	0
Withholding tax on income from deposits paid by households	0	1 206	6 223	2 823	8 402	5 440	8 994	10 076	7 488	7 671
Direct taxes refund (60%)	0	0	41	0	0	0	0	0	0	0
Other	0	53	123	0	534	681	501	581	816	962
1120 On capital gains	0	144	867	685	14	7	5	3	0	0
Tax on capital gains on land	..	0	0	0	0	0	0	0	..	..
Municipal capital gains tax on buildings paid by households (60%)	..	144	867	685	14	7	5	3	..	..
1200 Corporate	379	4 710	26 605	34 699	50 529	36 740	41 194	33 530	32 886	35 264
1210 On profits	379	4 494	26 027	34 242	50 520	36 736	41 190	33 528	32 881	35 260
Corporation tax	0	1 245	9 042	28 877	47 192	34 841	39 160	31 927	31 056	32 742
Municipal surcharge on buildings (60%)	37	8	0	32	0	0	0	0	0	0
Tax on income from investments (40%)	213	37	10	0	0	0	8	54	35	31
Company franchise and liabilities tax	88	12	2	0	0	0	0	0	0	0
Law 1177 proportional surcharge (40%)	26	0	0	0	0	0	0	0	0	0
Direct taxes 5% proportional surcharge (40%)	0	20	48	0	0	0	0	0	0	0
Decree 1132 revenues (40%)	0	0	0	0	0	0	0	0	0	0
Additional Treasury increase (40%)	15	4	0	0	0	0	0	0	0	0
Withholding tax on company dividends paid by firms	0	77	745	166	0	0	0	0	0	0
Withholding tax on income from deposits paid by firms	0	1 810	9 334	4 235	2 370	605	1 464	759	393	599
Local income tax paid by firms	0	1 245	6 738	100	15	13	12	12	14	6
Direct taxes refund (40%)	0	0	27	0	0	0	0	0	0	0
Other	0	36	82	832	943	1 277	546	776	1 383	1 882
1220 On capital gains	0	216	578	457	9	4	4	2	5	4
Municipal capital gains tax on buildings paid by firms (40%)	..	216	578	457	9	4	4	2	5	4
1300 Unallocable between 1100 and 1200	0	171	448	7 295	3 833	2 295	6 104	7 782	6 656	8 399
Refunds tax on income	..	-240	-1 768	-5 175	0	0	0	0	0	0
Other	..	412	2 216	12 470	3 833	2 295	6 104	7 782	6 656	8 399
2000 Social security contributions	**1 881**	**22 976**	**87 256**	**143 629**	**200 772**	**209 122**	**210 462**	**214 376**	**229 643**	**237 346**
2100 Employees	..	4 171	16 753	27 333	35 715	37 598	39 284	39 805	42 725	44 486
2110 On a payroll basis	..	..	..	27 333	35 715	37 598	39 284	39 805	42 725	44 486
2120 On an income tax basis	..	..	..	0	0	0	0	0	0	0
2200 Employers	..	17 152	62 540	99 904	137 924	144 281	141 629	143 273	153 908	158 611
2210 On a payroll basis	..	..	..	99 904	137 924	144 281	141 629	143 273	153 908	158 611
2220 On an income tax basis	..	..	..	0	0	0	0	0	0	0
2300 Self-employed or non-employed	..	1 654	7 962	16 392	27 133	27 243	29 549	31 298	33 010	34 249
2310 On a payroll basis	..	..	..	16 392	27 133	27 243	29 549	31 298	33 010	34 249
2320 On an income tax basis	..	..	..	0	0	0	0	0	0	0
2400 Unallocable between 2100, 2200 and 2300	1 881	0	0	0	0	0	0	0	0	0
2410 On a payroll basis	..	..	..	..	..	..	..	..	..	..
2420 On an income tax basis	..	..	..	..	..	..	..	..	..	..
3000 Taxes on payroll and workforce	**0**	**387**	**890**	**0**	**0**	**0**	**0**	**0**	**0**	**0**
Contributions to GESCAL	..	387	890	..	..	..	..	..	..	..
4000 Taxes on property	**397**	**2 248**	**5 983**	**23 360**	**32 646**	**32 441**	**43 883**	**46 259**	**44 086**	**43 220**

	1965	1980	1990	2000	2007	2010	2013	2015	2018	2019
4100 Recurrent taxes on immovable property	96	7	1	9 354	12 778	9 663	20 748	25 558	21 955	21 997
Income tax on landowners	2	0	0	0	0	0	0	0	0	0
Income tax on buildings	12	2	1	0	0	0	0	0	0	0
Income tax on luxury buildings	1	0	0	0	0	0	0	0	0	0
Surcharge on land (provincial)	16	0	0	0	0	0	0	0	0	0
Surcharge on land (municipal)	18	0	0	0	0	0	0	0	0	0
Surcharge on buildings (provincial)	26	2	0	0	0	0	0	0	0	0
Surcharge on buildings (municipal)	21	3	0	0	0	0	0	0	0	0
Municipal real estate tax	0	0	0	9 354	12 778	9 663	20 748	20 798	20 817	20 819
Tax on indivisible services (TASI)	0	0	0	0	0	0	0	4 760	1 138	1 178
4110 Households	..	..	..	..	..	..	..	..	..	..
4120 Others	..	..	..	..	..	..	..	..	..	..
4200 Recurrent taxes on net wealth	0	0	0	14	1	2 118	2 547	231	311	226
4210 Individual	..	..	..	5	0	0	0	0	0	0
4220 Corporate	..	..	..	9	1	2 118	2 547	231	311	226
4300 Estate, inheritance and gift taxes	47	128	376	1 005	149	483	622	674	820	798
Inheritance and gift duty	33	119	376	1 005	149	483	622	674	820	798
Estate duty	11	9	0	0	0	0	0	0	0	0
Proportional surcharge and premium	3	0	0	0	0	0	0	0	0	0
4310 Estate and inheritance taxes	..	..	..	..	..	..	..	..	..	..
4320 Gift taxes	..	..	..	..	..	..	..	..	..	..
4400 Taxes on financial and capital transactions	255	2 113	5 606	12 320	18 256	17 365	17 092	17 245	18 847	18 800
Registration tax	120	1 048	2 421	6 794	9 410	9 019	7 353	7 625	9 359	9 587
Mortgage taxes and land registry duties	22	190	469	1 067	2 525	2 071	1 841	1 529	1 657	1 625
5% proportional surcharge	6	0	0	0	0	0	0	0	0	0
Additional surcharge	4	0	0	0	0	0	0	0	0	0
Stamp duties and surcharges accruing on cadastral acts	104	751	2 185	4 459	6 321	6 275	7 898	7 600	7 376	7 190
Other	0	123	530	0	0	0	0	491	455	398
4500 Non-recurrent taxes	0	0	0	98	151	916	985	309	442	227
4510 On net wealth	..	..	..	0	0	0	0	0	0	0
4520 Other non-recurrent taxes	..	..	..	98	151	916	985	309	442	227
4600 Other recurrent taxes on property	0	0	0	569	1 311	1 896	1 889	2 242	1 711	1 172
5000 Taxes on goods and services	**2 173**	**15 990**	**74 280**	**141 852**	**171 869**	**178 863**	**187 210**	**196 473**	**212 057**	**214 990**
5100 Taxes on production, sale, transfer, etc.	2 037	15 251	67 083	127 281	155 191	160 775	164 597	174 443	184 729	187 723
Direct taxes refund	0	-73	-86	0	0	0	0	0	0	0
5110 General taxes	710	9 438	38 940	77 473	95 623	97 586	93 921	100 692	109 333	111 533
5111 Value added taxes	0	9 438	38 940	77 473	95 623	97 586	93 921	100 692	109 333	111 533
VAT	..	9 438	38 940	77 473	95 623	97 586	93 921	100 692	109 333	111 533
5112 Sales tax	0	0	0	0	0	0	0	0	0	0
5113 Other	710	0	0	0	0	0	0	0	0	0
General tax on receipts	662	..	..	..	..	..	..	..	..	..
Compensation tax on imported products	48	..	..	..	..	..	..	..	..	..
5120 Taxes on specific goods and services	1 327	5 886	28 048	49 808	59 568	63 189	70 676	73 751	75 396	76 190
5121 Excise duties	816	4 088	20 304	31 479	32 904	36 414	45 720	46 238	47 088	47 112
Duty on mineral oils	465	3 462	15 928	22 172	23 252	22 884	26 332	25 759	25 947	25 907
Duty on spirits	27	87	206	486	595	570	571	600	679	657
Duty on beer	12	54	172	242	489	476	532	633	818	710
Duty on sugars	22	25	68	120	0	5	10	5	-8	0
Duty on electricity	20	51	2 018	3 079	3 034	7 152	13 542	15 246	15 069	15 141
Duty on bananas	9	53	97	0	0	0	0	0	0	0
Duty on coffee	31	60	74	0	0	0	0	0	0	0
Duty on cocoa	3	4	7	0	0	0	0	0	0	0
Duty on olive oil	0	0	0	0	0	0	0	0	0	0
Other duty	44	190	1 037	5 201	5 385	5 268	4 659	3 898	4 556	4 673
Alcohol, spirits, liquor	5	0	0	0	0	0	0	0	0	0
On matches and flints	13	22	47	0	0	0	0	0	0	0
Meat	26	0	0	0	0	0	0	0	0	0
In-bond surcharge	0	81	650	174	143	54	67	90	20	17
Combustible materials	39	0	0	0	0	0	0	0	0	0
Construction materials	30	0	0	0	0	0	0	0	0	0
Excise duty on sound and video	3	0	0	0	0	0	0	0	0	0
Tax on phonograph records	1	0	0	0	0	0	0	0	0	0
Stamp duty on playing cards	1	0	0	0	0	0	0	0	0	0
Other	66	0	0	5	6	5	7	7	7	7
5122 Profits of fiscal monopolies	303	1 033	3 248	7 718	10 440	10 983	10 683	10 711	10 601	10 653
Duty on tobacco	292	1 033	3 248	7 712	10 436	10 978	10 679	10 710	10 600	10 652
On salt	10	0	0	0	0	0	0	0	0	0
Duty on products of Monopoli di Stato	1	0	0	6	4	5	4	1	1	1

	1965	1980	1990	2000	2007	2010	2013	2015	2018	2019
5123 Customs and import duties	142	261	1 164	1 536	2 261	2 225	1 890	2 246	2 295	2 314
Common Customs tariff (CEE)	0	0	836	1 536	2 261	2 225	1 890	2 246	2 295	2 314
Customs and shipping duties	115	14	0	0	0	0	0	0	0	0
Administrative services duties	11	0	0	0	0	0	0	0	0	0
Tax on agriculture	15	228	207	0	0	0	0	0	0	0
Other duties	0	9	68	0	0	0	0	0	0	0
Compensatory amounts	0	9	53	0	0	0	0	0	0	0
5124 Taxes on exports	0	0	0	0	0	0	0	0	0	0
5125 Taxes on investment goods	0	0	0	0	0	0	0	0	0	0
5126 Taxes on specific services	67	483	3 141	9 029	13 932	13 567	12 383	14 556	15 412	16 111
Entertainment tax	20	59	167	118	68	58	42	40	34	32
Stamp duty	6	0	0	0	0	0	0	0	0	0
Tax on advertisements	6	56	168	389	392	384	424	405	456	455
Tax on lotto, lotteries, betting and Totocalcio game	3	123	617	4 164	7 144	7 983	7 088	7 488	9 350	10 514
Casino takings, special duties, etc.	0	0	0	158	152	192	130	112	114	106
Single tax on games of skill and betting-levied indirectly	9	74	476	487	405	242	85	116	143	181
Aerotaxi passengers tax	0	0	0	0	0	0	7	8	11	9
Local tax (including insurance)	23	171	1 714	3 713	5 771	4 708	4 607	3 835	4 167	3 968
Bank levy for the National Resolution Fund	..	..	..	..	..	..	..	2 552	1 137	846
5127 Other taxes on internat. trade and transactions	0	0	0	0	0	0	0	0	0	0
Special Duty on foreign payments and currency selling	..	..	..	..	..	..	..	..	..	..
5128 Other taxes	0	21	192	46	31	0	0	0	0	0
ECSC taxes and contributions on sugar and other levies	..	21	121	0	0	..	..	..	..	..
Other	..	0	70	46	31	..	..	..	..	..
Bank cont. to the unique European Resolution Fund	..	0	0	0	0	..	..	..	..	..
5130 Unallocable between 5110 and 5120	0	0	180	0	0	0	0	0	0	0
5200 Taxes on use of goods and perform activities	136	456	4 474	8 479	10 550	10 531	11 352	11 130	14 498	14 093
5210 Recurrent taxes	136	456	4 474	8 479	10 550	1 155	1 359	1 653	1 873	1 856
Public motor vehicle register tax	64	152	967	1 034	1 326	1 155	1 359	1 653	1 873	1 856
Tax on vehicles 5% proportional surcharge	3	13	450	0	0	0	0	0	0	0
Surcharge on diesel cars	0	66	683	0	0	0	0	0	0	0
Surcharge on gas cars	0	0	171	0	0	0	0	0	0	0
5211 Paid by households: motor vehicles	..	..	..	3 433	4 652	4 628	4 487	4 710	5 468	5 362
5212 Paid by others: motor vehicles	..	..	..	1 006	1 332	1 300	1 395	1 446	1 426	1 394
Motor vehicle duty paid by firms	..	..	..	1 006	1 332	1 300	1 395	1 446	1 426	1 394
5213 Paid in respect of other goods	67	225	2 203	3 006	3 240	3 448	4 111	3 321	5 731	5 481
Law 1177 proportional surcharge	22	0	0	0	0	0	0	0	0	0
Taxes on signs	2	4	0	0	0	0	0	0	0	0
Tax on dog tags	0	7	12	0	0	0	0	0	0	0
Tax on hunting and fishing	0	0	0	0	0	0	0	0	0	0
Duty on official franchises	43	215	2 191	3 006	3 240	3 448	4 111	3 321	3 809	3 585
Television tax (households)	0	0	0	0	0	0	0	0	1 922	1 896
5220 Non-recurrent taxes	0	0	0	0	0	0	0	0	0	0
Motor vehicles, airplanes	..	..	..	..	..	..	..	..	..	..
Pro-Friuli tax on vehicles	..	..	..	..	..	..	..	..	..	..
5300 Unallocable between 5100 and 5200	0	283	2 724	6 092	6 128	7 557	11 261	10 900	12 830	13 174
Indirect taxes refund	..	0	160	288	616	693	477	715	954	859
Other	..	283	2 564	5 804	5 512	6 864	10 784	10 185	11 876	12 315
6000 Other taxes	**72**	**0**	**0**	**27 343**	**39 404**	**31 939**	**31 980**	**28 072**	**23 949**	**24 278**
6100 Paid solely by business	0	..	..	27 343	39 404	31 939	31 980	28 072	23 949	24 278
6200 Other	72	..	..	0	0	0	0	0	0	0
Capital levies	2	..	..	..	..	..	..	..	..	..
Other taxes	71	..	..	..	..	..	..	..	..	..
Memorandum items										
Customs duties collected on behalf of the EU	..	..	836	1 536	2 261	2 225	1 890	2 246	2 295	2 314
SRF contributions collected on behalf of the EU	..	..	..	..	..	..	..	2 346	1 137	846
Taxes and compulsory social security contributions paid by EU civil servants	..	..	..	..	..	..	55	61	69	72
Taxes paid by EU civil servants: income taxes	..	..	..	..	..	..	28	31	35	37
Taxes paid by EU civil servants: compulsory social security contributions	..	..	..	..	..	..	27	30	34	35
Non-wastable tax credits										
Non-wastable tax credits against 1110	..	..	..	..	0	0	357	9 793	10 303	10 071
Tax expenditure component	..	..	..	..	..	-109	206	8 615	9 142	8 932
Transfer component	..	..	..	..	..	109	151	1 178	1 162	1 139
Non-wastable tax credits against 1210	..	..	..	..	0	0	2 401	4 866	1 451	308
Tax expenditure component	..	..	..	..	..	0	0	0	0	0
Transfer component	..	..	..	..	..	0	2 401	4 866	1 451	308
Total tax revenue on cash basis	**5 505**	**60 422**	**265 116**	**488 738**	**653 836**	**659 704**	**689 299**	**711 837**	**734 051**	**754 185**
Total tax revenue on accrual basis	**..**	**..**	**..**	**503 096**	**671 189**	**671 912**	**706 829**	**711 114**	**739 193**	**759 633**

	1965	1980	1990	2000	2007	2010	2013	2015	2018	2019
Conciliation with National Accounts										
Additional taxes included in National Accounts	..	..	..	0	0	0	0	0	0	0
Taxes excluded from National Accounts	..	..	..	-5 416	-5 470	-6 538	-9 786	-9 801	-10 651	-10 949
The tax for the urban solid waste disposal (TARSU)	..	..	..	-4 387	-4 443	-5 519	-8 363	-8 519	-9 205	-9 459
Other	..	..	..	-1 029	-1 027	-1 019	-1 423	-1 282	-1 446	-1 490
Difference in treatment of tax credits	..	..	..	0	0	-109	206	8 615	9 142	8 932
Capital transfer for uncollected revenue	..	..	..	0	0	0	0	0	0	0
Voluntary social security contributions	..	..	..	464	567	561	738	750	771	708
Miscellaneous differences	..	..	..	0	0	0	0	0	0	0
National Accounts: Taxes and actual social contributions	..	..	..	498 144	666 286	665 826	697 987	710 678	738 455	758 324
Imputed social contributions	..	..	..	3 884	3 980	3 984	4 093	3 938	4 019	4 157
National Accounts: Taxes and all social contributions	..	..	..	502 028	670 266	669 810	702 080	714 616	742 474	762 481

.. Not available

Note: The tax year ends in December 31th.

As from 2000, revenues data are computed on accrual basis.

As from 1997, revenues data are based on data provided to the European Union as for the Treaty of Maastricht excessive deficit procedure.

Section 6000: Regional Tax on Productive Activities (IRAP); it is a tax on the value of production therefore its taxable base is different from other groups tax bases.

Regarding the section "Taxes excluded National Accounts" the item "Others" includes: tax on the public areas utilization and tax on the collection and disposal of waste water.

Source: Ministero dell'economia e delle finanze; Istituto nazionale di statistica.

StatLink https://stat.link/d96iqp

Table 5.20. Japan: Details of tax revenue, 1965-2019

Billion JPY

	1965	1980	1990	2000	2007	2010	2013	2015	2018	2019
Total tax revenue	**6 172**	**62 443**	**130 843**	**136 236**	**146 248**	**132 484**	**146 405**	**163 533**	**175 564**	**175 380**
1000 Taxes on income, profits and capital gains	**2 708**	**28 800**	**65 682**	**47 398**	**53 174**	**40 034**	**47 534**	**50 969**	**56 083**	**53 994**
1100 Of individuals	1 338	15 180	36 394	28 677	28 600	24 663	28 150	30 847	33 492	32 947
1110 On income and profits	1 338	15 180	36 394	28 677	28 600	24 663	28 150	30 847	33 492	32 947
Income tax	970	10 800	25 996	18 789	16 080	12 984	15 865	18 178	20 316	19 571
Prefectural inhabitants tax	123	1 415	3 675	3 621	5 008	4 699	5 090	5 252	4 863	4 840
Municipal inhabitants tax	220	2 890	6 475	6 044	7 294	6 795	7 015	7 224	8 106	8 325
Enterprise tax	25	75	249	223	218	184	181	194	207	211
1120 On capital gains	0	0	0	0	0	0	0	0	0	0
1200 Corporate	1 370	13 620	29 288	18 721	24 573	15 372	19 384	20 122	22 591	21 046
1210 On profits	1 370	13 620	29 288	18 721	24 573	15 372	19 384	20 122	22 591	21 046
Corporation tax	927	8 923	18 384	11 747	14 744	8 968	11 698	10 832	12 318	10 797
Prefectural inhabitants tax	53	557	1 414	879	1 206	777	854	859	835	821
Municipal inhabitants tax	85	1 297	3 198	2 176	3 015	1 954	2 157	2 324	2 427	2 395
Enterprise tax	305	2 843	6 293	3 918	5 608	2 253	2 674	3 510	4 243	4 385
Local special corporate tax	0	0	0	0	0	1 420	2 001	2 081	2 088	2 044
Local corporate tax	0	0	0	0	0	0	0	516	681	604
Special corporate enterprise tax	..	..	0	0	0	0	0	0	0	0
1220 On capital gains	0	0	0	0	0	0	0	0	0	0
1300 Unallocable between 1100 and 1200	0	0	0	0	0	0	0	0	0	0
2000 Social security contributions	**1 344**	**18 178**	**34 613**	**47 968**	**53 325**	**54 461**	**59 803**	**64 465**	**70 588**	**71 993**
2100 Employees	446	6 393	13 895	19 830	21 975	23 593	25 984	28 224	31 243	31 954
2110 On a payroll basis	..	..	13 895	19 830	21 975	23 593	25 984	28 224	31 243	31 954
2120 On an income tax basis	..	..	0	0	0	0	0	0	0	0
2200 Employers	588	9 267	16 649	22 456	24 243	24 674	27 143	29 479	32 664	33 488
2210 On a payroll basis	..	..	16 649	22 456	24 243	24 674	27 143	29 479	32 664	33 488
2220 On an income tax basis	..	..	0	0	0	0	0	0	0	0
2300 Self-employed or non-employed	107	2 518	4 069	5 683	7 108	6 194	6 676	6 763	6 681	6 552
2310 On a payroll basis	..	..	4 069	5 683	7 108	6 194	6 676	6 763	6 681	6 552
2320 On an income tax basis	..	..	0	0	0	0	0	0	0	0
2400 Unallocable between 2100, 2200 and 2300	203	0	0	0	0	0	0	0	0	0
2410 On a payroll basis	..	..	..	..	..	..	..	..	..	..
2420 On an income tax basis	..	..	..	..	..	..	..	..	..	..
3000 Taxes on payroll and workforce	**0**	**0**	**0**	**0**	**0**	**0**	**0**	**0**	**0**	**0**
4000 Taxes on property	**498**	**5 114**	**12 296**	**14 294**	**13 138**	**12 878**	**12 940**	**13 400**	**14 196**	**14 340**
4100 Recurrent taxes on immovable property	319	3 326	7 099	10 414	9 949	10 225	9 882	10 005	10 386	10 612
Prefectural property tax	4	8	15	11	14	5	2	2	11	8
Municipal property tax	296	2 784	6 023	9 041	8 729	8 961	8 653	8 755	9 083	9 286
City planning tax	19	469	942	1 318	1 202	1 256	1 227	1 244	1 291	1 318
Special landholding tax	0	65	118	43	4	3	1	3	0	0
Water and land utilization tax	0	0	0	0	0	0	0	0	0	0
Land value tax	0	0	0	1	0	0	0	0	0	0
4110 Households	..	..	..	..	..	..	..	..	..	..
4120 Others	..	..	..	..	..	..	..	..	..	..
4200 Recurrent taxes on net wealth	0	0	0	0	0	0	0	0	0	0
4210 Individual	..	..	..	..	..	..	..	..	..	..
4220 Corporate	..	..	..	..	..	..	..	..	..	..
4300 Estate, inheritance and gift taxes	44	441	1 918	1 782	1 503	1 250	1 574	1 968	2 333	2 301
4310 Estate and inheritance taxes	34	375	..	..	..	..	..	..	..	..
Inheritance tax	34	375	..	..	..	..	..	..	..	..
4320 Gift taxes	10	65	..	..	..	..	..	..	..	..
Tax on gifts	10	65	..	..	..	..	..	..	..	..
4400 Taxes on financial and capital transactions	135	1 347	3 280	2 099	1 686	1 403	1 483	1 426	1 477	1 427
Bourse tax	3	15	41	0	0	0	0	0	0	0
Securities transaction	8	209	748	0	0	0	0	0	0	0
Bank of Japan note issue tax	0	0	0	0	0	0	0	0	0	0
Stamp revenues	83	841	1 894	1 532	1 202	1 024	1 126	1 050	1 073	1 023
Real property acquisition tax	41	282	596	567	485	379	357	377	404	404
4500 Non-recurrent taxes	0	0	0	0	0	0	0	0	0	0
4510 On net wealth	..	..	..	..	..	..	..	..	..	..
4520 Other non-recurrent taxes	..	..	..	..	..	..	..	..	..	..
4600 Other recurrent taxes on property	0	0	0	0	0	0	0	0	0	0
5000 Taxes on goods and services	**1 620**	**10 200**	**17 917**	**26 227**	**26 256**	**24 730**	**25 744**	**34 286**	**34 252**	**34 599**
5100 Taxes on production, sale, transfer, etc.	1 544	8 822	15 647	23 180	23 241	22 160	23 313	31 871	31 754	32 046
5110 General taxes	0	0	5 778	12 350	12 841	12 675	13 479	22 400	22 496	23 148
5111 Value added taxes	..	..	5 778	12 350	12 841	12 675	13 479	22 400	22 496	23 148
5112 Sales tax	..	..	0	0	0	0	0	0	0	0
5113 Other	..	..	0	0	0	0	0	0	0	0
5120 Taxes on specific goods and services	1 544	8 822	9 868	10 830	10 400	9 485	9 834	9 470	9 258	8 898

	1965	1980	1990	2000	2007	2010	2013	2015	2018	2019
5121 Excise duties	1 062	6 674	8 637	9 837	9 374	8 622	8 728	8 351	8 121	7 891
Liquor tax	353	1 424	1 935	1 816	1 524	1 389	1 371	1 338	1 275	1 247
Sugar excises	29	43	0	0	0	0	0	0	0	0
Local gasoline tax	46	278	361	296	302	294	275	264	251	244
Gasoline tax	254	1 547	2 007	2 769	2 820	2 750	2 574	2 465	2 348	2 281
Liquefied petroleum gas tax	0	30	31	28	27	24	21	18	15	14
Aviation fuel tax	0	58	76	104	104	89	67	66	68	65
Commodity tax	138	1 038	5	0	0	0	0	0	0	0
Playing-card tax	1	1	0	0	0	0	0	0	0	0
Prefectural tobacco tax	44	229	361	282	278	256	173	153	139	140
Municipal tobacco tax	73	402	636	865	853	788	983	936	850	854
Timber delivery tax	3	3	0	0	0	0	0	0	0	0
Mineral product tax	2	5	3	2	2	2	2	2	2	2
Electricity and gas tax	54	386	0	0	0	0	0	0	0	0
Diesel oil tax	65	447	834	1 208	1 034	918	943	925	958	945
Vehicle acquisition tax	0	270	613	464	425	192	193	137	198	104
Promotion of power resources development tax	0	109	295	375	352	349	328	316	322	316
Petroleum and coal tax	0	404	487	489	513	502	600	630	701	638
Tobacco tax	0	0	996	876	925	908	1 038	954	861	874
Special tobacco tax	0	0	0	264	214	163	161	148	125	124
International tourist tax	..	..	0	0	0	0	0	0	7	44
5122 Profits of fiscal monopolies	179	808	0	0	0	0	0	0	0	0
Monopoly profits	179	808	..	..	..	..	..	..	..	..
5123 Customs and import duties	222	786	928	877	941	786	1 034	1 049	1 071	941
Customs duty	222	786	928	877	941	786	1 034	1 049	1 071	941
5124 Taxes on exports	0	0	0	0	0	0	0	0	0	0
5125 Taxes on investment goods	0	0	0	0	0	0	0	0	0	0
5126 Taxes on specific services	81	554	303	116	85	77	71	70	66	66
Travel tax	4	64	0	0	0	0	0	0	0	0
Admission tax	10	5	0	0	0	0	0	0	0	0
Local entertainment tax	10	74	0	0	0	0	0	0	0	0
Golf course utilization tax	0	0	90	81	60	55	49	48	43	43
Meal and lodging tax	56	398	0	0	0	0	0	0	0	0
Special local consumption tax	0	0	195	12	0	0	0	0	0	0
Bathing tax	1	13	18	23	25	22	22	23	22	23
5127 Other taxes on internat. trade and transactions	0	0	0	0	0	0	0	0	0	0
5128 Other taxes	0	0	0	0	0	0	0	0	0	0
5130 Unallocable between 5110 and 5120	0	0	0	0	0	0	0	0	0	0
5200 Taxes on use of goods and perform activities	76	1 378	2 270	3 047	3 015	2 570	2 431	2 416	2 498	2 553
5210 Recurrent taxes	69	1 358	2 250	3 027	2 993	2 548	2 409	2 393	2 475	2 530
Automobile tax	55	781	1 276	1 765	1 717	1 616	1 574	1 543	1 550	1 588
Light vehicle tax	13	43	88	125	164	178	189	200	258	269
Motor vehicle tonnage tax	0	527	881	1 134	1 110	753	643	649	665	671
Hunter licence tax	0	3	2	2	0	0	0	0	0	0
Hunting tax	0	3	2	1	2	2	2	1	1	1
Mine lot tax	1	1	1	1	0	0	0	0	0	0
5211 Paid by households: motor vehicles	..	..	..	..	..	..	..	..	..	..
5212 Paid by others: motor vehicles	..	..	..	..	..	..	..	..	..	..
5213 Paid in respect of other goods	..	..	..	..	..	..	..	..	..	..
5220 Non-recurrent taxes	7	20	20	20	22	21	22	22	23	23
5300 Unallocable between 5100 and 5200	0	0	0	0	0	0	0	0	0	0
6000 Other taxes	**2**	**151**	**335**	**348**	**356**	**381**	**384**	**413**	**445**	**454**
6100 Paid solely by business	0	139	288	324	313	330	348	361	378	387
Business office tax	..	139	288	324	313	330	348	361	378	387
6200 Other	2	12	47	24	43	52	36	52	67	68
Taxes not in local tax law	2	12	47	24	43	52	36	52	65	67
Other	0	0	0	0	0	0	0	0	2	1
Total tax revenue on cash basis	**6 172**	**62 443**	**..**	**..**	**..**	**..**	**..**	**..**	**..**	**..**
Total tax revenue on accrual basis	**..**	**..**	**130 843**	**136 236**	**146 248**	**132 484**	**146 405**	**163 533**	**175 564**	**175 380**
Conciliation with National Accounts										
Additional taxes included in National Accounts	..	..	..	..	..	..	..	..	..	..
Taxes excluded from National Accounts	..	..	..	..	..	..	..	..	..	..
Difference in treatment of tax credits	..	..	..	..	..	..	..	..	..	..
Capital transfer for uncollected revenue	..	..	..	..	..	..	..	..	..	..
Voluntary social security contributions	..	..	..	..	..	..	..	..	..	..
Miscellaneous differences	..	..	..	..	..	..	..	..	..	..
National Accounts: Taxes and actual social contributions	..	..	..	..	..	..	..	..	..	..
Imputed social contributions	..	..	..	..	..	..	..	..	..	..
National Accounts: Taxes and all social contributions	..	..	..	..	..	..	..	..	..	..

.. Not available

Note: Data are on a fiscal year basis beginning 1st April.
From 1990, data are on accrual basis.
The figures for different groups of taxes are reported on different reporting bases, namely: Social security contributions (heading 2000) : in principle accrual basis, Central government taxes : accrual basis (revenues accrued during the fiscal year plus cash receipts collected before the end of May (the end of April until 1977), Local government taxes : accrual basis (due to be paid during the fiscal year and cash receipts collected before the end of May).
The Japanese authorities take the view that the Enterprise tax (classified in 1100 and 1200) and the Mineral product tax (classified in 5121) should be classified in heading 6000 since under articles 72 and 519 of the Local Tax Law these taxes are regarded as levies on the business or mining activity itself.
Heading 2000 includes some unidentifiable voluntary contributions.
Heading 2300: Includes contibutions to the National pension, National Health Insurance and the Farmer's pension fund. Contributions to the Farmer's pension fund are not available for the years before 1999.
Heading 4100: Municipal property tax, includes Prefectural property tax from 1990 to 1994 because data is not available to provide a breakdown.
Heading 5121: Municipal tobacco tax, includes Prefectural tobacco tax from 1990 to 1994 because data is not available to provide a breakdown.
Heading 5121: In sub-item Petroleum and coal tax, the data before 2003 refer to petroleum tax.
Source: Tax Bureau, Ministry of Finance.

StatLink https://stat.link/ir6mq8

Table 5.21. Korea: Details of tax revenue, 1965-2019

Billion KRW

	1965	1980	1990	2000	2007	2010	2013	2015	2018	2019
Total tax revenue	..	**6 687**	**37 262**	**136 295**	**258 571**	**295 968**	**347 332**	**393 559**	**506 548**	**523 985**
1000 Taxes on income, profits and capital gains	..	**1 704**	**12 203**	**39 254**	**82 239**	**82 905**	**101 792**	**119 151**	**172 976**	**174 040**
1100 Of individuals	..	766	7 440	19 950	43 276	42 098	53 311	67 600	93 274	91 714
1110 On income and profits	..	766	6 327	18 569	31 984	33 935	46 654	55 744	75 251	75 613
Income tax	..	0	0	0	0	0	0	0	0	0
Dividends and interest income tax	..	0	0	0	4 682	4 425	4 889	4 561	4 982	5 577
Wages and salaries income tax	..	0	0	0	14 124	15 517	21 931	27 055	38 000	38 466
Other income tax	..	0	0	0	2 607	2 986	3 432	4 467	5 975	6 640
Global income tax	..	661	4 723	16 128	6 151	6 369	10 901	12 784	17 483	16 778
Defence tax on income tax	..	105	938	0	0	0	0	0	0	0
Education tax on income tax	..	0	325	0	0	0	0	0	0	0
Rural dev. tax on interest, bus. Inc. & cap. gains relief	..	0	0	156	160	179	124	105	111	139
Inhabitant tax on income tax (local)	..	0	341	2 285	4 260	4 459	5 377	6 772	8 700	8 013
1120 On capital gains	..	0	1 113	1 381	11 292	8 163	6 657	11 856	18 023	16 101
Capital gains tax	..	..	1 113	1 381	11 292	8 163	6 657	11 856	18 023	16 101
1200 Corporate	..	738	4 757	19 271	38 963	40 807	48 481	51 551	79 702	82 326
1210 On profits	..	738	4 757	19 271	38 963	40 807	48 481	51 551	79 702	82 326
Corporation tax - withholding	..	..	677	8 577	8 360	9 095	12 176	12 317	13 174	14 168
Corporation tax - final returns	..	..	2 549	9 302	27 057	28 173	31 679	32 713	57 763	58 006
Defence tax on corporation tax	..	..	1 323	0	0	0	0	0	0	0
Inhabitant tax on corporation tax (local)	..	..	207	1 142	3 152	3 094	4 118	6 217	8 307	9 729
Rural development tax corporate income	..	..	0	251	394	445	508	304	458	423
Excess profit tax	..	0	0	0	0	0	0	0	0	0
1220 On capital gains	..	0	0	0	0	0	0	0	0	0
Capital gains tax	..	..	..	..	..	..	..	..	..	..
1300 Unallocable between 1100 and 1200	..	199	6	33	0	0	0	0	0	0
Business income tax	..	0	0	0	..	..	..	..	..	..
Real estate income tax	..	0	0	0	..	..	..	..	..	..
Defence tax on real estate & business income	..	0	0	0	..	..	..	..	..	..
Rural dev. tax on bus. inc. & cap. gains relief	..	0	0	30	..	..	..	..	..	..
Inhabitant tax before 1990 (local)	..	117	0	0	..	..	..	..	..	..
Farm land tax (local)	..	83	6	3	..	..	..	..	..	..
Inhabitant tax on farm land tax (local)	..	0	0	0	..	..	..	..	..	..
2000 Social security contributions	..	**73**	**3 760**	**22 759**	**53 588**	**69 090**	**91 596**	**104 693**	**128 660**	**140 071**
2100 Employees	..	0	1 464	8 578	21 773	28 213	38 396	44 281	55 257	60 682
Veterans' relief fund	..	0	0	0	0	0	0	0	0	0
Soldiers' annuity fund	..	0	0	0	0	0	0	0	0	0
Unemployment assurance	..	0	0	598	1 164	1 358	2 418	3 076	3 666	4 027
National welfare pension fund	..	0	429	4 325	9 338	11 004	13 890	15 821	19 090	20 630
Social benefit fund	..	0	0	0	0	0	0	0	0	0
Health Insurance	..	0	483	2 066	8 180	11 783	17 128	19 868	24 920	27 911
Teachers' pensions	..	0	86	279	581	868	1 077	1 125	1 595	1 678
Government employees pensions	..	0	406	1 144	2 202	2 878	3 435	3 876	5 371	5 796
Military personal pensions	..	0	60	166	308	322	448	515	615	640
2110 On a payroll basis	..	..	..	8 578	21 773	28 213	38 396	44 281	55 257	60 682
2120 On an income tax basis	..	..	..	0	0	0	0	0	0	0
2200 Employers	..	73	1 694	9 409	23 557	30 856	41 518	47 846	58 712	63 780
Ind. works' insurance fund	..	73	550	1 876	4 431	4 632	5 436	6 062	7 346	7 539
Soldiers' annuity fund	..	0	0	0	0	0	0	0	0	0
Pneumoconiosis fund	..	0	0	0	0	0	0	0	0	0
Unemployment insurance	..	0	0	1 449	2 474	2 860	4 545	5 499	6 517	7 063
Veterans' relief fund	..	0	0	0	0	0	0	0	0	0
National welfare pension fund	..	0	430	4 340	9 383	11 052	13 958	15 895	19 155	20 631
Social benefit fund	..	0	0	0	0	0	0	0	0	0
Health Insurance	..	0	658	1 547	6 844	11 718	16 826	19 493	24 346	27 110
Teachers' pensions	..	0	56	197	425	594	753	897	1 348	1 437
Government employees pensions	..	0	0	0	0	0	0	0	0	0
2210 On a payroll basis	..	..	..	9 409	23 557	30 856	41 518	47 846	58 712	63 780
2220 On an income tax basis	..	..	..	0	0	0	0	0	0	0
2300 Self-employed or non-employed	..	0	602	4 772	8 258	10 021	11 682	12 566	14 691	15 609
2310 On a payroll basis	..	..	0	0	0	0	0	0	0	0
2320 On an income tax basis	..	..	602	4 772	8 258	10 021	11 682	12 566	14 691	15 609
2400 Unallocable between 2100, 2200 and 2300	..	0	0	0	0	0	0	0	0	0
2410 On a payroll basis	..	..	..	..	..	..	..	..	..	..
2420 On an income tax basis	..	..	..	..	..	..	..	..	..	..
3000 Taxes on payroll and workforce	..	**34**	**153**	**258**	**619**	**714**	**981**	**1 122**	**1 492**	**1 597**
Workshop tax on workforce (local)	..	31	124	258	619	714	981	1 122	1 492	1 597
Vocational training promotion fund	..	3	29	0	0	0	0	0	0	0
4000 Taxes on property	..	**537**	**4 389**	**16 846**	**33 109**	**33 516**	**35 847**	**48 625**	**58 811**	**59 732**

	1965	1980	1990	2000	2007	2010	2013	2015	2018	2019
4100 Recurrent taxes on immovable property	..	183	980	3 385	9 196	9 270	10 809	12 486	15 589	17 750
Property tax (local)	..	119	227	728	3 755	4 817	8 267	9 294	11 532	12 677
City planning tax on urban real estate (local)	..	51	244	815	1 883	2 465	0	0	0	0
Community facilities tax (local)	..	13	86	341	543	650	912	1 351	1 626	1 681
Tax on excessive land holdings (local)	..	0	1	0	0	0	0	0	0	0
Tax on aggregate land holdings (local)	..	0	400	1 282	5	0	0	0	0	0
Rural dev. tax on local agg. land holdings tax	..	0	0	81	1	0	0	0	0	0
Tax on excessively increased land value	..	0	0	0	0	0	0	0	0	0
Comprehensive real estate tax	..	0	0	0	2 414	1 029	1 224	1 399	1 873	2 671
Rural dev. tax on comprehensive real estate tax	..	0	0	0	483	208	250	267	356	505
4110 Households	..	..	0	0	0	0	0	0	0	0
4120 Others	..	..	22	138	112	101	156	175	202	216
Workshop tax on property (local)	..	..	22	138	112	101	156	175	202	216
4200 Recurrent taxes on net wealth	..	0	0	0	0	0	0	0	0	0
4210 Individual	..	..	..	..	..	..	..	..	..	..
4220 Corporate	..	..	..	..	..	..	..	..	..	..
4300 Estate, inheritance and gift taxes	..	12	354	989	2 842	3 076	4 290	5 044	7 359	8 329
4310 Estate and inheritance taxes	..	5	85	449	1 059	1 203	1 587	1 944	2 832	3 154
Inheritance tax	..	3	71	449	1 059	1 203	1 587	1 944	2 832	3 154
Defence tax on inheritance tax	..	2	14	0	0	0	0	0	0	0
4320 Gift taxes	..	7	269	540	1 783	1 873	2 703	3 100	4 527	5 175
Gift tax	..	7	225	540	1 783	1 873	2 703	3 100	4 527	5 175
Defence tax on gift tax	..	0	44	0	0	0	0	0	0	0
4400 Taxes on financial and capital transactions	..	319	2 960	11 935	21 071	21 170	20 748	31 095	35 863	33 653
Registration tax (local)	..	122	1 378	4 528	7 254	7 370	1 312	1 831	1 718	1 837
Registration tax	..	0	0	0	0	0	0	0	0	0
Defence tax on registration tax	..	0	0	0	0	0	0	0	0	0
Rural dev. tax on local acquisition tax	..	0	0	246	627	632	874	969	993	947
Rural dev. tax on local registration tax	..	0	0	66	143	144	1	1	0	0
Securities transactions tax	..	0	224	2 736	3 469	3 667	3 077	4 670	6 241	4 473
Rural dev. tax on securities transaction tax	..	0	0	823	1 729	2 010	1 529	1 861	2 217	1 635
Acquisition tax (local)	..	163	1 165	3 148	7 261	6 825	13 318	20 810	23 813	23 915
Stamp tax	..	34	193	388	588	522	637	953	881	846
4500 Non-recurrent taxes	..	22	95	537	0	0	0	0	0	0
Asset revaluation tax	..	22	95	537	..	..	..	..	..	..
4510 On net wealth	..	..	0	0	..	..	..	..	..	..
4520 Other non-recurrent taxes	..	..	0	0	..	..	..	..	..	..
4600 Other recurrent taxes on property	..	0	0	0	0	0	0	0	0	0
5000 Taxes on goods and services	**..**	**4 190**	**16 497**	**52 271**	**80 861**	**99 769**	**106 717**	**110 326**	**133 095**	**135 276**
5100 Taxes on production, sale, transfer, etc.	..	4 114	16 024	50 023	78 414	96 573	99 970	103 254	125 207	127 551
5110 General taxes	..	1 471	6 964	23 212	40 942	51 800	59 105	60 162	77 471	82 174
5111 Value added taxes	..	1 471	6 964	23 212	40 942	51 800	59 105	60 162	77 471	82 174
Value added tax	..	1 471	6 964	23 212	40 942	51 800	59 105	60 162	77 471	82 174
5112 Sales tax	..	0	0	0	0	0	0	0	0	0
Business tax	..	..	..	..	..	..	..	..	..	..
5113 Other	..	0	0	0	0	0	0	0	0	0
5120 Taxes on specific goods and services	..	2 643	9 059	26 811	37 472	44 773	40 865	43 092	47 736	45 377
5121 Excise duties	..	1 029	4 924	18 155	27 880	31 340	27 661	31 857	36 218	34 691
Commodity tax	..	0	0	0	0	0	0	0	0	0
Defence tax on commodity tax	..	0	0	0	0	0	0	0	0	0
Liquor tax	..	298	1 022	1 963	2 268	2 878	2 947	3 228	3 261	3 504
Defence tax on liquor tax	..	78	0	0	0	0	0	0	0	0
Education tax on liquor tax	..	0	81	516	580	724	764	808	788	844
Textile tax	..	0	0	0	0	0	0	0	0	0
Petroleum tax	..	0	0	0	0	0	0	0	0	0
Transport tax on petrol products	..	0	0	8 404	11 464	13 970	13 248	14 055	15 335	14 563
Education tax on transport tax	..	0	0	1 247	1 715	2 133	1 895	2 154	2 304	2 190
Electricity and gas tax	..	0	0	0	0	0	0	0	0	0
Special excise tax	..	583	1 912	2 985	5 161	5 066	5 484	8 001	10 451	9 719
Defence tax on special excise tax	..	70	337	0	0	0	0	0	0	0
Education tax on special excise tax	..	0	0	498	607	501	485	515	545	455
Rural development on special excise tax	..	0	0	37	54	24	56	61	56	58
Tobacco sales tax (local)	..	0	0	0	0	0	0	0	0	0
Tobacco consumption tax (local)	..	0	1 572	2 251	2 761	2 875	2 782	3 035	3 478	3 358
Motor fuel tax (local)	..	0	0	254	3 270	3 169	0	0	0	0
5122 Profits of fiscal monopolies	..	510	0	0	0	0	0	0	0	0
Monopoly profit	..	510	..	..	..	..	..	..	..	..

	1965	1980	1990	2000	2007	2010	2013	2015	2018	2019
5123 Customs and import duties	..	1 014	3 692	5 936	7 690	11 046	11 012	8 907	9 213	8 250
Customs duties	..	762	2 765	5 800	7 411	10 666	10 562	8 495	8 815	7 882
Defence tax on customs duties	..	248	919	0	0	0	0	0	0	0
Special customs duties	..	0	0	0	0	0	0	0	0	0
Tonnage tax	..	0	0	0	0	0	0	0	0	0
Education tax on imports	..	0	7	99	234	336	429	390	370	345
Rural dev. tax on customs exemptions	..	0	0	37	45	44	21	22	28	23
Previous year receipts	..	4	0	0	0	0	0	0	0	0
5124 Taxes on exports	..	0	0	0	0	0	0	0	0	0
5125 Taxes on investment goods	..	0	0	0	0	0	0	0	0	0
5126 Taxes on specific services	..	90	444	2 720	1 902	2 387	2 192	2 328	2 305	2 436
Telephone tax	..	50	262	1 457	0	0	0	0	0	0
Defence tax on telephone tax	..	33	0	0	0	0	0	0	0	0
Entertainment tax	..	0	0	0	0	0	0	0	0	0
Defence tax on entertainment tax	..	0	0	0	0	0	0	0	0	0
Entertainment tax (local)	..	0	0	0	0	0	0	0	0	0
Travel tax	..	0	0	0	0	0	0	0	0	0
Admission tax	..	0	0	0	0	0	0	0	0	0
Defence tax on admission tax	..	0	0	0	0	0	0	0	0	0
Education tax on banking & insurance	..	0	108	473	721	951	938	1 004	1 092	1 277
Horse race tax (local)	..	3	56	566	864	1 068	1 042	1 089	1 016	970
Rural dev. tax on horse race tax	..	0	0	84	165	215	212	235	197	189
Butchery tax (local)	..	5	18	51	52	58	0	0	0	0
Regional development tax (local)	..	0	0	89	100	95	0	0	0	0
5127 Other taxes on internat. trade and transactions	..	0	0	0	0	0	0	0	0	0
5128 Other taxes	..	0	0	0	0	0	0	0	0	0
5130 Unallocable between 5110 and 5120	..	0	0	0	0	0	0	0	0	0
5200 Taxes on use of goods and perform activities	..	75	474	2 248	2 447	3 196	6 747	7 072	7 888	7 725
5210 Recurrent taxes	..	75	474	2 248	2 447	3 196	6 747	7 072	7 888	7 725
License tax (local)	..	18	48	241	77	76	0	0	0	0
Automobile tax (local)	..	57	426	2 007	2 370	3 120	6 747	7 072	7 888	7 725
5211 Paid by households: motor vehicles	..	..	..	..	..	..	..	..	..	..
5212 Paid by others: motor vehicles	..	..	..	..	..	..	..	..	..	..
5213 Paid in respect of other goods	..	..	..	..	..	..	..	..	..	..
5220 Non-recurrent taxes	..	0	0	0	0	0	0	0	0	0
5300 Unallocable between 5100 and 5200	..	0	0	0	0	0	0	0	0	0
6000 Other taxes	..	**150**	**259**	**4 907**	**8 155**	**9 974**	**10 399**	**9 642**	**11 514**	**13 269**
6100 Paid solely by business	..	0	0	0	0	0	0	0	0	0
6200 Other	..	150	259	4 907	8 155	9 974	10 399	9 642	11 514	13 269
Unallocable tax revenue	..	143	0	0	0	0	0	0	0	0
Previous year tax	..	0	213	1 474	2 965	4 449	4 774	3 435	4 430	5 873
Previous year tax (local)	..	6	47	474	672	654	601	392	540	719
Unallocable defence tax	..	0	0	-3	0	0	0	0	0	0
Education tax on local taxes	..	0	0	2 962	4 518	4 871	5 024	5 815	6 544	6 677
Total tax revenue on cash basis	..	**6 687**	**37 262**	**136 295**	**258 571**	**295 968**	**347 332**	**393 559**	**506 548**	**523 985**
Total tax revenue on accrual basis	..	..	..	..	..	..	..	..	..	..
Conciliation with National Accounts										
Additional taxes included in National Accounts	..	..	..	..	..	..	..	..	..	..
Taxes excluded from National Accounts	..	..	..	..	..	..	..	..	..	..
Difference in treatment of tax credits	..	..	..	..	..	..	..	..	..	..
Capital transfer for uncollected revenue	..	..	..	..	..	..	..	..	..	..
Voluntary social security contributions	..	..	..	..	..	..	..	..	..	..
Miscellaneous differences	..	..	..	..	..	..	..	..	..	..
National Accounts: Taxes and actual social contributions	..	..	..	..	..	..	..	..	..	..
Imputed social contributions	..	..	..	..	..	..	..	..	..	..
National Accounts: Taxes and all social contributions	..	..	..	..	..	..	..	..	..	..

.. Not available

Note: Year ending 31st December.

Data are on cash basis.

Heading 2000: From 1997 the contributions to the three funds (civil servant pension fund, private school teachers pension fund and medical insurance fund) are classified as security social contributions. The reasons for the change are that the contributions either became mandatory or the fund started to be managed by public authorities in that year, thereby meeting the OECD definition of social security contributions.

Heading 2200: From 2007, this includes long-term care insurance.

Source: Ministry of Finance and Economy, Ministry of Home Affairs.

StatLink https://stat.link/689ehs

Table 5.22. Latvia: Details of tax revenue, 1965-2019

Million EUR

	1965	1980	1990	2000	2007	2010	2013	2015	2018	2019
Total tax revenue	..	..	..	**1 995**	**6 401**	**5 162**	**6 695**	**7 334**	**9 076**	**9 505**
Total tax revenue exclusive of taxes collected for the EU	..	..	..	**1 995**	**6 362**	**5 137**	**6 667**	**7 286**	**9 016**	**9 459**
1000 Taxes on income, profits and capital gains	..	..	..	**480**	**1 857**	**1 292**	**1 690**	**1 833**	**2 049**	**2 026**
1100 Of individuals	..	..	..	376	1 287	1 116	1 320	1 445	1 742	1 978
1110 On income and profits	..	..	..	376	1 287	1 116	1 320	1 445	1 742	1 978
Personal income tax	..	..	..	376	1 287	1 116	1 320	1 445	1 740	1 978
Solidarity tax	..	..	..	0	0	0	0	0	2	1
1120 On capital gains	..	..	..	0	0	0	0	0	0	0
1200 Corporate	..	..	..	105	570	175	370	389	308	48
1210 On profits	..	..	..	105	570	175	370	389	308	48
1220 On capital gains	..	..	..	0	0	0	0	0	0	0
1300 Unallocable between 1100 and 1200	..	..	..	0	0	0	0	0	0	0
2000 Social security contributions	..	..	..	**669**	**1 774**	**1 554**	**1 933**	**2 030**	**2 658**	**2 911**
2100 Employees	..	..	..	167	479	389	531	585	779	847
2110 On a payroll basis	..	..	..	167	479	389	531	585	779	847
2120 On an income tax basis	..	..	..	0	0	0	0	0	0	0
2200 Employers	..	..	..	501	1 283	1 155	1 391	1 432	1 855	2 037
2210 On a payroll basis	..	..	..	501	1 283	1 155	1 391	1 432	1 855	2 037
2220 On an income tax basis	..	..	..	0	0	0	0	0	0	0
2300 Self-employed or non-employed	..	..	..	1	12	9	11	12	25	27
2310 On a payroll basis	..	..	..	1	12	9	11	12	25	27
2320 On an income tax basis	..	..	..	0	0	0	0	0	0	0
2400 Unallocable between 2100, 2200 and 2300	..	..	..	0	0	0	0	0	0	0
2410 On a payroll basis	..	..	..	..	..	..	..	..	..	..
2420 On an income tax basis	..	..	..	..	..	..	..	..	..	..
3000 Taxes on payroll and workforce	..	..	..	**0**	**4**	**3**	**3**	**3**	**3**	**3**
Risk duty of business	..	..	..	..	4	3	3	3	3	3
4000 Taxes on property	..	..	..	**76**	**195**	**157**	**221**	**246**	**275**	**283**
4100 Recurrent taxes on immovable property	..	..	..	63	106	128	173	197	223	226
4110 Households	..	..	..	0	0	0	22	24	37	40
4120 Others	..	..	..	63	106	128	151	173	186	187
Tax on property	..	..	..	63	106	128	151	173	186	187
Tax on land	..	..	..	0	0	0	0	0	0	0
4200 Recurrent taxes on net wealth	..	..	..	0	0	0	0	0	0	0
4210 Individual	..	..	..	..	..	..	..	..	..	..
4220 Corporate	..	..	..	..	..	..	..	..	..	..
4300 Estate, inheritance and gift taxes	..	..	..	0	3	3	5	7	10	11
4310 Estate and inheritance taxes	..	..	..	..	3	3	5	7	10	11
Duty for legacies and donations	..	..	..	..	0	2	3	4	8	9
Stamp duty for transactions made in Land Register in relation to legacies and donations	..	..	..	..	1	0	0	1	1	1
Duty for consolidation of ownership and legal cliens in Land Register anent legacies and donations	..	..	..	..	2	2	2	2	2	2
4320 Gift taxes	..	..	..	..	0	0	0	0	0	0
4400 Taxes on financial and capital transactions	..	..	..	13	86	26	43	42	42	45
Duties on transactions with privatization vouchers	..	..	..	0	0	0	0	0	0	0
Stamp duty for transactions made in Land Register, which have been collected from juridical persons, except legacies and donations	..	..	..	0	1	1	1	1	1	1
Duty for consolidation of ownership and legal liens in Land Register, which have been collected from juridical persons, except legacies and donations	..	..	..	4	27	13	17	18	18	19
Stamp duty for transactions made in Land Register, which have been collected from physical persons, except legacies and donations	..	..	..	1	8	1	2	2	2	2
Duty for consolidation of ownership and legal liens in Land Register, which have been collected from physical persons, except legacies and donations	..	..	..	7	51	11	23	20	21	23
4500 Non-recurrent taxes	..	..	..	0	0	0	0	0	0	0
4510 On net wealth	..	..	..	..	..	..	..	..	..	..
4520 Other non-recurrent taxes	..	..	..	..	..	..	..	..	..	..
4600 Other recurrent taxes on property	..	..	..	0	0	0	0	0	0	0
5000 Taxes on goods and services	..	..	..	**770**	**2 572**	**2 157**	**2 849**	**3 222**	**4 090**	**4 281**
5100 Taxes on production, sale, transfer, etc.	..	..	..	739	2 515	2 031	2 695	3 052	3 875	3 977
5110 General taxes	..	..	..	476	1 753	1 301	1 855	2 130	2 698	2 783
5111 Value added taxes	..	..	..	476	1 727	1 202	1 690	1 876	2 449	2 632
5112 Sales tax	..	..	..	0	0	0	0	31	0	0
Subsidised electricity tax	..	..	..	..	..	..	..	31	..	..
5113 Other	..	..	..	0	27	99	165	223	249	150
Mandatory procurement public service obligation fee	..	..	..	..	27	99	165	223	249	150

	1965	1980	1990	2000	2007	2010	2013	2015	2018	2019
5120 Taxes on specific goods and services	..	..	..	262	761	730	840	922	1 177	1 194
5121 Excise duties	..	..	..	232	626	645	742	807	1 041	1 068
Excise duty on alcoholic beverages	..	..	..	63	127	111	124	128	194	200
Excise duty on beer	..	..	..	4	15	25	24	27	53	54
Excise duty on oil products	..	..	..	124	359	360	388	428	536	542
Excise duty on tobacco	..	..	..	27	92	130	160	178	213	228
Excise duty on other products	..	..	..	14	32	18	24	25	16	17
Excise duty on coffee and non alcoholic beverages	..	..	..	6	8	13	14	14	16	17
Excise duty / Tax on cars and motorcycles	..	..	..	8	24	5	10	11	0	0
Excise duty on natural gas	..	..	..	0	0	1	22	20	23	22
Tax on electricity	..	..	..	0	1	1	1	2	5	5
5122 Profits of fiscal monopolies	..	..	..	0	0	0	0	0	0	0
5123 Customs and import duties	..	..	..	21	70	38	29	43	58	52
Customs duties	..	..	..	21	40	25	28	40	53	50
Levies on imported agricultural products	..	..	..	0	2	0	0	0	0	0
Excise duty of imported goods for omission for free turnover	..	..	..	0	28	14	2	3	5	2
5124 Taxes on exports	..	..	..	0	0	0	0	0	0	0
5125 Taxes on investment goods	..	..	..	0	0	0	0	0	0	0
5126 Taxes on specific services	..	..	..	10	66	47	68	72	78	74
Taxes on lotteries and gambling	..	..	..	7	42	22	29	32	44	47
Financial stability fee	..	..	..	0	0	0	5	4	10	7
Passenger departure duty	..	..	..	3	0	0	0	0	0	0
Contributions to the EU Single Resolution Fund	..	..	..	0	0	0	0	8	7	6
Contributions to the fund for the protection of the insured	..	..	..	0	1	1	1	1	0	0
Contributions to the deposit guarantee fund	..	..	..	0	22	24	32	28	17	14
5127 Other taxes on internat. trade and transactions	..	..	..	0	0	0	0	0	0	0
5128 Other taxes	..	..	..	0	0	0	0	0	0	0
5130 Unallocable between 5110 and 5120	..	..	..	0	0	0	0	0	0	0
5200 Taxes on use of goods and perform activities	..	..	..	32	57	126	154	170	215	304
5210 Recurrent taxes	..	..	..	32	57	73	140	142	168	171
5211 Paid by households: motor vehicles	..	..	..	12	16	34	48	54	62	64
Vehicle tax for vehicles which have been registered on physical persons	..	..	..	0	0	0	48	54	62	64
Annual vehicle duty for vehicles which have been registered on physical persons	..	..	..	12	16	34	0	0	0	0
5212 Paid by others: motor vehicles	..	..	..	0	20	22	45	46	53	52
Tax on cars belonging to enterprises	..	..	..	..	0	0	21	20	21	21
Vehicle tax for vehicles which have been registered on judical persons	..	..	..	..	0	0	24	26	32	31
Annual vehicle duty for vehicles which have been registered on judical persons	..	..	..	..	20	22	0	0	0	0
5213 Paid in respect of other goods	..	..	..	20	21	17	47	42	52	55
Duty for keeping animals	..	..	..	0	0	0	0	0	0	0
Income from lease of reservoirs and fishing rights and non-production use of fishing rights (fishing cards)	..	..	..	0	0	0	1	1	1	1
Business and professional licences	..	..	..	5	6	4	27	20	21	23
State duties and payments for issue of special permits (licences) and registration of documents that commensurate correspondence of professional qualification	..	..	..	1	0	0	0	0	0	0
Lottery and gambling state duty	..	..	..	1	4	2	2	2	4	4
Gambling equipment marking duty	..	..	..	0	1	1	0	0	0	0
Payment for rental of commercial fishing rights	..	..	..	0	0	0	0	1	1	1
Lottery of goods and services organization duty	..	..	..	2	0	0	0	0	0	0
State duty for using numerative rights	..	..	..	0	0	0	0	0	0	0
State duty for keeping oil products` security reserves	..	..	..	0	0	0	24	16	16	19
Tax on natural resources	..	..	..	15	15	12	19	22	30	30
5220 Non-recurrent taxes	..	..	..	0	0	53	14	28	47	133
Revenue from state-owned greenhouse gas emission unit trade	..	..	..	..	..	53	14	0	0	0
Payment for emission quota trading	..	..	..	..	..	0	0	11	20	105
The fee for the appeal of procurement	..	..	..	..	..	0	0	0	0	0
Toll for the use of motorways	..	..	..	..	..	0	0	17	27	28
5300 Unallocable between 5100 and 5200	..	..	..	0	0	0	0	0	0	0
6000 Other taxes	**..**	**..**	**..**	**0**	**0**	**0**	**0**	**0**	**0**	**0**
6100 Paid solely by business	..	..	..	..	..	..	..	..	..	..
6200 Other	..	..	..	..	..	..	..	..	..	..
Memorandum items										
Customs duties collected on behalf of the EU	..	..	..	..	37	25	28	40	53	40
SRF contributions collected on behalf of the EU	..	..	..	..	..	..	..	8	7	6
Total tax revenue on cash basis	**..**	**..**	**..**	**..**	**..**	**..**	**..**	**..**	**..**	**..**

	1965	1980	1990	2000	2007	2010	2013	2015	2018	2019
Total tax revenue on accrual basis	..	..	..	**1 995**	**6 401**	**5 162**	**6 695**	**7 334**	**9 076**	**9 505**
Conciliation with National Accounts										
Additional taxes included in National Accounts	..	..	..	14	1	1	0	0	0	0
Taxes excluded from National Accounts	..	..	..	0	0	0	0	0	..	..
Difference in treatment of tax credits	..	..	..	0	0	0	0	0	..	..
Capital transfer for uncollected revenue	..	..	..	0	0	0	0	0	..	..
Voluntary social security contributions	..	..	..	0	0	0	0	0	0	0
Miscellaneous differences	..	..	..	0	0	0	0	0	..	..
National Accounts: Taxes and actual social contributions	..	..	..	2 009	6 402	5 163	6 695	7 334	9 076	9 505
Imputed social contributions	..	..	..	12	51	36	59	80	108	149
National Accounts: Taxes and all social contributions	..	..	..	2 022	6 453	5 199	6 754	7 415	9 184	9 653

.. Not available

Note: Year ending 31st December.

Data on accrual basis.

Source: Ministry of Finance.

StatLink https://stat.link/6gfeym

Table 5.23. Lithuania: Details of tax revenue, 1965-2019

Million EUR

	1965	1980	1990	2000	2007	2010	2013	2015	2018	2019
Total tax revenue	..	..	..	**4 154**	**8 730**	**7 961**	**9 377**	**10 727**	**13 759**	**14 780**
Total tax revenue exclusive of taxes collected for the EU	..	..	..	**4 154**	**8 656**	**7 908**	**9 370**	**10 716**	**13 637**	**14 650**
1000 Taxes on income, profits and capital gains	..	..	..	**1 111**	**2 625**	**1 281**	**1 726**	**2 013**	**2 625**	**4 288**
1100 Of individuals	..	..	..	1 020	1 891	1 005	1 250	1 440	1 933	3 529
1110 On income and profits	..	..	..	1 020	1 810	972	1 226	1 390	1 847	3 529
Tax on payroll and workforce	..	..	..	950	1 628	793	1 008	1 148	1 416	2 990
Tax on income from individual activities	..	..	..	40	81	36	48	55	83	110
Tax on capital income	..	..	..	31	102	143	170	187	348	429
1120 On capital gains	..	..	..	0	81	33	24	50	86	0
1200 Corporate	..	..	..	90	734	276	477	574	691	759
1210 On profits	..	..	..	90	734	276	477	574	691	759
1220 On capital gains	..	..	..	0	0	0	0	0	0	0
1300 Unallocable between 1100 and 1200	..	..	..	0	0	0	0	0	0	0
2000 Social security contributions	..	..	..	**1 362**	**2 643**	**3 293**	**3 791**	**4 338**	**5 752**	**4 706**
2100 Employees	..	..	..	107	233	641	763	873	1 156	3 574
2110 On a payroll basis	..	..	..	107	233	641	763	873	1 156	3 574
2120 On an income tax basis	..	..	..	0	0	0	0	0	0	0
2200 Employers	..	..	..	1 119	2 180	2 109	2 526	2 916	3 894	359
2210 On a payroll basis	..	..	..	1 119	2 180	2 109	2 526	2 916	3 894	359
2220 On an income tax basis	..	..	..	0	0	0	0	0	0	0
2300 Self-employed or non-employed	..	..	..	135	230	544	502	549	702	773
2310 On a payroll basis	..	..	..	135	230	544	502	549	702	773
2320 On an income tax basis	..	..	..	0	0	0	0	0	0	0
2400 Unallocable between 2100, 2200 and 2300	..	..	..	0	0	0	0	0	0	0
2410 On a payroll basis	..	..	..	..	..	..	..	..	..	..
2420 On an income tax basis	..	..	..	..	..	..	..	..	..	..
3000 Taxes on payroll and workforce	..	..	..	**0**	**0**	**0**	**0**	**0**	**0**	**0**
4000 Taxes on property	..	..	..	**62**	**83**	**103**	**97**	**126**	**137**	**145**
4100 Recurrent taxes on immovable property	..	..	..	61	82	102	96	125	135	143
4110 Households	..	..	..	3	6	7	8	17	36	39
4120 Others	..	..	..	58	76	95	88	108	99	105
Tax on land from corporations	..	..	..	3	8	9	10	10	5	6
Tax on immovable property	..	..	..	55	69	86	77	98	94	99
4200 Recurrent taxes on net wealth	..	..	..	0	0	0	0	0	0	0
4210 Individual	..	..	..	..	..	..	..	..	..	..
4220 Corporate	..	..	..	..	..	..	..	..	..	..
4300 Estate, inheritance and gift taxes	..	..	..	1	2	1	1	1	2	2
4310 Estate and inheritance taxes	..	..	..	1	2	1	1	1	2	2
4320 Gift taxes	..	..	..	0	0	0	0	0	0	0
4400 Taxes on financial and capital transactions	..	..	..	0	0	0	0	0	0	0
4500 Non-recurrent taxes	..	..	..	0	0	0	0	0	0	0
4510 On net wealth	..	..	..	..	..	..	..	..	..	..
4520 Other non-recurrent taxes	..	..	..	..	..	..	..	..	..	..
4600 Other recurrent taxes on property	..	..	..	0	0	0	0	0	0	0
5000 Taxes on goods and services	..	..	..	**1 619**	**3 378**	**3 284**	**3 762**	**4 249**	**5 246**	**5 640**
5100 Taxes on production, sale, transfer, etc.	..	..	..	1 556	3 298	3 202	3 685	4 176	5 150	5 541
5110 General taxes	..	..	..	1 086	2 339	2 183	2 611	2 913	3 552	3 876
5111 Value added taxes	..	..	..	1 005	2 330	2 180	2 611	2 889	3 522	3 850
5112 Sales tax	..	..	..	0	0	0	0	0	0	0
5113 Other	..	..	..	81	8	3	0	24	30	26
Deductions from revenue according to the RoL on the financing of road maintence and development	..	..	..	81	0	0	..	0	0	0
Deductions from revenue according to the RoL Forestry Law	..	..	..	0	0	0	..	24	30	26
Turnover tax on goods	..	..	..	0	0	0	..	0	0	0
Deductions from Ignalina nuclear power plant income generated by sales of electricity	..	..	..	0	8	3	..	0	0	0
Turnover tax on publications of erotic and violent nature	..	..	..	0	0	0	..	0	0	0
Turnover tax on motor cars	..	..	..	0	0	0	..	0	0	0
Turnover tax on goods containing ethyl	..	..	..	0	0	0	..	0	0	0
5120 Taxes on specific goods and services	..	..	..	470	960	1 019	1 073	1 263	1 598	1 665

	1965	1980	1990	2000	2007	2010	2013	2015	2018	2019
5121 Excise duties	..	..	..	428	835	903	996	1 165	1 444	1 503
Alcoholic beverages	..	..	..	10	2	10	12	6	17	20
Manufactured tabacco	..	..	..	41	121	170	209	270	293	300
Oil and other oil products	..	..	..	230	451	487	534	619	807	835
Electricity	..	..	..	2	0	3	3	4	2	2
Luxury cars	..	..	..	1	0	0	0	0	0	0
Sugar	..	..	..	25	13	1	7	1	0	0
Other former minor excises	..	..	..	5	0	0	0	0	0	0
Wine and sparkling wine	..	..	..	6	23	30	31	36	43	48
Beer	..	..	..	24	38	44	38	50	86	84
Other alcoholic beverages	..	..	..	84	186	158	162	179	196	213
5122 Profits of fiscal monopolies	..	..	..	0	0	0	0	0	0	0
5123 Customs and import duties	..	..	..	41	61	53	0	0	116	122
Taxes on international trades and transactions	..	..	..	41	0	0	..	..	0	0
Imported sugar tax	..	..	..	0	0	0	..	..	0	0
Custom duties collected for the EU	..	..	..	..	61	53	68	99	116	122
5124 Taxes on exports	..	..	..	0	0	0	0	0	0	0
5125 Taxes on investment goods	..	..	..	0	0	0	0	0	0	0
5126 Taxes on specific services	..	..	..	0	64	63	77	98	37	39
Tax on lotteries and gambling	..	..	..	..	9	8	12	15	17	19
Contributions to the Guarantee Fund	..	..	..	..	11	5	12	16	0	0
Deposit and investment insurance tax	..	..	..	..	43	48	52	56	12	11
Resolution Fund	..	..	..	..	..	..	..	10	7	8
Other taxes on specific services	..	..	..	..	0	1	2	1	1	2
5127 Other taxes on internat. trade and transactions	..	..	..	0	0	0	0	0	0	0
5128 Other taxes	..	..	..	0	0	0	0	0	0	0
5130 Unallocable between 5110 and 5120	..	..	..	0	0	0	0	0	0	0
5200 Taxes on use of goods and perform activities	..	..	..	64	80	83	78	74	96	99
5210 Recurrent taxes	..	..	..	64	80	83	78	74	96	99
5211 Paid by households: motor vehicles	..	..	..	0	0	0	0	0	0	0
5212 Paid by others: motor vehicles	..	..	..	7	30	13	31	32	39	38
Car registration taxes	..	..	..	0	0	0	15	15	17	18
Conveyance taxes	..	..	..	7	30	13	16	17	21	20
5213 Paid in respect of other goods	..	..	..	57	50	70	47	42	57	61
Pollution taxes	..	..	..	6	18	7	19	13	22	20
Payments by households for licences (not for business purposes)	..	..	..	5	3	6	2	2	2	2
Tax on market place	..	..	..	2	0	0	0	0	0	0
State-imposed fees and charges	..	..	..	34	22	44	6	5	5	6
Other taxes on production	..	..	..	10	6	13	21	22	28	33
5220 Non-recurrent taxes	..	..	..	0	0	0	0	0	0	0
5300 Unallocable between 5100 and 5200	..	..	..	0	0	0	0	0	0	0
6000 Other taxes	**..**	**..**	**..**	**0**	**0**	**0**	**0**	**0**	**0**	**0**
6100 Paid solely by business	..	..	..	..	..	..	..	..	..	..
6200 Other	..	..	..	..	..	..	..	..	..	..
Memorandum items										
Customs duties collected on behalf of the EU	..	..	..	..	61	53	68	99	116	122
SRF contributions collected on behalf of the EU	..	..	..	..	..	..	..	10	7	8
Total tax revenue on cash basis	**..**	**..**	**..**	**..**	**..**	**..**	**..**	**..**	**..**	**..**
Total tax revenue on accrual basis	**..**	**..**	**..**	**4 154**	**8 730**	**7 961**	**9 377**	**10 727**	**13 759**	**14 780**
Conciliation with National Accounts										
Additional taxes included in National Accounts	..	..	..	0	0	0	0	0	0	0
Taxes excluded from National Accounts	..	..	..	0	0	0	0	0	0	0
Difference in treatment of tax credits	..	..	..	0	0	0	0	0	0	0
Capital transfer for uncollected revenue	..	..	..	-39	-9	-32	-17	-18	-9	-2
Voluntary social security contributions	..	..	..	0	2	2	3	2	2	2
Miscellaneous differences	..	..	..	0	0	0	0	0	0	0
National Accounts: Taxes and actual social contributions	..	..	..	4 115	8 723	7 932	9 362	10 712	13 753	14 781
Imputed social contributions	..	..	..	3	91	103	99	116	138	160
National Accounts: Taxes and all social contributions	..	..	..	4 118	8 814	8 035	9 461	10 828	13 890	14 941

.. Not available

Note: Year ending 31st December.

Data on an accrual basis.

Source: Ministry of Finance.

StatLink https://stat.link/90ihrm

Table 5.24. Luxembourg: Details of tax revenue, 1965-2019

Million EUR

	1965	1980	1990	2000	2007	2010	2013	2015	2018	2019
Total tax revenue	**266**	**1 543**	**3 671**	**8 510**	**13 456**	**15 117**	**17 777**	**18 830**	**23 707**	**24 749**
Total tax revenue exclusive of taxes collected for the EU	..	..	**3 654**	**8 482**	**13 432**	**15 099**	**17 761**	**18 777**	**23 554**	**24 584**
1000 Taxes on income, profits and capital gains	**95**	**667**	**1 476**	**3 106**	**4 654**	**5 467**	**6 274**	**7 011**	**9 391**	**9 678**
1100 Of individuals	66	417	884	1 573	2 677	3 156	4 061	4 716	5 599	5 917
1110 On income and profits	66	417	884	1 573	2 677	3 156	4 061	4 716	5 599	5 917
Personal income tax - fixed by assessment	27	106	184	258	389	540	666	721	751	782
Supplementary solidarity income tax	0	10	41	37	59	74	268	305	362	381
Tax on wages and salaries	36	287	601	1 177	1 909	2 136	2 797	3 227	3 904	4 146
Withholding tax on income from capital	2	11	52	88	188	315	223	313	488	516
Special tax on company directors fees	1	2	5	11	20	26	38	44	57	57
Tax on certain income of non-residents	0	1	1	2	1	1	1	1	1	2
Tax withheld on savings income (non-residents)	0	0	0	0	51	33	40	0	0	0
Withholding tax on interest	0	0	0	0	60	31	28	20	31	30
Crisis tax	0	0	0	0	0	0	0	0	0	0
Temporary budgetary balance tax	0	0	0	0	0	0	0	85	5	2
Tax withheld on contributions to a registered supplementary pension plan for self-employed persons	..	..	0	0	0	0	0	0	0	1
1120 On capital gains	0	0	0	0	0	0	0	0	0	0
Tax on betting gains	..	..	..	..	..	..	..	..	..	..
1200 Corporate	29	250	592	1 533	1 977	2 311	2 213	2 295	3 793	3 761
1210 On profits	29	250	592	1 533	1 977	2 311	2 213	2 295	3 793	3 761
Corporation tax	18	168	376	1 031	1 381	1 646	1 530	1 569	2 616	2 460
Supplementary solidarity corporation tax	0	2	8	43	58	61	113	120	177	192
Trade tax	0	80	209	460	538	603	569	606	1 000	1 110
1220 On capital gains	0	0	0	0	0	0	0	0	0	0
1300 Unallocable between 1100 and 1200	0	0	0	0	0	0	0	0	0	0
2000 Social security contributions	**86**	**443**	**1 011**	**2 224**	**3 710**	**4 387**	**5 132**	**5 548**	**6 483**	**6 854**
2100 Employees	32	175	388	993	1 691	2 017	2 308	2 498	2 970	3 159
2110 On a payroll basis	..	175	388	993	1 691	2 017	2 308	2 498	2 970	3 159
2120 On an income tax basis	..	0	0	0	0	0	0	0	0	0
2200 Employers	49	243	494	964	1 580	1 888	2 157	2 335	2 707	2 844
2210 On a payroll basis	..	243	494	964	1 580	1 888	2 157	2 335	2 707	2 844
2220 On an income tax basis	..	0	0	0	0	0	0	0	0	0
2300 Self-employed or non-employed	5	25	129	266	438	482	667	715	806	851
2310 On a payroll basis	..	25	129	266	438	482	667	715	806	851
2320 On an income tax basis	..	0	0	0	0	0	0	0	0	0
2400 Unallocable between 2100, 2200 and 2300	0	0	0	0	0	0	0	0	0	0
2410 On a payroll basis	..	..	..	..	..	..	..	..	..	..
2420 On an income tax basis	..	..	..	..	..	..	..	..	..	..
3000 Taxes on payroll and workforce	**2**	**10**	**0**	**0**	**0**	**0**	**0**	**0**	**0**	**0**
Payroll tax	2	10	..	..	..	..	..	..	..	..
4000 Taxes on property	**16**	**87**	**309**	**910**	**1 294**	**1 062**	**1 296**	**1 715**	**2 315**	**2 416**
4100 Recurrent taxes on immovable property	4	9	14	21	27	29	33	36	38	38
Taxes on ownership of lands and buildings	4	9	14	21	27	29	33	36	38	38
4110 Households	..	..	0	0	0	0	0	0	0	0
4120 Others	..	..	0	0	0	0	0	0	0	0
4200 Recurrent taxes on net wealth	7	44	172	633	878	831	980	1 318	1 692	1 844
4210 Individual	0	0	0	0	0	0	0	0	0	0
Wealth tax	..	..	..	..	..	..	..	..	..	..
4220 Corporate	7	44	172	633	878	831	980	1 318	1 692	1 844
Wealth tax	2	15	58	152	172	208	269	385	682	771
Holding tax	3	29	114	481	706	622	710	933	1 010	1 073
4300 Estate, inheritance and gift taxes	1	5	11	23	47	50	72	74	91	114
4310 Estate and inheritance taxes	1	5	11	23	47	50	72	74	91	114
4320 Gift taxes	0	0	0	0	0	0	0	0	0	0
4400 Taxes on financial and capital transactions	4	30	112	232	343	152	212	287	494	420
Registration taxes	4	26	94	208	288	116	164	221	385	319
Mortgage taxes	1	3	9	12	29	21	28	39	66	64
Stamp duties	0	2	2	5	7	5	7	8	8	9
Tax on contruction in dense sectors	0	0	0	0	1	1	1	2	2	3
Tax on sale of real estate	0	0	6	7	17	8	10	16	30	23
Mortgage tax on salaries	0	0	1	1	1	1	1	1	1	1
Building permits	0	0	0	0	0	0	0	0	0	0
Infrastructure tax	0	0	0	0	0	0	0	0	0	0
Authorisation taxes on oil tanks	0	0	0	0	0	0	0	0	0	0
Tax on secondary residence	0	0	0	0	0	1	0	0	0	0
4500 Non-recurrent taxes	0	0	0	0	0	0	0	0	0	0
4510 On net wealth	..	..	..	..	..	..	..	..	..	..

	1965	1980	1990	2000	2007	2010	2013	2015	2018	2019
4520 Other non-recurrent taxes	..	..	..	..	..	..	..	..	..	..
4600 Other recurrent taxes on property	0	0	0	0	0	0	0	0	0	0
5000 Taxes on goods and services	**66**	**336**	**868**	**2 260**	**3 784**	**4 180**	**5 052**	**4 528**	**5 489**	**5 772**
5100 Taxes on production, sale, transfer, etc.	62	327	848	2 229	3 709	4 105	4 969	4 442	5 392	5 675
5110 General taxes	33	179	443	1 127	2 231	2 616	3 399	2 946	3 503	3 699
5111 Value added taxes	0	179	443	1 127	2 231	2 616	3 399	2 946	3 503	3 699
VAT own resources	..	18	75	92	50	41	49	45	59	64
5112 Sales tax	0	0	0	0	0	0	0	0	0	0
5113 Other	33	0	0	0	0	0	0	0	0	0
Turnover tax	33	..	..	..	..	..	..	..	..	..
5120 Taxes on specific goods and services	30	148	404	1 103	1 478	1 489	1 570	1 496	1 888	1 977
5121 Excise duties	26	134	365	1 036	1 394	1 401	1 484	1 374	1 556	1 674
Excise duties on mineral oils	1	1	10	100	135	145	197	184	197	221
Excise duties on tobacco (part on national production)	..	0	8	24	66	70	85	81	146	159
Autonomous excise duties on mineral oils	..	76	173	414	559	536	530	495	532	551
Tax on the consumption of national alcoholic beverages and spirits	1	5	19	20	21	20	25	28	42	46
Excise duties on tobacco	..	40	141	407	418	422	445	394	430	462
Supplementary tax on fuel	..	0	0	59	145	132	126	117	128	135
Tax on control of domestic fuel	..	0	0	2	3	3	2	2	2	2
Excise duty on liquefied petroleum	..	0	0	0	0	0	0	0	0	0
Excise duty on benzol	..	0	0	1	1	1	1	1	1	1
Excise duties on imported alcoholic beverages	..	3	5	5	6	5	7	8	11	13
Excise duties on beers (national production)	..	4	2	3	4	4	4	5	4	4
Excise duty on fermented fruit beverages	..	2	3	0	0	0	0	0	0	0
Excise duties on fermented sparkling beverages	..	0	1	0	0	0	0	0	0	0
Excise duty on sugar	..	0	1	0	0	0	0	0	0	0
Excise UEBL	..	0	0	0	0	0	0	0	0	0
Excise duties on nationally produced alcoholic beverages	..	1	1	0	0	0	0	0	0	0
Excise duty on Kyoto	..	0	0	0	37	62	62	58	62	80
Excise duty on alcopops	..	0	0	0	0	0	0	0	0	0
5122 Profits of fiscal monopolies	0	0	0	0	0	0	0	0	0	0
5123 Customs and import duties	1	5	11	27	24	18	16	23	24	26
Levies on imported agricultural products	1	0	0	0	1	0	0	0	0	0
Customs duty	0	0	0	0	0	0	0	0	0	0
Customs duty + mobiles + C.E.C.A. + anti-dumping	0	4	11	27	23	18	15	23	24	26
Agricultural compensatory amounts	0	0	0	0	0	0	0	0	0	0
5124 Taxes on exports	0	0	0	0	0	0	0	0	0	0
5125 Taxes on investment goods	0	0	0	0	0	0	0	0	0	0
5126 Taxes on specific services	2	6	22	39	60	69	70	98	308	277
Tax on betting stakes	0	0	0	0	0	0	0	0	0	0
Tax on insurance	1	5	15	23	32	40	45	46	53	59
Tax on transport	1	0	0	0	0	0	0	0	0	0
Tourist tax	0	0	1	1	2	2	2	3	3	3
Tax on national lottery	0	0	3	4	3	3	0	0	0	0
Tax on casino gambling	0	0	3	9	21	23	21	19	20	22
Tax on bank notes	0	0	0	0	0	0	0	0	0	0
Entertainment tax	0	1	1	2	2	1	2	2	1	1
Contributions to FGDL	0	0	0	0	0	0	0	0	95	45
Contributions to FRL	..	..	..	..	..	..	..	29	129	139
Special tax for insurers in the interest of the rescue service	0	0	0	0	0	0	0	0	7	6
5127 Other taxes on internat. trade and transactions	0	0	0	0	0	0	0	0	0	0
5128 Other taxes	0	4	6	1	0	1	1	1	0	0
C.E.C.A.	..	3	4	0	0	0	0	0	..	..
Co-responsibility tax on milk	..	1	2	1	0	1	1	1	..	..
Co-responsibility tax on cereals	..	0	0	0	0	0	0	0	..	..
5130 Unallocable between 5110 and 5120	0	0	0	0	0	0	0	0	0	0
5200 Taxes on use of goods and perform activities	3	9	20	30	75	75	83	86	97	97
5210 Recurrent taxes	3	8	18	28	68	68	72	71	70	70
5211 Paid by households: motor vehicles	2	4	9	16	39	39	40	41	40	40
5212 Paid by others: motor vehicles	1	4	7	11	26	26	27	28	27	27
5213 Paid in respect of other goods	0	0	1	2	2	3	4	3	3	3
Tax on licenced premises	0	0	0	0	1	1	1	1	1	1
Ship registration tax	0	0	0	1	1	1	2	1	1	1
Dog tax	0	0	1	1	1	1	1	1	1	1
Tax on peddling	0	0	0	0	0	0	0	0	0	0
Tax on ships	0	0	0	0	0	0	0	0	0	0
5220 Non-recurrent taxes	0	0	2	2	7	7	11	15	27	27
Emission permits	..	..	0	0	0	0	5	7	18	17
Car registration taxes	..	..	2	2	7	7	6	8	9	10

	1965	1980	1990	2000	2007	2010	2013	2015	2018	2019
5300 Unallocable between 5100 and 5200	0	0	0	0	0	0	0	0	0	0
6000 Other taxes	**0**	**0**	**7**	**11**	**14**	**22**	**23**	**28**	**29**	**29**
6100 Paid solely by business	..	0	6	11	13	16	15	28	29	29
Supplementary tax on electricity	..	0	0	2	2	2	2	2	2	2
Tax on distribution of electricity	..	0	3	4	1	1	1	1	1	1
Tax on production of electricity	..	0	2	2	1	1	1	0	4	2
Tax on natural gas consumption	..	0	0	0	3	4	5	4	5	5
Tax on enterprise register	..	0	1	1	0	0	0	0	0	0
Tax concerning foreign affairs departments	..	0	0	0	2	5	5	4	5	5
Chancellery stamps	..	0	1	2	4	3	2	1	1	2
VAT reclassified as tax on production	..	0	0	1	1	1	1	1	1	2
Under-compensation of VAT (flat rate system)	..	0	2	0	0	0	0	0	0	0
Tax on water	..	0	2	0	0	0	0	0	0	0
6200 Other	..	0	0	0	0	0	0	0	0	0
Memorandum items										
Customs duties collected on behalf of the EU	..	..	11	27	23	18	15	23	24	26
SRF contributions collected on behalf of the EU	..	..	..	..	..	..	..	29	129	139
Non-wastable tax credits										
Non-wastable tax credits against 1110	..	..	..	..	..	..	..	198	194	191
Tax expenditure component	..	..	..	..	..	..	..	..	..	..
Transfer component	..	..	..	..	..	..	..	..	..	..
Total tax revenue on cash basis	**266**	**1 543**	**3 722**	**8 612**	**13 385**	**14 746**	**17 800**	**19 087**	**23 584**	**25 170**
Total tax revenue on accrual basis	**..**	**..**	**3 671**	**8 510**	**13 456**	**15 117**	**17 777**	**18 830**	**23 707**	**24 749**
Conciliation with National Accounts										
Additional taxes included in national accounts	..	..	0	0	0	0	0	0	0	0
Tax excluded from national accounts	..	..	0	0	0	0	0	0	0	0
Difference in treatment of tax credits	..	..	0	0	0	0	0	0	0	0
Capital transfer for uncollected revenue	..	..	0	0	0	0	-13	-1	-6	-10
Voluntary social security contributions	..	..	4	18	18	28	33	38	46	48
Miscellaneous differences	..	..	0	0	0	0	0	0	0	0
National Accounts: taxes and actual social contributions	..	..	3 675	8 528	13 474	15 146	17 797	18 867	23 747	24 787
Imputed social contributions	..	..	267	288	429	505	605	669	775	813
National Accounts: taxes and all social contributions	..	..	3 941	8 816	13 903	15 651	18 402	19 536	24 523	25 600

.. Not available

Note: The civil year ends December 31st.

From 1990 onwards, data are on an accrual basis.

Under the heading 2000, the difference between the total social security contributions and those collected by the social security parastatals corresponds to the levy for realignment of pensions operated on the remuneration and pensions of employees and former agents of P&T and BCEE; one of these establishments belonging to the "non-corporate and quasi-corporate sector" and the other to the "credit institutions sector".

Source: General account of the State.

StatLink https://stat.link/0yn3d2

Table 5.25. Mexico: Details of tax revenue, 1965-2019

Million MXN

	1965	1980	1990	2000	2007	2010	2013	2015	2018	2019
Total tax revenue	..	**771**	**102 005**	**767 216**	**1 382 103**	**1 716 243**	**2 165 501**	**2 953 480**	**3 797 888**	**3 995 654**
1000 Taxes on income, profits and capital gains	..	**230**	**34 673**	**276 548**	**554 099**	**683 604**	**957 213**	**1 230 555**	**1 671 513**	**1 694 143**
1100 Of individuals	..	..	..	..	238 938	313 473	425 621	609 384	804 236	829 501
Tax on income of individuals	..	..	..	..	238 938	313 473	425 621	609 384	804 236	829 501
1110 On income and profits	..	..	..	..	..	..	..	..	..	..
1120 On capital gains	..	..	..	..	..	..	..	..	..	..
1200 Corporate	..	..	..	..	217 790	246 745	392 199	592 443	809 834	803 643
Tax on income of corporations	..	..	..	..	217 790	246 745	392 199	592 443	809 834	803 643
1210 On profits	..	..	..	..	..	..	..	..	..	..
1220 On capital gains	..	..	..	..	..	..	..	..	..	..
1300 Unallocable between 1100 and 1200	..	230	34 673	276 548	97 370	123 386	139 393	28 728	57 443	60 999
Tax on income	..	..	..	244 841	54 785	66 937	89 028	36 268	50 878	54 686
Tax on asset	..	..	..	13 913	15 670	-624	-1 325	-502	-396	-585
Credit on salary	..	..	..	17 794	23 177	9 708	1 274	993	1 172	1 290
Oil yields tax	..	..	..	0	3 738	2 296	3 210	0	0	0
IETU	..	..	..	0	0	45 069	47 205	-11 777	319	-195
Imposed by activity exploration and extraction of hydrocarbon	..	..	..	0	0	0	0	3 746	5 470	5 803
2000 Social security contributions	..	**109**	**17 165**	**138 223**	**236 727**	**277 459**	**351 993**	**409 249**	**509 087**	**552 058**
2100 Employees	..	..	..	..	..	..	..	..	..	..
2110 On a payroll basis	..	..	..	..	..	..	..	..	..	..
2120 On an income tax basis	..	..	..	..	..	..	..	..	..	..
2200 Employers	..	..	..	..	..	..	..	..	..	..
2210 On a payroll basis	..	..	..	..	..	..	..	..	..	..
2220 On an income tax basis	..	..	..	..	..	..	..	..	..	..
2300 Self-employed or non-employed	..	..	..	..	..	..	..	..	..	..
2310 On a payroll basis	..	..	..	..	..	..	..	..	..	..
2320 On an income tax basis	..	..	..	..	..	..	..	..	..	..
2400 Unallocable between 2100, 2200 and 2300	..	109	17 165	138 223	236 727	277 459	351 993	409 249	509 087	552 058
2410 On a payroll basis	..	..	..	138 223	236 727	277 459	351 993	409 249	509 087	552 058
2420 On an income tax basis	..	..	..	0	0	0	0	0	0	0
3000 Taxes on payroll and workforce	..	**8**	**1 797**	**11 217**	**28 071**	**36 911**	**53 042**	**70 221**	**93 303**	**101 284**
Substitute tax on salary	..	..	..	0	0	0	0	0	0	0
Payroll tax	..	..	..	11 101	20 277	27 813	41 184	69 866	92 833	100 798
Tax on remuneration to the personal work	..	..	..	65	7 578	8 841	11 645	152	270	298
Tax on professions and fees	..	..	..	36	68	71	50	106	111	121
Tax on operations by contract	..	..	..	15	148	186	163	96	90	67
4000 Taxes on property	..	**15**	**1 914**	**13 964**	**33 161**	**38 955**	**46 238**	**57 673**	**77 110**	**79 262**
4100 Recurrent taxes on immovable property	..	10	1 036	9 948	19 425	25 724	31 338	37 961	49 445	50 540
4110 Households	..	0	0	0	0	0	0	0	0	0
4120 Others	..	10	1 036	9 948	19 425	25 724	31 338	37 961	49 445	50 540
Property tax	..	..	..	9 948	19 425	25 724	31 338	37 961	49 445	50 540
4200 Recurrent taxes on net wealth	..	0	0	0	0	0	0	0	0	0
4210 Individual	..	..	..	..	..	..	..	..	..	..
4220 Corporate	..	..	..	..	..	..	..	..	..	..
4300 Estate, inheritance and gift taxes	..	0	8	0	0	0	0	0	0	0
4310 Estate and inheritance taxes	..	..	8	..	..	..	..	..	..	..
4320 Gift taxes	..	..	0	..	..	..	..	..	..	..
4400 Taxes on financial and capital transactions	..	5	870	4 017	13 736	13 231	14 900	19 712	27 665	28 722
Alienation of immovable property	..	..	..	1 763	1 076	1 122	1 271	1 595	1 823	1 939
Transfer of ownership of real estate	..	..	..	2 236	8 147	5 027	4 518	6 671	8 658	8 385
Purchasing property	..	..	..	18	4 513	7 082	9 110	11 447	17 184	18 397
4500 Non-recurrent taxes	..	0	0	0	0	0	0	0	0	0
4510 On net wealth	..	..	..	..	..	..	..	..	..	..
4520 Other non-recurrent taxes	..	..	..	..	..	..	..	..	..	..
4600 Other recurrent taxes on property	..	0	0	0	0	0	0	0	0	0
5000 Taxes on goods and services	..	**395**	**44 837**	**319 612**	**513 140**	**651 915**	**715 811**	**1 141 170**	**1 381 659**	**1 504 252**
5100 Taxes on production, sale, transfer, etc.	..	388	44 171	310 325	491 928	630 123	696 150	1 120 610	1 364 208	1 486 758
5110 General taxes	..	121	26 635	189 606	409 013	504 509	556 794	707 213	922 238	933 327
5111 Value added taxes	..	120	26 635	189 606	409 013	504 509	556 794	707 213	922 238	933 327
5112 Sales tax	..	0	0	0	0	0	0	0	0	0
5113 Other	..	1	0	0	0	0	0	0	0	0
5120 Taxes on specific goods and services	..	265	17 519	120 720	82 915	125 614	139 356	413 397	441 970	553 432
5121 Excise duties	..	45	10 072	86 163	47 008	86 098	104 111	361 538	358 577	470 993
Special tax on production and services	..	..	..	81 544	41 532	81 427	97 860	354 294	347 436	460 496
Tax on new automobiles	..	..	..	4 619	5 476	4 671	6 252	7 244	11 142	10 497
Tax on luxury goods and services	..	..	..	0	0	0	0	0	0	0
5122 Profits of fiscal monopolies	..	0	0	0	0	0	0	0	0	0

	1965	1980	1990	2000	2007	2010	2013	2015	2018	2019
5123 Customs and import duties	..	45	6 998	33 285	33 344	26 602	32 324	45 366	67 232	66 295
Step customs officer	..	..	..	423	1 156	2 071	3 065	1 270	1 690	1 554
Import taxes	..	..	..	32 861	32 188	24 531	29 260	44 096	65 543	64 741
5124 Taxes on exports	..	2	75	4	3	0	1	1	0	0
Tax on exports	..	..	..	4	3	0	1	1	0	0
5125 Taxes on investment goods	..	0	0	0	0	0	0	0	0	0
5126 Taxes on specific services	..	8	132	1 042	2 146	10 958	-967	1 763	8 692	9 196
IDE	..	8	..	0	0	8 022	-5 988	-3 323	-629	-405
Tax on lodging	..	0	..	504	1 059	1 384	1 890	2 561	3 945	4 254
Public entertainment tax	..	0	..	240	365	462	566	689	909	924
Tax on lotteries, raffles and gambling	..	0	..	267	705	923	1 213	1 416	2 947	3 403
Tax on commercials	..	0	..	4	17	166	203	210	1 231	376
Various indirect taxes	..	0	..	28	0	1	1 149	209	288	644
5127 Other taxes on internat. trade and transactions	..	0	0	0	0	0	0	0	0	0
5128 Other taxes	..	165	242	226	414	1 956	3 886	4 730	7 468	6 947
Mining fees	..	..	..	226	414	1 956	3 886	4 730	7 468	6 947
5130 Unallocable between 5110 and 5120	..	2	17	0	0	0	0	0	0	0
5200 Taxes on use of goods and perform activities	..	7	666	9 287	21 212	21 793	19 661	20 560	17 451	17 494
5210 Recurrent taxes	..	7	666	9 287	21 212	21 793	19 661	20 560	17 451	17 494
5211 Paid by households: motor vehicles	..	3	567	8 878	20 692	21 319	19 174	19 880	16 533	16 624
Tax on motor vehicules	..	..	..	8 878	20 692	21 319	19 174	19 880	16 533	16 624
5212 Paid by others: motor vehicles	..	0	0	301	275	281	357	439	640	645
Tax on federal auto transport	..	..	..	301	275	281	357	439	640	645
5213 Paid in respect of other goods	..	4	99	108	246	193	130	240	278	225
Sport fishing	..	..	..	40	98	59	50	62	73	73
Sport hunting	..	..	..	3	0	0	0	0	0	0
Tax on commercial activities	..	..	..	63	147	50	26	64	115	41
Trade in books and magazines	..	..	..	0	0	0	3	1	0	0
Tax on industrial activities	..	..	..	2	0	82	49	93	73	92
Mining	..	..	..	0	0	1	1	21	17	17
5220 Non-recurrent taxes	..	0	0	0	0	0	0	0	0	0
5300 Unallocable between 5100 and 5200	..	0	0	0	0	0	0	0	0	0
6000 Other taxes	..	**14**	**1 619**	**7 651**	**16 905**	**27 398**	**41 204**	**44 612**	**65 217**	**64 654**
6100 Paid solely by business	..	0	0	0	0	0	0	0	0	0
6200 Other	..	14	1 619	7 651	16 905	27 398	41 204	44 612	65 217	64 654
Accessories	..	..	..	5 504	12 403	22 206	25 301	23 211	45 864	41 063
Unallocable between 1000 and 5000 caused in exercices fiscal previous liquidation slopes or of payment	..	..	..	374	222	30	1 618	4 168	400	79
Additional state and local taxes	..	..	..	1 773	4 280	5 162	14 285	17 232	18 952	23 512
Non-wastable tax credits										
Non-wastable tax credits against 1000	..	..	..	..	59 065	40 344	41 800	43 806	49 101	50 649
Tax expenditure component	..	..	..	..	35 888	30 635	40 526	42 813	47 929	49 359
Transfer component	..	..	..	..	23 177	9 708	1 274	993	1 172	1 290
Total tax revenue on cash basis	..	**771**	**102 005**	**767 216**	**1 382 103**	**1 716 243**	**2 165 501**	**2 953 480**	**3 797 888**	**3 995 654**
Total tax revenue on accrual basis	..	..	..	..	..	..	..	..	..	..
Conciliation with National Accounts										
Additional taxes included in National Accounts	..	..	..	..	..	..	..	..	..	..
Taxes excluded from National Accounts	..	..	..	..	..	..	..	..	..	..
Difference in treatment of tax credits	..	..	..	..	..	..	..	..	..	..
Capital transfer for uncollected revenue	..	..	..	..	..	..	..	..	..	..
Voluntary social security contributions	..	..	..	..	..	..	..	..	..	..
Miscellaneous differences	..	..	..	..	..	..	..	..	..	..
National Accounts: Taxes and actual social contributions	..	..	..	..	..	..	..	..	..	..
Imputed social contributions	..	..	..	..	..	..	..	..	..	..
National Accounts: Taxes and all social contributions	..	..	..	..	..	..	..	..	..	..

.. Not available

Note: Year ending 31st December.

Data are on cash basis.

Source: Ministry of Finance, Economic Department.

StatLink https://stat.link/zap213

Table 5.26. Netherlands: Details of tax revenue, 1965-2019

Million EUR

	1965	1980	1990	2000	2007	2010	2013	2015	2018	2019
Total tax revenue	**10 860**	**69 982**	**104 419**	**166 824**	**220 950**	**227 911**	**238 488**	**255 348**	**300 298**	**319 236**
Total tax revenue exclusive of taxes collected for the EU	..	..	**102 926**	**165 227**	**218 926**	**225 943**	**236 479**	**252 272**	**296 931**	**315 652**
1000 Taxes on income, profits and capital gains	**3 884**	**22 998**	**33 689**	**43 256**	**62 463**	**63 581**	**59 085**	**70 849**	**88 769**	**99 003**
1100 Of individuals	3 008	18 383	25 806	25 116	41 414	48 992	44 830	52 405	61 660	68 968
1110 On income and profits	3 007	18 364	25 757	25 057	41 276	48 771	44 592	52 167	61 514	68 811
Income tax	1 359	2 895	2 455	-880	2 294	2 076	-1 337	-2 566	-1 082	4 858
Wage tax	1 466	14 984	22 258	24 433	37 729	46 102	45 546	53 953	61 573	61 757
Dividend tax	123	486	1 044	1 504	1 253	593	383	780	1 023	2 196
Directors tax	14	0	0	0	0	0	0	0	0	0
Inhabited house tax	45	0	0	0	0	0	0	0	0	0
1120 On capital gains	1	18	50	59	138	221	238	238	146	157
Tax on games of chance	1	18	50	59	138	221	238	238	146	157
1200 Corporate	876	4 615	7 882	18 140	21 049	14 589	14 255	18 444	27 109	30 035
1210 On profits	876	4 615	7 882	18 140	21 049	14 589	14 255	18 444	27 109	30 035
Corporate income and dividend taxes	876	4 615	7 882	18 140	21 049	14 589	14 255	18 444	27 109	30 035
1220 On capital gains	0	0	0	0	0	0	0	0	0	0
1300 Unallocable between 1100 and 1200	0	0	0	0	0	0	0	0	0	0
2000 Social security contributions	**3 342**	**26 641**	**39 075**	**64 522**	**77 072**	**82 732**	**97 372**	**96 426**	**108 049**	**109 298**
2100 Employees	1 659	11 018	24 109	35 305	40 918	41 637	49 327	48 213	41 775	40 695
2110 On a payroll basis	..	..	..	35 305	40 918	41 637	49 327	48 213	41 775	40 695
2120 On an income tax basis	..	..	..	0	0	0	0	0	0	0
2200 Employers	1 371	12 465	7 837	18 671	25 925	29 351	31 603	34 614	40 702	43 693
2210 On a payroll basis	..	..	..	18 671	25 925	29 351	31 603	34 614	40 702	43 693
2220 On an income tax basis	..	..	..	0	0	0	0	0	0	0
2300 Self-employed or non-employed	311	3 158	7 129	10 546	10 229	11 744	16 442	13 599	25 572	24 910
2310 On a payroll basis	..	..	..	0	0	0	0	0	0	0
2320 On an income tax basis	..	..	..	10 546	10 229	11 744	16 442	13 599	25 572	24 910
2400 Unallocable between 2100, 2200 and 2300	0	0	0	0	0	0	0	0	0	0
2410 On a payroll basis	..	..	..	..	..	..	..	..	..	..
2420 On an income tax basis	..	..	..	..	..	..	..	..	..	..
3000 Taxes on payroll and workforce	**0**	**0**	**0**	**0**	**0**	**0**	**0**	**0**	**0**	**0**
4000 Taxes on property	**476**	**2 509**	**3 816**	**8 797**	**10 363**	**8 770**	**8 084**	**9 768**	**12 142**	**12 179**
4100 Recurrent taxes on immovable property	111	1 021	1 711	3 094	3 488	4 241	5 249	6 382	7 370	7 385
Municipal immovable property tax	-59	821	1 398	..	..	..	..	..	..	..
Other municipal taxes	66	5	18	..	..	..	..	..	..	..
Contributions polder boards	44	195	295	..	..	..	..	..	..	..
Tax on land	59	0	0	..	..	..	..	..	..	..
4110 Households	..	..	..	1 806	1 642	2 058	2 802	3 741	4 513	4 417
Municipal immovable property tax	..	..	..	1 651	1 368	1 553	1 754	1 882	2 032	2 125
Contributions polder boards	..	..	..	155	274	429	492	514	584	606
Levies on social housing corporations	..	..	..	0	0	76	556	1 345	1 897	1 686
4120 Others	..	..	..	1 288	1 846	2 183	2 447	2 641	2 857	2 968
Municipal immovable property tax	..	..	..	893	1 319	1 488	1 686	1 809	1 952	2 041
Contributions polder boards	..	..	..	395	527	695	761	832	905	927
4200 Recurrent taxes on net wealth	86	517	554	824	30	23	1	0	0	0
4210 Individual	86	517	554	824	30	23	1	..	..	..
Property tax of individuals	86	517	554	824	30	23	1	..	..	..
4220 Corporate	0	0	0	0	0	0	0	..	..	..
4300 Estate, inheritance and gift taxes	117	336	522	1 483	1 877	1 721	1 730	1 614	1 731	1 777
4310 Estate and inheritance taxes	..	304	472	1 303	1 877	1 721	1 730	1 614	1 731	1 777
Estate tax	..	0	0	0	0	0	0	0	0	0
Inheritance tax	..	304	472	1 303	1 877	1 721	1 730	1 614	1 731	1 777
4320 Gift taxes	..	32	50	180	0	0	0	0	0	0
4400 Taxes on financial and capital transactions	162	635	1 030	3 396	4 968	2 785	1 104	1 772	3 041	3 017
Stamp duties	44	0	0	0	0	0	0	0	0	0
Registration duties	118	0	0	0	0	0	0	0	0	0
Tax on legal transactions	0	635	1 030	0	0	0	0	0	0	0
Real estate transfer tax	0	0	0	2 804	4 925	2 785	1 104	1 772	3 041	3 017
Tax on capital formation	0	0	0	592	43	0	0	0	0	0
4500 Non-recurrent taxes	0	0	0	0	0	0	0	0	0	0
4510 On net wealth	..	..	..	..	..	..	..	..	..	..
4520 Other non-recurrent taxes	..	..	..	..	..	..	..	..	..	..
4600 Other recurrent taxes on property	0	0	0	0	0	0	0	0	0	0
5000 Taxes on goods and services	**3 110**	**17 675**	**27 585**	**49 472**	**70 084**	**71 866**	**72 824**	**77 889**	**90 531**	**97 978**
5100 Taxes on production, sale, transfer, etc.	2 943	16 204	25 067	44 871	63 673	64 247	65 030	69 315	81 470	88 461
5110 General taxes	1 344	11 081	17 216	28 857	42 884	42 674	42 459	44 922	52 782	58 186
5111 Value added taxes	0	11 081	17 216	28 849	42 873	42 654	42 424	44 879	52 712	58 115
5112 Sales tax	0	0	0	0	0	0	0	0	0	0

	1965	1980	1990	2000	2007	2010	2013	2015	2018	2019
5113 Other	1 344	0	0	8	11	20	35	43	70	71
Turnover tax	1 344	..	..	..	..	..	..	..	..	..
5120 Taxes on specific goods and services	1 600	5 123	7 850	16 014	20 789	21 573	22 571	24 393	28 688	30 275
5121 Excise duties	880	3 789	5 985	13 755	17 724	18 392	17 309	18 020	20 995	22 039
Excise on spirits	129	463	422	397	335	331	306	314	342	331
Excise on beer	34	123	259	263	310	389	413	451	457	422
Excise on sugar	45	9	27	0	0	0	0	0	0	0
Excise on tobacco	307	839	948	1 590	2 136	2 437	2 228	2 222	2 669	2 547
Excise on wine	14	82	91	173	257	304	348	354	347	330
Registration tax on motor vehicles	0	613	1 189	2 875	3 647	2 096	1 159	1 462	2 270	2 347
Excise on soft drinks	0	59	186	216	155	156	154	207	278	269
Levies for nuclear reactor	0	0	0	0	0	0	0	0	0	0
Excise on petrol	310	1 280	1 684	3 151	4 010	4 086	3 960	4 109	4 472	4 574
Excise on other mineral oils	41	295	808	2 139	2 965	3 573	3 630	3 757	3 919	3 887
Levies on air pollution	0	27	304	0	0	0	0	0	0	0
Taxes on pollution/resources	0	0	68	462	456	655	144	345	379	502
Levies on energy	0	0	0	2 387	3 333	4 250	4 856	4 679	5 724	6 698
Other excise duties and consumption taxes	0	0	0	0	0	0	0	0	0	0
Other environmental taxes	0	0	0	34	35	15	10	14	27	22
Strategic stockpile tax on mineral oils	0	0	0	68	85	100	101	106	111	110
5122 Profits of fiscal monopolies	0	0	0	0	0	0	0	0	0	0
5123 Customs and import duties	702	971	1 375	1 310	1 679	1 732	1 756	2 266	2 504	2 709
EU levies on food products	338	295	168	0	0	0	0	0	0	0
MCA levy	0	9	0	0	0	0	0	0	0	0
Remaining import duties	364	667	1 207	0	0	0	0	0	0	0
Custom duties collected for the EU	..	..	..	1 310	1 679	1 732	1 756	2 266	2 504	2 709
5124 Taxes on exports	0	0	0	0	0	0	0	0	0	0
5125 Taxes on investment goods	0	77	0	0	0	0	0	0	0	0
Selective investment regulation levy	..	77	..	..	..	..	..	..	..	..
5126 Taxes on specific services	16	222	372	662	1 041	1 213	3 253	3 751	4 946	5 284
Tax on fire insurance	2	0	0	0	0	0	0	0	0	0
Entertainment tax	14	0	0	0	0	0	0	0	0	0
Tax on insurances	0	209	340	512	807	861	2 343	2 375	2 715	2 880
Tourist tax	0	14	32	83	125	131	164	206	288	342
Tax on games of chance	0	0	0	67	109	221	239	238	384	415
Flight tax	0	0	0	0	0	0	0	0	0	0
Bank levies	0	0	0	0	0	0	507	478	939	1 015
Contribution to EU Single Resolution Fund	..	..	..	..	..	..	..	454	620	632
5127 Other taxes on internat. trade and transactions	0	0	0	0	0	0	0	0	0	0
5128 Other taxes	1	64	118	287	345	236	253	356	243	243
ESCC levy	1	5	0	0	0	0	0	0	0	0
Sugar contribution	0	23	36	0	0	0	0	0	0	0
Milk levy	0	36	82	0	0	0	0	0	0	0
EU levies on food products	0	0	0	273	345	236	253	356	243	243
Sugar storage duty	0	0	0	14	0	0	0	0	0	0
5130 Unallocable between 5110 and 5120	0	0	0	0	0	0	0	0	0	0
5200 Taxes on use of goods and perform activities	167	1 470	2 518	4 601	6 411	7 619	7 794	8 574	9 061	9 517
5210 Recurrent taxes	165	1 470	2 518	4 601	6 411	7 619	7 751	8 410	8 800	8 993
5211 Paid by households: motor vehicles	27	463	799	2 288	3 211	4 084	4 008	4 470	4 686	4 752
Motor vehicle tax	27	427	744	2 288	3 211	4 084	4 008	4 470	4 686	4 752
Motor vehicle licence	0	36	54	0	0	0	0	0	0	0
5212 Paid by others: motor vehicles	132	604	1 044	554	760	976	959	1 069	1 121	1 137
Motor vehicle tax	132	590	1 026	554	760	976	959	1 069	1 121	1 137
Motor vehicle licence	0	14	18	0	0	0	0	0	0	0
Heavy motor vehicle tax	0	0	0	0	0	0	0	0	0	0
5213 Paid in respect of other goods	6	404	676	1 759	2 440	2 559	2 784	2 871	2 993	3 104
Dog licences	3	23	27	40	54	59	67	65	56	52
Commuter tax	0	5	5	12	21	25	29	29	28	35
Levies on water pollution	1	372	644	1 003	1 220	1 127	1 182	1 212	1 284	1 339
Permission to sell spirits	2	5	0	0	0	0	0	0	0	0
Sewerage charges	0	0	0	650	1 094	1 304	1 463	1 531	1 619	1 669
Levies on manure surplus	0	0	0	18	-4	2	4	3	4	7
Noise nuisance tax civil aviation	0	0	0	36	55	42	39	31	2	2
5220 Non-recurrent taxes	2	0	0	0	0	0	43	164	261	524
Emission permits	..	..	..	..	..	..	43	164	261	524
5300 Unallocable between 5100 and 5200	0	0	0	0	0	0	0	0	0	0
6000 Other taxes	**48**	**159**	**254**	**777**	**968**	**962**	**1 123**	**416**	**807**	**778**
6100 Paid solely by business	48	159	254	410	322	326	139	0	0	0
Administrative levies	48	159	254	410	322	326	139	..	..	..

	1965	1980	1990	2000	2007	2010	2013	2015	2018	2019
6200 Other	0	0	0	367	646	636	984	416	807	778
Employers tax	..	..	..	331	497	609	804	208	563	496
Tax revenue from Caribbean Netherlands	..	..	..	0	0	13	100	128	152	161
Other taxes on wealth	..	..	..	36	149	14	80	80	92	121
Memorandum items										
Customs duties collected on behalf of the EU	..	..	..	1 310	1 679	1 732	1 756	2 266	2 504	2 709
SRF contributions collected on behalf of the EU	..	..	..	..	..	..	..	454	620	632
Total tax revenue on cash basis	**10 860**	**69 982**	**104 419**	**165 503**	**..**	**..**	**..**	**..**	**..**	**..**
Total tax revenue on accrual basis	**..**	**..**	**..**	**166 824**	**220 950**	**227 911**	**238 488**	**255 348**	**300 298**	**319 236**
Conciliation with National Accounts										
Additional taxes included in National Accounts	..	..	..	1 400	0	0	0	0	0	0
Wage Tax reductions	..	..	..	1 400	..	..	..	..	..	..
Taxes excluded from National Accounts	..	..	..	0	0	0	0	0	0	0
Difference in treatment of tax credits	..	..	..	0	0	0	0	0	0	0
Capital transfer for uncollected revenue	..	..	..	0	0	0	0	0	0	0
Voluntary social security contributions	..	..	..	0	0	0	0	0	0	0
Miscellaneous differences	..	..	..	-70	0	0	0	0	0	0
National Accounts: Taxes and actual social contributions	..	..	..	168 154	220 950	227 911	238 488	255 348	300 298	319 236
Imputed social contributions	..	..	..	3 808	3 509	3 545	3 414	3 160	3 685	3 852
National Accounts: Taxes and all social contributions	..	..	..	171 962	224 459	231 456	241 902	258 508	303 983	323 088

.. Not available

Note: Year ending 31st December.

From 1999 data are on accrual basis.

Heading 2000: From 1998 the figures include some violuntary contributions and the breakdown between premiums paid by employees (2100) and by self-employed / non-employed has been estimated. This is also the case for the breakdown between premiums paid on a payroll or on an income tax basis for those years where both apply.

Heading 4100: From 1992, there was a structural break in the data for the 'municipal immovable property tax'. The tax ceased to be collected by the central government at that time and the figures are presented on a different type of statistical registration (no longer cash basis).

Heading 5110: Includes 358 millions of euros (1969) and 186 millions of euros (1970) in respect of deduction of turnover tax on stocks existing at 1st January 1969.

Heading 5213: Small amounts (less than 2.3 millions euros) of hunting and fishing licence receipts which should be classified here have been omitted.

Source: Social security contributions and local taxes: Central Bureau of Statistics.

Other taxes: Ministry of Finance.

StatLink https://stat.link/6v3gfz

Table 5.27. New Zealand: Details of tax revenue, 1965-2019

Million NZD

	1965	1980	1990	2000	2007	2010	2013	2015	2018	2019
Total tax revenue	**1 001**	**7 594**	**27 471**	**39 765**	**64 046**	**62 310**	**72 187**	**81 499**	**99 834**	**99 792**
1000 Taxes on income, profits and capital gains	**606**	**5 299**	**16 370**	**23 861**	**40 308**	**33 494**	**39 415**	**44 723**	**56 173**	**55 016**
1100 Of individuals	394	4 679	13 177	17 126	26 965	23 519	26 555	30 297	37 467	39 677
1110 On income and profits	394	4 679	13 177	17 126	26 965	23 519	26 555	30 297	37 467	39 677
1120 On capital gains	0	0	0	0	0	0	0	0	0	0
1200 Corporate	207	589	1 780	4 914	9 069	7 609	10 344	11 407	15 559	12 415
1210 On profits	207	589	1 780	4 914	9 069	7 609	10 344	11 407	15 559	12 415
1220 On capital gains	0	0	0	0	0	0	0	0	0	0
1300 Unallocable between 1100 and 1200	5	31	1 413	1 821	4 274	2 366	2 516	3 019	3 147	2 924
NRWT	5	24	277	760	1 506	467	427	733	651	570
Property speculation	0	0	0	0	0	0	0	0	0	0
Absentee income tax	0	7	0	0	0	0	0	0	0	0
Interest	0	0	1 028	990	2 699	1 704	1 643	1 660	1 659	1 528
Dividends	0	0	83	71	69	195	446	626	837	826
Other	0	0	25	0	0	0	0	0	0	0
2000 Social security contributions	**0**	**0**	**0**	**0**	**0**	**0**	**0**	**0**	**0**	**0**
2100 Employees	0	0	0	0	0	0	0	0	0	0
2110 On a payroll basis	..	..	..	..	..	..	..	..	..	..
2120 On an income tax basis	..	..	..	..	..	..	..	..	..	..
2200 Employers	0	0	0	0	0	0	0	0	0	0
2210 On a payroll basis	..	..	..	..	..	..	..	..	..	..
2220 On an income tax basis	..	..	..	..	..	..	..	..	..	..
2300 Self-employed or non-employed	0	0	0	0	0	0	0	0	0	0
2310 On a payroll basis	..	..	..	..	..	..	..	..	..	..
2320 On an income tax basis	..	..	..	..	..	..	..	..	..	..
2400 Unallocable between 2100, 2200 and 2300	0	0	0	0	0	0	0	0	0	0
2410 On a payroll basis	..	..	..	..	..	..	..	..	..	..
2420 On an income tax basis	..	..	..	..	..	..	..	..	..	..
3000 Taxes on payroll and workforce	**0**	**0**	**0**	**0**	**0**	**0**	**0**	**0**	**0**	**0**
4000 Taxes on property	**116**	**602**	**1 880**	**2 112**	**3 417**	**4 119**	**4 585**	**5 046**	**5 814**	**6 156**
4100 Recurrent taxes on immovable property	84	515	1 722	2 049	3 322	4 031	4 492	4 962	5 709	6 055
Local govt rates and services	81	503	1 550	2 049	3 322	4 031	4 492	4 962	5 709	6 055
Land tax	3	12	172	0	0	0	0	0	0	0
4110 Households	..	..	0	..	..	..	..	..	..	..
4120 Others	..	..	172	..	..	..	..	..	..	..
4200 Recurrent taxes on net wealth	0	0	0	0	0	0	0	0	0	0
4210 Individual	..	..	..	..	..	..	..	..	..	..
4220 Corporate	..	..	..	..	..	..	..	..	..	..
4300 Estate, inheritance and gift taxes	23	39	80	2	3	2	0	0	0	0
4310 Estate and inheritance taxes	21	37	74	0	0	0	..	..	..	..
4320 Gift taxes	2	2	6	2	3	2	..	..	..	..
4400 Taxes on financial and capital transactions	9	48	78	61	92	86	93	84	105	101
Instrument duty	7	40	62	51	85	82	91	84	105	101
Cheque duty	2	8	16	10	7	4	2	0	0	0
4500 Non-recurrent taxes	0	0	0	0	0	0	0	0	0	0
4510 On net wealth	..	..	..	..	..	..	..	..	..	..
4520 Other non-recurrent taxes	..	..	..	..	..	..	..	..	..	..
4600 Other recurrent taxes on property	0	0	0	0	0	0	0	0	0	0
5000 Taxes on goods and services	**280**	**1 693**	**9 220**	**13 792**	**20 290**	**24 692**	**28 184**	**31 728**	**37 845**	**38 618**
5100 Taxes on production, sale, transfer, etc.	262	1 624	8 680	12 887	18 832	23 107	26 344	29 584	35 271	36 004
5110 General taxes	77	776	6 163	9 885	15 046	19 143	22 063	24 587	29 521	30 259
5111 Value added taxes	0	0	6 163	9 885	15 046	19 143	22 063	24 587	29 521	30 259
5112 Sales tax	77	776	0	0	0	0	0	0	0	0
Motor vehicles	..	231	..	..	..	..	..	..	..	..
Other sales tax	..	544	..	..	..	..	..	..	..	..
5113 Other	0	0	0	0	0	0	0	0	0	0
5120 Taxes on specific goods and services	186	849	2 517	3 002	3 786	3 964	4 281	4 997	5 750	5 745
5121 Excise duties	124	548	1 929	2 148	1 627	1 782	1 854	2 280	2 622	2 468
On alcoholic beverages	37	84	411	436	573	622	650	672	722	710
Beer	33	64	0	201	290	207	250	262	274	268
Wine	0	0	0	100	163	181	204	216	225	221
Spirits	4	20	0	135	120	234	196	194	223	221
Tobacco	33	99	568	764	159	220	273	362	483	485
Motor vehicles	0	0	7	0	0	0	0	0	0	0
Refined sugar	2	0	0	0	0	0	0	0	0	0
CA petroleum fuels	0	140	835	810	819	872	865	1 185	1 201	1 075
NRF fuel excise	49	121	0	0	0	0	0	0	0	0
Local petroleum fuels	0	18	21	27	30	32	31	33	190	175
CA mileage tax	0	0	0	0	0	0	0	0	0	0

	1965	1980	1990	2000	2007	2010	2013	2015	2018	2019
NRF mileage tax	3	0	0	0	0	0	0	0	0	0
Road user charges	0	68	0	0	0	0	0	0	0	0
Energy resources levy	0	20	87	111	46	36	35	28	26	23
5122 Profits of fiscal monopolies	0	0	0	0	0	0	0	0	0	0
5123 Customs and import duties	49	231	505	648	1 857	1 916	2 160	2 442	2 814	3 001
5124 Taxes on exports	0	0	0	0	0	0	0	0	0	0
5125 Taxes on investment goods	0	0	0	0	0	0	0	0	0	0
5126 Taxes on specific services	13	57	83	206	302	266	267	275	314	276
Lottery (national)	1	6	26	167	290	253	254	260	299	266
Lottery (overseas)	0	0	0	0	0	0	0	0	0	0
Racing	12	46	57	39	12	13	13	15	15	10
Film hire tax	0	1	0	0	0	0	0	0	0	0
Domestic air travel tax	0	3	0	0	0	0	0	0	0	0
5127 Other taxes on internat. trade and transactions	0	12	0	0	0	0	0	0	0	0
Foreign fishing vessels tax	..	0	..	..	..	..	..	..	..	..
Foreign travel tax	..	0	..	..	..	..	..	..	..	..
International departure tax	..	12	..	..	..	..	..	..	..	..
5128 Other taxes	0	0	0	0	0	0	0	0	0	0
5130 Unallocable between 5110 and 5120	0	0	0	0	0	0	0	0	0	0
5200 Taxes on use of goods and perform activities	18	69	539	905	1 458	1 585	1 840	2 144	2 574	2 614
5210 Recurrent taxes	18	69	539	905	1 458	1 585	1 840	2 144	2 574	2 614
Motor vehicle registration	7	47	154	181	226	172	187	214	227	226
Heavy traffic fees	8	0	285	532	851	1 016	1 205	1 381	1 673	1 716
Accident compensation levies	0	0	0	0	0	0	0	0	0	0
5211 Paid by households: motor vehicles	0	0	0	0	0	0	0	0	0	0
5212 Paid by others: motor vehicles	0	0	0	0	0	0	0	0	0	0
5213 Paid in respect of other goods	3	23	100	192	381	397	448	549	674	672
Local authority fees and charges	3	23	100	192	381	397	448	549	674	672
5220 Non-recurrent taxes	0	0	0	0	0	0	0	0	0	0
5300 Unallocable between 5100 and 5200	0	0	0	0	0	0	0	0	0	0
6000 Other taxes	**0**	**0**	**1**	**0**	**31**	**5**	**3**	**2**	**2**	**2**
6100 Paid solely by business	..	..	0	..	0	0	0	0	0	0
6200 Other	..	..	1	..	31	5	3	2	2	2
Non-wastable tax credits										
Non-wastable tax credits against 1110	..	..	..	1 057	2 568	2 794	2 582	2 352	2 766	2 831
Tax expenditure component	..	..	..	311	873	950	1 349	1 254	1 518	1 429
Transfer component	..	..	..	746	1 695	1 844	1 233	1 098	1 248	1 402
Non-wastable tax credits against 1210	..	..	..	0	0	0	0	0	0	0
Tax expenditure component	..	..	..	..	..	..	..	..	..	..
Transfer component	..	..	..	..	..	..	..	..	..	..
Total tax revenue on cash basis	**1 001**	**7 594**	**27 471**	**39 276**	**64 273**	**62 053**	**73 172**	**82 481**	**98 586**	**100 173**
Total tax revenue on accrual basis	**..**	**..**	**..**	**39 765**	**64 046**	**62 310**	**72 187**	**81 499**	**99 834**	**99 792**
Conciliation with National Accounts										
Additional taxes included in National Accounts	..	..	..	..	0	0	2 397	3 858	4 944	5 380
Taxes excluded from National Accounts	..	..	..	..	0	0	-4 955	-6 903	-7 859	-9 155
Difference in treatment of tax credits	..	..	..	..	873	950	1 349	1 254	1 518	1 429
Capital transfer for uncollected revenue	..	..	..	..	0	0	0	0	0	0
Voluntary social security contributions	..	..	..	..	0	0	0	0	0	0
Miscellaneous differences	..	..	..	..	0	0	461	-1 602	-3 325	6 760
National Accounts: Taxes and actual social contributions	..	..	..	..	64 919	63 260	71 439	78 106	95 112	104 206
Imputed social contributions	..	..	..	..	0	0	2 617	2 063	2 060	2 199
National Accounts: Taxes and all social contributions	..	..	..	..	64 919	63 260	74 056	80 169	97 172	106 405

.. Not available

Note: For the years before 1989 data are on a fiscal year basis ending 31st March. The figures provided for 1989 and onwards relate to the financial year ending 30th June of the following year.

From 1993, data are on accrual basis.

Heading 1000: Tax credits to exporters under the export incentives schemes are non-wastable, but that part of the excess of tax liability paid out to taxpayers is not identifiable.

Heading 1100: The figures up to 1969 include revenues collected by a social security income tax. The base of this tax was the same as the ordinary income tax base and the two have now been incorporated into a single income tax.

Heading 5121: From October 1986 incorporates that portion of the selective impost on wine, spirits, tobacco and motor vehicles which was formerly collected and reported as sales tax. The revenue collected on those imported goods which are subject to the equivalent of the domestic excise has been classified as excise duty. In this respect, there is a discontinuity between the excises recorded before and after October 1986.

Heading 5210: The other local authority licence fees include some small items which could be regarded as non-tax revenues.

Heading for non-wastable tax credits 1110 comprises four Family assistance tax credits. The total in item 1100 is net of the tax expenditure component but not net of the transfer component.

Source: Local Authorities Statistics, Department of Statistics, Wellington.

StatLink https://stat.link/ozbcvl

Table 5.28. Norway: Details of tax revenue, 1965-2019

Million NOK

	1965	1980	1990	2000	2007	2010	2013	2015	2018	2019
Total tax revenue	**16 842**	**133 499**	**301 812**	**627 989**	**987 278**	**1 083 337**	**1 222 890**	**1 195 354**	**1 399 094**	**1 424 058**
1000 Taxes on income, profits and capital gains	**7 316**	**55 837**	**106 290**	**284 189**	**474 460**	**512 244**	**558 171**	**475 374**	**584 283**	**580 056**
1100 Of individuals	6 671	38 018	79 068	152 013	219 726	256 544	304 409	335 199	354 726	370 400
1110 On income and profits	6 671	38 018	79 068	152 013	219 726	256 544	304 409	335 199	354 726	370 400
Employee social security contributions	1 305	0	0	0	0	0	0	0	0	0
Income taxes	5 366	38 018	79 068	152 013	219 726	256 544	304 409	335 199	354 726	370 400
1120 On capital gains	0	0	0	0	0	0	0	0	0	0
1200 Corporate	645	17 819	27 222	132 176	254 734	255 700	253 762	140 175	229 557	209 656
1210 On profits	..	..	..	132 176	254 734	255 700	253 762	140 175	229 557	209 656
1220 On capital gains	..	..	..	0	0	0	0	0	0	0
1300 Unallocable between 1100 and 1200	0	0	0	0	0	0	0	0	0	0
2000 Social security contributions	**2 009**	**28 205**	**79 362**	**132 170**	**204 473**	**243 002**	**292 461**	**325 130**	**357 317**	**377 427**
2100 Employees	0	6 639	25 345	45 162	68 518	81 032	98 124	112 662	124 519	131 039
2110 On a payroll basis	..	..	..	45 162	68 518	81 032	98 124	112 662	124 519	131 039
2120 On an income tax basis	..	..	..	0	0	0	0	0	0	0
2200 Employers	1 716	20 454	50 116	79 242	124 178	148 047	177 458	190 923	208 840	221 175
2210 On a payroll basis	..	..	..	79 242	124 178	148 047	177 458	190 923	208 840	221 175
2220 On an income tax basis	..	..	..	0	0	0	0	0	0	0
2300 Self-employed or non-employed	293	1 112	3 901	7 766	11 777	13 923	16 879	21 545	23 958	25 213
2310 On a payroll basis	..	..	..	7 766	11 777	13 923	16 879	21 545	23 958	25 213
2320 On an income tax basis	..	..	..	0	0	0	0	0	0	0
2400 Unallocable between 2100, 2200 and 2300	0	0	0	0	0	0	0	0	0	0
2410 On a payroll basis	..	..	..	..	..	..	..	..	..	..
2420 On an income tax basis	..	..	..	..	..	..	..	..	..	..
3000 Taxes on payroll and workforce	**0**	**0**	**0**	**0**	**0**	**0**	**0**	**0**	**1 976**	**2 011**
4000 Taxes on property	**523**	**2 295**	**8 887**	**14 422**	**26 601**	**28 547**	**34 810**	**34 021**	**43 744**	**45 651**
4100 Recurrent taxes on immovable property	100	431	2 216	2 724	5 571	7 109	8 879	11 177	14 205	14 748
4110 Households	..	431	2 216	2 724	2 149	3 024	3 693	5 437	7 446	7 680
4120 Others	..	0	0	0	3 422	4 085	5 186	5 740	6 759	7 068
4200 Recurrent taxes on net wealth	341	1 450	5 118	7 703	12 900	13 193	16 376	14 123	19 897	20 549
4210 Individual	235	907	3 692	6 869	10 746	12 169	14 039	12 902	15 645	15 968
4220 Corporate	106	543	1 426	834	2 154	1 024	2 337	1 221	4 252	4 581
4300 Estate, inheritance and gift taxes	45	122	446	1 273	2 576	2 377	2 246	295	73	44
4310 Estate and inheritance taxes	..	122	446	1 273	2 576	2 377	2 246	295	73	44
4320 Gift taxes	..	0	0	0	0	0	0	0	0	0
4400 Taxes on financial and capital transactions	37	292	1 107	2 722	5 554	5 868	7 309	8 426	9 569	10 310
4500 Non-recurrent taxes	0	0	0	0	0	0	0	0	0	0
4510 On net wealth	..	..	..	..	..	..	..	..	..	..
4520 Other non-recurrent taxes	..	..	..	..	..	..	..	..	..	..
4600 Other recurrent taxes on property	0	0	0	0	0	0	0	0	0	0
5000 Taxes on goods and services	**6 928**	**47 154**	**107 262**	**197 208**	**281 744**	**299 544**	**337 448**	**360 829**	**411 774**	**418 913**
5100 Taxes on production, sale, transfer, etc.	6 720	45 882	102 901	185 921	266 456	284 646	321 557	342 410	392 783	399 022
5110 General taxes	3 622	24 350	56 656	124 985	189 424	201 802	235 771	256 029	297 918	308 280
5111 Value added taxes	0	24 350	56 656	124 166	188 705	201 184	234 941	255 182	296 900	307 000
Value added tax	..	24 350	56 656	124 166	188 705	201 184	234 941	255 182	296 900	307 000
5112 Sales tax	0	0	0	0	719	618	0	0	1 018	1 280
5113 Other	3 622	0	0	819	0	0	830	847	0	0
5120 Taxes on specific goods and services	3 098	21 532	46 245	60 936	77 032	82 844	85 786	86 381	94 865	90 742
5121 Excise duties	2 338	14 914	37 453	54 871	71 047	76 328	78 515	78 845	84 000	79 654
Stamp duty on tobacco	392	1 076	3 750	6 806	6 815	7 768	6 375	7 219	6 863	6 313
Taxes on spirits and wines	449	2 013	3 454	5 217	0	0	0	0	0	0
Excise on beer	162	605	2 195	3 650	0	0	0	0	0	0
Excise on petrol	480	2 310	7 057	9 756	8 132	7 373	6 417	5 711	5 535	5 239
Vehicles transfer tax	395	2 761	4 554	10 956	22 898	21 835	22 229	19 355	15 916	14 418
Chocolate and sweets	123	247	551	789	1 078	1 173	1 261	1 324	2 277	1 458
Sugar	0	0	217	230	192	196	201	206	186	191
Non-alcoholic beverages	38	120	487	1 113	1 024	1 739	1 803	1 972	2 964	3 071
Electric energy	89	1 515	3 414	5 091	7 079	8 110	8 656	9 233	12 000	11 393
Oil and gas products	0	3 703	8 729	88	92	98	108	103	114	112
Sales of radio and tv sets	0	163	220	920	0	0	0	0	0	0
Mineral oil	0	113	1 098	490	685	1 419	1 383	1 986	1 851	1 912
Cosmetics	0	0	0	159	0	0	0	0	0	0
Recording equipment	0	0	92	35	0	0	0	0	0	0
Others	210	288	1 635	1 249	1 821	1 965	2 060	2 535	3 015	2 915
Taxes on alcoholic beverages	0	0	0	0	10 338	11 317	12 602	12 969	14 103	14 518
Excise on diesel	0	0	0	4 802	6 424	8 653	10 507	10 267	10 432	10 040
Tax on Co2 emissions, petroleum sector excepted	0	0	0	3 520	4 469	4 682	4 913	5 965	8 744	8 074

	1965	1980	1990	2000	2007	2010	2013	2015	2018	2019
5122 Profits of fiscal monopolies	31	395	751	2 534	2 902	3 433	3 751	3 869	5 089	5 168
Profits state wine monopoly	31	30	67	41	32	44	36	0	0	0
Norsk tipping	0	365	684	2 493	2 870	3 389	3 715	3 869	5 089	5 168
5123 Customs and import duties	634	697	1 360	1 944	2 132	2 505	3 111	3 305	3 396	3 480
Customs revenue	615	689	1 305	1 944	2 132	2 505	3 111	3 305	3 396	3 480
Loading and lighthouse dues	11	0	0	0	0	0	0	0	0	0
Other import duties	8	8	55	0	0	0	0	0	0	0
5124 Taxes on exports	7	105	227	0	112	151	177	178	260	322
5125 Taxes on investment goods	0	4 274	4 454	0	0	0	0	0	0	0
5126 Taxes on specific services	88	195	1 233	1 386	131	114	140	138	2 060	2 058
Excise on race tracks	9	25	15	88	119	114	140	138	136	127
Taxes on specific services	34	49	150	1 298	0	0	0	0	1 924	1 931
Pengelotteriet (national lotteries)	45	121	462	0	0	0	0	0	0	0
Excise on lotto games	0	0	606	0	12	0	0	0	0	0
5127 Other taxes on internat. trade and transactions	0	0	0	0	0	0	0	0	0	0
5128 Other taxes	0	952	767	201	708	313	92	46	60	60
5130 Unallocable between 5110 and 5120	0	0	0	0	0	0	0	0	0	0
5200 Taxes on use of goods and perform activities	208	1 272	4 361	11 287	15 288	14 898	15 891	18 419	18 991	19 891
5210 Recurrent taxes	208	1 272	4 361	11 287	15 288	13 423	15 603	17 635	17 416	17 554
5211 Paid by households: motor vehicles	88	458	1 789	4 435	6 699	7 157	8 007	8 400	7 559	7 613
5212 Paid by others: motor vehicles	108	696	2 072	1 346	712	539	494	352	337	335
5213 Paid in respect of other goods	12	118	500	5 506	7 877	5 727	7 102	8 883	9 520	9 606
CO_2 tax	0	0	0	3 047	3 385	2 166	3 293	4 906	5 296	5 478
Excise on pharmacies	6	32	59	105	153	80	78	99	61	74
Others	6	86	441	2 354	3 132	3 394	3 666	3 809	4 105	3 989
Tax on emissions of NOX	0	0	0	0	1 207	87	65	69	58	65
5220 Non-recurrent taxes	0	0	0	0	0	1 475	288	784	1 575	2 337
5300 Unallocable between 5100 and 5200	0	0	0	0	0	0	0	0	0	0
6000 Other taxes	**66**	**8**	**11**	**0**	**0**	**0**	**0**	**0**	**0**	**0**
6100 Paid solely by business	0	3	2	..	..	..	..	..	..	..
6200 Other	66	5	9	..	..	..	..	..	..	..
Non-wastable tax credits										
Non-wastable tax credits against 1210	..	..	..	..	994	1 229	1 576	2 959	4 029	4 200
Tax expenditure component	..	..	..	..	350	75	307	484	811	847
Transfer component	..	..	..	..	644	1 154	1 269	2 475	3 218	3 353
Total tax revenue on cash basis	**16 842**	**133 499**	**301 812**	**575 989**	**0**	**0**	**0**	**0**	**1 354 365**	**1 434 405**
Total tax revenue on accrual basis	**..**	**..**	**..**	**627 989**	**987 278**	**1 083 337**	**1 222 890**	**1 195 354**	**1 399 094**	**1 424 058**
Conciliation with National Accounts										
Additional taxes included in National Accounts	..	..	1 485	2 773	3 288	4 022	4 560	4 674	4 821	4 904
Taxes excluded from National Accounts	..	..	..	0	0	0	0	0	0	0
Difference in treatment of tax credits	..	..	..	0	350	75	307	484	811	847
Capital transfer for uncollected revenue	..	..	..	0	0	0	0	0	0	0
Voluntary social security contributions	..	..	..	0	0	0	0	0	0	0
Miscellaneous differences	..	..	..	0	0	0	0	0	0	0
National Accounts: Taxes and actual social contributions	..	..	..	630 762	990 916	1 087 434	1 227 757	1 200 512	1 404 726	1 429 809
Imputed social contributions	..	..	..	2 076	2 931	3 164	3 628	3 870	5 467	5 516
National Accounts: Taxes and all social contributions	..	..	..	632 838	993 847	1 090 598	1 231 385	1 204 382	1 410 193	1 435 325

.. Not available

Note: Year ending 31st December.

From 2000, data are on accrual basis.

Heading 5211: Up to 1971 this item contains motor vehicle licences paid by both households and enterprises.

Heading 5121: From 2005, taxes on alcoholic beverages include both 'taxes on spirits and wines' and 'excise on beer'.

Heading 5125: From 1998, revenue from taxes on investments goods is included in item 5121 "Others".

Source: Statistics Norway; National Accounts.

https://stat.link/0fjlx1

Table 5.29. Poland: Details of tax revenue, 1965-2019

Million PLN

	1965	1980	1990	2000	2007	2010	2013	2015	2018	2019
Total tax revenue	..	..	..	**247 064**	**412 656**	**454 660**	**530 086**	**586 263**	**748 375**	**808 080**
Total tax revenue exclusive of taxes collected for the EU	..	..	..	**247 064**	**410 945**	**452 961**	**527 935**	**583 369**	**744 464**	**803 617**
1000 Taxes on income, profits and capital gains	..	..	..	**50 268**	**93 795**	**91 026**	**103 567**	**117 078**	**156 984**	**172 539**
1100 Of individuals	..	..	..	32 415	61 471	62 901	74 216	83 974	112 659	121 932
Individual income tax	..	..	..	32 415	61 403	62 818	74 124	83 861	112 503	121 755
Tax on winnings from lottery or gambling	..	..	..	0	68	83	92	113	156	177
1110 On income and profits	..	..	..	..	..	..	..	..	..	..
1120 On capital gains	..	..	..	..	..	..	..	..	..	..
1200 Corporate	..	..	..	17 853	32 324	28 125	29 351	33 104	44 325	50 607
1210 On profits	..	..	..	..	..	..	..	..	..	..
1220 On capital gains	..	..	..	..	..	..	..	..	..	..
1300 Unallocable between 1100 and 1200	..	..	..	0	0	0	0	0	0	0
2000 Social security contributions	..	..	..	**97 411**	**141 457**	**157 432**	**204 600**	**225 711**	**280 462**	**305 354**
2100 Employees	..	..	..	42 808	52 437	60 790	83 405	92 046	116 919	127 377
2110 On a payroll basis	..	..	..	..	..	..	..	..	..	..
2120 On an income tax basis	..	..	..	..	..	..	..	..	..	..
2200 Employers	..	..	..	41 570	54 874	65 942	80 311	88 490	109 761	118 629
2210 On a payroll basis	..	..	..	..	..	..	..	..	..	..
2220 On an income tax basis	..	..	..	..	..	..	..	..	..	..
2300 Self-employed or non-employed	..	..	..	13 033	34 146	30 700	40 884	45 175	53 782	59 348
2310 On a payroll basis	..	..	..	..	..	..	..	..	..	..
2320 On an income tax basis	..	..	..	..	..	..	..	..	..	..
2400 Unallocable between 2100, 2200 and 2300	..	..	..	0	0	0	0	0	0	0
2410 On a payroll basis	..	..	..	..	..	..	..	..	..	..
2420 On an income tax basis	..	..	..	..	..	..	..	..	..	..
3000 Taxes on payroll and workforce	..	..	..	**1 628**	**3 081**	**3 720**	**3 998**	**4 028**	**4 720**	**5 928**
Rehabilitation fund contribution	..	..	..	1 508	2 860	3 370	3 633	3 621	4 344	4 737
Wage guarantee fund contribution	..	..	..	120	221	350	365	407	376	424
Receipts from employers' obligatory payments to the Fundusz Solidarnościowy	..	..	..	0	0	0	0	0	0	767
4000 Taxes on property	..	..	..	**10 584**	**17 116**	**19 068**	**23 120**	**24 637**	**27 850**	**28 993**
4100 Recurrent taxes on immovable property	..	..	..	8 404	13 515	16 399	20 747	22 206	24 325	25 201
Agricultural tax-local	..	..	..	720	906	969	1 666	1 579	1 486	1 527
Forest tax-local	..	..	..	96	157	165	228	230	304	298
Real estate tax-local	..	..	..	7 588	12 452	15 265	18 853	20 397	22 535	23 376
4110 Households	..	..	..	2 348	3 613	4 555	6 289	6 549	7 157	7 436
4120 Others	..	..	..	6 056	9 902	11 844	14 458	15 657	17 168	17 765
4200 Recurrent taxes on net wealth	..	..	..	0	0	0	0	0	0	0
4210 Individual	..	..	..	..	..	..	..	..	..	..
4220 Corporate	..	..	..	..	..	..	..	..	..	..
4300 Estate, inheritance and gift taxes	..	..	..	172	328	290	252	246	299	325
Inheritance and gift tax-local	..	..	..	172	328	290	252	246	299	325
4310 Estate and inheritance taxes	..	..	..	..	..	..	..	..	..	..
4320 Gift taxes	..	..	..	..	..	..	..	..	..	..
4400 Taxes on financial and capital transactions	..	..	..	2 008	3 273	2 379	2 121	2 185	3 226	3 467
Tax on civil law transactions and stamp tax	..	..	..	2 008	3 273	2 379	2 121	2 185	3 226	3 467
4500 Non-recurrent taxes	..	..	..	0	0	0	0	0	0	0
4510 On net wealth	..	..	..	..	..	..	..	..	..	..
4520 Other non-recurrent taxes	..	..	..	..	..	..	..	..	..	..
4600 Other recurrent taxes on property	..	..	..	0	0	0	0	0	0	0
5000 Taxes on goods and services	..	..	..	**86 880**	**156 683**	**182 820**	**193 776**	**214 162**	**277 278**	**294 143**
5100 Taxes on production, sale, transfer, etc.	..	..	..	84 885	151 804	176 044	188 331	206 197	268 295	281 787
5110 General taxes	..	..	..	51 615	97 848	109 717	116 607	125 895	172 264	182 147
5111 Value added taxes	..	..	..	51 615	97 848	109 717	116 607	125 895	172 264	182 147
5112 Sales tax	..	..	..	0	0	0	0	0	0	0
5113 Other	..	..	..	0	0	0	0	0	0	0
Turnover tax, of which:	..	..	..	..	..	..	..	..	..	..
On spirits	..	..	..	..	..	..	..	..	..	..
On fuels	..	..	..	..	..	..	..	..	..	..
On tobacco	..	..	..	..	..	..	..	..	..	..
5120 Taxes on specific goods and services	..	..	..	33 270	53 956	66 327	71 724	80 302	96 031	99 640
5121 Excise duties	..	..	..	27 170	49 376	62 016	66 310	70 632	82 140	83 854
On domestic excise products, of which:	..	..	..	24 213	45 752	58 935	60 774	62 442	77 377	79 127
On spirits	..	..	..	4 309	5 000	6 154	7 393	6 655	7 420	8 202
On fuels	..	..	..	11 056	22 128	26 545	28 184	29 874	41 434	43 078
On tobacco	..	..	..	6 143	11 973	17 348	18 126	17 788	19 574	20 752
On beer	..	..	..	1 758	2 975	3 303	3 473	3 547	3 414	3 328
On wine	..	..	..	459	378	315	219	246	213	218

	1965	1980	1990	2000	2007	2010	2013	2015	2018	2019
On other products	..	..	..	488	3 298	5 270	3 379	4 332	9 104	3 549
On imported excise products, of which:	..	..	..	2 957	3 624	3 081	5 536	8 190	4 763	4 727
On spirits	..	..	..	90	253	311	279	267	339	400
On fuels	..	..	..	2 031	2 045	1 051	3 481	5 650	1 233	966
On tobacco	..	..	..	18	214	114	62	86	41	45
On beer	..	..	..	26	12	14	43	53	52	64
On wine	..	..	..	71	106	133	149	139	172	181
On other products	..	..	..	721	994	1 458	1 522	1 995	2 926	3 071
5122 Profits of fiscal monopolies	..	..	..	0	0	0	0	0	0	0
5123 Customs and import duties	..	..	..	5 038	1 711	1 627	1 977	2 823	3 911	4 463
5124 Taxes on exports	..	..	..	0	0	0	0	0	0	0
5125 Taxes on investment goods	..	..	..	0	0	0	0	0	0	0
5126 Taxes on specific services	..	..	..	1 062	1 297	1 974	2 534	5 795	8 915	10 211
Taxes and payments of financial institutions	..	..	..	443	189	375	1 077	4 472	2 491	3 076
Gambling tax	..	..	..	619	1 108	1 599	1 457	1 323	1 900	2 319
Tax from some financial institutions	..	..	..	0	0	0	0	0	4 525	4 816
5127 Other taxes on internat. trade and transactions	..	..	..	0	0	0	0	0	0	0
5128 Other taxes	..	..	..	0	1 572	710	903	1 052	1 065	1 112
5130 Unallocable between 5110 and 5120	..	..	..	0	0	0	0	0	0	0
5200 Taxes on use of goods and perform activities	..	..	..	1 995	4 879	6 776	5 445	7 965	8 983	12 356
5210 Recurrent taxes	..	..	..	433	2 383	3 667	3 432	4 317	4 013	4 377
5211 Paid by households: motor vehicles	..	..	..	0	0	0	0	0	0	0
5212 Paid by others: motor vehicles	..	..	..	0	0	0	0	0	0	0
5213 Paid in respect of other goods	..	..	..	433	2 383	3 667	3 432	4 317	4 013	4 377
5220 Non-recurrent taxes	..	..	..	1 562	2 496	3 109	2 013	3 648	4 970	7 979
5300 Unallocable between 5100 and 5200	..	..	..	0	0	0	0	0	0	0
6000 Other taxes	**..**	**..**	**..**	**293**	**524**	**594**	**1 025**	**647**	**1 081**	**1 123**
Abolished taxes	..	..	..	0	0	0	0	0	0	0
6100 Paid solely by business	..	..	..	0	0	0	0	0	0	0
6200 Other	..	..	..	293	524	594	1 025	647	1 081	1 123
Memorandum item										
Customs duties collected on behalf of the EU	..	..	..	..	1 711	1 627	1 977	2 823	3 911	4 463
Total tax revenue on cash basis	**..**	**..**	**..**	**..**	**..**	**..**	**..**	**..**	**..**	**..**
Total tax revenue on accrual basis	**..**	**..**	**..**	**247 064**	**412 656**	**454 660**	**530 086**	**586 263**	**748 375**	**808 080**
Conciliation with National Accounts										
Additional taxes included in National Accounts	..	..	..	..	..	..	..	..	..	..
Taxes excluded from National Accounts	..	..	..	..	..	..	..	..	..	..
Difference in treatment of tax credits	..	..	..	..	..	..	..	..	..	..
Capital transfer for uncollected revenue	..	..	..	1 025	1 371	1 406	2 005	2 229	2 792	3 035
Voluntary social security contributions	..	..	..	..	..	..	34	49	45	46
Miscellaneous differences	..	..	..	..	..	..	..	..	..	..
National Accounts: Taxes and actual social contributions	..	..	..	246 039	411 285	453 254	528 115	584 083	745 628	805 091
Imputed social contributions	..	..	..	777	10 848	13 841	16 603	17 423	18 322	19 464
National Accounts: Taxes and all social contributions	..	..	..	252 943	422 133	467 095	544 718	601 506	763 950	824 555

.. Not available

Note: Year ending 31st December.

From 2002, data are on accrual basis.

Source: Ministry of Finance, Economic Department.

StatLink https://stat.link/cyn08i

Table 5.30. Portugal: Details of tax revenue, 1965-2019

Million EUR

	1965	1980	1990	2000	2007	2010	2013	2015	2018	2019
Total tax revenue	**99**	**1 798**	**14 825**	**39 705**	**55 885**	**54 541**	**57 913**	**61 788**	**71 109**	**73 818**
Total tax revenue exclusive of taxes collected for the EU	..	..	**14 675**	**39 501**	**55 695**	**54 363**	**57 769**	**61 630**	**70 752**	**73 465**
1000 Taxes on income, profits and capital gains	**24**	**355**	**3 805**	**11 691**	**15 546**	**14 585**	**18 664**	**18 762**	**20 114**	**20 242**
1100 Of individuals	..	..	2 350	6 768	9 328	9 637	13 119	13 149	13 312	13 580
Individual income tax	..	..	2 350	6 768	9 328	9 637	13 119	13 149	13 312	13 580
1110 On income and profits	..	..	0	0	0	0	0	0	0	0
1120 On capital gains	..	..	0	0	0	0	0	0	0	0
1200 Corporate	..	..	1 182	4 744	6 128	4 936	5 545	5 614	6 802	6 662
Corporate income tax	..	..	1 088	4 457	5 815	4 670	5 327	5 405	6 494	6 308
Local corporate income tax ("Derrama")	..	..	84	287	313	266	217	208	308	354
Other	..	..	11	0	0	0	0	0	0	0
1210 On profits	..	..	0	0	0	0	0	0	0	0
1220 On capital gains	..	..	0	0	0	0	0	0	0	0
1300 Unallocable between 1100 and 1200	24	355	273	178	90	12	0	0	0	0
Tax on wages and professional income	2	93	9	0	0	0	0	0	..	..
Industrial tax	7	108	129	0	0	0	0	0	..	..
Tax on income from movable capital	2	71	1	0	0	0	0	0	..	..
Property income tax	3	23	17	0	0	0	0	0	..	..
Agricultural income tax	0	0	1	0	0	0	0	0	..	..
Complementary income ax	4	43	58	0	0	0	0	0	..	..
Tax on capital gains	0	3	1	0	0	0	0	0	..	..
Taxes abolished by DL 442-A/88 and DL 442-B/88	0	0	0	0	0	0	0	0	..	..
Other	6	15	58	178	90	12	0	0	..	..
2000 Social security contributions	**22**	**531**	**4 026**	**10 168**	**14 305**	**15 462**	**15 139**	**16 182**	**19 131**	**20 550**
2100 Employees	8	203	1 470	4 286	6 344	6 670	6 403	6 992	7 691	8 172
2110 On a payroll basis	8	203	1 470	4 286	6 344	6 670	6 403	6 992	7 691	8 172
Compulsory employee's social contributions	8	203	1 470	4 286	6 344	6 670	6 403	6 992	7 691	8 172
2120 On an income tax basis	0	0	0	0	0	0	0	0	0	0
2200 Employers	13	318	2 413	5 882	7 961	8 792	8 736	9 191	11 441	12 377
2210 On a payroll basis	13	318	2 413	5 882	7 961	8 792	8 736	9 191	11 441	12 377
Employers' social contributions	13	318	2 413	5 882	7 961	8 792	8 736	9 191	11 441	12 377
2220 On an income tax basis	0	0	0	0	0	0	0	0	0	0
2300 Self-employed or non-employed	0	10	143	0	0	0	0	0	0	0
Compulsory social contributions by self-employed	0	10	143	..	..	..	..	..	..	..
2310 On a payroll basis	..	..	0	..	..	..	..	..	..	..
2320 On an income tax basis	..	..	0	..	..	..	..	..	..	..
2400 Unallocable between 2100, 2200 and 2300	0	0	0	0	0	0	0	0	0	0
2410 On a payroll basis	..	..	..	..	..	..	..	..	..	..
2420 On an income tax basis	..	..	..	..	..	..	..	..	..	..
3000 Taxes on payroll and workforce	**1**	**47**	**0**	**0**	**0**	**0**	**0**	**0**	**0**	**0**
Contributions for Unemployment Fund	1	47	..	..	..	..	..	..	..	..
Stamp duty on wages and salaries	0	0	..	..	..	..	..	..	..	..
4000 Taxes on property	**5**	**26**	**402**	**1 468**	**2 330**	**2 028**	**1 915**	**2 307**	**2 965**	**3 046**
4100 Recurrent taxes on immovable property	0	0	133	508	1 008	1 112	1 339	1 535	1 644	1 664
Real estate tax	..	..	133	508	1 008	1 112	1 339	1 535	1 644	1 664
4110 Households	..	..	0	0	0	0	0	0	0	0
4120 Others	..	..	0	0	0	0	0	0	0	0
4200 Recurrent taxes on net wealth	0	0	0	0	0	0	0	0	0	0
4210 Individual	..	..	..	..	..	..	..	..	..	..
4220 Corporate	..	..	..	..	..	..	..	..	..	..
4300 Estate, inheritance and gift taxes	2	4	74	103	10	85	2	0	0	0
Inheritance and gift taxes	2	4	74	103	10	85	2	..	0	0
4310 Estate and inheritance taxes	..	..	0	103	10	85	2	..	0	0
4320 Gift taxes	..	..	0	0	0	0	0	..	0	0
4400 Taxes on financial and capital transactions	2	21	195	857	1 312	831	575	772	1 321	1 383
Real estate transfer tax	2	21	195	674	973	595	356	569	976	1 011
Stamp duty on registrations and mortgages	0	0	0	34	45	35	28	49	15	17
Stamp duty on the raising of capital	0	0	0	0	9	1	0	0	0	0
Stamp duty on real estate transactions	0	0	0	150	285	201	191	154	330	355
4500 Non-recurrent taxes	0	0	0	0	0	0	0	0	0	0
4510 On net wealth	..	..	..	..	..	..	..	..	..	..
4520 Other non-recurrent taxes	..	..	..	..	..	..	..	..	..	..
4600 Other recurrent taxes on property	0	0	0	0	0	0	0	0	0	0
5000 Taxes on goods and services	**47**	**837**	**6 555**	**16 155**	**23 166**	**22 023**	**21 554**	**23 957**	**28 224**	**29 407**
5100 Taxes on production, sale, transfer, etc.	44	810	6 440	15 847	22 708	21 433	20 727	23 094	27 022	28 070
5110 General taxes	0	290	2 906	9 733	14 333	13 527	13 710	15 368	17 868	18 786
5111 Value added taxes	0	0	2 899	9 733	14 333	13 527	13 710	15 368	17 868	18 786
VAT	..	..	2 899	9 733	14 333	13 527	13 710	15 368	17 868	18 786

	1965	1980	1990	2000	2007	2010	2013	2015	2018	2019
5112 Sales tax	0	290	7	0	0	0	0	0	0	0
General sales tax	..	290	7	..	..	..	..	..	..	..
5113 Other	0	0	0	0	0	0	0	0	0	0
5120 Taxes on specific goods and services	44	519	3 534	6 113	8 374	7 906	7 017	7 726	9 154	9 284
5121 Excise duties	15	295	2 052	4 496	5 937	5 653	4 677	5 211	6 230	6 195
Excise duties on tobacco	3	62	362	1 077	1 165	1 496	1 387	1 357	1 577	1 484
Excise duties on beer	1	0	55	87	97	80	75	75	90	95
Tax on motor vehicle sales	1	59	304	1 239	1 221	832	360	585	785	743
Tax on oil products	6	166	1 251	1 969	3 320	3 126	2 740	3 069	3 546	3 642
Excise duties on alcoholic beverages	0	0	23	123	126	112	108	115	137	145
Excise duties on alcohol	0	0	0	1	1	1	1	0	1	1
Tax on sugary soft drinks	0	0	0	0	0	0	0	0	74	60
Other	4	7	59	0	6	6	4	11	21	25
5122 Profits of fiscal monopolies	0	0	0	261	521	425	538	582	746	775
5123 Customs and import duties	21	96	511	204	190	177	144	158	224	229
Import levies	14	36	392	0	0	0	0	0	0	0
Import surtax	0	26	1	0	0	0	0	0	0	0
Agricultural Levies	..	..	0	30	29	20	25	0	0	0
Levy on sugar and isoglucse	..	..	0	4	5	0	0	0	0	0
Other	6	34	119	0	0	0	0	0	0	0
Custom duties collected for the EU	..	..	0	170	156	157	119	158	224	229
5124 Taxes on exports	0	0	0	0	0	0	0	0	0	0
Taxes on Oporto wine exports	0	0	..	..	..	..	..	..	..	..
Other	0	0	..	..	..	..	..	..	..	..
5125 Taxes on investment goods	0	0	0	0	0	0	0	0	0	0
5126 Taxes on specific services	1	38	547	1 116	1 679	1 539	1 493	1 523	1 738	1 852
Tax on insurance premiums	0	6	47	131	170	215	200	218	259	281
Stamp duty on bank transactions	1	24	405	330	694	619	508	464	539	581
Stamp duty on debt related operations, interest and leasing of buildings	0	0	22	258	386	293	212	144	132	142
Stamp duty on insurance premiums	0	0	0	248	335	325	308	313	373	402
Bank levies	0	0	0	100	48	46	238	353	380	378
Other	2	8	73	47	46	40	29	30	55	69
5127 Other taxes on internat. trade and transactions	0	0	0	0	0	0	0	0	0	0
5128 Other taxes	6	91	424	36	48	111	166	251	216	233
Stamp taxes (miscellaneous)	6	91	424	36	48	111	166	251	216	233
Other	0	0	0	0	0	0	0	0	0	0
5130 Unallocable between 5110 and 5120	0	0	0	0	0	0	0	0	0	0
5200 Taxes on use of goods and perform activities	4	27	115	267	427	573	802	850	1 188	1 331
5210 Recurrent taxes	4	27	115	267	427	573	768	770	970	1 090
5211 Paid by households: motor vehicles	0	4	15	55	94	139	225	209	226	235
Local tax on vehicles	..	4	15	55	94	139	225	209	226	235
5212 Paid by others: motor vehicles	2	10	20	67	132	180	303	330	424	460
Local tax on vehicles	0	2	6	0	0	0	0	0	0	0
Road taxes	2	8	14	67	132	180	303	330	424	460
5213 Paid in respect of other goods	2	13	80	145	202	255	240	232	320	396
Gambling tax	0	3	72	110	140	143	107	108	163	221
Tax on the use, carrying and possession of weapons	0	0	1	3	6	4	7	5	9	8
Tax on motor vehicles - compensation	2	8	0	0	0	0	0	0	0	0
Hunting and fishery licenses	0	1	4	1	7	12	12	13	14	13
Fee for the use of water resources	0	0	0	0	2	19	23	19	20	36
Other	0	1	2	31	47	76	92	88	114	117
5220 Non-recurrent taxes	0	0	0	0	0	0	34	80	218	240
Special tax on motor vehicles	..	..	0	..	..	..	0	0	0	0
Emissions Permits	..	..	0	..	..	..	34	80	218	240
5300 Unallocable between 5100 and 5200	0	0	0	41	31	17	25	13	14	6
Miscellaneous taxes on production	..	..	..	41	31	17	25	13	14	6
6000 Other taxes	**0**	**3**	**37**	**224**	**539**	**442**	**641**	**580**	**675**	**573**
6100 Paid solely by business	0	2	17	90	200	210	214	341	410	317
General services and licenses granted to corporations	0	2	17	90	200	210	214	341	410	317
6200 Other	0	0	20	134	339	231	427	239	265	256
Fees collected by courts of justice	0	0	0	128	328	215	401	237	264	254
Miscellaneous taxes	0	0	20	5	11	17	25	1	1	2
Memorandum items										
Customs duties collected on behalf of the EU	..	..	..	170	156	157	119	158	224	229
SRF contributions collected on behalf of the EU	..	..	..	..	..	..	..	..	132	124
Total tax revenue on cash basis	**99**	**1 798**	**14 825**	..	..	..	..	..	..	..
Total tax revenue on accrual basis	..	..	..	**39 705**	**55 885**	**54 541**	**57 913**	**61 788**	**71 109**	**73 818**

	1965	1980	1990	2000	2007	2010	2013	2015	2018	2019
Conciliation with National Accounts										
Additional taxes included in National Accounts	..	..	..	5	7	14	14	18	19	20
Taxes excluded from National Accounts	..	..	0	0	0	0	0	0	0	0
Difference in treatment of tax credits	..	..	0	0	0	0	0	0	0	0
Capital transfer for uncollected revenue	..	..	0	0	0	0	0	0	0	0
Voluntary social security contributions	..	..	0	0	0	0	0	0	0	0
Miscellaneous differences	..	..	0	0	0	0	0	0	0	0
National Accounts: Taxes and actual social contributions	..	..	..	39 710	55 892	54 555	57 927	61 806	71 127	73 838
Imputed social contributions	..	..	..	3 292	5 592	5 906	5 311	4 602	4 728	4 725
National Accounts: Taxes and all social contributions	..	..	..	43 002	61 484	60 461	63 238	66 408	75 856	78 563

.. Not available

Note: Fiscal year ending 31 December.
From 1995, data are on accrual basis.

Source: Instituto Nacionale de Estatistica; Conta do Estado, Contas de Gerência dos Fundos e Serviços Autonomos da Administraçao Central; Estatisticas das Financas publicas; Relatorio do Instituto de Gestao Financeira da Seguranta Social, Contas de Gerência das Regioes Autonomas da Madeira e dos Atores.

StatLink https://stat.link/y3qaj6

Table 5.31. Slovak Republic: Details of tax revenue, 1965-2019

Million EUR

	1965	1980	1990	2000	2007	2010	2013	2015	2018	2019
Total tax revenue	..	..	..	**10 648**	**18 456**	**19 159**	**23 082**	**26 049**	**30 558**	**32 462**
Total tax revenue exclusive of taxes collected for the EU	..	..	..	**10 648**	**18 321**	**19 016**	**22 967**	**25 930**	**30 402**	**32 316**
1000 Taxes on income, profits and capital gains	..	..	..	**2 181**	**3 844**	**3 601**	**4 471**	**5 542**	**6 370**	**6 628**
1100 Of individuals	..	..	..	1 055	1 820	1 790	2 175	2 464	3 218	3 535
1110 On income and profits	..	..	..	1 055	1 820	1 790	2 175	2 464	3 218	3 535
Wages and salaries withholding	..	..	..	0	0	0	0	0	0	0
Of unicorporated individuals	..	..	..	0	0	0	0	0	0	0
1120 On capital gains	..	..	..	0	0	0	0	0	0	0
1200 Corporate	..	..	..	813	1 835	1 659	2 118	2 917	2 943	2 848
1210 On profits	..	..	..	0	0	0	0	0	0	0
1220 On capital gains	..	..	..	0	0	0	0	0	0	0
1300 Unallocable between 1100 and 1200	..	..	..	314	189	152	178	162	209	246
2000 Social security contributions	..	..	..	**4 409**	**7 244**	**8 154**	**9 847**	**10 897**	**13 147**	**14 085**
2100 Employees	..	..	..	901	1 700	2 077	2 238	2 410	3 263	3 435
Retirement	..	..	..	0	0	0	0	0	0	0
State employment policy	..	..	..	0	0	0	0	0	0	0
Health insurance	..	..	..	0	0	0	0	0	0	0
Sick leave	..	..	..	0	0	0	0	0	0	0
2110 On a payroll basis	..	..	..	901	1 700	2 077	2 238	2 410	3 263	3 435
2120 On an income tax basis	..	..	..	0	0	0	0	0	0	0
2200 Employers	..	..	..	2 850	3 914	4 579	5 556	6 319	7 782	8 539
Retirement	..	..	..	0	0	0	0	0	0	0
State employment policy	..	..	..	0	0	0	0	0	0	0
Health insurance	..	..	..	0	0	0	0	0	0	0
Sick leave	..	..	..	0	0	0	0	0	0	0
2210 On a payroll basis	..	..	..	2 850	3 914	4 579	5 556	6 319	7 782	8 539
2220 On an income tax basis	..	..	..	0	0	0	0	0	0	0
2300 Self-employed or non-employed	..	..	..	658	1 631	1 498	2 054	2 168	2 103	2 111
Retirement	..	..	..	0	0	0	0	0	0	0
State employment policy	..	..	..	0	0	0	0	0	0	0
Health insurance	..	..	..	0	0	0	0	0	0	0
Sick leave	..	..	..	0	0	0	0	0	0	0
2310 On a payroll basis	..	..	..	658	1 631	1 498	2 054	2 168	2 103	2 111
2320 On an income tax basis	..	..	..	0	0	0	0	0	0	0
2400 Unallocable between 2100, 2200 and 2300	..	..	..	0	0	0	0	0	0	0
2410 On a payroll basis	..	..	..	..	..	..	..	..	..	..
2420 On an income tax basis	..	..	..	..	..	..	..	..	..	..
3000 Taxes on payroll and workforce	..	..	..	**0**	**0**	**0**	**0**	**0**	**0**	**0**
4000 Taxes on property	..	..	..	**194**	**245**	**277**	**327**	**335**	**369**	**378**
4100 Recurrent taxes on immovable property	..	..	..	143	243	277	327	335	369	378
4110 Households	..	..	..	28	22	25	28	29	31	35
4120 Others	..	..	..	114	222	252	299	306	338	343
4200 Recurrent taxes on net wealth	..	..	..	0	0	0	0	0	0	0
4210 Individual	..	..	..	..	..	..	..	..	..	..
4220 Corporate	..	..	..	..	..	..	..	..	..	..
4300 Estate, inheritance and gift taxes	..	..	..	8	0	0	0	0	0	0
4310 Estate and inheritance taxes	..	..	..	3	0	0	0	0	0	..
4320 Gift taxes	..	..	..	5	0	0	0	0	0	..
4400 Taxes on financial and capital transactions	..	..	..	43	1	0	0	0	0	0
Real property transfer tax	..	..	..	30	1	0	0	0	0	0
4500 Non-recurrent taxes	..	..	..	0	0	0	0	0	0	0
4510 On net wealth	..	..	..	..	..	..	..	..	..	..
4520 Other non-recurrent taxes	..	..	..	..	..	..	..	..	..	..
4600 Other recurrent taxes on property	..	..	..	0	0	0	0	0	0	0
5000 Taxes on goods and services	..	..	..	**3 864**	**7 123**	**7 127**	**8 436**	**9 275**	**10 671**	**11 371**
5100 Taxes on production, sale, transfer, etc.	..	..	..	3 631	6 580	6 573	7 780	8 573	9 913	10 525
5110 General taxes	..	..	..	2 168	4 147	4 182	4 696	5 423	6 319	6 830
5111 Value added taxes	..	..	..	2 168	4 147	4 182	4 696	5 423	6 319	6 830
5112 Sales tax	..	..	..	0	0	0	0	0	0	0
5113 Other	..	..	..	0	0	0	0	0	0	0
5120 Taxes on specific goods and services	..	..	..	1 464	2 433	2 391	3 084	3 151	3 594	3 695

	1965	1980	1990	2000	2007	2010	2013	2015	2018	2019
5121 Excise duties	..	..	..	971	2 171	2 081	2 462	2 567	2 810	2 839
On hydrocarbon fuels and lubricants	..	..	..	617	1 118	1 032	1 045	1 139	1 267	1 289
On alcohol and liquers	..	..	..	143	201	197	201	205	221	218
On beer	..	..	..	43	66	56	56	57	60	59
On wine	..	..	..	12	4	4	4	4	5	5
On tobacco products	..	..	..	156	783	602	636	665	728	767
On electricity	..	..	..	0	0	16	17	13	11	12
On coal	..	..	..	0	0	1	1	0	0	0
On natural gas	..	..	..	0	0	24	25	23	24	23
5122 Profits of fiscal monopolies	..	..	..	0	0	0	0	0	0	0
5123 Customs and import duties	..	..	..	437	136	143	115	119	137	127
Customs duties	..	..	..	122	136	143	115	119	137	127
Import surcharges	..	..	..	315	0	0	0	0	0	0
Other customs revenues	..	..	..	0	0	0	0	0	0	0
5124 Taxes on exports	..	..	..	0	0	0	0	0	0	0
5125 Taxes on investment goods	..	..	..	0	0	0	6	2	3	3
5126 Taxes on specific services	..	..	..	55	125	167	501	462	644	726
5127 Other taxes on internat. trade and transactions	..	..	..	0	0	0	0	0	0	0
5128 Other taxes	..	..	..	0	0	0	0	0	0	0
5130 Unallocable between 5110 and 5120	..	..	..	0	0	0	0	0	0	0
5200 Taxes on use of goods and perform activities	..	..	..	231	438	421	505	549	597	666
5210 Recurrent taxes	..	..	..	219	372	384	466	470	506	523
5211 Paid by households: motor vehicles	..	..	..	0	0	0	0	0	0	0
5212 Paid by others: motor vehicles	..	..	..	93	153	153	198	204	232	233
5213 Paid in respect of other goods	..	..	..	127	219	231	268	266	273	290
5220 Non-recurrent taxes	..	..	..	12	66	37	39	79	92	142
5300 Unallocable between 5100 and 5200	..	..	..	2	105	134	151	153	161	181
6000 Other taxes	**..**	**..**	**..**	**0**	**0**	**0**	**0**	**0**	**0**	**0**
6100 Paid solely by business	..	..	..	..	..	..	..	..	..	..
6200 Other	..	..	..	..	..	..	..	..	..	..
Memorandum items										
Customs duties collected on behalf of the EU	..	..	..	..	136	143	115	119	137	127
SRF contributions collected on behalf of the EU	..	..	..	..	..	..	..	..	19	19
Non-wastable tax credits										
Non-wastable tax credits against 1110	..	..	..	..	252	276	265	261	269	338
Tax expenditure component	..	..	..	..	..	..	..	..	..	..
Transfer component	..	..	..	..	..	..	..	..	..	..
Non-wastable tax credits against 1210	..	..	..	..	0	0	0	0	0	0
Tax expenditure component	..	..	..	..	..	..	..	..	..	..
Transfer component	..	..	..	..	..	..	..	..	..	..
Total tax revenue on cash basis	**..**	**..**	**..**	**10 843**	**18 033**	**18 358**	**22 082**	**25 757**	**29 647**	**31 308**
Total tax revenue on accrual basis	**..**	**..**	**..**	**10 648**	**18 456**	**19 159**	**23 082**	**26 049**	**30 558**	**32 462**
Conciliation with National Accounts										
Additional taxes included in National Accounts	..	..	..	53	33	47	0	43	3	4
Taxes excluded from National Accounts	..	..	..	0	-103	-131	-148	-149	-158	-178
Difference in treatment of tax credits	..	..	..	0	0	0	0	0	0	0
Capital transfer for uncollected revenue	..	..	..	0	0	0	0	0	0	0
Voluntary social security contributions	..	..	..	0	22	31	17	11	11	11
Miscellaneous differences	..	..	..	0	0	0	0	0	0	0
National Accounts: Taxes and actual social contributions	..	..	..	10 702	18 409	19 106	22 951	25 953	30 414	32 300
Imputed social contributions	..	..	..	19	80	143	147	171	188	219
National Accounts: Taxes and all social contributions	..	..	..	10 721	18 488	19 250	23 098	26 124	30 602	32 518

.. Not available

Note: Year ending 31st December.

Data are on accrual basis.

Source: Ministry of Finance.

StatLink https://stat.link/au2df3

Table 5.32. Slovenia: Details of tax revenue, 1965-2019

Million EUR

	1965	1980	1990	2000	2007	2010	2013	2015	2018	2019
Total tax revenue	..	..	..	**7 117**	**13 352**	**13 756**	**13 576**	**14 496**	**17 094**	**17 988**
Total tax revenue exclusive of taxes collected for the EU	..	..	..	**7 117**	**13 267**	**13 696**	**13 524**	**14 428**	**17 026**	**17 917**
1000 Taxes on income, profits and capital gains	..	..	..	**1 280**	**3 041**	**2 692**	**2 285**	**2 547**	**3 348**	**3 505**
1100 Of individuals	..	..	..	1 041	1 919	2 020	1 849	1 977	2 460	2 548
1110 On income and profits	..	..	..	1 039	1 916	2 017	1 847	1 974	2 457	2 545
Personal income tax	..	..	..	1 039	1 916	2 017	1 847	1 974	2 457	2 545
Special contribution for the reconstruction of the Posocje region	..	..	..	0	0	0	0	0	0	0
1120 On capital gains	..	..	..	2	3	3	3	3	3	3
Taxes on winnings from lottery and gambling	..	..	..	2	3	3	3	3	3	3
1200 Corporate	..	..	..	216	1 116	668	433	568	886	954
1210 On profits	..	..	..	216	1 116	668	433	568	886	954
1220 On capital gains	..	..	..	0	0	0	0	0	0	0
1300 Unallocable between 1100 and 1200	..	..	..	24	5	4	3	2	2	3
Tax on income - copy rights, patents and trademarks	..	..	..	24	5	4	2	2	2	2
Tax on profits due to changes in land use	..	..	..	0	0	0	0	0	0	0
2000 Social security contributions	..	..	..	**2 824**	**5 046**	**5 761**	**5 647**	**5 983**	**7 081**	**7 587**
2100 Employees	..	..	..	1 447	2 490	2 785	2 637	2 910	3 490	3 751
2110 On a payroll basis	..	..	..	1 447	2 490	2 785	2 637	2 910	3 490	3 751
2120 On an income tax basis	..	..	..	0	0	0	0	0	0	0
2200 Employers	..	..	..	1 012	1 852	2 070	2 022	2 135	2 590	2 781
2210 On a payroll basis	..	..	..	1 012	1 852	2 070	2 022	2 135	2 590	2 781
2220 On an income tax basis	..	..	..	0	0	0	0	0	0	0
2300 Self-employed or non-employed	..	..	..	365	705	906	988	938	1 001	1 055
2310 On a payroll basis	..	..	..	365	705	906	988	938	1 001	1 055
2320 On an income tax basis	..	..	..	0	0	0	0	0	0	0
2400 Unallocable between 2100, 2200 and 2300	..	..	..	0	0	0	0	0	0	0
2410 On a payroll basis	..	..	..	..	..	..	..	..	..	..
2420 On an income tax basis	..	..	..	..	..	..	..	..	..	..
3000 Taxes on payroll and workforce	..	..	..	**289**	**418**	**28**	**23**	**20**	**22**	**23**
Payroll tax	..	..	..	272	391	0	0	0	0	0
Tax on work contracts	..	..	..	18	27	28	23	20	22	23
4000 Taxes on property	..	..	..	**120**	**206**	**222**	**232**	**241**	**276**	**299**
4100 Recurrent taxes on immovable property	..	..	..	81	140	173	199	199	223	235
4110 Households	..	..	..	17	38	46	61	56	65	70
Property tax on weekend cottages	..	..	..	1	1	1	1	1	0	1
Compensation on the use of building ground - paid by individuals	..	..	..	16	37	45	48	56	64	68
Tax on immovable property of higher value	..	..	..	0	0	0	13	0	0	0
4120 Others	..	..	..	65	102	127	138	142	158	165
Property tax on buildings	..	..	..	2	3	3	4	4	3	9
Compensation on the use of building ground - paid by legal entities	..	..	..	63	100	124	134	139	155	156
4200 Recurrent taxes on net wealth	..	..	..	4	0	0	0	0	0	0
4210 Individual	..	..	..	0	..	..	..	..	..	..
4220 Corporate	..	..	..	4	..	..	..	..	..	..
Tax on balance wealth paid by banks	..	..	..	4	..	..	..	..	..	..
4300 Estate, inheritance and gift taxes	..	..	..	2	9	14	8	8	10	16
4310 Estate and inheritance taxes	..	..	..	..	..	..	..	..	..	..
4320 Gift taxes	..	..	..	..	..	..	..	..	..	..
4400 Taxes on financial and capital transactions	..	..	..	23	57	32	23	29	40	44
Taxes on the sale of immovable property - from legal entities	..	..	..	11	19	7	5	7	7	9
Taxes on the sale of immovable property - from individuals	..	..	..	12	38	25	18	23	33	36
4500 Non-recurrent taxes	..	..	..	10	0	2	1	4	3	3
4510 On net wealth	..	..	..	0	..	0	0	0	0	0
4520 Other non-recurrent taxes	..	..	..	10	..	2	1	4	3	3
Payments for the change of use of agricultural and forest land	..	..	..	10	..	0	1	2	1	2
Granting of easements and the creation of building rights	..	..	..	0	..	2	1	3	2	1
4600 Other recurrent taxes on property	..	..	..	0	0	0	0	0	0	0
Property tax on boats	..	..	..	0	0	0	0	0	0	0
5000 Taxes on goods and services	..	..	..	**2 602**	**4 641**	**5 053**	**5 389**	**5 706**	**6 367**	**6 575**
5100 Taxes on production, sale, transfer, etc.	..	..	..	2 481	4 426	4 838	5 049	5 329	5 969	6 113
5110 General taxes	..	..	..	1 641	2 916	2 927	3 048	3 222	3 768	3 891
5111 Value added taxes	..	..	..	1 610	2 916	2 927	3 048	3 222	3 768	3 891
Value added tax	..	..	..	1 598	2 898	2 924	3 044	3 218	3 763	3 886
Negative compensation of farmers in a VAT flat rate	..	..	..	12	18	3	4	4	4	5

	1965	1980	1990	2000	2007	2010	2013	2015	2018	2019
system										
5112 Sales tax	..	..	..	8	0	0	0	0	0	0
Customs duties paid by individuals	..	..	..	1	..	..	..	..	..	..
Special import duties and customs charges	..	..	..	7	..	..	..	..	..	..
5113 Other	..	..	..	23	0	0	0	0	0	0
Turnover tax on goods	..	..	..	11	..	..	..	..	..	..
Turnover tax on services	..	..	..	12	..	..	..	..	..	..
Special turnover tax on alcohol	..	..	..	0	..	..	..	..	..	..
5120 Taxes on specific goods and services	..	..	..	841	1 510	1 911	2 001	2 107	2 202	2 223
5121 Excise duties	..	..	..	581	1 196	1 555	1 579	1 626	1 679	1 671
Alcohol and alcoholic drinks	..	..	..	39	71	89	96	108	119	122
Mineral oil and gas	..	..	..	405	758	1 016	998	1 033	1 066	1 053
Tobacco	..	..	..	97	301	391	425	419	420	419
Duty free shops - alcohol and alcoholic drinks	..	..	..	3	0	0	0	0	0	0
Duty free shops - tobacco	..	..	..	17	0	0	0	0	0	0
Electric power and coal	..	..	..	0	4	19	31	34	32	32
Tax on the sales of new motor vehicles	..	..	..	18	60	40	26	26	34	37
Tax on the sales of used motor vehicles	..	..	..	2	2	0	0	0	0	0
Additional tax on motor vehicles	..	..	..	0	0	0	3	6	8	8
5122 Profits of fiscal monopolies	..	..	..	0	0	0	0	0	0	0
5123 Customs and import duties	..	..	..	158	85	60	53	53	58	62
Import duties	..	..	..	151	0	0	0	0	0	0
Levies on imported agricultural products	..	..	..	7	0	0	0	0	0	0
Custom duties collected for the EU	..	..	..	0	85	60	53	53	58	62
5124 Taxes on exports	..	..	..	0	0	0	0	0	0	0
5125 Taxes on investment goods	..	..	..	0	0	0	0	0	0	0
5126 Taxes on specific services	..	..	..	102	230	296	369	428	464	490
Tax on special gambling (gambling in casinos)	..	..	..	25	64	53	41	48	45	46
Tax on classical gambling (lottery...)	..	..	..	1	3	3	3	3	3	3
Special tax on slot machines	..	..	..	4	0	0	0	0	0	0
Tax on insurance services	..	..	..	37	65	69	65	82	94	101
Sojourn tax	..	..	..	3	7	7	8	11	18	25
Concessions	..	..	..	1	29	40	90	79	67	77
Concessions duties on special gambling (in casinos)	..	..	..	26	55	47	38	37	38	39
Fire protection tax	..	..	..	4	6	7	8	8	8	9
Tax on lottery tickets	..	..	..	0	0	0	3	17	18	20
Tax on financial services	..	..	..	0	0	0	32	57	76	71
FIHO, FSO	..	..	..	0	0	25	26	27	25	26
SOS	..	..	..	0	0	23	10	11	12	12
Tax on balance wealth paid by banks	..	..	..	0	0	0	18	2	0	0
Commodity reserve fund	..	..	..	0	0	21	27	32	30	31
Deposit guarantee Fund, Single Resolution Fund	..	..	..	..	..	..	..	16	29	30
5127 Other taxes on internat. trade and transactions	..	..	..	0	0	0	0	0	0	0
5128 Other taxes	..	..	..	0	0	0	0	0	0	0
Sugar levy	..	..	..	..	0	..	..	..	..	..
5130 Unallocable between 5110 and 5120	..	..	..	0	0	0	0	0	0	0
5200 Taxes on use of goods and perform activities	..	..	..	121	215	215	340	377	398	462
5210 Recurrent taxes	..	..	..	121	215	215	321	353	373	395
5211 Paid by households: motor vehicles	..	..	..	49	87	86	109	118	125	127
Registration fees on motor vehicles, boats and airplanes paid by individuals	..	..	..	49	87	86	109	118	125	127
5212 Paid by others: motor vehicles	..	..	..	12	21	20	24	27	31	33
Registration fees on motor vehicles, boats and airplanes paid by legal entities	..	..	..	12	21	20	24	27	31	33
Registration fees on tractors	..	..	..	0	0	0	0	0	0	0
5213 Paid in respect of other goods	..	..	..	59	107	110	187	208	217	236
Charges on the use of water	..	..	..	4	22	23	29	32	31	32
Taxes on waste pollution	..	..	..	7	10	3	2	2	1	1
Taxes on air pollution - caused by gas and hard fuels	..	..	..	3	8	10	10	13	15	15
Cont. of nuclear power plant to finance its de-composition	..	..	..	16	8	8	8	8	8	8
Indemnity for the restricted use of area on the territory of nuclear power plant	..	..	..	0	7	10	11	12	12	12
Taxes on air pollution	..	..	..	29	21	23	98	114	126	145
Special water tax	..	..	..	0	30	33	29	27	23	22
5220 Non-recurrent taxes	..	..	..	0	0	0	19	24	25	66
Emission permits	..	..	..	..	..	..	19	24	25	66
5300 Unallocable between 5100 and 5200	..	..	..	0	0	0	0	0	0	0
6000 Other taxes	**..**	**..**	**..**	**0**	**0**	**0**	**0**	**0**	**0**	**0**
6100 Paid solely by business	..	..	..	..	..	..	..	..	..	..
Memorandum items										
Customs duties collected on behalf of the EU	..	..	..	..	85	60	53	53	58	62
SRF contributions collected on behalf of the EU	..	..	..	..	..	..	..	16	10	9

	1965	1980	1990	2000	2007	2010	2013	2015	2018	2019
Total tax revenue on cash basis	..	..	..	**7 135**	**13 140**	**13 605**	**13 485**	**14 560**	**17 135**	**18 126**
Total tax revenue on accrual basis	..	..	..	**7 117**	**13 352**	**13 756**	**13 576**	**14 496**	**17 094**	**17 988**
Conciliation with National Accounts										
Additional taxes included in National Accounts	..	..	..	..	..	87	90	94	95	96
Radio and television licence fee	..	..	..	..	..	87	90	94	95	96
Taxes excluded from National Accounts	..	..	..	..	..	..	..	..	..	..
Difference in treatment of tax credits	..	..	..	0	0	0	0	0	0	0
Capital transfer for uncollected revenue	..	..	..	0	0	0	0	0	0	0
Voluntary social security contributions	..	..	..	0	0	0	0	0	0	0
Miscellaneous differences	..	..	..	0	0	0	0	0	0	0
National Accounts: Taxes and actual social contributions	..	..	..	7 117	13 352	13 842	13 667	14 590	17 188	18 084
Imputed social contributions	..	..	..	39	81	100	117	118	126	136
National Accounts: Taxes and all social contributions	..	..	..	7 156	13 433	13 943	13 784	14 708	17 314	18 220

.. Not available

Note: Year ending 31st December.

Data are on accrual basis.

Source: Statistical Office of the Republic of Slovenia.

StatLink https://stat.link/bv7yhd

Table 5.33. Spain: Details of tax revenue, 1965-2019

Million EUR

	1965	1980	1990	2000	2007	2010	2013	2015	2018	2019
Total tax revenue	**1 238**	**22 002**	**103 662**	**214 114**	**391 648**	**335 563**	**337 891**	**364 683**	**417 076**	**431 575**
Total tax revenue exclusive of taxes collected for the EU	..	..	..	**213 067**	**389 927**	**334 019**	**336 567**	**362 175**	**414 423**	**428 901**
1000 Taxes on income, profits and capital gains	**304**	**5 714**	**31 763**	**60 145**	**130 081**	**93 798**	**97 664**	**102 645**	**122 042**	**123 678**
1100 Of individuals	177	4 481	22 527	41 248	80 719	74 118	77 230	78 896	92 376	97 960
Personal income tax	..	..	22 527	40 366	79 973	73 534	76 690	78 586	91 859	97 499
Income tax of non-residents	..	..	0	882	746	584	540	310	517	461
1110 On income and profits	..	..	..	..	..	..	..	..	..	..
1120 On capital gains	..	..	..	..	..	..	..	..	..	..
1200 Corporate	114	1 119	9 146	18 897	49 362	19 680	20 434	23 749	29 666	25 718
Corporate income tax	..	..	9 146	18 597	47 499	17 567	19 516	22 471	27 490	23 757
Income tax of non-residents (legal persons)	..	..	0	300	1 863	2 113	918	1 278	2 176	1 961
1210 On profits	..	..	..	..	..	..	..	..	..	..
Tax on commercial activity	..	..	..	..	..	..	..	..	..	..
Special tax 4 percent	..	..	..	..	..	..	..	..	..	..
Taxes on profits	..	..	..	..	..	..	..	..	..	..
1220 On capital gains	..	..	..	..	..	..	..	..	..	..
1300 Unallocable between 1100 and 1200	13	114	91	0	0	0	0	0	0	0
Local taxes	13	114	0	..	..	..	..	..	..	..
Other taxes	..	..	..	..	..	..	..	..	..	..
2000 Social security contributions	**350**	**10 682**	**36 722**	**74 683**	**127 088**	**127 235**	**116 875**	**122 835**	**141 283**	**152 527**
2100 Employees	81	2 376	5 976	11 711	19 625	19 423	16 603	18 783	21 647	23 272
2110 On a payroll basis	..	..	5 976	11 711	19 625	19 423	16 603	18 783	21 647	23 272
2120 On an income tax basis	..	..	0	..	..	..	..	..	..	..
2200 Employers	269	8 306	26 385	54 226	93 234	89 666	82 224	87 988	103 358	112 274
2210 On a payroll basis	..	..	26 385	54 226	93 234	89 666	82 224	87 988	103 358	112 274
2220 On an income tax basis	..	..	0	..	..	..	..	..	..	..
2300 Self-employed or non-employed	0	0	4 361	8 746	14 229	18 146	18 048	16 064	16 278	16 981
Self-employment	..	..	2 492	6 788	10 120	10 119	10 244	10 872	11 714	11 501
Unemployment	..	..	1 869	1 958	4 109	8 027	7 804	5 192	4 564	5 480
2310 On a payroll basis	..	..	..	..	..	..	..	..	..	..
2320 On an income tax basis	..	..	..	..	..	..	..	..	..	..
2400 Unallocable between 2100, 2200 and 2300	0	0	0	0	0	0	0	0	0	0
2410 On a payroll basis	..	..	..	..	..	..	..	..	..	..
2420 On an income tax basis	..	..	..	..	..	..	..	..	..	..
3000 Taxes on payroll and workforce	**0**	**0**	**0**	**0**	**0**	**0**	**0**	**0**	**0**	**0**
4000 Taxes on property	**79**	**1 004**	**5 718**	**13 827**	**32 133**	**22 178**	**24 250**	**27 855**	**30 549**	**30 497**
4100 Recurrent taxes on immovable property	6	41	1 478	3 988	7 281	9 666	11 829	12 623	13 426	13 444
Real State tax (IBI)/Real State tax surcharge	..	41	1 478	3 982	7 267	9 657	11 755	12 581	13 384	13 393
Special Real State tax for non-residents	..	0	0	6	6	8	8	4	4	2
Other taxes on property, land or building use	..	0	0	0	3	0	1	1	0	0
4110 Households	..	..	..	..	..	..	..	..	..	..
4120 Others	..	..	..	0	5	1	65	37	38	49
Tax on large commercial establishments	..	..	..	..	5	1	65	37	38	49
4200 Recurrent taxes on net wealth	0	107	637	1 413	2 479	688	2 049	1 904	2 220	2 241
4210 Individual	..	107	637	1 413	2 479	688	2 049	1 904	2 220	2 241
Wealth tax	..	..	637	1 199	2 054	104	1 339	1 144	1 395	1 417
Real State tax (unoccupied dwellings) and others	..	..	0	214	425	584	710	760	825	824
4220 Corporate	..	0	0	0	0	0	0	0	0	0
4300 Estate, inheritance and gift taxes	13	90	440	1 379	2 901	2 412	2 492	2 790	2 686	2 513
Inheritance and gift tax	..	..	440	1 379	2 901	2 412	2 492	2 790	2 686	2 513
4310 Estate and inheritance taxes	..	..	..	..	..	..	..	..	..	..
4320 Gift taxes	..	..	..	..	..	..	..	..	..	..
4400 Taxes on financial and capital transactions	60	767	2 478	5 939	17 025	7 603	5 301	6 984	9 308	9 327
Taxes on property transactions	60	767	2 478	5 939	17 025	7 603	5 301	6 984	9 308	9 327
4500 Non-recurrent taxes	0	0	646	1 108	2 447	1 809	2 579	3 554	2 909	2 972
4510 On net wealth	..	..	467	0	495	192	325	1 006	354	334
Tax on land holding gains	..	..	467	..	..	..	..	0	0	..
Urban use tax	..	..	..	..	495	192	90	73	120	100
Extraordinary resource of FGD	..	..	..	..	0	0	235	933	234	234
4520 Other non-recurrent taxes	..	..	179	1 108	1 952	1 617	2 254	2 548	2 555	2 638
Special duties	..	..	179	180	168	129	84	70	80	78
Land development contributions	..	..	0	223	368	225	71	61	59	59
Tax on the increase in value of urban terrains	..	..	0	705	1 416	1 263	1 711	2 417	2 416	2 501
Others	..	..	0	0	0	0	2	0	0	0
Levy on "Revaluation of Reserve Account"	..	..	..	0	0	0	386	0	0	0
4600 Other recurrent taxes on property	0	0	38	0	0	0	0	0	0	0
5000 Taxes on goods and services	**506**	**4 553**	**29 437**	**65 456**	**102 334**	**92 344**	**99 026**	**111 159**	**123 004**	**124 720**
5100 Taxes on production, sale, transfer, etc.	503	4 552	26 732	59 383	93 814	84 985	91 122	102 912	113 796	115 049

	1965	1980	1990	2000	2007	2010	2013	2015	2018	2019
5110 General taxes	275	2 234	16 611	37 800	62 778	55 629	60 488	69 478	79 433	81 086
5111 Value added taxes	0	0	16 304	37 785	62 743	55 318	60 314	69 294	79 239	80 896
Value added tax (VAT)	..	..	16 304	37 045	61 472	54 509	59 207	67 913	77 536	79 308
Canary Islands general indirect tax	..	..	0	740	1 271	809	1 107	1 381	1 703	1 588
5112 Sales tax	0	0	0	15	35	311	174	184	194	190
Fees for RTVE (since 2010)	..	..	..	0	0	278	174	184	194	190
Fees from Nat. Commission of Telecomms. Market	..	..	..	15	35	33	0	0	0	0
5113 Other	275	2 234	307	0	0	0	0	0	0	0
Cascade tax	118	1 483	197	..	..	..	..	..	..	..
Excises on luxury expenditure	96	939	15	..	..	..	..	..	..	..
Other import duties	94	832	128	..	..	..	..	..	..	..
Refund of internal taxes	-33	-1 020	-33	..	..	..	..	..	..	..
5120 Taxes on specific goods and services	228	2 317	10 120	21 583	31 036	29 356	30 634	33 434	34 363	33 963
5121 Excise duties	69	1 239	6 048	17 952	25 581	24 384	24 550	25 908	26 790	26 222
Special excises	69	1 239	10	0	0	0	0	0	0	0
On beer	0	0	87	202	307	302	302	316	346	355
On wine	0	0	0	0	0	0	0	0	0	0
On alcohol	0	0	481	785	1 008	876	775	843	881	882
On hydrocarbon	0	0	4 222	9 977	11 787	10 907	11 949	12 465	13 409	13 758
On tobacco	0	0	1 123	4 507	7 258	7 976	7 114	7 213	7 173	6 971
On electricity bills	0	0	0	703	1 153	1 483	1 558	1 458	1 439	1 460
On carbon	0	0	0	0	0	0	148	308	271	139
Tax on retail sales of specific hydrocarbons	0	0	0	0	1 356	1 238	453	7	0	0
Tax on oil derived fuels	0	0	120	237	253	220	267	314	331	332
Petrol tax	0	0	0	6	5	5	13	22	25	23
Production and storage of electricity	0	0	0	0	0	0	1 261	1 576	1 585	717
Tax Greenhouse Effect Flourinated	0	0	0	0	0	0	0	99	110	81
Other taxes	0	0	5	17	21	18	17	22	21	22
Canary Islands taxes on national products	0	0	0	51	86	71	75	85	86	84
Taxes on national products in Ceuta and Melilla	0	0	0	108	110	105	103	115	114	112
Fees from the National Energy Commission	0	0	0	13	27	35	0	0	0	0
Contribution to the National Energy Efficiency Fund	0	0	0	0	0	366	150	207	207	204
Special tax on certain means of transport	0	0	0	1 317	2 158	735	325	358	609	697
Fee for use of continental waters for electricity production	0	0	0	0	0	0	0	453	110	317
Special duties and other taxes on imported products	0	0	0	29	52	47	40	47	31	33
Other taxes on products	0	0	0	0	0	0	0	0	42	35
5122 Profits of fiscal monopolies	66	132	546	0	0	0	0	0	0	0
Tobacco	21	77	0	..	..	..	..	..	..	..
Petroleum	45	55	546	..	..	..	..	..	..	..
5123 Customs and import duties	87	561	2 078	1 044	1 816	1 593	1 401	1 899	2 019	2 062
Import duties	87	561	1 394	0	0	0	0	0	0	0
Tax on Imports of Goods in the Canary Islands	0	0	137	33	51	44	45	53	55	54
Tax on Imports in Ceuta and Melilla	0	0	36	41	42	40	39	43	43	42
Customs duties collected for the EU	..	..	511	970	1 723	1 509	1 317	1 803	1 921	1 966
5124 Taxes on exports	0	0	0	0	0	0	0	0	0	0
5125 Taxes on investment goods	0	0	0	0	0	0	0	0	0	0
5126 Taxes on specific services	7	385	1 427	2 497	3 633	3 166	4 469	5 408	5 297	5 462
Taxes on betting and gambling	0	232	1 307	1 649	2 051	1 635	1 249	1 164	1 327	1 362
Taxes on other specific services	6	153	120	0	0	0	0	0	0	0
Taxes on insurance premiums	0	0	0	848	1 581	1 531	1 417	1 446	1 604	1 714
Tax on deposits of credit institution	0	0	0	0	1	0	227	421	377	381
Ordinary resource DGF	0	0	0	0	0	0	1 576	1 644	1 074	1 101
Tourist tax	0	0	0	0	0	0	0	43	180	196
EU SRF contribution	..	..	..	..	..	..	..	690	735	708
5127 Other taxes on internat. trade and transactions	0	0	0	0	0	0	0	0	0	0
5128 Other taxes	0	0	22	90	6	213	214	219	257	217
EU levies	..	..	22	77	-2	35	7	15	-3	0
Others	..	..	0	13	8	9	20	37	107	65
Resource CORES	..	..	0	0	0	169	187	167	153	152
5130 Unallocable between 5110 and 5120	0	0	0	0	0	0	0	0	0	0
5200 Taxes on use of goods and perform activities	3	1	2 633	6 073	8 520	7 359	7 904	8 247	9 208	9 671
5210 Recurrent taxes	3	1	1 616	4 306	5 311	5 782	6 493	6 420	6 788	6 823
Other taxes on luxury expenses	..	..	..	2	7	4	3	3	3	3
5211 Paid by households: motor vehicles	..	0	461	1 117	1 626	1 770	1 848	1 725	1 767	1 771
Car registration tax	..	..	461	1 117	1 626	1 770	1 848	1 725	1 767	1 771
5212 Paid by others: motor vehicles	..	0	117	298	502	498	503	470	489	490
Car registration tax	..	..	117	298	502	498	503	470	489	490

	1965	1980	1990	2000	2007	2010	2013	2015	2018	2019
5213 Paid in respect of other goods	..	1	1 038	2 889	3 176	3 510	4 139	4 222	4 529	4 559
Hunting and fishing taxes	..	..	0	28	28	34	34	30	30	30
Economic activity tax	..	..	925	1 934	1 633	1 785	1 701	1 794	1 922	1 879
Advertising	..	..	27	0	0	0	0	0	0	0
Taxes on environment and pollution	..	..	0	42	91	141	616	563	619	674
Tax on effluent, use of hydrocarbon and mines	..	..	0	51	83	67	158	184	195	187
Other fees paid by households for licences	..	..	0	179	264	228	206	245	331	328
Compensation for local taxes	..	..	86	140	176	165	129	118	134	130
Vehicle inspection duty	..	..	0	6	18	17	20	19	16	16
Municipal fees for private use of public space	..	..	0	509	883	1 073	1 275	1 269	1 282	1 315
5220 Non-recurrent taxes	0	0	1 017	1 767	3 209	1 577	1 411	1 827	2 420	2 848
Tax and building permits	..	..	327	1 117	2 227	859	519	575	983	1 076
Urban licenses	..	..	0	451	490	260	157	200	326	329
Greenhouse gas emission trading	..	..	0	0	0	0	138	412	723	1 015
Parafiscal taxes	..	..	690	199	492	458	597	640	388	428
5300 Unallocable between 5100 and 5200	0	0	72	0	0	0	0	0	0	0
6000 Other taxes	**0**	**49**	**22**	**3**	**12**	**8**	**76**	**189**	**198**	**153**
6100 Paid solely by business	..	49	0	0	0	0	0	0	0	0
6200 Other	..	0	22	3	12	8	76	189	198	153
Other taxes on production	..	..	..	3	12	8	76	189	198	153
Memorandum items										
Customs duties collected on behalf of the EU	..	..	..	970	1 723	1 509	1 317	1 803	1 921	1 966
SRF contributions collected on behalf of the EU	..	..	..	..	..	..	..	690	735	708
Non-wastable tax credits										
Non-wastable tax credits against 1110	..	..	..	..	1 323	1 897	774	1 093	1 852	2 379
Tax expenditure component	..	..	..	..	522	729	432	546	872	1 070
Transfer component	..	..	..	..	801	1 168	342	547	980	1 309
Non-wastable tax credits against 1210	..	..	..	..	0	0	0	46	1 257	177
Tax expenditure component	..	..	..	..	0	0	0	12	34	39
Transfer component	..	..	..	..	0	0	0	34	1 223	138
Total tax revenue on cash basis	**1 238**	**22 002**	**103 662**	**210 565**	**385 676**	**330 362**	**335 663**	**357 575**	**409 352**	**426 102**
Total tax revenue on accrual basis	**..**	**..**	**..**	**214 114**	**391 648**	**335 563**	**337 891**	**364 683**	**417 076**	**431 575**
Conciliation with National Accounts										
Additional taxes included in National Accounts	..	..	..	0	0	0	0	0	0	0
Taxes excluded from National Accounts	..	..	..	0	0	0	0	0	0	0
Difference in treatment of tax credits	..	..	..	0	522	729	432	558	906	1 109
Capital transfer for uncollected revenue	..	..	..	0	0	0	0	0	0	0
Voluntary social security contributions	..	..	..	447	937	1 155	2 209	1 170	1 038	987
Miscellaneous differences	..	..	..	0	0	0	0	0	0	0
National Accounts: Taxes and actual social contributions	..	..	..	214 561	393 107	337 447	340 532	366 411	419 020	433 671
Imputed social contributions	..	..	..	5 379	7 618	8 585	7 772	7 503	7 129	7 153
National Accounts: Taxes and all social contributions	..	..	..	219 940	400 725	346 032	348 304	373 914	426 149	440 824

.. Not available

Note: Year ending 31st December.

From 2000, data are on accrual basis.

From 1981 the figures take into account the classification procedures set out in the OECD Interpretative Guide. Consequently they are not completely comparable with the figures for earlier years though the amounts involved are quite small.

Heading 1000: Includes a tax on property 'Contribucion Rustica' which would be more appropriately classified in 4110, and the 'Licencia fiscal industrial and professionales' which, because it is a tax levied by reference to the size of the firm, energy input, etc, would be more appropriately classified in 6000. The data necessary to provide a breakdown is not available.

All subdivisions are estimated.

Heading 2300: Contributions paid by self-employed were shown under heading 2100 until 1982.

Heading 4100: Most of these receipts fall under 4110.

Heading 4400: In 1988 revenues from taxes on legal Acts issued by Autonomous Communities (Local) are included in 4400.

Heading 5121 comprises certain local levies which may include non-tax revenues.

Source: Informacion Estatistica del Ministerio de Hacienda (for national taxes).

Cuentas de las Administraciones Publicas (for local taxes and social security) both published by Secretaria General Tecnica del Ministerio de Hacienda.

StatLink https://stat.link/lic7fb

Table 5.34. Sweden: Details of tax revenue, 1965-2019

Million SEK

	1965	1980	1990	2000	2007	2010	2013	2015	2018	2019
Total tax revenue	**40 003**	**259 216**	**755 953**	**1 204 794**	**1 491 190**	**1 532 259**	**1 624 632**	**1 816 204**	**2 113 548**	**2 162 928**
Total tax revenue exclusive of taxes collected for the EU	..	..	**755 953**	**1 200 999**	**1 485 306**	**1 526 585**	**1 619 411**	**1 809 928**	**2 107 050**	**2 156 064**
1000 Taxes on income, profits and capital gains	**21 956**	**112 730**	**314 797**	**514 729**	**580 372**	**546 696**	**566 234**	**657 539**	**761 048**	**772 121**
1100 Of individuals	19 500	106 376	291 146	426 956	464 435	430 896	466 286	533 660	623 602	620 161
1110 On income and profits	19 390	105 866	289 598	392 532	414 728	396 353	433 985	464 596	554 257	550 584
Coupon tax	9	44	233	2 040	6 306	3 047	4 108	4 615	8 527	7 216
Duties on foreign artists	4	3	3	50	86	89	-1	2	0	0
National income tax individual	8 676	31 682	70 755	66 850	44 326	42 595	44 664	52 480	63 632	57 083
Local income tax individual	9 294	78 134	220 072	336 304	479 068	522 850	581 934	635 719	726 221	748 197
Tax reduction individual	0	-3 997	-1 465	-18 872	-122 029	-179 890	-204 632	-236 613	-253 181	-271 871
Public service tax	..	..	0	5 061	6 674	6 981	7 208	7 759	8 171	9 028
Other	1 407	0	0	1 098	296	681	704	635	886	931
1120 On capital gains	110	510	1 548	34 425	49 707	34 543	32 301	69 064	69 345	69 577
Lottery prize tax	110	510	1 548	60	0	0	0	0	0	0
1200 Corporate	2 456	6 354	23 651	87 772	115 937	115 800	99 948	123 878	137 447	151 960
1210 On profits	2 456	6 354	23 651	87 772	115 937	115 800	99 948	123 878	137 447	151 960
Tax on profits not distributed	1	10	3	0	0	0	0	0	0	0
National income tax b.c. list	1 425	2 078	19 774	74 501	103 150	103 944	93 097	115 507	132 089	146 652
Local income tax b.c. list	1 030	4 266	0	0	0	0	0	0	0	0
Special tax on profits	0	0	3 874	0	0	0	0	0	0	0
Taxes on pension insurance savings	0	0	0	13 271	12 787	11 856	6 850	8 371	5 358	5 308
1220 On capital gains	0	0	0	0	0	0	0	0	0	0
1300 Unallocable between 1100 and 1200	0	0	0	0	0	0	0	0	0	0
2000 Social security contributions	**4 851**	**74 647**	**205 867**	**306 974**	**388 505**	**384 668**	**376 684**	**404 851**	**463 338**	**462 860**
2100 Employees	743	254	823	63 074	81 088	89 175	100 861	108 356	123 661	128 161
Health insurance fees	743	9	5	0	0	0	0	0	0	0
Unemployment insurance fees	0	245	818	0	0	0	0	0	0	0
Pension fees	0	0	0	63 074	81 088	89 175	100 861	108 356	123 661	128 161
2110 On a payroll basis	..	..	..	63 074	81 088	89 175	100 861	108 356	123 661	128 161
2120 On an income tax basis	..	..	..	0	0	0	0	0	0	0
2200 Employers	3 568	71 602	196 905	237 576	300 010	288 310	271 449	291 646	335 354	331 065
Survivors pension fees	0	20 343	44 181	14 847	19 611	20 362	15 693	17 305	12 534	11 159
Health insurance fees	717	26 005	58 334	74 097	100 979	71 292	58 365	64 332	77 890	66 015
Unemployment insurance fees	0	0	0	0	0	0	0	0	0	0
Labour market fees	0	982	12 516	45 975	48 471	55 443	39 007	37 926	45 972	47 682
Industrial injury insurance fees	132	1 201	4 663	12 030	7 844	8 146	4 022	4 431	3 585	3 718
Seamen's pension fees	0	10	26	30	0	0	0	0	0	0
Part pension fees	0	1 119	2 897	0	0	0	0	0	0	0
Supplementary pension fees	2 719	21 458	73 129	71 384	97 748	106 712	119 508	129 204	148 819	154 165
Parent insurance fees	0	484	1 159	19 215	25 356	26 355	34 854	38 448	46 554	48 326
2210 On a payroll basis	..	..	..	237 576	300 010	288 310	271 449	291 646	335 354	331 065
2220 On an income tax basis	..	..	..	0	0	0	0	0	0	0
2300 Self-employed or non-employed	540	2 791	8 139	5 569	8 391	7 584	5 607	5 058	4 832	4 297
Survivors pension fees	0	943	1 580	451	662	687	442	443	256	158
Health insurance fees	260	992	1 702	1 988	3 297	2 082	550	256	291	152
Industrial injury insurance fees	0	64	191	365	264	275	113	84	59	51
Parent insurance fees	0	58	106	573	856	888	960	603	636	518
Supplementary pension fees	280	734	4 560	2 192	3 312	3 652	3 542	3 672	3 590	3 420
Reduction	0	0	0	0	0	0	0	0	0	0
2310 On a payroll basis	..	..	..	5 569	8 391	7 584	5 607	5 058	4 832	4 297
2320 On an income tax basis	..	..	..	0	0	0	0	0	0	0
2400 Unallocable between 2100, 2200 and 2300	0	0	0	756	-984	-401	-1 233	-209	-509	-662
2410 On a payroll basis	..	..	..	756	-984	-401	-1 233	-209	-509	-662
2420 On an income tax basis	..	..	..	0	0	0	0	0	0	0
3000 Taxes on payroll and workforce	**13**	**6 759**	**18 686**	**50 106**	**83 279**	**107 515**	**172 170**	**194 121**	**245 036**	**268 832**
Special wage tax	0	61	0	22 391	30 225	33 090	36 832	40 283	49 185	49 367
Child care fees	0	4 740	13 080	0	0	0	0	0	0	0
Adult education fees	0	614	1 555	0	0	0	0	0	0	0
Building research fees	13	105	0	0	0	0	0	0	0	0
Labour welfare fees	0	257	2 033	0	0	0	0	0	0	0
Labour education fees	0	982	0	0	0	0	0	0	0	0
Labour market fees	0	0	0	112	156	219	7	-1	1	1
General wage fees	0	0	2 018	27 603	52 898	74 207	135 331	153 839	195 849	219 464
4000 Taxes on property	**712**	**2 424**	**26 630**	**39 890**	**36 228**	**36 509**	**41 182**	**43 852**	**45 842**	**47 265**
4100 Recurrent taxes on immovable property	10	16	8 946	23 286	25 899	26 402	31 596	32 444	33 217	34 391
4110 Households	0	0	3 877	13 321	13 474	11 666	12 936	13 320	14 972	15 387
Special tax on real estate	..	..	3 877	13 321	13 474	11 666	12 936	13 320	14 972	15 387

	1965	1980	1990	2000	2007	2010	2013	2015	2018	2019
4120 Others	10	16	5 069	9 965	12 424	14 736	18 660	19 124	18 245	19 003
Forestry levy	10	16	423	22	34	18	37	19	10	9
Special tax on real estate	0	0	4 646	9 943	12 390	14 718	18 623	19 105	18 235	18 995
4200 Recurrent taxes on net wealth	366	717	3 200	8 223	0	0	0	0	0	0
4210 Individual	361	702	3 135	8 043	..	..	..	..	..	..
4220 Corporate	5	15	65	180	..	..	..	..	..	..
4300 Estate, inheritance and gift taxes	155	545	1 433	2 549	23	9	-4	0	0	0
4310 Estate and inheritance taxes	143	495	1 118	2 088	15	9	-4	0	..	..
4320 Gift taxes	12	50	315	460	8	0	0	0	..	..
4400 Taxes on financial and capital transactions	181	1 146	13 051	5 833	10 305	10 097	9 590	11 408	12 625	12 874
Taxes on financial and capital transactions	181	1 146	6 946	4 878	9 414	8 968	8 913	10 895	12 059	12 276
Turnover tax on securities	0	0	6 105	0	0	0	0	0	0	0
Tax on life group insurances	0	0	0	955	891	1 129	678	513	566	598
4500 Non-recurrent taxes	0	0	0	0	0	0	0	0	0	0
4510 On net wealth	..	..	..	..	..	..	..	..	..	..
4520 Other non-recurrent taxes	..	..	..	..	..	..	..	..	..	..
4600 Other recurrent taxes on property	0	0	0	0	0	0	0	0	0	0
5000 Taxes on goods and services	**12 471**	**62 234**	**188 709**	**291 615**	**401 038**	**455 450**	**466 556**	**514 485**	**596 358**	**610 185**
5100 Taxes on production, sale, transfer, etc.	11 808	58 474	181 587	284 182	387 956	439 050	450 054	495 733	576 524	589 535
5110 General taxes	4 147	34 643	112 399	199 606	286 211	326 685	341 952	383 002	445 489	459 825
5111 Value added taxes	0	34 643	112 399	197 483	282 586	322 603	337 822	379 120	445 361	459 699
5112 Sales tax	4 147	0	0	0	0	0	0	0	0	0
5113 Other	0	0	0	2 123	3 625	4 082	4 130	3 882	128	126
5120 Taxes on specific goods and services	7 661	23 831	69 188	84 576	101 745	112 365	108 102	112 731	131 035	129 710
5121 Excise duties	5 953	19 941	55 332	70 313	84 873	91 470	88 168	91 572	102 112	104 451
Taxes on petrol and fuel	1 420	4 229	17 171	39 011	44 501	47 426	43 869	44 906	48 198	48 718
Special sales tax	390	585	1 098	0	0	0	0	0	0	0
Sales tax on motor vehicles	325	553	1 983	195	3	0	0	0	0	0
Tobacco tax	1 150	3 087	5 636	7 747	9 742	10 588	11 136	11 825	12 374	11 892
Tax on spirits	1 548	4 431	6 205	4 902	4 250	4 324	4 001	4 208	4 466	4 532
Tax on wine	149	930	2 922	3 567	4 001	4 589	4 887	5 654	6 110	6 143
Tax on beer and soft drinks	242	964	2 532	2 355	2 773	3 219	3 329	3 895	4 344	4 313
Tax on energy consumption	729	5 162	16 352	11 451	18 994	21 035	20 827	20 787	25 009	27 130
Taxes on electricity from certain sources	0	0	1 018	0	0	0	0	0	0	0
Tax on wastes	0	0	0	1 085	609	289	119	297	234	252
Tax on cassette tapes	0	0	194	0	0	0	0	0	0	0
Tax on video recorders	0	0	221	0	0	0	0	0	0	0
Tax on chemicals	0	0	0	0	0	0	0	0	1 377	1 469
5122 Profits of fiscal monopolies	72	204	332	3 641	3 952	5 068	5 385	5 001	4 658	1 817
Alcohol monopoly wholesale	23	116	98	0	0	0	0	0	0	0
Alcohol monopoly retailing	49	88	234	80	296	302	116	198	180	240
Gaming monopoly retailing	0	0	0	3 561	3 657	4 766	5 269	4 803	4 478	1 577
5123 Customs and import duties	1 419	2 433	8 308	3 450	5 099	5 412	4 976	6 243	6 498	6 865
Customs	1 080	1 300	3 115	3 450	5 099	5 412	4 976	6 243	6 498	6 865
Agricultural levies	339	1 133	5 193	0	0	0	0	0	0	0
5124 Taxes on exports	0	0	0	0	0	0	0	0	0	0
5125 Taxes on investment goods	0	0	40	0	0	0	0	0	0	0
Investment tax	..	..	40	..	..	..	..	..	..	..
5126 Taxes on specific services	217	1 253	5 176	5 834	3 361	4 712	6 594	7 120	13 618	13 730
Betting tax	79	223	616	0	0	0	0	0	0	0
Advertisement tax	0	202	1 073	1 116	657	335	244	200	146	151
Tax on gambling	0	69	88	1 245	1 315	1 378	1 309	1 353	1 467	3 801
Other specific services	138	656	2 938	3 473	1 388	2 999	5 041	5 567	10 737	7 993
Tax on charter travelling	0	103	461	0	0	0	0	0	0	0
Tax on air travel	..	..	0	0	0	0	0	0	1 268	1 785
5127 Other taxes on internat. trade and transactions	0	0	0	0	0	0	0	0	0	0
5128 Other taxes	0	0	0	1 339	4 460	5 702	2 980	2 795	4 149	2 847
5130 Unallocable between 5110 and 5120	0	0	0	0	0	0	0	0	0	0
5200 Taxes on use of goods and perform activities	663	3 760	7 122	7 433	13 083	16 400	16 502	18 752	19 835	20 650
5210 Recurrent taxes	663	3 760	7 122	7 433	13 083	16 400	16 502	18 752	19 835	20 650
5211 Paid by households: motor vehicles	336	1 241	2 003	4 969	7 414	8 550	8 275	10 897	9 856	10 067
5212 Paid by others: motor vehicles	313	2 476	5 055	2 464	5 669	7 850	8 227	7 855	9 979	10 584
5213 Paid in respect of other goods	14	43	64	0	0	0	0	0	0	0
5220 Non-recurrent taxes	0	0	0	0	0	0	0	0	0	0
5300 Unallocable between 5100 and 5200	0	0	0	0	0	0	0	0	0	0
6000 Other taxes	**0**	**422**	**1 264**	**1 479**	**1 768**	**1 421**	**1 806**	**1 356**	**1 926**	**1 665**
6100 Paid solely by business	..	0	0	0	0	0	0	0	0	0
6200 Other	..	422	1 264	1 479	1 768	1 421	1 806	1 356	1 926	1 665
Memorandum item										
Customs duties collected on behalf of the EU	..	..	..	3 450	5 099	5 412	4 976	6 243	6 498	6 865
Total tax revenue on cash basis	**40 003**	**259 216**	**755 953**	**1 144 233**	**1 465 382**	**1 496 374**	**1 611 798**	**1 762 187**	**0**	**0**
Total tax revenue on accrual basis	**..**	**..**	**..**	**1 204 794**	**1 491 190**	**1 532 259**	**1 624 632**	**1 816 204**	**2 113 548**	**2 162 928**

	1965	1980	1990	2000	2007	2010	2013	2015	2018	2019
Conciliation with National Accounts										
Additional taxes included in National Accounts	..	..	..	0	0	0	0	0	0	0
Taxes excluded from National Accounts	..	..	..	0	0	0	0	0	0	0
Difference in treatment of tax credits	..	..	..	0	0	0	0	0	0	0
Capital transfer for uncollected revenue	..	..	..	0	0	0	0	0	0	0
Voluntary social security contributions	..	..	..	7 951	12 376	13 167	15 909	16 726	23 457	24 966
Miscellaneous differences	..	..	..	0	0	0	0	0	0	0
National Accounts: Taxes and actual social contributions	..	..	..	1 212 745	1 503 566	1 545 426	1 640 541	1 832 930	2 137 005	2 187 894
Imputed social contributions	..	..	..	0	0	0	0	0	0	0
National Accounts: Taxes and all social contributions	..	..	..	1 212 745	1 503 566	1 545 426	1 640 541	1 832 930	2 137 005	2 187 894

.. Not available

Note: Year ending 31st December.

From 2000 data are on accrual basis.

Figures prior to 1970 are not strictly comparable with those of later years, though the amounts involved are insignificant.

Heading 1000: Receipts are on accrual and not on a cash basis for all years.

Heading 2000 includes some voluntary contributions.

Source: Monthly reports of central Government Revenues (unpublished) National Audit Bureau, Stockholm. Local Government Finance (SOS), Tax assessment statistics (SOS) , National Central Bureau of Statistics, Stockholm.National Accounts (Statistical Reports), National Bureau of Statistics, Stockholm.

StatLink https://stat.link/0ouvmb

Table 5.35. Switzerland: Details of tax revenue, 1965-2019

Million CHF

	1965	1980	1990	2000	2007	2010	2013	2015	2018	2019
Total tax revenue	**11 237**	**46 385**	**85 774**	**128 205**	**151 404**	**162 356**	**173 121**	**181 128**	**193 879**	**199 971**
1000 Taxes on income, profits and capital gains	**4 616**	**21 022**	**40 203**	**56 411**	**69 790**	**74 439**	**79 267**	**84 362**	**92 596**	**96 634**
1100 Of individuals	3 748	18 056	27 824	37 948	47 994	51 835	53 801	56 375	59 749	61 335
1110 On income and profits	3 547	17 622	27 824	37 948	47 994	51 835	53 801	56 375	59 749	61 335
Direct federal tax	245	2 525	4 432	5 713	8 589	9 880	9 655	10 394	11 157	11 455
Military service exemption tax	35	103	135	163	138	155	163	173	167	168
Cantonal tax individuals	1 473	7 510	12 856	17 592	23 094	24 957	26 253	27 156	28 743	29 672
Municipal tax individuals	1 322	6 235	10 402	14 481	16 174	16 844	17 731	18 651	19 683	20 040
Withholding tax	358	1 249	0	0	0	0	0	0	0	0
Coupons	114	0	0	0	0	0	0	0	0	0
1120 On capital gains	201	434	0	0	0	0	0	0	0	0
Cantonal tax individuals	84	229	..	..	..	..	..	..	..	..
Municipal tax individuals	112	190	..	..	..	..	..	..	..	..
Direct federal tax	5	15	..	..	..	..	..	..	..	..
1200 Corporate	868	2 966	6 300	11 323	16 161	16 378	17 814	19 432	22 046	22 707
1210 On profits	801	2 818	6 300	11 323	16 161	16 378	17 814	19 432	22 046	22 707
Direct federal tax	153	781	2 214	4 928	6 800	8 006	8 698	9 731	11 289	11 813
Corporate cantonal tax	363	1 230	2 576	3 989	6 098	5 445	5 985	6 294	7 015	6 900
Corporate municipal tax	285	807	1 510	2 406	3 263	2 927	3 130	3 407	3 742	3 994
Withholding tax	0	0	0	0	0	0	0	0	0	0
1220 On capital gains	67	148	..	..	..	..	..	..	..	..
Corporate tax on gains	2	7	..	..	..	..	..	..	..	..
Corporate cantonal tax	28	77	..	..	..	..	..	..	..	..
Corporate municipal tax	37	64	..	..	..	..	..	..	..	..
1300 Unallocable between 1100 and 1200	0	0	6 079	7 140	5 635	6 226	7 652	8 556	10 801	12 592
Withholding tax	..	..	4 044	6 202	4 211	4 723	5 619	6 543	8 347	9 842
Property gains tax	..	..	2 035	938	1 424	1 502	2 033	2 013	2 454	2 751
Other	..	..	..	..	..	..	..	..	..	..
2000 Social security contributions	**1 670**	**10 844**	**19 952**	**30 961**	**34 974**	**38 385**	**42 862**	**44 285**	**46 072**	**47 234**
2100 Employees	716	4 833	9 341	14 491	16 369	17 579	19 720	20 445	21 364	21 906
2110 On a payroll basis	716	4 833	9 341	14 491	16 369	17 579	19 720	20 445	21 364	21 906
2120 On an income tax basis	0	0	..	..	..	..	..	..	..	..
2200 Employers	747	4 897	9 350	14 504	16 383	17 610	19 940	20 671	21 598	22 197
2210 On a payroll basis	747	4 897	9 350	14 504	16 383	17 610	19 940	20 671	21 598	22 197
2220 On an income tax basis	0	0	..	..	..	..	..	..	..	..
2300 Self-employed or non-employed	208	1 046	1 261	1 967	2 222	3 197	3 202	3 169	3 111	3 131
2310 On a payroll basis	209	1 046	1 261	1 967	2 222	3 197	3 202	3 169	3 111	3 131
2320 On an income tax basis	0	0	..	..	..	..	..	..	..	..
2400 Unallocable between 2100, 2200 and 2300	0	68	0	0	0	0	0	0	0	0
2410 On a payroll basis	..	68	..	..	..	..	..	..	..	..
2420 On an income tax basis	..	0	..	..	..	..	..	..	..	..
3000 Taxes on payroll and workforce	**0**	**0**	**0**	**0**	**0**	**0**	**0**	**0**	**0**	**0**
4000 Taxes on property	**1 108**	**3 830**	**7 586**	**12 333**	**12 223**	**12 402**	**12 041**	**13 140**	**14 508**	**15 343**
4100 Recurrent taxes on immovable property	78	304	447	735	895	968	1 052	1 138	1 204	1 329
4110 Households	78	304	447	735	895	968	1 052	1 138	1 204	1 329
Cantonal tax on buildings	20	71	125	187	265	286	303	349	347	395
Municipal tax on buildings	58	233	322	548	630	682	748	789	857	934
4120 Others	0	0	..	..	..	..	..	..	..	..
4200 Recurrent taxes on net wealth	692	2 201	3 382	5 254	7 002	7 105	7 406	8 096	9 327	9 994
4210 Individual	420	1 383	2 194	3 972	5 309	5 576	5 787	6 606	7 535	7 927
Cantonal wealth tax	206	739	1 232	2 241	3 145	3 324	3 532	4 044	4 593	4 855
Municipal wealth tax	214	644	962	1 731	2 164	2 252	2 255	2 562	2 942	3 071
4220 Corporate	272	818	1 188	1 282	1 693	1 529	1 619	1 490	1 792	2 067
Direct federal tax on capital	21	92	0	0	0	0	0	0	0	0
Cantonal tax on capital	142	436	760	821	1 107	969	1 032	947	1 117	1 325
Municipal tax on capital	109	290	428	461	586	561	586	542	674	742
4300 Estate, inheritance and gift taxes	142	393	896	1 215	869	974	966	1 088	1 212	1 232
4310 Estate and inheritance taxes	142	393	896	1 215	869	974	966	1 088	1 212	1 232
Cantonal inheritance tax	128	361	820	1 118	774	886	854	964	1 058	1 065
Municipal inheritance tax	14	32	76	97	96	88	112	124	154	168
4320 Gift taxes	0	0	..	..	..	..	..	..	..	..
4400 Taxes on financial and capital transactions	196	932	2 245	4 342	2 562	2 428	1 671	1 902	1 684	1 705
Cantonal transfer tax	48	245	115	144	182	182	185	177	212	207
Municipal transfer tax	21	103	39	52	42	50	52	52	59	64
Securities issuance	99	175	0	0	405	779	182	360	248	173
Securities trading	19	409	0	0	1 933	1 417	1 253	1 314	1 166	1 262
Currency effects	9	0	0	0	0	0	0	0	0	0
Securities issuance and trading	0	0	2 091	4 146	0	0	0	0	0	0
4500 Non-recurrent taxes	0	0	0	0	0	0	0	0	0	0

	1965	1980	1990	2000	2007	2010	2013	2015	2018	2019
4510 On net wealth	..	..	..	..	..	..	..	..	..	..
4520 Other non-recurrent taxes	..	..	..	..	..	..	..	..	..	..
4600 Other recurrent taxes on property	0	0	616	786	895	927	946	915	1 082	1 083
5000 Taxes on goods and services	**3 843**	**10 689**	**17 894**	**28 285**	**34 168**	**36 539**	**38 287**	**38 542**	**39 674**	**39 711**
5100 Taxes on production, sale, transfer, etc.	3 582	9 863	15 975	25 302	30 669	32 264	33 861	33 771	34 485	34 338
5110 General taxes	1 191	4 772	9 871	16 917	19 962	21 035	22 870	22 791	23 042	22 915
5111 Value added taxes	0	0	9 871	16 594	19 604	20 662	22 501	22 397	22 644	22 508
5112 Sales tax	1 191	4 772	0	323	358	373	369	393	398	407
Automobile duty	..	..	..	323	358	373	369	393	398	407
Other sales taxes	..	..	..	0	0	0	0	0	0	0
5113 Other	0	0	..	..	..	..	..	..	..	..
5120 Taxes on specific goods and services	2 391	5 091	6 058	8 337	10 663	11 191	10 936	10 912	11 340	11 307
5121 Excise duties	1 016	3 427	4 604	6 810	7 805	8 295	8 099	8 056	8 457	8 353
Beer tax	26	33	0	0	107	112	113	114	115	117
Excises on tobacco	190	634	15	32	2 247	2 417	2 354	2 255	2 135	2 095
Other price supplements	104	542	1 503	1 783	3	0	0	3	3	3
Fuel tax	467	955	1 334	2 975	3 076	3 110	3 034	2 864	2 785	2 746
Additional fuel tax	229	1 263	1 753	2 020	2 071	2 082	2 025	1 905	1 847	1 821
Road tax	0	0	0	0	0	0	0	0	0	0
Mineral oil tax on combustibles	0	0	0	0	20	20	23	19	15	17
Automobile duty	0	0	0	0	0	0	0	0	0	0
Tax on distilled spirits	0	0	0	1	281	296	292	279	268	275
Electricity consumption tax	0	0	0	0	0	259	258	617	1 288	1 281
5122 Profits of fiscal monopolies	158	472	..	..	..	..	..	..	..	..
Alcohol monopoly	111	354	..	..	..	..	..	..	..	..
Salt monopoly	16	25	..	..	..	..	..	..	..	..
Water monopoly	30	90	..	..	..	..	..	..	..	..
Other	1	3	..	..	..	..	..	..	..	..
5123 Customs and import duties	1 104	953	1 201	1 096	1 040	1 079	1 059	1 056	1 103	1 143
Import duties	972	923	1 201	1 096	1 040	1 079	1 059	1 056	1 103	1 143
Tobacco duty	114	6	0	0	0	0	0	0	0	0
Additional duties	18	24	0	0	0	0	0	0	0	0
5124 Taxes on exports	0	0	..	..	..	..	..	..	..	..
5125 Taxes on investment goods	0	0	..	..	..	..	..	..	..	..
5126 Taxes on specific services	113	239	253	431	1 818	1 816	1 778	1 800	1 780	1 812
Games in B casinos Confederation	2	2	2	37	449	381	308	272	281	311
Cantonal entertainment tax	17	37	23	27	39	101	73	67	66	73
Municipal entertainment tax	11	19	46	26	18	17	15	15	15	15
Other cantonal expenditure taxes	24	63	0	0	0	0	0	0	0	0
Other municipal expenditure taxes	19	6	0	0	0	0	0	0	0	0
Premium stamp duty	40	112	0	0	645	659	700	715	703	717
Lottery taxes	0	0	181	320	474	459	466	527	512	493
Other	0	0	0	20	193	199	216	204	202	203
5127 Other taxes on internat. trade and transactions	0	0	..	..	..	..	..	..	..	..
5128 Other taxes	0	0	..	..	..	..	..	..	..	..
5130 Unallocable between 5110 and 5120	0	0	46	47	44	38	55	68	104	116
5200 Taxes on use of goods and perform activities	261	826	1 918	2 983	3 499	4 276	4 426	4 771	5 188	5 373
5210 Recurrent taxes	261	826	1 918	2 983	3 499	4 276	4 426	4 767	5 184	5 365
5211 Paid by households: motor vehicles	152	501	921	1 336	1 580	1 667	1 685	1 768	1 841	1 863
Paid by households in respect of motor vehicles	..	..	921	1 336	1 580	1 667	1 685	1 768	1 841	1 863
Paid by households in respect of motorway tax sticker	..	..	0	0	0	0	0	0	0	0
5212 Paid by others: motor vehicles	76	251	230	334	395	417	421	442	460	466
Paid by others in respect of motor vehicles	..	..	230	334	395	417	421	442	460	466
Paid by others in respect of motorway tax sticker	..	..	0	0	0	0	0	0	0	0
Paid by others in respect of heavy vehicle charge	..	..	0	0	0	0	0	0	0	0
5213 Paid in respect of other goods	33	74	768	1 314	1 524	2 192	2 319	2 556	2 882	3 036
Hunting and fishing	9	20	0	0	0	0	0	0	0	0
Cantonal dog license	3	9	6	9	8	8	10	9	10	11
Municipal dog license	2	8	14	21	25	30	33	35	41	41
Cantonal inns	12	24	0	0	0	0	0	0	0	0
Cantonal royalties	5	12	0	0	0	0	0	0	0	0
Other	2	1	0	33	33	30	31	24	13	12
Environmental incentive fees	0	0	3	73	166	755	833	1 036	1 294	1 447
Royalties and concessions	0	0	42	53	64	84	100	101	130	134
Radio and television licences	..	..	703	1 124	1 228	1 285	1 313	1 351	1 394	1 391
5220 Non-recurrent taxes	0	0	0	0	0	0	0	5	4	9
5300 Unallocable between 5100 and 5200	0	0	0	0	0	0	0	0	0	0
6000 Other taxes	**0**	**0**	**140**	**215**	**249**	**590**	**664**	**799**	**1 029**	**1 049**
6100 Paid solely by business	..	..	42	65	75	274	300	342	383	397
6200 Other	..	..	98	151	174	316	364	457	646	652
Exemption tax	..	..	98	151	174	187	191	190	200	201
Other	..	..	0	0	0	130	173	267	445	450

	1965	1980	1990	2000	2007	2010	2013	2015	2018	2019
Total tax revenue on cash basis	**11 237**	**46 385**	..	..	..	..	..	..	..	..
Total tax revenue on accrual basis	..	..	**85 774**	**128 205**	**151 404**	**162 356**	**173 121**	**181 128**	**193 879**	**199 971**
Conciliation with National Accounts										
Additional taxes included in national accounts	..	..	0	0	0	0	0	0	0	0
Tax excluded from national accounts	..	..	0	0	0	0	0	0	0	0
Difference in treatment of tax credits	..	..	0	0	0	0	0	0	0	0
Capital transfer for uncollected revenue	..	..	-242	-733	-936	-1 121	-1 309	-1 058	-1 036	-1 023
Voluntary social security contributions	..	..	0	0	0	0	0	0	0	0
Miscellaneous differences	..	..	0	0	0	0	0	0	0	0
National Accounts: taxes and actual social contributions	..	..	85 533	127 472	150 468	161 235	171 812	180 070	192 842	198 948
Imputed social contributions	..	..	362	502	467	455	483	337	370	390
National Accounts: taxes and all social contributions	..	..	85 895	127 974	150 935	161 690	172 295	180 407	193 212	199 338

.. Not available

Note: Calendar year ending on 31 December.

The data is on an accrual basis.

The pre-1970 figures are not strictly comparable with those from the following years which were revised slightly.

"Parish taxes" are not reported in these statistics from 1985 onward.

In section 1100: payments made in consideration for exemption from military service could be classed under nontax receipts.

Section 2000 (Social security contributions) has been revised from 1985 onward to take account of the sectoring of government units adopted when switching to the ESA 95 system of accounts (currently ESA 2010). Consequently, health insurance contributions and those to the Swiss National Accident Insurance Fund are now excluded from section 2000.

Source: Financial Statistics, Federal Finance Administration.

StatLink https://stat.link/8du5b2

Table 5.36. Turkey: Details of tax revenue, 1965-2019

Million TRY

	1965	1980	1990	2000	2007	2010	2013	2015	2018	2019
Total tax revenue	**0**	**1**	**79**	**40 263**	**203 053**	**287 873**	**458 698**	**586 722**	**901 485**	**997 551**
1000 Taxes on income, profits and capital gains	**0**	**0**	**26**	**11 890**	**48 197**	**61 317**	**92 749**	**119 144**	**217 666**	**241 533**
1100 Of individuals	0	0	21	8 954	34 447	40 392	63 761	85 756	138 992	162 704
1110 On income and profits	0	0	21	8 954	34 447	40 392	63 761	85 756	138 992	162 704
Income tax	0	0	21	8 954	34 447	40 392	63 761	85 756	138 992	162 704
1120 On capital gains	0	0	0	0	0	0	0	0	0	0
1200 Corporate	0	0	5	2 935	13 751	20 925	28 988	33 388	78 673	78 829
1210 On profits	0	0	5	2 935	13 751	20 925	28 988	33 388	78 673	78 829
Corporation tax	0	0	5	2 935	13 751	20 925	28 988	33 388	78 673	78 829
1220 On capital gains	0	0	0	0	0	0	0	0	0	0
1300 Unallocable between 1100 and 1200	0	0	0	0	0	0	0	0	0	0
Fiscal balance tax	..	0	..	..	..	..	..	..	..	..
Capital gains tax on real estate sales	..	0	..	..	..	..	..	..	..	..
2000 Social security contributions	**0**	**0**	**15**	**7 543**	**44 052**	**71 696**	**125 871**	**170 282**	**269 932**	**312 808**
2100 Employees	0	0	6	2 712	17 867	26 934	49 831	64 214	101 666	120 108
2110 On a payroll basis	..	..	..	2 712	17 867	26 934	49 831	64 214	101 666	120 108
2120 On an income tax basis	..	..	..	0	0	0	0	0	0	0
2200 Employers	0	0	9	3 619	20 442	39 363	71 184	95 067	151 373	178 345
2210 On a payroll basis	..	..	..	3 619	20 442	39 363	71 184	95 067	151 373	178 345
2220 On an income tax basis	..	..	..	0	0	0	0	0	0	0
2300 Self-employed or non-employed	0	0	1	1 211	5 743	5 399	4 856	11 001	16 893	14 356
2310 On a payroll basis	..	..	..	1 211	5 743	5 399	4 856	11 001	16 893	14 356
2320 On an income tax basis	..	..	..	0	0	0	0	0	0	0
2400 Unallocable between 2100, 2200 and 2300	0	0	0	0	0	0	0	0	0	0
2410 On a payroll basis	..	..	..	..	..	..	..	..	..	..
2420 On an income tax basis	..	..	..	..	..	..	..	..	..	..
3000 Taxes on payroll and workforce	**0**	**0**	**0**	**0**	**0**	**0**	**0**	**0**	**0**	**0**
4000 Taxes on property	**0**	**0**	**2**	**1 272**	**7 621**	**11 684**	**21 280**	**28 582**	**38 941**	**41 721**
4100 Recurrent taxes on immovable property	0	0	0	191	1 464	2 669	3 847	5 882	8 703	9 681
Real estate tax	0	0	..	191	1 464	2 669	3 847	5 882	8 703	9 681
4110 Households	..	..	..	..	..	..	..	..	..	..
4120 Others	..	..	..	..	..	..	..	..	..	..
4200 Recurrent taxes on net wealth	0	0	0	0	0	0	0	0	0	0
4210 Individual	..	..	..	..	..	..	..	..	..	..
4220 Corporate	..	..	..	..	..	..	..	..	..	..
4300 Estate, inheritance and gift taxes	0	0	0	15	125	215	340	435	921	1 104
Gift and inheritance tax	0	0	0	15	125	215	340	435	921	1 104
4310 Estate and inheritance taxes	..	..	..	..	..	..	..	..	..	..
4320 Gift taxes	..	..	..	..	..	..	..	..	..	..
4400 Taxes on financial and capital transactions	0	0	2	1 065	6 032	8 800	17 093	22 265	29 318	30 937
Stamp tax	0	0	2	818	3 642	5 083	9 416	12 045	16 961	18 853
Real estate purchase tax	0	0	0	0	0	0	0	0	0	0
Title deed fees	0	0	0	207	2 000	3 329	7 072	9 530	11 534	11 213
Notary fees	0	0	0	40	389	388	606	690	822	872
4500 Non-recurrent taxes	0	0	0	0	0	0	0	0	0	0
4510 On net wealth	..	..	..	..	..	..	..	..	..	..
4520 Other non-recurrent taxes	..	..	..	..	..	..	..	..	..	..
4600 Other recurrent taxes on property	0	0	0	0	0	0	0	0	0	0
5000 Taxes on goods and services	**0**	**0**	**22**	**16 901**	**96 766**	**137 252**	**211 257**	**259 964**	**364 982**	**389 092**
5100 Taxes on production, sale, transfer, etc.	0	0	22	16 328	92 605	131 878	203 364	250 261	351 455	373 692
5110 General taxes	0	0	16	9 735	43 285	62 533	100 723	121 070	178 616	180 729
5111 Value added taxes	..	..	14	9 735	43 285	62 533	100 723	121 070	178 616	180 729
5112 Sales tax	..	..	0	0	0	0	0	0	0	0
5113 Other	..	..	1	0	0	0	0	0	0	0
5120 Taxes on specific goods and services	0	0	6	6 593	49 320	69 345	102 641	129 191	172 839	192 963
5121 Excise duties	0	0	1	4 718	39 111	57 285	85 462	105 922	133 904	147 131
Sales taxes	0	0	0	0	0	0	0	0	0	0
Domestic production tax	0	0	0	0	0	0	0	0	0	0
Domestic production tax on petrol	0	0	0	0	0	0	0	0	0	0
Production tax on monopoly goods	0	0	0	0	0	0	0	0	0	0
Sugar consumption taxes	0	0	0	0	0	0	0	0	0	0
Motor vehicles purchase tax (Total)	0	0	1	916	4 293	6 193	10 565	17 027	17 328	13 807
Motor vehicles purchase tax	0	0	0	498	4 293	6 193	10 565	17 027	17 328	13 807
Additional motor vehicle purchase tax	0	0	0	418	0	0	0	0	0	0
Revenue from other excises	0	0	0	533	12 765	19 395	29 739	38 066	60 982	72 328
Petroleum consumption tax	0	0	0	3 269	22 052	31 697	45 158	50 830	55 593	60 997
5122 Profits of fiscal monopolies	0	0	0	0	0	0	0	0	0	0

	1965	1980	1990	2000	2007	2010	2013	2015	2018	2019
5123 Customs and import duties	0	0	4	462	2 478	3 319	5 542	8 521	15 959	17 460
Customs duty	0	0	1	449	2 441	3 240	5 409	8 280	15 276	16 832
Customs duty on petrol	0	0	0	0	0	0	0	0	0	0
Production tax on imports	0	0	0	0	0	0	0	0	0	0
Production tax on petrol imports	0	0	0	0	0	0	0	0	0	0
Stamp duty on imports	0	0	2	0	0	0	0	0	0	0
Wharf duty	0	0	1	0	0	0	0	0	0	0
Other	0	0	0	13	37	80	133	240	683	628
5124 Taxes on exports	0	0	0	0	0	0	0	0	0	0
5125 Taxes on investment goods	0	0	0	0	0	0	0	0	0	0
5126 Taxes on specific services	0	0	1	997	7 686	4 005	6 853	10 014	19 340	24 352
Bank, insurance transaction tax	0	0	1	997	3 149	3 571	6 160	9 172	18 184	22 670
Transportation tax	0	0	0	0	0	0	0	0	0	0
PTT service tax	0	0	0	0	4 211	0	0	0	0	0
Tax on football pool	0	0	0	0	0	0	0	0	0	0
Lottery tax	0	0	0	0	327	434	692	842	1 155	1 681
5127 Other taxes on internat. trade and transactions	0	0	0	0	0	0	0	0	0	0
Foreign travel expenditures tax	0	0	..	..	..	..	..	..	..	..
5128 Other taxes	0	0	0	416	46	4 736	4 785	4 734	3 637	4 019
5130 Unallocable between 5110 and 5120	0	0	0	0	0	0	0	0	0	0
5200 Taxes on use of goods and perform activities	0	0	0	572	4 161	5 374	7 894	9 703	13 527	15 400
5210 Recurrent taxes	0	0	0	359	4 161	5 374	7 894	9 703	13 527	15 400
Motor vehicles tax	0	0	0	359	0	5 374	7 894	9 703	13 527	15 400
5211 Paid by households: motor vehicles	..	..	..	0	0	0	0	0	0	0
5212 Paid by others: motor vehicles	..	..	..	359	4 161	5 374	7 894	9 703	13 527	15 400
Motor vehicles tax	..	..	..	302	3 521	5 033	7 353	8 949	12 844	14 503
Traffic fees	..	..	..	58	640	341	540	754	683	897
5213 Paid in respect of other goods	..	..	..	0	0	0	0	0	0	0
5220 Non-recurrent taxes	0	0	0	213	0	0	0	0	0	0
Building construction tax	..	0	..	0	..	..	..	..	..	..
5300 Unallocable between 5100 and 5200	0	0	0	0	0	0	0	0	0	0
6000 Other taxes	**0**	**0**	**13**	**2 658**	**6 417**	**5 924**	**7 541**	**8 750**	**9 963**	**12 397**
6100 Paid solely by business	..	0	0	0	0	0	0	0	0	0
6200 Other	..	0	13	2 658	6 417	5 924	7 541	8 750	9 963	12 397
Funds	..	..	..	1 938	0	0	0	0	0	0
Vocatial Train Pro.F.	..	..	..	67	0	0	0	0	0	0
Tax penalties and fines	..	..	..	548	4 191	2 689	3 175	3 779	4 159	6 361
Municipalities revenue	..	..	..	106	2 227	3 235	4 366	4 971	5 805	6 035
Total tax revenue on cash basis	**0**	**1**	**79**	**40 263**	**203 053**	**287 873**	**458 698**	**586 722**	**901 485**	**997 551**
Total tax revenue on accrual basis	..	..	..	..	..	..	..	..	..	..
Conciliation with National Accounts										
Additional taxes included in National Accounts	..	..	..	..	..	..	..	..	..	..
Taxes excluded from National Accounts	..	..	..	..	..	..	..	..	..	..
Difference in treatment of tax credits	..	..	..	..	..	..	..	..	..	..
Capital transfer for uncollected revenue	..	..	..	..	..	..	..	..	..	..
Voluntary social security contributions	..	..	..	..	..	..	..	..	..	..
Miscellaneous differences	..	..	..	..	..	..	..	..	..	..
National Accounts: Taxes and actual social contributions	..	..	..	..	..	..	..	..	..	..
Imputed social contributions	..	..	..	..	..	..	..	..	..	..
National Accounts: Taxes and all social contributions	..	..	..	..	..	..	..	..	..	..

.. Not available

Note: From 1982 the data are based on the fiscal year ending 31st December. Before that the data are on a fiscal year basis beginning 1st March.

Revenue is reported on a cash basis except for social security contributions which are reported on an assessment basis.

The figures under the local tax collections include taxes under "Municipalities Revenues Law" and Property tax. They also include transfers to the local authorities from central budget tax revenues under the revenue sharing system.

Heading 2000: Before 2003, contributions to some private social security schemes are included in this heading.

Source: Bulletin of national accounts and the Budget revenue Bulletin.

StatLink https://stat.link/8gpikv

Table 5.37. United Kingdom: Details of tax revenue, 1965-2019

Million GBP

	1965	1980	1990	2000	2007	2010	2013	2015	2018	2019
Total tax revenue	**10 945**	**81 153**	**202 368**	**359 370**	**508 724**	**514 797**	**568 769**	**611 151**	**704 364**	**725 615**
Total tax revenue exclusive of taxes collected for the EU	..	..	**200 520**	**357 240**	**506 309**	**511 852**	**565 843**	**608 064**	**700 792**	**721 936**
1000 Taxes on income, profits and capital gains	**4 050**	**30 651**	**79 576**	**142 197**	**201 316**	**192 771**	**199 745**	**212 633**	**247 764**	**251 489**
1100 Of individuals	3 618	23 868	59 506	104 136	151 157	147 019	156 570	168 873	192 765	200 486
1110 On income and profits	3 615	23 376	57 614	101 925	147 309	144 502	152 668	163 291	184 968	191 299
Income tax	..	23 370	57 614	101 925	147 309	144 502	152 668	163 291	184 968	191 299
Surtax	..	6	0	0	0	0	0	0	0	0
1120 On capital gains	3	492	1 892	2 211	3 848	2 517	3 902	5 582	7 797	9 187
1200 Corporate	484	6 783	20 070	38 061	50 159	45 752	43 175	43 760	54 999	51 003
1210 On profits	484	6 510	18 994	35 730	46 841	44 857	42 172	42 344	53 226	49 308
Petroleum revenue tax	..	1 799	941	1 540	1 387	1 349	1 296	-552	-817	-319
Supplementary petroleum duty	..	0	0	0	0	0	0	0	0	0
Corporation tax	..	4 712	18 053	34 190	44 740	42 865	40 209	42 276	53 351	48 813
Corporation tax overspill relief	..	-1	0	0	0	0	0	0	0	0
Profits tax	..	0	0	0	0	0	0	0	0	0
Windfall tax	..	0	0	0	0	0	0	0	0	0
Betting tax	..	0	0	0	590	568	605	595	692	814
Non fossil fuel obligation levy	..	0	0	0	124	75	62	25	0	0
1220 On capital gains	0	273	1 076	2 331	3 318	895	1 003	1 416	1 773	1 695
1300 Unallocable between 1100 and 1200	-52	0	0	0	0	0	0	0	0	0
2000 Social security contributions	**1 685**	**13 531**	**34 457**	**60 252**	**93 210**	**97 346**	**106 085**	**114 173**	**135 225**	**143 255**
2100 Employees	770	5 228	13 296	24 175	36 585	38 703	41 481	44 488	52 137	56 200
2110 On a payroll basis	..	..	13 296	24 175	36 585	38 703	41 481	44 488	52 137	56 200
2120 On an income tax basis	..	..	0	0	0	0	0	0	0	0
2200 Employers	831	8 210	19 984	34 028	53 765	55 887	62 019	66 491	79 240	82 699
2210 On a payroll basis	..	..	19 984	34 028	53 765	55 887	62 019	66 491	79 240	82 699
2220 On an income tax basis	..	..	0	0	0	0	0	0	0	0
2300 Self-employed or non-employed	75	317	1 177	2 049	2 860	2 756	2 585	3 194	3 848	4 356
2310 On a payroll basis	..	..	1 177	2 049	2 860	2 756	2 585	3 194	3 848	4 356
2320 On an income tax basis	..	..	0	0	0	0	0	0	0	0
2400 Unallocable between 2100, 2200 and 2300	9	-224	0	0	0	0	0	0	0	0
2410 On a payroll basis	..	..	..	..	..	..	..	..	..	..
2420 On an income tax basis	..	..	..	..	..	..	..	..	..	..
3000 Taxes on payroll and workforce	**0**	**3 498**	**0**	**0**	**0**	**0**	**0**	**0**	**2 604**	**2 764**
Selective employment tax	..	0	..	..	..	..	..	..	0	0
National insurance surcharge	..	3 498	..	..	..	..	..	..	0	0
Apprenticeship Levy	..	0	..	..	..	..	..	..	2 604	2 764
4000 Taxes on property	**1 591**	**9 774**	**16 538**	**41 134**	**63 392**	**61 768**	**70 094**	**76 565**	**88 664**	**90 258**
4100 Recurrent taxes on immovable property	1 228	8 665	13 462	30 552	44 891	50 028	55 139	58 185	66 407	68 748
4110 Households	539	3 687	2 373	14 205	23 609	25 919	27 640	29 355	34 733	36 537
Northern Ireland rates paid to CG	..	37	113	141	265	335	409	384	351	334
Council tax	..	0	0	13 991	23 217	25 438	27 061	28 777	34 153	35 957
Rates paid to LA	..	3 650	2 260	73	127	146	170	194	229	246
4120 Others	689	4 978	11 089	16 347	21 282	24 109	27 499	28 830	31 674	32 211
National non-domestic rates	..	0	7 542	14 966	19 358	21 602	24 611	25 834	28 410	28 928
Rates paid to LA	..	4 925	2 869	149	267	497	567	601	690	689
Northern Ireland rates paid to CG	..	53	115	207	353	361	373	398	431	448
London Regional Transport levy	..	0	47	0	0	0	0	0	0	0
LA payments of NNDR	..	0	469	889	1 111	1 236	1 389	1 389	1 389	1 389
NPISH payments of NNDR	..	0	47	136	193	245	342	384	478	489
Crossrail Business rates supplement	..	0	0	0	0	168	217	224	276	268
4200 Recurrent taxes on net wealth	0	0	0	0	0	0	0	0	0	0
4210 Individual	..	..	..	..	..	..	..	..	..	..
4220 Corporate	..	..	..	..	..	..	..	..	..	..
4300 Estate, inheritance and gift taxes	287	479	1 321	2 215	3 867	2 642	3 379	4 442	5 301	5 165
4310 Estate and inheritance taxes	287	479	1 321	2 215	3 867	2 642	3 379	4 442	5 301	5 165
Death duties	..	423	1 278	2 156	3 764	2 592	3 293	4 359	5 198	5 097
Development land tax	..	42	6	0	0	0	0	0	0	0
Taxes on other capital transfers	..	14	37	59	50	50	50	50	50	50
Special tax on bank deposits	..	0	0	0	0	0	0	0	0	0
Betterment duty	..	0	0	0	0	0	0	0	0	0
Special charges	..	0	0	0	0	0	0	0	0	0
Special contribution	..	0	0	0	0	0	0	0	0	0
Equal pay on capital transfers	..	0	0	0	53	0	36	33	53	18
4320 Gift taxes	0	0	0	0	0	0	0	0	0	0
4400 Taxes on financial and capital transactions	76	630	1 755	8 367	14 634	9 098	11 540	13 791	16 654	15 962
Stamp duties	..	630	1 755	8 367	14 634	9 098	11 540	13 791	16 654	15 962
4500 Non-recurrent taxes	0	0	0	0	0	0	36	147	302	383

	1965	1980	1990	2000	2007	2010	2013	2015	2018	2019
4510 On net wealth	..	..	..	..	..	..	0	0	0	0
4520 Other non-recurrent taxes	..	..	..	..	..	..	36	147	302	383
4600 Other recurrent taxes on property	0	0	0	0	0	0	0	0	0	0
5000 Taxes on goods and services	**3 619**	**23 699**	**62 780**	**115 787**	**150 806**	**162 912**	**192 845**	**207 780**	**230 107**	**237 849**
5100 Taxes on production, sale, transfer, etc.	3 406	22 677	59 379	110 804	144 752	155 471	185 262	200 337	222 059	229 312
5110 General taxes	647	11 897	34 136	65 018	93 374	97 646	121 460	133 064	149 104	154 754
5111 Value added taxes	0	11 897	34 136	65 018	93 374	97 646	121 460	133 064	149 104	154 754
Value added tax	..	11 893	33 620	64 918	93 348	97 565	121 650	132 948	149 254	154 781
Adj. to VAT contribution	..	4	516	100	26	81	-190	116	-150	-27
Purchase tax	..	0	0	0	0	0	0	0	0	0
5112 Sales tax	647	0	0	0	0	0	0	0	0	0
5113 Other	0	0	0	0	0	0	0	0	0	0
5120 Taxes on specific goods and services	2 759	10 780	25 243	45 786	51 378	57 825	63 802	67 273	72 955	74 558
5121 Excise duties	2 383	8 616	19 707	37 315	40 427	45 454	46 588	47 294	49 125	49 285
Beer	..	1 029	2 220	2 813	3 042	3 278	3 337	3 294	3 638	3 659
Wines, spirits, cider and perry	..	1 513	2 627	3 751	5 008	6 075	7 063	7 385	8 355	8 457
Tobacco	..	2 735	5 541	7 666	7 862	9 076	9 479	9 190	8 976	9 038
Hydrocarbon oil	..	3 327	9 302	23 041	24 512	27 013	26 697	27 415	27 919	27 795
Other excise duties	..	12	17	0	0	0	0	0	0	0
Sugar levy	..	12	0	44	3	12	12	10	0	0
Soft Drinks Levy	..	..	0	0	0	0	0	0	237	336
5122 Profits of fiscal monopolies	0	0	0	0	0	0	0	0	0	0
5123 Customs and import duties	343	1 109	1 837	2 086	2 522	3 058	3 042	3 219	3 480	3 488
Custom duties	..	..	..	1 800	2 074	2 933	2 914	3 077	3 335	3 343
Import duties	..	855	1 722	0	0	0	0	0	0	0
Agricultural levies	..	254	115	286	338	0	0	0	0	0
Temporary charges of import	..	0	0	0	0	0	0	0	0	0
British Transport Police	..	0	0	0	110	125	128	142	145	145
5124 Taxes on exports	0	-1	36	0	0	0	0	0	0	0
Levies on exports	..	-1	36	..	..	..	..	..	..	..
5125 Taxes on investment goods	0	0	0	0	0	0	0	0	0	0
5126 Taxes on specific services	33	456	1 022	5 826	6 523	7 292	11 601	13 626	16 320	17 043
Betting and gaming	..	456	1 022	1 522	959	1 092	1 538	2 053	2 202	2 502
National Lottery contributions to fund	..	0	0	1 590	1 310	1 625	1 644	1 713	1 713	1 713
Air passenger duty	..	0	0	940	1 883	2 094	2 960	3 119	3 513	3 810
Insurance premium tax	..	0	0	1 707	2 306	2 401	3 018	3 294	6 201	6 417
Bank Levy - Stability Fee Scheme	..	0	0	0	0	0	2 352	3 369	2 613	2 523
Light Dues	..	0	0	67	65	80	89	78	78	78
5127 Other taxes on internat. trade and transactions	0	0	0	0	0	0	0	0	0	0
5128 Other taxes	0	600	2 641	559	1 906	2 021	2 571	3 134	4 030	4 742
Fossil fuel levy	..	0	875	56	0	0	0	0	0	0
European coal and steel levy	..	21	11	0	0	0	0	0	0	0
Gas levy	..	12	291	0	0	0	0	0	0	0
Car tax	..	83	1 464	0	0	0	0	0	0	0
Landfill tax	..	484	0	461	877	1 065	1 191	1 028	842	784
Climate change levy	..	0	0	0	690	666	1 098	1 752	1 911	2 091
Aggregates levy	..	0	0	0	339	290	282	354	366	396
Hydro benefit	..	0	0	42	0	0	0	0	0	0
Renewable energy obligations	..	0	0	0	0	0	0	0	0	0
Channel 4 advertising formula	..	0	0	0	0	0	0	0	0	0
Milk super levy	..	0	0	0	0	0	0	0	0	0
Contracts for Difference	..	0	0	0	0	0	0	0	911	1 471
5130 Unallocable between 5110 and 5120	0	0	0	0	0	0	0	0	0	0
5200 Taxes on use of goods and perform activities	212	1 378	3 401	4 983	6 054	7 441	7 583	7 443	8 048	8 537
5210 Recurrent taxes	212	1 378	3 401	4 983	6 054	7 441	7 583	7 443	7 963	8 452
5211 Paid by households: motor vehicles	118	729	1 841	2 996	4 096	4 561	4 312	3 970	4 512	4 998
Motor vehicle duty	..	726	1 837	2 992	4 096	4 561	4 312	3 970	4 512	4 998
Boat licences	..	3	4	4	0	0	0	0	0	0
5212 Paid by others: motor vehicles	74	588	1 134	1 614	1 288	1 279	1 789	1 929	2 001	2 007
Motor vehicle levy	..	588	1 134	1 614	1 288	1 279	1 789	1 929	2 001	2 007
5213 Paid in respect of other goods	20	61	426	373	670	1 601	1 482	1 544	1 450	1 447
IBA levy	..	..	134	0	0	0	0	0	0	0
Telecommunications regulator fees	..	..	7	12	17	12	0	0	0	0
Gas regulator fees	..	..	2	0	0	0	0	0	0	0
Electricity regulator fees	..	..	5	0	0	0	0	0	0	0
Water regulator fees	..	..	6	11	11	12	24	27	33	36
Rail regulator fees	..	..	0	14	12	12	12	12	12	12
Company registration surplus fees	..	..	12	0	0	0	0	0	0	0
Consumer and credit act fees	..	..	163	119	281	480	480	480	480	480
Levy funded bodies	..	..	97	217	349	1 040	922	970	859	853
1936 Tithe Act payments	..	..	0	0	0	0	0	0	0	0
Recurrent taxes paid in respect of other goods	..	..	0	0	0	45	44	55	66	66

	1965	1980	1990	2000	2007	2010	2013	2015	2018	2019
5220 Non-recurrent taxes	0	0	0	0	0	0	0	0	85	85
Immigration Skills Charge	..	..	..	..	..	..	..	..	85	85
5300 Unallocable between 5100 and 5200	1	-356	0	0	0	0	0	0	0	0
6000 Other taxes	**0**	**0**	**9 017**	**0**	**0**	**0**	**0**	**0**	**0**	**0**
6100 Paid solely by business	..	..	0	..	..	..	..	..	..	..
6200 Other	..	..	9 017	..	..	..	..	..	..	..
Community charge	..	..	9 017	..	..	..	..	..	..	..
Memorandum item										
Customs duties collected on behalf of the EU	..	..	..	1 800	2 074	2 933	2 914	3 077	3 335	3 343
Non-wastable tax credits										
Non-wastable tax credits against 1110	..	..	7 454	4 651	20 030	28 879	29 710	28 539	22 878	18 003
Tax expenditure component	..	..	6 973	1 233	4 414	5 542	2 538	2 571	2 061	1 622
Transfer component	..	..	481	3 418	15 617	23 338	27 172	25 968	20 817	16 381
Non-wastable tax credits against 1210	..	..	0	0	918	1 313	1 156	3 273	6 262	7 314
Tax expenditure component	..	..	0	0	654	915	626	1 136	2 002	2 309
Transfer component	..	..	0	0	264	398	530	2 137	4 260	5 005
Total tax revenue on cash basis	**10 945**	**81 153**	**202 400**	**356 070**	**509 032**	**509 500**	**562 359**	**601 426**	**689 586**	**708 100**
Total tax revenue on accrual basis	**..**	**..**	**202 368**	**359 370**	**508 724**	**514 797**	**568 769**	**611 151**	**704 364**	**725 615**
Conciliation with National Accounts										
Additional taxes included in National Accounts	..	..	1 323	2 062	4 072	4 731	5 816	7 261	9 657	9 895
Taxes excluded from National Accounts	..	..	0	0	0	0	0	0	0	0
Difference in treatment of tax credits	..	..	6 973	1 233	5 068	6 457	3 164	3 707	4 063	3 931
Capital transfer for uncollected revenue	..	..	0	0	0	0	0	0	0	0
Voluntary social security contributions	..	..	3 288	8 103	18 629	21 217	22 438	25 025	27 546	33 474
Miscellaneous differences	..	..	0	0	0	0	0	0	0	0
National Accounts: Taxes and actual social contributions	..	..	213 952	370 768	536 493	547 202	600 187	647 144	745 630	772 915
Imputed social contributions	..	..	3 966	4 234	1 391	1 616	1 568	1 565	1 499	1 953
National Accounts: Taxes and all social contributions	..	..	217 918	375 002	537 884	548 818	601 755	648 709	747 129	774 868

.. Not available

Note: Year ending 31st December.

From 1990 data are on accrual basis.

Supranational taxes reported by the United Kingdom continue to be reported for 2020 in Revenue Statistics as in previous years. From 2021, at the end of the Brexit transition period, this will come to an end and taxes subsequently introduced by the United Kingdom will be reflected in the appropriate tax category at the national or subnational levels of government, as appropriate.

Heading 1210: The corporate tax figures include company income tax from 1990 onwards.

Heading 2000: Includes some voluntary contributions which cannot be separately identified.

Heading 6200: The community charge replaced domestic rates in Scotland in April 1989 and was extended to England and Wales in April 1990. This tax has been classified in heading 6200 as it is a lump-sum tax levied on each adult in a household (domestic rates are classified in heading 4100). Headings for non-wastable tax credits 1110 and 1210 are consistent with the guidelines, and the figures in the data are treated accordingly. The following method is adopted separately for Working Families 'Tax Credit and Disabled Persons Tax Credit' paid from 1999 to 2003. For each calendar, a random sample of awards over-lapping the quarter is taken. Each recipient family's income tax liability for the fiscal year within which the quarter falls is calculated , based on the earned income reported for the award (uprated to the middle of the overlap period). And the result multiplied by the number of days in the overlap period divided by 365. The tax expenditure component is defined as the minimum of this amount and the total amount of award paid in the overlap period. The total amount of award paid and the tax expenditure component are each summed over the sample cases, and the ratio is taken as the tax expenditure ration for the quarter. From 2003, the equivalent breakdown for Child and Working tax credits is based on household survey data. Survey data is used to estimate the breakdown into the tax expenditure and the transfer components for the other smaller tax credits.

The United Kingdom Personal Tax Credit information presented in Revenue Statistics is on a cash basis (rather than an accrual basis as for the rest of the data). PTC information on a financial year basis has been used as a proxy for calendar year. Please note that since 2015-16 tax credits is no longer split into tax expenditure and transfer component. The split for years after 2014-15 is estimated by applying the 2014-15 split to total personal tax credits expenditure. The sum of tax expenditure and transfer components may not match the total due to rounding. Total values are consistent with published figures available here: https://www.gov.uk/government/statistics/hmrc-tax-and-nics-receipts-for-the-uk.

Please note that the sum of the corporate tax credit (CTC) components in the United Kingdom may not match total CTC's due to rounding. The CTC information presented in Revenue Statistics is on a cash basis (rather than an accrual basis as for the rest of the data). CTC information on a financial year basis has been used as a proxy for calendar year. Please note that the breakdown of total CTCs from 2002/03 to 2010/11 have been estimated using historic proportional splits applied to total published CTC information. Total values are consistent with published figures available here: https://www.gov.uk/government/statistics/hmrc-tax-and-nics-receipts-for-the-uk.

Source: National Income and Expenditure; Central Statistical Office; Annual reports of Her Majesty's Revenue and Customs.

StatLink https://stat.link/p2xqej

Table 5.38. United States: Details of tax revenue, 1965-2019

Million USD

	1965	1980	1990	2000	2007	2010	2013	2015	2018	2019
Total tax revenue	**167 022**	**730 672**	**1 552 413**	**2 900 519**	**3 868 612**	**3 517 144**	**4 291 752**	**4 773 680**	**5 109 964**	**5 336 458**
1000 Taxes on income, profits and capital gains	**80 284**	**364 137**	**701 731**	**1 453 865**	**1 865 205**	**1 488 699**	**2 016 390**	**2 314 542**	**2 344 668**	**2 478 497**
1100 Of individuals	52 894	285 513	584 733	1 224 538	1 479 085	1 223 218	1 664 074	1 929 215	2 073 662	2 191 677
1110 On income and profits	50 401	272 879	552 859	1 088 967	1 326 736	1 163 737	1 556 113	1 753 783	1 872 662	1 980 150
Individual income tax federal	46 492	233 269	449 239	895 677	1 062 755	910 874	1 235 275	1 413 376	1 484 440	1 572 684
Individual income tax state and local govt.	3 909	39 610	103 620	193 290	263 981	252 863	320 838	340 407	388 222	407 466
1120 On capital gains	2 493	12 634	31 874	135 571	152 349	59 481	107 961	175 432	201 000	211 527
Capital gains federal	2 300	10 800	25 900	111 507	122 036	46 557	85 702	141 381	159 331	168 000
Capital gains tax state and local govt.	193	1 834	5 974	24 064	30 313	12 924	22 259	34 051	41 669	43 527
1200 Corporate	27 390	78 624	116 998	229 327	386 119	265 481	352 316	385 327	271 006	286 820
1210 On profits	26 745	73 586	106 134	170 835	330 597	240 445	313 172	337 786	231 155	239 625
Corporate income tax federal	24 861	60 525	85 736	144 590	281 040	198 698	265 274	288 486	179 592	181 550
Corporate income tax state and local govt.	1 884	13 061	20 398	26 245	49 556	41 747	47 898	49 300	51 563	58 075
1220 On capital gains	645	5 038	10 864	58 492	55 523	25 036	39 144	47 541	39 852	47 195
Capital gains tax corp. federal	600	4 143	8 776	49 506	47 200	20 689	33 157	40 602	30 962	35 757
Capital gains tax corp. state and local govt.	45	895	2 088	8 986	8 323	4 347	5 987	6 939	8 890	11 438
1300 Unallocable between 1100 and 1200	0	0	0	0	0	0	0	0	0	0
2000 Social security contributions	**22 192**	**159 763**	**396 972**	**683 104**	**907 357**	**917 409**	**1 030 099**	**1 125 493**	**1 254 375**	**1 305 959**
2100 Employees	8 459	67 022	173 860	305 555	400 941	406 404	456 777	502 103	570 080	595 561
Federal insurance contribution Act tax	8 084	66 221	..	..	..	..	..	..	..	..
Less refund federal	-192	-507	..	..	..	..	..	..	..	..
Railroad retirement taxes federal	322	590	..	..	..	..	..	..	..	..
Fed. hosp. insur. recpts from railroad retir.	0	111	..	..	..	..	..	..	..	..
Unemployment state tax federal	20	127	..	..	..	..	..	..	..	..
Temp. disability insurance state and local	225	480	..	..	..	..	..	..	..	..
2110 On a payroll basis	..	..	..	..	..	..	..	..	..	..
2120 On an income tax basis	..	..	..	..	..	..	..	..	..	..
2200 Employers	12 703	87 019	204 102	343 184	456 602	461 702	519 064	561 936	618 519	642 189
Federal insurance contributions act tax	7 802	64 768	..	..	..	..	..	..	..	..
Railroad retirement taxes federal	314	1 722	..	..	..	..	..	..	..	..
Fed. hosp. insur. recpts from railroad retir.	0	111	..	..	..	..	..	..	..	..
Military service credit federal	14	652	..	..	..	..	..	..	..	..
Old-age dis. hosp. insur. fed. employer contr.	282	1 453	..	..	..	..	..	..	..	..
Unemployment state tax federal	3 032	11 788	..	..	..	..	..	..	..	..
Federal unemployment tax Act	615	3 246	..	..	..	..	..	..	..	..
Railroad unempl. insurance Act tax federal	152	175	..	..	..	..	..	..	..	..
Workmen's compensation state and local	484	3 039	..	..	..	..	..	..	..	..
Temp. disability insurance state and local	8	65	..	..	..	..	..	..	..	..
2210 On a payroll basis	..	..	..	..	..	..	..	..	..	..
2220 On an income tax basis	..	..	..	..	..	..	..	..	..	..
2300 Self-employed or non-employed	1 030	5 722	19 010	34 365	49 814	49 303	54 258	61 454	65 776	68 209
Federal old-age survivors trust	0	4 250	..	..	..	..	..	..	..	..
Federal disability insurance trust	1 030	733	..	..	..	..	..	..	..	..
Federal hospital insurance trust	0	739	..	..	..	..	..	..	..	..
2310 On a payroll basis	..	..	..	..	..	..	..	..	..	..
2320 On an income tax basis	..	..	..	..	..	..	..	..	..	..
2400 Unallocable between 2100, 2200 and 2300	0	0	0	0	0	0	0	0	0	0
2410 On a payroll basis	..	..	..	..	..	..	..	..	..	..
2420 On an income tax basis	..	..	..	..	..	..	..	..	..	..
3000 Taxes on payroll and workforce	**0**	**0**	**0**	**0**	**285**	**2 285**	**1 591**	**1 751**	**2 167**	**2 760**
4000 Taxes on property	**26 529**	**77 913**	**182 408**	**299 546**	**463 052**	**473 422**	**503 220**	**539 732**	**603 792**	**612 875**
4100 Recurrent taxes on immovable property	22 918	68 499	161 533	254 669	403 688	438 588	456 790	490 410	549 156	564 026
4110 Households	8 548	28 975	..	..	..	..	..	..	..	..
Property tax state and local	8 548	28 975	..	..	..	..	..	..	..	..
Other	0	0	..	..	..	..	..	..	..	..
4120 Others	14 370	39 524	..	..	..	..	..	..	..	..
Property tax state and local	14 370	39 524	..	..	..	..	..	..	..	..
Other	0	0	..	..	..	..	..	..	..	..
4200 Recurrent taxes on net wealth	0	0	0	0	0	0	0	0	0	0
4210 Individual	..	..	..	..	..	..	..	..	..	..
4220 Corporate	..	..	..	..	..	..	..	..	..	..
4300 Estate, inheritance and gift taxes	3 447	8 425	15 755	35 640	31 927	19 699	26 178	25 582	28 251	21 709
4310 Estate and inheritance taxes	3 080	8 149	..	..	..	..	..	..	..	..
Estate tax less refund federal	2 427	6 181	..	..	..	..	..	..	..	..
Estate tax state and local govt.	653	1 968	..	..	..	..	..	..	..	..
4320 Gift taxes	367	276	..	..	..	..	..	..	..	..
Gift tax less refund federal	289	209	..	..	..	..	..	..	..	..
Gift tax calculate state and local govt.	78	67	..	..	..	..	..	..	..	..

	1965	1980	1990	2000	2007	2010	2013	2015	2018	2019
4400 Taxes on financial and capital transactions	164	989	2 148	4 389	20 503	7 460	12 171	14 896	16 406	16 906
Interest equalisation tax federal	15	0	..	..	..	..	..	..	..	..
Document and stock transfer state and local	149	989	2 148	4 389	20 503	7 460	12 171	14 896	16 406	16 906
4500 Non-recurrent taxes	0	0	0	0	0	0	0	0	0	0
4510 On net wealth	..	..	..	..	..	..	..	..	0	0
4520 Other non-recurrent taxes	..	..	..	..	..	..	..	..	..	..
4600 Other recurrent taxes on property	0	0	2 972	4 848	6 934	7 675	8 081	8 844	9 979	10 234
5000 Taxes on goods and services	**38 017**	**128 844**	**271 301**	**464 004**	**632 713**	**635 329**	**740 452**	**792 162**	**904 961**	**936 366**
5100 Taxes on production, sale, transfer, etc.	33 300	111 810	235 233	404 093	540 291	546 710	640 249	695 784	789 032	816 923
5110 General taxes	8 016	51 328	125 575	221 358	301 403	295 123	343 853	374 173	421 150	434 796
5111 Value added taxes	0	0	0	0	0	0	0	0	0	0
5112 Sales tax	8 016	51 328	125 575	221 358	301 403	295 123	343 853	374 173	421 150	434 796
General sales - general receipts state and local	7 981	51 328	125 575	221 358	301 403	295 123	343 853	374 173	421 150	434 796
Other state and local	35	0	0	0	0	0	0	0	0	0
5113 Other	0	0	0	0	0	0	0	0	0	0
5120 Taxes on specific goods and services	25 284	60 482	109 658	182 735	238 888	251 587	296 396	321 611	367 882	382 127
5121 Excise duties	21 209	45 471	64 953	108 600	137 373	146 582	154 390	156 902	164 243	163 625
Alcohol taxes federal govt.	3 689	5 601	5 228	7 281	8 571	8 848	9 026	9 514	9 562	9 178
Tobacco taxes federal govt.	2 142	2 443	4 217	6 741	8 377	17 487	15 830	14 265	12 186	10 909
Airport, airway, highway federal	3 559	6 411	0	0	0	0	0	0	0	0
Manufacturer's excise taxes federal govt.	2 867	6 122	0	0	0	0	0	0	0	0
Sugar tax federal govt.	97	0	0	0	0	0	0	0	0	0
Other taxes excise federal govt.	889	2	0	0	0	0	0	0	0	0
Undistributed tax deposits federal government	-11	152	0	0	0	0	0	0	0	0
Other taxes excise and undist. fed.govt. -	0	0	13 316	32 005	31 747	26 913	33 746	35 287	36 740	35 992
Less special tax liquor occupations federal	-22	-21	0	0	0	0	0	0	0	0
Other federal (refunds)	-7	-32	0	0	0	0	0	0	0	0
Alcohol taxes state and local govt.	949	2 642	3 577	4 485	5 684	6 197	6 706	7 260	7 600	7 859
Tobacco taxes state and local govt.	1 386	3 874	6 009	8 726	16 433	18 611	18 464	18 002	18 764	18 792
Public utilities state and local govt.	871	5 888	11 814	17 989	27 879	28 892	28 544	27 834	27 674	27 767
Motor fuel taxes state and local govt.	4 331	9 822	20 792	31 373	38 682	39 634	42 074	44 740	51 716	53 127
Other state and local taxes	469	2 295	0	0	0	0	0	0	0	0
Coal tonnage tax federal govt.	0	272	0	0	0	0	0	0	0	0
Hazardous substances tax federal	0	0	0	0	0	0	0	0	0	0
Transportation fuels tax federal	0	0	0	0	0	0	0	0	0	0
Boat fuels and equipment tax federal	0	0	0	0	0	0	0	0	0	0
Waste site deposits tax federal	0	0	0	0	0	0	0	0	0	0
Leaking underground storage federal	0	0	0	0	0	0	0	0	0	0
Vaccine injury compens. federal	0	0	0	0	0	0	0	0	0	0
Ozone depletion tax federal	0	0	0	0	0	0	0	0	0	0
Oil spill liability federal	0	0	0	0	0	0	0	0	0	0
Luxury tax federal govt.	0	0	0	0	0	0	0	0	0	0
5122 Profits of fiscal monopolies	275	608	..	..	..	..	..	..	..	..
Liquor store revenue state and local govt.	1 447	3 200	..	..	..	..	..	..	..	..
Liquor store expend. state and local govt.	-1 172	-2 592	..	..	..	..	..	..	..	..
5123 Customs and import duties	1 442	7 436	17 490	21 123	28 793	28 603	35 468	38 123	53 284	77 752
Custom duties federal	1 442	7 436	17 490	21 123	28 793	28 603	35 468	38 123	53 284	77 752
Petroleum import fees federal govt.	0	0	0	0	0	0	0	0	0	0
5124 Taxes on exports	0	0	0	0	0	0	0	0	0	0
5125 Taxes on investment goods	0	0	0	0	0	0	0	0	0	0
5126 Taxes on specific services	2 358	6 967	8 895	13 857	23 639	23 642	26 899	30 153	34 510	34 218
Amusements state and local govt.	23	234	671	3 668	7 105	7 082	7 784	8 202	9 051	9 415
Parimutuels state and local govt.	386	731	659	326	328	206	193	182	194	193
Transportation of persons federal	126	1 601	0	0	0	0	0	0	0	0
Transport of property	0	92	0	0	0	0	0	0	0	0
General and toll telephone federal	1 079	1 118	0	0	0	0	0	0	0	0
Foreign insurance policies federal	0	75	0	0	0	0	0	0	0	0
Insurance state and local govt.	744	3 113	7 565	9 863	16 206	16 354	18 922	21 769	25 266	24 611
Employee pension plans federal	0	3	0	0	0	0	0	0	0	0
Inland waterway tax federal	0	0	0	0	0	0	0	0	0	0
Ship departure tax federal	0	0	0	0	0	0	0	0	0	0
5127 Other taxes on internat. trade and transactions	0	0	0	0	0	0	0	0	0	0
5128 Other taxes	0	0	18 320	39 155	49 083	52 760	79 639	96 433	115 845	106 532
5130 Unallocable between 5110 and 5120	0	0	0	0	0	0	0	0	0	0
5200 Taxes on use of goods and perform activities	4 717	17 034	36 068	59 910	92 422	88 619	100 203	96 377	115 929	119 443
5210 Recurrent taxes	3 490	9 501	21 262	37 114	68 547	66 440	70 557	74 447	85 431	88 025
5211 Paid by households: motor vehicles	1 211	3 370	8 104	11 409	14 996	16 294	17 781	18 809	21 143	21 463
Motor vehicle regis. license st. and loc.	1 056	2 981	..	..	..	..	..	..	..	..
Motor vehicle oper. license st. and loc.	152	389	..	..	..	..	..	..	..	..
Other motor vehicle	3	0	..	..	..	..	..	..	..	..

	1965	1980	1990	2000	2007	2010	2013	2015	2018	2019
5212 Paid by others: motor vehicles	937	2 343	3 564	6 688	8 484	9 108	10 071	10 702	12 155	12 312
Motor vehicle regis. license st. and loc.	937	2 343	..	..	..	..	..	..	..	..
Motor vehicle oper. license st. and loc.	0	0	..	..	..	..	..	..	..	..
5213 Paid in respect of other goods	1 342	3 788	9 594	19 017	45 067	41 038	42 705	44 936	52 133	54 250
Misc. fees permit license federal	19	0	0	0	0	0	0	0	0	0
Special tax liquor occupations federal	22	21	0	0	0	0	0	0	0	0
Use tax of certain vehicles federal	99	277	0	0	0	0	0	0	0	0
Use of internat. travel facilities federal	0	92	0	0	0	0	0	0	0	0
Use tax of aircraft federal	0	21	0	0	0	0	0	0	0	0
Corporation in general license st. and loc.	528	1 388	3 147	6 736	10 658	9 473	7 560	6 678	7 372	7 907
Alcoholic beverage license tax st. and loc.	133	179	264	308	608	596	899	824	928	939
Public utilities license tax st. and loc.	30	130	270	395	1 903	1 468	1 432	1 665	1 825	1 850
Amusements license taxes st. and loc.	7	69	202	196	966	638	604	740	903	875
Occupation and business license st. and loc.	349	1 113	3 512	7 651	16 484	17 812	19 284	20 423	22 105	22 948
Wagering occupation tax federal	7	12	0	0	0	0	0	0	0	0
Other license taxes st. and loc.	10	69	2 118	3 619	14 302	10 900	12 772	14 445	18 825	19 557
Hunting and fishing license taxes st. and loc.	138	417	82	112	146	151	155	162	174	175
Other	0	0	0	0	0	0	0	0	0	0
5220 Non-recurrent taxes	1 227	7 533	14 806	22 796	23 875	22 179	29 645	21 930	30 499	31 417
Severance state and local govt.	503	4 167	5 224	5 285	12 895	11 751	18 266	9 755	14 778	15 450
Poll taxes state and local govt.	9	0	0	0	0	0	0	0	0	0
Other taxes state and local govt.	715	3 366	9 582	17 511	10 980	10 428	11 379	12 175	15 721	15 968
5300 Unallocable between 5100 and 5200	0	0	0	0	0	0	0	0	0	0
6000 Other taxes	**0**	**15**	**0**	**0**	**0**	**0**	**0**	**0**	**0**	**0**
6100 Paid solely by business	..	0	..	..	..	..	..	..	..	..
6200 Other	..	15	..	..	..	..	..	..	..	..
Non-wastable tax credits										
Non-wastable tax credits against 1110	..	..	6 155	36 511	90 439	171 630	158 160	156 656	194 270	255 580
Tax expenditure component	..	..	1 800	9 602	35 910	69 870	41 560	42 826	57 340	102 660
Transfer component	..	..	4 355	26 909	54 529	101 760	116 600	113 830	136 930	152 920
Non-wastable tax credits against 1210	..	..	..	..	..	250	630	577	440	440
Tax expenditure component	..	..	..	..	..	240	610	527	380	380
Transfer component	..	..	..	..	..	10	20	50	60	60
Unallocable transfer component	..	..	..	..	..	2 420	4 280	4 890	4 795	4 230
Total tax revenue on cash basis	**167 022**	**730 672**	**..**	**..**	**..**	**..**	**..**	**..**	**..**	**..**
Total tax revenue on accrual basis	**..**	**..**	**..**	**..**	**..**	**..**	**..**	**..**	**..**	**..**
Conciliation with National Accounts										
Additional taxes included in National Accounts	..	..	..	..	..	..	..	..	..	..
Taxes excluded from National Accounts	..	..	..	..	..	..	..	..	..	..
Difference in treatment of tax credits	..	..	..	..	..	..	..	..	..	..
Capital transfer for uncollected revenue	..	..	..	..	..	..	..	..	..	..
Voluntary social security contributions	..	..	11 719	22 562	51 635	61 833	69 903	74 886	102 411	108 999
Miscellaneous differences	..	..	..	..	..	..	..	..	..	..
National Accounts: Taxes and actual social contributions	..	..	1 564 132	2 923 081	3 920 247	3 578 977	4 361 655	4 848 566	5 212 375	5 445 457
Imputed social contributions	..	..	3 384	3 727	7 134	9 428	9 438	9 636	8 811	9 018
National Accounts: Taxes and all social contributions	..	..	1 567 516	2 926 808	3 927 381	3 588 405	4 371 093	4 858 202	5 221 186	5 454 475

.. Not available

Note: From 1990, data are on a year ending 31st December basis. For years up to and including 1976 the dated covered fiscal years ending 30th June. Between 1977 and 1989, Federal government data covered fiscal years ending 30th September and State & Local government data covered fiscal years ending 30th June.

From 1990, data are on accrual basis. There are no separate estimates for the State and Local capital gains tax revenues.

Heading 5121: In 1994 through 1996, some Federal excise taxes formerly shown separately were included in 'Other taxes,excises and undistributed, Federal government'.

Source: Federal estimates are derived from the US Budget, the Final Monthly Treasury Statement and the Annual Report of the US Treasury Department. The State and Local estimates are derived from Government Finances, published by the Bureau of the Census.

StatLink https://stat.link/1tezab

5.2. Memorandum tables

Table 5.39 shows different sources for financing social benefits, beyond compulsory social security contributions reported in section 5.1. In addition, this table shows also data on other taxes, on voluntary contributions to government and on compulsory contributions to private sector.

Table 5.40 shows social security contributions and payroll taxes paid by government. During the revision of the Interpretative Guide in 1984, the question arose of how to treat taxes paid by government. The two most prominent examples of such taxes are social security contributions and payroll taxes paid by government in respect of its employees. After a long discussion it was decided that the data shown in this publication should continue to include taxes paid by government (see §7 of the Interpretative Guide in annex A).

Whilst it was recognised that for certain purposes (e.g. to show the cash flow to the government sector from the private sector) it would be appropriate to eliminate taxes paid by one sector of government to another or tax payments between different units of the same sector of government, the view was taken that to record tax flows in the context of the economy as a whole required that taxes paid by government should be included in the data. This treatment ensures that the different resource flows of an economy, including the calculation of the output of government, are measured consistently in after-tax units. Nevertheless, it was decided that data on identifiable taxes paid by government should be separately identified in a memorandum item and this is the purpose of the country tables which follow.

The data that are reproduced in the following tables refer to actual compulsory payments made by general government in respect of their employees. Fictive, voluntary and imputed contributions are excluded from these data. The definitions of social security contributions, payroll taxes and general government are those set out in §40 to §46, §47 and §3 to §4 of the Interpretative Guide. Information on the other taxes paid by government (namely property taxes and consumption taxes) is not available in most countries, although it is believed that in all countries taxes based upon payroll are the most important taxes paid by government. In many cases, the data are estimates and are not always constructed on a basis consistent with that used in the main tables.

Table 5.39. Financing social benefits

	1965	1980	1990	2000	2007	2010	2013	2015	2018	2019
Australia, million AUD										
Contribution under 2000 heading	..	..	..	..	..	..	..	..	..	..
Other taxes	..	..	..	..	..	..	..	..	..	..
Voluntary contributions to government	..	..	..	..	..	..	..	..	..	..
Compulsory contributions to private sector	..	..	..	..	..	..	..	..	..	..
Total	**0**	**0**	**0**	**0**	**0**	**0**	**0**	**0**	**0**	**0**
Austria, million EUR										
Contribution under 2000 heading	1 548	9 200	17 763	30 510	38 453	41 423	46 845	49 867	56 671	59 077
Other taxes	0	0	0	0	0	0	0	0	0	0
Voluntary contributions to government	32	135	141	206	256	339	299	321	321	336
Compulsory contributions to private sector	0	0	0	0	0	0	0	0	0	0
Total	**1 580**	**9 335**	**17 904**	**30 716**	**38 709**	**41 762**	**47 144**	**50 188**	**56 992**	**59 412**
Belgium, million EUR										
Contribution under 2000 heading	2 018	10 798	23 386	34 865	45 929	50 674	56 527	58 812	61 105	63 203
Other taxes	0	171	644	5 375	13 659	16 772	18 390	12 347	18 321	19 758
Voluntary contributions to government	0	41	52	58	57	59	77	70	85	84
Compulsory contributions to private sector	0	0	0	0	0	0	0	0	0	0
Total	**2 018**	**11 009**	**24 082**	**40 298**	**59 644**	**67 505**	**74 994**	**71 228**	**79 510**	**83 045**
Canada, million CAD										
Contribution under 2000 heading	854	10 649	29 653	53 109	73 722	76 787	90 394	96 371	103 502	108 364
Other taxes	1 199	0	0	0	0	0	0	0	0	0
Voluntary contributions to government	0	0	0	0	0	0	0	0	0	0
Compulsory contributions to private sector	0	0	0	0	0	0	0	0	0	0
Total	**2 053**	**10 649**	**29 653**	**53 109**	**73 722**	**76 787**	**90 394**	**96 371**	**103 502**	**108 364**
Chile, million CLP										
Contribution under 2000 heading	..	..	159 559	576 758	1 148 647	1 493 987	1 968 973	2 252 489	2 786 173	2 994 906
Other taxes	..	..	0	0	0	0	0	0	0	0
Voluntary contributions to government	..	..	0	0	0	0	0	0	0	0
Compulsory contributions to private sector	..	..	328 102	2 021 631	3 808 658	5 408 703	7 583 251	8 914 415	11 077 114	11 975 273
Total	**..**	**..**	**487 661**	**2 598 389**	**4 957 305**	**6 902 690**	**9 552 224**	**11 166 904**	**13 863 286**	**14 970 179**
Colombia, million COP										
Contribution under 2000 heading	..	..	203 596	4 989 000	9 694 000	11 478 085	16 644 445	13 585 138	18 192 049	19 875 398
Other taxes	..	..	0	0	0	0	0	0	0	0
Voluntary contributions to government	..	..	0	0	0	0	0	0	0	0
Compulsory contributions to private sector	..	..	0	0	18 667 073	27 354 493	30 808 731	31 112 566	39 712 117	43 732 211
Total	**..**	**..**	**203 596**	**4 989 000**	**28 361 073**	**38 832 579**	**47 453 177**	**44 697 703**	**57 904 167**	**63 607 609**
Costa Rica, million CRC										
Contribution under 2000 heading	..	..	33 990	297 069	885 053	1 450 531	1 928 082	2 305 133	2 859 467	3 026 691
Other taxes	..	..	..	..	..	..	..	..	..	..
Voluntary contributions to government	..	..	..	..	..	..	..	..	..	..
Compulsory contributions to private sector	..	..	..	..	..	..	..	..	..	..
Total	**..**	**..**	**33 990**	**297 069**	**885 053**	**1 450 531**	**1 928 082**	**2 305 133**	**2 859 467**	**3 026 691**
Czech Republic, million CZK										
Contribution under 2000 heading	..	..	..	341 544	573 417	576 029	603 072	659 743	829 702	889 237
Other taxes	..	..	..	0	0	0	0	0	0	0
Voluntary contributions to government	..	..	..	1 099	974	661	337	386	523	578
Compulsory contributions to private sector	..	..	..	2 837	5 757	6 094	6 424	6 741	8 322	8 921
Total	**..**	**..**	**..**	**345 480**	**580 148**	**582 784**	**609 833**	**666 871**	**838 547**	**898 736**
Denmark, million DKK										
Contribution under 2000 heading	690	710	101	8 453	1 286	1 815	1 618	1 378	1 061	991
Other taxes	0	0	0	0	0	0	0	0	0	0
Voluntary contributions to government	0	1 673	8 087	16 633	17 061	17 192	14 655	14 721	14 751	14 792
Compulsory contributions to private sector	145	554	1 278	1 445	4 526	3 847	3 068	2 964	2 771	2 828
Total	**835**	**2 937**	**9 466**	**26 531**	**22 874**	**22 854**	**19 341**	**19 063**	**18 583**	**18 611**
Estonia, million EUR										
Contribution under 2000 heading	..	..	..	674	1 683	1 879	2 077	2 300	2 978	3 256
Other taxes	..	..	..	0	0	0	0	0	0	0
Voluntary contributions to government	..	..	..	0	0	0	0	0	0	0
Compulsory contributions to private sector	..	..	..	1	341	38	268	389	392	299
Total	**..**	**..**	**..**	**674**	**2 024**	**1 918**	**2 346**	**2 689**	**3 370**	**3 556**

	1965	1980	1990	2000	2007	2010	2013	2015	2018	2019
Finland, million EUR										
Contribution under 2000 heading	93	2 776	10 012	15 756	21 384	22 648	25 632	26 639	27 647	28 295
Other taxes	47	22	0	404	0	0	0	0	0	0
Voluntary contributions to government	0	262	632	236	228	254	270	303	269	246
Compulsory contributions to private sector	0	123	431	532	653	619	694	673	645	655
Total	**140**	**3 183**	**11 075**	**16 928**	**22 265**	**23 521**	**26 596**	**27 615**	**28 561**	**29 196**
France, million EUR										
Contribution under 2000 heading	8 804	76 235	191 141	231 875	307 663	323 816	356 934	370 375	381 230	363 817
Other taxes	0	895	2 950	81 001	127 511	137 383	162 838	170 210	199 736	232 687
Voluntary contributions to government	0	0	0	0	0	0	0	0	0	0
Compulsory contributions to private sector	0	0	0	0	0	0	0	0	0	0
Total	**8 804**	**77 130**	**194 091**	**312 876**	**435 174**	**461 199**	**519 772**	**540 585**	**580 966**	**596 504**
Germany, million EUR										
Contribution under 2000 heading	19 876	98 659	170 449	299 440	320 750	354 320	392 378	424 841	487 654	508 124
Other taxes	0	0	0	0	0	0	0	0	0	0
Voluntary contributions to government	1 946	8 441	13 002	23 329	21 409	5 102	5 352	6 068	7 490	7 262
Compulsory contributions to private sector	107	690	1 462	6 120	8 243	9 386	10 444	11 202	12 929	13 780
Total	**21 929**	**107 791**	**184 914**	**328 889**	**350 402**	**368 808**	**408 174**	**442 111**	**508 073**	**529 166**
Greece, million EUR										
Contribution under 2000 heading	37	485	3 466	14 284	24 940	24 748	19 354	18 807	21 473	22 293
Other taxes	8	0	0	0	0	0	0	0	0	0
Voluntary contributions to government	0	0	0	0	0	0	0	0	0	0
Compulsory contributions to private sector	0	0	0	0	0	0	0	0	0	0
Total	**44**	**485**	**3 466**	**14 284**	**24 940**	**24 748**	**19 354**	**18 807**	**21 473**	**22 293**
Hungary, million HUF										
Contribution under 2000 heading	..	..	..	1 506 755	3 402 194	3 179 509	3 899 154	4 433 464	5 049 751	5 544 824
Other taxes	..	..	..	188 413	85 058	78 629	246 574	294 313	328 876	145 025
Voluntary contributions to government	..	..	..	1 273	1 762	1 693	1 523	1 229	1 090	983
Compulsory contributions to private sector	..	..	..	62 836	190 331	279 814	0	0	0	0
Total	**..**	**..**	**..**	**1 759 277**	**3 679 344**	**3 539 645**	**4 147 251**	**4 729 006**	**5 379 717**	**5 690 832**
Iceland, million ISK										
Contribution under 2000 heading	5	102	3 607	19 680	39 594	63 599	69 899	79 707	98 230	97 423
Other taxes	0	1 047	20 571	26 732	52 444	77 472	90 895	97 987	146 810	187 636
Voluntary contributions to government	0	0	0	0	0	0	0	0	0	0
Compulsory contributions to private sector	0	459	13 454	48 847	118 117	95 438	117 903	139 792	209 341	187 003
Total	**5**	**1 608**	**37 632**	**95 260**	**210 155**	**236 509**	**278 697**	**317 486**	**454 381**	**472 062**
Ireland, million EUR										
Contribution under 2000 heading	21	578	1 729	3 966	8 143	8 458	8 854	9 992	12 085	13 140
Other taxes	0	0	0	0	0	0	0	0	0	0
Voluntary contributions to government	0	0	0	0	0	0	0	0	0	0
Compulsory contributions to private sector	0	0	0	0	0	0	0	0	0	0
Total	**21**	**578**	**1 729**	**3 966**	**8 143**	**8 458**	**8 854**	**9 992**	**12 085**	**13 140**
Israel, million ILS										
Contribution under 2000 heading	..	..	..	27 565	37 909	45 343	53 364	59 561	70 635	74 420
Other taxes	..	..	..	0	0	0	0	0	0	0
Voluntary contributions to government	..	..	..	0	0	0	0	0	0	0
Compulsory contributions to private sector	..	..	..	0	0	9 100	22 400	28 700	36 000	37 700
Total	**..**	**..**	**..**	**27 565**	**37 909**	**54 443**	**75 764**	**88 261**	**106 635**	**112 120**
Italy, million EUR										
Contribution under 2000 heading	1 881	22 976	87 256	143 629	200 772	209 122	210 462	214 376	229 643	237 346
Other taxes	0	0	0	0	0	0	0	0	0	0
Voluntary contributions to government	0	0	0	464	567	561	738	750	771	708
Compulsory contributions to private sector	0	0	0	0	0	0	0	0	0	0
Total	**1 881**	**22 976**	**87 256**	**144 093**	**201 339**	**209 683**	**211 200**	**215 126**	**230 414**	**238 054**
Japan, billion JPY										
Contribution under 2000 heading	1 344	18 178	34 613	47 968	53 325	54 461	59 803	64 465	70 588	71 993
Other taxes	0	0	0	0	0	0	0	0	0	0
Voluntary contributions to government	0	0	0	0	0	0	0	0	0	0
Compulsory contributions to private sector	0	0	0	0	0	0	0	0	0	0
Total	**1 344**	**18 178**	**34 613**	**47 968**	**53 325**	**54 461**	**59 803**	**64 465**	**70 588**	**71 993**

	1965	1980	1990	2000	2007	2010	2013	2015	2018	2019
Korea, billion KRW										
Contribution under 2000 heading	..	73	3 760	22 759	53 588	69 090	91 596	104 693	128 660	140 071
Other taxes	..	0	0	0	0	0	0	0	0	0
Voluntary contributions to government	..	0	0	0	0	0	0	0	0	0
Compulsory contributions to private sector	..	0	0	0	0	0	0	0	0	0
Total	**..**	**73**	**3 760**	**22 759**	**53 588**	**69 090**	**91 596**	**104 693**	**128 660**	**140 071**
Latvia, million EUR										
Contribution under 2000 heading	..	..	..	669	1 774	1 554	1 933	2 030	2 658	2 911
Other taxes	..	..	..	12	51	36	59	80	108	149
Voluntary contributions to government	..	..	..	0	0	0	0	0	0	0
Compulsory contributions to private sector	..	..	..	0	0	0	0	0	0	0
Total	**..**	**..**	**..**	**682**	**1 825**	**1 590**	**1 992**	**2 111**	**2 767**	**3 060**
Lithuania, million EUR										
Contribution under 2000 heading	..	..	..	1 362	2 643	3 293	3 791	4 338	5 752	4 706
Other taxes	..	..	..	0	0	0	0	0	0	0
Voluntary contributions to government	..	..	..	0	2	2	3	2	2	2
Compulsory contributions to private sector	..	..	..	0	247	95	149	140	192	3
Total	**..**	**..**	**..**	**1 362**	**2 892**	**3 391**	**3 943**	**4 480**	**5 947**	**4 711**
Luxembourg, million EUR										
Contribution under 2000 heading	86	443	1 011	2 224	3 710	4 387	5 132	5 548	6 483	6 854
Other taxes	0	0	0	0	0	0	0	0	0	0
Voluntary contributions to government	0	0	4	18	18	28	33	38	46	48
Compulsory contributions to private sector	0	0	0	0	0	0	0	0	0	0
Total	**86**	**443**	**1 015**	**2 241**	**3 728**	**4 415**	**5 166**	**5 587**	**6 529**	**6 902**
Mexico, million MXN										
Contribution under 2000 heading	..	109	17 165	138 223	236 727	277 459	351 993	409 249	509 087	552 058
Other taxes	..	0	0	0	0	0	0	0	0	0
Voluntary contributions to government	..	0	0	0	0	0	0	0	0	0
Compulsory contributions to private sector	..	25	3 840	67 352	144 331	146 110	168 111	206 824	269 500	303 426
Total	**..**	**134**	**21 005**	**205 575**	**381 057**	**423 569**	**520 104**	**616 073**	**778 587**	**855 484**
Netherlands, million EUR										
Contribution under 2000 heading	3 342	26 641	39 075	64 522	77 072	82 732	97 372	96 426	108 049	109 298
Other taxes	0	0	0	0	0	0	0	0	0	0
Voluntary contributions to government	168	1 139	163	0	0	0	0	0	0	0
Compulsory contributions to private sector	1 266	7 642	5 727	37 088	..	..	..	..	..	..
Total	**4 776**	**35 422**	**44 965**	**101 610**	**77 072**	**82 732**	**97 372**	**96 426**	**108 049**	**109 298**
New Zealand, million NZD										
Contribution under 2000 heading	..	..	..	..	..	..	..	..	..	..
Other taxes	..	..	..	..	..	..	..	..	..	..
Voluntary contributions to government	..	..	..	..	..	..	..	..	..	..
Compulsory contributions to private sector	..	..	..	..	..	..	..	..	..	..
Total	**0**	**0**	**0**	**0**	**0**	**0**	**0**	**0**	**0**	**0**
Norway, million NOK										
Contribution under 2000 heading	2 009	28 205	79 362	132 170	204 473	243 002	292 461	325 130	357 317	377 427
Other taxes	1 305	4 256	0	0	0	0	0	0	0	0
Voluntary contributions to government	0	0	0	0	0	0	0	0	0	0
Compulsory contributions to private sector	0	242	339	0	0	0	0	0	0	0
Total	**3 314**	**32 703**	**79 701**	**132 170**	**204 473**	**243 002**	**292 461**	**325 130**	**357 317**	**377 427**
Poland, million PLN										
Contribution under 2000 heading	..	..	..	97 411	141 457	157 432	204 600	225 711	280 462	305 354
Other taxes	..	..	..	0	0	0	0	0	0	0
Voluntary contributions to government	..	..	..	0	0	0	34	49	45	46
Compulsory contributions to private sector	..	..	..	0	0	0	0	0	0	0
Total	**..**	**..**	**..**	**97 411**	**141 457**	**157 432**	**204 634**	**225 760**	**280 507**	**305 400**
Portugal, million EUR										
Contribution under 2000 heading	22	531	4 026	10 168	14 305	15 462	15 139	16 182	19 131	20 550
Other taxes	0	1	29	434	658	698	970	994	824	854
Voluntary contributions to government	0	0	0	0	0	0	0	0	0	0
Compulsory contributions to private sector	0	0	0	0	0	0	0	0	0	0
Total	**22**	**532**	**4 055**	**10 602**	**14 963**	**16 160**	**16 109**	**17 176**	**19 955**	**21 404**

	1965	1980	1990	2000	2007	2010	2013	2015	2018	2019
Slovak Republic, million EUR										
Contribution under 2000 heading	..	..	..	4 409	7 244	8 154	9 847	10 897	13 147	14 085
Other taxes	..	..	..	0	0	0	0	0	0	0
Voluntary contributions to government	..	..	..	0	22	31	17	11	11	11
Compulsory contributions to private sector	..	..	..	0	701	719	385	413	606	713
Total	**..**	**..**	**..**	**4 409**	**7 968**	**8 904**	**10 249**	**11 321**	**13 765**	**14 809**
Slovenia, million EUR										
Contribution under 2000 heading	..	..	..	2 824	5 046	5 761	5 647	5 983	7 081	7 587
Other taxes	..	..	..	0	0	0	0	0	0	0
Voluntary contributions to government	..	..	..	0	0	0	0	0	0	0
Compulsory contributions to private sector	..	..	..	0	0	0	0	0	0	0
Total	**..**	**..**	**..**	**2 824**	**5 046**	**5 761**	**5 647**	**5 983**	**7 081**	**7 587**
Spain, million EUR										
Contribution under 2000 heading	350	10 682	36 722	74 683	127 088	127 235	116 875	122 835	141 283	152 527
Other taxes	0	49	0	0	0	0	0	0	0	0
Voluntary contributions to government	0	0	0	447	937	1 155	2 209	1 170	1 038	987
Compulsory contributions to private sector	0	0	0	0	0	0	0	0	0	0
Total	**350**	**10 731**	**36 722**	**75 130**	**128 025**	**128 390**	**119 084**	**124 005**	**142 321**	**153 514**
Sweden, million SEK										
Contribution under 2000 heading	4 851	74 647	205 867	306 974	388 505	384 668	376 684	404 851	463 338	462 860
Other taxes	1 407	0	0	0	0	0	0	0	0	0
Voluntary contributions to government	0	0	0	7 951	12 376	13 167	15 909	16 726	23 457	24 966
Compulsory contributions to private sector	0	0	0	0	0	0	0	0	0	0
Total	**6 258**	**74 647**	**205 867**	**314 925**	**400 881**	**397 835**	**392 593**	**421 577**	**486 795**	**487 826**
Switzerland, million CHF										
Contribution under 2000 heading	1 670	10 844	19 952	30 961	34 974	38 385	42 862	44 285	46 072	47 234
Other taxes	336	778	1 176	4 509	6 342	6 644	7 760	7 590	6 507	6 260
Voluntary contributions to government	95	431	0	0	0	0	0	0	0	0
Compulsory contributions to private sector	2 505	9 674	20 797	29 532	42 219	45 974	49 965	52 890	58 589	59 357
Total	**4 606**	**21 727**	**41 924**	**65 002**	**83 535**	**91 004**	**100 587**	**104 765**	**111 168**	**112 852**
Turkey, million TRY										
Contribution under 2000 heading	0	0	15	7 543	44 052	71 696	125 871	170 282	269 932	312 808
Other taxes	0	0	0	0	0	0	0	0	0	0
Voluntary contributions to government	0	0	0	0	0	0	0	0	0	0
Compulsory contributions to private sector	0	0	0	0	0	0	0	0	0	0
Total	**0**	**0**	**15**	**7 543**	**44 052**	**71 696**	**125 871**	**170 282**	**269 932**	**312 808**
United Kingdom, million GBP										
Contribution under 2000 heading	1 685	13 531	34 457	60 252	93 210	97 346	106 085	114 173	135 225	143 255
Other taxes	0	0	0	0	0	0	0	0	0	0
Voluntary contributions to government	0	11	3 288	8 103	18 629	21 217	22 438	25 025	27 546	33 474
Compulsory contributions to private sector	1 148	13 350	7 945	8 308	9 969	9 656	6 074	5 495	0	0
Total	**2 833**	**26 892**	**45 690**	**76 663**	**121 808**	**128 219**	**134 597**	**144 693**	**162 771**	**170 801**
United States, million USD										
Contribution under 2000 heading	22 192	159 763	396 972	683 104	907 357	917 409	1 030 099	1 125 493	1 254 375	1 305 959
Other taxes	0	0	0	0	0	0	0	0	0	0
Voluntary contributions to government	488	3 407	11 719	22 562	51 635	61 833	69 903	74 886	102 411	108 999
Compulsory contributions to private sector	0	0	0	0	0	0	0	0	0	0
Total	**22 680**	**163 170**	**408 691**	**705 666**	**958 992**	**979 242**	**1 100 002**	**1 200 379**	**1 356 786**	**1 414 958**

.. Not available

StatLink https://stat.link/2qvy4j

Table 5.40. Social security contributions and payroll taxes paid by government, details

	1965	1980	1990	2000	2007	2010	2013	2015	2018	2019
Australia, million AUD										
2000 Social security contributions										
Federal or Central government	..	..	..	..	..	..	..	..	..	..
State/Regional	..	..	..	..	..	..	..	..	..	..
Local government	..	..	..	..	..	..	..	..	..	..
Social Security Funds	..	..	..	..	..	..	..	..	..	..
Total	**0**	**0**	**0**	**0**	**0**	**0**	**0**	**0**	**0**	**0**
3000 Taxes on payroll and workforce										
Federal or Central government	0	4	0	0	0	0	0	0	0	0
State/Regional	15	302	0	0	0	0	0	0	0	0
Local government	0	0	2	19	44	32	37	38	38	42
Social Security Funds	0	0	0	0	0	0	0	0	0	0
Multi-jurisdictional (University) sector[1]	..	..	..	..	..	..	..	..	..	..
Total	**15**	**306**	**92**	**301**	**499**	**580**	**702**	**765**	**889**	**922**
2000+3000 Total	**15**	**306**	**92**	**301**	**499**	**580**	**702**	**765**	**889**	**922**
Austria, million EUR[2]										
2000 Social security contributions										
Federal or Central government	48	230	337	620	1 244	1 532	1 664	1 825	2 112	2 206
State/Regional	13	166	337	692	988	1 179	1 255	1 376	1 631	1 708
Local government	17	145	292	699	1 036	1 277	1 379	1 515	1 690	1 815
Social Security Funds	11	79	48	176	203	226	250	264	284	293
Total	**88**	**619**	**1 015**	**2 186**	**3 471**	**4 213**	**4 547**	**4 980**	**5 717**	**6 022**
3000 Taxes on payroll and workforce										
Federal or Central government	0	49	134	186	337	533	558	624	645	648
State/Regional	0	48	74	232	351	458	485	492	490	506
Local government	1	29	79	301	262	359	396	428	464	455
Social Security Funds	0	0	39	44	51	55	61	65	68	71
Total	**1**	**125**	**326**	**763**	**1 000**	**1 405**	**1 500**	**1 609**	**1 667**	**1 680**
2000+3000 Total	**89**	**745**	**1 341**	**2 949**	**4 471**	**5 618**	**6 047**	**6 589**	**7 384**	**7 703**
Belgium, million EUR										
2000 Social security contributions										
Federal or Central government	..	536	211	259	434	493	532	859	904	934
State/Regional	..	0	614	1 218	1 600	1 873	2 089	2 440	2 608	2 696
Local government	..	434	768	1 376	2 151	2 655	3 641	3 973	4 317	4 462
Social Security Funds	..	89	176	252	308	360	416	415	434	449
Total	**..**	**1 059**	**1 769**	**3 105**	**4 493**	**5 381**	**6 678**	**7 686**	**8 263**	**8 541**
3000 Taxes on payroll and workforce										
Federal or Central government	..	..	..	..	..	..	..	..	..	..
State/Regional	..	..	..	..	..	..	..	..	..	..
Local government	..	..	..	..	..	..	..	..	..	..
Social Security Funds	..	..	..	..	..	..	..	..	..	..
Total	**..**	**0**	**0**	**0**	**0**	**0**	**0**	**0**	**0**	**0**
2000+3000 Total	**..**	**1 059**	**1 769**	**3 105**	**4 493**	**5 381**	**6 678**	**7 686**	**8 263**	**8 541**
Canada, million CAD										
2000 Social security contributions										
Federal or Central government	..	..	..	944	1 198	1 397	1 449	1 515	1 666	1 779
State/Regional	..	..	..	3 023	4 269	5 071	5 825	6 349	6 754	6 814
Local government	..	..	..	2 225	2 806	3 390	3 912	4 205	4 489	4 529
Social Security Funds	..	..	..	0	0	0	0	0	0	0
Total	**..**	**..**	**..**	**6 192**	**8 273**	**9 857**	**11 186**	**12 070**	**12 908**	**13 122**
3000 Taxes on payroll and workforce										
Federal or Central government	..	..	..	0	0	0	0	0	0	0
State/Regional	..	..	..	173	234	328	362	362	394	402
Local government	..	..	..	0	0	0	0	0	0	0
Social Security Funds	..	..	..	0	0	0	0	0	0	0
Total	**..**	**..**	**..**	**173**	**234**	**328**	**362**	**362**	**394**	**402**
2000+3000 Total	**..**	**..**	**..**	**6 365**	**8 507**	**10 185**	**11 548**	**12 432**	**13 302**	**13 524**

	1965	1980	1990	2000	2007	2010	2013	2015	2018	2019
Chile, million CLP										
2000 Social security contributions										
Federal or Central government	..	..	..	43 210	107 911	148 006	186 652	205 125	254 883	270 571
State/Regional	..	..	..	..	..	..	..	..	..	..
Local government	..	..	..	11 317	30 218	41 518	51 114	63 603	95 270	104 484
Social Security Funds	..	..	..	106	263	449	550	600	815	825
Total	**..**	**..**	**..**	**54 633**	**138 392**	**189 974**	**238 315**	**269 328**	**350 968**	**375 881**
3000 Taxes on payroll and workforce										
Federal or Central government	..	..	..	..	..	..	..	..	..	..
State/Regional	..	..	..	..	..	..	..	..	..	..
Local government	..	..	..	..	..	..	..	..	..	..
Social Security Funds	..	..	..	..	..	..	..	..	..	..
Total	**..**	**..**	**..**	**..**	**..**	**..**	**..**	**..**	**..**	**..**
2000+3000 Total	**..**	**..**	**..**	**54 633**	**138 392**	**189 974**	**238 315**	**269 328**	**350 968**	**375 881**
Colombia, million COP										
2000 Social security contributions										
Federal or Central government	..	..	..	..	..	..	0	0	0	0
State/Regional	..	..	..	..	..	..	0	0	0	0
Local government	..	..	..	..	..	..	0	0	0	0
Social Security Funds	..	..	..	..	..	..	1 007 283	1 255 666	1 778 257	1 889 685
Total	**..**	**..**	**..**	**..**	**..**	**..**	**1 007 283**	**1 255 666**	**1 778 257**	**1 889 685**
3000 Taxes on payroll and workforce										
Federal or Central government	..	..	..	..	..	..	372 476	436 646	563 148	589 456
State/Regional	..	..	..	..	..	..	0	0	0	0
Local government	..	..	..	..	..	..	0	0	0	0
Social Security Funds	..	..	..	..	..	..	0	0	0	0
Total	**..**	**..**	**..**	**..**	**..**	**..**	**372 476**	**436 646**	**563 148**	**589 456**
2000+3000 Total	**..**	**..**	**..**	**..**	**..**	**..**	**1 379 759**	**1 692 312**	**2 341 405**	**2 479 141**
Costa Rica, million CRC										
2000 Social security contributions										
Federal or Central government	..	..	3 219	35 099	102 041	197 340	258 663	301 475	347 115	358 848
State/Regional	..	..	0	0	0	0	0	0	0	0
Local government	..	..	228	2 214	5 357	9 866	14 042	17 177	21 750	23 092
Social Security Funds	..	..	0	0	0	0	0	0	0	0
Total	**..**	**..**	**3 447**	**37 313**	**107 398**	**207 206**	**272 706**	**318 652**	**368 865**	**381 940**
3000 Taxes on payroll and workforce										
Federal or Central government	..	..	91	2 666	5 320	12 405	15 059	17 321	20 054	20 795
State/Regional	..	..	0	0	0	0	0	0	0	0
Local government	..	..	0	0	0	0	0	0	0	0
Social Security Funds	..	..	0	0	0	0	0	0	0	0
Total	**..**	**..**	**91**	**2 666**	**5 320**	**12 405**	**15 059**	**17 321**	**20 054**	**20 795**
2000+3000 Total	**..**	**..**	**3 538**	**39 979**	**112 718**	**219 611**	**287 765**	**335 973**	**388 918**	**402 736**
Czech Republic, million CZK										
2000 Social security contributions										
Federal or Central government	..	..	..	28 050	44 437	45 439	46 360	37 553	48 579	52 185
State/Regional	..	..	..	..	..	..	..	..	..	..
Local government	..	..	..	5 660	8 253	9 394	9 448	41 954	54 940	61 791
Social Security Funds	..	..	..	510	791	938	881	975	1 148	1 275
Total	**..**	**..**	**..**	**34 220**	**53 481**	**55 771**	**56 689**	**80 482**	**104 666**	**115 252**
3000 Taxes on payroll and workforce										
Federal or Central government	..	..	..	..	..	..	..	..	..	..
State/Regional	..	..	..	..	..	..	..	..	..	..
Local government	..	..	..	..	..	..	..	..	..	..
Social Security Funds	..	..	..	..	..	..	..	..	..	..
Total	**..**	**..**	**..**	**0**	**0**	**0**	**0**	**0**	**0**	**0**
2000+3000 Total	**..**	**..**	**..**	**34 220**	**53 481**	**55 771**	**56 689**	**80 482**	**104 666**	**115 252**

	1965	1980	1990	2000	2007	2010	2013	2015	2018	2019
Denmark, million DKK										
2000 Social security contributions										
Federal or Central government	..	179	..	..	..	..	..	..	..	..
State/Regional	..	..	..	..	..	..	..	..	..	..
Local government	..	0	..	..	..	..	..	..	..	..
Social Security Funds	..	0	..	..	..	..	..	..	..	..
Total	**..**	**179**	**0**	**0**	**0**	**0**	**0**	**0**	**0**	**0**
3000 Taxes on payroll and workforce										
Federal or Central government	..	..	..	..	..	..	..	..	..	..
State/Regional	..	..	..	..	..	..	..	..	..	..
Local government	..	..	..	..	..	..	..	..	..	..
Social Security Funds	..	..	..	..	..	..	..	..	..	..
Total	**..**	**0**	**0**	**0**	**0**	**0**	**0**	**0**	**0**	**0**
2000+3000 Total	**..**	**179**	**0**	**0**	**0**	**0**	**0**	**0**	**0**	**0**
Estonia, million EUR										
2000 Social security contributions										
Federal or Central government	..	..	..	129	257	315	371	451	531	577
State/Regional	..	..	..	..	..	..	..	..	..	..
Local government	..	..	..	48	156	175	206	235	304	338
Social Security Funds	..	..	..	0	3	41	24	24	76	88
Total	**..**	**..**	**..**	**177**	**417**	**532**	**601**	**710**	**911**	**1 003**
3000 Taxes on payroll and workforce										
Federal or Central government	..	..	..	..	..	..	..	..	..	..
State/Regional	..	..	..	..	..	..	..	..	..	..
Local government	..	..	..	..	..	..	..	..	..	..
Social Security Funds	..	..	..	..	..	..	..	..	..	..
Total	**..**	**..**	**..**	**0**	**0**	**0**	**0**	**0**	**0**	**0**
2000+3000 Total	**..**	**..**	**..**	**177**	**417**	**532**	**601**	**710**	**911**	**1 003**
Finland, million EUR										
2000 Social security contributions										
Federal or Central government	..	61	196	908	1 057	1 138	1 227	1 229	1 055	1 104
State/Regional	..	..	..	..	..	..	..	..	..	..
Local government	..	170	1 709	2 786	4 061	4 352	4 881	4 868	4 251	4 270
Social Security Funds	..	9	34	75	88	89	101	109	121	114
Total	**..**	**239**	**1 939**	**3 769**	**5 206**	**5 579**	**6 209**	**6 206**	**5 427**	**5 488**
3000 Taxes on payroll and workforce										
Federal or Central government	..	1	..	..	..	..	..	..	..	..
State/Regional	..	..	..	..	..	..	..	..	..	..
Local government	..	4	..	..	..	..	..	..	..	..
Social Security Funds	..	0	..	..	..	..	..	..	..	..
Total	**..**	**5**	**0**	**0**	**0**	**0**	**0**	**0**	**0**	**0**
2000+3000 Total	**..**	**245**	**1 939**	**3 769**	**5 206**	**5 579**	**6 209**	**6 206**	**5 427**	**5 488**
France, million EUR										
2000 Social security contributions										
Federal or Central government	..	3 816	8 063	10 466	12 426	12 841	12 825	12 999	14 107	14 275
State/Regional	..	..	..	..	..	..	..	..	..	..
Local government	..	2 369	5 542	10 372	15 925	18 065	20 050	21 553	21 911	22 157
Social Security Funds	..	2 594	6 940	10 827	14 035	15 427	16 614	17 399	17 790	17 548
Total	**..**	**8 779**	**20 545**	**31 665**	**42 386**	**46 333**	**49 489**	**51 951**	**53 808**	**53 980**
3000 Taxes on payroll and workforce										
Federal or Central government	..	836	494	854	1 558	1 611	1 697	1 768	1 927	1 968
State/Regional	..	..	..	..	..	..	..	..	..	..
Local government	..	27	107	324	549	698	791	852	921	962
Social Security Funds	..	629	2 234	3 413	4 531	5 028	5 374	5 522	5 681	5 782
Total	**..**	**1 492**	**2 835**	**4 591**	**6 638**	**7 337**	**7 862**	**8 142**	**8 529**	**8 712**
2000+3000 Total	**..**	**10 271**	**23 380**	**36 256**	**49 024**	**53 670**	**57 351**	**60 093**	**62 337**	**62 692**

	1965	1980	1990	2000	2007	2010	2013	2015	2018	2019
Germany, million EUR										
2000 Social security contributions										
Federal or Central government	775	1 324	2 376	1 554	1 377	1 649	1 631	1 766	2 080	2 283
State/Regional	293	2 611	4 647	5 664	6 045	6 781	7 231	7 749	8 746	9 272
Local government	325	3 140	5 791	6 920	8 296	9 499	9 967	10 767	12 701	13 672
Social Security Funds	1 495	456	767	1 806	2 131	2 446	2 614	2 840	3 150	3 327
Total	**2 887**	**7 531**	**13 581**	**15 945**	**17 849**	**20 374**	**21 443**	**23 123**	**26 677**	**28 553**
3000 Taxes on payroll and workforce										
Federal or Central government	..	..	..	..	..	..	..	..	..	..
State/Regional	..	..	..	..	..	..	..	..	..	..
Local government	..	..	..	..	..	..	..	..	..	..
Social Security Funds	..	..	..	..	..	..	..	..	..	..
Total	**0**	**0**	**0**	**0**	**0**	**0**	**0**	**0**	**0**	**0**
2000+3000 Total	**2 887**	**7 531**	**13 581**	**15 945**	**17 849**	**20 374**	**21 443**	**23 123**	**26 677**	**28 553**
Greece, million EUR										
2000 Social security contributions										
Federal or Central government	..	..	124	1 542	2 888	3 217	2 372	2 337	1 469	1 745
State/Regional	..	..	..	..	..	..	..	..	..	..
Local government	..	..	0	0	0	0	0	0	0	0
Social Security Funds	..	..	0	200	440	387	350	265	392	403
Total	**..**	**..**	**124**	**1 742**	**3 328**	**3 604**	**2 722**	**2 602**	**1 861**	**2 148**
3000 Taxes on payroll and workforce										
Federal or Central government	..	..	..	..	..	..	..	..	..	..
State/Regional	..	..	..	..	..	..	..	..	..	..
Local government	..	..	..	..	..	..	..	..	..	..
Social Security Funds	..	..	..	..	..	..	..	..	..	..
Total	**..**	**..**	**0**	**0**	**0**	**0**	**0**	**0**	**0**	**0**
2000+3000 Total	**..**	**..**	**124**	**1 742**	**3 328**	**3 604**	**2 722**	**2 602**	**1 861**	**2 148**
Hungary, million HUF										
2000 Social security contributions										
Federal or Central government	..	..	..	148 251	293 684	352 354	449 428	539 106	521 151	530 607
State/Regional	..	..	..	..	..	..	..	..	..	..
Local government	..	..	..	173 475	343 306	291 375	124 111	152 189	142 851	147 213
Social Security Funds	..	..	..	4 936	8 052	6 763	2 781	2 977	730	876
Total	**..**	**..**	**..**	**326 661**	**645 042**	**650 492**	**576 320**	**694 272**	**664 732**	**678 696**
3000 Taxes on payroll and workforce										
Federal or Central government	..	..	..	13 901	7 287	5 419	12 435	12 876	18 145	19 481
State/Regional	..	..	..	..	..	..	..	..	..	..
Local government	..	..	..	25 990	11 928	9 275	4 224	3 357	4 134	4 617
Social Security Funds	..	..	..	406	162	194	101	110	38	37
Total	**..**	**..**	**..**	**40 297**	**19 377**	**14 888**	**16 760**	**16 342**	**22 317**	**24 135**
2000+3000 Total	**..**	**..**	**..**	**366 958**	**664 420**	**665 380**	**593 080**	**710 614**	**687 049**	**702 831**
Iceland, million ISK										
2000 Social security contributions										
Federal or Central government	..	..	..	..	..	..	..	..	..	..
State/Regional	..	..	..	..	..	..	..	..	..	..
Local government	..	..	..	..	..	..	..	..	..	..
Social Security Funds	..	..	..	..	..	..	..	..	..	..
Total	**..**	**..**	**..**	**..**	**..**	**..**	**..**	**..**	**..**	**..**
3000 Taxes on payroll and workforce										
Federal or Central government	..	..	..	..	..	..	..	..	..	..
State/Regional	..	..	..	..	..	..	..	..	..	..
Local government	..	..	..	..	..	..	..	..	..	..
Social Security Funds	..	..	..	..	..	..	..	..	..	..
Total	**..**	**..**	**..**	**..**	**..**	**..**	**..**	**..**	**..**	**..**
2000+3000 Total	**..**	**..**	**..**	**..**	**..**	**..**	**..**	**..**	**..**	**..**

	1965	1980	1990	2000	2007	2010	2013	2015	2018	2019
Ireland, million EUR										
2000 Social security contributions										
Federal or Central government	..	21	65	166	460	395	426	497	619	680
State/Regional	..	..	..	..	..	..	..	..	..	..
Local government	..	25	83	277	862	740	799	932	1 160	1 274
Social Security Funds	..	0	1	4	6	6	6	6	6	6
Total	**..**	**46**	**149**	**447**	**1 328**	**1 140**	**1 231**	**1 435**	**1 785**	**1 960**
3000 Taxes on payroll and workforce										
Federal or Central government	..	..	..	..	..	..	..	..	..	..
State/Regional	..	..	..	..	..	..	..	..	..	..
Local government	..	..	..	..	..	..	..	..	..	..
Social Security Funds	..	..	..	..	..	..	..	..	..	..
Total	**..**	**0**	**0**	**0**	**0**	**0**	**0**	**0**	**0**	**0**
2000+3000 Total	**..**	**46**	**149**	**447**	**1 328**	**1 140**	**1 231**	**1 435**	**1 785**	**1 960**
Israel, million ILS										
2000 Social security contributions										
Federal or Central government	..	..	..	840	1 030	1 180	1 550	1 780	2 240	2 380
State/Regional	..	..	..	..	..	..	..	..	..	..
Local government	..	..	..	280	340	390	510	590	740	790
Social Security Funds	..	..	..	5	12	15	0	0	0	0
Total	**..**	**..**	**..**	**1 120**	**1 370**	**1 570**	**2 060**	**2 370**	**2 980**	**3 170**
3000 Taxes on payroll and workforce										
Federal or Central government	..	..	..	2 330	3 600	4 180	5 220	5 650	6 540	6 850
State/Regional	..	..	..	..	..	..	..	..	..	..
Local government	..	..	..	660	880	960	1 190	1 290	1 490	1 570
Social Security Funds	..	..	..	5	12	15	0	0	0	0
Total	**..**	**..**	**..**	**2 990**	**4 480**	**5 140**	**6 410**	**6 940**	**8 030**	**8 420**
2000+3000 Total	**..**	**..**	**..**	**4 110**	**5 850**	**6 710**	**8 470**	**9 310**	**11 010**	**11 590**
Italy, million EUR										
2000 Social security contributions										
Federal or Central government	..	..	..	0	0	0	0	0	0	0
State/Regional	..	..	..	..	..	..	..	..	..	..
Local government	..	..	..	0	0	0	0	0	0	0
Social Security Funds	..	..	..	36 679	47 394	50 627	49 827	49 251	52 194	52 364
Total	**..**	**..**	**..**	**36 679**	**47 394**	**50 627**	**49 827**	**49 251**	**52 194**	**52 364**
3000 Taxes on payroll and workforce										
Federal or Central government	..	..	..	..	..	..	..	..	..	..
State/Regional	..	..	..	..	..	..	..	..	..	..
Local government	..	..	..	..	..	..	..	..	..	..
Social Security Funds	..	..	..	..	..	..	..	..	..	..
Total	**..**	**..**	**..**	**0**	**0**	**0**	**0**	**0**	**0**	**0**
2000+3000 Total	**..**	**..**	**..**	**36 679**	**47 394**	**50 627**	**49 827**	**49 251**	**52 194**	**52 364**
Japan, billion JPY										
2000 Social security contributions										
Federal or Central government	..	..	507	732	766	758	810	881	928	932
State/Regional	..	..	..	..	..	..	..	..	..	..
Local government	..	..	1 510	2 168	2 216	2 223	2 392	2 524	2 607	2 615
Social Security Funds	..	..	0	0	0	0	0	0	0	0
Total	**..**	**..**	**2 017**	**2 900**	**2 982**	**2 981**	**3 202**	**3 405**	**3 535**	**3 547**
3000 Taxes on payroll and workforce										
Federal or Central government	..	..	..	..	..	..	..	..	..	..
State/Regional	..	..	..	..	..	..	..	..	..	..
Local government	..	..	..	..	..	..	..	..	..	..
Social Security Funds	..	..	..	..	..	..	..	..	..	..
Total	**..**	**..**	**0**	**0**	**0**	**0**	**0**	**0**	**0**	**0**
2000+3000 Total	**..**	**..**	**2 017**	**2 900**	**2 982**	**2 981**	**3 202**	**3 405**	**3 535**	**3 547**

	1965	1980	1990	2000	2007	2010	2013	2015	2018	2019
Korea, billion KRW										
2000 Social security contributions										
Federal or Central government	..	..	..	..	..	..	..	..	..	..
State/Regional	..	..	..	..	..	..	..	..	..	..
Local government	..	..	..	..	..	..	..	..	..	..
Social Security Funds	..	..	..	..	..	..	..	..	..	..
Total	**..**	**..**	**..**	**..**	**..**	**..**	**..**	**..**	**..**	**..**
3000 Taxes on payroll and workforce										
Federal or Central government	..	..	..	..	..	..	..	..	..	..
State/Regional	..	..	..	..	..	..	..	..	..	..
Local government	..	..	..	..	..	..	..	..	..	..
Social Security Funds	..	..	..	..	..	..	..	..	..	..
Total	**..**	**..**	**..**	**..**	**..**	**..**	**..**	**..**	**..**	**..**
2000+3000 Total	**..**	**..**	**..**	**..**	**..**	**..**	**..**	**..**	**..**	**..**
Latvia, million EUR										
2000 Social security contributions										
Federal or Central government	..	..	..	..	..	..	..	..	..	..
State/Regional	..	..	..	..	..	..	..	..	..	..
Local government	..	..	..	..	..	..	..	..	..	..
Social Security Funds	..	..	..	..	..	..	..	..	..	..
Total	**..**	**..**	**..**	**40**	**156**	**174**	**228**	**262**	**339**	**358**
3000 Taxes on payroll and workforce										
Federal or Central government	..	..	..	..	..	..	..	..	..	..
State/Regional	..	..	..	..	..	..	..	..	..	..
Local government	..	..	..	..	..	..	..	..	..	..
Social Security Funds	..	..	..	..	..	..	..	..	..	..
Total	**..**	**..**	**..**	**0**	**0**	**0**	**0**	**0**	**0**	**0**
2000+3000 Total	**..**	**..**	**..**	**40**	**156**	**174**	**228**	**262**	**339**	**358**
Lithuania, million EUR										
2000 Social security contributions										
Federal or Central government	..	..	..	179	327	335	395	426	529	50
State/Regional	..	..	..	..	..	..	..	..	..	..
Local government	..	..	..	174	294	351	348	375	462	40
Social Security Funds	..	..	..	5	14	16	15	16	16	1
Total	**..**	**..**	**..**	**358**	**635**	**701**	**758**	**818**	**1 006**	**91**
3000 Taxes on payroll and workforce										
Federal or Central government	..	..	..	..	..	..	..	..	..	..
State/Regional	..	..	..	..	..	..	..	..	..	..
Local government	..	..	..	..	..	..	..	..	..	..
Social Security Funds	..	..	..	..	..	..	..	..	..	..
Total	**..**	**..**	**..**	**0**	**0**	**0**	**0**	**0**	**0**	**0**
2000+3000 Total	**..**	**..**	**..**	**358**	**635**	**701**	**758**	**818**	**1 006**	**91**
Luxembourg, million EUR										
2000 Social security contributions										
Federal or Central government	..	..	257	273	413	488	587	648	751	787
State/Regional	..	..	..	..	..	..	..	..	..	..
Local government	..	..	2	4	4	4	4	4	4	4
Social Security Funds	..	..	7	11	12	13	14	17	21	22
Total	**..**	**..**	**267**	**288**	**429**	**505**	**605**	**669**	**775**	**813**
3000 Taxes on payroll and workforce										
Federal or Central government	..	..	..	..	..	..	..	..	..	..
State/Regional	..	..	..	..	..	..	..	..	..	..
Local government	..	..	..	..	..	..	..	..	..	..
Social Security Funds	..	..	..	..	..	..	..	..	..	..
Total	**..**	**..**	**0**	**0**	**0**	**0**	**0**	**0**	**0**	**0**
2000+3000 Total	**..**	**..**	**267**	**288**	**429**	**505**	**605**	**669**	**775**	**813**

	1965	1980	1990	2000	2007	2010	2013	2015	2018	2019
Mexico, million MXN										
2000 Social security contributions										
Federal or Central government	..	25	2 952	44 879	94 251	103 440	126 518	145 329	169 788	183 462
State/Regional	..	0	0	0	0	0	0	0	0	0
Local government	..	0	0	0	0	0	0	0	0	0
Social Security Funds	..	0	0	0	0	0	0	0	0	0
Total	**..**	**25**	**2 952**	**44 879**	**94 251**	**103 440**	**126 518**	**145 329**	**169 788**	**183 462**
3000 Taxes on payroll and workforce										
Federal or Central government	..	..	..	..	..	..	..	..	..	..
State/Regional	..	..	..	..	..	..	..	..	..	..
Local government	..	..	..	..	..	..	..	..	..	..
Social Security Funds	..	..	..	..	..	..	..	..	..	..
Total	**..**	**0**	**0**	**0**	**0**	**0**	**0**	**0**	**0**	**0**
2000+3000 Total	**..**	**25**	**2 952**	**44 879**	**94 251**	**103 440**	**126 518**	**145 329**	**169 788**	**183 462**
Netherlands, million EUR										
2000 Social security contributions										
Federal or Central government	63	1 366	286	..	..	..	..	..	..	..
State/Regional	..	..	..	..	..	..	..	..	..	..
Local government	0	0	0	..	..	..	..	..	..	..
Social Security Funds	7	91	59	..	..	..	..	..	..	..
Total	**70**	**1 457**	**345**	**2 006**	**4 310**	**..**	**..**	**..**	**..**	**..**
3000 Taxes on payroll and workforce										
Federal or Central government	..	..	..	..	..	..	..	..	..	..
State/Regional	..	..	..	..	..	..	..	..	..	..
Local government	..	..	..	..	..	..	..	..	..	..
Social Security Funds	..	..	..	..	..	..	..	..	..	..
Total	**0**	**0**	**0**	**0**	**0**	**0**	**0**	**0**	**0**	**0**
2000+3000 Total	**70**	**1 457**	**345**	**2 006**	**4 310**	**0**	**0**	**0**	**0**	**0**
New Zealand, million NZD										
2000 Social security contributions										
Federal or Central government	..	..	..	..	..	..	..	..	..	..
State/Regional	..	..	..	..	..	..	..	..	..	..
Local government	..	..	..	..	..	..	..	..	..	..
Social Security Funds	..	..	..	..	..	..	..	..	..	..
Total	**0**	**0**	**0**	**0**	**0**	**0**	**0**	**0**	**0**	**0**
3000 Taxes on payroll and workforce										
Federal or Central government	..	..	..	..	..	..	..	..	..	..
State/Regional	..	..	..	..	..	..	..	..	..	..
Local government	..	..	..	..	..	..	..	..	..	..
Social Security Funds	..	..	..	..	..	..	..	..	..	..
Total	**0**	**0**	**0**	**0**	**0**	**0**	**0**	**0**	**0**	**0**
2000+3000 Total	**0**	**0**	**0**	**0**	**0**	**0**	**0**	**0**	**0**	**0**
Norway, million NOK										
2000 Social security contributions										
Federal or Central government	..	1 242	2 859	11 895	28 233	33 746	40 145	46 487	50 073	52 458
State/Regional	..	..	..	..	..	..	..	..	..	..
Local government	..	4 538	11 964	24 831	32 110	41 024	53 123	59 556	67 171	71 600
Social Security Funds	..	1 222	3 064	0	0	0	0	0	0	0
Total	**..**	**7 002**	**17 887**	**36 726**	**60 343**	**74 770**	**93 268**	**106 043**	**117 244**	**124 058**
3000 Taxes on payroll and workforce										
Federal or Central government	..	..	..	..	..	..	..	..	..	..
State/Regional	..	..	..	..	..	..	..	..	..	..
Local government	..	..	..	..	..	..	..	..	..	..
Social Security Funds	..	..	..	..	..	..	..	..	..	..
Total	**..**	**0**	**0**	**0**	**0**	**0**	**0**	**0**	**0**	**0**
2000+3000 Total	**..**	**7 002**	**17 887**	**36 726**	**60 343**	**74 770**	**93 268**	**106 043**	**117 244**	**124 058**

	1965	1980	1990	2000	2007	2010	2013	2015	2018	2019
Poland, million PLN										
2000 Social security contributions										
Federal or Central government	..	..	..	4 566	6 023	6 643	8 145	9 840	11 693	12 587
State/Regional	..	..	..	..	..	..	..	..	..	..
Local government	..	..	..	6 756	9 856	11 411	13 702	14 796	17 308	18 662
Social Security Funds	..	..	..	279	426	499	536	518	627	658
Total	**..**	**..**	**..**	**11 601**	**16 305**	**18 553**	**22 383**	**25 154**	**29 628**	**31 907**
3000 Taxes on payroll and workforce										
Federal or Central government	..	..	..	..	..	..	..	..	..	..
State/Regional	..	..	..	..	..	..	..	..	..	..
Local government	..	..	..	..	..	..	..	..	..	..
Social Security Funds	..	..	..	..	..	..	..	..	..	..
Total	**..**	**..**	**..**	**0**	**0**	**0**	**0**	**0**	**0**	**0**
2000+3000 Total	**..**	**..**	**..**	**11 601**	**16 305**	**18 553**	**22 383**	**25 154**	**29 628**	**31 907**
Portugal, million EUR										
2000 Social security contributions										
Federal or Central government	..	0	0	0	..	..	..	..	..	..
State/Regional	..	..	..	..	..	..	..	..	..	..
Local government	..	0	33	197	..	..	..	..	..	..
Social Security Funds	..	4	0	0	..	..	..	..	..	..
Total	**..**	**4**	**33**	**197**	**0**	**0**	**0**	**0**	**0**	**0**
3000 Taxes on payroll and workforce										
Federal or Central government	..	..	..	..	..	..	..	..	..	..
State/Regional	..	..	..	..	..	..	..	..	..	..
Local government	..	..	..	..	..	..	..	..	..	..
Social Security Funds	..	..	..	..	..	..	..	..	..	..
Total	**..**	**0**	**0**	**0**	**0**	**0**	**0**	**0**	**0**	**0**
2000+3000 Total	**..**	**4**	**33**	**197**	**0**	**0**	**0**	**0**	**0**	**0**
Slovak Republic, million EUR										
2000 Social security contributions										
Federal or Central government	..	..	..	489	602	797	944	1 069	1 126	1 340
State/Regional	..	..	..	..	..	..	..	..	..	..
Local government	..	..	..	130	427	515	587	658	769	921
Social Security Funds	..	..	..	22	26	43	33	36	43	49
Total	**..**	**..**	**..**	**642**	**1 056**	**1 354**	**1 564**	**1 763**	**1 937**	**2 310**
3000 Taxes on payroll and workforce										
Federal or Central government	..	..	..	..	..	..	..	..	..	..
State/Regional	..	..	..	..	..	..	..	..	..	..
Local government	..	..	..	..	..	..	..	..	..	..
Social Security Funds	..	..	..	..	..	..	..	..	..	..
Total	**..**	**..**	**..**	**0**	**0**	**0**	**0**	**0**	**0**	**0**
2000+3000 Total	**..**	**..**	**..**	**642**	**1 056**	**1 354**	**1 564**	**1 763**	**1 937**	**2 310**
Slovenia, million EUR										
2000 Social security contributions										
Federal or Central government	..	..	..	178	339	409	387	375	449	488
State/Regional	..	..	..	..	..	..	..	..	..	..
Local government	..	..	..	94	175	195	187	189	225	243
Social Security Funds	..	..	..	3	7	8	7	6	8	8
Total	**..**	**..**	**..**	**275**	**521**	**612**	**582**	**571**	**682**	**739**
3000 Taxes on payroll and workforce										
Federal or Central government	..	..	..	56	77	6	7	7	7	9
State/Regional	..	..	..	..	..	..	..	..	..	..
Local government	..	..	..	29	36	3	4	4	4	4
Social Security Funds	..	..	..	1	2	0	0	0	0	0
Total	**..**	**..**	**..**	**86**	**114**	**9**	**11**	**11**	**12**	**13**
2000+3000 Total	**..**	**..**	**..**	**361**	**636**	**621**	**593**	**582**	**693**	**752**

	1965	1980	1990	2000	2007	2010	2013	2015	2018	2019
Spain, million EUR										
2000 Social security contributions										
Federal or Central government	..	387	989	1 408	1 966	2 201	2 014	2 234	2 486	2 700
State/Regional	..	2	0	4 411	9 426	10 996	10 212	11 245	12 987	14 126
Local government	..	252	1 819	2 524	4 098	4 781	4 617	4 797	5 128	5 552
Social Security Funds	..	396	1 202	1 284	484	527	498	496	494	517
Total	**..**	**1 037**	**4 010**	**9 627**	**15 974**	**18 505**	**17 341**	**18 772**	**21 095**	**22 895**
3000 Taxes on payroll and workforce										
Federal or Central government	..	..	..	..	..	..	..	..	..	..
State/Regional	..	..	..	..	..	..	..	..	..	..
Local government	..	..	..	..	..	..	..	..	..	..
Social Security Funds	..	..	..	..	..	..	..	..	..	..
Total	**..**	**0**	**0**	**0**	**0**	**0**	**0**	**0**	**0**	**0**
2000+3000 Total	**..**	**1 037**	**4 010**	**9 627**	**15 974**	**18 505**	**17 341**	**18 772**	**21 095**	**22 895**
Sweden, million SEK										
2000 Social security contributions										
Federal or Central government	..	7 543	12 430	21 153	25 164	24 729	24 595	25 707	28 594	28 554
State/Regional	..	..	..	..	..	..	..	..	..	..
Local government	..	18 149	49 298	66 215	83 877	82 141	78 774	85 373	98 662	98 072
Social Security Funds	..	0	0	0	0	0	0	0	0	0
Total	**..**	**25 692**	**61 728**	**87 367**	**109 040**	**106 870**	**103 370**	**111 079**	**127 256**	**126 625**
3000 Taxes on payroll and workforce										
Federal or Central government	..	..	1 527	3 453	5 394	6 912	11 242	12 326	15 122	16 584
State/Regional	..	..	..	..	..	..	..	..	..	..
Local government	..	..	6 060	10 808	17 980	22 958	36 005	40 935	52 177	56 961
Social Security Funds	..	..	0	0	0	0	0	0	0	0
Total	**..**	**0**	**7 587**	**14 261**	**23 374**	**29 870**	**47 247**	**53 261**	**67 299**	**73 545**
2000+3000 Total	**..**	**25 692**	**69 315**	**101 628**	**132 414**	**136 740**	**150 616**	**164 340**	**194 555**	**200 170**
Switzerland, million CHF										
2000 Social security contributions										
Federal or Central government	13	91	224	293	381	448	494	530	553	584
State/Regional	34	380	770	971	1 269	1 520	1 695	1 766	1 898	1 943
Local government	22	270	460	595	745	823	867	911	957	947
Social Security Funds	2	21	4	14	18	23	25	26	26	28
Total	**71**	**762**	**1 458**	**1 873**	**2 413**	**2 813**	**3 080**	**3 234**	**3 434**	**3 502**
3000 Taxes on payroll and workforce										
Federal or Central government	..	..	..	..	..	..	..	..	..	..
State/Regional	..	..	..	..	..	..	..	..	..	..
Local government	..	..	..	..	..	..	..	..	..	..
Social Security Funds	..	..	..	..	..	..	..	..	..	..
Total	**0**	**0**	**0**	**0**	**0**	**0**	**0**	**0**	**0**	**0**
2000+3000 Total	**71**	**762**	**1 458**	**1 873**	**2 413**	**2 813**	**3 080**	**3 234**	**3 434**	**3 502**
Turkey, million TRY										
2000 Social security contributions										
Federal or Central government	..	..	9	3 619	20 442	39 363	71 184	95 067	151 373	178 345
State/Regional	..	..	..	..	..	..	..	..	..	..
Local government	..	..	0	0	0	0	0	0	0	0
Social Security Funds	..	..	0	0	0	0	0	0	0	0
Total	**..**	**..**	**9**	**3 619**	**20 442**	**39 363**	**71 184**	**95 067**	**151 373**	**178 345**
3000 Taxes on payroll and workforce										
Federal or Central government	..	..	..	..	..	..	..	..	..	..
State/Regional	..	..	..	..	..	..	..	..	..	..
Local government	..	..	..	..	..	..	..	..	..	..
Social Security Funds	..	..	..	..	..	..	..	..	..	..
Total	**..**	**..**	**0**	**0**	**0**	**0**	**0**	**0**	**0**	**0**
2000+3000 Total	**..**	**..**	**9**	**3 619**	**20 442**	**39 363**	**71 184**	**95 067**	**151 373**	**178 345**

	1965	1980	1990	2000	2007	2010	2013	2015	2018	2019
United Kingdom, million GBP										
2000 Social security contributions										
Federal or Central government	87	920	2 134	3 146	5 842	6 456	7 052	7 814	9 579	10 287
State/Regional	..	..	..	..	..	..	..	..	..	..
Local government	83	926	1 957	2 924	4 862	5 340	4 667	4 536	4 810	4 951
Social Security Funds	0	0	0	0	0	0	0	0	0	0
Total	**170**	**1 846**	**4 091**	**6 070**	**10 704**	**11 796**	**11 719**	**12 350**	**14 389**	**15 238**
3000 Taxes on payroll and workforce										
Federal or Central government	..	360	..	..	..	..	..	..	..	..
State/Regional	..	..	..	..	..	..	..	..	..	..
Local government	..	410	..	..	..	..	..	..	..	..
Social Security Funds	..	0	..	..	..	..	..	..	..	..
Total	**0**	**770**	**0**	**0**	**0**	**0**	**0**	**0**	**0**	**0**
2000+3000 Total	**170**	**2 616**	**4 091**	**6 070**	**10 704**	**11 796**	**11 719**	**12 350**	**14 389**	**15 238**
United States, million USD										
2000 Social security contributions										
Federal or Central government	301	2 053	9 059	11 323	19 628	25 434	25 938	26 722	27 793	28 755
State/Regional	699	7 585	19 802	32 814	44 061	45 936	46 832	49 105	54 050	55 966
Local government	0	0	0	0	0	0	0	0	0	0
Social Security Funds	0	0	0	0	0	0	0	0	0	0
Total	**1 000**	**9 638**	**28 861**	**44 137**	**63 689**	**71 370**	**72 770**	**75 827**	**81 843**	**84 721**
3000 Taxes on payroll and workforce										
Federal or Central government	..	..	..	..	..	..	..	..	..	..
State/Regional	..	..	..	..	..	..	..	..	..	..
Local government	..	..	..	..	..	..	..	..	..	..
Social Security Funds	..	..	..	..	..	..	..	..	..	..
Total	**0**	**0**	**0**	**0**	**0**	**0**	**0**	**0**	**0**	**0**
2000+3000 Total	**1 000**	**9 638**	**28 861**	**44 137**	**63 689**	**71 370**	**72 770**	**75 827**	**81 843**	**84 721**

.. Not available

1. The multi-jurisdictional sector contains units where jurisdiction is shared between two or more governments, or classification of a unit to a jurisdiction is otherwise unclear. The main type of units currently falling into this category is public universities.
2. There is a break in the series in 1990. The data are based on ESA 2010 from that year onwards.

StatLink https://stat.link/i7sbuq

6 Tax revenues by subsectors of general government

Chapter 6 provides information on tax revenues by subsectors of general government for each OECD country.

6.1. Country tables 1975, 1985, 1995, 2005 and 2019

This chapter presents detailed country information on tax revenues by level of government. The data have been attributed to the sub-sectors of general government identified in section A.12 of the Interpretative Guide (see Annex A) and the attribution criteria used are those set out in that guide.

Table 6.1. Australia, tax revenues by sub-sectors of government

Million AUD

	Federal government					State/Regional				
	1975	1995	2005	2015	2019	1975	1995	2005	2015	2019
1000 Taxes on income, profits and capital gains	**11 831**	**82 615**	**175 695**	**261 345**	**325 116**	**0**	**0**	**0**	**0**	**0**
1100 Of individuals	9 213	60 602	118 239	191 720	230 932	..	..	..	..	..
1200 Corporate	2 618	22 013	57 456	69 625	94 184	..	..	..	..	..
1300 Unallocable between 1100 and 1200	0	0	0	0	0	0	..	..	..	..
2000 Social security contributions	**0**	**0**	**0**	**0**	**0**	**0**	**0**	**0**	**0**	**0**
2100 Employees	0	0	0	0	0	0	0	0	0	0
2200 Employers	0	0	0	0	0	0	0	0	0	0
2300 Self-employed or non-employed	0	0	0	0	0	0	0	0	0	0
2400 Unallocable between 2100, 2200 and 2300	0	0	0	0	0	0	0	0	0	0
3000 Taxes on payroll and workforce	**54**	**3 065**	**369**	**670**	**1 034**	**1 171**	**7 120**	**13 095**	**22 684**	**24 993**
4000 Taxes on property	**103**	**8**	**14**	**15**	**15**	**883**	**7 988**	**16 940**	**32 533**	**34 389**
4100 Recurrent taxes on immovable property	12	0	0	0	0	217	1 840	4 559	10 029	14 225
4200 Recurrent taxes on net wealth	0	0	0	0	0	0	0	0	0	0
4300 Estate, inheritance and gift taxes	87	0	0	0	0	227	0	0	0	0
4400 Taxes on financial and capital transactions	4	8	14	15	15	439	6 148	12 381	22 504	20 164
4500 Non-recurrent taxes	0	0	0	0	0	0	0	0	0	0
4600 Other recurrent taxes on property	0	0	0	0	0	0	0	0	0	0
5000 Taxes on goods and services	**4 932**	**30 004**	**68 710**	**103 455**	**117 978**	**1 262**	**13 295**	**14 479**	**23 407**	**26 433**
5100 Taxes on production, sale, transfer, etc	4 919	29 613	67 172	97 166	110 772	532	4 923	8 188	11 884	12 867
5110 General taxes	1 408	12 970	39 436	60 680	65 720	0	0	0	0	0
5120 Taxes on specific goods and services	3 511	16 643	27 736	36 486	45 052	532	4 923	8 188	11 884	12 867
5130 Unallocable between 5110 and 5120	0	0	0	0	0	0	0	0	0	0
5200 Taxes on use of goods and perform activities	13	391	1 538	6 289	7 206	730	8 372	6 291	11 523	13 566
5300 Unallocable between 5100 and 5200	0	0	0	0	0	0	0	0	0	0
6000 Other taxes	**0**	**0**	**0**	**0**	**0**	**0**	**0**	**0**	**0**	**0**
6100 Paid solely by business	..	..	..	..	..	..	..	..	..	..
6200 Other	..	..	..	..	..	..	..	..	..	..
Total tax revenue	**16 920**	**115 692**	**244 788**	**365 485**	**444 143**	**3 316**	**28 403**	**44 514**	**78 624**	**85 815**

	Local government					Social Security Funds				
	1975	1995	2005	2015	2019	1975	1995	2005	2015	2019
1000 Taxes on income, profits and capital gains	**0**	**0**	**0**	**0**	**0**	**0**	**0**	**0**	**0**	**0**
1100 Of individuals	..	..	..	..	..	..	..	..	..	..
1200 Corporate	..	..	..	..	..	..	..	..	..	..
1300 Unallocable between 1100 and 1200	0	..	..	..	..	0	..	..	..	..
2000 Social security contributions	**0**	**0**	**0**	**0**	**0**	**0**	**0**	**0**	**0**	**0**
2100 Employees	0	0	0	0	0	0	0	0	0	0
2200 Employers	0	0	0	0	0	0	0	0	0	0
2300 Self-employed or non-employed	0	0	0	0	0	0	0	0	0	0
2400 Unallocable between 2100, 2200 and 2300	0	0	0	0	0	0	0	0	0	0
3000 Taxes on payroll and workforce	**0**	**0**	**0**	**0**	**0**	**0**	**0**	**0**	**0**	**0**
4000 Taxes on property	**883**	**5 134**	**8 726**	**16 620**	**19 578**	**0**	**0**	**0**	**0**	**0**
4100 Recurrent taxes on immovable property	883	5 134	8 726	16 620	19 578	..	..	..	..	..
4200 Recurrent taxes on net wealth	0	0	0	0	0	..	..	..	..	..
4300 Estate, inheritance and gift taxes	0	0	0	0	0	..	..	..	..	..
4400 Taxes on financial and capital transactions	0	0	0	0	0	..	..	..	..	..
4500 Non-recurrent taxes	0	0	0	0	0	..	..	..	..	..
4600 Other recurrent taxes on property	0	0	0	0	0	..	..	..	..	..
5000 Taxes on goods and services	**0**	**0**	**0**	**0**	**0**	**0**	**0**	**0**	**0**	**0**
5100 Taxes on production, sale, transfer, etc	0	0	0	0	0	0	0	0	0	0
5110 General taxes	0	0	0	0	0	0	0	0	0	0
5120 Taxes on specific goods and services	0	0	0	0	0	0	0	0	0	0
5130 Unallocable between 5110 and 5120	0	0	0	0	0	0	0	0	0	0
5200 Taxes on use of goods and perform activities	0	0	0	0	0	0	0	0	0	0
5300 Unallocable between 5100 and 5200	0	0	0	0	0	0	0	0	0	0
6000 Other taxes	**0**	**0**	**0**	**0**	**0**	**0**	**0**	**0**	**0**	**0**
6100 Paid solely by business	..	..	..	..	..	..	..	..	..	..
6200 Other	..	..	..	..	..	..	..	..	..	..
Total tax revenue	**883**	**5 134**	**8 726**	**16 620**	**19 578**	**0**	**0**	**0**	**0**	**0**

.. Not available

StatLink https://stat.link/b1kwgr

Table 6.2. Austria, tax revenues by sub-sectors of government

Million EUR

	Federal government					State/Regional				
	1975	1995	2005	2015	2019	1975	1995	2005	2015	2019
1000 Taxes on income, profits and capital gains	**3 064**	**18 452**	**28 781**	**43 714**	**48 600**	**865**	**547**	**742**	**1 081**	**1 264**
1100 Of individuals	2 381	14 649	22 126	34 901	37 123	834	459	637	941	1 116
1200 Corporate	655	2 267	5 341	7 519	10 647	31	88	104	141	148
1300 Unallocable between 1100 and 1200	27	1 536	1 313	1 295	830	0	0	0	0	0
2000 Social security contributions	**352**	**4 243**	**5 720**	**7 547**	**8 535**	**34**	**311**	**409**	**496**	**465**
2100 Employees	225	2 379	2 978	3 911	4 404	34	310	395	465	435
2200 Employers	127	1 830	2 498	3 350	3 852	0	0	0	0	0
2300 Self-employed or non-employed	0	34	243	286	279	0	1	14	31	29
2400 Unallocable between 2100, 2200 and 2300	0	0	0	0	0	0	0	0	0	0
3000 Taxes on payroll and workforce	**1 217**	**3 394**	**4 384**	**6 861**	**5 845**	**0**	**132**	**156**	**203**	**1 101**
4000 Taxes on property	**282**	**655**	**801**	**1 247**	**1 383**	**35**	**31**	**36**	**44**	**51**
4100 Recurrent taxes on immovable property	18	32	32	43	54	15	31	36	44	51
4200 Recurrent taxes on net wealth	226	58	0	0	0	10	0	0	0	0
4300 Estate, inheritance and gift taxes	24	82	140	12	1	10	0	0	0	0
4400 Taxes on financial and capital transactions	14	483	629	1 116	1 318	0	0	0	0	0
4500 Non-recurrent taxes	0	0	0	76	11	0	0	0	0	0
4600 Other recurrent taxes on property	0	0	0	0	0	0	0	0	0	0
5000 Taxes on goods and services	**4 554**	**19 894**	**29 646**	**39 720**	**44 992**	**1 013**	**222**	**234**	**362**	**464**
5100 Taxes on production, sale, transfer, etc	4 549	18 639	27 613	36 693	41 407	926	158	139	216	288
5110 General taxes	2 545	13 436	19 421	26 282	30 426	662	0	0	0	0
5120 Taxes on specific goods and services	1 991	5 159	8 148	10 408	10 977	264	158	139	216	288
5130 Unallocable between 5110 and 5120	14	44	45	4	5	0	0	0	0	0
5200 Taxes on use of goods and perform activities	5	1 255	2 033	3 027	3 585	87	64	95	146	176
5300 Unallocable between 5100 and 5200	0	0	0	0	0	0	0	0	0	0
6000 Other taxes	**52**	**486**	**699**	**517**	**554**	**8**	**50**	**61**	**91**	**99**
6100 Paid solely by business	..	..	..	..	..	..	..	..	..	..
6200 Other	..	..	..	..	..	..	..	..	..	..
Total tax revenue	**9 521**	**47 124**	**70 031**	**99 606**	**109 910**	**1 955**	**1 294**	**1 638**	**2 277**	**3 444**

	Local government					Social Security Funds				
	1975	1995	2005	2015	2019	1975	1995	2005	2015	2019
1000 Taxes on income, profits and capital gains	**887**	**46**	**0**	**0**	**0**	**0**	**0**	**0**	**0**	**0**
1100 Of individuals	771	19	0	0	0	..	..	..	..	..
1200 Corporate	115	26	0	0	0	..	..	..	..	..
1300 Unallocable between 1100 and 1200	0	0	0	0	0	..	..	..	..	..
2000 Social security contributions	**29**	**258**	**267**	**266**	**245**	**4 667**	**21 173**	**28 912**	**41 557**	**49 832**
2100 Employees	29	207	240	241	226	1 840	8 110	10 751	15 499	18 706
2200 Employers	0	50	27	26	20	2 375	10 912	14 037	19 906	23 955
2300 Self-employed or non-employed	0	0	0	0	0	453	2 151	4 125	6 153	7 171
2400 Unallocable between 2100, 2200 and 2300	0	0	0	0	0	0	0	0	0	0
3000 Taxes on payroll and workforce	**262**	**1 492**	**2 035**	**2 977**	**3 833**	**0**	**0**	**0**	**0**	**0**
4000 Taxes on property	**254**	**395**	**539**	**675**	**724**	**0**	**0**	**0**	**0**	**0**
4100 Recurrent taxes on immovable property	139	395	539	675	724	..	..	..	..	..
4200 Recurrent taxes on net wealth	35	0	0	0	0	..	..	..	..	..
4300 Estate, inheritance and gift taxes	0	0	0	0	0	..	..	..	..	..
4400 Taxes on financial and capital transactions	81	0	0	0	0	..	..	..	..	..
4500 Non-recurrent taxes	0	0	0	0	0	..	..	..	..	..
4600 Other recurrent taxes on property	0	0	0	0	0	..	..	..	..	..
5000 Taxes on goods and services	**792**	**738**	**302**	**353**	**392**	**0**	**0**	**0**	**0**	**0**
5100 Taxes on production, sale, transfer, etc	769	582	134	96	101	..	..	..	..	..
5110 General taxes	448	0	0	0	0	..	..	..	..	..
5120 Taxes on specific goods and services	321	582	134	96	101	..	..	..	..	..
5130 Unallocable between 5110 and 5120	0	0	0	0	0	..	..	..	..	..
5200 Taxes on use of goods and perform activities	24	155	168	258	291	..	..	..	..	..
5300 Unallocable between 5100 and 5200	0	0	0	0	0	..	..	..	..	..
6000 Other taxes	**55**	**60**	**103**	**129**	**155**	**0**	**0**	**0**	**0**	**0**
6100 Paid solely by business	..	..	..	..	..	..	..	..	..	..
6200 Other	..	..	..	..	..	..	..	..	..	..
Total tax revenue	**2 279**	**2 987**	**3 246**	**4 400**	**5 349**	**4 667**	**21 173**	**28 912**	**41 557**	**49 832**

.. Not available

Note: Including taxes collected on behalf of the European Union.

StatLink https://stat.link/mzytpu

Table 6.3. Belgium, tax revenues by sub-sectors of government

Million EUR

	Federal government					State/Regional				
	1975	1995	2005	2015	2019	1975	1995	2005	2015	2019
1000 Taxes on income, profits and capital gains	**8 534**	**30 905**	**45 859**	**57 131**	**57 006**	**..**	**79**	**0**	**4 283**	**10 013**
1100 Of individuals	6 929	25 997	36 007	43 436	39 199	..	79	..	4 283	10 013
1200 Corporate	1 596	4 867	9 811	13 644	17 736	..	0	..	0	0
1300 Unallocable between 1100 and 1200	10	41	42	51	71	..	0	..	0	0
2000 Social security contributions	**299**	**1 181**	**1 904**	**2 336**	**65**	**..**	**0**	**34**	**11**	**255**
2100 Employees	264	854	1 125	1 372	0	..	..	7	2	246
2200 Employers	36	228	608	715	65	..	..	27	9	9
2300 Self-employed or non-employed	0	99	171	249	0	..	..	0	0	0
2400 Unallocable between 2100, 2200 and 2300	0	0	0	0	0	..	..	0	0	0
3000 Taxes on payroll and workforce	**0**	**0**	**0**	**0**	**0**	**..**	**0**	**0**	**0**	**0**
4000 Taxes on property	**583**	**1 340**	**873**	**1 861**	**2 245**	**..**	**1 168**	**4 669**	**7 087**	**8 085**
4100 Recurrent taxes on immovable property	12	25	41	41	47	..	83	192	249	374
4200 Recurrent taxes on net wealth	0	8	189	661	922	..	0	0	0	0
4300 Estate, inheritance and gift taxes	178	42	0	0	0	..	647	1 749	2 996	2 936
4400 Taxes on financial and capital transactions	393	1 193	521	596	623	..	438	2 728	3 763	4 755
4500 Non-recurrent taxes	0	73	123	563	435	..	0	0	79	20
4600 Other recurrent taxes on property	0	0	0	0	217	..	0	0	0	0
5000 Taxes on goods and services	**5 813**	**20 951**	**29 984**	**39 004**	**44 465**	**..**	**412**	**2 044**	**2 678**	**3 172**
5100 Taxes on production, sale, transfer, etc	5 562	19 767	29 742	38 985	44 415	..	58	76	227	355
5110 General taxes	3 776	13 894	21 533	27 952	32 181	..	0	0	0	0
5120 Taxes on specific goods and services	1 785	5 872	8 208	11 034	12 234	..	58	76	227	355
5130 Unallocable between 5110 and 5120	0	0	0	0	0	..	0	0	0	0
5200 Taxes on use of goods and perform activities	249	1 178	234	10	37	..	355	1 968	2 451	2 817
5300 Unallocable between 5100 and 5200	3	6	8	9	13	..	0	0	0	0
6000 Other taxes	**0**	**0**	**0**	**0**	**0**	**..**	**0**	**68**	**40**	**0**
6100 Paid solely by business	..	..	..	..	..	..	..	0	0	..
6200 Other	..	..	..	..	..	..	..	68	40	..
Total tax revenue	**15 230**	**54 377**	**78 621**	**100 332**	**103 780**	**..**	**1 659**	**6 816**	**14 099**	**21 526**

	Local government					Social Security Funds				
	1975	1995	2005	2015	2019	1975	1995	2005	2015	2019
1000 Taxes on income, profits and capital gains	**683**	**3 058**	**2 249**	**3 052**	**3 517**	**0**	**335**	**825**	**1 106**	**1 267**
1100 Of individuals	675	3 058	2 249	3 052	3 517	..	335	825	1 106	1 267
1200 Corporate	8	0	0	0	0	..	0	0	0	0
1300 Unallocable between 1100 and 1200	0	0	0	0	0	..	0	0	0	0
2000 Social security contributions	**27**	**80**	**20**	**27**	**19**	**6 709**	**28 479**	**39 537**	**56 438**	**62 864**
2100 Employees	27	80	18	21	19	1 749	8 268	11 558	15 640	18 806
2200 Employers	0	0	3	6	0	4 347	17 746	24 613	35 510	37 828
2300 Self-employed or non-employed	0	0	0	0	0	612	2 465	3 366	5 289	6 230
2400 Unallocable between 2100, 2200 and 2300	0	0	0	0	0	0	0	0	0	0
3000 Taxes on payroll and workforce	**0**	**0**	**0**	**0**	**0**	**0**	**0**	**5**	**8**	**9**
4000 Taxes on property	**154**	**815**	**3 599**	**5 142**	**5 724**	**0**	**121**	**229**	**318**	**305**
4100 Recurrent taxes on immovable property	154	815	3 599	5 142	5 724	..	0	0	0	0
4200 Recurrent taxes on net wealth	0	0	0	0	0	..	0	0	0	0
4300 Estate, inheritance and gift taxes	0	0	0	0	0	..	0	0	0	0
4400 Taxes on financial and capital transactions	0	0	0	0	0	..	0	0	0	0
4500 Non-recurrent taxes	0	0	0	0	0	..	0	0	0	0
4600 Other recurrent taxes on property	0	0	0	0	0	..	121	229	318	305
5000 Taxes on goods and services	**166**	**332**	**523**	**715**	**739**	**14**	**330**	**1 237**	**1 575**	**2 330**
5100 Taxes on production, sale, transfer, etc	150	295	437	694	716	14	330	1 237	1 575	2 330
5110 General taxes	0	0	0	0	0	0	29	373	219	381
5120 Taxes on specific goods and services	150	295	437	694	716	14	301	865	1 356	1 949
5130 Unallocable between 5110 and 5120	0	0	0	0	0	0	0	0	0	0
5200 Taxes on use of goods and perform activities	16	37	87	22	23	0	0	0	0	0
5300 Unallocable between 5100 and 5200	0	0	0	0	0	0	0	0	0	0
6000 Other taxes	**0**	**0**	**0**	**0**	**0**	**0**	**0**	**0**	**0**	**0**
6100 Paid solely by business	..	..	..	..	..	..	..	..	..	..
6200 Other	..	..	..	..	..	..	..	..	..	..
Total tax revenue	**1 029**	**4 284**	**6 392**	**8 937**	**9 999**	**6 723**	**29 265**	**41 833**	**59 445**	**66 775**

.. Not available

Note: Including taxes collected on behalf of the European Union.

StatLink https://stat.link/7vkf13

Table 6.4. Canada, tax revenues by sub-sectors of government

Million CAD

	Federal government					State/Regional				
	1975	1995	2005	2015	2019	1975	1995	2005	2015	2019
1000 Taxes on income, profits and capital gains	**19 047**	**82 237**	**140 013**	**191 684**	**239 115**	**8 165**	**52 373**	**78 331**	**123 157**	**148 453**
1100 Of individuals	12 822	65 384	102 366	143 315	169 476	6 074	43 428	62 435	96 989	111 898
1200 Corporate	5 741	14 739	32 197	41 726	59 605	2 091	8 944	15 896	26 168	36 555
1300 Unallocable between 1100 and 1200	484	2 114	5 450	6 643	10 034	0	0	0	0	0
2000 Social security contributions	**0**	**0**	**17 936**	**23 603**	**23 403**	**0**	**0**	**11 759**	**13 892**	**14 587**
2100 Employees	..	..	7 429	9 772	9 680	..	..	1 858	1 128	1 357
2200 Employers	..	..	10 507	13 831	13 723	..	..	9 901	12 764	13 230
2300 Self-employed or non-employed	..	..	0	0	0	..	..	0	0	0
2400 Unallocable between 2100, 2200 and 2300	..	..	0	0	0	..	..	0	0	0
3000 Taxes on payroll and workforce	**0**	**0**	**0**	**0**	**0**	**0**	**6 498**	**9 230**	**13 256**	**17 245**
4000 Taxes on property	**13**	**0**	**0**	**0**	**0**	**428**	**6 492**	**9 298**	**11 809**	**15 019**
4100 Recurrent taxes on immovable property	0	..	..	..	..	85	2 960	2 934	5 410	7 050
4200 Recurrent taxes on net wealth	0	..	..	..	..	200	2 914	3 456	372	441
4300 Estate, inheritance and gift taxes	13	..	..	..	..	143	3	0	268	347
4400 Taxes on financial and capital transactions	0	..	..	..	..	0	0	1 965	3 912	5 087
4500 Non-recurrent taxes	0	..	..	..	..	0	615	943	1 847	2 094
4600 Other recurrent taxes on property	0	..	..	..	..	0	0	0	0	0
5000 Taxes on goods and services	**8 180**	**31 160**	**48 551**	**53 837**	**63 133**	**10 128**	**42 076**	**67 537**	**95 289**	**113 502**
5100 Taxes on production, sale, transfer, etc	8 180	31 136	48 506	53 797	63 095	6 800	37 961	61 316	86 827	103 631
5110 General taxes	3 504	19 167	35 069	36 958	43 337	3 664	21 328	33 353	53 577	66 287
5120 Taxes on specific goods and services	4 676	11 969	13 437	16 839	19 758	3 136	16 633	27 963	33 250	37 344
5130 Unallocable between 5110 and 5120	0	0	0	0	0	0	0	0	0	0
5200 Taxes on use of goods and perform activities	0	24	45	40	38	3 328	4 115	6 221	8 462	9 871
5300 Unallocable between 5100 and 5200	0	0	0	0	0	0	0	0	0	0
6000 Other taxes	**198**	**0**	**0**	**0**	**0**	**0**	**0**	**0**	**0**	**0**
6100 Paid solely by business	0	..	..	..	..	..	..	..	..	..
6200 Other	198	..	..	..	..	..	..	..	..	..
Total tax revenue	**27 438**	**113 397**	**206 500**	**269 124**	**325 651**	**18 721**	**107 439**	**176 156**	**257 403**	**308 806**

	Local government					Social Security Funds				
	1975	1995	2005	2015	2019	1975	1995	2005	2015	2019
1000 Taxes on income, profits and capital gains	**0**	**0**	**0**	**0**	**0**	**0**	**0**	**0**	**0**	**0**
1100 Of individuals	..	..	..	..	..	..	..	..	..	..
1200 Corporate	..	..	..	..	..	..	..	..	..	..
1300 Unallocable between 1100 and 1200	..	..	..	..	..	..	..	..	..	..
2000 Social security contributions	**0**	**0**	**0**	**0**	**0**	**5 787**	**40 559**	**38 834**	**58 876**	**70 374**
2100 Employees	..	..	..	..	..	2 142	15 028	18 328	27 785	33 220
2200 Employers	..	..	..	..	..	3 527	24 765	18 328	27 785	33 220
2300 Self-employed or non-employed	..	..	..	..	..	118	766	2 177	3 307	3 933
2400 Unallocable between 2100, 2200 and 2300	..	..	..	..	..	0	0	0	0	0
3000 Taxes on payroll and workforce	**0**	**0**	**0**	**0**	**0**	**0**	**0**	**0**	**0**	**0**
4000 Taxes on property	**5 018**	**24 415**	**40 495**	**65 969**	**74 074**	**0**	**0**	**0**	**0**	**0**
4100 Recurrent taxes on immovable property	4 770	23 150	37 409	57 241	63 386	..	..	..	..	..
4200 Recurrent taxes on net wealth	0	0	0	0	0	..	..	..	..	..
4300 Estate, inheritance and gift taxes	0	0	0	0	0	..	..	..	..	..
4400 Taxes on financial and capital transactions	0	0	375	1 063	1 702	..	..	..	..	..
4500 Non-recurrent taxes	248	1 265	2 711	7 665	8 986	..	..	..	..	..
4600 Other recurrent taxes on property	0	0	0	0	0	..	..	..	..	..
5000 Taxes on goods and services	**142**	**406**	**833**	**1 149**	**1 401**	**0**	**0**	**0**	**0**	**0**
5100 Taxes on production, sale, transfer, etc	22	51	104	126	206	..	..	..	..	..
5110 General taxes	10	40	88	63	76	..	..	..	..	..
5120 Taxes on specific goods and services	12	11	16	63	130	..	..	..	..	..
5130 Unallocable between 5110 and 5120	0	0	0	0	0	..	..	..	..	..
5200 Taxes on use of goods and perform activities	120	355	729	1 023	1 195	..	..	..	..	..
5300 Unallocable between 5100 and 5200	0	0	0	0	0	..	..	..	..	..
6000 Other taxes	**525**	**3 662**	**1 483**	**748**	**894**	**0**	**0**	**0**	**0**	**0**
6100 Paid solely by business	437	2 946	541	0	0	..	..	..	..	..
6200 Other	88	716	942	748	894	..	..	..	..	..
Total tax revenue	**5 685**	**28 483**	**42 811**	**67 866**	**76 369**	**5 787**	**40 559**	**38 834**	**58 876**	**70 374**

.. Not available

StatLink https://stat.link/173z9i

Table 6.5. Chile, tax revenues by sub-sectors of government

Million CLP

	Central government					State/Regional				
	1975	1995	2005	2015	2019	1975	1995	2005	2015	2019
1000 Taxes on income, profits and capital gains	..	**1 359 694**	**5 171 293**	**11 840 521**	**14 283 183**	..	..	..	..	..
1100 Of individuals	..	281 293	738 620	3 199 876	2 937 532	..	..	..	..	..
1200 Corporate	..	836 725	3 155 480	6 839 133	9 597 472	..	..	..	..	..
1300 Unallocable between 1100 and 1200	..	241 676	1 277 193	1 801 512	1 748 179	..	..	..	..	..
2000 Social security contributions	..	**155 855**	**287 422**	**434 658**	**495 073**	..	..	..	..	..
2100 Employees	..	142 001	249 526	370 744	394 892	..	..	..	..	..
2200 Employers	..	13 854	37 896	63 914	100 181	..	..	..	..	..
2300 Self-employed or non-employed	..	0	0	0	0	..	..	..	..	..
2400 Unallocable between 2100, 2200 and 2300	..	0	0	0	0	..	..	..	..	..
3000 Taxes on payroll and workforce	..	**0**	**0**	**0**	**0**	..	..	..	..	..
4000 Taxes on property	..	**181 432**	**490 120**	**379 603**	**759 291**	..	..	..	..	..
4100 Recurrent taxes on immovable property	..	13 044	4 909	15 249	23 912	..	..	..	..	..
4200 Recurrent taxes on net wealth	..	0	0	0	0	..	..	..	..	..
4300 Estate, inheritance and gift taxes	..	13 245	23 184	92 236	62 824	..	..	..	..	..
4400 Taxes on financial and capital transactions	..	155 143	462 027	272 118	672 555	..	..	..	..	..
4500 Non-recurrent taxes	..	0	0	0	0	..	..	..	..	..
4600 Other recurrent taxes on property	..	0	0	0	0	..	..	..	..	..
5000 Taxes on goods and services	..	**3 179 304**	**6 831 482**	**16 181 720**	**19 837 629**	..	..	..	..	..
5100 Taxes on production, sale, transfer, etc	..	3 169 645	6 811 389	16 129 953	19 656 251	..	..	..	..	..
5110 General taxes	..	2 187 602	5 391 285	13 273 958	16 348 944	..	..	..	..	..
5120 Taxes on specific goods and services	..	982 043	1 420 104	2 855 995	3 307 307	..	..	..	..	..
5130 Unallocable between 5110 and 5120	..	0	0	0	0	..	..	..	..	..
5200 Taxes on use of goods and perform activities	..	9 659	20 094	51 767	181 379	..	..	..	..	..
5300 Unallocable between 5100 and 5200	..	0	0	0	0	..	..	..	..	..
6000 Other taxes	..	**-29 554**	**-85 954**	**-579 308**	**-250 523**	..	..	..	..	..
6100 Paid solely by business	..	0	0	0	0	..	..	..	..	..
6200 Other	..	-29 554	-85 954	-579 308	-250 523	..	..	..	..	..
Total tax revenue	..	**4 846 730**	**12 694 362**	**28 257 194**	**35 124 653**	..	..	..	..	..

	Local government					Social Security Funds				
	1975	1995	2005	2015	2019	1975	1995	2005	2015	2019
1000 Taxes on income, profits and capital gains	..	**0**	**0**	**0**	**0**	..	**0**	**0**	**0**	**0**
1100 Of individuals	..	..	..	..	..	..	..	..	..	..
1200 Corporate	..	..	..	..	..	..	..	..	..	..
1300 Unallocable between 1100 and 1200	..	..	..	..	..	..	..	..	..	..
2000 Social security contributions	..	**0**	**0**	**0**	**0**	..	**193 269**	**644 295**	**1 817 831**	**2 499 833**
2100 Employees	..	..	..	..	..	..	193 269	644 295	1 817 831	2 499 833
2200 Employers	..	..	..	..	..	..	0	0	0	0
2300 Self-employed or non-employed	..	..	..	..	..	..	0	0	0	0
2400 Unallocable between 2100, 2200 and 2300	..	..	..	..	..	..	0	0	0	0
3000 Taxes on payroll and workforce	..	**0**	**0**	**0**	**0**	..	**0**	**0**	**0**	**0**
4000 Taxes on property	..	**157 193**	**411 656**	**1 041 671**	**1 483 271**	..	**0**	**0**	**0**	**0**
4100 Recurrent taxes on immovable property	..	157 193	411 656	1 041 671	1 483 271	..	..	..	..	..
4200 Recurrent taxes on net wealth	..	0	0	0	0	..	..	..	..	..
4300 Estate, inheritance and gift taxes	..	0	0	0	0	..	..	..	..	..
4400 Taxes on financial and capital transactions	..	0	0	0	0	..	..	..	..	..
4500 Non-recurrent taxes	..	0	0	0	0	..	..	..	..	..
4600 Other recurrent taxes on property	..	0	0	0	0	..	..	..	..	..
5000 Taxes on goods and services	..	**192 325**	**514 952**	**1 415 658**	**1 917 752**	..	**0**	**0**	**0**	**0**
5100 Taxes on production, sale, transfer, etc	..	52 690	140 703	385 532	510 761	..	..	..	..	..
5110 General taxes	..	0	0	0	0	..	..	..	..	..
5120 Taxes on specific goods and services	..	52 690	140 703	385 532	510 761	..	..	..	..	..
5130 Unallocable between 5110 and 5120	..	0	0	0	0	..	..	..	..	..
5200 Taxes on use of goods and perform activities	..	139 635	374 249	1 030 126	1 406 990	..	..	..	..	..
5300 Unallocable between 5100 and 5200	..	0	0	0	0	..	..	..	..	..
6000 Other taxes	..	**0**	**0**	**0**	**0**	..	**0**	**0**	**0**	**0**
6100 Paid solely by business	..	..	..	..	..	..	..	..	..	..
6200 Other	..	..	..	..	..	..	..	..	..	..
Total tax revenue	..	**349 518**	**926 608**	**2 457 329**	**3 401 022**	..	**193 269**	**644 295**	**1 817 831**	**2 499 833**

.. Not available

StatLink https://stat.link/2wxq4t

Table 6.6. Colombia, tax revenues by sub-sectors of government

Million COP

	Federal government					State/Regional				
	1975	1995	2005	2015	2019	1975	1995	2005	2015	2019
1000 Taxes on income, profits and capital gains	..	**3 393 700**	**17 348 618**	**52 656 876**	**67 519 599**	..	**0**	**0**	**0**	**0**
1100 Of individuals	..	131 405	3 594 441	9 215 137	14 155 111	..	..	..	..	..
1200 Corporate	..	988 082	13 044 361	41 401 857	50 242 515	..	..	..	..	..
1300 Unallocable between 1100 and 1200	..	2 274 213	709 816	2 039 882	3 121 974	..	..	..	..	..
2000 Social security contributions	..	**0**	**0**	**0**	**0**	..	**0**	**0**	**0**	**0**
2100 Employees	..	..	..	..	..	..	..	..	..	..
2200 Employers	..	..	..	..	..	..	..	..	..	..
2300 Self-employed or non-employed	..	..	..	..	..	..	..	..	..	..
2400 Unallocable between 2100, 2200 and 2300	..	..	..	..	..	..	..	..	..	..
3000 Taxes on payroll and workforce	..	**599 198**	**2 179 842**	**2 797 308**	**3 604 071**	..	**0**	**0**	**0**	**0**
4000 Taxes on property	..	**0**	**2 863 946**	**12 094 140**	**10 241 299**	..	**0**	**0**	**0**	**0**
4100 Recurrent taxes on immovable property	..	..	0	0	0	..	..	..	..	..
4200 Recurrent taxes on net wealth	..	..	462 720	5 352 940	923 255	..	..	..	..	..
4300 Estate, inheritance and gift taxes	..	..	0	0	0	..	..	..	..	..
4400 Taxes on financial and capital transactions	..	..	2 401 226	6 741 200	8 190 516	..	..	..	..	..
4500 Non-recurrent taxes	..	..	0	0	1 127 528	..	..	..	..	..
4600 Other recurrent taxes on property	..	..	0	0	0	..	..	..	..	..
5000 Taxes on goods and services	..	**4 773 500**	**21 645 318**	**51 831 190**	**70 637 076**	..	**771 560**	**2 507 423**	**4 986 314**	**7 496 594**
5100 Taxes on production, sale, transfer, etc	..	4 773 500	21 645 318	51 831 190	70 637 076	..	771 560	2 228 909	4 456 650	6 494 522
5110 General taxes	..	3 427 600	17 427 948	41 659 696	61 936 282	..	0	0	0	0
5120 Taxes on specific goods and services	..	1 345 900	4 217 370	10 171 494	8 700 794	..	771 560	2 228 909	4 456 650	6 494 522
5130 Unallocable between 5110 and 5120	..	0	0	0	0	..	0	0	0	0
5200 Taxes on use of goods and perform activities	..	0	0	0	0	..	0	278 514	529 665	1 002 072
5300 Unallocable between 5100 and 5200	..	0	0	0	0	..	0	0	0	0
6000 Other taxes	..	**17 900**	**682 084**	**419 939**	**619 651**	..	**0**	**575 919**	**2 624 769**	**2 975 868**
6100 Paid solely by business	..	0	0	0	0	..	..	0	0	0
6200 Other	..	17 900	682 084	419 939	619 651	..	..	575 919	2 624 769	2 975 868
Total tax revenue	..	**8 784 297**	**44 719 808**	**119 799 453**	**152 621 696**	..	**771 560**	**3 083 342**	**7 611 084**	**10 472 462**

	Local government					Social Security Funds				
	1975	1995	2005	2015	2019	1975	1995	2005	2015	2019
1000 Taxes on income, profits and capital gains	..	**0**	**0**	**0**	**0**	..	**0**	**0**	**0**	**0**
1100 Of individuals	..	..	..	..	..	..	..	..	..	..
1200 Corporate	..	..	..	..	..	..	..	..	..	..
1300 Unallocable between 1100 and 1200	..	..	..	..	..	..	..	..	..	..
2000 Social security contributions	..	**0**	**0**	**0**	**0**	..	**3 159 328**	**7 845 000**	**13 585 138**	**19 875 398**
2100 Employees	..	..	..	..	..	..	..	..	..	..
2200 Employers	..	..	..	..	..	..	..	..	..	..
2300 Self-employed or non-employed	..	..	..	..	..	..	..	..	..	..
2400 Unallocable between 2100, 2200 and 2300	..	..	..	..	..	..	3 159 328	7 845 000	13 585 138	19 875 398
3000 Taxes on payroll and workforce	..	**0**	**0**	**0**	**0**	..	**0**	**0**	**0**	**0**
4000 Taxes on property	..	**365 051**	**1 974 213**	**6 061 965**	**8 743 115**	..	**0**	**0**	**0**	**0**
4100 Recurrent taxes on immovable property	..	365 051	1 974 213	6 061 965	8 743 115	..	..	..	..	..
4200 Recurrent taxes on net wealth	..	0	0	0	0	..	..	..	..	..
4300 Estate, inheritance and gift taxes	..	0	0	0	0	..	..	..	..	..
4400 Taxes on financial and capital transactions	..	0	0	0	0	..	..	..	..	..
4500 Non-recurrent taxes	..	0	0	0	0	..	..	..	..	..
4600 Other recurrent taxes on property	..	0	0	0	0	..	..	..	..	..
5000 Taxes on goods and services	..	**471 710**	**3 496 411**	**8 899 062**	**11 664 256**	..	**0**	**0**	**0**	**0**
5100 Taxes on production, sale, transfer, etc	..	471 710	3 496 411	8 400 241	10 932 488	..	..	..	..	..
5110 General taxes	..	471 710	2 506 452	7 025 204	9 298 856	..	..	..	..	..
5120 Taxes on specific goods and services	..	0	989 959	1 375 037	1 633 632	..	..	..	..	..
5130 Unallocable between 5110 and 5120	..	0	0	0	0	..	..	..	..	..
5200 Taxes on use of goods and perform activities	..	0	0	498 821	731 768	..	..	..	..	..
5300 Unallocable between 5100 and 5200	..	0	0	0	0	..	..	..	..	..
6000 Other taxes	..	**355 943**	**588 614**	**4 200 992**	**5 694 388**	..	**0**	**0**	**0**	**0**
6100 Paid solely by business	..	0	0	0	0	..	..	..	..	..
6200 Other	..	355 943	588 614	4 200 992	5 694 388	..	..	..	..	..
Total tax revenue	..	**1 192 705**	**6 059 238**	**19 162 019**	**26 101 758**	..	**3 159 328**	**7 845 000**	**13 585 138**	**19 875 398**

.. Not available

StatLink https://stat.link/1omf8e

Table 6.7. Costa Rica, tax revenues by sub-sectors of government

Million CRC

	Central government					State/Regional				
	1975	1995	2005	2015	2019	1975	1995	2005	2015	2019
1000 Taxes on income, profits and capital gains	..	**47 678**	**324 224**	**1 247 308**	**1 854 866**	..	..	..	..	..
1100 Of individuals	..	..	16 438	386 241	540 954	..	..	..	..	..
1200 Corporate	..	..	288 355	659 951	1 058 086	..	..	..	..	..
1300 Unallocable between 1100 and 1200	..	47 678	19 430	201 116	255 827	..	..	..	..	..
2000 Social security contributions	..	**11 096**	**30 854**	**63 458**	**77 472**	..	..	..	..	..
2100 Employees	..	..	..	..	..	..	..	..	..	..
2200 Employers	..	0	0	0	0	..	..	..	..	..
2300 Self-employed or non-employed	..	..	..	..	..	..	..	..	..	..
2400 Unallocable between 2100, 2200 and 2300	..	11 096	30 854	63 458	77 472	..	..	..	..	..
3000 Taxes on payroll and workforce	..	**0**	**0**	**0**	**0**	..	..	..	..	..
4000 Taxes on property	..	**2 023**	**10 846**	**37 334**	**47 254**	..	..	..	..	..
4100 Recurrent taxes on immovable property	..	440	0	4 076	4 699	..	..	..	..	..
4200 Recurrent taxes on net wealth	..	0	0	0	0	..	..	..	..	..
4300 Estate, inheritance and gift taxes	..	0	0	0	0	..	..	..	..	..
4400 Taxes on financial and capital transactions	..	1 583	10 846	33 258	42 554	..	..	..	..	..
4500 Non-recurrent taxes	..	0	0	0	0	..	..	..	..	..
4600 Other recurrent taxes on property	..	0	0	0	0	..	..	..	..	..
5000 Taxes on goods and services	..	**185 943**	**917 118**	**2 536 562**	**2 940 121**	..	..	..	..	..
5100 Taxes on production, sale, transfer, etc	..	177 808	884 359	2 385 807	2 752 919	..	..	..	..	..
5110 General taxes	..	84 034	485 168	1 368 601	1 662 503	..	..	..	..	..
5120 Taxes on specific goods and services	..	93 774	399 192	1 017 206	1 090 415	..	..	..	..	..
5130 Unallocable between 5110 and 5120	..	0	0	0	0	..	..	..	..	..
5200 Taxes on use of goods and perform activities	..	8 135	32 758	150 755	187 202	..	..	..	..	..
5300 Unallocable between 5100 and 5200	..	0	0	0	0	..	..	..	..	..
6000 Other taxes	..	**11 010**	**54 338**	**162 200**	**201 844**	..	..	..	..	..
6100 Paid solely by business	..	0	0	0	0	..	..	..	..	..
6200 Other	..	11 010	54 338	162 200	201 844	..	..	..	..	..
Total tax revenue	..	**257 751**	**1 337 380**	**4 046 862**	**5 121 557**	..	..	..	..	..

	Local government					Social Security Funds				
	1975	1995	2005	2015	2019	1975	1995	2005	2015	2019
1000 Taxes on income, profits and capital gains	..	**0**	**0**	**0**	**0**	..	**0**	**0**	**0**	**0**
1100 Of individuals	..	..	..	..	..	..	..	..	..	..
1200 Corporate	..	..	..	..	..	..	..	..	..	..
1300 Unallocable between 1100 and 1200	..	..	..	..	..	..	..	..	..	..
2000 Social security contributions	..	**0**	**0**	**0**	**0**	..	**106 727**	**586 829**	**2 241 674**	**2 949 219**
2100 Employees	..	..	..	..	..	..	..	..	..	..
2200 Employers	..	..	..	..	..	..	14 654	84 988	318 652	381 940
2300 Self-employed or non-employed	..	..	..	..	..	..	..	..	..	..
2400 Unallocable between 2100, 2200 and 2300	..	..	..	..	..	..	92 073	501 841	1 923 022	2 567 279
3000 Taxes on payroll and workforce	..	**0**	**0**	**0**	**0**	..	**22 992**	**115 730**	**423 616**	**522 529**
4000 Taxes on property	..	**2 037**	**14 264**	**85 927**	**120 698**	..	**0**	**0**	**0**	**0**
4100 Recurrent taxes on immovable property	..	2 037	14 264	85 927	120 698	..	..	..	..	..
4200 Recurrent taxes on net wealth	..	0	0	0	0	..	..	..	..	..
4300 Estate, inheritance and gift taxes	..	0	0	0	0	..	..	..	..	..
4400 Taxes on financial and capital transactions	..	0	0	0	0	..	..	..	..	..
4500 Non-recurrent taxes	..	0	0	0	0	..	..	..	..	..
4600 Other recurrent taxes on property	..	0	0	0	0	..	..	..	..	..
5000 Taxes on goods and services	..	**1 214**	**27 506**	**125 341**	**141 820**	..	**0**	**0**	**0**	**0**
5100 Taxes on production, sale, transfer, etc	..	0	94	3 093	3 841	..	..	..	..	..
5110 General taxes	..	..	0	0	0	..	..	..	..	..
5120 Taxes on specific goods and services	..	..	94	3 093	3 841	..	..	..	..	..
5130 Unallocable between 5110 and 5120	..	..	0	0	0	..	..	..	..	..
5200 Taxes on use of goods and perform activities	..	1 214	27 411	122 248	137 979	..	..	..	..	..
5300 Unallocable between 5100 and 5200	..	0	0	0	0	..	..	..	..	..
6000 Other taxes	..	**2 935**	**3 207**	**155**	**62**	..	**0**	**0**	**0**	**0**
6100 Paid solely by business	..	0	0	0	0	..	..	..	..	..
6200 Other	..	2 935	3 207	155	62	..	..	..	..	..
Total tax revenue	..	**6 185**	**44 976**	**211 422**	**262 580**	..	**129 718**	**702 559**	**2 665 291**	**3 471 748**

.. Not available

StatLink https://stat.link/f5teu6

Table 6.8. Czech Republic, tax revenues by sub-sectors of government

Million CZK

	Central government[1]					State/Regional				
	1975	1995	2005	2015	2019	1975	1995	2005	2015	2019
1000 Taxes on income, profits and capital gains	..	**137 616**	**273 549**	**329 768**	**458 514**	..	..	..	..	..
1100 Of individuals	..	70 361	137 937	164 678	255 398	..	..	..	..	..
1200 Corporate	..	67 255	135 611	165 090	203 116	..	..	..	..	..
1300 Unallocable between 1100 and 1200	..	0	0	0	0	..	..	..	..	..
2000 Social security contributions	..	**0**	**0**	**0**	**0**	..	..	..	..	..
2100 Employees	..	..	..	..	..	..	..	..	..	..
2200 Employers	..	..	..	..	..	..	..	..	..	..
2300 Self-employed or non-employed	..	..	..	..	..	..	..	..	..	..
2400 Unallocable between 2100, 2200 and 2300	..	..	..	..	..	..	..	..	..	..
3000 Taxes on payroll and workforce	..	**0**	**0**	**0**	**0**	..	..	..	..	..
4000 Taxes on property	..	**3 857**	**8 050**	**11 607**	**13 145**	..	..	..	..	..
4100 Recurrent taxes on immovable property	..	0	5	20	32	..	..	..	..	..
4200 Recurrent taxes on net wealth	..	0	0	0	0	..	..	..	..	..
4300 Estate, inheritance and gift taxes	..	393	728	20	1	..	..	..	..	..
4400 Taxes on financial and capital transactions	..	3 464	7 317	11 566	13 113	..	..	..	..	..
4500 Non-recurrent taxes	..	0	0	0	0	..	..	..	..	..
4600 Other recurrent taxes on property	..	0	0	0	0	..	..	..	..	..
5000 Taxes on goods and services	..	**175 869**	**343 554**	**505 085**	**624 512**	..	..	..	..	..
5100 Taxes on production, sale, transfer, etc	..	162 913	325 662	487 086	603 852	..	..	..	..	..
5110 General taxes	..	91 673	215 118	333 274	435 463	..	..	..	..	..
5120 Taxes on specific goods and services	..	71 240	110 544	153 812	168 389	..	..	..	..	..
5130 Unallocable between 5110 and 5120	..	0	0	0	0	..	..	..	..	..
5200 Taxes on use of goods and perform activities	..	12 956	17 892	17 999	20 660	..	..	..	..	..
5300 Unallocable between 5100 and 5200	..	0	0	0	0	..	..	..	..	..
6000 Other taxes	..	**545**	**55**	**387**	**220**	..	..	..	..	..
6100 Paid solely by business	..	0	0	0	0	..	..	..	..	..
6200 Other	..	545	55	387	220	..	..	..	..	..
Total tax revenue	..	**317 887**	**625 207**	**846 847**	**1 096 391**	..	..	..	..	..

	Local government					Social Security Funds				
	1975	1995	2005	2015	2019	1975	1995	2005	2015	2019
1000 Taxes on income, profits and capital gains	..	**0**	**0**	**0**	**0**	..	**0**	**0**	**0**	**0**
1100 Of individuals	..	..	..	..	..	..	..	..	..	..
1200 Corporate	..	..	..	..	..	..	..	..	..	..
1300 Unallocable between 1100 and 1200	..	..	..	..	..	..	..	..	..	..
2000 Social security contributions	..	**0**	**0**	**0**	**0**	..	**227 871**	**481 626**	**659 743**	**889 237**
2100 Employees	..	..	..	..	..	..	54 536	108 316	133 878	184 563
2200 Employers	..	..	..	..	..	..	148 342	307 618	417 778	569 522
2300 Self-employed or non-employed	..	..	..	..	..	..	24 993	65 692	108 088	135 153
2400 Unallocable between 2100, 2200 and 2300	..	..	..	..	..	..	0	0	0	0
3000 Taxes on payroll and workforce	..	**0**	**0**	**0**	**0**	..	**0**	**0**	**0**	**0**
4000 Taxes on property	..	**3 778**	**4 987**	**10 313**	**10 935**	..	**0**	**0**	**0**	**0**
4100 Recurrent taxes on immovable property	..	3 778	4 987	10 313	10 935	..	..	..	..	..
4200 Recurrent taxes on net wealth	..	0	0	0	0	..	..	..	..	..
4300 Estate, inheritance and gift taxes	..	0	0	0	0	..	..	..	..	..
4400 Taxes on financial and capital transactions	..	0	0	0	0	..	..	..	..	..
4500 Non-recurrent taxes	..	0	0	0	0	..	..	..	..	..
4600 Other recurrent taxes on property	..	0	0	0	0	..	..	..	..	..
5000 Taxes on goods and services	..	**1 150**	**7 395**	**7 749**	**8 584**	..	**0**	**0**	**0**	**0**
5100 Taxes on production, sale, transfer, etc	..	124	199	292	380	..	..	..	..	..
5110 General taxes	..	0	0	0	0	..	..	..	..	..
5120 Taxes on specific goods and services	..	124	199	292	380	..	..	..	..	..
5130 Unallocable between 5110 and 5120	..	0	0	0	0	..	..	..	..	..
5200 Taxes on use of goods and perform activities	..	1 026	7 196	7 457	8 204	..	..	..	..	..
5300 Unallocable between 5100 and 5200	..	0	0	0	0	..	..	..	..	..
6000 Other taxes	..	**0**	**0**	**0**	**0**	..	**0**	**0**	**0**	**0**
6100 Paid solely by business	..	..	..	..	..	..	..	..	..	..
6200 Other	..	..	..	..	..	..	..	..	..	..
Total tax revenue	..	**4 928**	**12 382**	**18 063**	**19 519**	..	**227 871**	**481 626**	**659 743**	**889 237**

.. Not available

Note: Including taxes collected on behalf of the European Union.

1. Tax revenues of the regions are reported under the heading of central government up to and including 1995 and under local government thereafter.

StatLink https://stat.link/50mrcq

Table 6.9. Denmark, tax revenues by sub-sectors of government

Million DKK

	Central government					State/Regional				
	1975	1995	2005	2015	2019	1975	1995	2005	2015	2019
1000 Taxes on income, profits and capital gains	**28 694**	**164 962**	**258 922**	**384 883**	**457 825**	**..**	**..**	**..**	**..**	**..**
1100 Of individuals	25 904	124 613	167 082	304 329	321 690	..	..	..	..	..
1200 Corporate	2 790	23 803	54 597	57 723	72 724	..	..	..	..	..
1300 Unallocable between 1100 and 1200	0	16 546	37 244	22 832	63 411	..	..	..	..	..
2000 Social security contributions	**143**	**562**	**1 180**	**836**	**686**	**..**	**..**	**..**	**..**	**..**
2100 Employees	0	559	1 177	826	684	..	..	..	..	..
2200 Employers	142	3	3	10	3	..	..	..	..	..
2300 Self-employed or non-employed	0	0	0	0	0	..	..	..	..	..
2400 Unallocable between 2100, 2200 and 2300	0	0	0	0	0	..	..	..	..	..
3000 Taxes on payroll and workforce	**0**	**2 262**	**2 907**	**5 894**	**6 534**	**..**	**..**	**..**	**..**	**..**
4000 Taxes on property	**1 779**	**7 094**	**11 801**	**11 084**	**15 785**	**..**	**..**	**..**	**..**	**..**
4100 Recurrent taxes on immovable property	16	170	0	0	0	..	..	..	..	..
4200 Recurrent taxes on net wealth	414	930	0	0	0	..	..	..	..	..
4300 Estate, inheritance and gift taxes	336	2 372	3 154	5 177	8 571	..	..	..	..	..
4400 Taxes on financial and capital transactions	936	3 584	8 613	5 907	7 214	..	..	..	..	..
4500 Non-recurrent taxes	77	38	34	0	0	..	..	..	..	..
4600 Other recurrent taxes on property	0	0	0	0	0	..	..	..	..	..
5000 Taxes on goods and services	**29 014**	**156 578**	**253 352**	**301 504**	**330 244**	**..**	**..**	**..**	**..**	**..**
5100 Taxes on production, sale, transfer, etc	27 338	149 393	239 951	277 791	304 823	..	..	..	..	..
5110 General taxes	15 117	94 368	154 654	191 479	222 730	..	..	..	..	..
5120 Taxes on specific goods and services	12 221	55 026	85 298	86 312	82 093	..	..	..	..	..
5130 Unallocable between 5110 and 5120	0	0	0	0	0	..	..	..	..	..
5200 Taxes on use of goods and perform activities	1 676	4 739	9 379	16 537	16 099	..	..	..	..	..
5300 Unallocable between 5100 and 5200	0	2 446	4 021	7 177	9 322	..	..	..	..	..
6000 Other taxes	**0**	**0**	**203**	**320**	**289**	**..**	**..**	**..**	**..**	**..**
6100 Paid solely by business	..	..	203	320	289	..	..	..	..	..
6200 Other	..	..	0	0	0	..	..	..	..	..
Total tax revenue	**59 630**	**331 457**	**528 366**	**704 520**	**811 362**	**..**	**..**	**..**	**..**	**..**

	Local government					Social Security Funds				
	1975	1995	2005	2015	2019	1975	1995	2005	2015	2019
1000 Taxes on income, profits and capital gains	**22 171**	**140 762**	**214 581**	**220 815**	**247 583**	**0**	**0**	**0**	**0**	**0**
1100 Of individuals	22 170	140 758	214 581	220 815	247 583	..	..	..	..	..
1200 Corporate	1	5	0	0	0	..	..	..	..	..
1300 Unallocable between 1100 and 1200	0	0	0	0	0	..	..	..	..	..
2000 Social security contributions	**0**	**0**	**0**	**0**	**0**	**58**	**0**	**529**	**542**	**305**
2100 Employees	..	..	..	..	..	0	..	0	0	0
2200 Employers	..	..	..	..	..	58	..	529	542	305
2300 Self-employed or non-employed	..	..	..	..	..	0	..	0	0	0
2400 Unallocable between 2100, 2200 and 2300	..	..	..	..	..	0	..	0	0	0
3000 Taxes on payroll and workforce	**0**	**0**	**0**	**0**	**0**	**0**	**0**	**0**	**0**	**0**
4000 Taxes on property	**3 518**	**10 155**	**17 466**	**28 085**	**30 567**	**0**	**0**	**0**	**0**	**0**
4100 Recurrent taxes on immovable property	3 518	10 155	17 466	28 085	30 567	..	..	..	..	..
4200 Recurrent taxes on net wealth	0	0	0	0	0	..	..	..	..	..
4300 Estate, inheritance and gift taxes	0	0	0	0	0	..	..	..	..	..
4400 Taxes on financial and capital transactions	0	0	0	0	0	..	..	..	..	..
4500 Non-recurrent taxes	0	0	0	0	0	..	..	..	..	..
4600 Other recurrent taxes on property	0	0	0	0	0	..	..	..	..	..
5000 Taxes on goods and services	**0**	**0**	**0**	**0**	**0**	**0**	**0**	**0**	**0**	**0**
5100 Taxes on production, sale, transfer, etc	0	..	..	..	..	..	..	..	..	..
5110 General taxes	0	..	..	..	..	..	..	..	..	..
5120 Taxes on specific goods and services	0	..	..	..	..	..	..	..	..	..
5130 Unallocable between 5110 and 5120	0	..	..	..	..	..	..	..	..	..
5200 Taxes on use of goods and perform activities	..	..	..	..	..	..	..	..	..	..
5300 Unallocable between 5100 and 5200	0	..	..	..	..	..	..	..	..	..
6000 Other taxes	**0**	**0**	**0**	**0**	**0**	**0**	**0**	**0**	**0**	**0**
6100 Paid solely by business	..	..	..	..	..	..	..	..	..	..
6200 Other	..	..	..	..	..	..	..	..	..	..
Total tax revenue	**25 689**	**150 918**	**232 047**	**248 900**	**278 150**	**58**	**0**	**529**	**542**	**305**

.. Not available

Note: Including taxes collected on behalf of the European Union.

StatLink https://stat.link/nwifpr

Table 6.10. Estonia, tax revenues by sub-sectors of government

Million EUR

	Central government					State/Regional				
	1975	1995	2005	2015	2019	1975	1995	2005	2015	2019
1000 Taxes on income, profits and capital gains	**..**	**301**	**782**	**1 607**	**2 041**	**..**	**..**	**..**	**..**	**..**
1100 Of individuals	..	234	622	1 182	1 532	..	..	..	..	..
1200 Corporate	..	67	160	424	509	..	..	..	..	..
1300 Unallocable between 1100 and 1200	..	0	0	0	0	..	..	..	..	..
2000 Social security contributions	**..**	**191**	**636**	**1 191**	**1 716**	**..**	**..**	**..**	**..**	**..**
2100 Employees	..	0	0	0	0	..	..	..	..	..
2200 Employers	..	191	636	1 179	1 704	..	..	..	..	..
2300 Self-employed or non-employed	..	0	0	12	12	..	..	..	..	..
2400 Unallocable between 2100, 2200 and 2300	..	0	0	0	0	..	..	..	..	..
3000 Taxes on payroll and workforce	**..**	**0**	**0**	**0**	**0**	**..**	**..**	**..**	**..**	**..**
4000 Taxes on property	**..**	**3**	**0**	**0**	**0**	**..**	**..**	**..**	**..**	**..**
4100 Recurrent taxes on immovable property	..	3	..	..	..	..	..	..	..	..
4200 Recurrent taxes on net wealth	..	0	..	..	..	..	..	..	..	..
4300 Estate, inheritance and gift taxes	..	0	..	..	..	..	..	..	..	..
4400 Taxes on financial and capital transactions	..	0	..	..	..	..	..	..	..	..
4500 Non-recurrent taxes	..	0	..	..	..	..	..	..	..	..
4600 Other recurrent taxes on property	..	0	..	..	..	..	..	..	..	..
5000 Taxes on goods and services	**..**	**350**	**1 385**	**2 864**	**3 871**	**..**	**..**	**..**	**..**	**..**
5100 Taxes on production, sale, transfer, etc	..	345	1 348	2 790	3 660	..	..	..	..	..
5110 General taxes	..	266	908	1 873	2 483	..	..	..	..	..
5120 Taxes on specific goods and services	..	79	440	917	1 177	..	..	..	..	..
5130 Unallocable between 5110 and 5120	..	0	0	0	0	..	..	..	..	..
5200 Taxes on use of goods and perform activities	..	5	37	74	211	..	..	..	..	..
5300 Unallocable between 5100 and 5200	..	0	0	0	0	..	..	..	..	..
6000 Other taxes	**..**	**0**	**0**	**0**	**0**	**..**	**..**	**..**	**..**	**..**
6100 Paid solely by business	..	..	..	..	..	..	..	..	..	..
6200 Other	..	..	..	..	..	..	..	..	..	..
Total tax revenue	**..**	**845**	**2 803**	**5 662**	**7 628**	**..**	**..**	**..**	**..**	**..**

	Local government					Social Security Funds				
	1975	1995	2005	2015	2019	1975	1995	2005	2015	2019
1000 Taxes on income, profits and capital gains	**..**	**0**	**0**	**0**	**0**	**..**	**0**	**0**	**0**	**0**
1100 Of individuals	..	0	0	0	0	..	0	0	0	0
1200 Corporate	..	0	0	0	0	..	0	0	0	0
1300 Unallocable between 1100 and 1200	..	0	0	0	0	..	0	0	0	0
2000 Social security contributions	**..**	**0**	**0**	**0**	**0**	**..**	**149**	**511**	**1 110**	**1 541**
2100 Employees	..	..	..	..	..	..	0	31	99	136
2200 Employers	..	..	..	..	..	..	143	466	1 002	1 397
2300 Self-employed or non-employed	..	..	..	..	..	..	6	14	8	8
2400 Unallocable between 2100, 2200 and 2300	..	..	..	..	..	..	0	0	0	0
3000 Taxes on payroll and workforce	**..**	**0**	**0**	**0**	**0**	**..**	**0**	**0**	**0**	**0**
4000 Taxes on property	**..**	**7**	**32**	**58**	**58**	**..**	**0**	**0**	**0**	**0**
4100 Recurrent taxes on immovable property	..	7	32	58	58	..	..	..	..	..
4200 Recurrent taxes on net wealth	..	0	0	0	0	..	..	..	..	..
4300 Estate, inheritance and gift taxes	..	0	0	0	0	..	..	..	..	..
4400 Taxes on financial and capital transactions	..	0	0	0	0	..	..	..	..	..
4500 Non-recurrent taxes	..	0	0	0	0	..	..	..	..	..
4600 Other recurrent taxes on property	..	0	0	0	0	..	..	..	..	..
5000 Taxes on goods and services	**..**	**1**	**7**	**11**	**13**	**..**	**0**	**0**	**0**	**0**
5100 Taxes on production, sale, transfer, etc	..	0	2	4	6	..	..	..	..	..
5110 General taxes	..	0	0	0	0	..	..	..	..	..
5120 Taxes on specific goods and services	..	0	2	4	6	..	..	..	..	..
5130 Unallocable between 5110 and 5120	..	0	0	0	0	..	..	..	..	..
5200 Taxes on use of goods and perform activities	..	1	5	7	6	..	..	..	..	..
5300 Unallocable between 5100 and 5200	..	0	0	0	0	..	..	..	..	..
6000 Other taxes	**..**	**0**	**0**	**0**	**0**	**..**	**0**	**0**	**0**	**0**
6100 Paid solely by business	..	..	..	..	..	..	..	..	..	..
6200 Other	..	..	..	..	..	..	..	..	..	..
Total tax revenue	**..**	**8**	**40**	**69**	**71**	**..**	**149**	**511**	**1 110**	**1 541**

.. Not available

Note: Including taxes collected on behalf of the European Union.

StatLink https://stat.link/hd0mwg

Table 6.11. Finland, tax revenues by sub-sectors of government

Million EUR

	Central government					State/Regional				
	1975	1995	2005	2015	2019	1975	1995	2005	2015	2019
1000 Taxes on income, profits and capital gains	**1 304**	**6 538**	**12 885**	**12 127**	**14 176**	**..**	**..**	**..**	**..**	**..**
1100 Of individuals	1 146	5 320	8 791	9 248	10 025	..	..	..	..	..
1200 Corporate	157	1 218	4 094	2 879	4 151	..	..	..	..	..
1300 Unallocable between 1100 and 1200	0	0	0	0	0	..	..	..	..	..
2000 Social security contributions	**0**	**25**	**0**	**0**	**0**	**..**	**..**	**..**	**..**	**..**
2100 Employees	..	0	..	..	..	..	..	..	..	..
2200 Employers	..	25	..	..	..	..	..	..	..	..
2300 Self-employed or non-employed	..	0	..	..	..	..	..	..	..	..
2400 Unallocable between 2100, 2200 and 2300	..	0	..	..	..	..	..	..	..	..
3000 Taxes on payroll and workforce	**153**	**0**	**0**	**0**	**0**	**..**	**..**	**..**	**..**	**..**
4000 Taxes on property	**127**	**533**	**1 169**	**1 414**	**1 606**	**..**	**..**	**..**	**..**	**..**
4100 Recurrent taxes on immovable property	0	0	0	0	0	..	..	..	..	..
4200 Recurrent taxes on net wealth	33	35	129	0	0	..	..	..	..	..
4300 Estate, inheritance and gift taxes	14	167	486	631	749	..	..	..	..	..
4400 Taxes on financial and capital transactions	80	331	554	783	857	..	..	..	..	..
4500 Non-recurrent taxes	0	0	0	0	0	..	..	..	..	..
4600 Other recurrent taxes on property	0	0	0	0	0	..	..	..	..	..
5000 Taxes on goods and services	**2 099**	**13 241**	**21 768**	**29 650**	**33 746**	**..**	**..**	**..**	**..**	**..**
5100 Taxes on production, sale, transfer, etc	2 082	12 937	21 178	28 592	32 267	..	..	..	..	..
5110 General taxes	1 030	7 621	13 748	18 974	21 974	..	..	..	..	..
5120 Taxes on specific goods and services	1 052	5 316	7 430	9 618	10 293	..	..	..	..	..
5130 Unallocable between 5110 and 5120	0	0	0	0	0	..	..	..	..	..
5200 Taxes on use of goods and perform activities	16	304	590	1 058	1 479	..	..	..	..	..
5300 Unallocable between 5100 and 5200	0	0	0	0	0	..	..	..	..	..
6000 Other taxes	**10**	**90**	**68**	**81**	**51**	**..**	**..**	**..**	**..**	**..**
6100 Paid solely by business	0	0	0	0	0	..	..	..	..	..
6200 Other	10	90	68	81	51	..	..	..	..	..
Total tax revenue	**3 693**	**20 427**	**35 890**	**43 272**	**49 579**	**..**	**..**	**..**	**..**	**..**

	Local government					Social Security Funds				
	1975	1995	2005	2015	2019	1975	1995	2005	2015	2019
1000 Taxes on income, profits and capital gains	**1 547**	**9 313**	**13 574**	**20 244**	**21 294**	**0**	**0**	**0**	**0**	**0**
1100 Of individuals	1 393	8 319	12 420	18 576	19 376	..	..	..	..	..
1200 Corporate	154	994	1 154	1 668	1 918	..	..	..	..	..
1300 Unallocable between 1100 and 1200	0	0	0	0	0	..	..	..	..	..
2000 Social security contributions	**0**	**0**	**0**	**0**	**0**	**1 347**	**13 493**	**18 879**	**26 639**	**28 295**
2100 Employees	..	..	..	..	..	278	2 537	3 464	6 364	8 546
2200 Employers	..	..	..	..	..	990	9 447	14 127	18 232	17 778
2300 Self-employed or non-employed	..	..	..	..	..	79	1 509	1 288	2 043	1 971
2400 Unallocable between 2100, 2200 and 2300	..	..	..	..	..	0	0	0	0	0
3000 Taxes on payroll and workforce	**0**	**0**	**0**	**0**	**0**	**0**	**0**	**0**	**0**	**0**
4000 Taxes on property	**0**	**441**	**725**	**1 603**	**1 871**	**0**	**0**	**0**	**0**	**0**
4100 Recurrent taxes on immovable property	0	441	725	1 603	1 871	..	..	..	..	..
4200 Recurrent taxes on net wealth	0	0	0	0	0	..	..	..	..	..
4300 Estate, inheritance and gift taxes	0	0	0	0	0	..	..	..	..	..
4400 Taxes on financial and capital transactions	0	0	0	0	0	..	..	..	..	..
4500 Non-recurrent taxes	0	0	0	0	0	..	..	..	..	..
4600 Other recurrent taxes on property	0	0	0	0	0	..	..	..	..	..
5000 Taxes on goods and services	**3**	**7**	**8**	**2**	**1**	**0**	**0**	**0**	**0**	**0**
5100 Taxes on production, sale, transfer, etc	1	1	4	1	1	..	..	..	..	..
5110 General taxes	0	0	0	0	0	..	..	..	..	..
5120 Taxes on specific goods and services	1	1	4	1	1	..	..	..	..	..
5130 Unallocable between 5110 and 5120	0	0	0	0	0	..	..	..	..	..
5200 Taxes on use of goods and perform activities	2	6	4	1	0	..	..	..	..	..
5300 Unallocable between 5100 and 5200	0	0	0	0	0	..	..	..	..	..
6000 Other taxes	**0**	**0**	**0**	**0**	**0**	**0**	**0**	**0**	**0**	**0**
6100 Paid solely by business	..	..	..	..	..	..	..	..	..	..
6200 Other	..	..	..	..	..	..	..	..	..	..
Total tax revenue	**1 550**	**9 761**	**14 307**	**21 849**	**23 166**	**1 347**	**13 493**	**18 879**	**26 639**	**28 295**

.. Not available

Note: Including taxes collected on behalf of the European Union.

StatLink https://stat.link/odq8b0

Table 6.12. France, tax revenues by sub-sectors of government

Million EUR

	Central government					State/Regional				
	1975	1995	2005	2015	2019	1975	1995	2005	2015	2019
1000 Taxes on income, profits and capital gains	**13 106**	**69 134**	**98 623**	**121 529**	**144 069**	**..**	**..**	**..**	**..**	**..**
1100 Of individuals	8 743	43 963	56 862	75 366	89 804	..	..	..	..	..
1200 Corporate	4 282	25 172	41 761	46 163	54 265	..	..	..	..	..
1300 Unallocable between 1100 and 1200	80	0	0	0	0	..	..	..	..	..
2000 Social security contributions	**419**	**3 733**	**5 796**	**7 941**	**8 101**	**..**	**..**	**..**	**..**	**..**
2100 Employees	419	3 733	4 812	6 048	6 973	..	..	..	..	..
2200 Employers	0	0	984	1 893	1 128	..	..	..	..	..
2300 Self-employed or non-employed	0	0	0	0	0	..	..	..	..	..
2400 Unallocable between 2100, 2200 and 2300	0	0	0	0	0	..	..	..	..	..
3000 Taxes on payroll and workforce	**1 194**	**10 299**	**13 117**	**4 796**	**11 257**	**..**	**..**	**..**	**..**	**..**
4000 Taxes on property	**1 372**	**7 356**	**13 945**	**20 362**	**20 510**	**..**	**..**	**..**	**..**	**..**
4100 Recurrent taxes on immovable property	26	9	30	100	124	..	..	..	..	..
4200 Recurrent taxes on net wealth	0	1 309	3 053	5 224	2 054	..	..	..	..	..
4300 Estate, inheritance and gift taxes	616	4 261	9 006	12 317	15 252	..	..	..	..	..
4400 Taxes on financial and capital transactions	731	1 777	1 856	2 721	3 080	..	..	..	..	..
4500 Non-recurrent taxes	0	0	0	0	0	..	..	..	..	..
4600 Other recurrent taxes on property	0	0	0	0	0	..	..	..	..	..
5000 Taxes on goods and services	**26 154**	**129 457**	**167 750**	**178 755**	**172 398**	**..**	**..**	**..**	**..**	**..**
5100 Taxes on production, sale, transfer, etc	25 618	126 699	163 729	173 782	166 286	..	..	..	..	..
5110 General taxes	19 077	89 768	127 096	141 371	124 777	..	..	..	..	..
5120 Taxes on specific goods and services	6 540	36 931	36 633	32 411	41 509	..	..	..	..	..
5130 Unallocable between 5110 and 5120	0	0	0	0	0	..	..	..	..	..
5200 Taxes on use of goods and perform activities	536	2 758	4 021	4 973	6 112	..	..	..	..	..
5300 Unallocable between 5100 and 5200	..	0	0	0	0	..	..	..	..	..
6000 Other taxes	**49**	**924**	**3 522**	**1 683**	**1 122**	**..**	**..**	**..**	**..**	**..**
6100 Paid solely by business	32	871	3 502	1 677	1 099	..	..	..	..	..
6200 Other	17	53	21	6	23	..	..	..	..	..
Total tax revenue	**42 294**	**220 903**	**302 753**	**335 066**	**357 457**	**..**	**..**	**..**	**..**	**..**

	Local government					Social Security Funds				
	1975	1995	2005	2015	2019	1975	1995	2005	2015	2019
1000 Taxes on income, profits and capital gains	**0**	**0**	**0**	**20**	**28**	**0**	**14 997**	**80 173**	**112 983**	**137 989**
1100 Of individuals	0	0	0	13	13	0	14 997	80 173	112 978	137 989
1200 Corporate	0	0	0	7	15	0	0	0	5	0
1300 Unallocable between 1100 and 1200	0	0	0	0	0	0	0	0	0	0
2000 Social security contributions	**0**	**0**	**0**	**0**	**0**	**33 089**	**217 995**	**275 433**	**362 434**	**355 716**
2100 Employees	..	..	..	..	..	6 683	65 964	65 369	87 719	80 967
2200 Employers	..	..	..	..	..	24 236	135 892	190 090	246 280	246 309
2300 Self-employed or non-employed	..	..	..	..	..	2 170	16 139	19 975	28 435	28 440
2400 Unallocable between 2100, 2200 and 2300	..	..	..	..	..	0	0	0	0	0
3000 Taxes on payroll and workforce	**299**	**2 529**	**5 437**	**9 278**	**11 101**	**107**	**36**	**1 767**	**20 500**	**21 164**
4000 Taxes on property	**2 876**	**27 105**	**44 534**	**68 949**	**74 292**	**0**	**0**	**0**	**0**	**0**
4100 Recurrent taxes on immovable property	2 626	23 117	35 989	57 331	57 448	..	..	..	..	..
4200 Recurrent taxes on net wealth	..	0	0	0	0	..	..	..	..	..
4300 Estate, inheritance and gift taxes	0	0	0	0	0	..	..	..	..	..
4400 Taxes on financial and capital transactions	250	3 988	8 545	11 618	16 844	..	..	..	..	..
4500 Non-recurrent taxes	0	0	0	0	0	..	..	..	..	..
4600 Other recurrent taxes on property	..	0	0	0	0	..	..	..	..	..
5000 Taxes on goods and services	**496**	**8 056**	**14 708**	**43 987**	**52 521**	**301**	**5 708**	**12 776**	**36 159**	**72 895**
5100 Taxes on production, sale, transfer, etc	297	4 168	12 233	39 742	47 740	301	5 429	12 393	35 202	71 827
5110 General taxes	0	0	0	12 973	19 483	248	1 810	4 271	15 569	50 001
5120 Taxes on specific goods and services	297	4 168	12 233	26 769	28 257	53	3 620	8 122	19 633	21 826
5130 Unallocable between 5110 and 5120	..	0	0	0	0	..	0	0	0	0
5200 Taxes on use of goods and perform activities	198	3 888	2 475	4 245	4 781	0	279	383	957	1 068
5300 Unallocable between 5100 and 5200	..	0	0	0	0	..	0	0	0	0
6000 Other taxes	**2 577**	**18 971**	**22 334**	**9 120**	**10 489**	**0**	**0**	**0**	**568**	**639**
6100 Paid solely by business	2 577	18 970	22 334	9 120	10 489	..	..	..	568	639
6200 Other	0	1	0	0	0	..	..	..	0	0
Total tax revenue	**6 248**	**56 661**	**87 013**	**131 354**	**148 431**	**33 497**	**238 737**	**370 149**	**532 644**	**588 403**

.. Not available

Note: Including taxes collected on behalf of the European Union.

StatLink https://stat.link/knmxeb

Table 6.13. Germany, tax revenues by sub-sectors of government

Million EUR

	Federal government					State/Regional				
	1975	1995	2005	2015	2019	1975	1995	2005	2015	2019
1000 Taxes on income, profits and capital gains	**26 782**	**90 688**	**89 383**	**143 677**	**179 603**	**26 428**	**77 258**	**83 503**	**133 880**	**166 705**
1100 Of individuals	23 469	83 710	77 468	129 731	159 432	23 267	71 598	70 916	118 873	145 891
1200 Corporate	3 314	6 978	11 915	13 946	20 171	3 160	5 659	12 587	15 007	20 814
1300 Unallocable between 1100 and 1200	0	0	0	0	..	0	0	0	0	..
2000 Social security contributions	**0**	**0**	**0**	**0**	**0**	**0**	**0**	**0**	**0**	**0**
2100 Employees	..	..	..	..	..	..	..	..	..	..
2200 Employers	..	..	..	..	..	..	..	..	..	..
2300 Self-employed or non-employed	..	..	..	..	..	..	..	..	..	..
2400 Unallocable between 2100, 2200 and 2300	..	..	..	..	..	..	..	..	..	..
3000 Taxes on payroll and workforce	**0**	**0**	**0**	**0**	**0**	**0**	**0**	**0**	**0**	**0**
4000 Taxes on property	**1 225**	**175**	**0**	**324**	**1 466**	**2 606**	**9 080**	**8 985**	**17 537**	**24 280**
4100 Recurrent taxes on immovable property	0	0	..	0	0	0	0	0	0	1 505
4200 Recurrent taxes on net wealth	920	147	..	324	1 466	1 993	4 163	97	-2	0
4300 Estate, inheritance and gift taxes	0	0	..	0	0	271	1 815	4 097	6 290	6 986
4400 Taxes on financial and capital transactions	305	28	..	0	0	342	3 102	4 791	11 249	15 789
4500 Non-recurrent taxes	0	0	..	0	0	0	0	0	0	0
4600 Other recurrent taxes on property	0	0	..	0	..	0	0	0	0	..
5000 Taxes on goods and services	**35 370**	**125 377**	**147 967**	**199 445**	**212 527**	**13 082**	**62 564**	**82 093**	**107 822**	**128 093**
5100 Taxes on production, sale, transfer, etc	35 370	125 377	147 967	188 868	200 404	10 371	55 506	66 406	99 805	120 246
5110 General taxes	18 458	67 178	74 361	110 451	119 184	9 194	52 783	62 851	96 751	116 924
5120 Taxes on specific goods and services	16 913	58 200	73 170	78 125	80 932	1 177	2 723	3 555	3 054	3 322
5130 Unallocable between 5110 and 5120	0	0	436	292	288	0	0	0	0	0
5200 Taxes on use of goods and perform activities	0	0	0	10 577	12 123	2 711	7 058	15 687	8 017	7 847
5300 Unallocable between 5100 and 5200	0	0	0	0	0	0	0	0	0	0
6000 Other taxes	**0**	**0**	**-1**	**0**	**0**	**0**	**0**	**0**	**0**	**0**
6100 Paid solely by business	..	..	0	..	..	..	..	..	..	..
6200 Other	..	..	-1	0	0	..	..	0	0	0
Total tax revenue	**63 378**	**216 240**	**237 349**	**343 446**	**393 596**	**42 116**	**148 902**	**174 581**	**259 239**	**319 078**

	Local government					Social Security Funds				
	1975	1995	2005	2015	2019	1975	1995	2005	2015	2019
1000 Taxes on income, profits and capital gains	**11 819**	**40 295**	**46 725**	**73 916**	**90 454**	**0**	**0**	**0**	**0**	**0**
1100 Of individuals	9 931	33 761	31 261	50 775	61 999	..	..	..	..	..
1200 Corporate	1 888	6 534	15 464	23 141	28 455	..	..	..	..	..
1300 Unallocable between 1100 and 1200	0	0	0	0	..	..	..	..	..	..
2000 Social security contributions	**0**	**0**	**0**	**0**	**0**	**64 290**	**268 052**	**311 530**	**424 841**	**508 124**
2100 Employees	..	..	..	..	..	28 106	117 916	134 939	186 305	220 204
2200 Employers	..	..	..	..	..	34 609	133 120	148 507	196 679	238 358
2300 Self-employed or non-employed	..	..	..	..	..	1 575	17 016	28 084	41 857	49 562
2400 Unallocable between 2100, 2200 and 2300	..	..	..	..	..	0	0	0	0	0
3000 Taxes on payroll and workforce	**1 533**	**0**	**0**	**0**	**0**	**0**	**0**	**0**	**0**	**0**
4000 Taxes on property	**3 461**	**9 794**	**10 247**	**13 215**	**12 934**	**0**	**0**	**0**	**0**	**0**
4100 Recurrent taxes on immovable property	2 122	7 027	10 247	13 215	12 934	..	..	..	..	..
4200 Recurrent taxes on net wealth	911	2 615	0	0	0	..	..	..	..	..
4300 Estate, inheritance and gift taxes	0	0	0	0	0	..	..	..	..	..
4400 Taxes on financial and capital transactions	428	151	0	0	0	..	..	..	..	..
4500 Non-recurrent taxes	0	0	0	0	0	..	..	..	..	..
4600 Other recurrent taxes on property	0	0	0	0	..	..	..	..	..	..
5000 Taxes on goods and services	**162**	**448**	**3 395**	**5 947**	**9 700**	**0**	**0**	**0**	**0**	**0**
5100 Taxes on production, sale, transfer, etc	94	271	3 136	5 615	9 322	..	..	..	..	..
5110 General taxes	0	0	2 909	4 734	8 325	..	..	..	..	..
5120 Taxes on specific goods and services	94	271	227	881	997	..	..	..	..	..
5130 Unallocable between 5110 and 5120	0	0	0	0	0	..	..	..	..	..
5200 Taxes on use of goods and perform activities	68	176	259	332	378	..	..	..	..	..
5300 Unallocable between 5100 and 5200	0	0	0	0	0	..	..	..	..	..
6000 Other taxes	**67**	**130**	**79**	**216**	**319**	**0**	**0**	**0**	**0**	**0**
6100 Paid solely by business	0	0	0	0	..	..	..	..	..	..
6200 Other	67	130	79	216	319	..	..	..	..	..
Total tax revenue	**17 042**	**50 666**	**60 446**	**93 294**	**113 407**	**64 290**	**268 052**	**311 530**	**424 841**	**508 124**

.. Not available

Note: Including taxes collected on behalf of the European Union.

StatLink https://stat.link/djvcki

Table 6.14. Greece, tax revenues by sub-sectors of government

Million EUR

	Central government					State/Regional				
	1975	1995	2005	2015	2019	1975	1995	2005	2015	2019
1000 Taxes on income, profits and capital gains	**64**	**5 456**	**16 101**	**14 577**	**15 632**	..	..	..	..	..
1100 Of individuals	43	3 011	8 719	10 146	10 991	..	..	..	..	..
1200 Corporate	17	2 067	6 487	3 800	4 071	..	..	..	..	..
1300 Unallocable between 1100 and 1200	4	378	895	631	570	..	..	..	..	..
2000 Social security contributions	**0**	**380**	**1 048**	**745**	**58**	..	..	..	..	..
2100 Employees	..	380	1 031	744	58	..	..	..	..	..
2200 Employers	..	0	17	1	0	..	..	..	..	..
2300 Self-employed or non-employed	..	0	0	0	0	..	..	..	..	..
2400 Unallocable between 2100, 2200 and 2300	..	0	0	0	0	..	..	..	..	..
3000 Taxes on payroll and workforce	**1**	**0**	**0**	**0**	**0**	..	..	..	..	..
4000 Taxes on property	**47**	**1 060**	**2 263**	**3 931**	**3 977**	..	..	..	..	..
4100 Recurrent taxes on immovable property	1	0	0	3 046	2 646	..	..	..	..	..
4200 Recurrent taxes on net wealth	0	138	284	180	190	..	..	..	..	..
4300 Estate, inheritance and gift taxes	5	274	258	134	244	..	..	..	..	..
4400 Taxes on financial and capital transactions	41	641	1 469	509	869	..	..	..	..	..
4500 Non-recurrent taxes	0	0	73	0	0	..	..	..	..	..
4600 Other recurrent taxes on property	0	7	179	62	28	..	..	..	..	..
5000 Taxes on goods and services	**224**	**10 586**	**21 526**	**25 088**	**28 266**	..	..	..	..	..
5100 Taxes on production, sale, transfer, etc	205	9 953	19 454	20 899	24 296	..	..	..	..	..
5110 General taxes	90	5 504	13 605	12 904	15 395	..	..	..	..	..
5120 Taxes on specific goods and services	114	4 413	5 772	7 901	8 867	..	..	..	..	..
5130 Unallocable between 5110 and 5120	0	36	77	94	34	..	..	..	..	..
5200 Taxes on use of goods and perform activities	20	385	1 780	3 187	3 237	..	..	..	..	..
5300 Unallocable between 5100 and 5200	0	248	292	1 002	733	..	..	..	..	..
6000 Other taxes	**0**	**0**	**0**	**0**	**0**	..	..	..	..	..
6100 Paid solely by business	..	..	..	..	..	..	..	..	..	..
6200 Other	..	..	..	..	..	..	..	..	..	..
Total tax revenue	**337**	**17 482**	**40 938**	**44 341**	**47 933**	..	..	..	..	..

	Local government					Social Security Funds				
	1975	1995	2005	2015	2019	1975	1995	2005	2015	2019
1000 Taxes on income, profits and capital gains	**3**	**0**	**0**	**0**	**0**	**0**	**0**	**0**	**9**	**10**
1100 Of individuals	2	..	..	..	..	0	..	..	9	10
1200 Corporate	0	..	..	..	..	0	..	..	0	0
1300 Unallocable between 1100 and 1200	1	..	..	..	..	0	..	..	0	0
2000 Social security contributions	**0**	**0**	**0**	**0**	**0**	**148**	**7 991**	**20 288**	**18 062**	**22 235**
2100 Employees	..	..	..	..	..	62	4 181	10 206	10 351	12 022
2200 Employers	..	..	..	..	..	62	3 810	10 082	7 711	10 213
2300 Self-employed or non-employed	..	..	..	..	..	0	0	0	0	0
2400 Unallocable between 2100, 2200 and 2300	..	..	..	..	..	24	0	0	0	0
3000 Taxes on payroll and workforce	**0**	**0**	**0**	**0**	**0**	**0**	**0**	**0**	**0**	**0**
4000 Taxes on property	**1**	**447**	**1 208**	**1 449**	**1 625**	**0**	**66**	**361**	**38**	**0**
4100 Recurrent taxes on immovable property	0	180	420	546	622	..	32	83	0	..
4200 Recurrent taxes on net wealth	0	267	788	903	1 003	..	0	0	0	..
4300 Estate, inheritance and gift taxes	0	0	0	0	0	..	0	0	0	..
4400 Taxes on financial and capital transactions	0	0	0	0	0	..	34	278	38	..
4500 Non-recurrent taxes	0	0	0	0	0	..	0	0	0	..
4600 Other recurrent taxes on property	0	0	0	0	0	..	0	0	0	..
5000 Taxes on goods and services	**10**	**89**	**197**	**96**	**118**	**0**	**124**	**248**	**240**	**115**
5100 Taxes on production, sale, transfer, etc	7	87	185	82	102	..	102	195	224	111
5110 General taxes	2	32	26	3	2	..	86	85	170	77
5120 Taxes on specific goods and services	6	55	159	79	100	..	16	110	47	23
5130 Unallocable between 5110 and 5120	0	0	0	0	0	..	0	0	7	11
5200 Taxes on use of goods and perform activities	3	2	12	14	16	..	22	53	16	4
5300 Unallocable between 5100 and 5200	0	0	0	0	0	..	0	0	0	0
6000 Other taxes	**0**	**0**	**0**	**0**	**0**	**0**	**0**	**0**	**0**	**0**
6100 Paid solely by business	..	..	..	..	..	..	..	..	..	..
6200 Other	..	..	..	..	..	..	..	..	..	..
Total tax revenue	**17**	**536**	**1 405**	**1 545**	**1 743**	**148**	**8 181**	**20 897**	**18 349**	**22 360**

.. Not available

Note: Including taxes collected on behalf of the European Union.

StatLink https://stat.link/rswemi

Table 6.15. Hungary, tax revenues by sub-sectors of government

Million HUF

	Central government					State/Regional				
	1975	1995	2005	2015	2019	1975	1995	2005	2015	2019
1000 Taxes on income, profits and capital gains	..	**498 608**	**1 915 178**	**2 299 697**	**3 059 375**	..	..	..	..	..
1100 Of individuals	..	383 744	1 449 552	1 698 410	2 445 549	..	..	..	..	..
1200 Corporate	..	106 259	465 626	601 287	613 826	..	..	..	..	..
1300 Unallocable between 1100 and 1200	..	8 605	0	0	0	..	..	..	..	..
2000 Social security contributions	..	**69 554**	**235 148**	**148 044**	**286 910**	..	..	..	..	..
2100 Employees	..	18 468	53 611	144 868	285 475	..	..	..	..	..
2200 Employers	..	51 086	175 013	3 176	1 435	..	..	..	..	..
2300 Self-employed or non-employed	..	0	0	0	0	..	..	..	..	..
2400 Unallocable between 2100, 2200 and 2300	..	0	6 524	0	0	..	..	..	..	..
3000 Taxes on payroll and workforce	..	**5 474**	**39 459**	**231 467**	**484 827**	..	..	..	..	..
4000 Taxes on property	..	**11 463**	**63 007**	**292 329**	**279 539**	..	..	..	..	..
4100 Recurrent taxes on immovable property	..	0	0	55 906	54 509	..	..	..	..	..
4200 Recurrent taxes on net wealth	..	0	0	135 661	44 894	..	..	..	..	..
4300 Estate, inheritance and gift taxes	..	1 364	7 678	7 373	11 428	..	..	..	..	..
4400 Taxes on financial and capital transactions	..	10 099	55 329	93 389	168 708	..	..	..	..	..
4500 Non-recurrent taxes	..	0	0	0	0	..	..	..	..	..
4600 Other recurrent taxes on property	..	0	0	0	0	..	..	..	..	..
5000 Taxes on goods and services	..	**924 906**	**2 870 189**	**5 168 034**	**6 723 041**	..	..	..	..	..
5100 Taxes on production, sale, transfer, etc	..	919 500	2 854 738	5 060 613	6 543 339	..	..	..	..	..
5110 General taxes	..	423 954	1 972 998	3 485 479	4 683 055	..	..	..	..	..
5120 Taxes on specific goods and services	..	495 546	881 740	1 575 134	1 860 284	..	..	..	..	..
5130 Unallocable between 5110 and 5120	..	0	0	0	0	..	..	..	..	..
5200 Taxes on use of goods and perform activities	..	5 406	15 451	107 421	179 702	..	..	..	..	..
5300 Unallocable between 5100 and 5200	..	0	0	0	0	..	..	..	..	..
6000 Other taxes	..	**8 901**	**25 403**	**30 665**	**25 780**	..	..	..	..	..
6100 Paid solely by business	..	0	4 240	9 156	8 143	..	..	..	..	..
6200 Other	..	0	0	0	0	..	..	..	..	..
Total tax revenue	..	**1 518 905**	**5 148 383**	**8 170 236**	**10 859 472**	..	..	..	..	..

	Local government					Social Security Funds				
	1975	1995	2005	2015	2019	1975	1995	2005	2015	2019
1000 Taxes on income, profits and capital gains	..	**0**	**173**	**45**	**27**	..	**0**	**26 307**	**126 216**	**11 991**
1100 Of individuals	..	0	173	45	27	..	0	26 307	126 216	11 991
1200 Corporate	..	0	0	0	0	..	0	0	0	0
1300 Unallocable between 1100 and 1200	..	0	0	0	0	..	0	0	0	0
2000 Social security contributions	..	**0**	**0**	**0**	**0**	..	**778 467**	**2 452 562**	**4 285 420**	**5 257 914**
2100 Employees	..	..	..	..	..	..	116 824	530 098	1 626 055	2 485 557
2200 Employers	..	..	..	..	..	..	632 478	1 894 306	2 634 154	2 744 392
2300 Self-employed or non-employed	..	..	..	..	..	..	27 466	2 080	0	0
2400 Unallocable between 2100, 2200 and 2300	..	..	..	..	..	..	1 699	26 078	25 211	27 965
3000 Taxes on payroll and workforce	..	**1 075**	**1 153**	**0**	**0**	..	**0**	**44 397**	**10 283**	**10 179**
4000 Taxes on property	..	**17 531**	**123 929**	**145 000**	**166 932**	..	**0**	**0**	**0**	**0**
4100 Recurrent taxes on immovable property	..	6 068	58 836	145 000	166 932	..	..	..	..	..
4200 Recurrent taxes on net wealth	..	0	0	0	0	..	..	..	..	..
4300 Estate, inheritance and gift taxes	..	1 364	7 932	0	0	..	..	..	..	..
4400 Taxes on financial and capital transactions	..	10 099	57 162	0	0	..	..	..	..	..
4500 Non-recurrent taxes	..	0	0	0	0	..	..	..	..	..
4600 Other recurrent taxes on property	..	0	0	0	0	..	..	..	..	..
5000 Taxes on goods and services	..	**41 970**	**388 385**	**625 571**	**839 233**	..	**0**	**0**	**103 105**	**111 355**
5100 Taxes on production, sale, transfer, etc	..	39 240	337 935	594 855	804 557	..	..	..	103 105	111 355
5110 General taxes	..	38 472	334 077	584 380	788 308	..	..	..	29 882	54 912
5120 Taxes on specific goods and services	..	768	3 858	10 475	16 249	..	..	..	73 223	56 443
5130 Unallocable between 5110 and 5120	..	0	0	0	0	..	..	..	0	0
5200 Taxes on use of goods and perform activities	..	2 730	50 450	30 716	34 676	..	..	..	0	0
5300 Unallocable between 5100 and 5200	..	0	0	0	0	..	..	..	0	0
6000 Other taxes	..	**0**	**0**	**0**	**0**	..	**21 605**	**9 616**	**14 021**	**8 114**
6100 Paid solely by business	..	..	..	..	..	..	0	0	0	0
6200 Other	..	..	..	..	..	..	0	0	0	0
Total tax revenue	..	**60 576**	**513 641**	**770 616**	**1 006 192**	..	**800 072**	**2 532 882**	**4 539 045**	**5 399 553**

.. Not available

Note: Including taxes collected on behalf of the European Union.

StatLink https://stat.link/zas5hm

Table 6.16. Iceland, tax revenues by sub-sectors of government

Million ISK

	Central government					State/Regional				
	1975	1995	2005	2015	2019	1975	1995	2005	2015	2019
1000 Taxes on income, profits and capital gains	**68**	**27 156**	**105 705**	**210 536**	**288 811**	**..**	**..**	**..**	**..**	**..**
1100 Of individuals	55	22 914	70 944	127 535	193 971	..	..	..	..	..
1200 Corporate	13	4 242	20 297	52 544	62 972	..	..	..	..	..
1300 Unallocable between 1100 and 1200	0	0	14 464	30 457	31 868	..	..	..	..	..
2000 Social security contributions	**17**	**11 452**	**32 777**	**79 707**	**97 423**	**..**	**..**	**..**	**..**	**..**
2100 Employees	0	460	..	..	..	..	..	..	..	..
2200 Employers	17	10 992	..	..	..	..	..	..	..	..
2300 Self-employed or non-employed	0	0	..	..	..	..	..	..	..	..
2400 Unallocable between 2100, 2200 and 2300	0	0	32 777	79 707	97 423	..	..	..	..	..
3000 Taxes on payroll and workforce	**27**	**0**	**324**	**6 638**	**9 124**	**..**	**..**	**..**	**..**	**..**
4000 Taxes on property	**15**	**7 198**	**13 340**	**8 786**	**11 353**	**..**	**..**	**..**	**..**	**..**
4100 Recurrent taxes on immovable property	0	47	0	178	240	..	..	..	..	..
4200 Recurrent taxes on net wealth	5	3 191	2 887	657	10	..	..	..	..	..
4300 Estate, inheritance and gift taxes	0	389	866	2 919	4 668	..	..	..	..	..
4400 Taxes on financial and capital transactions	9	3 571	9 073	4 327	5 269	..	..	..	..	..
4500 Non-recurrent taxes	0	0	248	362	623	..	..	..	..	..
4600 Other recurrent taxes on property	0	0	266	343	542	..	..	..	..	..
5000 Taxes on goods and services	**392**	**66 356**	**168 295**	**259 996**	**335 801**	**..**	**..**	**..**	**..**	**..**
5100 Taxes on production, sale, transfer, etc	387	62 140	157 941	250 095	320 533	..	..	..	..	..
5110 General taxes	182	42 358	113 897	183 674	243 285	..	..	..	..	..
5120 Taxes on specific goods and services	205	19 782	44 044	66 421	77 248	..	..	..	..	..
5130 Unallocable between 5110 and 5120	0	0	0	0	0	..	..	..	..	..
5200 Taxes on use of goods and perform activities	5	4 216	10 354	9 901	15 268	..	..	..	..	..
5300 Unallocable between 5100 and 5200	0	0	0	0	0	..	..	..	..	..
6000 Other taxes	**0**	**0**	**1 504**	**38 364**	**18 594**	**..**	**..**	**..**	**..**	**..**
6100 Paid solely by business	..	..	565	32 477	11 629	..	..	..	..	..
6200 Other	..	..	939	5 887	6 966	..	..	..	..	..
Total tax revenue	**519**	**112 162**	**321 944**	**604 026**	**761 108**	**..**	**..**	**..**	**..**	**..**

	Local government					Social Security Funds				
	1975	1995	2005	2015	2019	1975	1995	2005	2015	2019
1000 Taxes on income, profits and capital gains	**78**	**21 170**	**74 455**	**170 443**	**241 350**	**0**	**0**	**0**	**0**	**0**
1100 Of individuals	74	21 170	74 455	170 443	241 350	..	..	..	..	..
1200 Corporate	4	0	0	0	0	..	..	..	..	..
1300 Unallocable between 1100 and 1200	0	0	0	0	0	..	..	..	..	..
2000 Social security contributions	**0**	**0**	**0**	**0**	**0**	**0**	**0**	**0**	**0**	**0**
2100 Employees	..	..	..	..	..	..	..	..	..	..
2200 Employers	..	..	..	..	..	..	..	..	..	..
2300 Self-employed or non-employed	..	..	..	..	..	..	..	..	..	..
2400 Unallocable between 2100, 2200 and 2300	..	..	..	..	..	..	..	..	..	..
3000 Taxes on payroll and workforce	**0**	**0**	**0**	**0**	**0**	**0**	**0**	**0**	**0**	**0**
4000 Taxes on property	**18**	**5 674**	**13 931**	**34 701**	**52 282**	**0**	**0**	**0**	**0**	**0**
4100 Recurrent taxes on immovable property	18	5 674	13 931	34 701	52 282	..	..	..	..	..
4200 Recurrent taxes on net wealth	0	0	0	0	0	..	..	..	..	..
4300 Estate, inheritance and gift taxes	0	0	0	0	0	..	..	..	..	..
4400 Taxes on financial and capital transactions	0	0	0	0	0	..	..	..	..	..
4500 Non-recurrent taxes	0	0	0	0	0	..	..	..	..	..
4600 Other recurrent taxes on property	0	0	0	0	0	..	..	..	..	..
5000 Taxes on goods and services	**9**	**2 585**	**6 904**	**2 832**	**7 208**	**0**	**0**	**0**	**0**	**0**
5100 Taxes on production, sale, transfer, etc	9	2 585	0	0	0	..	..	..	..	..
5110 General taxes	0	2 585	..	..	..	..	..	..	..	..
5120 Taxes on specific goods and services	9	0	..	..	..	..	..	..	..	..
5130 Unallocable between 5110 and 5120	0	0	..	..	..	..	..	..	..	..
5200 Taxes on use of goods and perform activities	0	0	6 904	2 832	7 208	..	..	..	..	..
5300 Unallocable between 5100 and 5200	0	0	0	0	0	..	..	..	..	..
6000 Other taxes	**14**	**0**	**93**	**0**	**0**	**0**	**0**	**0**	**0**	**0**
6100 Paid solely by business	14	..	93	..	..	..	..	..	..	..
6200 Other	0	..	0	..	..	..	..	..	..	..
Total tax revenue	**119**	**29 429**	**95 383**	**207 976**	**300 840**	**0**	**0**	**0**	**0**	**0**

.. Not available

StatLink https://stat.link/4l3mkq

Table 6.17. Ireland, tax revenues by sub-sectors of government

Million EUR

	Central government					State/Regional				
	1975	1995	2005	2015	2019	1975	1995	2005	2015	2019
1000 Taxes on income, profits and capital gains	**456**	**7 022**	**21 186**	**26 599**	**35 646**	..	..	..	..	..
1100 Of individuals	382	5 563	15 674	19 722	24 753	..	..	..	..	..
1200 Corporate	73	1 458	5 511	6 873	10 894	..	..	..	..	..
1300 Unallocable between 1100 and 1200	0	0	0	4	0	..	..	..	..	..
2000 Social security contributions	**11**	**87**	**217**	**1 340**	**1 355**	..	..	..	..	..
2100 Employees	10	87	217	1 340	1 355	..	..	..	..	..
2200 Employers	0	0	0	0	0	..	..	..	..	..
2300 Self-employed or non-employed	1	0	0	0	0	..	..	..	..	..
2400 Unallocable between 2100, 2200 and 2300	0	0	0	0	0	..	..	..	..	..
3000 Taxes on payroll and workforce	**0**	**209**	**332**	**357**	**774**	..	..	..	..	..
4000 Taxes on property	**37**	**370**	**2 741**	**2 530**	**2 976**	..	..	..	..	..
4100 Recurrent taxes on immovable property	0	15	0	475	474	..	..	..	..	..
4200 Recurrent taxes on net wealth	5	0	0	169	0	..	..	..	..	..
4300 Estate, inheritance and gift taxes	17	76	255	401	531	..	..	..	..	..
4400 Taxes on financial and capital transactions	15	279	2 486	1 484	1 971	..	..	..	..	..
4500 Non-recurrent taxes	0	0	0	0	0	..	..	..	..	..
4600 Other recurrent taxes on property	0	0	0	0	0	..	..	..	..	..
5000 Taxes on goods and services	**671**	**6 763**	**19 122**	**19 686**	**23 632**	..	..	..	..	..
5100 Taxes on production, sale, transfer, etc	639	6 419	18 106	17 709	21 816	..	..	..	..	..
5110 General taxes	223	3 666	12 373	11 831	15 281	..	..	..	..	..
5120 Taxes on specific goods and services	416	2 753	5 733	5 878	6 535	..	..	..	..	..
5130 Unallocable between 5110 and 5120	0	0	0	0	0	..	..	..	..	..
5200 Taxes on use of goods and perform activities	33	344	1 015	1 977	1 815	..	..	..	..	..
5300 Unallocable between 5100 and 5200	0	0	0	0	0	..	..	..	..	..
6000 Other taxes	**0**	**0**	**0**	**12**	**5**	..	..	..	..	..
6100 Paid solely by business	..	..	..	0	0	..	..	..	..	..
6200 Other	..	..	..	12	5	..	..	..	..	..
Total tax revenue	**1 175**	**14 451**	**43 598**	**50 525**	**64 388**	..	..	..	..	..

	Local government					Social Security Funds				
	1975	1995	2005	2015	2019	1975	1995	2005	2015	2019
1000 Taxes on income, profits and capital gains	**0**	**0**	**0**	**0**	**0**	**0**	**0**	**0**	**0**	**0**
1100 Of individuals	..	..	..	..	..	..	..	..	..	..
1200 Corporate	..	..	..	..	..	..	..	..	..	..
1300 Unallocable between 1100 and 1200	0	..	..	..	..	0	..	..	..	..
2000 Social security contributions	**0**	**56**	**90**	**125**	**82**	**198**	**2 215**	**6 230**	**8 527**	**11 702**
2100 Employees	..	56	90	125	82	73	576	1 415	1 856	2 575
2200 Employers	..	0	0	0	0	125	1 528	4 427	6 211	8 495
2300 Self-employed or non-employed	..	0	0	0	0	0	111	388	460	632
2400 Unallocable between 2100, 2200 and 2300	..	0	0	0	0	0	0	0	0	0
3000 Taxes on payroll and workforce	**0**	**0**	**0**	**0**	**0**	**0**	**0**	**0**	**0**	**0**
4000 Taxes on property	**110**	**408**	**1 020**	**1 389**	**1 459**	..	**0**	**0**	**0**	**0**
4100 Recurrent taxes on immovable property	110	408	1 020	1 389	1 459	..	..	..	..	..
4200 Recurrent taxes on net wealth	0	0	0	0	0	..	..	..	..	..
4300 Estate, inheritance and gift taxes	0	0	0	0	0	..	..	..	..	..
4400 Taxes on financial and capital transactions	0	0	0	0	0	..	..	..	..	..
4500 Non-recurrent taxes	0	0	0	0	0	..	..	..	..	..
4600 Other recurrent taxes on property	0	0	0	0	0	..	..	..	..	..
5000 Taxes on goods and services	**0**	**0**	**0**	**0**	**0**	**0**	**0**	**0**	**0**	**0**
5100 Taxes on production, sale, transfer, etc	..	..	..	..	..	..	..	..	..	..
5110 General taxes	..	..	..	..	..	..	..	..	..	..
5120 Taxes on specific goods and services	..	..	..	..	..	..	..	..	..	..
5130 Unallocable between 5110 and 5120	0	..	..	..	..	0	..	..	..	..
5200 Taxes on use of goods and perform activities	..	..	..	..	..	0	..	..	..	..
5300 Unallocable between 5100 and 5200	0	..	..	..	..	0	..	..	..	..
6000 Other taxes	**0**	**0**	**0**	**0**	**0**	**0**	**0**	**0**	**0**	**0**
6100 Paid solely by business	..	..	..	..	..	..	..	..	..	..
6200 Other	..	..	..	..	..	..	..	..	..	..
Total tax revenue	**110**	**464**	**1 110**	**1 513**	**1 541**	**198**	**2 215**	**6 230**	**8 527**	**11 702**

.. Not available

Note: Including taxes collected on behalf of the European Union. The personal income tax data shown for the country table for Ireland is different to the ESA2010 presentation as the expenditure component of the payable tax credits are excluded in accordance with the OECD Interpretative Guide.

StatLink https://stat.link/ar2iy0

Table 6.18. Israel, tax revenues by sub-sectors of government

Million ILS

	Central government					State/Regional				
	1975	1995	2005	2015	2019	1975	1995	2005	2015	2019
1000 Taxes on income, profits and capital gains	..	**37 422**	**73 082**	**113 966**	**140 453**	..	..	..	..	..
1100 Of individuals	..	28 399	47 062	70 885	89 493	..	..	..	..	..
1200 Corporate	..	8 514	21 909	34 676	43 291	..	..	..	..	..
1300 Unallocable between 1100 and 1200	..	509	4 111	8 405	7 669	..	..	..	..	..
2000 Social security contributions	..	**0**	**0**	**0**	**0**	..	..	..	..	..
2100 Employees	..	..	..	..	..	..	..	..	..	..
2200 Employers	..	..	..	..	..	..	..	..	..	..
2300 Self-employed or non-employed	..	..	..	..	..	..	..	..	..	..
2400 Unallocable between 2100, 2200 and 2300	..	..	..	..	..	..	..	..	..	..
3000 Taxes on payroll and workforce	..	**5 007**	**9 920**	**13 770**	**16 168**	..	..	..	..	..
4000 Taxes on property	..	**4 122**	**5 547**	**10 593**	**11 426**	..	..	..	..	..
4100 Recurrent taxes on immovable property	..	786	322	44	25	..	..	..	..	..
4200 Recurrent taxes on net wealth	..	0	0	0	0	..	..	..	..	..
4300 Estate, inheritance and gift taxes	..	0	0	0	0	..	..	..	..	..
4400 Taxes on financial and capital transactions	..	2 049	3 591	6 732	6 923	..	..	..	..	..
4500 Non-recurrent taxes	..	1 287	1 634	3 817	4 478	..	..	..	..	..
4600 Other recurrent taxes on property	..	0	0	0	0	..	..	..	..	..
5000 Taxes on goods and services	..	**38 673**	**75 877**	**136 829**	**152 118**	..	..	..	..	..
5100 Taxes on production, sale, transfer, etc	..	36 637	70 741	128 277	143 066	..	..	..	..	..
5110 General taxes	..	31 975	59 374	107 765	120 541	..	..	..	..	..
5120 Taxes on specific goods and services	..	4 662	11 367	20 512	22 525	..	..	..	..	..
5130 Unallocable between 5110 and 5120	..	0	0	0	0	..	..	..	..	..
5200 Taxes on use of goods and perform activities	..	2 036	5 137	8 552	9 052	..	..	..	..	..
5300 Unallocable between 5100 and 5200	..	0	0	0	0	..	..	..	..	..
6000 Other taxes	..	**0**	**0**	**0**	**0**	..	..	..	..	..
6100 Paid solely by business	..	..	..	..	..	..	..	..	..	..
6200 Other	..	..	..	..	..	..	..	..	..	..
Total tax revenue	..	**85 224**	**164 426**	**275 158**	**320 165**	..	..	..	..	..

	Local government					Social Security Funds				
	1975	1995	2005	2015	2019	1975	1995	2005	2015	2019
1000 Taxes on income, profits and capital gains	..	**0**	**0**	**0**	**0**	..	**0**	**0**	**0**	**0**
1100 Of individuals	..	0	0	0	0	..	0	0	0	0
1200 Corporate	..	..	..	..	..	..	..	..	..	..
1300 Unallocable between 1100 and 1200	..	0	0	0	0	..	0	0	0	0
2000 Social security contributions	..	**0**	**0**	**0**	**0**	..	**14 958**	**34 597**	**59 561**	**74 420**
2100 Employees	..	..	..	..	..	..	7 953	19 720	34 692	41 852
2200 Employers	..	..	..	..	..	..	4 672	10 679	17 247	23 105
2300 Self-employed or non-employed	..	..	..	..	..	..	2 334	4 198	7 622	9 464
2400 Unallocable between 2100, 2200 and 2300	..	..	..	..	..	..	0	0	0	0
3000 Taxes on payroll and workforce	..	**0**	**0**	**0**	**0**	..	**0**	**0**	**0**	**0**
4000 Taxes on property	..	**6 445**	**15 689**	**28 148**	**32 347**	..	**0**	**0**	**0**	**0**
4100 Recurrent taxes on immovable property	..	5 489	13 962	23 658	27 080	..	..	..	..	..
4200 Recurrent taxes on net wealth	..	0	0	0	0	..	..	..	..	..
4300 Estate, inheritance and gift taxes	..	0	0	0	0	..	..	..	..	..
4400 Taxes on financial and capital transactions	..	0	0	0	0	..	..	..	..	..
4500 Non-recurrent taxes	..	956	1 727	4 490	5 267	..	..	..	..	..
4600 Other recurrent taxes on property	..	0	0	0	0	..	..	..	..	..
5000 Taxes on goods and services	..	**361**	**650**	**1 314**	**1 601**	..	**0**	**0**	**0**	**0**
5100 Taxes on production, sale, transfer, etc	..	0	0	0	0	..	..	..	..	..
5110 General taxes	..	0	0	0	0	..	..	..	..	..
5120 Taxes on specific goods and services	..	0	0	0	0	..	..	..	..	..
5130 Unallocable between 5110 and 5120	..	0	0	0	0	..	..	..	..	..
5200 Taxes on use of goods and perform activities	..	361	650	1 314	1 601	..	..	..	..	..
5300 Unallocable between 5100 and 5200	..	0	0	0	0	..	..	..	..	..
6000 Other taxes	..	**0**	**0**	**0**	**0**	..	**0**	**0**	**0**	**0**
6100 Paid solely by business	..	..	..	..	..	..	..	..	..	..
6200 Other	..	..	..	..	..	..	..	..	..	..
Total tax revenue	..	**6 806**	**16 339**	**29 462**	**33 948**	..	**14 958**	**34 597**	**59 561**	**74 420**

.. Not available

StatLink https://stat.link/okx0qr

Table 6.19. Italy, tax revenues by sub-sectors of government

Million EUR

	Central government					State/Regional				
	1975	1995	2005	2015	2019	1975	1995	2005	2015	2019
1000 Taxes on income, profits and capital gains	**3 897**	**128 458**	**165 580**	**195 451**	**222 961**	**..**	**..**	**..**	**..**	**..**
1100 Of individuals	2 767	98 695	131 047	156 320	179 297	..	..	..	..	..
1200 Corporate	1 131	32 890	31 969	31 421	35 264	..	..	..	..	..
1300 Unallocable between 1100 and 1200	0	-3 127	2 564	7 710	8 399	..	..	..	..	..
2000 Social security contributions	**0**	**0**	**0**	**0**	**0**	**..**	**..**	**..**	**..**	**..**
2100 Employees	..	..	..	..	..	..	..	..	..	..
2200 Employers	..	..	..	..	..	..	..	..	..	..
2300 Self-employed or non-employed	..	..	..	..	..	..	..	..	..	..
2400 Unallocable between 2100, 2200 and 2300	..	..	..	..	..	..	..	..	..	..
3000 Taxes on payroll and workforce	**0**	**1 136**	**0**	**0**	**0**	**..**	**..**	**..**	**..**	**..**
4000 Taxes on property	**587**	**13 546**	**15 717**	**22 226**	**24 490**	**..**	**..**	**..**	**..**	**..**
4100 Recurrent taxes on immovable property	4	0	0	3 892	3 866	..	..	..	..	..
4200 Recurrent taxes on net wealth	0	4 494	0	231	226	..	..	..	..	..
4300 Estate, inheritance and gift taxes	39	587	56	638	798	..	..	..	..	..
4400 Taxes on financial and capital transactions	544	8 464	13 794	16 310	18 800	..	..	..	..	..
4500 Non-recurrent taxes	0	0	1 322	303	137	..	..	..	..	..
4600 Other recurrent taxes on property	0	0	545	852	663	..	..	..	..	..
5000 Taxes on goods and services	**5 506**	**95 323**	**123 870**	**157 330**	**185 302**	**..**	**..**	**..**	**..**	**..**
5100 Taxes on production, sale, transfer, etc	5 306	92 042	121 824	154 713	179 199	..	..	..	..	..
5110 General taxes	2 685	52 531	80 619	93 282	111 533	..	..	..	..	..
5120 Taxes on specific goods and services	2 621	39 245	41 205	61 431	67 666	..	..	..	..	..
5130 Unallocable between 5110 and 5120	0	323	0	0	0	..	..	..	..	..
5200 Taxes on use of goods and perform activities	200	2 802	1 535	2 191	4 739	..	..	..	..	..
5300 Unallocable between 5100 and 5200	0	479	511	426	1 364	..	..	..	..	..
6000 Other taxes	**1**	**0**	**0**	**0**	**0**	**..**	**..**	**..**	**..**	**..**
6100 Paid solely by business	0	..	..	..	..	..	..	..	..	..
6200 Other	1	..	..	..	..	..	..	..	..	..
Total tax revenue	**9 991**	**238 462**	**305 167**	**375 007**	**432 753**	**..**	**..**	**..**	**..**	**..**

	Local government					Social Security Funds				
	1975	1995	2005	2015	2019	1975	1995	2005	2015	2019
1000 Taxes on income, profits and capital gains	**134**	**5 658**	**18 494**	**30 483**	**16 838**	**0**	**0**	**0**	**0**	**0**
1100 Of individuals	81	145	16 995	28 302	16 838	..	..	..	..	..
1200 Corporate	54	97	1 491	2 109	0	..	..	..	..	..
1300 Unallocable between 1100 and 1200	0	5 416	8	72	0	..	..	..	..	..
2000 Social security contributions	**0**	**0**	**0**	**0**	**0**	**8 607**	**119 612**	**179 362**	**214 376**	**237 346**
2100 Employees	..	..	..	..	..	1 692	23 036	31 998	39 805	44 486
2200 Employers	..	..	..	..	..	6 915	79 716	125 099	143 273	158 611
2300 Self-employed or non-employed	..	..	..	..	..	0	16 860	22 265	31 298	34 249
2400 Unallocable between 2100, 2200 and 2300	..	..	..	..	..	0	0	0	0	0
3000 Taxes on payroll and workforce	**0**	**0**	**0**	**0**	**0**	**0**	**0**	**0**	**0**	**0**
4000 Taxes on property	**29**	**7 915**	**13 484**	**24 033**	**18 730**	**0**	**0**	**0**	**0**	**0**
4100 Recurrent taxes on immovable property	29	7 449	11 736	21 666	18 131	..	..	..	..	..
4200 Recurrent taxes on net wealth	0	0	0	0	0	..	..	..	..	..
4300 Estate, inheritance and gift taxes	0	0	5	36	0	..	..	..	..	..
4400 Taxes on financial and capital transactions	0	466	904	935	0	..	..	..	..	..
4500 Non-recurrent taxes	0	0	481	6	90	..	..	..	..	..
4600 Other recurrent taxes on property	0	0	358	1 390	509	..	..	..	..	..
5000 Taxes on goods and services	**4**	**6 941**	**30 231**	**34 551**	**26 528**	**0**	**0**	**0**	**0**	**0**
5100 Taxes on production, sale, transfer, etc	0	1 505	17 114	15 138	5 364	..	..	..	..	..
5110 General taxes	..	0	4 698	7 410	0	..	..	..	..	..
5120 Taxes on specific goods and services	..	1 505	12 416	7 728	5 364	..	..	..	..	..
5130 Unallocable between 5110 and 5120	..	0	0	0	0	..	..	..	..	..
5200 Taxes on use of goods and perform activities	4	2 838	7 512	8 939	9 354	..	..	..	..	..
5300 Unallocable between 5100 and 5200	0	2 597	5 605	10 474	11 810	..	..	..	..	..
6000 Other taxes	**0**	**0**	**34 690**	**28 072**	**24 278**	**0**	**0**	**0**	**0**	**0**
6100 Paid solely by business	..	..	34 690	28 072	24 278	..	..	..	..	..
6200 Other	..	..	0	0	0	..	..	..	..	..
Total tax revenue	**168**	**20 514**	**96 899**	**117 139**	**86 374**	**8 607**	**119 612**	**179 362**	**214 376**	**237 346**

.. Not available

Note: Including taxes collected on behalf of the European Union.

StatLink https://stat.link/nsk5fm

Table 6.20. Japan, tax revenues by sub-sectors of government

Billion JPY

	Central government					State/Regional				
	1975	1995	2005	2015	2019	1975	1995	2005	2015	2019
1000 Taxes on income, profits and capital gains	**9 747**	**33 255**	**29 975**	**31 607**	**33 016**	**..**	**..**	**..**	**..**	**..**
1100 Of individuals	5 482	19 515	16 702	18 178	19 571	..	..	..	..	..
1200 Corporate	4 265	13 740	13 274	13 429	13 445	..	..	..	..	..
1300 Unallocable between 1100 and 1200	0	0	0	0	0	..	..	..	..	..
2000 Social security contributions	**0**	**0**	**0**	**0**	**0**	**..**	**..**	**..**	**..**	**..**
2100 Employees	..	..	..	..	..	..	..	..	..	..
2200 Employers	..	..	..	..	..	..	..	..	..	..
2300 Self-employed or non-employed	..	..	..	..	..	..	..	..	..	..
2400 Unallocable between 2100, 2200 and 2300	..	..	..	..	..	..	..	..	..	..
3000 Taxes on payroll and workforce	**0**	**0**	**0**	**0**	**0**	**..**	**..**	**..**	**..**	**..**
4000 Taxes on property	**871**	**5 561**	**2 735**	**3 018**	**3 324**	**..**	**..**	**..**	**..**	**..**
4100 Recurrent taxes on immovable property	0	406	0	0	0	..	..	..	..	..
4200 Recurrent taxes on net wealth	0	0	0	0	0	..	..	..	..	..
4300 Estate, inheritance and gift taxes	310	2 690	1 566	1 968	2 301	..	..	..	..	..
4400 Taxes on financial and capital transactions	561	2 464	1 169	1 050	1 023	..	..	..	..	..
4500 Non-recurrent taxes	0	0	0	0	0	..	..	..	..	..
4600 Other recurrent taxes on property	0	0	0	0	0	..	..	..	..	..
5000 Taxes on goods and services	**3 888**	**16 147**	**19 580**	**25 345**	**25 835**	**..**	**..**	**..**	**..**	**..**
5100 Taxes on production, sale, transfer, etc	3 579	15 083	18 424	24 673	25 141	..	..	..	..	..
5110 General taxes	0	7 238	10 583	17 426	18 353	..	..	..	..	..
5120 Taxes on specific goods and services	3 579	7 845	7 840	7 247	6 788	..	..	..	..	..
5130 Unallocable between 5110 and 5120	0	0	0	0	0	..	..	..	..	..
5200 Taxes on use of goods and perform activities	309	1 065	1 157	671	694	..	..	..	..	..
5300 Unallocable between 5100 and 5200	0	0	0	0	0	..	..	..	..	..
6000 Other taxes	**0**	**0**	**0**	**0**	**1**	**..**	**..**	**..**	**..**	**..**
6100 Paid solely by business	..	..	..	..	0	..	..	..	..	..
6200 Other	..	..	..	..	1	..	..	..	..	..
Total tax revenue	**14 506**	**54 963**	**52 290**	**59 969**	**62 175**	**..**	**..**	**..**	**..**	**..**

	Local government					Social Security Funds				
	1975	1995	2005	2015	2019	1975	1995	2005	2015	2019
1000 Taxes on income, profits and capital gains	**4 472**	**17 752**	**16 655**	**19 362**	**20 978**	**0**	**0**	**0**	**0**	**0**
1100 Of individuals	2 147	10 283	8 520	12 669	13 376	..	..	..	..	..
1200 Corporate	2 325	7 470	8 135	6 693	7 602	..	..	..	..	..
1300 Unallocable between 1100 and 1200	0	0	0	0	0	..	..	..	..	..
2000 Social security contributions	**0**	**0**	**0**	**0**	**0**	**9 253**	**44 794**	**50 848**	**64 465**	**71 993**
2100 Employees	..	..	..	..	..	3 436	18 404	20 982	28 224	31 954
2200 Employers	..	..	..	..	..	4 825	21 432	23 154	29 479	33 488
2300 Self-employed or non-employed	..	..	..	..	..	992	4 958	6 712	6 763	6 552
2400 Unallocable between 2100, 2200 and 2300	..	..	..	..	..	0	0	0	0	0
3000 Taxes on payroll and workforce	**0**	**0**	**0**	**0**	**0**	**0**	**0**	**0**	**0**	**0**
4000 Taxes on property	**2 029**	**10 653**	**10 593**	**10 382**	**11 016**	**0**	**0**	**0**	**0**	**0**
4100 Recurrent taxes on immovable property	1 848	9 865	10 116	10 005	10 612	..	..	..	..	..
4200 Recurrent taxes on net wealth	0	0	0	0	0	..	..	..	..	..
4300 Estate, inheritance and gift taxes	0	0	0	0	0	..	..	..	..	..
4400 Taxes on financial and capital transactions	181	788	477	377	404	..	..	..	..	..
4500 Non-recurrent taxes	0	0	0	0	0	..	..	..	..	..
4600 Other recurrent taxes on property	0	0	0	0	0	..	..	..	..	..
5000 Taxes on goods and services	**1 636**	**4 941**	**7 206**	**8 942**	**8 764**	**0**	**0**	**0**	**0**	**0**
5100 Taxes on production, sale, transfer, etc	1 234	3 245	5 299	7 198	6 905	..	..	..	..	..
5110 General taxes	0	0	2 551	4 974	4 796	..	..	..	..	..
5120 Taxes on specific goods and services	1 234	3 245	2 747	2 223	2 110	..	..	..	..	..
5130 Unallocable between 5110 and 5120	0	0	0	0	0	..	..	..	..	..
5200 Taxes on use of goods and perform activities	402	1 697	1 907	1 744	1 858	..	..	..	..	..
5300 Unallocable between 5100 and 5200	0	0	0	0	0	..	..	..	..	..
6000 Other taxes	**20**	**329**	**351**	**413**	**454**	**0**	**0**	**0**	**0**	**0**
6100 Paid solely by business	15	307	297	361	387	..	..	..	..	..
6200 Other	5	22	54	52	67	..	..	..	..	..
Total tax revenue	**8 157**	**33 675**	**34 805**	**39 099**	**41 211**	**9 253**	**44 794**	**50 848**	**64 465**	**71 993**

.. Not available

StatLink https://stat.link/e640zr

Table 6.21. Korea, tax revenues by sub-sectors of government

Billion KRW

	Central government					State/Regional				
	1975	1995	2005	2015	2019	1975	1995	2005	2015	2019
1000 Taxes on income, profits and capital gains	**344**	**23 000**	**55 109**	**106 162**	**156 298**	..	..	..	..	..
1100 Of individuals	134	13 713	24 766	60 828	83 701	..	..	..	..	..
1200 Corporate	139	8 988	30 343	45 334	72 597	..	..	..	..	..
1300 Unallocable between 1100 and 1200	71	300	0	0	0	..	..	..	..	..
2000 Social security contributions	**0**	**0**	**0**	**0**	**0**	..	..	..	..	..
2100 Employees	..	..	..	..	..	..	..	..	..	..
2200 Employers	..	..	..	..	..	..	..	..	..	..
2300 Self-employed or non-employed	..	..	..	..	..	..	..	..	..	..
2400 Unallocable between 2100, 2200 and 2300	..	..	..	..	..	..	..	..	..	..
3000 Taxes on payroll and workforce	**0**	**0**	**0**	**0**	**0**	..	..	..	..	..
4000 Taxes on property	**65**	**2 482**	**6 769**	**15 164**	**19 406**	..	..	..	..	..
4100 Recurrent taxes on immovable property	0	106	535	1 666	3 176	..	..	..	..	..
4200 Recurrent taxes on net wealth	0	0	0	0	0	..	..	..	..	..
4300 Estate, inheritance and gift taxes	11	1 029	1 873	5 044	8 329	..	..	..	..	..
4400 Taxes on financial and capital transactions	49	1 258	4 363	8 454	7 901	..	..	..	..	..
4500 Non-recurrent taxes	5	89	-2	0	0	..	..	..	..	..
4600 Other recurrent taxes on property	0	0	0	0	0	..	..	..	..	..
5000 Taxes on goods and services	**920**	**29 170**	**63 480**	**93 127**	**111 877**	..	..	..	..	..
5100 Taxes on production, sale, transfer, etc	920	29 170	63 480	93 127	111 877	..	..	..	..	..
5110 General taxes	198	14 637	36 118	54 159	70 828	..	..	..	..	..
5120 Taxes on specific goods and services	722	14 533	27 362	38 968	41 049	..	..	..	..	..
5130 Unallocable between 5110 and 5120	0	0	0	0	0	..	..	..	..	..
5200 Taxes on use of goods and perform activities	0	0	0	0	0	..	..	..	..	..
5300 Unallocable between 5100 and 5200	0	0	0	0	0	..	..	..	..	..
6000 Other taxes	**64**	**2 121**	**2 108**	**3 435**	**5 873**	..	..	..	..	..
6100 Paid solely by business	0	0	0	0	0	..	..	..	..	..
6200 Other	64	2 121	2 108	3 435	5 873	..	..	..	..	..
Total tax revenue	**1 393**	**56 774**	**127 466**	**217 888**	**293 454**	..	..	..	..	..

	Local government					Social Security Funds				
	1975	1995	2005	2015	2019	1975	1995	2005	2015	2019
1000 Taxes on income, profits and capital gains	**36**	**1 704**	**5 500**	**12 989**	**17 742**	**0**	**0**	**0**	**0**	**0**
1100 Of individuals	0	1 137	2 804	6 772	8 013	..	..	..	..	..
1200 Corporate	0	565	2 696	6 217	9 729	..	..	..	..	..
1300 Unallocable between 1100 and 1200	36	3	0	0	0	..	..	..	..	..
2000 Social security contributions	**0**	**0**	**0**	**0**	**0**	**13**	**9 913**	**43 902**	**104 693**	**140 071**
2100 Employees	..	..	..	..	..	0	4 539	17 632	44 281	60 682
2200 Employers	..	..	..	..	..	13	3 918	18 486	47 846	63 780
2300 Self-employed or non-employed	..	..	..	..	..	0	1 456	7 784	12 566	15 609
2400 Unallocable between 2100, 2200 and 2300	..	..	..	..	..	0	0	0	0	0
3000 Taxes on payroll and workforce	**0**	**237**	**514**	**1 122**	**1 597**	**0**	**0**	**0**	**0**	**0**
4000 Taxes on property	**87**	**8 960**	**17 928**	**33 461**	**40 326**	**0**	**0**	**0**	**0**	**0**
4100 Recurrent taxes on immovable property	45	2 636	4 495	10 820	14 574	..	..	..	..	..
4200 Recurrent taxes on net wealth	0	0	0	0	0	..	..	..	..	..
4300 Estate, inheritance and gift taxes	0	0	0	0	0	..	..	..	..	..
4400 Taxes on financial and capital transactions	42	6 324	13 433	22 641	25 752	..	..	..	..	..
4500 Non-recurrent taxes	0	0	0	0	0	..	..	..	..	..
4600 Other recurrent taxes on property	0	0	0	0	0	..	..	..	..	..
5000 Taxes on goods and services	**36**	**4 218**	**7 561**	**17 199**	**23 399**	**0**	**0**	**0**	**0**	**0**
5100 Taxes on production, sale, transfer, etc	19	2 464	5 589	10 127	15 674	..	..	..	..	..
5110 General taxes	0	0	0	6 003	11 346	..	..	..	..	..
5120 Taxes on specific goods and services	19	2 464	5 589	4 124	4 328	..	..	..	..	..
5130 Unallocable between 5110 and 5120	0	0	0	0	0	..	..	..	..	..
5200 Taxes on use of goods and perform activities	17	1 754	1 972	7 072	7 725	..	..	..	..	..
5300 Unallocable between 5100 and 5200	0	0	0	0	0	..	..	..	..	..
6000 Other taxes	**0**	**198**	**4 474**	**6 207**	**7 396**	**0**	**0**	**0**	**0**	**0**
6100 Paid solely by business	..	0	0	0	0	..	..	..	..	..
6200 Other	..	198	4 474	6 207	7 396	..	..	..	..	..
Total tax revenue	**159**	**15 316**	**35 977**	**70 978**	**90 460**	**13**	**9 913**	**43 902**	**104 693**	**140 071**

.. Not available

StatLink https://stat.link/velpcw

Table 6.22. Latvia, tax revenues by sub-sectors of government

Million EUR

	Central government					State/Regional				
	1975	1995	2005	2015	2019	1975	1995	2005	2015	2019
1000 Taxes on income, profits and capital gains	**..**	**68**	**453**	**677**	**438**	**..**	**..**	**..**	**..**	**..**
1100 Of individuals	..	0	195	289	390	..	..	..	..	..
1200 Corporate	..	68	258	389	48	..	..	..	..	..
1300 Unallocable between 1100 and 1200	..	0	0	0	0	..	..	..	..	..
2000 Social security contributions	**..**	**0**	**0**	**0**	**100**	**..**	**..**	**..**	**..**	**..**
2100 Employees	..	..	..	..	100	..	..	..	..	..
2200 Employers	..	..	..	..	0	..	..	..	..	..
2300 Self-employed or non-employed	..	..	..	..	0	..	..	..	..	..
2400 Unallocable between 2100, 2200 and 2300	..	..	..	..	0	..	..	..	..	..
3000 Taxes on payroll and workforce	**..**	**0**	**4**	**3**	**3**	**..**	**..**	**..**	**..**	**..**
4000 Taxes on property	**..**	**4**	**48**	**44**	**48**	**..**	**..**	**..**	**..**	**..**
4100 Recurrent taxes on immovable property	..	0	0	0	0	..	..	..	..	..
4200 Recurrent taxes on net wealth	..	0	0	0	0	..	..	..	..	..
4300 Estate, inheritance and gift taxes	..	0	0	3	3	..	..	..	..	..
4400 Taxes on financial and capital transactions	..	4	48	42	45	..	..	..	..	..
4500 Non-recurrent taxes	..	0	0	0	0	..	..	..	..	..
4600 Other recurrent taxes on property	..	0	0	0	0	..	..	..	..	..
5000 Taxes on goods and services	**..**	**453**	**1 553**	**3 156**	**4 213**	**..**	**..**	**..**	**..**	**..**
5100 Taxes on production, sale, transfer, etc	..	453	1 510	2 997	3 921	..	..	..	..	..
5110 General taxes	..	343	1 002	2 130	2 783	..	..	..	..	..
5120 Taxes on specific goods and services	..	110	508	867	1 139	..	..	..	..	..
5130 Unallocable between 5110 and 5120	..	0	0	0	0	..	..	..	..	..
5200 Taxes on use of goods and perform activities	..	1	43	159	291	..	..	..	..	..
5300 Unallocable between 5100 and 5200	..	0	0	0	0	..	..	..	..	..
6000 Other taxes	**..**	**0**	**0**	**0**	**0**	**..**	**..**	**..**	**..**	**..**
6100 Paid solely by business	..	..	..	..	..	..	..	..	..	..
6200 Other	..	..	..	..	..	..	..	..	..	..
Total tax revenue	**..**	**525**	**2 058**	**3 881**	**4 801**	**..**	**..**	**..**	**..**	**..**

	Local government					Social Security Funds				
	1975	1995	2005	2015	2019	1975	1995	2005	2015	2019
1000 Taxes on income, profits and capital gains	**..**	**197**	**538**	**1 156**	**1 588**	**..**	**0**	**0**	**0**	**0**
1100 Of individuals	..	197	538	1 156	1 588	..	..	..	..	..
1200 Corporate	..	0	0	0	0	..	..	..	..	..
1300 Unallocable between 1100 and 1200	..	0	0	0	0	..	..	..	..	..
2000 Social security contributions	**..**	**0**	**0**	**0**	**0**	**..**	**445**	**1 079**	**2 030**	**2 811**
2100 Employees	..	..	..	..	..	..	12	292	585	747
2200 Employers	..	..	..	..	..	..	433	781	1 432	2 037
2300 Self-employed or non-employed	..	..	..	..	..	..	1	7	12	27
2400 Unallocable between 2100, 2200 and 2300	..	..	..	..	..	..	0	0	0	0
3000 Taxes on payroll and workforce	**..**	**0**	**0**	**0**	**0**	**..**	**0**	**0**	**0**	**0**
4000 Taxes on property	**..**	**37**	**88**	**197**	**226**	**..**	**0**	**0**	**4**	**9**
4100 Recurrent taxes on immovable property	..	37	88	197	226	..	..	0	0	0
4200 Recurrent taxes on net wealth	..	0	0	0	0	..	..	0	0	0
4300 Estate, inheritance and gift taxes	..	0	0	0	0	..	..	0	4	9
4400 Taxes on financial and capital transactions	..	0	0	0	0	..	..	0	0	0
4500 Non-recurrent taxes	..	0	0	0	0	..	..	0	0	0
4600 Other recurrent taxes on property	..	0	0	0	0	..	..	0	0	0
5000 Taxes on goods and services	**..**	**2**	**8**	**18**	**23**	**..**	**0**	**0**	**0**	**0**
5100 Taxes on production, sale, transfer, etc	..	0	5	7	10	..	..	..	..	..
5110 General taxes	..	0	0	0	0	..	..	..	..	..
5120 Taxes on specific goods and services	..	0	5	7	10	..	..	..	..	..
5130 Unallocable between 5110 and 5120	..	0	0	0	0	..	..	..	..	..
5200 Taxes on use of goods and perform activities	..	2	3	11	13	..	..	..	..	..
5300 Unallocable between 5100 and 5200	..	0	0	0	0	..	..	..	..	..
6000 Other taxes	**..**	**0**	**0**	**0**	**0**	**..**	**0**	**0**	**0**	**0**
6100 Paid solely by business	..	..	..	..	..	..	..	..	..	..
6200 Other	..	..	..	..	..	..	..	..	..	..
Total tax revenue	**..**	**236**	**634**	**1 371**	**1 838**	**..**	**445**	**1 079**	**2 034**	**2 820**

.. Not available

Note: Including taxes collected on behalf of the European Union.

StatLink https://stat.link/xshwlz

Table 6.23. Lithuania, tax revenues by sub-sectors of government

Million EUR

	Central government					State/Regional				
	1975	1995	2005	2015	2019	1975	1995	2005	2015	2019
1000 Taxes on income, profits and capital gains	..	**646**	**1 871**	**2 013**	**4 288**	..	..	..	..	..
1100 Of individuals	..	487	1 435	1 440	3 529	..	..	..	..	..
1200 Corporate	..	160	437	574	759	..	..	..	..	..
1300 Unallocable between 1100 and 1200	..	0	0	0	0	..	..	..	..	..
2000 Social security contributions	..	**0**	**0**	**0**	**0**	..	..	..	..	..
2100 Employees	..	..	..	..	..	..	..	..	..	..
2200 Employers	..	..	..	..	..	..	..	..	..	..
2300 Self-employed or non-employed	..	..	..	..	..	..	..	..	..	..
2400 Unallocable between 2100, 2200 and 2300	..	..	..	..	..	..	..	..	..	..
3000 Taxes on payroll and workforce	..	**0**	**0**	**0**	**0**	..	..	..	..	..
4000 Taxes on property	..	**0**	**0**	**1**	**3**	..	..	..	..	..
4100 Recurrent taxes on immovable property	..	..	..	1	3	..	..	..	..	..
4200 Recurrent taxes on net wealth	..	..	..	0	0	..	..	..	..	..
4300 Estate, inheritance and gift taxes	..	..	..	0	0	..	..	..	..	..
4400 Taxes on financial and capital transactions	..	..	..	0	0	..	..	..	..	..
4500 Non-recurrent taxes	..	..	..	0	0	..	..	..	..	..
4600 Other recurrent taxes on property	..	..	..	0	0	..	..	..	..	..
5000 Taxes on goods and services	..	**892**	**2 273**	**4 220**	**5 484**	..	..	..	..	..
5100 Taxes on production, sale, transfer, etc	..	869	2 235	4 164	5 411	..	..	..	..	..
5110 General taxes	..	635	1 584	2 913	3 876	..	..	..	..	..
5120 Taxes on specific goods and services	..	234	651	1 252	1 535	..	..	..	..	..
5130 Unallocable between 5110 and 5120	..	0	0	0	0	..	..	..	..	..
5200 Taxes on use of goods and perform activities	..	24	38	56	73	..	..	..	..	..
5300 Unallocable between 5100 and 5200	..	0	0	0	0	..	..	..	..	..
6000 Other taxes	..	**0**	**0**	**0**	**0**	..	..	..	..	..
6100 Paid solely by business	..	..	..	..	..	..	..	..	..	..
6200 Other	..	..	..	..	..	..	..	..	..	..
Total tax revenue	..	**1 539**	**4 145**	**6 235**	**9 775**	..	..	..	..	..

	Local government					Social Security Funds				
	1975	1995	2005	2015	2019	1975	1995	2005	2015	2019
1000 Taxes on income, profits and capital gains	..	**0**	**0**	**0**	**0**	..	**0**	**0**	**0**	**0**
1100 Of individuals	..	..	..	..	..	..	..	..	..	..
1200 Corporate	..	..	..	..	..	..	..	..	..	..
1300 Unallocable between 1100 and 1200	..	..	..	..	..	..	..	..	..	..
2000 Social security contributions	..	**0**	**0**	**0**	**0**	..	**559**	**1 864**	**4 338**	**4 706**
2100 Employees	..	..	..	..	..	..	17	154	873	3 574
2200 Employers	..	..	..	..	..	..	537	1 522	2 916	359
2300 Self-employed or non-employed	..	..	..	..	..	..	4	188	549	773
2400 Unallocable between 2100, 2200 and 2300	..	..	..	..	..	..	0	0	0	0
3000 Taxes on payroll and workforce	..	**0**	**0**	**0**	**0**	..	**0**	**0**	**0**	**0**
4000 Taxes on property	..	**25**	**72**	**125**	**143**	..	**0**	**0**	**0**	**0**
4100 Recurrent taxes on immovable property	..	25	71	124	141	..	..	..	..	..
4200 Recurrent taxes on net wealth	..	0	0	0	0	..	..	..	..	..
4300 Estate, inheritance and gift taxes	..	0	1	1	2	..	..	..	..	..
4400 Taxes on financial and capital transactions	..	0	0	0	0	..	..	..	..	..
4500 Non-recurrent taxes	..	0	0	0	0	..	..	..	..	..
4600 Other recurrent taxes on property	..	0	0	0	0	..	..	..	..	..
5000 Taxes on goods and services	..	**23**	**17**	**18**	**27**	..	**0**	**0**	**0**	**0**
5100 Taxes on production, sale, transfer, etc	..	0	0	0	0	..	..	..	..	..
5110 General taxes	..	..	..	..	..	..	..	..	..	..
5120 Taxes on specific goods and services	..	..	..	..	..	..	..	..	..	..
5130 Unallocable between 5110 and 5120	..	..	..	..	..	..	..	..	..	..
5200 Taxes on use of goods and perform activities	..	23	17	18	27	..	..	..	..	..
5300 Unallocable between 5100 and 5200	..	0	0	0	0	..	..	..	..	..
6000 Other taxes	..	**0**	**0**	**0**	**0**	..	**0**	**0**	**0**	**0**
6100 Paid solely by business	..	..	..	..	..	..	..	..	..	..
6200 Other	..	..	..	..	..	..	..	..	..	..
Total tax revenue	..	**48**	**89**	**143**	**169**	..	**559**	**1 864**	**4 338**	**4 706**

.. Not available

Note: Including taxes collected on behalf of the European Union.

StatLink https://stat.link/njbw1l

Table 6.24. Luxembourg, tax revenues by sub-sectors of government

Million EUR

	Central government					State/Regional				
	1975	1995	2005	2015	2019	1975	1995	2005	2015	2019
1000 Taxes on income, profits and capital gains	**353**	**1 873**	**3 454**	**6 405**	**8 568**	..	..	..	..	..
1100 Of individuals	254	1 214	2 161	4 716	5 917	..	..	..	..	..
1200 Corporate	99	659	1 293	1 689	2 652	..	..	..	..	..
1300 Unallocable between 1100 and 1200	0	0	0	0	0	..	..	..	..	..
2000 Social security contributions	**4**	**20**	**89**	**150**	**180**	..	..	..	..	..
2100 Employees	3	15	89	150	180	..	..	..	..	..
2200 Employers	0	0	0	0	0	..	..	..	..	..
2300 Self-employed or non-employed	1	5	0	0	0	..	..	..	..	..
2400 Unallocable between 2100, 2200 and 2300	0	0	0	0	0	..	..	..	..	..
3000 Taxes on payroll and workforce	**0**	**0**	**0**	**0**	**0**	..	..	..	..	..
4000 Taxes on property	**42**	**371**	**928**	**1 661**	**2 351**	..	..	..	..	..
4100 Recurrent taxes on immovable property	0	0	0	0	0	..	..	..	..	..
4200 Recurrent taxes on net wealth	21	268	698	1 318	1 844	..	..	..	..	..
4300 Estate, inheritance and gift taxes	3	15	44	74	114	..	..	..	..	..
4400 Taxes on financial and capital transactions	18	88	186	269	393	..	..	..	..	..
4500 Non-recurrent taxes	0	0	0	0	0	..	..	..	..	..
4600 Other recurrent taxes on property	0	0	0	0	0	..	..	..	..	..
5000 Taxes on goods and services	**189**	**1 374**	**3 241**	**4 466**	**5 596**	..	..	..	..	..
5100 Taxes on production, sale, transfer, etc	182	1 350	3 202	4 381	5 501	..	..	..	..	..
5110 General taxes	112	670	1 812	2 946	3 699	..	..	..	..	..
5120 Taxes on specific goods and services	70	680	1 390	1 435	1 803	..	..	..	..	..
5130 Unallocable between 5110 and 5120	0	0	0	0	0	..	..	..	..	..
5200 Taxes on use of goods and perform activities	7	23	39	85	95	..	..	..	..	..
5300 Unallocable between 5100 and 5200	0	0	0	0	0	..	..	..	..	..
6000 Other taxes	**0**	**6**	**11**	**27**	**28**	..	..	..	..	..
6100 Paid solely by business	..	6	10	27	28	..	..	..	..	..
6200 Other	..	0	0	0	0	..	..	..	..	..
Total tax revenue	**588**	**3 644**	**7 722**	**12 708**	**16 724**	..	..	..	..	..

	Local government					Social Security Funds				
	1975	1995	2005	2015	2019	1975	1995	2005	2015	2019
1000 Taxes on income, profits and capital gains	**46**	**331**	**460**	**606**	**1 110**	**0**	**0**	**0**	**0**	**0**
1100 Of individuals	0	0	0	0	0	..	..	..	..	..
1200 Corporate	46	331	460	606	1 110	..	..	..	..	..
1300 Unallocable between 1100 and 1200	0	0	0	0	0	..	..	..	..	..
2000 Social security contributions	**0**	**0**	**0**	**0**	**0**	**268**	**1 460**	**3 086**	**5 399**	**6 674**
2100 Employees	..	..	..	..	..	102	577	1 321	2 348	2 979
2200 Employers	..	..	..	..	..	150	684	1 378	2 335	2 844
2300 Self-employed or non-employed	..	..	..	..	..	16	200	387	715	851
2400 Unallocable between 2100, 2200 and 2300	..	..	..	..	..	0	0	0	0	0
3000 Taxes on payroll and workforce	**9**	**0**	**0**	**0**	**0**	**0**	**0**	**0**	**0**	**0**
4000 Taxes on property	**6**	**21**	**35**	**54**	**65**	**0**	**0**	**0**	**0**	**0**
4100 Recurrent taxes on immovable property	6	17	26	36	38	..	..	..	..	..
4200 Recurrent taxes on net wealth	0	0	0	0	0	..	..	..	..	..
4300 Estate, inheritance and gift taxes	0	0	0	0	0	..	..	..	..	..
4400 Taxes on financial and capital transactions	0	4	10	18	27	..	..	..	..	..
4500 Non-recurrent taxes	0	0	0	0	0	..	..	..	..	..
4600 Other recurrent taxes on property	0	0	0	0	0	..	..	..	..	..
5000 Taxes on goods and services	**1**	**4**	**8**	**10**	**11**	**0**	**0**	**0**	**0**	**0**
5100 Taxes on production, sale, transfer, etc	1	3	7	8	9	..	..	..	..	..
5110 General taxes	0	0	0	0	0	..	..	..	..	..
5120 Taxes on specific goods and services	1	3	7	8	9	..	..	..	..	..
5130 Unallocable between 5110 and 5120	0	0	0	0	0	..	..	..	..	..
5200 Taxes on use of goods and perform activities	0	1	1	1	1	..	..	..	..	..
5300 Unallocable between 5100 and 5200	0	0	0	0	0	..	..	..	..	..
6000 Other taxes	**0**	**1**	**2**	**1**	**2**	**0**	**0**	**0**	**0**	**0**
6100 Paid solely by business	..	1	2	1	2	..	..	..	..	..
6200 Other	..	0	0	0	0	..	..	..	..	..
Total tax revenue	**62**	**357**	**505**	**671**	**1 186**	**268**	**1 460**	**3 086**	**5 399**	**6 674**

.. Not available

Note: Including taxes collected on behalf of the European Union.

StatLink https://stat.link/fwux3i

Table 6.25. Mexico, tax revenues by sub-sectors of government

Million MXN

	Federal government					State/Regional				
	1975	1995	2005	2015	2019	1975	1995	2005	2015	2019
1000 Taxes on income, profits and capital gains	..	**76 148**	**402 036**	**1 230 555**	**1 694 143**	..	**1**	**0**	**0**	**0**
1100 Of individuals	..	..	195 869	609 384	829 501	..	..	..	..	..
1200 Corporate	..	..	135 840	592 443	803 643	..	..	..	..	..
1300 Unallocable between 1100 and 1200	..	76 148	70 327	28 728	60 999	..	1	..	..	..
2000 Social security contributions	..	**0**	**0**	**0**	**0**	..	**0**	**0**	**0**	**0**
2100 Employees	..	..	..	..	..	..	..	..	..	..
2200 Employers	..	..	..	..	..	..	..	..	..	..
2300 Self-employed or non-employed	..	..	..	..	..	..	..	..	..	..
2400 Unallocable between 2100, 2200 and 2300	..	..	..	..	..	..	..	..	..	..
3000 Taxes on payroll and workforce	..	**0**	**0**	**0**	**0**	..	**2 976**	**20 429**	**70 221**	**101 284**
4000 Taxes on property	..	**0**	**0**	**0**	**0**	..	**2 927**	**10 905**	**22 481**	**29 206**
4100 Recurrent taxes on immovable property	..	..	..	..	..	..	2 198	6 544	14 245	19 059
4200 Recurrent taxes on net wealth	..	..	..	..	..	..	0	0	0	0
4300 Estate, inheritance and gift taxes	..	..	..	..	..	..	2	0	0	0
4400 Taxes on financial and capital transactions	..	..	..	..	..	..	727	4 361	8 235	10 147
4500 Non-recurrent taxes	..	..	..	..	..	..	0	0	0	0
4600 Other recurrent taxes on property	..	..	..	..	..	..	0	0	0	0
5000 Taxes on goods and services	..	**91 452**	**416 533**	**1 116 026**	**1 477 876**	..	**441**	**2 124**	**24 355**	**25 198**
5100 Taxes on production, sale, transfer, etc	..	88 372	401 580	1 115 525	1 477 157	..	22	1 364	4 357	8 443
5110 General taxes	..	51 785	318 432	707 213	933 327	..	0	0	0	0
5120 Taxes on specific goods and services	..	36 587	83 148	408 312	543 831	..	22	1 364	4 357	8 443
5130 Unallocable between 5110 and 5120	..	0	0	0	0	..	0	0	0	0
5200 Taxes on use of goods and perform activities	..	3 080	14 954	501	719	..	419	760	19 998	16 754
5300 Unallocable between 5100 and 5200	..	0	0	0	0	..	0	0	0	0
6000 Other taxes	..	**5 149**	**8 616**	**27 379**	**41 142**	..	**228**	**1 537**	**6 489**	**8 061**
6100 Paid solely by business	..	0	0	0	0	..	0	0	0	0
6200 Other	..	5 149	8 616	27 379	41 142	..	228	1 537	6 489	8 061
Total tax revenue (collecting government)	..	**172 749**	**827 186**	**2 373 960**	**3 213 161**	..	**6 573**	**34 995**	**123 545**	**163 749**
Adjustment[1]	..	**-49 115**	**-278 892**	**-629 130**	**0**	..	**39 225**	**218 291**	**494 239**	**688 920**
Total tax revenue (beneficiary government)	..	..	..	..	..	..	..	..	..	..

	Local government					Social Security Funds				
	1975	1995	2005	2015	2019	1975	1995	2005	2015	2019
1000 Taxes on income, profits and capital gains	..	**16**	**0**	**0**	**0**	..	**0**	**0**	**0**	**0**
1100 Of individuals	..	..	..	..	..	..	..	..	..	..
1200 Corporate	..	..	..	..	..	..	..	..	..	..
1300 Unallocable between 1100 and 1200	..	16	..	..	..	..	..	..	..	..
2000 Social security contributions	..	**0**	**0**	**0**	**0**	..	**50 871**	**206 551**	**409 249**	**552 058**
2100 Employees	..	..	..	..	..	..	..	..	..	..
2200 Employers	..	..	..	..	..	..	..	..	..	..
2300 Self-employed or non-employed	..	..	..	..	..	..	..	..	..	..
2400 Unallocable between 2100, 2200 and 2300	..	..	..	..	..	..	50 871	206 551	409 249	552 058
3000 Taxes on payroll and workforce	..	**6**	**32**	**1**	**0**	..	**0**	**0**	**0**	**0**
4000 Taxes on property	..	**2 702**	**15 891**	**35 193**	**50 056**	..	**0**	**0**	**0**	**0**
4100 Recurrent taxes on immovable property	..	1 854	10 098	23 715	31 481	..	..	..	..	..
4200 Recurrent taxes on net wealth	..	0	0	0	0	..	..	..	..	..
4300 Estate, inheritance and gift taxes	..	0	0	0	0	..	..	..	..	..
4400 Taxes on financial and capital transactions	..	848	5 793	11 477	18 575	..	..	..	..	..
4500 Non-recurrent taxes	..	0	0	0	0	..	..	..	..	..
4600 Other recurrent taxes on property	..	0	0	0	0	..	..	..	..	..
5000 Taxes on goods and services	..	**582**	**288**	**789**	**1 179**	..	**0**	**0**	**0**	**0**
5100 Taxes on production, sale, transfer, etc	..	575	214	728	1 158	..	..	..	..	..
5110 General taxes	..	0	0	0	0	..	..	..	..	..
5120 Taxes on specific goods and services	..	572	214	728	1 158	..	..	..	..	..
5130 Unallocable between 5110 and 5120	..	3	0	0	0	..	..	..	..	..
5200 Taxes on use of goods and perform activities	..	7	74	61	21	..	..	..	..	..
5300 Unallocable between 5100 and 5200	..	0	0	0	0	..	..	..	..	..
6000 Other taxes	..	**179**	**1 539**	**10 743**	**15 451**	..	**0**	**0**	**0**	**0**
6100 Paid solely by business	..	0	0	0	0	..	..	..	..	..
6200 Other	..	179	1 539	10 743	15 451	..	..	..	..	..
Total tax revenue (collecting government)	..	**3 485**	**17 750**	**46 726**	**66 686**	..	**50 871**	**206 551**	**409 249**	**552 058**
Adjustment[1]	..	**9 890**	**60 601**	**134 892**	**190 425**	..	**0**	**0**	**0**	**0**
Total tax revenue (beneficiary government)	..	..	..	..	..	..	..	..	..	..

.. Not available

1. This adjustment is for taxes collected by Federal government in which States and Local governments have a share. Sub-central government's shares cannot be identified by type of tax.

StatLink https://stat.link/vs7wgo

Table 6.26. Netherlands, tax revenues by sub-sectors of government

Million EUR

	Central government					State/Regional				
	1975	1995	2005	2015	2019	1975	1995	2005	2015	2019
1000 Taxes on income, profits and capital gains	**15 075**	**33 520**	**52 640**	**70 849**	**99 003**	**..**	**..**	**..**	**..**	**..**
1100 Of individuals	11 713	23 557	33 905	52 405	68 968	..	..	..	..	..
1200 Corporate	3 361	9 963	18 735	18 444	30 035	..	..	..	..	..
1300 Unallocable between 1100 and 1200	0	0	0	0	0	..	..	..	..	..
2000 Social security contributions	**0**	**0**	**0**	**0**	**0**	**..**	**..**	**..**	**..**	**..**
2100 Employees	..	..	..	..	..	..	..	..	..	..
2200 Employers	..	..	..	..	..	..	..	..	..	..
2300 Self-employed or non-employed	..	..	..	..	..	..	..	..	..	..
2400 Unallocable between 2100, 2200 and 2300	..	..	..	..	..	..	..	..	..	..
3000 Taxes on payroll and workforce	**0**	**0**	**0**	**0**	**0**	**..**	**..**	**..**	**..**	**..**
4000 Taxes on property	**767**	**2 880**	**6 235**	**4 731**	**6 480**	**..**	**..**	**..**	**..**	**..**
4100 Recurrent taxes on immovable property	50	0	0	1 345	1 686	..	..	..	..	..
4200 Recurrent taxes on net wealth	231	671	60	0	0	..	..	..	..	..
4300 Estate, inheritance and gift taxes	163	773	1 709	1 614	1 777	..	..	..	..	..
4400 Taxes on financial and capital transactions	323	1 436	4 466	1 772	3 017	..	..	..	..	..
4500 Non-recurrent taxes	0	0	0	0	0	..	..	..	..	..
4600 Other recurrent taxes on property	0	0	0	0	0	..	..	..	..	..
5000 Taxes on goods and services	**9 716**	**31 892**	**57 116**	**70 161**	**89 225**	**..**	**..**	**..**	**..**	**..**
5100 Taxes on production, sale, transfer, etc	9 113	29 728	54 658	65 990	84 464	..	..	..	..	..
5110 General taxes	6 257	19 832	36 950	44 879	58 115	..	..	..	..	..
5120 Taxes on specific goods and services	2 856	9 896	17 708	21 111	26 349	..	..	..	..	..
5130 Unallocable between 5110 and 5120	0	0	0	0	0	..	..	..	..	..
5200 Taxes on use of goods and perform activities	604	2 164	2 458	4 171	4 761	..	..	..	..	..
5300 Unallocable between 5100 and 5200	0	0	0	0	0	..	..	..	..	..
6000 Other taxes	**109**	**491**	**989**	**416**	**778**	**..**	**..**	**..**	**..**	**..**
6100 Paid solely by business	109	448	372	0	0	..	..	..	..	..
6200 Other	0	43	617	416	778	..	..	..	..	..
Total tax revenue	**25 667**	**68 783**	**116 980**	**146 157**	**195 486**	**..**	**..**	**..**	**..**	**..**

	Local government					Social Security Funds				
	1975	1995	2005	2015	2019	1975	1995	2005	2015	2019
1000 Taxes on income, profits and capital gains	**77**	**0**	**0**	**0**	**0**	**0**	**0**	**0**	**0**	**0**
1100 Of individuals	77	0	0	0	0	0	0	0	0	0
1200 Corporate	0	0	0	0	0	0	0	0	0	0
1300 Unallocable between 1100 and 1200	0	0	0	0	0	0	0	0	0	0
2000 Social security contributions	**0**	**0**	**0**	**0**	**0**	**16 732**	**48 532**	**66 547**	**96 426**	**109 298**
2100 Employees	..	..	..	..	..	7 139	32 795	35 383	48 213	40 695
2200 Employers	..	..	..	..	..	7 687	5 941	20 595	34 614	43 693
2300 Self-employed or non-employed	..	..	..	..	..	1 905	9 796	10 569	13 599	24 910
2400 Unallocable between 2100, 2200 and 2300	..	..	..	..	..	0	0	0	0	0
3000 Taxes on payroll and workforce	**0**	**0**	**0**	**0**	**0**	**0**	**0**	**0**	**0**	**0**
4000 Taxes on property	**272**	**2 287**	**4 341**	**5 037**	**5 699**	**0**	**0**	**0**	**0**	**0**
4100 Recurrent taxes on immovable property	272	2 287	4 341	5 037	5 699	..	..	..	..	..
4200 Recurrent taxes on net wealth	0	0	0	0	0	..	..	..	..	..
4300 Estate, inheritance and gift taxes	0	0	0	0	0	..	..	..	..	..
4400 Taxes on financial and capital transactions	0	0	0	0	0	..	..	..	..	..
4500 Non-recurrent taxes	0	0	0	0	0	..	..	..	..	..
4600 Other recurrent taxes on property	0	0	0	0	0	..	..	..	..	..
5000 Taxes on goods and services	**153**	**1 533**	**3 330**	**4 652**	**5 169**	**0**	**0**	**0**	**0**	**0**
5100 Taxes on production, sale, transfer, etc	14	59	118	249	413	..	..	..	..	..
5110 General taxes	0	6	10	43	71	..	..	..	..	..
5120 Taxes on specific goods and services	14	53	108	206	342	..	..	..	..	..
5130 Unallocable between 5110 and 5120	0	0	0	0	0	..	..	..	..	..
5200 Taxes on use of goods and perform activities	139	1 474	3 212	4 403	4 756	..	..	..	..	..
5300 Unallocable between 5100 and 5200	0	0	0	0	0	..	..	..	..	..
6000 Other taxes	**0**	**0**	**0**	**0**	**0**	**0**	**0**	**0**	**0**	**0**
6100 Paid solely by business	..	..	..	..	..	..	..	..	..	..
6200 Other	..	..	..	..	..	..	..	..	..	..
Total tax revenue	**502**	**3 820**	**7 671**	**9 689**	**10 868**	**16 732**	**48 532**	**66 547**	**96 426**	**109 298**

.. Not available

Note: Including taxes collected on behalf of the European Union.

StatLink https://stat.link/xyji6d

Table 6.27. New Zealand, tax revenues by sub-sectors of government

Million NZD

	Central government					State/Regional				
	1975	1995	2005	2015	2019	1975	1995	2005	2015	2019
1000 Taxes on income, profits and capital gains	**2 296**	**21 253**	**37 379**	**44 723**	**55 016**	..	..	..	..	..
1100 Of individuals	1 874	15 626	24 373	30 297	39 677	..	..	..	..	..
1200 Corporate	407	4 122	9 957	11 407	12 415	..	..	..	..	..
1300 Unallocable between 1100 and 1200	16	1 505	3 049	3 019	2 924	..	..	..	..	..
2000 Social security contributions	**0**	**0**	**0**	**0**	**0**	..	..	..	..	..
2100 Employees	..	0	0	0	0	..	..	..	..	..
2200 Employers	..	0	0	0	0	..	..	..	..	..
2300 Self-employed or non-employed	..	0	0	0	0	..	..	..	..	..
2400 Unallocable between 2100, 2200 and 2300	..	0	0	0	0	..	..	..	..	..
3000 Taxes on payroll and workforce	**0**	**0**	**0**	**0**	**0**	..	..	..	..	..
4000 Taxes on property	**83**	**218**	**86**	**84**	**101**	..	..	..	..	..
4100 Recurrent taxes on immovable property	3	-1	0	0	0	..	..	..	..	..
4200 Recurrent taxes on net wealth	0	0	0	0	0	..	..	..	..	..
4300 Estate, inheritance and gift taxes	54	3	3	0	0	..	..	..	..	..
4400 Taxes on financial and capital transactions	25	216	83	84	101	..	..	..	..	..
4500 Non-recurrent taxes	0	0	0	0	0	..	..	..	..	..
4600 Other recurrent taxes on property	0	0	0	0	0	..	..	..	..	..
5000 Taxes on goods and services	**807**	**11 395**	**18 744**	**31 146**	**37 771**	..	..	..	..	..
5100 Taxes on production, sale, transfer, etc	770	10 833	17 792	29 551	35 829	..	..	..	..	..
5110 General taxes	311	7 895	14 133	24 587	30 259	..	..	..	..	..
5120 Taxes on specific goods and services	459	2 938	3 659	4 964	5 570	..	..	..	..	..
5130 Unallocable between 5110 and 5120	0	0	0	0	0	..	..	..	..	..
5200 Taxes on use of goods and perform activities	37	562	952	1 595	1 942	..	..	..	..	..
5300 Unallocable between 5100 and 5200	0	0	0	0	0	..	..	..	..	..
6000 Other taxes	**0**	**0**	**14**	**2**	**2**	..	..	..	..	..
6100 Paid solely by business	..	..	0	0	0	..	..	..	..	..
6200 Other	..	..	14	2	2	..	..	..	..	..
Total tax revenue	**3 186**	**32 866**	**56 223**	**75 955**	**92 890**	..	..	..	..	..

	Local government					Social Security Funds				
	1975	1995	2005	2015	2019	1975	1995	2005	2015	2019
1000 Taxes on income, profits and capital gains	**0**	**0**	**0**	**0**	**0**	**0**	**0**	**0**	**0**	**0**
1100 Of individuals	0	..	..	..	..	0	..	..	..	..
1200 Corporate	0	..	..	..	..	0	..	..	..	..
1300 Unallocable between 1100 and 1200	0	..	..	..	..	0	..	..	..	..
2000 Social security contributions	**0**	**0**	**0**	**0**	**0**	**0**	**0**	**0**	**0**	**0**
2100 Employees	..	0	0	0	0	..	0	0	0	0
2200 Employers	..	0	0	0	0	..	0	0	0	0
2300 Self-employed or non-employed	..	0	0	0	0	..	0	0	0	0
2400 Unallocable between 2100, 2200 and 2300	..	0	0	0	0	..	0	0	0	0
3000 Taxes on payroll and workforce	**0**	**0**	**0**	**0**	**0**	**0**	**0**	**0**	**0**	**0**
4000 Taxes on property	**237**	**1 646**	**2 825**	**4 962**	**6 055**	**0**	**0**	**0**	**0**	**0**
4100 Recurrent taxes on immovable property	237	1 646	2 825	4 962	6 055	..	..	..	..	..
4200 Recurrent taxes on net wealth	0	0	0	0	0	..	..	..	..	..
4300 Estate, inheritance and gift taxes	0	0	0	0	0	..	..	..	..	..
4400 Taxes on financial and capital transactions	0	0	0	0	0	..	..	..	..	..
4500 Non-recurrent taxes	0	0	0	0	0	..	..	..	..	..
4600 Other recurrent taxes on property	0	0	0	0	0	..	..	..	..	..
5000 Taxes on goods and services	**29**	**184**	**310**	**582**	**847**	**0**	**0**	**0**	**0**	**0**
5100 Taxes on production, sale, transfer, etc	18	33	30	33	175	..	..	..	..	..
5110 General taxes	0	0	0	0	0	..	..	..	..	..
5120 Taxes on specific goods and services	18	33	30	33	175	..	..	..	..	..
5130 Unallocable between 5110 and 5120	0	0	0	0	0	..	..	..	..	..
5200 Taxes on use of goods and perform activities	11	151	280	549	672	..	..	..	..	..
5300 Unallocable between 5100 and 5200	0	0	0	0	0	..	..	..	..	..
6000 Other taxes	**0**	**0**	**0**	**0**	**0**	**0**	**0**	**0**	**0**	**0**
6100 Paid solely by business	..	..	..	..	..	..	..	..	..	..
6200 Other	..	..	..	..	..	..	..	..	..	..
Total tax revenue	**266**	**1 830**	**3 135**	**5 544**	**6 902**	**0**	**0**	**0**	**0**	**0**

.. Not available

StatLink https://stat.link/0t91up

Table 6.28. Norway, tax revenues by sub-sectors of government

Million NOK

	Central government[1]					State/Regional				
	1975	1995	2005	2015	2019	1975	1995	2005	2015	2019
1000 Taxes on income, profits and capital gains	**6 495**	**67 402**	**316 851**	**314 792**	**389 115**	..	..	..	..	..
1100 Of individuals	5 424	38 059	87 503	174 617	179 459	..	..	..	..	..
1200 Corporate	1 071	29 343	229 348	140 175	209 656	..	..	..	..	..
1300 Unallocable between 1100 and 1200	0	0	0	0	0	..	..	..	..	..
2000 Social security contributions	**1 341**	**6 013**	**173 151**	**325 130**	**377 427**	..	..	..	..	..
2100 Employees	331	1 233	58 320	112 662	131 039	..	..	..	..	..
2200 Employers	1 010	4 780	104 794	190 923	221 175	..	..	..	..	..
2300 Self-employed or non-employed	0	0	10 037	21 545	25 213	..	..	..	..	..
2400 Unallocable between 2100, 2200 and 2300	0	0	0	0	0	..	..	..	..	..
3000 Taxes on payroll and workforce	**0**	**0**	**0**	**0**	**2 011**	..	..	..	..	..
4000 Taxes on property	**771**	**3 497**	**11 178**	**12 209**	**17 741**	..	..	..	..	..
4100 Recurrent taxes on immovable property	0	0	0	0	0	..	..	..	..	..
4200 Recurrent taxes on net wealth	490	1 172	4 741	3 488	7 387	..	..	..	..	..
4300 Estate, inheritance and gift taxes	146	975	1 768	295	44	..	..	..	..	..
4400 Taxes on financial and capital transactions	135	1 350	4 669	8 426	10 310	..	..	..	..	..
4500 Non-recurrent taxes	0	0	0	0	0	..	..	..	..	..
4600 Other recurrent taxes on property	0	0	0	0	0	..	..	..	..	..
5000 Taxes on goods and services	**25 056**	**141 645**	**232 462**	**359 255**	**417 237**	..	..	..	..	..
5100 Taxes on production, sale, transfer, etc	24 367	134 965	220 898	342 410	399 022	..	..	..	..	..
5110 General taxes	13 670	81 772	153 820	256 029	308 280	..	..	..	..	..
5120 Taxes on specific goods and services	10 697	53 193	67 078	86 381	90 742	..	..	..	..	..
5130 Unallocable between 5110 and 5120	0	0	0	0	0	..	..	..	..	..
5200 Taxes on use of goods and perform activities	689	6 680	11 564	16 845	18 215	..	..	..	..	..
5300 Unallocable between 5100 and 5200	0	0	0	0	0	..	..	..	..	..
6000 Other taxes	**130**	**15**	**0**	**0**	**0**	..	..	..	..	..
6100 Paid solely by business	124	1	..	..	..	..	..	..	..	..
6200 Other	6	14	..	..	..	..	..	..	..	..
Total tax revenue	**33 793**	**218 572**	**733 642**	**1 011 386**	**1 203 531**	..	..	..	..	..

	Local government					Social Security Funds				
	1975	1995	2005	2015	2019	1975	1995	2005	2015	2019
1000 Taxes on income, profits and capital gains	**13 725**	**67 978**	**100 512**	**160 582**	**190 941**	**2 728**	**0**	**0**	**0**	**0**
1100 Of individuals	12 877	61 784	100 512	160 582	190 941	2 728	..	..	..	..
1200 Corporate	848	6 194	0	0	0	0	..	..	..	..
1300 Unallocable between 1100 and 1200	0	0	0	0	0	0	..	..	..	..
2000 Social security contributions	**0**	**0**	**0**	**0**	**0**	**15 224**	**84 563**	**0**	**0**	**0**
2100 Employees	..	..	..	..	..	2 949	30 417	..	..	..
2200 Employers	..	..	..	..	..	11 315	48 396	..	..	..
2300 Self-employed or non-employed	..	..	..	..	..	960	5 750	..	..	..
2400 Unallocable between 2100, 2200 and 2300	..	..	..	..	..	0	0	..	..	..
3000 Taxes on payroll and workforce	**0**	**0**	**0**	**0**	**0**	**0**	**0**	**0**	**0**	**0**
4000 Taxes on property	**772**	**7 352**	**10 283**	**21 812**	**27 910**	**0**	**0**	**0**	**0**	**0**
4100 Recurrent taxes on immovable property	278	2 792	4 324	11 177	14 748	..	..	..	..	..
4200 Recurrent taxes on net wealth	494	4 560	5 959	10 635	13 162	..	..	..	..	..
4300 Estate, inheritance and gift taxes	0	0	0	0	0	..	..	..	..	..
4400 Taxes on financial and capital transactions	0	0	0	0	0	..	..	..	..	..
4500 Non-recurrent taxes	0	0	0	0	0	..	..	..	..	..
4600 Other recurrent taxes on property	0	0	0	0	0	..	..	..	..	..
5000 Taxes on goods and services	**0**	**431**	**2 281**	**1 574**	**1 676**	**51**	**267**	**0**	**0**	**0**
5100 Taxes on production, sale, transfer, etc	0	0	0	0	0	51	267	..	..	..
5110 General taxes	0	..	..	..	..	0	0	..	..	..
5120 Taxes on specific goods and services	0	..	..	..	..	51	267	..	..	..
5130 Unallocable between 5110 and 5120	0	..	..	..	..	0	0	..	..	..
5200 Taxes on use of goods and perform activities	0	431	2 281	1 574	1 676	0	0	..	..	..
5300 Unallocable between 5100 and 5200	0	0	0	0	0	0	0	..	..	..
6000 Other taxes	**432**	**0**	**0**	**0**	**0**	**0**	**0**	**0**	**0**	**0**
6100 Paid solely by business	0	..	..	..	..	..	..	..	..	..
6200 Other	432	..	..	..	..	..	..	..	..	..
Total tax revenue	**14 929**	**75 761**	**113 076**	**183 968**	**220 527**	**18 003**	**84 830**	**0**	**0**	**0**

.. Not available

1. The Norwegian National Insurance has been integrated into the Central government sector from the year 2000 onwards.

StatLink https://stat.link/dsv0he

Table 6.29. Poland, tax revenues by sub-sectors of government

Million PLN

	Central government					State/Regional				
	1975	1995	2005	2015	2019	1975	1995	2005	2015	2019
1000 Taxes on income, profits and capital gains	**..**	**32 774**	**40 398**	**71 381**	**105 141**	**..**	**..**	**..**	**..**	**..**
1100 Of individuals	..	23 937	24 518	45 462	65 386	..	..	..	..	..
1200 Corporate	..	8 837	15 880	25 919	39 755	..	..	..	..	..
1300 Unallocable between 1100 and 1200	..	0	0	0	0	..	..	..	..	..
2000 Social security contributions	**..**	**0**	**0**	**0**	**0**	**..**	**..**	**..**	**..**	**..**
2100 Employees	..	..	..	..	..	..	..	..	..	..
2200 Employers	..	..	..	..	..	..	..	..	..	..
2300 Self-employed or non-employed	..	..	..	..	..	..	..	..	..	..
2400 Unallocable between 2100, 2200 and 2300	..	..	..	..	..	..	..	..	..	..
3000 Taxes on payroll and workforce	**..**	**831**	**2 555**	**4 028**	**5 928**	**..**	**..**	**..**	**..**	**..**
4000 Taxes on property	**..**	**0**	**0**	**0**	**0**	**..**	**..**	**..**	**..**	**..**
4100 Recurrent taxes on immovable property	..	..	..	..	..	..	..	..	..	..
4200 Recurrent taxes on net wealth	..	..	..	..	..	..	..	..	..	..
4300 Estate, inheritance and gift taxes	..	..	..	..	..	..	..	..	..	..
4400 Taxes on financial and capital transactions	..	..	..	..	..	..	..	..	..	..
4500 Non-recurrent taxes	..	..	..	..	..	..	..	..	..	..
4600 Other recurrent taxes on property	..	..	..	..	..	..	..	..	..	..
5000 Taxes on goods and services	**..**	**43 483**	**120 207**	**207 129**	**285 675**	**..**	**..**	**..**	**..**	**..**
5100 Taxes on production, sale, transfer, etc	..	42 863	119 805	203 303	277 324	..	..	..	..	..
5110 General taxes	..	21 051	75 783	125 895	182 147	..	..	..	..	..
5120 Taxes on specific goods and services	..	21 812	44 022	77 408	95 177	..	..	..	..	..
5130 Unallocable between 5110 and 5120	..	0	0	0	0	..	..	..	..	..
5200 Taxes on use of goods and perform activities	..	620	402	3 826	8 351	..	..	..	..	..
5300 Unallocable between 5100 and 5200	..	0	0	0	0	..	..	..	..	..
6000 Other taxes	**..**	**99**	**18**	**0**	**0**	**..**	**..**	**..**	**..**	**..**
6100 Paid solely by business	..	0	0	..	..	..	..	..	..	..
6200 Other	..	99	18	..	..	..	..	..	..	..
Total tax revenue	**..**	**77 187**	**163 178**	**282 538**	**396 744**	**..**	**..**	**..**	**..**	**..**
	Local government					Social Security Funds				
	1975	1995	2005	2015	2019	1975	1995	2005	2015	2019
1000 Taxes on income, profits and capital gains	**..**	**4 896**	**23 093**	**45 697**	**67 398**	**..**	**0**	**0**	**0**	**0**
1100 Of individuals	..	4 427	17 916	38 512	56 546	..	..	..	..	..
1200 Corporate	..	469	5 177	7 185	10 852	..	..	..	..	..
1300 Unallocable between 1100 and 1200	..	0	0	0	0	..	..	..	..	..
2000 Social security contributions	**..**	**0**	**0**	**0**	**0**	**..**	**38 808**	**121 522**	**225 711**	**305 354**
2100 Employees	..	..	..	..	..	..	16 722	50 150	92 046	127 377
2200 Employers	..	..	..	..	..	..	19 370	46 738	88 490	118 629
2300 Self-employed or non-employed	..	..	..	..	..	..	2 716	24 634	45 175	59 348
2400 Unallocable between 2100, 2200 and 2300	..	..	..	..	..	..	0	0	0	0
3000 Taxes on payroll and workforce	**..**	**0**	**0**	**0**	**0**	**..**	**0**	**0**	**0**	**0**
4000 Taxes on property	**..**	**4 370**	**14 723**	**24 637**	**28 993**	**..**	**0**	**0**	**0**	**0**
4100 Recurrent taxes on immovable property	..	3 579	12 718	22 206	25 201	..	..	..	..	..
4200 Recurrent taxes on net wealth	..	0	0	0	0	..	..	..	..	..
4300 Estate, inheritance and gift taxes	..	44	242	246	325	..	..	..	..	..
4400 Taxes on financial and capital transactions	..	747	1 763	2 185	3 467	..	..	..	..	..
4500 Non-recurrent taxes	..	0	0	0	0	..	..	..	..	..
4600 Other recurrent taxes on property	..	0	0	0	0	..	..	..	..	..
5000 Taxes on goods and services	**..**	**1 340**	**3 492**	**4 139**	**4 005**	**..**	**0**	**0**	**0**	**0**
5100 Taxes on production, sale, transfer, etc	..	0	0	0	0	..	..	..	..	..
5110 General taxes	..	..	..	..	..	..	..	..	..	..
5120 Taxes on specific goods and services	..	..	..	..	..	..	..	..	..	..
5130 Unallocable between 5110 and 5120	..	..	..	..	..	..	..	..	..	..
5200 Taxes on use of goods and perform activities	..	1 340	3 492	4 139	4 005	..	..	..	..	..
5300 Unallocable between 5100 and 5200	..	0	0	0	0	..	..	..	..	..
6000 Other taxes	**..**	**158**	**278**	**647**	**1 123**	**..**	**0**	**0**	**0**	**0**
6100 Paid solely by business	..	0	0	0	0	..	..	..	..	..
6200 Other	..	158	278	647	1 123	..	..	..	..	..
Total tax revenue	**..**	**10 764**	**41 586**	**75 120**	**101 519**	**..**	**38 808**	**121 522**	**225 711**	**305 354**

.. Not available

Note: Including taxes collected on behalf of the European Union.

StatLink https://stat.link/sneyqi

Table 6.30. Portugal, tax revenues by sub-sectors of government

Million EUR

	Central government					State/Regional				
	1975	1995	2005	2015	2019	1975	1995	2005	2015	2019
1000 Taxes on income, profits and capital gains	**81**	**6 557**	**11 576**	**17 516**	**18 896**	..	..	..	..	..
1100 Of individuals	..	4 691	7 694	12 316	12 760	..	..	..	..	..
1200 Corporate	..	1 866	3 761	5 199	6 136	..	..	..	..	..
1300 Unallocable between 1100 and 1200	81	0	121	0	0	..	..	..	..	..
2000 Social security contributions	**0**	**1 560**	**1 887**	**2 064**	**2 052**	..	..	..	..	..
2100 Employees	..	941	1 629	1 867	1 939	..	..	..	..	..
2200 Employers	..	619	259	198	114	..	..	..	..	..
2300 Self-employed or non-employed	..	0	0	0	0	..	..	..	..	..
2400 Unallocable between 2100, 2200 and 2300	..	0	0	0	0	..	..	..	..	..
3000 Taxes on payroll and workforce	**12**	**0**	**0**	**0**	**0**	..	..	..	..	..
4000 Taxes on property	**12**	**226**	**308**	**202**	**508**	..	..	..	..	..
4100 Recurrent taxes on immovable property	0	0	0	6	152	..	..	..	..	..
4200 Recurrent taxes on net wealth	0	0	0	0	0	..	..	..	..	..
4300 Estate, inheritance and gift taxes	4	57	68	0	0	..	..	..	..	..
4400 Taxes on financial and capital transactions	7	169	240	196	356	..	..	..	..	..
4500 Non-recurrent taxes	0	0	0	0	0	..	..	..	..	..
4600 Other recurrent taxes on property	0	0	0	0	0	..	..	..	..	..
5000 Taxes on goods and services	**198**	**10 402**	**19 495**	**21 488**	**26 533**	..	..	..	..	..
5100 Taxes on production, sale, transfer, etc	187	10 195	19 233	20 881	25 501	..	..	..	..	..
5110 General taxes	52	5 481	11 846	13 745	17 170	..	..	..	..	..
5120 Taxes on specific goods and services	135	4 714	7 387	7 136	8 331	..	..	..	..	..
5130 Unallocable between 5110 and 5120	0	0	0	0	0	..	..	..	..	..
5200 Taxes on use of goods and perform activities	12	178	235	594	1 025	..	..	..	..	..
5300 Unallocable between 5100 and 5200	0	30	27	13	6	..	..	..	..	..
6000 Other taxes	**2**	**98**	**431**	**570**	**560**	..	..	..	..	..
6100 Paid solely by business	1	18	143	333	305	..	..	..	..	..
6200 Other	0	81	288	237	255	..	..	..	..	..
Total tax revenue	**304**	**18 844**	**33 697**	**41 840**	**48 549**	..	..	..	..	..
	Local government					Social Security Funds				
	1975	1995	2005	2015	2019	1975	1995	2005	2015	2019
1000 Taxes on income, profits and capital gains	**0**	**307**	**725**	**1 246**	**1 346**	**0**	**0**	**0**	**0**	**0**
1100 Of individuals	..	156	298	832	820	..	..	..	..	..
1200 Corporate	..	151	427	414	526	..	..	..	..	..
1300 Unallocable between 1100 and 1200	0	0	0	0	0	..	..	..	..	..
2000 Social security contributions	**0**	**2**	**7**	**19**	**0**	**161**	**5 267**	**11 133**	**14 099**	**18 497**
2100 Employees	..	2	7	19	..	62	2 100	4 053	5 106	6 234
2200 Employers	..	0	0	0	..	97	3 167	7 080	8 993	12 264
2300 Self-employed or non-employed	..	0	0	0	..	2	0	0	0	0
2400 Unallocable between 2100, 2200 and 2300	..	0	0	0	..	0	0	0	0	0
3000 Taxes on payroll and workforce	**0**	**0**	**0**	**0**	**0**	**0**	**0**	**0**	**0**	**0**
4000 Taxes on property	**0**	**599**	**1 541**	**2 105**	**2 538**	**0**	**0**	**0**	**0**	**0**
4100 Recurrent taxes on immovable property	..	310	827	1 529	1 512	..	..	..	..	..
4200 Recurrent taxes on net wealth	..	0	0	0	0	..	..	..	..	..
4300 Estate, inheritance and gift taxes	..	0	1	0	0	..	..	..	..	..
4400 Taxes on financial and capital transactions	..	289	713	576	1 026	..	..	..	..	..
4500 Non-recurrent taxes	..	0	0	0	0	..	..	..	..	..
4600 Other recurrent taxes on property	..	0	0	0	0	..	..	..	..	..
5000 Taxes on goods and services	**0**	**499**	**962**	**1 132**	**1 420**	**0**	**335**	**823**	**1 179**	**1 102**
5100 Taxes on production, sale, transfer, etc	0	442	827	876	1 123	..	335	823	1 179	1 093
5110 General taxes	0	318	563	629	761	..	276	592	994	854
5120 Taxes on specific goods and services	0	124	264	247	362	..	59	231	184	239
5130 Unallocable between 5110 and 5120	0	0	0	0	0	..	0	0	0	0
5200 Taxes on use of goods and perform activities	0	57	133	256	297	..	0	0	0	9
5300 Unallocable between 5100 and 5200	0	0	1	0	0	..	0	0	0	0
6000 Other taxes	**0**	**3**	**28**	**10**	**13**	**0**	**1**	**0**	**0**	**0**
6100 Paid solely by business	..	0	25	8	11	..	0	..	..	..
6200 Other	..	3	3	2	2	..	1	..	..	..
Total tax revenue	**0**	**1 410**	**3 262**	**4 512**	**5 317**	**161**	**5 603**	**11 956**	**15 278**	**19 599**

.. Not available

Note: Including taxes collected on behalf of the European Union.

StatLink https://stat.link/7t2hxv

Table 6.31. Slovak Republic, tax revenues by sub-sectors of government

Million EUR

	Central government					State/Regional				
	1975	1995	2005	2015	2019	1975	1995	2005	2015	2019
1000 Taxes on income, profits and capital gains	..	**1 993**	**2 968**	**5 542**	**6 628**	..	..	..	..	..
1100 Of individuals	..	695	1 496	2 464	3 535	..	..	..	..	..
1200 Corporate	..	1 166	1 345	2 917	2 848	..	..	..	..	..
1300 Unallocable between 1100 and 1200	..	132	128	162	246	..	..	..	..	..
2000 Social security contributions	..	**85**	**240**	**253**	**367**	..	..	..	..	..
2100 Employees	..	10	104	58	113	..	..	..	..	..
2200 Employers	..	75	136	195	252	..	..	..	..	..
2300 Self-employed or non-employed	..	0	0	0	1	..	..	..	..	..
2400 Unallocable between 2100, 2200 and 2300	..	0	0	0	0	..	..	..	..	..
3000 Taxes on payroll and workforce	..	**0**	**0**	**0**	**0**	..	..	..	..	..
4000 Taxes on property	..	**27**	**28**	**0**	**0**	..	..	..	..	..
4100 Recurrent taxes on immovable property	..	8	9	0	0	..	..	..	..	..
4200 Recurrent taxes on net wealth	..	0	0	0	0	..	..	..	..	..
4300 Estate, inheritance and gift taxes	..	2	1	0	0	..	..	..	..	..
4400 Taxes on financial and capital transactions	..	16	18	0	0	..	..	..	..	..
4500 Non-recurrent taxes	..	0	0	0	0	..	..	..	..	..
4600 Other recurrent taxes on property	..	0	0	0	0	..	..	..	..	..
5000 Taxes on goods and services	..	**2 782**	**6 031**	**8 974**	**11 010**	..	..	..	..	..
5100 Taxes on production, sale, transfer, etc	..	2 594	5 773	8 442	10 362	..	..	..	..	..
5110 General taxes	..	1 616	3 880	5 423	6 830	..	..	..	..	..
5120 Taxes on specific goods and services	..	978	1 893	3 020	3 532	..	..	..	..	..
5130 Unallocable between 5110 and 5120	..	0	0	0	0	..	..	..	..	..
5200 Taxes on use of goods and perform activities	..	189	256	532	648	..	..	..	..	..
5300 Unallocable between 5100 and 5200	..	0	2	0	0	..	..	..	..	..
6000 Other taxes	..	**0**	**0**	**0**	**0**	..	..	..	..	..
6100 Paid solely by business	..	..	..	..	..	..	..	..	..	..
6200 Other	..	..	..	..	..	..	..	..	..	..
Total tax revenue	..	**4 887**	**9 267**	**14 770**	**18 005**	..	..	..	..	..

	Local government					Social Security Funds				
	1975	1995	2005	2015	2019	1975	1995	2005	2015	2019
1000 Taxes on income, profits and capital gains	..	**0**	**0**	**0**	**0**	..	**0**	**0**	**0**	**0**
1100 Of individuals	..	..	..	..	..	..	..	..	..	..
1200 Corporate	..	..	..	..	..	..	..	..	..	..
1300 Unallocable between 1100 and 1200	..	..	..	..	..	..	..	..	..	..
2000 Social security contributions	..	**0**	**0**	**0**	**0**	..	**2 817**	**6 037**	**10 643**	**13 718**
2100 Employees	..	..	..	0	0	..	540	1 377	2 352	3 322
2200 Employers	..	..	..	0	0	..	1 774	3 356	6 124	8 286
2300 Self-employed or non-employed	..	..	..	0	0	..	503	1 304	2 168	2 109
2400 Unallocable between 2100, 2200 and 2300	..	..	..	0	0	..	0	0	0	0
3000 Taxes on payroll and workforce	..	**0**	**0**	**0**	**0**	..	**0**	**0**	**0**	**0**
4000 Taxes on property	..	**84**	**220**	**335**	**378**	..	**0**	**0**	**0**	**0**
4100 Recurrent taxes on immovable property	..	72	220	335	378	..	..	..	..	..
4200 Recurrent taxes on net wealth	..	0	0	0	0	..	..	..	..	..
4300 Estate, inheritance and gift taxes	..	0	0	0	0	..	..	..	..	..
4400 Taxes on financial and capital transactions	..	12	0	0	0	..	..	..	..	..
4500 Non-recurrent taxes	..	0	0	0	0	..	..	..	..	..
4600 Other recurrent taxes on property	..	0	0	0	0	..	..	..	..	..
5000 Taxes on goods and services	..	**17**	**198**	**182**	**215**	..	**0**	**0**	**0**	**0**
5100 Taxes on production, sale, transfer, etc	..	10	9	12	17	..	..	..	..	..
5110 General taxes	..	0	0	0	0	..	..	..	..	..
5120 Taxes on specific goods and services	..	10	9	12	17	..	..	..	..	..
5130 Unallocable between 5110 and 5120	..	0	0	0	0	..	..	..	..	..
5200 Taxes on use of goods and perform activities	..	1	94	17	17	..	..	..	..	..
5300 Unallocable between 5100 and 5200	..	6	95	153	181	..	..	..	..	..
6000 Other taxes	..	**0**	**0**	**0**	**0**	..	**0**	**0**	**0**	**0**
6100 Paid solely by business	..	..	..	..	..	..	..	..	..	..
6200 Other	..	..	..	..	..	..	..	..	..	..
Total tax revenue	..	**101**	**418**	**517**	**593**	..	**2 817**	**6 037**	**10 643**	**13 718**

.. Not available

Note: Including taxes collected on behalf of the European Union.

StatLink https://stat.link/1f9mxn

Table 6.32. Slovenia, tax revenues by sub-sectors of government

Million EUR

	Central government					State/Regional				
	1975	1995	2005	2015	2019	1975	1995	2005	2015	2019
1000 Taxes on income, profits and capital gains	**..**	**479**	**1 828**	**1 528**	**2 301**	**..**	**..**	**..**	**..**	**..**
1100 Of individuals	..	413	1 029	958	1 345	..	..	..	..	..
1200 Corporate	..	54	795	568	954	..	..	..	..	..
1300 Unallocable between 1100 and 1200	..	12	5	2	3	..	..	..	..	..
2000 Social security contributions	**..**	**38**	**42**	**59**	**77**	**..**	**..**	**..**	**..**	**..**
2100 Employees	..	20	24	31	40	..	..	..	..	..
2200 Employers	..	17	15	23	31	..	..	..	..	..
2300 Self-employed or non-employed	..	1	3	5	6	..	..	..	..	..
2400 Unallocable between 2100, 2200 and 2300	..	0	0	0	0	..	..	..	..	..
3000 Taxes on payroll and workforce	**..**	**14**	**521**	**20**	**23**	**..**	**..**	**..**	**..**	**..**
4000 Taxes on property	**..**	**5**	**3**	**2**	**3**	**..**	**..**	**..**	**..**	**..**
4100 Recurrent taxes on immovable property	..	0	0	0	0	..	..	..	..	..
4200 Recurrent taxes on net wealth	..	0	3	0	0	..	..	..	..	..
4300 Estate, inheritance and gift taxes	..	0	0	0	0	..	..	..	..	..
4400 Taxes on financial and capital transactions	..	0	0	0	0	..	..	..	..	..
4500 Non-recurrent taxes	..	5	0	2	2	..	..	..	..	..
4600 Other recurrent taxes on property	..	0	0	0	0	..	..	..	..	..
5000 Taxes on goods and services	**..**	**1 554**	**3 805**	**5 541**	**6 399**	**..**	**..**	**..**	**..**	**..**
5100 Taxes on production, sale, transfer, etc	..	1 524	3 624	5 203	5 972	..	..	..	..	..
5110 General taxes	..	1 192	2 467	3 222	3 891	..	..	..	..	..
5120 Taxes on specific goods and services	..	332	1 156	1 981	2 081	..	..	..	..	..
5130 Unallocable between 5110 and 5120	..	0	0	0	0	..	..	..	..	..
5200 Taxes on use of goods and perform activities	..	31	181	338	427	..	..	..	..	..
5300 Unallocable between 5100 and 5200	..	0	0	0	0	..	..	..	..	..
6000 Other taxes	**..**	**0**	**0**	**0**	**0**	**..**	**..**	**..**	**..**	**..**
6100 Paid solely by business	..	..	..	..	..	..	..	..	..	..
6200 Other	..	..	..	..	..	..	..	..	..	..
Total tax revenue	**..**	**2 090**	**6 199**	**7 150**	**8 803**	**..**	**..**	**..**	**..**	**..**

	Local government					Social Security Funds				
	1975	1995	2005	2015	2019	1975	1995	2005	2015	2019
1000 Taxes on income, profits and capital gains	**..**	**194**	**559**	**1 019**	**1 204**	**..**	**0**	**0**	**0**	**0**
1100 Of individuals	..	192	556	1 019	1 204	..	..	..	..	..
1200 Corporate	..	0	0	0	0	..	..	..	..	..
1300 Unallocable between 1100 and 1200	..	2	2	0	0	..	..	..	..	..
2000 Social security contributions	**..**	**0**	**0**	**0**	**0**	**..**	**1 795**	**4 354**	**5 924**	**7 510**
2100 Employees	..	..	..	..	..	..	812	2 124	2 879	3 710
2200 Employers	..	..	..	..	..	..	806	1 579	2 112	2 750
2300 Self-employed or non-employed	..	..	..	..	..	..	177	652	933	1 049
2400 Unallocable between 2100, 2200 and 2300	..	..	..	..	..	..	0	0	0	0
3000 Taxes on payroll and workforce	**..**	**2**	**0**	**0**	**0**	**..**	**0**	**0**	**0**	**0**
4000 Taxes on property	**..**	**53**	**167**	**239**	**296**	**..**	**0**	**0**	**0**	**0**
4100 Recurrent taxes on immovable property	..	37	122	199	234	..	..	..	..	..
4200 Recurrent taxes on net wealth	..	0	0	0	0	..	..	..	..	..
4300 Estate, inheritance and gift taxes	..	1	5	8	16	..	..	..	..	..
4400 Taxes on financial and capital transactions	..	12	40	29	44	..	..	..	..	..
4500 Non-recurrent taxes	..	3	0	3	1	..	..	..	..	..
4600 Other recurrent taxes on property	..	0	0	0	0	..	..	..	..	..
5000 Taxes on goods and services	**..**	**7**	**91**	**96**	**105**	**..**	**0**	**0**	**0**	**0**
5100 Taxes on production, sale, transfer, etc	..	7	43	57	70	..	..	..	..	..
5110 General taxes	..	0	0	0	0	..	..	..	..	..
5120 Taxes on specific goods and services	..	7	43	57	70	..	..	..	..	..
5130 Unallocable between 5110 and 5120	..	0	0	0	0	..	..	..	..	..
5200 Taxes on use of goods and perform activities	..	0	48	39	34	..	..	..	..	..
5300 Unallocable between 5100 and 5200	..	0	0	0	0	..	..	..	..	..
6000 Other taxes	**..**	**0**	**0**	**0**	**0**	**..**	**0**	**0**	**0**	**0**
6100 Paid solely by business	..	..	..	..	..	..	..	..	..	..
6200 Other	..	..	..	..	..	..	..	..	..	..
Total tax revenue	**..**	**256**	**817**	**1 354**	**1 604**	**..**	**1 795**	**4 354**	**5 924**	**7 510**

.. Not available

Note: Including taxes collected on behalf of the European Union.

StatLink https://stat.link/am71gv

Table 6.33. Spain, tax revenues by sub-sectors of government

Million EUR

	Federal government					State/Regional				
	1975	1995	2005	2015	2019	1975	1995	2005	2015	2019
1000 Taxes on income, profits and capital gains	**1 388**	**38 846**	**71 598**	**62 198**	**69 612**	**..**	**588**	**19 503**	**34 814**	**46 997**
1100 Of individuals	897	31 789	38 219	39 659	45 510	..	457	19 104	34 600	46 726
1200 Corporate	490	7 057	33 379	22 539	24 102	..	131	399	214	271
1300 Unallocable between 1100 and 1200	1	0	0	0	0	..	0	0	0	0
2000 Social security contributions	**0**	**2 027**	**3 027**	**3 505**	**3 481**	**..**	**0**	**0**	**0**	**0**
2100 Employees	..	1 017	1 369	1 541	1 406	..	..	..	..	..
2200 Employers	..	1 010	1 658	1 964	2 075	..	..	..	..	..
2300 Self-employed or non-employed	..	0	0	0	0	..	..	..	..	..
2400 Unallocable between 2100, 2200 and 2300	..	0	0	0	0	..	..	..	..	..
3000 Taxes on payroll and workforce	**0**	**0**	**0**	**0**	**0**	**..**	**0**	**0**	**0**	**0**
4000 Taxes on property	**421**	**405**	**77**	**1 197**	**284**	**..**	**4 050**	**19 031**	**10 286**	**12 772**
4100 Recurrent taxes on immovable property	1	3	5	4	2	..	0	2	38	49
4200 Recurrent taxes on net wealth	0	166	38	32	61	..	419	1 246	961	1 202
4300 Estate, inheritance and gift taxes	56	1	24	222	-19	..	835	2 315	2 454	2 410
4400 Taxes on financial and capital transactions	364	235	10	6	6	..	2 796	15 468	6 833	9 111
4500 Non-recurrent taxes	0	0	0	933	234	..	0	0	0	0
4600 Other recurrent taxes on property	0	0	0	0	0	..	0	0	0	0
5000 Taxes on goods and services	**1 609**	**32 388**	**71 536**	**89 031**	**100 156**	**..**	**2 556**	**7 956**	**6 553**	**6 890**
5100 Taxes on production, sale, transfer, etc	1 599	32 206	70 895	87 536	98 077	..	2 387	7 637	6 022	6 279
5110 General taxes	990	20 331	51 583	61 839	72 145	..	786	1 980	2 571	2 912
5120 Taxes on specific goods and services	608	11 875	19 312	25 697	25 932	..	1 601	5 657	3 451	3 367
5130 Unallocable between 5110 and 5120	0	0	0	0	0	..	0	0	0	0
5200 Taxes on use of goods and perform activities	10	182	641	1 495	2 079	..	169	319	531	611
5300 Unallocable between 5100 and 5200	0	0	0	0	0	..	0	0	0	0
6000 Other taxes	**0**	**0**	**0**	**101**	**116**	**..**	**0**	**1**	**19**	**12**
6100 Paid solely by business	0	..	..	0	0	..	..	0	0	0
6200 Other	0	..	..	101	116	..	..	1	19	12
Total tax revenue	**3 418**	**73 666**	**146 238**	**156 032**	**173 649**	**..**	**7 194**	**46 491**	**51 672**	**66 671**

	Local government					Social Security Funds				
	1975	1995	2005	2015	2019	1975	1995	2005	2015	2019
1000 Taxes on income, profits and capital gains	**175**	**2 514**	**4 892**	**5 633**	**7 069**	**0**	**0**	**0**	**0**	**0**
1100 Of individuals	131	2 137	3 426	4 637	5 724	..	..	..	..	..
1200 Corporate	0	377	1 466	996	1 345	..	..	..	..	..
1300 Unallocable between 1100 and 1200	44	0	0	0	0	..	..	..	..	..
2000 Social security contributions	**0**	**0**	**0**	**0**	**0**	**3 367**	**49 851**	**106 040**	**119 330**	**149 046**
2100 Employees	..	..	..	..	..	645	7 372	15 332	17 242	21 866
2200 Employers	..	..	..	..	..	2 722	35 137	77 989	86 024	110 199
2300 Self-employed or non-employed	..	..	..	..	..	0	7 342	12 719	16 064	16 981
2400 Unallocable between 2100, 2200 and 2300	..	..	..	..	..	0	0	0	0	0
3000 Taxes on payroll and workforce	**0**	**0**	**0**	**0**	**0**	**0**	**0**	**0**	**0**	**0**
4000 Taxes on property	**26**	**3 759**	**8 869**	**16 372**	**17 441**	**0**	**0**	**0**	**0**	**0**
4100 Recurrent taxes on immovable property	26	2 754	6 038	12 581	13 393	..	..	..	..	..
4200 Recurrent taxes on net wealth	0	177	431	911	978	..	..	..	..	..
4300 Estate, inheritance and gift taxes	0	19	79	114	122	..	..	..	..	..
4400 Taxes on financial and capital transactions	0	166	423	145	210	..	..	..	..	..
4500 Non-recurrent taxes	0	643	1 898	2 621	2 738	..	..	..	..	..
4600 Other recurrent taxes on property	0	0	0	0	0	..	..	..	..	..
5000 Taxes on goods and services	**104**	**6 072**	**12 810**	**13 067**	**15 000**	**0**	**0**	**0**	**0**	**0**
5100 Taxes on production, sale, transfer, etc	104	1 976	5 946	6 846	8 019	..	..	..	..	..
5110 General taxes	95	1 805	4 186	5 068	6 029	..	..	..	..	..
5120 Taxes on specific goods and services	10	171	1 760	1 778	1 990	..	..	..	..	..
5130 Unallocable between 5110 and 5120	0	0	0	0	0	..	..	..	..	..
5200 Taxes on use of goods and perform activities	0	4 096	6 864	6 221	6 981	..	..	..	..	..
5300 Unallocable between 5100 and 5200	0	0	0	0	0	..	..	..	..	..
6000 Other taxes	**0**	**8**	**6**	**69**	**25**	**0**	**0**	**0**	**0**	**0**
6100 Paid solely by business	..	0	0	0	0	..	..	..	..	..
6200 Other	..	8	6	69	25	..	..	..	..	..
Total tax revenue	**305**	**12 353**	**26 577**	**35 141**	**39 535**	**3 367**	**49 851**	**106 040**	**119 330**	**149 046**

.. Not available

Note: Including taxes collected on behalf of the European Union.

StatLink https://stat.link/kvd3gn

Table 6.34. Sweden, tax revenues by sub-sectors of government

Million SEK

	Central government					State/Regional				
	1975	1995	2005	2015	2019	1975	1995	2005	2015	2019
1000 Taxes on income, profits and capital gains	**28 216**	**72 342**	**123 698**	**21 820**	**23 924**	..	..	..	..	..
1100 Of individuals	25 626	22 541	21 708	-102 059	-128 036	..	..	..	..	..
1200 Corporate	2 590	49 801	101 989	123 878	151 960	..	..	..	..	..
1300 Unallocable between 1100 and 1200	0	0	0	0	0	..	..	..	..	..
2000 Social security contributions[1]	**0**	**50 560**	**212 964**	**180 723**	**196 344**	..	..	..	..	..
2100 Employees	..	0	0	0	0	..	..	..	..	..
2200 Employers	..	49 222	209 370	179 056	195 686	..	..	..	..	..
2300 Self-employed or non-employed	..	1 338	4 639	1 875	1 321	..	..	..	..	..
2400 Unallocable between 2100, 2200 and 2300	..	0	-1 044	-209	-662	..	..	..	..	..
3000 Taxes on payroll and workforce	**5 723**	**17 800**	**62 432**	**194 121**	**268 832**	..	..	..	..	..
4000 Taxes on property	**1 469**	**23 260**	**40 116**	**27 917**	**28 633**	..	..	..	..	..
4100 Recurrent taxes on immovable property	11	15 263	25 139	16 509	15 758	..	..	..	..	..
4200 Recurrent taxes on net wealth	647	3 583	4 998	0	0	..	..	..	..	..
4300 Estate, inheritance and gift taxes	335	1 388	1 092	0	0	..	..	..	..	..
4400 Taxes on financial and capital transactions	476	3 026	8 887	11 408	12 874	..	..	..	..	..
4500 Non-recurrent taxes	0	0	0	0	0	..	..	..	..	..
4600 Other recurrent taxes on property	0	0	0	0	0	..	..	..	..	..
5000 Taxes on goods and services	**31 985**	**237 720**	**354 724**	**508 210**	**603 320**	..	..	..	..	..
5100 Taxes on production, sale, transfer, etc	29 820	233 671	343 704	489 458	582 670	..	..	..	..	..
5110 General taxes	15 806	166 557	250 470	383 002	459 825	..	..	..	..	..
5120 Taxes on specific goods and services	14 014	67 114	93 234	106 456	122 845	..	..	..	..	..
5130 Unallocable between 5110 and 5120	0	0	0	0	0	..	..	..	..	..
5200 Taxes on use of goods and perform activities	2 165	4 049	11 019	18 752	20 650	..	..	..	..	..
5300 Unallocable between 5100 and 5200	0	0	0	0	0	..	..	..	..	..
6000 Other taxes	**260**	**1 438**	**1 347**	**1 356**	**1 665**	..	..	..	..	..
6100 Paid solely by business	0	0	0	0	0	..	..	..	..	..
6200 Other	260	1 438	1 347	1 356	1 665	..	..	..	..	..
Total tax revenue	**67 653**	**403 120**	**795 281**	**934 146**	**1 122 719**	..	..	..	..	..

	Local government					Social Security Funds				
	1975	1995	2005	2015	2019	1975	1995	2005	2015	2019
1000 Taxes on income, profits and capital gains	**38 415**	**265 068**	**435 577**	**635 719**	**748 197**	**0**	**0**	**0**	**0**	**0**
1100 Of individuals	35 269	265 068	435 577	635 719	748 197	..	..	..	..	..
1200 Corporate	3 146	0	0	0	0	..	..	..	..	..
1300 Unallocable between 1100 and 1200	0	0	0	0	0	..	..	..	..	..
2000 Social security contributions[1]	**0**	**0**	**0**	**0**	**0**	**25 756**	**186 992**	**151 019**	**224 129**	**266 516**
2100 Employees	..	..	..	..	..	0	28 989	74 178	108 356	128 161
2200 Employers	..	..	..	..	..	24 203	154 154	74 438	112 589	135 379
2300 Self-employed or non-employed	..	..	..	..	..	1 553	3 849	2 403	3 183	2 977
2400 Unallocable between 2100, 2200 and 2300	..	..	..	..	..	0	0	0	0	0
3000 Taxes on payroll and workforce	**0**	**0**	**0**	**0**	**0**	**0**	**0**	**0**	**0**	**0**
4000 Taxes on property	**0**	**0**	**0**	**15 935**	**18 632**	**0**	**0**	**0**	**0**	**0**
4100 Recurrent taxes on immovable property	..	..	..	15 935	18 632	..	..	..	..	..
4200 Recurrent taxes on net wealth	..	..	..	0	0	..	..	..	..	..
4300 Estate, inheritance and gift taxes	..	..	..	0	0	..	..	..	..	..
4400 Taxes on financial and capital transactions	..	..	..	0	0	..	..	..	..	..
4500 Non-recurrent taxes	..	..	..	0	0	..	..	..	..	..
4600 Other recurrent taxes on property	..	..	..	0	0	..	..	..	..	..
5000 Taxes on goods and services	**149**	**786**	**0**	**0**	**0**	**0**	**0**	**0**	**0**	**0**
5100 Taxes on production, sale, transfer, etc	119	732	0	0	0	..	..	..	..	..
5110 General taxes	0	0	0	0	0	..	..	..	..	..
5120 Taxes on specific goods and services	119	732	0	0	0	..	..	..	..	..
5130 Unallocable between 5110 and 5120	0	0	0	0	0	..	..	..	..	..
5200 Taxes on use of goods and perform activities	30	54	0	0	0	..	..	..	..	..
5300 Unallocable between 5100 and 5200	0	0	0	0	0	..	..	..	..	..
6000 Other taxes	**0**	**0**	**0**	**0**	**0**	**0**	**0**	**0**	**0**	**0**
6100 Paid solely by business	..	..	..	..	..	..	..	..	..	..
6200 Other	..	..	..	..	..	..	..	..	..	..
Total tax revenue	**38 564**	**265 854**	**435 577**	**651 654**	**766 829**	**25 756**	**186 992**	**151 019**	**224 129**	**266 516**

.. Not available

Note: Including taxes collected on behalf of the European Union.

1. From 1985, social security contributions are classified using the SNA definition of Social security Funds which means that a proportion of these payments are shown under the heading of Central Government. Prior to that year, all such payments were classified under the heading of Social Security.

StatLink https://stat.link/56dsav

Table 6.35. Switzerland, tax revenues by sub-sectors of government

Million CHF

	Federal government					State/Regional				
	1975	1995	2005	2015	2019	1975	1995	2005	2015	2019
1000 Taxes on income, profits and capital gains	**3 422**	**10 468**	**16 341**	**26 841**	**33 278**	**7 756**	**19 408**	**26 544**	**34 657**	**38 075**
1100 Of individuals	2 712	5 699	7 823	10 567	11 622	6 342	16 182	21 289	27 156	29 672
1200 Corporate	710	2 678	4 519	9 731	11 813	1 414	2 628	4 627	6 294	6 900
1300 Unallocable between 1100 and 1200	0	2 092	4 000	6 543	9 842	0	598	628	1 207	1 503
2000 Social security contributions	**0**	**0**	**0**	**0**	**0**	**0**	**0**	**0**	**0**	**0**
2100 Employees	..	..	..	..	..	..	..	..	..	..
2200 Employers	..	..	..	..	..	..	..	..	..	..
2300 Self-employed or non-employed	..	..	..	..	..	..	..	..	..	..
2400 Unallocable between 2100, 2200 and 2300	..	..	..	..	..	..	..	..	..	..
3000 Taxes on payroll and workforce	**0**	**0**	**0**	**0**	**0**	**0**	**0**	**0**	**0**	**0**
4000 Taxes on property	**463**	**1 703**	**2 703**	**1 674**	**1 434**	**1 428**	**4 116**	**5 523**	**7 191**	**8 674**
4100 Recurrent taxes on immovable property	0	0	0	0	0	60	162	230	349	395
4200 Recurrent taxes on net wealth	89	0	0	0	0	988	2 467	3 683	4 992	6 180
4300 Estate, inheritance and gift taxes	0	0	0	0	0	270	974	824	964	1 065
4400 Taxes on financial and capital transactions	374	1 703	2 703	1 674	1 434	110	103	157	177	207
4500 Non-recurrent taxes	0	0	0	0	0	0	0	0	0	0
4600 Other recurrent taxes on property	0	0	0	0	0	0	411	629	709	827
5000 Taxes on goods and services	**7 431**	**20 854**	**28 489**	**35 508**	**36 500**	**795**	**1 706**	**2 373**	**2 901**	**3 000**
5100 Taxes on production, sale, transfer, etc	7 431	19 763	27 114	33 093	33 641	154	266	447	615	584
5110 General taxes	3 205	12 428	18 429	22 791	22 915	0	0	0	0	0
5120 Taxes on specific goods and services	4 226	7 335	8 685	10 302	10 727	154	236	410	594	565
5130 Unallocable between 5110 and 5120	0	0	0	0	0	0	29	37	20	19
5200 Taxes on use of goods and perform activities	0	1 092	1 375	2 415	2 859	641	1 440	1 927	2 286	2 416
5300 Unallocable between 5100 and 5200	0	0	0	0	0	0	0	0	0	0
6000 Other taxes	**0**	**0**	**0**	**0**	**71**	**0**	**19**	**23**	**230**	**344**
6100 Paid solely by business	..	..	..	..	0	..	6	7	64	72
6200 Other	..	..	..	..	71	..	13	16	165	272
Total tax revenue	**11 316**	**33 026**	**47 533**	**64 023**	**71 283**	**9 979**	**25 249**	**34 462**	**44 979**	**50 093**

	Local government					Social Security Funds				
	1975	1995	2005	2015	2019	1975	1995	2005	2015	2019
1000 Taxes on income, profits and capital gains	**6 403**	**15 575**	**18 091**	**22 865**	**25 281**	**0**	**0**	**0**	**0**	**0**
1100 Of individuals	5 398	13 340	15 326	18 651	20 040	..	..	..	..	..
1200 Corporate	1 005	1 624	2 316	3 407	3 994	..	..	..	..	..
1300 Unallocable between 1100 and 1200	0	611	450	806	1 248	..	..	..	..	..
2000 Social security contributions	**0**	**0**	**0**	**0**	**0**	**8 111**	**28 019**	**32 332**	**44 285**	**47 234**
2100 Employees	..	..	..	..	..	3 589	13 115	15 133	20 445	21 906
2200 Employers	..	..	..	..	..	3 618	13 126	15 146	20 671	22 197
2300 Self-employed or non-employed	..	..	..	..	..	840	1 778	2 053	3 169	3 131
2400 Unallocable between 2100, 2200 and 2300	..	..	..	..	..	64	0	0	0	0
3000 Taxes on payroll and workforce	**0**	**0**	**0**	**0**	**0**	**0**	**0**	**0**	**0**	**0**
4000 Taxes on property	**1 068**	**2 614**	**3 251**	**4 275**	**5 235**	**0**	**0**	**0**	**0**	**0**
4100 Recurrent taxes on immovable property	182	443	588	789	934	..	..	..	..	..
4200 Recurrent taxes on net wealth	809	1 873	2 393	3 104	3 813	..	..	..	..	..
4300 Estate, inheritance and gift taxes	27	89	79	124	168	..	..	..	..	..
4400 Taxes on financial and capital transactions	50	42	38	52	64	..	..	..	..	..
4500 Non-recurrent taxes	0	0	0	0	0	..	..	..	..	..
4600 Other recurrent taxes on property	0	168	153	206	256	..	..	..	..	..
5000 Taxes on goods and services	**22**	**97**	**78**	**132**	**210**	**0**	**0**	**0**	**0**	**0**
5100 Taxes on production, sale, transfer, etc	17	55	26	63	112	..	..	..	..	..
5110 General taxes	0	0	0	0	0	..	..	..	..	..
5120 Taxes on specific goods and services	17	29	20	15	15	..	..	..	..	..
5130 Unallocable between 5110 and 5120	0	25	6	48	97	..	..	..	..	..
5200 Taxes on use of goods and perform activities	5	42	52	70	98	..	..	..	..	..
5300 Unallocable between 5100 and 5200	0	0	0	0	0	..	..	..	..	..
6000 Other taxes	**0**	**164**	**223**	**569**	**634**	**0**	**0**	**0**	**0**	**0**
6100 Paid solely by business	..	49	67	277	325	..	..	..	..	..
6200 Other	..	115	156	292	309	..	..	..	..	..
Total tax revenue	**7 493**	**18 451**	**21 643**	**27 841**	**31 361**	**8 111**	**28 019**	**32 332**	**44 285**	**47 234**

.. Not available

StatLink https://stat.link/b6sfgv

Table 6.36. Turkey, tax revenues by sub-sectors of government

Million TRY

	Central government					State/Regional				
	1975	1995	2005	2015	2019	1975	1995	2005	2015	2019
1000 Taxes on income, profits and capital gains	..	**433**	**30 324**	**104 699**	**212 320**	..	..	..	..	..
1100 Of individuals	..	330	20 458	75 426	143 163	..	..	..	..	..
1200 Corporate	..	103	9 866	29 272	69 157	..	..	..	..	..
1300 Unallocable between 1100 and 1200	..	0	0	0	0	..	..	..	..	..
2000 Social security contributions	..	**0**	**0**	**0**	**0**	..	..	..	..	..
2100 Employees	..	..	..	..	..	..	..	..	..	..
2200 Employers	..	..	..	..	..	..	..	..	..	..
2300 Self-employed or non-employed	..	..	..	..	..	..	..	..	..	..
2400 Unallocable between 2100, 2200 and 2300	..	..	..	..	..	..	..	..	..	..
3000 Taxes on payroll and workforce	..	**0**	**0**	**0**	**0**	..	..	..	..	..
4000 Taxes on property	..	**49**	**3 626**	**20 211**	**28 288**	..	..	..	..	..
4100 Recurrent taxes on immovable property	..	0	0	0	0	..	..	..	..	..
4200 Recurrent taxes on net wealth	..	0	0	0	0	..	..	..	..	..
4300 Estate, inheritance and gift taxes	..	1	78	379	982	..	..	..	..	..
4400 Taxes on financial and capital transactions	..	29	3 548	19 832	27 306	..	..	..	..	..
4500 Non-recurrent taxes	..	19	0	0	0	..	..	..	..	..
4600 Other recurrent taxes on property	..	0	0	0	0	..	..	..	..	..
5000 Taxes on goods and services	..	**574**	**71 956**	**231 227**	**346 102**	..	..	..	..	..
5100 Taxes on production, sale, transfer, etc	..	567	69 266	222 702	332 559	..	..	..	..	..
5110 General taxes	..	475	30 343	107 451	159 379	..	..	..	..	..
5120 Taxes on specific goods and services	..	92	38 923	115 251	173 180	..	..	..	..	..
5130 Unallocable between 5110 and 5120	..	0	0	0	0	..	..	..	..	..
5200 Taxes on use of goods and perform activities	..	8	2 691	8 526	13 543	..	..	..	..	..
5300 Unallocable between 5100 and 5200	..	0	0	0	0	..	..	..	..	..
6000 Other taxes	..	**259**	**4 181**	**3 779**	**6 361**	..	..	..	..	..
6100 Paid solely by business	..	0	0	0	0	..	..	..	..	..
6200 Other	..	259	4 181	3 779	6 361	..	..	..	..	..
Total tax revenue	..	**1 316**	**110 088**	**359 915**	**593 072**	..	..	..	..	..

	Local government					Social Security Funds				
	1975	1995	2005	2015	2019	1975	1995	2005	2015	2019
1000 Taxes on income, profits and capital gains	..	**63**	**4 011**	**14 445**	**29 213**	..	**0**	**0**	**0**	**0**
1100 Of individuals	..	48	2 706	10 330	19 541	..	..	..	..	..
1200 Corporate	..	15	1 305	4 116	9 672	..	..	..	..	..
1300 Unallocable between 1100 and 1200	..	0	0	0	0	..	..	..	..	..
2000 Social security contributions	..	**0**	**0**	**0**	**0**	..	**212**	**35 321**	**170 282**	**312 808**
2100 Employees	..	..	..	..	..	..	82	12 128	64 214	120 108
2200 Employers	..	..	..	..	..	..	110	16 132	95 067	178 345
2300 Self-employed or non-employed	..	..	..	..	..	..	19	7 061	11 001	14 356
2400 Unallocable between 2100, 2200 and 2300	..	..	..	..	..	..	0	0	0	0
3000 Taxes on payroll and workforce	..	**0**	**0**	**0**	**0**	..	**0**	**0**	**0**	**0**
4000 Taxes on property	..	**4**	**1 627**	**8 371**	**13 433**	..	**0**	**0**	**0**	**0**
4100 Recurrent taxes on immovable property	..	0	1 148	5 882	9 681	..	..	..	..	..
4200 Recurrent taxes on net wealth	..	0	0	0	0	..	..	..	..	..
4300 Estate, inheritance and gift taxes	..	0	10	56	121	..	..	..	..	..
4400 Taxes on financial and capital transactions	..	4	469	2 433	3 631	..	..	..	..	..
4500 Non-recurrent taxes	..	0	0	0	0	..	..	..	..	..
4600 Other recurrent taxes on property	..	0	0	0	0	..	..	..	..	..
5000 Taxes on goods and services	..	**84**	**5 649**	**28 737**	**42 990**	..	**0**	**0**	**0**	**0**
5100 Taxes on production, sale, transfer, etc	..	82	5 295	27 560	41 132	..	..	..	..	..
5110 General taxes	..	69	4 014	13 619	21 350	..	..	..	..	..
5120 Taxes on specific goods and services	..	13	1 281	13 940	19 782	..	..	..	..	..
5130 Unallocable between 5110 and 5120	..	0	0	0	0	..	..	..	..	..
5200 Taxes on use of goods and perform activities	..	1	354	1 177	1 857	..	..	..	..	..
5300 Unallocable between 5100 and 5200	..	0	0	0	0	..	..	..	..	..
6000 Other taxes	..	**73**	**721**	**4 971**	**6 035**	..	**0**	**0**	**0**	**0**
6100 Paid solely by business	..	0	0	0	0	..	..	..	..	..
6200 Other	..	73	721	4 971	6 035	..	..	..	..	..
Total tax revenue	..	**224**	**12 008**	**56 525**	**91 670**	..	**212**	**35 321**	**170 282**	**312 808**

.. Not available

StatLink https://stat.link/wtg201

Table 6.37. United Kingdom, tax revenues by sub-sectors of government

Million GBP

	Central government					State/Regional				
	1975	1995	2005	2015	2019	1975	1995	2005	2015	2019
1000 Taxes on income, profits and capital gains	**16 716**	**92 147**	**177 149**	**212 633**	**251 489**	..	..	..	..	..
1100 Of individuals	14 936	71 973	130 135	168 873	200 486	..	..	..	..	..
1200 Corporate	2 310	20 174	47 014	43 760	51 003	..	..	..	..	..
1300 Unallocable between 1100 and 1200	-530	0	0	0	0	..	..	..	..	..
2000 Social security contributions	**0**	**0**	**0**	**0**	**0**	..	..	..	..	..
2100 Employees	..	..	..	..	..	..	..	..	..	..
2200 Employers	..	..	..	..	..	..	..	..	..	..
2300 Self-employed or non-employed	..	..	..	..	..	..	..	..	..	..
2400 Unallocable between 2100, 2200 and 2300	..	..	..	..	..	..	..	..	..	..
3000 Taxes on payroll and workforce	**-1**	**0**	**0**	**0**	**2 764**	..	..	..	..	..
4000 Taxes on property	**619**	**15 730**	**32 583**	**46 622**	**52 715**	..	..	..	..	..
4100 Recurrent taxes on immovable property	44	12 369	19 523	28 389	31 588	..	..	..	..	..
4200 Recurrent taxes on net wealth	0	0	0	0	0	..	..	..	..	..
4300 Estate, inheritance and gift taxes	307	1 441	3 150	4 442	5 165	..	..	..	..	..
4400 Taxes on financial and capital transactions	266	1 920	9 910	13 791	15 962	..	..	..	..	..
4500 Non-recurrent taxes	2	0	0	0	0	..	..	..	..	..
4600 Other recurrent taxes on property	0	0	0	0	0	..	..	..	..	..
5000 Taxes on goods and services	**8 982**	**85 507**	**136 758**	**204 693**	**234 170**	..	..	..	..	..
5100 Taxes on production, sale, transfer, etc	8 502	81 175	131 362	197 250	225 633	..	..	..	..	..
5110 General taxes	3 515	47 539	84 649	133 064	154 754	..	..	..	..	..
5120 Taxes on specific goods and services	4 987	33 636	46 713	64 186	70 879	..	..	..	..	..
5130 Unallocable between 5110 and 5120	0	0	0	0	0	..	..	..	..	..
5200 Taxes on use of goods and perform activities	698	4 332	5 396	7 443	8 537	..	..	..	..	..
5300 Unallocable between 5100 and 5200	-218	0	0	0	0	..	..	..	..	..
6000 Other taxes	**0**	**0**	**0**	**0**	**0**	..	..	..	..	..
6100 Paid solely by business	..	..	..	..	..	..	..	..	..	..
6200 Other	..	..	..	..	..	..	..	..	..	..
Total tax revenue	**26 316**	**193 384**	**346 490**	**463 948**	**541 138**	..	..	..	..	..

	Local government					Social Security Funds				
	1975	1995	2005	2015	2019	1975	1995	2005	2015	2019
1000 Taxes on income, profits and capital gains	**0**	**0**	**0**	**0**	**0**	**0**	**0**	**0**	**0**	**0**
1100 Of individuals	0	..	..	..	..	0	..	..	..	..
1200 Corporate	0	..	..	..	..	0	..	..	..	..
1300 Unallocable between 1100 and 1200	0	..	..	..	..	0	..	..	..	..
2000 Social security contributions	**0**	**0**	**0**	**0**	**0**	**6 540**	**44 397**	**84 459**	**114 173**	**143 255**
2100 Employees	..	..	..	..	..	2 562	18 646	35 159	44 488	56 200
2200 Employers	..	..	..	..	..	4 068	24 210	46 475	66 491	82 699
2300 Self-employed or non-employed	..	..	..	..	..	195	1 541	2 825	3 194	4 356
2400 Unallocable between 2100, 2200 and 2300	..	..	..	..	..	-285	0	0	0	0
3000 Taxes on payroll and workforce	**0**	**0**	**0**	**0**	**0**	**0**	**0**	**0**	**0**	**0**
4000 Taxes on property	**4 127**	**9 303**	**21 255**	**29 943**	**37 543**	**0**	**0**	**0**	**0**	**0**
4100 Recurrent taxes on immovable property	3 978	9 303	21 255	29 796	37 160	..	..	..	..	..
4200 Recurrent taxes on net wealth	0	0	0	0	0	..	..	..	..	..
4300 Estate, inheritance and gift taxes	0	0	0	0	0	..	..	..	..	..
4400 Taxes on financial and capital transactions	0	0	0	0	0	..	..	..	..	..
4500 Non-recurrent taxes	0	0	0	147	383	..	..	..	..	..
4600 Other recurrent taxes on property	149	0	0	0	0	..	..	..	..	..
5000 Taxes on goods and services	**0**	**0**	**0**	**0**	**0**	**0**	**0**	**0**	**0**	**0**
5100 Taxes on production, sale, transfer, etc	..	..	..	..	..	..	..	..	..	..
5110 General taxes	..	..	..	..	..	..	..	..	..	..
5120 Taxes on specific goods and services	..	..	..	..	..	..	..	..	..	..
5130 Unallocable between 5110 and 5120	..	..	..	..	..	..	..	..	..	..
5200 Taxes on use of goods and perform activities	..	..	..	..	..	..	..	..	..	..
5300 Unallocable between 5100 and 5200	..	..	..	..	..	..	..	..	..	..
6000 Other taxes	**0**	**0**	**0**	**0**	**0**	**0**	**0**	**0**	**0**	**0**
6100 Paid solely by business	..	..	..	..	..	..	..	..	..	..
6200 Other	..	..	..	..	..	..	..	..	..	..
Total tax revenue	**4 127**	**9 303**	**21 255**	**29 943**	**37 543**	**6 540**	**44 397**	**84 459**	**114 173**	**143 255**

.. Not available

Note: Including taxes collected on behalf of the European Union.

StatLink https://stat.link/zj78h4

Table 6.38. United States, tax revenues by sub-sectors of government

Million USD

	Federal government					State/Regional				
	1975	1995	2005	2015	2019	1975	1995	2005	2015	2019
1000 Taxes on income, profits and capital gains	**163 072**	**750 144**	**1 268 412**	**1 883 845**	**1 957 991**	**25 509**	**157 598**	**275 728**	**391 166**	**476 013**
1100 Of individuals	122 386	594 213	948 921	1 554 757	1 740 684	..	128 429	226 576	343 101	415 361
1200 Corporate	40 686	155 931	319 490	329 088	217 307	..	29 169	49 152	48 065	60 652
1300 Unallocable between 1100 and 1200	0	0	0	0	0	..	0	0	0	0
2000 Social security contributions	**0**	**0**	**0**	**0**	**0**	**0**	**0**	**0**	**0**	**0**
2100 Employees	..	..	..	..	..	..	..	..	..	..
2200 Employers	..	..	..	..	..	..	..	..	..	..
2300 Self-employed or non-employed	..	..	..	..	..	..	..	..	..	..
2400 Unallocable between 2100, 2200 and 2300	..	..	..	..	..	..	..	..	..	..
3000 Taxes on payroll and workforce	**0**	**0**	**0**	**0**	**0**	**0**	**0**	**0**	**1 751**	**2 760**
4000 Taxes on property	**4 613**	**14 948**	**24 989**	**20 191**	**16 177**	**3 284**	**16 880**	**28 808**	**31 133**	**35 975**
4100 Recurrent taxes on immovable property	0	0	0	0	0	1 451	7 240	9 037	13 286	15 494
4200 Recurrent taxes on net wealth	0	0	0	0	0	0	0	0	0	0
4300 Estate, inheritance and gift taxes	4 611	14 948	24 989	20 191	16 177	1 418	5 061	5 322	5 143	5 216
4400 Taxes on financial and capital transactions	2	0	0	0	0	415	2 386	11 711	8 679	10 572
4500 Non-recurrent taxes	0	0	0	0	0	0	0	0	0	0
4600 Other recurrent taxes on property	0	0	0	0	0	0	2 193	2 738	4 025	4 694
5000 Taxes on goods and services	**20 773**	**75 553**	**99 411**	**140 319**	**173 679**	**52 032**	**232 033**	**377 795**	**502 682**	**586 830**
5100 Taxes on production, sale, transfer, etc	20 442	75 553	99 411	140 319	173 679	43 960	200 495	323 137	438 463	508 797
5110 General taxes	0	0	0	0	0	24 916	135 132	218 917	289 600	337 356
5120 Taxes on specific goods and services	20 442	75 553	99 411	140 319	173 679	19 044	65 363	104 220	148 863	171 441
5130 Unallocable between 5110 and 5120	0	0	0	0	0	0	0	0	0	0
5200 Taxes on use of goods and perform activities	331	0	0	0	0	8 072	31 538	54 658	64 219	78 033
5300 Unallocable between 5100 and 5200	0	0	0	0	0	0	0	0	0	0
6000 Other taxes	**0**	**0**	**0**	**0**	**0**	**0**	**0**	**0**	**0**	**0**
6100 Paid solely by business	..	..	..	..	..	..	..	..	..	..
6200 Other	..	..	..	..	..	..	..	..	..	..
Total tax revenue	**188 458**	**840 645**	**1 392 812**	**2 044 356**	**2 147 847**	**80 825**	**406 511**	**682 331**	**926 733**	**1 101 578**

	Local government					Social Security Funds				
	1975	1995	2005	2015	2019	1975	1995	2005	2015	2019
1000 Taxes on income, profits and capital gains	**2 635**	**15 795**	**28 272**	**39 531**	**44 493**	**0**	**0**	**0**	**0**	**0**
1100 Of individuals	..	13 308	22 481	31 357	35 632	..	..	..	..	..
1200 Corporate	..	2 487	5 791	8 174	8 861	..	..	..	..	..
1300 Unallocable between 1100 and 1200	..	0	0	0	0	..	..	..	..	..
2000 Social security contributions	**0**	**0**	**0**	**0**	**0**	**85 039**	**510 476**	**831 410**	**1 125 493**	**1 305 959**
2100 Employees	..	..	..	..	..	36 382	221 800	362 829	502 103	595 561
2200 Employers	..	..	..	..	..	45 241	261 805	423 936	561 936	642 189
2300 Self-employed or non-employed	..	..	..	..	..	3 416	26 871	44 645	61 454	68 209
2400 Unallocable between 2100, 2200 and 2300	..	..	..	..	..	0	0	0	0	0
3000 Taxes on payroll and workforce	**0**	**0**	**0**	**0**	**0**	**0**	**0**	**0**	**0**	**0**
4000 Taxes on property	**50 040**	**197 392**	**359 344**	**488 409**	**560 723**	**0**	**0**	**0**	**0**	**0**
4100 Recurrent taxes on immovable property	50 040	195 339	342 203	477 124	548 532	..	..	..	..	..
4200 Recurrent taxes on net wealth	0	0	0	0	0	..	..	..	..	..
4300 Estate, inheritance and gift taxes	0	30	114	249	316	..	..	..	..	..
4400 Taxes on financial and capital transactions	0	50	13 570	6 217	6 334	..	..	..	..	..
4500 Non-recurrent taxes	0	0	0	0	0	..	..	..	..	..
4600 Other recurrent taxes on property	0	1 973	3 457	4 819	5 541	..	..	..	..	..
5000 Taxes on goods and services	**8 389**	**57 507**	**108 696**	**149 160**	**175 857**	**0**	**0**	**0**	**0**	**0**
5100 Taxes on production, sale, transfer, etc	6 518	42 269	76 976	117 002	134 447	..	..	..	..	..
5110 General taxes	4 322	29 316	53 842	84 573	97 440	..	..	..	..	..
5120 Taxes on specific goods and services	2 196	12 953	23 134	32 429	37 007	..	..	..	..	..
5130 Unallocable between 5110 and 5120	0	0	0	0	0	..	..	..	..	..
5200 Taxes on use of goods and perform activities	1 871	15 238	31 720	32 158	41 410	..	..	..	..	..
5300 Unallocable between 5100 and 5200	0	0	0	0	0	..	..	..	..	..
6000 Other taxes	**0**	**0**	**0**	**0**	**0**	**0**	**0**	**0**	**0**	**0**
6100 Paid solely by business	..	..	..	..	..	..	..	..	..	..
6200 Other	..	..	..	..	..	..	..	..	..	..
Total tax revenue	**61 064**	**270 695**	**496 313**	**677 099**	**781 073**	**85 039**	**510 476**	**831 410**	**1 125 493**	**1 305 959**

.. Not available

StatLink https://stat.link/te35fd

Annex A. The OECD classification of taxes and interpretative guide

Table of Contents

A.1 The OECD Classification of Taxes

1. **1000. Taxes on income, profits and capital gains**
    - 1100. Taxes on income, profits and capital gains of individuals
        - 1110. On income and profits
        - 1120. On capital gains
    - 1200. Corporate taxes on income, profits and capital gains
        - 1210. On income and profits
        - 1220. On capital gains
    - 1300. Unallocable as between 1100 and 1200
2. **2000. Social security contributions**
    - 2100. Employees
        - 2110. On a payroll basis
        - 2120. On an income tax basis
    - 2200. Employers
        - 2210. On a payroll basis
        - 2220. On an income tax basis
    - 2300. Self-employed or non-employed
        - 2310. On a payroll basis
        - 2320. On an income tax basis
    - 2400 Unallocable as between 2100, 2200 and 2300
        - 2410. On a payroll basis
        - 2420. On an income tax basis
3. **3000. Taxes on payroll and workforce**
4. **4000. Taxes on property**
    - 4100. Recurrent taxes on immovable property
        - 4110. Households
        - 4120. Other
    - 4200 Recurrent taxes on net wealth
        - 4210. Individual
        - 4220. Corporate
    - 4300. Estate, inheritance and gift taxes
        - 4310. Estate and inheritance taxes
        - 4320. Gift taxes
    - 4400. Taxes on financial and capital transactions

4500. Other non-recurrent taxes on property

4510. On net wealth

4520. Other non-recurrent taxes

4600. Other recurrent taxes on property

5. **5000. Taxes on goods and services**

5100. Taxes on production, sale, transfer, leasing and delivery of goods and rendering of services

5110. General taxes

5111. Value added taxes

5112. Sales taxes

5113. Turnover and other general taxes on goods and services

5120. Taxes on specific goods and services

5121. Excises

5122. Profits of fiscal monopolies

5123. Customs and import duties

5124. Taxes on exports

5125. Taxes on investment goods

5126 . Taxes on specific services

5127. Other taxes on international trade and transactions

5128. Other taxes on specific goods and services

5130. Unallocable as between 5110 and 5120

5200. Taxes on use of goods, or on permission to use goods or perform activities

5210. Recurrent taxes

5211. Paid by households in respect of motor vehicles

5212. Paid by others in respect of motor vehicles

5213. Other recurrent taxes

5220. Non-recurrent taxes

5300. Unallocable as between 5100 and 5200

6. **6000. Other taxes**

6100. Paid solely by business

6200. Paid by other than business or unidentifiable

A.2 Coverage

General criteria

1. In the OECD classification, the term "taxes" is confined to compulsory unrequited payments to the general government or to a supranational authority. Taxes are unrequited in the sense that benefits provided by government to taxpayers are not normally in proportion to their payments.

2. The term "tax" does not include fines, penalties and compulsory loans paid to government. Borderline cases between tax and non-tax revenues in relation to certain fees and charges are discussed in §12–15.

3. General government consists of the central administration, agencies whose operations are under its effective control, state and local governments and their administrations, certain social security schemes and autonomous governmental entities, excluding public enterprises. This definition of government follows that of the 2008 *System of National Accounts* (SNA).[1] In that publication, the general government sector and its sub-sectors are defined in Chapter 4, paragraphs 4.117 to 4.165.

4. Extra-budgetary units are part of the general government system. These are general government entities with individual budgets that are not fully covered by the main or general budget. These entities operate under the authority or control of a central, state, or local government. Extra-budgetary entities may have their own revenue sources, which may be supplemented by grants (transfers) from the general budget or from other sources. Even though their budgets may be subject to approval by the legislature, similar to that of budgetary accounts, they have discretion over the volume and composition of their spending. Such entities may be established to carry out specific government functions, such as road construction, or the nonmarket production of health or education services. Budgetary arrangements vary widely across countries, and various terms are used to describe these entities, but they are often referred to as "extra-budgetary funds" or "decentralised agencies."

5. Compulsory, unrequited payments collected by national governments and paid to supranational authorities are also included as taxes under the definition in paragraph 1. Taxes that are collected by national governments and paid to a supranational authority are included as tax revenues at the level of the supranational authority in the SNA2008 (paragraphs 22.60-61, 22.88 and 22.99 refer) and the ESA2010 (paragraph 20.165 refers). In Revenue Statistics, these taxes include customs duties, contributions to the EU Single Resolution Fund, and any other taxes collected by EU member states on behalf of the European Union. They are included in the tax revenue amounts in the country tables (Chapter 5) of the country in which they are collected and are attributed to the supranational level of government (see §101).

6. In countries where the church forms part of general government, church taxes are included, provided they meet the criteria set out in §1 above. As the data refer to receipts of general government and to supranational authorities, levies paid to non-government bodies, welfare agencies or social insurance schemes outside general government, trade unions or trade associations, even where such levies are compulsory, are excluded. Compulsory payments to general government earmarked for such bodies are, however, included, provided that the government is not simply acting in an agency capacity.[2] Profits from fiscal monopolies are distinguished from those of other public enterprises and are treated as taxes because they reflect the exercise of the taxing power of the state by the use of monopoly powers (see §66–68), as are profits received by the government from the purchase and sale of foreign exchange at different rates (see §76).

7. Taxes paid by governments (e.g., social security contributions and payroll taxes paid by governments in their capacity as an employer, consumption taxes on their purchases or taxes on their property) are not excluded from the data provided. However, where it is possible to identify the amounts of revenue involved,[3] they are shown in Table 5.40 of this Report.

8. The relationship between this classification and that of the System of National Accounts (SNA) is set out in Sections A.9 and A.11 below. Because of the differences between the two classifications, the data shown in national accounts are sometimes calculated or classified differently from the practice set out in this guide. These and other differences are mentioned where appropriate (e.g., in §31 below) but it is not possible to refer to all of them. There may also be some differences between this classification and that employed domestically by certain national administrations (e.g., see §13 below), so that OECD and national statistics data may not always be consistent: any such differences, however, are likely to be very slight in terms of amounts of revenues involved.

Social security contributions

9. Compulsory social security contributions, as defined in §40, and paid to general government, are treated here as tax revenues. They may, however, differ from other taxes in that the receipt of social security benefits depends, in most countries, upon appropriate contributions having been made, although the size of the benefits is not necessarily related to the amount of the contributions. Better comparability between countries is obtained by treating social security contributions as taxes, but they are listed under a separate heading so that they can be distinguished in any analysis.

10. The strict dividing line between tax revenues (compulsory unrequited payments to general government or a supranational authority) and non-tax compulsory payments (NTCPs) (payments that are either requited or made to other institutions) is clearly defined. However, within the range of different compulsory payments to governments existing across countries, it is not always straightforward in practice to decide whether specific payments are either taxes or NTCPs. For example, compulsory pension savings that are controlled by general government and that accumulate on an individual account earning a market return or a rate that compensates for inflation would at first sight be categorised as NTCPs as opposed to taxes. However, even these payments might still be ‘unrequited’ and therefore classify as taxes instead of NTCPs (for example if these pension savings are not paid out when the taxpayer dies before reaching the pension age and the funds are then used to provide a minimum pension to all taxpayers that are insured). These issues result in the social security revenue figures reported for most countries being based on the premise that all types of compulsory payments to general government are judged to some extent to have a re-distributional element. It should be noted that this conclusion is based on a typically broad interpretation of the term ‘unrequited’ in the tax definition.

11. Social security contributions which are either voluntary or not payable to general government (see §1) are not treated as taxes, though in some countries, as indicated in the country footnotes, there are difficulties in completely eliminating voluntary contributions and certain compulsory payments to the private sector from the revenue figures. Imputed social security contributions are also not treated as taxes.

Fees, user charges and licence fees

12. Apart from vehicle licence fees, which are universally regarded as taxes, it is not easy to distinguish between those fees and user charges which are to be treated as taxes and those which are not, since, whilst a fee or charge is levied in connection with a specific service or activity, the strength of the link between the fee and the service provided may vary considerably, as may the relation between the amount of the fee and the cost of providing the service. Where the recipient of a service pays a fee clearly related to the cost of providing the service, the levy may be regarded as requited and under the definition of §1 would not be considered as a tax. In the following cases, however, a levy could be considered as ‘unrequited’:

- *a)* where the charge greatly exceeds the cost of providing the service;
- *b)* where the payer of the levy is not the receiver of the benefit (e.g., a fee collected from slaughterhouses to finance a service which is provided to farmers);

c) where government is not providing a specific service in return for the levy which it receives even though a licence may be issued to the payer (e.g., where the government grants a hunting, fishing or shooting licence which is not accompanied by the right to use a specific area of government land);

d) where benefits are received only by those paying the levy but the benefits received by each individual are not necessarily in proportion to his payments (e.g., a milk marketing levy paid by dairy farmers and used to promote the consumption of milk).

13. In marginal cases, however, the application of the criteria set out in §1 can be particularly difficult. The solution adopted — given the desirability of international uniformity and the relatively small amounts of revenue usually involved — is to follow the predominant practice among tax administrations rather than to allow each country to adopt its own view as to whether such levies are regarded as taxes or as non-tax revenue.[4]

14. A list of the main fees and charges in question and their normal[5] treatment in this publication is as follows:

Non-tax revenues:	court fees; driving licence fees; harbour fees; passport fees; radio and television licence fees where public authorities provide the service
Taxes within heading 5200	permission to perform such activities as distributing films; hunting, fishing and shooting; providing entertainment or gambling facilities; selling alcohol or tobacco; permission to own dogs or to use or own motor vehicles or guns; severance taxes

15. In practice, it may not always be possible to isolate tax receipts from non-tax revenue receipts when they are recorded together. If it is estimated that the bulk of the receipts derive from non-tax revenues, the whole amount involved is treated as a non-tax revenue; otherwise, such government receipts are included and classified according to the rules provided in §33 below.

Royalties

16. The ownership of subsoil assets in the form of deposits of minerals or fossil fuels (coal, oil, or natural gas) depends upon the way in which property rights are defined by law and also on international agreements in the case of deposits below international waters. In some cases, either the ground below which the mineral deposits are located, the deposits themselves or both may belong to a local or central government unit.

17. In such cases, these general government units may grant leases to other institutional units that permit them to extract these deposits over a specified period of time in return for a payment or series of payments. These payments are often described as 'royalties' but they are essentially rent that accrues to owners of natural resources in return for putting these assets at the disposal of other units for specified periods of time. The rent may take the form of periodic payments of fixed amounts, irrespective of the rate of extraction, or, more commonly, they may be a function of the quantity, volume, or value of the asset extracted. Enterprises engaged in exploration on government land may make payments to general government units in exchange for the right to undertake test drilling or otherwise investigate the existence and location of subsoil assets. Such payments are also recorded as rents even though no extraction may take place. These payments are therefore classified as non-tax revenues.

18. The same principles apply when other institutional units are granted leases that permit them to fell timber in natural forests on land owned by general government units. These payments are also classified as non-tax revenues.

19. These rents or royalties paid to general government should not be confused with taxes on income and profits, severance taxes, business licenses, or other taxes. If the payments are levied on the profits from the extraction activity, then they should be classified as taxes on incomes, profits and gains (1000).

In addition, any severance payments that are imposed on the extraction of minerals and fossil fuels from reserves owned privately or by another government should be classified as taxes. Payments related to the gross value of production should be classified as other taxes on goods and services (5128). Payments for a license or permit to conduct extraction operations should be classified as taxes on use of goods and on permission to use goods or perform activities (5213).

Fines and penalties

20. In principle, fines and penalties charged on overdue taxes or penalties imposed for the attempted evasion of taxes should not be recorded as tax revenues. However, it may not be possible to separate payments of fines or other penalties from the revenues from the taxes to which they relate. In this case, the fines and penalties relating to a particular tax are recorded together with the revenues from that tax and fines and penalties paid with revenue from unidentifiable taxes are classified as other taxes in Category 6000. Fines not relating to tax offences (e.g., for parking offences), or not identifiable as relating to tax offences, are also not treated as tax revenues.

A.3 Basis of reporting

Accrual reporting

21. The data reported in this publication for recent years are predominantly recorded on an accrual basis, i.e. recorded at the time that the tax liability was created. Further information is provided in the footnotes to the country table in Chapter 5 of the Report.

22. However, data for earlier years are still predominantly recorded on a cash basis, i.e. at the time at which the payment was received by government. Thus, for example, taxes withheld by employers in one year but paid to the government in the following year and taxes due in one year but actually paid in the following year are both included in the receipts of the second year. Corrective transactions, such as refunds, repayments and drawbacks, are deducted from gross revenues of the period in which they are made.

23. Data on tax revenues are recorded without offsets for the administrative expenses connected with tax collection. Similarly, where the proceeds of tax are used to subsidise particular members of the community, the subsidy is not deducted from the yield of the tax, though the tax may be shown net of subsidies in the national records of some countries.

24. As regards fiscal monopolies (heading 5122), only the amount actually transferred to the government is included in government revenues. However, if any expenditures of fiscal monopolies are considered to be government expenditures (e.g., social expenditures undertaken by fiscal monopolies at the direction of the government) they are added back for the purpose of arriving at tax revenue figures (see §66 below).

The distinction between tax and expenditure provisions[6]

25. Because this publication is concerned only with the revenue side of government operations, no account being taken of the expenditure side, a distinction has to be made between tax and expenditure provisions. Normally there is no difficulty in making this distinction as expenditures are made outside the tax system and the tax accounts and under legislation separate from the tax legislation. In borderline cases, cash flow is used to distinguish between tax provisions and expenditure provisions. Insofar as a provision affects the flow of tax payments from the taxpayer to the government, it is regarded as a tax provision and is taken into account in the data shown in this publication. A provision which does not affect this flow is seen as an expenditure provision and is disregarded in the data recorded in this publication.

26. Tax allowances, exemptions and deductions against the tax base clearly affect the amount of tax paid to the government and are therefore considered as tax provisions. At the other extreme, those subsidies which cannot be offset against tax liability and which are clearly not connected with the assessment process, do not reduce tax revenues as recorded in this publication. Tax credits are amounts deductible from tax payable (as distinct from deductions from the tax base). Two types of tax credits are distinguished, those (referred to here as wastable tax credits) which are limited to the amount of the tax liability and therefore cannot give rise to a payment by the authorities to the taxpayer, and those (referred to as non-wastable tax credits) which are not so limited, so that the excess of the credit over the tax liability can be paid to the taxpayer.[7] A wastable tax credit, like a tax allowance, clearly affects the amount of tax paid to the government, and is therefore considered as a tax provision. The practice followed for non-wastable tax credits[8] is to distinguish between the 'tax expenditure component',[9] which is that portion of the credit that is used to reduce or eliminate a taxpayer's liability, and the 'transfer component', which is the portion that exceeds the taxpayer's liability and is paid to that taxpayer. Reported tax revenues should be reduced by the amount of the tax expenditure component but not by the amount of the transfer component. In addition, the amounts of the tax expenditure and transfer components should be reported as memorandum items in the country tables. Countries that are unable to distinguish between the tax expenditure and transfer components should indicate whether or not the tax revenues have been reduced by the total of these components, and provide any available estimates of the amounts of the two components. Further information is given in Chapter 1 of the Report, which illustrates the effect of alternative treatments of non-wastable tax credits on tax to GDP.

Calendar and fiscal years

27. National authorities whose fiscal years do not correspond to the calendar year show data, where possible, on a calendar year basis to permit maximum comparability with the data of other countries. There remain a few countries where data refer to fiscal years. For these the GDP data used in the comparative tables also correspond to the fiscal years.

A.4 General classification criteria

The main classification criteria

28. The classification of receipts among the main headings (1000, 2000, 3000, 4000, 5000 and 6000) is generally governed by the base on which the tax is levied: 1000 income, profits and capital gains; 2000 and 3000 earnings, payroll or number of employees; 4000 property; 5000 goods and services; 6000 multiple bases, other bases or unidentifiable bases. Where a tax is calculated on more than one base, the receipts are, where possible, split among the various headings (see §33 and §83). The headings 4000 and 5000 cover not only taxes where the tax base is the property, goods or services themselves but also certain related taxes. Thus, taxes on the transfer of property are included in 4400[10] and taxes on the use of goods or on permission to perform activities in 5200. In headings 4000 and 5000 a distinction is made in certain sub-headings between recurrent and non-recurrent taxes: recurrent taxes are defined as those levied at regular intervals (usually annually) and non-recurrent taxes are levied once and for all (see also §48 to §51, §54, §55 and §81 for particular applications of this distinction).

29. Earmarking of a tax for specific purposes does not affect the classification of tax receipts. However, as explained in §40 on the classification of social security contributions, the conferment of an entitlement to social benefits is crucial to the definition of the 2000 main heading.

30. The way that a tax is levied or collected (e.g., by use of stamps) does not affect classification.

Classification of taxpayers

31. In certain sub-headings, distinctions are made between different categories of taxpayers. These distinctions vary from tax to tax:

a) *Between individuals and corporations in relation to income and net wealth taxes*

The basic distinction is that corporation income taxes, as distinct from individual income taxes, are levied on the corporation as an entity, not on the individuals who own it, and without regard to the personal circumstances of these individuals. The same distinction applies to net wealth taxes on corporations and those on individuals. Taxes paid on the profits of partnerships and the income of institutions, such as life insurance or pension funds, are classified according to the same rule. They are classified as corporate taxes (1200) if they are charged on the partnership or institution as an entity without regard to the personal circumstances of the owners. Otherwise, they are treated as individual taxes (1100). Usually, there is different legislation for the corporation taxes and for the individual taxes.[11] The distinction made here between individuals and corporations does not follow the sector classification between households, enterprises, and so on of the System of National Accounts for income and outlay accounts. The SNA classification requires certain unincorporated businesses[12] to be excluded from the household sector and included with non-financial enterprises and financial institutions. The tax on the profits of these businesses, however, cannot always be separated from the tax on the other income of their owners, or can be separated only on an arbitrary basis. No attempt at this separation is made here and the whole of the individual income tax is shown together without regard to the nature of the income chargeable.

b) *Between households and others in relation to taxes on immovable property*

Here the distinction is that adopted by the SNA for the production and consumption expenditure accounts. The distinction is between households as consumers (i.e. excluding non-incorporated business) on the one hand and producers on the other hand. However, taxes on dwellings occupied by households, whether paid by owner-occupiers, tenants or landlords, are classified under households. This follows the common distinction made between taxes on domestic property versus taxes on business property. Some countries are not, however, in a position to make this distinction.

c) *Between households and others in relation to motor vehicle licences*

Here the distinction is between households as consumers on the one hand and producers on the other, as in the production and consumption expenditure accounts of the SNA.

d) *Between business and others in relation to the residual taxes (6000)*

The distinction is the same as in c) above between producers on the one hand and households as consumers on the other hand. Taxes which are included under the heading 6000 because they involve more than one tax base or because the tax base does not fall within any of the previous categories but which are identifiable as levyable only on producers and not on households are included under 'business'. The rest of the taxes which are included under the heading 6000 are shown as 'other' or non-identified.

Surcharges

32. Receipts from surcharges in respect of particular taxes are usually classified with the receipts from the relevant tax whether or not the surcharge is temporary. If, however, the surcharge has a characteristic which would render it classifiable in a different heading of the OECD list, receipts from the surcharge are classified under that heading separately from the relevant tax.

Unidentifiable tax receipts and residual sub-headings

33. A number of cases arise where taxes cannot be identified as belonging entirely to a heading or sub-heading of the OECD classification and the following practices are applied in such cases:

a) The heading is known, but it is not known how receipts should be allocated between sub-headings: receipts are classified in the appropriate residual sub-heading (1300, 2400, 4520, 4600, 5130, 5300 or 6200).

b) It is known that the bulk of receipts from a group of taxes (usually local taxes) is derived from taxes within a particular heading or sub-heading, but some of the taxes in the group whose amount cannot be precisely ascertained may be classifiable in other headings or sub-headings: receipts are shown in the heading or sub-heading under which most of the receipts fall.

c) Neither the heading nor sub-heading of a tax (usually local) can be identified: the tax is classified in 6200 unless it is known that it is a tax on business in which case it is classified in 6100.

A.5 Commentaries on items of the list

1000 — Taxes on income, profits and capital gains

34. This heading covers taxes levied on the net income or profits (i.e. gross income minus allowable tax reliefs) of individuals and enterprises. Also covered are taxes levied on the capital gains of individuals and enterprises, and gains from gambling.

35. Included in the heading are:

a) taxes levied predominantly on income or profits, though partially on other bases. Taxes on various bases which are not predominantly income or profits are classified according to the principles laid down in §33 and §83;

b) taxes on property, which are levied on a presumed or estimated income as part of an income tax (see also §48(a), (c) and (d));

c) compulsory payments to social security fund contributions that are levied on income but do not confer an entitlement to social benefits. When such contributions do confer an entitlement to social benefits, they are included in heading 2000 (see §40);

d) receipts from integrated scheduler income tax systems are classified as a whole in this heading, even though certain of the scheduler taxes may be based upon gross income and may not take into account the personal circumstances of the taxpayer.

36. The main subdivision of this heading is between levies on individuals (1100) and those on corporate enterprises (1200). Under each subdivision a distinction is made between taxes on income and profits (1110 and 1210), and taxes on capital gains (1120 and 1220). If certain receipts cannot be identified as appropriate to either 1100 or 1200, or if in practice this distinction cannot be made (e.g., because there are no reliable data on the recipients of payments from which withholding taxes are deducted) they are classified in 1300 as not-allocable.

Treatment of credits under imputation systems

37. Under imputation systems of corporate income tax, a company's shareholders are wholly or partly relieved of their liability to income tax on dividends paid by the company out of income or profits liable to corporate income tax. In countries with such systems,[13] part of the tax on the company's profits is available

to provide relief against the shareholders' own tax liability. The relief to the shareholder takes the form of a tax credit, the amount of which may be less than, equal to, or more than the shareholder's overall tax liability. If the tax credit exceeds this tax liability the excess may be payable to the shareholder. As this type of tax credit is an integral part of the imputation system of corporate income tax, any payment to the shareholders is treated as a repayment of tax and not as expenditure (compare the treatment of other tax credits described in §26).

38. As the tax credit under imputation systems (even when exceeding tax liability) is to be regarded as a tax provision, the question arises whether it should be deducted from individual income tax receipts (1110) or corporate income tax receipts (1210). In this Report, the full amount of corporate income tax paid is shown under 1210 and no imputed tax is included under 1110. Thus, the full amount of the credit reduces the amount of 1110 whether the credit results in a reduction of personal income tax liability or whether an actual refund is made because the credit exceeds the income tax liability. (Where, however, such tax credits are deducted from corporation tax in respect of dividends paid to corporations the amounts are deducted from the receipts of 1210).

1120 and 1220 — Taxes on capital gains

39. These sub-headings comprise taxes imposed on capital gains, 1120 covering those levied on the gains of individuals and 1220 those levied on the gains of corporate enterprises, where receipts from such taxes can be separately identified. In many countries, this is not the case and the receipts from such taxes are then classified with those from the income tax. Heading 1120 also includes taxes on gains from gambling.

2000 — Social security contributions

40. Classified here are all compulsory payments to general government that confer an entitlement to receive a (contingent) future social benefit. Such payments are usually earmarked to finance social benefits and are often paid to institutions of general government that provide such benefits. However, such earmarking is not part of the definition of social security contributions and is not required for a tax to be classified here. However, conferment of an entitlement is required for a tax to be classified under this heading. So, levies on income or payroll that are earmarked for social security funds but do not confer an entitlement to benefit are excluded from this heading and shown under personal income taxes (1100) or taxes on payroll and workforce (3000). Taxes on other bases, such as goods and services, which are earmarked for social security benefits are not shown here but are classified according to their respective bases because they generally confer no entitlement to social security benefits.

41. Contributions for the following types of social security benefits would, *inter alia*, be included: unemployment insurance benefits and supplements, accident, injury and sickness benefits, old-age, disability and survivors' pensions, family allowances, reimbursements for medical and hospital expenses or provision of hospital or medical services. Contributions may be levied on both employees and employers.

42. Contributions may be based on earnings or payroll ('on a payroll basis') or on net income after deductions and exemptions for personal circumstances ('on an income tax basis'), and the revenues from the two bases should be separately identified if possible. However, where contributions to a general social security scheme are on a payroll basis, but the contributions of particular groups (such as the self-employed) cannot be assessed on this basis and net income is used as a proxy for gross earnings, the receipts may still be classified as being on a payroll basis. In principle, this heading excludes voluntary contributions paid to social security schemes. When separately identifiable these are shown in the memorandum item on the financing of social security benefits. In practice, however, they cannot always be separately identified from compulsory contributions, in which case they are included in this heading.

43. Contributions to social insurance schemes which are not institutions of general government and to other types of insurance schemes, provident funds, pension funds, friendly societies or other saving schemes are not considered as social security contributions. Provident funds are arrangements under which the contributions of each employee and of the corresponding employer on his/her behalf are kept in a separate account earning interest and withdrawable under specific circumstances. Pension funds are separately organised schemes negotiated between employees and employers and carry provisions for different contributions and benefits, sometimes more directly tied to salary levels and length of service than under social security schemes. When contributions to these schemes are compulsory or quasi-compulsory (e.g., by virtue of agreement with professional and union organisations) they are shown in the memorandum item (refer to Table 5.39 of the Report).

44. Contributions by government employees and by governments in respect of their employees, to social security schemes classified within general government are included in this heading. Contributions to separate schemes for government employees, which can be regarded as replacing general social security schemes, are also regarded as taxes.[14] Where, however, a separate scheme is not seen as replacing a general scheme and has been negotiated between the government, in its role as an employer, and its employees, it is not regarded as social security and contributions to it are not regarded as taxes, even though the scheme may have been established by legislation.

45. This heading excludes 'imputed' contributions, which correspond to social benefits paid directly by employers to their employees or former employees or to their representatives (e.g., when employers are legally obliged to pay sickness benefits for a certain period).

46. Contributions are divided into those of employees (2100), employers (2200), and self-employed or non-employed (2300), and then further sub-divided according to the basis on which they are levied. Employees are defined for this purpose as all persons engaged in activities of business units, government bodies, private non-profit institutions, or other paid employment, except the proprietors and their unpaid family members in the case of unincorporated businesses. Members of the armed forces are included, irrespective of the duration and type of their service, if they contribute to social security schemes. The contributions of employers are defined as their payments on account of their employees to social security schemes. Where employees or employers are required to continue the payment of social security contributions when the employee becomes unemployed these contributions, data permitting, are shown in 2100 and 2200 respectively. Accordingly, the sub-heading 2300 is confined to contributions paid by the self-employed and by those outside of the labour force (e.g., disabled or retired individuals).

3000 — Taxes on payroll and workforce

47. These consist of taxes payable by enterprises assessed either as a proportion of the wages or salaries paid or as a fixed amount per person employed. They do not include compulsory social security contributions paid by employers or any taxes paid by employees themselves out of their wages or salaries

4000 — Taxes on property

48. This heading covers recurrent and non-recurrent taxes on the use, ownership or transfer of property. These include taxes on immovable property or net wealth, taxes on the change of ownership of property through inheritance or gift and taxes on financial and capital transactions. The following kinds of tax are excluded from this heading:

a) taxes on capital gains resulting from the sale of a property (1120 or 1220);

b) taxes on the use of goods or on permission to use goods or perform activities (5200); see §78;

c) taxes on immovable property levied on the basis of a presumed net income which take into account the personal circumstances of the taxpayer. They are classified as income taxes along with taxes on income and capital gains derived from property (1100);

d) taxes on the use of property for residence, where the tax is payable by either proprietor or tenant and the amount payable is a function of the user's personal circumstances (pay, dependants, and so on). They are classified as taxes on income (1100);

e) taxes on building in excess of permitted maximum density, taxes on the enlargement, construction or alteration of certain buildings beyond a permitted value and taxes on building construction. They are classified as taxes on permission to perform activities (5200);

f) taxes on the use of one's own property for special trading purposes like selling alcohol, tobacco, meat or for exploitation of land resources (e.g., United States severance taxes). They are classified as taxes on permission to perform activities (5200).

4100 — Recurrent taxes on immovable property

49. This sub-heading covers taxes levied regularly in respect of the use or ownership of immovable property.

- these taxes are levied on land and buildings;
- they can be in the form of a percentage of an assessed property value based on a national rental income, sales price, or capitalised yield; or in terms of other characteristics of real property, (for example size or location) from which a presumed rent or capital value can be derived.
- such taxes can be levied on proprietors, tenants, or both. They can also be paid by one level of government to another level of government in respect of property under the jurisdiction of the latter.
- debts are not taken into account in the assessment of these taxes, and they differ from taxes on net wealth in this respect.

50. Taxes on immovable property are further sub-divided into those paid by households (4110) and those paid by other entities (4120), according to the criteria set out in §31(*b*) above.

4200 — Recurrent taxes on net wealth

51. This sub-heading covers taxes levied regularly (in most cases annually) on net wealth, i.e. taxes on a wide range of movable and immovable property, net of debt. It is sub-divided into taxes paid by individuals (4210) and taxes paid by corporate enterprises (4220) according to the criteria set out in §31(*a*) above. If separate figures exist for receipts paid by institutions, the tax payments involved are added to those paid by corporations.

4300 — Estate, inheritance and gift taxes

52. This sub-heading is divided into taxes on estates and inheritances (4310) and taxes on gifts (4320).[15] Estate taxes are charged on the amount of the total estate whereas inheritance taxes are charged on the shares of the individual recipients; in addition the latter may take into account the relationship of the individual recipients to the deceased.

4400 — Taxes on financial and capital transactions

53. This sub-heading comprises, *inter alia*, taxes on the issue, transfer, purchase and sale of securities, taxes on cheques, and taxes levied on specific legal transactions such as validation of contracts and the sale of immovable property. The heading does not include:

a) taxes on the use of goods or property or permission to perform certain activities (5200);
b) fees paid to cover court charges, charges for birth, marriage or death certificates, which are normally regarded as non-tax revenues (see §12);
c) taxes on capital gains (1000);
d) recurrent taxes on immovable property (4100);
e) recurrent taxes on net wealth (4200);
f) once-and-for-all levies on property or wealth (4500).

4500 — Other non-recurrent taxes on property

54. This sub-heading covers once-and-for-all, as distinct from recurrent, levies on property. It is divided into taxes on net wealth (4510) and other non-recurrent taxes on property (4520). Heading 4510 would include taxes levied to meet emergency expenditures, or for redistribution purposes. Heading 4520 would cover taxes levied to take account of increases in land value due to permission given to develop or provision of additional local facilities by general government, any taxes on the revaluation of capital and once-and-for-all taxes on particular items of property.

4600 — Other recurrent taxes on property

55. These rarely exist in OECD member countries, but the heading would include taxes on goods such as cattle, jewellery, windows, and other external signs of wealth.

5000 — Taxes on goods and services

56. All taxes and duties levied on the production, extraction, sale, transfer, leasing or delivery of goods, and the rendering of services (5100), or in respect of the use of goods or permission to use goods or to perform activities (5200) are included here. The heading thus covers:

a) multi-stage cumulative taxes;
b) general sales taxes — whether levied at manufacture/production, wholesale or retail level;
c) value-added taxes;
d) excises;
e) taxes levied on the import and export of goods;
f) taxes levied in respect of the use of goods and taxes on permission to use goods, or perform certain activities;
g) taxes on the extraction, processing or production of minerals and other products.

57. Borderline cases between this heading and heading 4000 (taxes on property) and 6100 (other taxes on business) are referred to in §48, §53 and §80. Residual sub-headings (5300) and (5130) cover tax receipts which cannot be allocated between 5100 and 5200 and between 5110 and 5120, respectively; see §33.

5100 — Taxes on the production, sale, transfer, leasing and delivery of goods and rendering of services

58. This sub-heading consists of all taxes, levied on transactions in goods and services on the basis of their intrinsic characteristics (e.g., value, weight of tobacco, strength of alcohol, and so on) as distinct from taxes imposed on the use of goods, or permission to use goods or perform activities, which fall under 5200.

5110 — General taxes on goods and services

59. This sub-heading includes all taxes, other than import and export duties (5123 and 5124), levied on the production, leasing, transfer, delivery or sales of a wide range of goods and/or the rendering of a wide range of services, irrespective of whether they are domestically produced or imported and irrespective of the stage of production or distribution at which they are levied. It thus covers value-added taxes, sales taxes and multi-stage cumulative taxes. Receipts from border adjustments in respect of such taxes when goods are imported are added to gross receipts for this category, and repayments of such taxes when goods are exported are deducted. These taxes are subdivided into 5111 value-added taxes, 5112 sales taxes, 5113 turnover and other general taxes on goods and services.

60. Borderline cases arise between this heading and taxes on specific goods (5120) when taxes are levied on a large number of goods, for example, the United Kingdom purchase tax (repealed in 1973) and the Japanese commodity tax (repealed in 1988). In conformity with national views, the former United Kingdom purchase tax is classified as a general tax (5112) and the former Japanese commodity tax as excises (5121).

5111 — Value-added taxes

61. All general consumption taxes charged on value-added are classified in this sub-heading, irrespective of the method of deduction and the stages at which the taxes are levied. In practice, all OECD countries with value-added taxes normally allow immediate deduction of taxes on purchases by all but the final consumer and impose tax at all stages. In some countries the heading may include certain taxes, such as those on financial and insurance activities, either because receipts from them cannot be identified separately from those from the value-added tax, or because they are regarded as an integral part of the value-added tax, even though similar taxes in other countries might be classified elsewhere (e.g., 5126 as taxes on services or 4400 as taxes on financial and capital transactions).

5112 — Sales taxes

62. All general taxes levied at one stage only, whether at manufacturing or production, wholesale or retail stage are classified here.

5113 — Turnover and other general taxes on goods and services

63. These are multi-stage cumulative taxes and taxes where elements of consumption taxes are combined with multistage taxes. These taxes are levied each time a transaction takes place without deduction for taxes paid on inputs. Multi-stage taxes can be combined with elements of value-added or sales taxes.

5120 — Taxes on specific goods and services

64. Excises, profits generated and transferred from fiscal monopolies, and customs and imports duties as well as taxes on exports, foreign exchange transactions, investment goods and betting stakes and special taxes on services, which do not form part of a general tax of 5110, are included in this category.

5121 — Excises

65. Excises are taxes levied as a product specific unit tax on a predefined limited range of goods. Excises are usually levied at differentiated rates on nonessential or luxury goods, alcoholic beverages, tobacco, and energy. Excises may be imposed at any stage of production or distribution and are usually assessed as a specific charge per unit based on characteristics by reference to the value, weight, strength,

or quantity of the product. Included are special taxes on individual products such as sugar, sugar beets, matches, and chocolates; taxes levied at varying rates on a certain range of goods; and taxes levied on tobacco goods, alcoholic drinks, motor fuels, and hydrocarbon oils. If a tax collected principally on imported goods also applies, or would apply, under the same law to comparable domestically produced goods, then the revenue from this tax is classified as arising from excises rather than from import duties. This principle applies even if there is no comparable domestic production or no possibility of such production. Taxes on the use of utilities such as water, electricity, gas, and energy are regarded as excises rather than taxes on specific services (5126). Excises exclude those taxes that are levied as general taxes on goods and services (5110); profits of fiscal monopolies (5122); customs and other import duties (5123); or taxes on exports (5124).

5122 — Profits of fiscal monopolies

66. This sub-heading covers that part of the profits of fiscal monopolies which is transferred to general government or which is used to finance any expenditures considered to be government expenditures (see §24). Amounts are shown when they are transferred to general government or used to make expenditures considered to be government expenditures.

67. Fiscal monopolies reflect the exercise of the taxing power of government by the use of monopoly powers. Fiscal monopolies are non-financial public enterprises exercising a monopoly in most cases over the production or distribution of tobacco, alcoholic beverages, salt, matches, playing cards and petroleum or agricultural products (i.e. on the kind of products which are likely to be, alternatively or additionally, subject to the excises of 5121), to raise the government revenues which in other countries are gathered through taxes on dealings in such commodities by private business units. The government monopoly may be at the production stage or, as in the case of government-owned and controlled liquor stores, at the distribution stage.

68. Fiscal monopolies are distinguished from public utilities such as rail transport, electricity, post offices, and other communications, which may enjoy a monopoly or quasi-monopoly position but where the primary purpose is normally to provide basic services rather than to raise revenue for government. Transfers from such other public enterprises to the government are considered as non-tax revenues. The traditional concept of fiscal monopoly is not generally extended to include state lotteries, the profits of which are usually accordingly regarded as non-tax revenues. However, they can be included as tax revenues if the prime reason for their operation is to raise revenues to finance government expenditure. Fiscal monopoly profits are distinguished from export and import monopoly profits (5127) transferred from marketing boards or other enterprises dealing with international trade.

5123 — Customs and other import duties

69. Taxes, stamp duties and surcharges restricted by law to imported products are included here. Also included are levies on imported agricultural products which are imposed in member countries of the European Union and amounts paid by certain of these countries under the Monetary Compensation Accounts (MCA) system.[16] Customs duties collected by European Union member states on behalf of the European Union are reported under this heading at the supranational level of government in the country tables (in Chapter 5 of the Report). Excluded here are taxes collected on imports as part of a general tax on goods and services, or an excise applicable to both imported and domestically produced goods.

5124 — Taxes on exports

70. In the 1970s, export duties were levied in Australia, Canada and Portugal as a regular measure and they have been used in Finland for counter-cyclical purposes. Some member countries of the European Union pay, as part of the MCA system, a levy on exports (see note 16 to §69). Where these

amounts are identifiable, they are shown in this heading. This heading does not include repayments of general consumption taxes or excises or customs duties on exported goods, which should be deducted from the gross receipts under 5110, 5121 or 5123, as appropriate.

5125 — Taxes on investment goods

71. This sub-heading covers taxes on investment goods, such as machinery. These taxes may be imposed for a number of years or temporarily for counter-cyclical purposes. Taxes on industrial inputs which are also levied on consumers [e.g., the Swedish energy tax which is classified under (5121)] are not included here.

5126 — Taxes on specific services

72. All taxes assessed on the payment for specific services, such as taxes on insurance premiums, banking services, gambling and betting stakes (e.g., from horse races, football pools, lottery tickets), transport, entertainment, restaurant and advertising charges, fall into this category. Taxes levied on the gross income of companies providing the service (e.g., gross insurance premiums or gambling stakes received by the company) are also classified under this heading.

73. Tax revenues from bank levies and payments to deposit insurance and financial stability schemes are also included here:

- Compulsory payments of stability fees, bank levies and deposit insurance should generally be treated as tax revenues where the payments are made to general government or supranational authorities and are allocated to the governments' consolidated or general funds so that the government is free to make immediate use of the money for the purposes that it chooses. This principle would apply regardless of whether the government is promising to make payments to guarantee the banks' customer deposits in some future contingency.
- If the compulsory payments are made to general government and placed in funds that are earmarked to be entirely channelled back to the sector of the economy that comprises the companies that are subject to the payment, they would still generally be treated as tax revenues on the grounds that the funds would be available for the government and would reduce its budget deficit, the fee is unrequited for an individual entity and the amounts raised could be unrelated to any eventual pay out to depositors or expenditure on wider support for the financial sector.
- Payments to made to the smaller long-standing schemes for insuring 'retail' deposits, where the payment levels are consistent with the costs of insurance should be classified as fee for service.
- Any payments which involve governments realising the assets of a failed institution or receiving a priority claim on its assets in liquidation in order to fund payments of compensation to customers for their lost deposits would be treated as a fee for a service as opposed to tax revenues.
- Compulsory payments that are made to funds operated outside the government sector and non-state institutions backed by the deposit takers and all payments to voluntary schemes should not be treated as tax revenues.

- Contributions made to the EU Single Resolution Fund are also included here and recorded under the supranational level of government in the country tables.

74. Excluded from this sub-heading are:

a) taxes on services forming part of a general tax on goods and services (5110);

b) taxes on electricity, gas and energy (5121 as excises);

c) taxes on individual gains from gambling (1120 as taxes on capital gains of individuals and non-corporate enterprises) and lump-sum taxes on the transfer of private lotteries or on the permission to set up lotteries (5200);[17]

d) taxes on cheques and on the issue, transfer or redemption of securities (4400 as taxes on financial and capital transactions).

5127 — Other taxes on international trade and transactions

75. This sub-heading covers revenue received by the government from the purchase and sale of foreign exchange at different rates. When the government exercises monopoly powers to extract a margin between the purchase and sales price of foreign exchange, other than to cover administrative costs, the revenue derived constitutes a compulsory levy exacted in indeterminate proportions from both purchaser and seller of foreign exchange. It is the common equivalent of an import duty and export duty levied in a single exchange rate system or of a tax on the sale or purchase of foreign exchange. Like the profits of fiscal monopolies and import or export monopolies transferred to government, it represents the exercise of monopoly powers for tax purposes and is included in tax revenues.

76. The sub-heading covers also the profits of export or import monopolies, which do not however exist in OECD countries, taxes on purchase or sale of foreign exchange, and any other taxes levied specifically on international trade or transactions.

5128 — Other taxes on specific goods and services

77. This item includes taxes on the extraction of minerals, fossil fuels and other exhaustible resources from deposits owned privately or by another government together with any other unidentifiable receipts from taxes on specific goods and services. Taxes on the extraction of exhaustible resources are usually a fixed amount per unit of quality or weight, but can be a percentage of value. The taxes are recorded when the resources are extracted. Payments from the extraction of exhaustible resources from deposits owned by the government unit receiving the payment are classified as rent.

5200 — Taxes on use of goods or on permission to use goods or perform activities

78. This sub-heading covers taxes which are levied in respect of the use of goods as distinct from taxes on the goods themselves. Unlike the latter taxes – reported under 5100 –, they are not assessed on the value of the goods but usually as fixed amounts. Taxes on permission to use goods or to perform activities are also included here, as are pollution taxes not based upon the value of particular goods. It is sometimes difficult to distinguish between compulsory user charges and licence fees which are regarded as taxes and those which are excluded as non-tax revenues. The criteria which are employed are noted in §12–13.

79. Although the sub-heading refers to the 'use' of goods, registration of ownership rather than use may be what generates liability to tax, so that the taxes of this heading may apply to the ownership of animals or goods rather than their use (e.g., race horses, dogs and motor vehicles) and may apply even to unusable goods (e.g., unusable motor vehicles or guns).

80. Borderline cases arise with:

a) taxes on the permission to perform business activities which are levied on a combined income, payroll or turnover base and, accordingly, are classified following the rules in §83;

b) taxes on the ownership or use of property of headings 4100, 4200 and 4600. The heading 4100 is confined to taxes on the ownership or tenancy of immovable property and – unlike the taxes of 5200 – they are related to the value of the property. The net wealth taxes and taxes on chattels of 4200 and 4600 respectively are confined to the ownership rather than the use of assets, apply to groups of assets rather than particular goods and again are related to the value of the assets,

5210 — Recurrent taxes on use of goods and on permission to use goods or perform activities

81. The principal characteristic of taxes classified here is that they are levied at regular intervals and that they are usually fixed amounts. The most important item in terms of revenue receipts is vehicle licence taxes. This sub-heading also covers taxes on permission to hunt, shoot, fish or to sell certain products and taxes on the ownership of dogs and on the performance of certain services, provided that they meet the criteria set out in §12–13. The sub-divisions of 5210 are user taxes on motor vehicles paid by households (5211) and those paid by others (5212). Sub-heading 5213 covers dog licences and user charges for permission to perform activities such as selling meat or liquor when the levies are on a recurring basis. It also covers recurrent general licences for hunting, shooting and fishing where the right to carry out these activities is not granted as part of a normal commercial transaction (e.g., the granting of the licence is not accompanied by the right to use a specific area which is owned by government).

5220 — Non-recurrent taxes on use of goods and on permission to use goods or perform activities

82. This section covers non-recurrent taxes levied on the use of goods or on permission to use goods or perform activities and taxes levied each time goods are used. It includes taxes levied on the emission or discharge into the environment of noxious gases, liquids or other harmful substances.

- Payments for tradable emission permits issued by governments under cap and trade schemes should be recorded here at the time the emissions occur. No revenue should be recorded for permits that governments issue free of charge. The accrual basis of recording means that there can be a timing difference between the cash being received by government for the permits and the time the emission occurs. In the national accounts, this timing gives rise to a financial liability for government during the period.
- Payments made for the collection and disposal of waste or noxious substances by public authorities should be excluded as they constitute a sale of services to enterprises.

83. Other taxes falling under heading 5200 that are not levied recurrently are also included here. Thus, once-and-for-all payments for permission to sell liquor or tobacco or to set up betting shops are included provided they meet the criteria set out in §12–13.

6000 — Other taxes

84. Taxes levied on a base, or bases, other than those described under headings 1000, 3000, 4000 and 5000, or on bases of which cannot be considered to be related to any one of these headings, are included here. Where taxes are levied on a multiple base and it is possible to estimate the receipts related to each base the separate amounts are included under the appropriate headings. If separate amounts cannot be estimated and it is known that most of the receipts are derived from one base, the whole of the receipts are classified according to that base. Otherwise, they are classified here. Other revenues included here are presumptive taxes not included elsewhere in the classification system, taxes on individuals in the form of a poll tax or capitation tax, stamp taxes not related to financial and capital transactions nor falling exclusively on a single category of transaction, expenditure taxes where personal deductions or exemptions are applied and unidentifiable tax receipts. A subdivision is made between taxes levied wholly or predominantly on business (6100) and those levied on others (6200).

A.6 Conciliation with National Accounts

85. This section of the tables provides a re-conciliation between the OECD calculation of total tax revenues and the total of all taxes and social contributions paid to general government as recorded in the country's National Accounts. Where the country is a member of the European Union (EU), the comparison is between the OECD calculation of total tax revenues and the sum of tax revenues and social contributions recorded in the combination of the general government and the institutions of the EU sectors of the National Accounts.

A.7 Memorandum item on the financing of social security benefits

86. In view of the varying relationship between taxation and social security contributions and the cases referred to in §40 to §46, a memorandum item collects together all payments earmarked for social security-type benefits, other than voluntary payments to the private sector. Data are presented as follows (refer Table 5.39 of the Report):

a) Taxes of 2000 series.

b) Taxes earmarked for social security benefits.

c) Voluntary contributions to the government.

d) Compulsory contributions to the private sector.

Guidance on the breakdown of (a) to (d) above is provided in §40 to §46.

A.8 Memorandum item on identifiable taxes paid by government

87. Identifiable taxes actually paid by government are presented in a memorandum item classified by the main headings of the OECD classification of taxes. In the vast majority of countries, only social security contributions and payroll taxes paid by government can be identified. These are, however, usually the most important taxes paid by governments (refer to Table 5.40 of the Report).

A.9 Relation of OECD classification of taxes to national accounting systems

88. A system of national accounts (SNA) seeks to provide a coherent framework for recording and presenting the main flows relating respectively to production, consumption, accumulation and external transactions of a given economic area, usually a country or a major region within a country. Government revenues are an important part of the transactions recorded in SNA. The final version of the 2008 SNA was jointly published by five international organisations: the United Nations, the International Monetary Fund, the European Union, the Organisation for Economic Co-operation and Development, and the World Bank in August 2009. The *System* is a comprehensive, consistent and flexible set of macroeconomic accounts. It is designed for use in countries with market economies, whatever their stage of economic development, and also in countries in transition to market economies. The important parts of the SNA's conceptual framework and its definitions of the various sectors of the economy have been reflected in the OECD's classification of taxes.

89. There are, however, some differences between the OECD classification of taxes and SNA concepts that are listed below. They arise because the aim of the former is to provide the maximum disaggregation of statistical data on what are generally regarded as taxes by tax administrations.

a) OECD includes compulsory social security contributions paid to general government in total tax revenues. Imputed and voluntary contributions plus those paid to private funds are not treated as taxes (§9 and §11 above);

b) there are different points of view on whether or not some levies and fees are classified as taxes (§12 and §13 above);

c) OECD excludes imputed taxes or subsidies resulting from the operation of official multiple exchange rates or from the central bank paying a rate of interest on required reserves that is different from other market rates;

d) there are differences in the treatment of non-wastable tax credits

90. As noted in §1 and §2, headings 1000 to 6000 of the OECD list of taxes cover all unrequited payments to general government or to a supranational authority, other than compulsory loans and fines. Such unrequited payments including fines, but excluding compulsory loans can be obtained from adding together the following figures in the 2008 SNA

- value-added type taxes (D.211);
- taxes and duties on imports, excluding VAT (D.212);
- export taxes (D.213);
- taxes on products, excluding VAT, import and export taxes (D.214);
- other taxes on production (D.29);
- taxes on income (D.51);
- other current taxes (D.59);
- actual social contributions (D.611 and D613), excluding voluntary contributions and payments to employment-related schemes that are not social security schemes
- capital taxes (D.91).

A.10 The OECD classification of taxes and the International Monetary Fund (GFS) system

91. The coverage and valuation of tax revenues in the GFS system and the 2008 SNA are very similar. Therefore, the differences between the OECD classification and that of the 2008 SNA (see §89 above) also apply to the GFS. In addition the International Monetary Fund subdivides the OECD 5000 heading into section IV (Domestic Taxes on Goods and Services) and section V (Taxes on International Trade and Transactions). This reflects the fact that while the latter usually yield insignificant amounts of revenue in OECD countries, this is not the case in many non-OECD countries.

A.11 Comparison of the OECD classification of taxes with other international classifications

92. The table below describes an item by item comparison of the OECD classification of taxes and the classifications used in the following:

a) System of National Accounts (2008 SNA);

b) European System of Accounts (2010 ESA);

c) IMF Government Finance Statistics Manual (GFSM2014).

93. These comparisons represent those that would be expected to apply in the majority of cases. However in practice some flexibility should be used in their application. This is because in particular cases, countries can adopt varying approaches to the classification of revenues in National Accounts.

OECD Classification					2008 SNA	2010 ESA	GFSM2014
1000				Taxes on income, profits and capital gains			
	1100			Individuals			
		1110		Income and profits	D51-8.61a	D51A	1111
		1120		Capital gains	D51-8.61c, d	D51C, D	1111
	1200			Corporations			
		1210		Income and profits	D51-8.61b	D51B	1112
		1220		Capital gains	D51-8.61c	D51C	1112
	1300			Unallocable as between 1100 and 1200			1113
2000				Social security contributions			
	2100			Employees	D613-8.85	D613	1211
	2200			Employers	D611-8.83	D611	1212
	2300			Self-employed, non-employed	D613-8.85	D613	1213
	2400			Unallocable as between 2100, 2200 and 2300			1214
3000				Taxes on payroll and workforce	D29-7.97a	D29C	112
4000				Taxes on property			
	4100			Recurrent taxes on immovable property			
		4110		Households	D59-8.63a	D59A	1131
		4120		Other	D29-7.97b	D29A	1131
	4200			Recurrent net wealth taxes			
		4210		Individual	D59-8.63b	D59A	1132
		4220		Corporations	D59-8.63b	D59A	1132
	4300			Estate, inheritance and gift taxes			
		4310		Estate and inheritance taxes	D91-10.207b	D91A	1133
		4320		Gift taxes	D91-10.207b	D91A	1133
	4400			Taxes on financial and capital transactions	D59-7.96d; D29-7.97e	D214B, C	114114; 1161
	4500			Other non-recurrent taxes on property	D91-10.207a	D91B	1135
	4600			Other recurrent taxes on property	D59-8.63c	D59A	1136
5000				Taxes on goods and services			
	5100			Taxes on production, sale and transfer of goods and services			
		5110		General taxes on goods and services			
			5111	Value-added taxes	D211-7.89	D211; D29G	11411
			5112	Sales taxes	D2122-7.94a; D214-7.96a	D21224; D214I	11412
			5113	Other general taxes on goods and services	D214-7.96a	D214I	11413
		5120		Taxes on specific goods and services			
			5121	Excises	D2122-7.94b; D214-7.96b	D21223; D214A, B, D	1142
			5122	Profits of fiscal monopolies	D214-7.96e	D214J	1143
			5123	Customs and other import duties	D2121-7.93	D2121; D21221, 2	1151
			5124	On exports	D213-7.95a	D214K	1152-4
			5125	On investment goods			
			5126	On specific services	D2122-7.94c; D214-7.96c	D21225; D214E, F, G, H; D29F	1144; 1156
			5127	Other taxes on international trade and transactions	D2122-7.94d D29-7.95b D29-7.97g D59-8.64d	D21226; D29D; D59E	1153; 1155-6

			5128	Other taxes on specific goods and services			1146
		5130		Unallocable between 5110 and 5120			
	5200			Taxes on use of goods and on permission to use goods or perform activities			
		5210		Recurrent taxes on use of goods and on permission to use goods or perform activities			
			5211	Motor vehicle taxes households	D59-8.64c	D59D	11451
			5212	Motor vehicles taxes others	D29-7.97d	D214D; D29B	11451
			5213	Other recurrent taxes on use of goods and on permission to use goods or perform activities	D29-7.97c, d, f D59-8.64c	D29B, E, F; D59D	11452
		5220		Non-recurrent taxes on permission to use goods or perform activities			11452
	5300			Unallocable as between 5100 and 5200			
6000				Other taxes			
	6100			Payable solely by business			1161
	6200			Payable by other than business, or unidentifiable	D59-8.64a, b	D59B, C	1162

A.12 Attribution of tax revenues by sub-sectors of general government

94. The OECD classification requires a breakdown of tax revenues by sub-sectors of government. The definition of each sub-sector and the criteria to be used to attribute tax revenues between these sub-sectors are set out below. They follow the guidance of the 2008 SNA and GFSM 2014.

Sub-sectors of general government to be identified

a) Central government

95. The central government sub-sector includes all governmental departments, offices, establishments and other bodies which are agencies or instruments of the central authority whose competence extends over the whole territory, with the exception of the administration of social security funds. Central government therefore has the authority to impose taxes on all resident and non-resident units engaged in economic activities within the country.

b) State, provincial or regional government

96. This sub-sector consists of intermediate units of government exercising a competence at a level below that of central government. It includes all such units operating independently of central government in a part of a country's territory encompassing a number of smaller localities, with the exception of the administration of social security funds. In unitary countries, regional governments may be considered to have a separate existence where they have substantial autonomy to raise a significant proportion of their revenues from sources within their control and their officers are independent of external administrative control in the actual operation of the unit's activities.

97. At present, federal countries comprise the majority of cases where revenues attributed to intermediate units of government are identified separately. Colombia and Spain are the only two unitary countries in this position. In the remaining unitary countries, regional revenues are included with those of local governments.

c) *Local* government

98. This sub-sector includes all other units of government exercising an independent competence in part of the territory of a country, with the exception of the administration of social security funds. It

encompasses various urban and/or rural jurisdictions (e.g., local authorities, municipalities, cities, boroughs, districts).

d) Social security funds

99. Social security funds form a separate sub-sector of general government. The social security sub-sector is defined in the 2008 SNA by the following extracts from paragraphs 4.124 to 4.126 and 4.147:

"Social security schemes are social insurance schemes covering the community as a whole or large section of the community that are imposed and controlled by government units. The schemes cover a wide variety of programmes, providing benefits in cash or in kind for old age, invalidity or death, survivors, sickness and maternity, work injury, unemployment, family allowance, health care, etc. There is not necessarily a direct link between the amount of the contribution paid by an individual and the benefits he or she may receive." (Paragraph 4.124).

"When social security schemes are separately organised from the other activities of government units and hold their assets and liabilities separately from the latter and engage in financial transactions on their own account they qualify as institutional units that are described as social security funds." (Paragraph 4.125).

"The amounts raised, and paid out, in social security contributions and benefits may be deliberately varied in order to achieve objectives of government policy that have no direct connection with the concept of social security as a scheme to provide social benefits to members of the community. They may be raised or lowered in order to influence the level of aggregate demand in the economy, for example. Nevertheless, so long as they remain separately constituted funds, they must be treated as separate institutional units in the SNA. (Paragraph 4.126).

"The social security funds sub-sector (of general government) consists of the social security funds operating at all levels of government. Such funds are social insurance schemes covering the community as a whole or large section of the community that are imposed by government units." (Paragraph 4.147).

100. This definition of social security funds is followed in the OECD classification with the two following exceptions which are excluded

- Schemes imposed by government and operated by bodies outside the general government sector, as defined in §3 of this manual; and
- Schemes to which all contributions are voluntary.

Supranational Authorities

101. This sub-sector covers the revenue-raising operations of supra-national authorities within a country. In practice, the only relevant supranational authority in the OECD area is that of the institutions of the European Union (EU). Tax revenues collected by member countries and paid to the EU are included in the *Revenue Statistics* at the supranational level of government. Income taxes and social security contributions collected by European Institutions and paid by European civil servants who are resident of EU member countries should not be included.

Criteria to be used for the attribution of tax revenues

102. When a government collects taxes and pays them over in whole or in part to other governments, it is necessary to determine whether the revenues should be considered to be those of the collecting government which it distributes to others as grants, or those of the beneficiary governments which the collecting government receives and passes on only as their agent. The criteria to be used in the attribution of revenues are set out in §103 to §106 which replicate paragraphs 3.70 to 3.73 from the 2008 SNA.

103. In general, a tax is attributed to the government unit that

a) exercises the authority to impose the tax (either as a principal or through the delegated authority of the principal),

b) has final discretion to set and vary the rate of the tax

104. Where an amount is collected by one government for and on behalf of another government, and the latter government has the authority to impose the tax, and set and vary its rate, then the former is acting as an agent for the latter and the tax is reassigned. Any amount retained by the collecting government as a collection charge should be treated as a payment for a service. Any other amount retained by the collecting government, such as under a tax-sharing arrangement, should be treated as a current grant. If the collecting government was delegated the authority to set and vary the rate, then the amount collected should be treated as tax revenue of this government.

105. Where different governments jointly and equally set the rate of a tax and jointly and equally decide on the distribution of the proceeds, with no individual government having ultimate overriding authority, then the tax revenues are attributed to each government according to its respective share of the proceeds. If an arrangement allows one government unit to exercise ultimate overriding authority, then all of the tax revenue is attributed to that unit.

106. There may also be the circumstance where a tax is imposed under the constitutional or other authority of one government, but other governments individually set the tax rate in their jurisdictions. The proceeds of the tax generated in each respective government's jurisdiction are attributed as tax revenues of that government.

107. The levies paid by the member states of the EU take the form specific levies which include

a) custom duties and levies on agricultural goods (5123),

b) gross monetary compensation accounts (5123 if relating to imports and 5124 if relating to exports);

c) contributions to the Single Resolution Fund (5126); and

d) Steel, coal, sugar and milk levies (5128).

108. The custom duties collected by member states on behalf of the EU are recorded

- on a gross of collection fee basis;
- using figures adjusted so that duties are shown on a 'final destination' as opposed to a 'country of first entry' basis where such adjustments can be made. These adjustments concern in particular duties collected at important (sea) ports. Although the EU duties are collected by the authorities of the country of first entry, when possible these duties should be excluded from the revenue of the collecting country and be included in the revenue of the country of final destination

109. These are the specific EU levies that most clearly conform to the attribution criterion described in §101 above. Consequently, these amounts are footnoted as a memorandum item to the EU member state country tables (in Chapter 5) and are shown as supranational revenues against each of the tax headings identified in §107.

Notes

1. All references to SNA are to the 2008 edition.

2. See section A.12 of this guide for a discussion of the concept of agency capacity.

3. It is usually possible to identify amounts of social security contributions and payroll taxes, but not other taxes paid by government.

4. If, however, a levy which is considered as non-tax revenue by most countries is regarded as a tax — or raises substantial revenue — in one or more countries, the amounts collected are footnoted at the end of the relevant country tables, even though the amounts are not included in total tax revenues.

5. Names, however, can frequently be misleading. For example, though a passport fee would normally be considered a non-tax revenue, if a supplementary levy on passports (as is the case in Portugal) were imposed in order to raise substantial amounts of revenue relative to the cost of providing the passport, the levy would be regarded as a tax under 5200.

6. A more detailed explanation of this distinction can be found in the special feature, 'Current issues in reporting tax revenues', in the 2001 edition of the *Revenue Statistics*.

7. Sometimes the terms 'non-refundable' and 'refundable' are used, but it may be considered illogical to talk of 'refundable' when nothing has been paid.

8. A different treatment, however, is accorded to non-wastable tax credits under imputation systems of corporate income tax (§37–39).

9. This is not strictly a true tax expenditure in the formal sense. Such tax expenditures require identification of a benchmark tax system for each country or, preferably, a common international benchmark. In practice it has not been possible to reach agreement on a common international benchmark.

10. Unless based on the profit made on a sale, in which case they would be classified as capital gains taxes under 1120 or 1220.

11. In some countries the same legislation applies to both individual and corporate enterprises for particular taxes on income. However, the receipts from such taxes are usually allocable between individuals and enterprises and can therefore be shown in the appropriate sub-heading.

12. For example, "... sufficiently self-contained and independent that they behave in the same way as corporations... (including) keeping a complete set of accounts" (2008 SNA, section 4.44).

13. In Canada — a country also referred to as having an imputation system — the (wastable) tax credit for the shareholder is in respect of domestic corporation tax deemed to have been paid whether or not a corporation tax liability has arisen. As there is no integral connection between the corporation tax liability and the credit given against income tax under such systems, these credits for dividends are treated, along with other tax credits, on the lines described in §26.

14. This may also apply where a scheme for government employees existed prior to the introduction of a general social security scheme.

15. In the 2008 SNA these are regarded as capital transfers and not as taxes (see section A.8).

16. This is the system by which the European Union adjusts for differences between the exchange rates used to determine prices under the Common Market Agricultural Policy and actual exchange rates. Payments under the system may relate to imports or exports and where these amounts are separately identifiable they are shown under the appropriate heading (5123 or 5124). In this Report, these amounts are shown gross (i.e. without deducting any subsidies paid out under the MCA system).

17. Transfers of profits of State lotteries are regarded as non-tax revenues (see also §68).

www.ingramcontent.com/pod-product-compliance
Lightning Source LLC
Chambersburg PA
CBHW061157240926
51846CB00006B/1043